THE IRISH SUPREME COURT

The Irish Supreme Court

Historical and Comparative Perspectives

BRICE DICKSON

OXFORD
UNIVERSITY PRESS

OXFORD
UNIVERSITY PRESS

Great Clarendon Street, Oxford, OX2 6DP,
United Kingdom

Oxford University Press is a department of the University of Oxford.
It furthers the University's objective of excellence in research, scholarship,
and education by publishing worldwide. Oxford is a registered trade mark of
Oxford University Press in the UK and in certain other countries

First Edition published in 2019

Published in the United States of America by Oxford University Press
198 Madison Avenue, New York, NY 10016, United States of America

British Library Cataloguing in Publication Data
Data available

Library of Congress Control Number: 2018961826

ISBN 978–0–19–879373–1

Foreword

The Irish Supreme Court and its predecessor, the Supreme Court of the Irish Free State, enjoyed a distinction denied to all other courts in these islands. They alone could, and can, rule that duly enacted legislation was of no legal affect because it was repugnant to the relevant Constitution, whether of the Free State or of Ireland. It is a distinction which, as Professor Dickson's impressive study amply demonstrates, seemed of little practical significance in the early years of Irish independence, but in later times has resulted in a significant body of case law entitled to an honourable place in international constitutional jurisprudence.

Professor Dickson's book is not the first full length study of the Supreme Court. That distinction belongs to a history of the court by Mr Ruadhan Mac Cormaic which was published in 2016. While it is a highly enjoyable and interesting work, it does not profess to be a comprehensive and scholarly examination of the court's jurisprudence. Professor Dickson has now filled a major lacuna in Irish legal studies by presenting us with the results of such an examination and placing them in their historical and comparative perspective. The industry and erudition which his work displays are indeed remarkable, but so too is the readable and frequently provocative style in which it is written.

For most of the 94 years covered by this book, the Supreme Court of the Irish Free State and its successors worked under difficulties not experienced in at least some of the courts of final appeal in other common law countries, notably the House of Lords in the United Kingdom and the Supreme Court in the United States. There was no filtering mechanism which enabled the court to ensure that only cases sufficiently important to warrant a hearing at the highest level reached their calendar. Since, with some exceptions, there was a constitutional right of appeal in every case to the court from decisions of the High Court, its ability to deal with its case load in an efficient and timely fashion was seriously impaired. In recent years, after decades in which the problem was ignored at the executive and legislative levels, it has at last been tackled by the creation of a Court of Appeal. Since the amendment of the Constitution in 2014, that court has replaced the Supreme Court as the final court of appeal in all cases, save where the latter court is satisfied that the decision involves a matter of general public importance or that an appeal to them is necessary in the interests of justice. Where the court is satisfied that it is warranted by exceptional circumstances and the same two preconditions are met, there can also be a direct appeal from the High Court to the Supreme Court.

This is rightly described by Professor Dickson as the most important alteration in Irish legal structures since independence. However, the change has not been effected without difficulty. The transfer to the Court of Appeal of the huge backlog of arrears from the Supreme Court means that it is now the new court which has major difficulties in dealing with its caseload. It is to be hoped that the government and legislature will recognise the importance of assisting the Court of Appeal in its difficulties, if necessary by substantially increasing its size.

It has often been said that the Supreme Court showed little enthusiasm for exercising its role of ensuring that the legislature and executive observed the requirements of the Constitution in the decades before Ó Dálaigh CJ became chief justice in 1961. But it also has to be said that the court was not solely responsible for what could be fairly described as an era of judicial stagnation at the highest level. Judges can only deal with cases that come before them and, in those cases, can only respond to the arguments which litigants and advocates choose to advance. The tendency to treat parliamentary sovereignty as a critical element of the political system which should be preserved in all but the rarest cases was widely shared in those days.

While acknowledging that the many seminal decisions of the court in the sixties and seventies which he discusses reflected a remarkable change from the previous era of judicial deference, Professor Dickson also takes the view that there has, in recent times, been a return to a more cautious and conservative approach. He is certainly not alone in that belief. I have no doubt myself that judges should not hesitate to use their power to develop the common law so that it reflects the mores of the time in which we live. But that is not to say that they should also use it to change the law in areas of policy which are the exclusive domain of the legislature. This is an issue with which, we can be sure, the Supreme Court will have to grapple again in times to come.

Professor Dickson's valuable and ground-breaking work is certain to be welcomed by judges, counsel, solicitors, lecturers and researchers and, of course, students of law of every age.

Ronan Keane
19 September 2018

Preface

This book has been long in the making, partly because of other pressing commitments but also because the project was a more ambitious one than I originally realised. I had been aware that academic literature on Irish law had mushroomed in recent years, and that the Supreme Court was churning out decisions at a much faster rate than the United Kingdom's Supreme Court, whose jurisprudence I was much more familiar with. However I did not know that the literature and case law were quite so extensive as they are. I had always planned to compile a study that would span the full history of the Supreme Court from its creation in 1924 until today, and in doing so to give a flavour of the developments it had initiated in a large number of fields of law, but my research soon convinced me that I would not be able to be as comprehensive as I had hoped.

What follows, therefore, is a highly selective survey of the output of the Irish Supreme Court over the past 94 years. It can only scratch the surface of the fields of law that it covers, and it leaves some areas completely untouched. In particular it largely neglects the jurisprudence of the Court in realms of private law, such as contract law, commercial law, tort law and property law. Perhaps there will be an opportunity to explore the Court's work in such fields in contributions to journals at a later stage. Moreover the book is more in the business of telling a story than of defending a theory. It does not purport to superimpose some grand design on the jurisprudence of the Court to date. Instead it focuses on series of decisions in various fields of law and attempts to evaluate whether, overall, the Court has developed the law in a coherent and defensible fashion.

I have sought to measure the Supreme Court's performance in accordance with criteria such as clarity, fairness and efficiency, and where appropriate I have drawn upon the experience of Supreme Courts in other common law jurisdictions to help evaluate the Irish Court's judgments. Of course every country's judicial system is unique, not least because it exists within a constitutional framework which inevitably determines what it can and cannot do. In this book I identify what constraints seem to have operated on the Irish Supreme Court to date and whether any of them could have been avoided without the Court losing the people's respect and, in a wider sense, its own legitimacy.

Anyone writing in this area, especially someone based in a different jurisdiction, is hugely indebted to the large cadre of commentators who have done Ireland proud in the attention they have already devoted to the Supreme Court's jurisprudence. Invidious though it may be to do so, I feel it necessary to highlight the work of Gerard Hogan, whose seemingly inexhaustible energy as an academic, barrister, judge and (since 2018) Advoctae General, is astonishing. I am more directly grateful to a number of people who, whether they are aware of it or not, have helped me in various ways to make progress with the book during the past five years. They include Gordon Anthony, Louis Blom-Cooper, Paul Daly, Fiona de Londras, Suzanne Egan, Neil Faris, Robin Hickey, Aileen Kavanagh, Muiris MacCarthaigh, Donncha O'Connell and Dermot Walsh. Several readers of chapters pointed out errors, for which I am truly appreciative. Remaining mistakes are entirely my own responsibility.

Librarians and archivists at Queen's University Belfast, Trinity College Dublin, University College Dublin, the National Archives of Ireland and the National Library of Ireland all assisted in various ways. The Irish Society of Comparative Law and the Institute of Irish Studies generously allowed me to make presentations about the Irish Supreme Court at the National University of Ireland Galway and Queen's University Belfast respectively. At Oxford University Press I am grateful to Jamie Berezin, Natasha Flemming, Nicole Leyland,

John Louth and Eve Ryle-Hodges. Thanks too to all at Newgen who helped with the book's production, especially Afrose. My wife, Patricia Mallon, has given her customary unstinting support throughout the project and the book is dedicated to her. Particular thanks go to Ronan Keane, a former Chief Justice of Ireland, for contributing such a generous Foreword. I also acknowledge the invaluable financial support of the Leverhulme Trust, which granted me a six-month Research Fellowship in 2013–14 that relieved me of university teaching duties for a semester and defrayed some expenses associated with the project. Without this kick-start I doubt if the plan to produce the book would ever have come to fruition.

For purists I should point out that in two respects I have departed from Irish legal conventions: I have not inserted a comma before the date of Acts of the Oireachtas and I have not used a superscript symbol to indicate subsections of Articles in the Constitution.

Brice Dickson
Queen's University Belfast, 14 November 2018

Contents

Table of Cases

IRISH CASES

CASES AT THE EUROPEAN COURT OF HUMAN RIGHTS AND THE COURT OF JUSTICE OF THE EUROPEAN UNION

OTHER NATIONAL CASES

United Kingdom

Australia

Canada

Germany

New Zealand

South Africa

United States

INTERNATIONAL CASES

Table of Legislative Provisions and Treaties

IRISH LEGISLATION

Constitutional Provisions

Statutes

Secondary Legislation

INTERNATIONAL LAW

International Treaties, Agreements and Conventions

UN Resolutions

Rules and Guidelines

EUROPEAN LAW

Conventions and Treaties

Secondary Legislation

United States

1
Introduction

The Aims of this Study

Each independent country has its own way of governing itself. Most modern liberal democracies opt to have one body of elected people who enact laws through a parliament, a second body of people who propose laws for enactment and take responsibility for implementing those which are enacted, and a third body of people who adjudicate upon disputes over how laws, once enacted, should be interpreted and applied. Ireland, which became an almost completely independent country in 1922, is no exception to that pattern. It has a parliament (the Oireachtas), a government and a judiciary. Since 1924 the top court within the judiciary has been the Supreme Court. This book is an attempt to evaluate the performance of the Supreme Court in the 94 years of its existence to date.

In making this evaluation the book seeks to analyse the contribution the Court has made to the development of Irish law. Beyond that, given that a country's law reflects the nature of the society governed by that law, the book is an assessment of the contribution made by the Supreme Court to the development of Irish nationhood. To what extent have fundamental features of Irish society been created or sustained by the Court? Conversely, what features do not exist because the Supreme Court has prevented them from taking a foothold? In addition the book attempts to assess the impact of external influences on the Supreme Court, the leadership displayed by particular judges who have served on the Court, the mechanisms which have operated to facilitate or obstruct its work and the awareness of the Court itself concerning the expectations which others have of it. Where it is deemed appropriate the study draws upon experiences of supreme courts in other parts of the world by way of comparison.

Reasons of space preclude comprehensive coverage of the total output of the Court. Instead the study focuses on how the Court has performed during certain periods and in certain areas of law. Naturally the Court's judges have always been conscious of the times in which they are living, so any analysis of their decisions should take into account the social, economic and political context of the day. As judges are not elected, they do not have a direct mandate to develop new laws. However they are tasked with interpreting and applying not just legislation but also the common law, that is, the law which has emerged over centuries as a result of previous courts' decisions and the acceptance of those decisions by elected law-makers. This gives judges in the top court some discretion as to how to develop the law. The book seeks to critique the principal occasions on which such developments have been made. In doing so it builds on the growing literature concerning supreme courts as institutions, a brief résumé of which is therefore appropriate.

Evaluating Supreme Courts

The task of assessing the contribution which a nation's apex court has made to the nation's development is a challenging one. It requires careful delineation between the matters which the court has power to control and those which it does not. The drawing of this line will depend on which powers have been granted to the court by the nation's Constitution and other legislation. It will also depend on how much latitude the court is acknowledged to have as regards the exercise of its 'inherent' powers and on whether other institutions have been given powers which may interfere with or even trump those of the court. Beyond this, criteria need to be developed to facilitate an assessment of how the apex court has exercised the powers it does possess. In turn those criteria will reflect what a nation can reasonably expect from the court.

It is submitted that there are four main expectations which a nation is entitled to hold regarding the performance of its top court. The first is *clarity* in decision-making, not just when it is ruling on which party to a legal dispute should win but also when it is setting out the rules and principles on which those rulings are based. Above all a country wants its top judges to firmly engage in rule-based and principle-based decision-making. It needs to avoid vagueness and arbitrariness, relying solely on the persuasiveness of its reasoning to convince the litigants, their legal representatives and society as a whole that the decisions it has reached are appropriate.

The second expectation is that the apex court will conduct its business with *fairness*. This means that it must give all parties to the litigation a full opportunity to make their points. It should also take proper account of the context within which it is reaching its decisions, for it must be able to explain why it is, or is not, changing the law as hitherto understood, and how its decisions in one area of law are consistent with those it has taken in another area even if at first sight they appear not to be. Many would argue that fairness presupposes an open-mindedness to arguments that are based not so much on legislation or precedent as on other relevant considerations such as justice, morality, international comity or even affordability.

Thirdly, a nation is entitled to expect that its apex court operates with *efficiency*. Decisions should be reached and published within a reasonable time of the dispute being brought to the court, users of the court should be treated as customers who deserve a high quality of service that is good value for money, and staff of the court—officials as well as judges—should behave as if they are public servants rather than some special class of people who do not need to be accountable for the way they go about their business.

Fourthly, and perhaps most importantly, the top court should be one which has earned respect. Respect will flow from the attributes already mentioned—clarity, fairness and efficiency—but it will also be dependent on the independence, objectivity and integrity of the judges who sit on the court, on their understanding and empathy, and above all on their honesty and incorruptibility. Judges everywhere are expected to be upright; those appointed to sit in the highest national courts need to display that characteristic in spades.

Assessments Elsewhere

The most studied court in the world is the Supreme Court of the United States. Books about that Court are legion and can be divided into three broad categories: those focusing on judgments of particular Justices,[1] those examining the Court's output during the tenure of particular Chief Justices,[2] and those looking more generally at the Court's work over a period of time[3] or in relation to a particular area of law.[4] There are also several reference books about the Court[5] and countless articles in prestigious academic law

[1] eg Dunne (1970); Greenhouse (2005).
[2] eg Schwartz (ed) (2002); Graetz and Greenhouse (2016).
[3] Classics include Chemerinsky (2014); Toobin (2007); Irons (2006); Lazarus (2005); Schwartz (1993); Woodward and Armstrong (1979).
[4] eg Thomas (2008); Klarman (2004); Cox (1987).
[5] The most encyclopaedic is Hall (2005). See too Ward, Brough and Arnold (2015).

journals.[6] For almost half a century the first of each year's eight issues of the *Harvard Law Review* has been entirely devoted to an overview of the previous year's decisions by the US Supreme Court. The Supreme Court Historical Society has been publishing the scholarly *Journal of Supreme Court History* since 1975.

Three features of their Supreme Court make it particularly fascinating to Americans. The first is that the Court is extremely powerful: it can declare any Act of the US Congress or of any State legislature to be unconstitutional and therefore invalid and, because the process for changing the US Constitution is so hard to complete, the Supreme Court's views tend to settle the constitutional position for a considerable period, until the Court decides to overrule its previous decision. Nothing better illustrates the power of the Court than its role in the law on abortion. In 1973 it ruled in *Roe v Wade*,[7] by a vote of seven to two, that during the first trimester of a woman's pregnancy she has what amounts to an unrestricted right, after consulting with her doctor, to choose to have an abortion. That has remained the basic position ever since.

The second crucial feature of the US Supreme Court is that the right to nominate persons to vacancies on the Court rests with the President, though the nominee can be appointed only 'by and with the advice of the Senate'.[8] Usually the Senate confirms the President's nomination, but Robert Bork failed to be endorsed when nominated by President Reagan in 1987, supposedly on account of Bork's very conservative views. President Trump is on record as wanting to see *Roe v Wade* reversed and this may indeed occur if the persons he nominates as Supreme Court Justices are eventually approved by the Senate.[9] This highlights the third significant feature of the US Court, which is that the nine persons[10] appointed to be Justices are appointed for life: if they wish to, they can continue in office until they die. Of the 113 Justices who have served on the Court to date (September 2018), 56 continued in office until they died or are still serving, while only 57 retired.[11] Two of the current Justices are already in their 80s.[12]

Assessment of the work of the Justices takes many forms. Most of it is doctrinal, meaning that commentators evaluate a Justice's legal reasoning by comparing it with that of other Justices. But a great deal of it is political in that commentators try to determine where each Justice sits on the political spectrum: how Republican or Democratic are they, how conservative or liberal? The work of Lee Epstein and his associates is noteworthy in this context.[13] Complex statistical analyses are often conducted to provide support for labelling a Justice in a particular way. Moreover the Justices themselves have been more than willing to write about their own and their colleagues' approaches to law-making: in 2012 one blog post listed 353 books written by Supreme Court Justices to date.[14]

Nothing comparable to the scale of judicial studies found in the USA exists anywhere else. But all of the leading common law jurisdictions—those ultimately deriving from the Anglo-Saxon tradition—have some books and other studies devoted to their top courts. Canada's pedigree is second only to that of the USA. As well as full-length monographs[15] there is

[6] For recent symposia see Barnes et al (2016); Sherry et al (2016); Shapiro and Schmidt (2013). See too Orentlicher (2018); Schauer (2017); Carlson, Livermore and Rockmore (2015).

[7] 410 US 113 (1973). For contextual background see Irons (2006) 436–49.

[8] Art II, s 2, of the Constitution. The Senate holds hearings in its Judicial Committee.

[9] His first nominee, Neil Gorsuch, was approved by the Senate in April 2017.

[10] The Judiciary Act 1866 provided for the number of Justices to be reduced to seven, but this provision was repealed by the Judiciary Act 1869.

[11] See Hall (2005), App 2, 1141–44. Anthony Kennedy retired on 31 July 2018. The nomination of Brett Kavanaugh (b 1965) was approved by the Senate in October 2018 after bitterly contested hearings.

[12] Ruth Bader Ginsburg (b 1933) and Stephen Breyer (b 1938).

[13] Epstein et al (1998) and (2007).

[14] See http://www.scotusblog.com/2012/03/351-books-by-supreme-court-justices.

[15] Roach (2016); Schertzer (2016); Songer (2008); Muttart (2007); McCormick (2000).

a whole journal devoted to the Canadian Supreme Court (the *Supreme Court Law Review*) and many articles elsewhere on specific judges or on the Court's attitude to specific issues.[16] The enactment of Canada's Charter of Rights and Freedoms, through the Constitution Act 1982, gave a huge impetus to these studies. The fact that the Canadian Supreme Court, like its US neighbour, usually sits *en banc*, with its full complement of nine judges, means that the role of the Chief Justice, who presides in almost every case, becomes very significant.[17] Just as Americans refer to the Warren Court (1953–69), the Burger Court (1969–86) or the Rehnquist Court (1986–2005), so Canadians refer to the Dickson Court (1984–90), the Lamer Court (1990–2000) and the McLachlin Court (2000–17).[18] Many studies focus on what in Canada is called 'attitudinal' decision-making, where judges supposedly decide cases in accordance with their conscious or subconscious attitudes rather than with existing law.[19]

Australia's top court—the High Court—has also been the subject of close examination. There is an excellent reference work on the Court[20] and several studies of its constitutional jurisprudence, including more than a dozen detailed annual overviews by Andrew Lynch and George Williams.[21] But the fact that the High Court sits in panels and not *en banc* perhaps makes it a less attractive focus of attention. The same can be said, perhaps surprisingly, for the United Kingdom's highest court, formerly the Appellate Committee of the House of Lords but now, since 2009, the Supreme Court. The classic study of the House of Lords is by Blom-Cooper and Drewry,[22] and there are impressive sequels by Robert Stevens,[23] Alan Paterson[24] and David Robertson.[25] Replacement of the Appellate Committee by the Supreme Court has led to subsequent books on the work of the judges involved[26] and a number of statistical studies.[27] A *UK Supreme Court Yearbook* is also published[28] and there is an excellent blog dedicated to the Court's decisions.[29] What has been lacking has been any systematic analysis of whether judges on the top UK court have allowed their personal political convictions to influence their decision-making. John Griffith attempted this in 1977,[30] but his analysis remains controversial and cannot be said to have stood the test of time.

The Supreme Court of India has been the subject of academic attention too, though most of it has focused on the work of particular judges[31] rather than on the court as an institution.[32] A study of its decisions was included in an edited collection on judicial activism published in 2007,[33] where a comparison was made of the extent to which top courts in nine common law countries had adopted an activist approach to law-making.[34] The merits and demerits of judicial activism have also been at the centre of studies of the two major European courts, the Court of Justice of the European Union in Luxembourg[35] and the European Court of Human Rights in Strasbourg.[36] As international courts, when those

[16] See eg the articles marking the Court's 125th anniversary in (2000) 79(2) *Can Bar Rev*; Greschner (47–76) makes a case for viewing the Canadian Court as an umpire rather than an institution in dialogue with others. For a broader historical account see Hogg (2006).

[17] eg McCormick (1993).

[18] On the legacy of McLachlin CJ see the six-part symposium on the I-CON website, 4–9 December 2017.

[19] eg Ostberg and Wetstein (2007).

[20] Blackshield, Coper and Williams (eds) (2001).

[21] Published in the *University of New South Wales Law Journal* since 2004.

[22] Blom-Cooper and Drewry (1972).

[23] Stevens (1979).

[24] Paterson (1982).

[25] Robertson (1998).

[26] eg Blom-Cooper, Dickson and Drewry (eds) (2009); Lee (ed) (2011); Dickson (2013); Paterson (2013).

[27] eg Poole and Shah (2009) and (2011); Shah, Poole and Blackwell (2014).

[28] Currently published by Wildy & Sons Ltd.

[29] www.ukscblog.com.

[30] Griffith (1997). Griffith did not focus only on the apex court, and nor did Lee (1988).

[31] eg Gadbois (2011).

[32] eg Verma and Kusum (eds) (2004).

[33] Iyer (2007).

[34] The countries were Australia, Canada, India, Ireland, Israel, New Zealand, South Africa, the UK and the USA.

[35] eg Vilhena de Freitas (2015); Dawson, de Witte and Muir (eds) (2013); Rasmussen (1986).

[36] eg Flogaitis, Zwart and Fraser (eds) (2013); Christoffersen and Madsen (eds) (2011).

institutions are reaching decisions they clearly have to take into account a range of considerations different from those which face national supreme courts, but the accusation that they are stepping beyond their remit and developing the law in ways for which they have no democratic mandate is still one which they wish to avoid, for fear of losing their legitimacy in the eyes of those affected by their decisions. As regards the Strasbourg court, the discrete analyses by Dothan and Voeten show that the outcome of a case can depend on the background and ideology of the particular judges who happen to deal with it.[37] Another study shows that natural language processing can predict the outcome of the Strasbourg Court's decisions with an average accuracy of 79 per cent.[38]

The Approach of this Book

The Supreme Court of Ireland is a relatively under-studied court by comparison withthose which have just been reviewed. There are many commentaries on particular decisions of the Court and on its powers and duties,[39] but relatively little literature on how the Court has developed as an institution over time, the tenor of its decisions in particular branches of law or how its contribution to the value-system of the State compares with that made by apex courts in other countries.[40] It is a measure of the degree to which the Court and its judges were largely ignored by scholars that the first revelatory piece about the workings of the Court was written for *Magill* magazine by Colm Tóibin in 1985.[41] The piece was prompted by the role being played by the Supreme Court in the extradition of suspected terrorists to Northern Ireland.[42]

The 'bible' on constitutional law in Ireland—John Kelly's great tome first published in 1980 and now in its fifth edition—devotes more than thirty pages to the Supreme Court, but these focus mainly on jurisdictional issues.[43] In 2001 a short but penetrating critique was published by David Gwynn Morgan, who was critical of the Supreme Court's judgments in a number of fields, mainly on the basis of their allegedly poor and at times inconsistent reasoning.[44] In 2004 Morgan argued that in Ireland the main way in which the separation of powers doctrine traditionally manifests itself is through a 'judicial-o-centric' approach, but in recent case law he detected (and approved of) 'a fairly consistent development of respect for the notion that some "space" must be left to the expertise and legitimacy of the political organs'.[45] A few years later William Binchy contributed an insightful overview of the Court's approach to law-making in the comparative collection on judicial activism mentioned above.[46] His assessment was more generous than that of Morgan, but still guarded. He concluded that the Supreme Court had not yet developed 'a contemporary philosophical perspective which will provide, if not clearly ordained solutions, at least a convincing framework for resolution of crucial issues'.[47] He thought that it had failed to produce 'some grand jurisprudential theory' to reconcile 'deep inconsistencies' in the Irish Constitution

[37] Dothan (2011–12) and (2015); Voeten (2008). [38] Aletras et al (2016).

[39] On its powers and duties see Byrne and McCutcheon (2014) 346–69; Forde and Leonard (2013) 162–70; Hogan et al (2018) 1146-80.

[40] An exception is McGuckian (2005), who discusses the legal, political and attitudinal models of decision-making. She maintains (at 319) that, notwithstanding the power of constitutional review enjoyed by senior Irish judges, '[t]he political role assumed by the judiciary in Ireland occupies a middle space between the proactive stance adopted by senior members of the American judiciary and the more passive approach that [has] been traditionally taken by the English judiciary'.

[41] Tóibin (1985). [42] See Chap 7 below,151-70. [43] Hogan et al (2018) 1146-80.

[44] Morgan (2001). [45] Morgan (2004) 143. [46] Binchy (2007). [47] Ibid, 214.

and he bemoaned the fact that, unlike the High Court of Australia for example, the Irish Supreme Court had yet to 'broaden its interest in the jurisprudence of common law jurisdictions beyond Britain'.[48]

Following the appearance of a short book primarily describing the Four Courts building in Dublin where the Supreme Court is located but also summarising some of the Court's key decisions,[49] and a series of commentaries reflecting more generally—and provocatively—on the Irish legal system, during which decisions of the Supreme Court featured prominently,[50] a ground-breaking and highly readable account of the workings and 'performance' of the Irish Supreme Court was published in 2016, the first wholescale monograph devoted to the institution,[51] parts of which were presaged in a series of newspaper articles by the same author three years earlier.[52] Ruadhán Mac Cormaic's study is a thoroughly researched account of critical turning points in the Court's history, enlivened at frequent intervals by excerpts from interviews he conducted with over 140 individuals, as well as by materials drawn from archives and personal correspondence. The current study does not attempt to duplicate Mac Cormaic's impressive work, which is animated by a journalist's instinct for the telling phrase and the pivotal moment. Instead it adopts a more legalistic perspective, using as its core research database the words used by Supreme Court judges in some of the thousands of judgments they have issued to date and attempting to evaluate the quality of those utterances as legal rules and principles. The book's publication coincides with a welcome initiative by the School of Law at Trinity College Dublin to hold an annual conference on the output of the Irish Supreme Court, the papers at which are then to be published.[53]

Chapter 2 looks in detail at the antecedents of the Supreme Court and at how it emerged out of the chaos that Ireland experienced during the period 1919–23. It is only by understanding what preceded the Court—in particular the 'British' character of the institutions then in place—that a true appreciation of the role of the Supreme Court during the years of the Irish Free State (1922–37) can be gained, which is the subject-matter of Chapter 3. Chapters 4 and 5 conclude what is essentially the first of three sections in the book by looking at developments in the powers (or 'jurisdiction') of the Supreme Court from 1924 until today (Chapter 4) and at the system for appointing individuals to serve as judges on the Court (Chapter 5). Those two chapters serve as a backdrop to the following five chapters, each of which assesses the output of the Supreme Court in a specific field of law. They begin with the crucial field of constitutional law (Chapter 6), continue with an analysis of how the Court has dealt with issues relating to Northern Ireland (Chapter 7) and then look at the cognate field of administrative law (Chapter 8). The next two chapters focus on the discrete areas of criminal justice (Chapter 9) and family law (Chapter 10), two fields which have proved fertile ground for Supreme Court judges who have wanted to leave their mark on the Irish legal system. The final section of the book is devoted to a study of the relationship between the Supreme Court of Ireland and the two main bodies of European law—European Union law (Chapter 11) and European human rights law (Chapter 12). The book concludes with an attempt to sum up how the Supreme Court has exercised its powers during the course of its history to date and what might lie ahead for it in the near future (Chapter 13).

[48] Ibid, 215. [49] Kennedy et al (eds) (2003).
[50] eg Bacik and Rogan (2016); Williams (2015); Bacik (2004). [51] Mac Cormaic (2016).
[52] Mac Cormaic (2013).
[53] The first such conference took placeon 6 October 2018 and the papers are due to be published by Clarus Press in the *Irish Supreme Court Review* early in 2019. Decisions by the Supreme Court are also regularly analysed on the Irish Legal News website: www.irishlegal.com.

2

The Origins of the Supreme Court

The Birth of an Independent Ireland

It was in 1169 that the Norman rulers of England first came to Ireland with a view to conquering its people and making the island an English possession. In 1177 King Henry II of England made his young son, the future King John, the first Lord of Ireland, and all subsequent English monarchs held that title until the Parliament of Ireland, by the Crown of Ireland Act 1542, conferred the kingship of Ireland on the then English monarch, Henry VIII. From then until 1801 the same individual was King of England and King of Ireland but there was no political union between the two countries. Such a union was created between Scotland and England in 1707, forming the Kingdom of Great Britain, and in 1800 a further Act of Union added Ireland to that political union to form the United Kingdom of Great Britain and Ireland. This meant that from 1 January 1801 the powers to make legislation for Ireland rested solely with the Parliament at Westminster in London and the highest court dealing with Irish cases was the House of Lords in London—more specifically the Appellate Committee of the House of Lords, which was eventually put on a statutory footing in 1876.[1]

Following substantial clamour in favour of 'home rule' for Ireland, which had already led to three previous attempts to enact legislation,[2] devolution was eventually brought about by the Government of Ireland Act 1920. This was achieved, however, at the cost of dividing the island into two separate jurisdictions because the predominantly Protestant population in the north-east did not want as broad a degree of home rule as the predominantly Catholic population in the rest of the island. The six counties in the north-east were therefore renamed Northern Ireland and continued to form a constituent part of the United Kingdom, albeit with their own Parliament to which substantial law-making powers were transferred. The remaining 26 counties on the island became Southern Ireland. They too were to be given their own Parliament with substantial devolved powers. The original plan was that Southern Ireland would also remain a part of the United Kingdom, but ongoing civil unrest in the 26 counties put paid to that idea.

In the 1918 general election to the Westminster Parliament, 73 of the 105 seats in Ireland had been won by representatives of Sinn Féin, a party which favoured the complete independence of Ireland from Great Britain.[3] Rather than take their seats in London, these elected representatives established their own Irish Parliament in Dublin, which they called the first Dáil Éireann ('Assembly of Ireland'). They also set up a separate court system from that which already existed—the Dáil Éireann courts.[4] An armed struggle to achieve a greater degree of autonomy—the War of Independence—was then waged from 1919 to

[1] Appellate Jurisdiction Act 1876; Jones (2009); Osborough (1996) 244–7.

[2] These were the Government of Ireland Bills of 1886 and 1893, which failed to get the approval of the House of Lords in its capacity as the second chamber of Parliament, and the Government of Ireland Act 1914, which, although receiving Royal Assent, was never brought into force because of the outbreak of the First World War in August 1914 and the Easter Rising in Dublin in April 1916.

[3] For details of this crucial election see www.ark.ac.uk/elections/h1918.htm. Each of three Sinn Féin candidates stood, and were elected, in two different constituencies.

[4] Costello (2003) Chap 6. See too 10-12 below.

1921, resulting in approximately 1,230 fatalities.[5] A truce was called on 11 July 1921 and a peace settlement, the Anglo-Irish Treaty, was signed on 6 December 1921. Under this treaty, Southern Ireland was to be renamed the Irish Free State (Saorstát Éireann) and to become a self-governing dominion within the British Empire, a status comparable to that of Australia, Canada, Newfoundland, New Zealand and South Africa. The status of Northern Ireland was unaffected.

As a result of the Anglo-Irish Treaty the devolution arrangements provided for in the Government of Ireland Act 1920 were abandoned as far as the south of Ireland was concerned. The Treaty was ratified by Parliament at Westminster on 16 December 1921 and narrowly approved by the second Dáil Éireann[6] on 7 January 1922 (by 64 votes to 57), but since the British government did not recognise the Dáil as a legitimate parliamentary assembly it insisted that the Treaty also be put before a meeting of the members entitled to sit in the House of Commons of Southern Ireland, that is, the 128 persons who had been elected in May 1921 when, as required by the 1920 Act, elections were held throughout the island. Only the 64 pro-Treaty members of the Dáil, together with the four MPs for Dublin University who were unwilling to attend the Dáil, were present at that meeting on 14 January 1922 and the Treaty was unanimously approved. It was given the force of law by the Westminster Parliament through the Irish Free State (Agreement) Act 1922, which received Royal Assent on 31 March 1922. This Act authorised the establishment of a provisional government[7] as well as a provisional parliament in Dublin, and later that year the former asked the latter—the third Dáil Éireann, elected on 16 June 1922,[8] but sitting as a Constituent Assembly rather than as a law-making body—to approve the draft Constitution of the Irish Free State.

The draft Constitution had been produced by a committee which first met on 24 January 1922 and was published on 15 June 1922.[9] The third Dáil conferred its approval on 25 October 1922 and on 5 December 1922 the Westminster Parliament passed the Irish Free State (Constitution) Act 1922 to confirm the adoption of the new Constitution. King George V issued a Royal Proclamation on 6 December 1922 formally bringing the Constitution into force. That was exactly a year after the signing of the Anglo-Irish Treaty, the maximum time which the Treaty had allowed for the formation of the new State. Irish independence, therefore, can be said to formally date from 6 December 1922.[10] On that day the former provisional government became known as the Executive Council. The original head of the provisional government, Michael Collins, had been assassinated by anti-Treaty forces on 22 August 1922, so the position of President of the Executive Council was taken up by William Cosgrave, Collins' successor as Chairman of the provisional government.

[5] Gray (1994) 81.

[6] This parliament comprised the 125 Sinn Féin MPs who on 24 May 1921 had won seats in the proposed parliaments for Northern Ireland (six) and Southern Ireland (119).

[7] It had already been functioning since 16 January 1922.

[8] Of the 128 persons elected, 35 were anti-Treaty Sinn Féin candidates led by Éamon de Valera, and they refused to take their seats.

[9] For details of the drafting process see Farrell (1970–71); more generally onthe creation of the Free State see Curran (1980); for the pre-1922 constitutional history of Ireland see Donaldson (1957) Chap 2.

[10] The 'illegal' first Dáil proclaimed its own Declaration of Independence at its inaugural meeting on 21 January 1919, so many Sinn Féin supporters consider that to be the founding date of Ireland's independence. For a fascinating exploration of what is Ireland's 'Independence Day' see Mohr (2018).

The Evolution of the Court System in Ireland

The intention of the Government of Ireland Act 1920 was that after partition the court systems in each part of Ireland would remain very much as they had been since the rationalisation introduced in the 1870s by the Supreme Court of Judicature (Ireland) Act 1877, which mirrored legislation introduced a few years earlier for England and Wales.[11] Before the 1920 Act came into force on 3 May 1921 the highest court sitting in Ireland was the Court of Appeal, but on that date it was divided into the Court of Appeal of Northern Ireland and the Court of Appeal of Southern Ireland. Final appeals from either court could lie to the High Court of Appeal for Ireland and thence to the House of Lords in London.[12] Although all of these appeal courts tended to adhere quite strictly to the doctrine of precedent, they were not obliged to do so by law: 'the following of precedent in former superior Irish courts did not originate as a common law or statutory rule—it was in fact a custom that derived from judicial comity (as in England)'.[13] They would depart from previous decisions if those decisions failed to refer to relevant legislation or other authorities, but the need to avoid an intolerable degree of uncertainty in the law was also a strong motivating factor for following their predecessors.

Irish influence in the House of Lords

It is worth noting that Irish influence in the House of Lords was still significant: between the statutory recognition of the House's appellate jurisdiction in 1876 and the partition of Ireland in 1921 seven of the 22 judges appointed as Lords of Appeal were men who had qualified as Irish barristers.[14]

The first three of the seven were all graduates of Trinity College Dublin: Lord FitzGerald, a former Liberal Party MP for Ennis in County Clare, served from 1882 to 1889; Lord Macnaghten, a former Conservative MP for Antrim in the North of Ireland, served from 1887 to 1913; and Lord Morris, a former Liberal Party MP for Galway, served from 1889 to 1899. The next Irishman to be appointed was Lord Russell of Killowen, from County Down in the North of Ireland: he was another former Liberal MP, first for Dundalk and then for South Hackney in London, before becoming the Attorney General for England and Wales. In 1894, after just a month as a Lord of Appeal, he was appointed as Lord Chief Justice of England.

The fifth Irish man appointed, in 1905, was Lord Atkinson, a Northerner who was a Conservative MP for Londonderry; he served for 23 years. Lord Collins, yet another Northerner, was Master of the Rolls in Ireland (head of the Court of Appeal) before being appointed a Lord of Appeal in 1907 and serving until 1910. The final Irishman appointed before the partition of Ireland was Lord Edward Carson, a prominent Ulster unionist, who sat as a Lord of Appeal from 1921 to 1929. At partition, therefore, two of the six Lords of Appeal then in office were from Ireland—Lords Atkinson and Carson, both very much of a unionist disposition.[15] No openly nationalist person with an Irish background was ever appointed to the Appellate Committee.

[11] Supreme Court of Judicature Acts 1873–75.

[12] See too Chap 4 below, 46-7. For more on Ireland's legal systems between 1916 and 1926, see Osborough (1972).

[13] Walsh (2005) 185. Walsh maintains that this was also so for the 'first' Irish Supreme Court (1924–61).

[14] Lowry (2001); on the Irish House of Lords as a judicial body at the end of the 18th century see Lyall (1993–95).

[15] The other four Lords of Appeal were Lord Shaw and Lord Dunedin from Scotland and Viscount Cave and Lord Sumner from England and Wales.

The Constitution and the Dáil Éireann courts

Article 64 of the Constitution of the Irish Free State, which came into force on 6 December 1922, provided that the Oireachtas (the Irish Parliament) must establish public courts comprising 'Courts of First Instance and a Court of Final Appeal to be called the Supreme Court'. The Courts of First Instance were to include a High Court, with full original jurisdiction in all civil and criminal matters, and also courts of local and limited jurisdiction. By Article 66 the Supreme Court was, 'with such exceptions (not including cases which involve questions as to the validity of any law) and subject to such regulations as may be prescribed by law', to have appellate jurisdiction from all decisions of the High Court. Moreover by the same provision all decisions of the Supreme Court were to be final and conclusive, incapable of being reviewed by any other authority. By Article 75, one of the transitory provisions in the Constitution, pending the establishment of the new courts existing courts were to continue to exercise the same jurisdiction as before, and any judge of any such court, unless wanting to resign, was to continue to hold office on the same terms. The provisions of Article 66 concerning the finality of decisions taken by the proposed new Supreme Court were in the interim to be applied to decisions of the Court of Appeal.

In fact, no legislation was enacted setting out the exact powers and duties of the proposed new courts until the Courts of Justice Act was passed in 1924, taking effect on 6 June. For part of the interim period, operating illegally alongside the official courts, there was a remarkable system of 'republican courts'.[16] As Casey has shown, the process by which these came to be established in various parts of the country after the first meeting of Dáil Éireann on 21 January 1919 is rather obscure, as so few contemporary records survive, but in May 1920 'rules of arbitration' were finalised for use within parish and district republican courts.[17] Kotsonouris has charted developments thereafter, highlighting the issuing of a decree by Dáil Éireann on 29 June 1920 which authorised the sitting of civil and criminal courts throughout the country, even though they often had to be held in secret for fear of attracting the attention of the police.[18] The (unofficial) Department of Home Affairs then issued a document entitled *Judiciary*, which primarily contained rules and forms for the parish and district courts but also made several references to a Supreme Court.[19] The Supreme Court was to sit in Dublin and have jurisdiction 'over the Republic'. It was to consist of not less than three judges who, after the first appointments, were to be legally qualified persons of at least 12 years' standing (unless the Department of Home Affairs determined otherwise 'for special reasons'). They were to hold office for life and be removable only by special decree of the Dáil passed by a two-thirds majority. Where a case of exceptional public importance came before the Court it could direct that it be heard by a full Court, consisting of not less than two judges of the Supreme Court and two Circuit Court judges. In such cases, if there was an equality of votes, the President of the Supreme Court was to have a casting vote.

By September 1920 four senior professional judges were in place to help regularise the Dáil Éireann courts. They were James Creed Meredith (a King's Counsel with a doctorate in philosophy), Arthur Clery (a professor of law at University College Dublin), Cahir Davitt (an enthusiastic young barrister practising mainly in Connaught) and Diarmuid Crowley (a contemporary of Davitt practising mainly in Munster). Meredith and Clery were made members of the Supreme Court of the Irish Republic and allocated an annual salary of

[16] Foxton (2008) 187–97. [17] Casey (1974).
[18] Kotsonouris (2004) 7–232; see too Casey (1970).
[19] The information here is at pp 4 and 8 of the document.

£750; Meredith, indeed, was made President of the Supreme Court. Davitt and Crowley were Circuit Court judges, hearing cases mainly outside Dublin. On one occasion Judge Crowley was arrested and prosecuted for participating in the courts, serving two years in prison as a result. Davitt occasionally sat with Meredith and Clery in the Supreme Court in Dublin.[20] As the intensity of the War of Independence wound down in the early months of 1921 the Dáil Éireann courts began to operate more openly and continued to do so up until the completion of negotiations leading to the Anglo-Irish Treaty in December. Kotsonouris notes that immediately after being released from prison in November Crowley returned to his job as a republican judge.[21]

The Dáil Éireann Supreme Court was given both an appellate jurisdiction and an original jurisdiction. The former catered for appeals from the Circuit Court on questions of law in civil cases, equity cases, criminal cases (if the appellant was convicted by a Circuit Court Judge in an earlier appeal) and Land Commission cases. The Supreme Court's original jurisdiction was to be exercised either by the whole Court or by any member of it and covered matters such as applications for an order of *habeas corpus* or bail, applications from any party or District Judge to hear a civil or criminal case or applications to change the venue of any civil or criminal case. Sadly, there is a lack of surviving evidence as to how frequently the Supreme Court sat and what kind of legal reasoning its judges engaged in.

The Anglo-Irish Treaty did not mention the outlawed courts and after Dáil Éireann voted to approve the Treaty on 7 January 1922 the Provisional Government directed that all pre-existing *official* courts should continue to carry out their functions 'unless and until otherwise ordered'.[22] Yet at the same time instructions were sent to those operating the *unofficial* courts to keep them running. What's more, additional judges were appointed to sit in those courts, such as Cecil Lavery, a future Supreme Court judge. As a high number of litigants insisted on taking advantage of the republican Supreme Court, Dáil Éireann itself had to direct, in April 1922, that an application by a litigant to prevent his or her opponent from proceeding with a case in the official courts should be granted only if the full Supreme Court approved of it.[23]

As tensions rose between the pro-Treaty and anti-Treaty factions of Sinn Féin and the prospect of a civil war beckoned, the provisional government attempted to crack down on the unofficial courts. Judge Meredith, presiding in the Supreme Court, announced on 13 July 1922 that the Dáil Éireann cabinet had advised that no further sittings of the Supreme Court should take place until the judicial system could be properly reconstructed, presumably as intended in the draft Constitution published a month earlier. Less than two weeks later, on 25 July 1922, the Provisional Government decided to repeal the decree of Dáil Éireann of 29 June 1920, thereby marking the end of this separate system of unofficial courts.[24] The process for completing the cases already begun, and for dealing with appeals against decisions by unofficial parish and district courts outside Dublin which the decision of 29 June 1920 had exempted from abolition, has been painstakingly detailed elsewhere and need not divert us now.[25] Suffice it to note that one of the principal architects of the process was none other than James Creed Meredith, the former President of the Dáil

[20] Davitt served as President of the High Court from 1951 to 1966. He lived on until 1986.

[21] Kotsonouris (2004) 14.

[22] *Iris Oifigiúil* (Official Bulletin), no 4, 14 February 1922.

[23] Kotsonouris (2004) 15–6, citing Minutes of the Dáil Éireann cabinet, 15 March 1922.

[24] *Iris Oifigiúil*, no 55, 1 August 1922.

[25] Under the Dáil Éireann Courts (Winding Up) Act 1923; see Kotsonouris (1994) and (2004). Kennedy et al (2003) say of the Dáil Éireann courts: 'Given the relative inexperience of the judges who conducted the courts and the extremely constrained and sometimes dangerous conditions in which they were endeavouring to administer justice, the experiment was remarkably successful' (33).

Éireann Supreme Court. It fell to him, as Chief Judicial Commissioner of Ireland, to wind up the Dáil courts efficiently. When the Courts of Justice Act 1924 came into force he was appointed a judge of the High Court, where he remained for 13 years before serving for an additional five years as a judge of what was by then the *official* Supreme Court of Ireland. In 1925 the Dáil even provided pensions for outgoing members of the Dáil Supreme Court.[26]

The Judiciary Committee 1923

The Courts of Justice Act 1924 was largely the result of work carried out by a Committee appointed by the Executive Council (ie, the government). As announced to the Dáil by William Cosgrave on 30 January 1923, the precise terms of reference of the Committee were:

> To advise the Executive Council of Saorstát Éireann in relation to the establishment in accordance with the Constitution of Courts for the exercise of the judicial power and the administration of justice in Saorstát Éireann, and the setting up of the offices and other machinery necessary or expedient for the official conduct of legal business.[27]

The Judiciary Committee, as it became known, consisted of 12 members, including the chairman Lord Glenavy, formerly known as Sir James Campbell. Campbell had served as the Lord Chief Justice of Ireland from 1916 to 1918 and as the last Lord Chancellor of Ireland from 1918 to 1921. He was therefore very much a member of the British establishment but he let it be known that he was sympathetic to home rule for Ireland. He was undoubtedly a hugely experienced legal practitioner with an intimate knowledge of the details of the Irish legal system.[28] He later claimed that without hesitation he found his experience as Chair of the Judiciary Committee to be the happiest of the many curious experiences he had had in a long and varied career,[29] although he was certainly not universally admired.[30] The other members of the Committee were the head of the Court of Appeal (Charles O'Connor MR), four other judges (James Creed Meredith and Cathaoir Mac Dáibhid [Cahir Davitt] of the Supreme Court of Dáil Éireann, Judge Johnston from the High Court and District Justice Lughaidh Breathnach [Louis Walsh]), the Attorney General (Aodh Ua Cinneidigh [Hugh Kennedy]), two practising barristers (Timothy Sullivan and John O'Byrne), two solicitors (Patrick Brady and Henry Murphy) and the President of the Dublin Chamber of Commerce (William Hewat). In his letter to each of these members, written the day before his announcement in the Dáil and published at the start of the Committee's report, William Cosgrave (named as Liam Mac Cosgair) stressed that 'there is nothing more prized among our newly won liberties than the liberty to construct a system of judiciary and an administration of law and justice according to the dictates of our own needs and after a pattern of our own designing'.[31] Cosgrave added that the current system for administering law and justice was 'a standing monument of alien government' and he urged the Committee to approach their task 'untrammelled by any regard to any of the existing system of judicature in

[26] Dáil Supreme Court (Pensions) Act 1925. [27] Dáil Debs, vol 2, col 1088.

[28] On the formation of the Irish Free State Cosgrave nominated him as a member of the Seanad (Senate); the other members then elected him as their chairperson.

[29] Seanad Debs, vol 2 no 11, p 4, 16 January 1924.

[30] Hugh Kennedy, Ireland's first Chief Justice, said of Glenavy in a letter to Louis Walsh that '[he] stops at nothing to gain his own end' and '[h]is advocacy is of the most thoroughly dishonest and disreputable character' (Hugh Kennedy Archive, UCD, P4/1125, 8 February 1924). Kennedy annotated Walsh's reply to this letter with 'Glenavy is a terrible old cod' (P4/1126, 9 February 1924).

[31] Cited by the All Party Oireachtas Committee on the Constitution in its *Fourth Progress Report: Courts and the Judiciary* (2003), Stationery Office, Dublin, para 10.

this country'. As it turned out, however, 'the pattern of our own designing' was in the end not very different from the pattern of British designing.

The Committee had its first sitting on 2 February 1923 and signed off its report on 25 May 1923. Its report was unanimous, but comprised just 26 pages, including preliminary documents. It recommended the establishment of a District Court (to replace the petty sessions courts), a Circuit Court (to replace the County Courts), a High Court and a Criminal Appeal Court (to replace the former Supreme Court of Judicature) and a Supreme Court of Appeal (to replace civil appeals to the Court of Appeal and any further appeals to the House of Lords or Privy Council). Somewhat disingenuously, and very unhelpfully, the report used the fact that its conclusions were agreed unanimously to support its statement that 'we have not thought it necessary to set out the reasons upon which our recommendations are based'.[32]

The section of the report on 'the Supreme Court of Appeal' covers just over two pages.[33] It proposed that the Supreme Court should consist of a President and two Judges, with the President of the High Court being an additional *ex officio* member,[34] and that one or more High Court judges should be eligible and required to sit in the Supreme Court if the President of that Court so requested because, owing to its difficulty or importance, an appeal needed to be heard by a court of five judges. The report also recommended that a member of the Supreme Court should preside in the Criminal Appeal Court, sitting alongside two High Court judges.[35] The Supreme Court itself should hear appeals from decisions of the High Court and deal directly with motions for a new trial or judgment in '*nisi prius*' cases, that is, cases heard by the High Court outside Dublin. To be appointed a judge of the High Court or Supreme Court a person should have practised at the Bar for at least 12 years, although time served as a Circuit judge would be deemed to be practice at the Bar. The proposed salary for Supreme Court judges was £3,000 per year, with the President of the Court receiving an additional £1,000.[36]

On none of these matters is the Committee's report at all detailed. There is absolutely no discussion of how any other country—least of all other British dominions—had chosen to organise their court systems. Neither the long experience of the USA nor the much shorter experience of the new democracies which emerged from the peace treaties following the First World War[37] was alluded to. More generally, the Committee does not appear to have considered what role the new Supreme Court might be encouraged to play in the development of the Irish Free State. This was despite the fact that Article 65 of the Constitution expressly conferred on the High Court the power to rule on 'the validity of any law having regard to the provisions of the Constitution', and Article 66 presumed that the Supreme Court would be able to consider appeals against all such rulings. This meant that the Supreme Court would be the final arbiter of whether any law, even one enacted by the national parliament, was valid. This was a notion which was completely alien to the British legal tradition, where Diceyan logic maintained that supreme power lay with Parliament and not with any court. It is not clear to what extent members of the Committee considered the experience of other common law countries before deciding what option to take on this issue.

[32] Judicial Committee (1923) 26. [33] Ibid, 23–5.

[34] The report recommended that the High Court should consist of six judges, one of whom would be designated as its President: ibid, 19.

[35] Ibid, 23.

[36] Elsewhere (at 22) the report suggests that the annual salary of the President of the High Court should be £3,000 and that of High Court judges should be £2,500.

[37] Austria, Estonia, Finland, Hungary, Latvia, Lithuania and Yugoslavia.

Supreme Courts Elsewhere at this Time

By 1924 none of the five other British dominions had created legal systems which gave the last word on the constitutionality of legislation to a domestic court. But nor did the Constitutions of those jurisdictions confer complete sovereignty on domestic legislatures. The essence of 'dominion' status was that such entities were still subject, in legal theory at least, to the mother country—the United Kingdom. The dominion legislatures had power to make laws for 'the peace, order and good government' of the territories,[38] but some residual law-making power was retained in London. More particularly, changes to the Constitutions of the dominions could occur only if Westminster consented to those changes. In addition, if a dispute arose within a dominion as to whether a law was valid or not the body which would ultimately decide the question was not the highest court in the dominion but the Judicial Committee of the Privy Council in London. That was the court, statutorily recognised since 1833,[39] which traditionally heard appeals from jurisdictions created by British overseas expansionism.[40] The one foreign common law court which had retained for itself the supreme authority over its country's legislature and government was the US Supreme Court. Yet the report of the Irish Free State's Judiciary Committee made no reference to that or any other overseas court.

Canada

In 1924 the Supreme Court of Canada was approaching its fiftieth birthday.[41] From 1875 it had comprised six judges, two of whom were drawn from the civil law system of Quebec. A seventh seat would be created in 1927, and two more in 1949, the year in which appeals to the Privy Council from Canada were finally abolished. The size of the Canadian Supreme Court has remained unchanged since then. But it took some time for the Court to win credibility after it was first created. In MacKinnon's words, its early years were 'extremely troublesome'.[42] By the mid-1920s it had still not found its feet, primarily because the shadow of the Privy Council still hung over it. In addition, most of its judges were not particularly activist. More to the point, if anyone in Ireland had been keen to model the Irish Supreme Court on its Canadian equivalent, there was little literature on the latter around which to fashion such imitation. Even as late as 1964 a future Chief Justice of Canada, Bora Laskin, was still lamenting the lack of attention given to its work:

> ... it is clear that the Court has not hitherto been regarded by the public at large as a potent element in Canadian self-government ... It is a fact that hardly anything has been written about its doctrine, and only recently has there been any professional curiosity manifested about its jurisdiction ... Indeed, neither the Court itself nor (with a few exceptions) its judges have been subjected to appraisal in any book or article.[43]

Laskin did add, perhaps disingenuously, that in the area of constitutional doctrine the Court 'has given adequate proof of responsible utterances',[44] but in his subsequent exegesis he makes it clear that only after the abolition of appeals to the Privy Council was

[38] On the significance of this phrase see the valuable study by Yusuf (2014).
[39] The Judicial Committee Act 1833, largely still in force.
[40] See the written history and useful video presentation on the Judicial Committee's website.
[41] Much of what follows derives from Iacobucci (2002) 28–33. [42] MacKinnon (1964) 122.
[43] Laskin (1964), 127, footnote omitted. [44] Ibid, 128.

the Canadian Supreme Court truly 'free to adopt its own canons of judicial behaviour'.[45] Prior to then:

> The Court as a whole appeared loath to strike out in new directions except where the Judicial Committee itself had given a lead ... The task of the Supreme Court was not to interpret the constitution but rather to interpret what the Privy Council said the constitution meant.[46]

Similar concerns were raised by others. Cheffins described the Supreme Court as 'playing a rather moderate role'; he thought it was 'being by-passed as an important arena for the making of vital constitutional decisions'.[47] Weiler was more severe in his critique, which he summed up in one short sentence: 'Our judges share an outmoded and unduly narrow conception of the role of law in courts.'[48] McCormick writes that in 1950 'the Supreme Court of Canada was a minor blip on the Canadian political scene ... The 1950s and 1960s saw flickering moments of promise but little in the way of substantial change'.[49]

The disregard of the Canadian Supreme Court by the Irish Free State's Judiciary Committee is nevertheless surprising given that the Anglo-Irish Treaty of 1921 makes several references to Canada as the constitutional model which the Irish Free State should follow. Article 2, for example, provided that:

> Subject to the provisions hereinafter set out the position of the Irish Free State in relation to the Imperial Parliament and Government and otherwise shall be that of the Dominion of Canada, and the law, practice and constitutional usage governing the relationship of the Crown or the representative of the Crown and of the Imperial Parliament to the Dominion of Canada shall govern their relationship to the Irish Free State.

The first Chief Justice of Ireland, Hugh Kennedy, was to pay tribute to the Canadian model when he addressed the Canadian Bar Association in 1928, but his remarks relate more to the role of the Crown, parliament and government than to the judiciary.[50]

Australia

By the Commonwealth of Australia Constitution Act 1900, enacted by the Westminster Parliament, the name given to the country's Federal Supreme Court was 'the High Court'.[51] Its first judges were sworn in on 6 October 1903. They were granted original jurisdiction, usually exercised by a single judge, as well as appellate jurisdiction, usually exercised by all the judges. From 1903 to 1906 the Court had three judges, from 1906 to 1912 it had five, and from 1912, except for the period from 1931 to 1942 when it was reduced to six, it had seven, the number which it still maintains today.

The High Court's original jurisdiction included matters in which the Commonwealth of Australia itself was suing or being sued and matters between States within the Commonwealth, between residents of different States or between a State and a resident of another State.[52] Its appellate jurisdiction included appeals from any decision of the High Court itself when exercising its original jurisdiction, from any other federal court, from the Supreme Court of any Australian State and from the Inter-State Commission.[53] The 1900 Act added that, until the Australian Parliament provided otherwise, conditions already attaching to appeals to the Privy Council from Supreme Courts of Australian States should

[45] Ibid, 150. [46] Ibid, 143. [47] Cheffins (1966) 259. [48] Weiler (1974) 4.
[49] McCormick (2000) 3.
[50] Kennedy (1928b). He also addressed the American Bar Association during the same trip: Kennedy (1928a).
[51] s 71. [52] Ibid s 73. [53] Ibid s 75. This Commission is explained in the next paragraph.

apply to appeals from the High Court,[54] but unless the High Court itself gave leave to appeal no appeal was to lie to the Privy Council against decisions on the limits of the constitutional powers of the Commonwealth compared with those of any State or on the limits of the constitutional powers of any two or more States.[55] In other cases the Crown's prerogative to grant special leave to appeal from the High Court to the Privy Council was preserved, as it had been in Canada.[56]

In the years leading up to the mid-1920s the Australian High Court exerted its authority more ostentatiously than the Canadian Supreme Court managed to do. This mostly manifested itself in decisions on what constituted 'judicial power' for the purposes of the 1900 Constitution.[57] Thus, in *New South Wales v The Commonwealth* (the Wheat case) the High Court found that the conferment of adjudicatory powers relating to inter-State trade and commerce on the Inter-State Commission, an institution provided for by section 101 of the Constitution, was unconstitutional,[58] and in *In re Judiciary and Navigation Acts* the High Court struck down a provision in the Judiciary Act 1903 purporting to confer on the High Court the power to issue advisory opinions on whether any Act of the Commonwealth Parliament was valid.[59] More generally, in *R v Kidman* the High Court held that the Federal Parliament had the power to make even criminal laws operate retrospectively.[60] In addition, in the landmark case of *Amalgamated Society of Engineers v Adelaide Steamship Co Ltd* (the Engineers case) the High Court departed from established case law concerning the powers and immunities of State governments in order to hold that the Commonwealth of Australia, representing the Crown, was bound to adhere to the Constitution, which should be interpreted in a traditional common law fashion, that is, literally.[61] In this decision the relevance of precedents from the US Supreme Court was denied and the Australian Constitution came of age as a fundamental law. This was just four years before Ireland enacted its Courts of Justice Act 1924.

South Africa

Ellison Kahn, writing in 1960,[62] gives a clear account of the structure and powers accorded to the Supreme Court of South Africa by the South Africa Act 1909.[63] The supreme courts of the former colonies of Cape Colony, Natal, Orange River Colony and Transvaal became provincial divisions of the Supreme Court of South Africa, which comprised an Appellate Division, Provincial Divisions and Local Divisions. The seat of the Appellate Division, controversially, was placed in Bloemfontein, the relatively remote capital of the province of Orange Free State (formerly Orange River Colony). The Appellate Division at first comprised a Chief Justice, two permanent 'ordinary judges of appeal' and two additional judges of appeal who would be assigned to the Court as required from its Provincial or Local Divisions, but in 1920 the labels of 'ordinary' and 'additional' judges were dropped[64] and the Supreme Court simply comprised the Chief Justice and four judges of appeal. The normal quorum was three judges, but in appeals from a court where two or more judges had sat, the quorum was first set at five and then, after 1927,[65] at four. The number of seats on the Court

[54] Ibid, s 73 (final sentence). [55] Ibid, s 74. [56] Ibid, final paragraph.

[57] Section 71 of the Constitution. See Kirk (2001); Paton (1952); Sawer (1948). The High Court also sought to treat Australian State Constitutions as a form of higher law which could not be impliedly repealed or amended, but the Privy Council overturned that approach in *McCawley v The King* [1920] AC 69.

[58] (1915) 20 CLR 54. [59] (1921) 29 CLR 257. [60] (1915) 20 CLR 425.

[61] (1920) 28 CLR 129. See Mason (2003) and Paton (1952) 61–9. [62] Kahn (1960) 249–67.

[63] Pt VI (ss 95–116). [64] Appellate Division Act, No 12 of 1920, s 3.

[65] Administration of Justice (Further Amendment) Act, No 11 of 1927, s 1.

was gradually increased over the years and in 1996 the Appellate Division was renamed the Supreme Court of Appeal of South Africa. Today it has a President, a Deputy President and 23 other judges.[66]

In line with British Diceyan tradition, the South Africa Act 1909 did not confer any powers on South African judges to review legislation. Section 59 declared that the country's Parliament 'shall have full power to make laws for the peace, order, and good government of the Union', but the Supreme Court soon issued a self-denying ordinance in *R v McChlery*, where it held that whether an Act of Parliament met that criterion was a matter to be determined by Parliament itself and not by any court.[67] By the mid-1920s the Supreme Court had not issued any decisions which would have illuminated the path for Irish politicians who were seeking a special role for the Irish Supreme Court. Following the ending of apartheid in 1994 and the adoption of a new Constitution in 1996, the Supreme Court of Appeal of South Africa no longer deals with constitutional issues at all. Instead these are reserved for the Constitutional Court some 400 miles away in Johannesburg.[68]

Newfoundland and New Zealand

The two remaining dominions, although more similar to Ireland in terms of size of population, would have had little to offer the Irish Free State's Judiciary Committee during its deliberations in 1923. They became dominions in 1907 and their courts were no more powerful than those in the other dominions. In 1924 appeals from Newfoundland still went to the Judicial Committee of the Privy Council and indeed in that year the Council was in the midst of dealing with a long-running dispute between Newfoundland and Quebec as to where exactly the boundary should be drawn between them.[69] New Zealand preserved its links with the Privy Council until the twenty-first century. A Supreme Court was set up in 2004 to replace the role of the Privy Council[70] but the final decision by the Privy Council in a dispute originating in New Zealand was made as recently as 2015.[71] The relationship of New Zealand and of Ireland to the former colonial power has always been very different.

European nations and the USA

As Leo Kohn points out, by 1924 the power to judicially review legislation was still a relatively recent development anywhere in Europe:

> ... until the new era of constitution-making which followed the European war, the conception of the review of legislation, judicial or otherwise, was not generally accepted on the Continent ... It was essentially the American Courts—heirs to the traditions of the Common Law Judiciary—which established the doctrine that the Acts of the Legislature could be reviewed by an independent agency as to their conformity with the Constitution and that this power was vested in the civil Courts.[72]

[66] See the description at www.justice.gov.za/sca/aboutsca.htm.

[67] 1912 AD 199, 219–20, cited in Kahn (1960) 146, n 49.

[68] See www.constitutionalcourt.org.za/home.htm. See too Hadjigeorgiu (2014); Roux (2013); Klug (2009).

[69] The Privy Council ruled in favour of Newfoundland: see www.bailii.org/uk/cases/UKPC/1927/1927_25.html.

[70] Supreme Court Act 2002 (NZ).

[71] *Pora v The Queen* [2015] UKPC 9, [2016] 1 NZLR 277 (where a man's convictions for rape and murder were quashed after he had served 22 years in prison).

[72] Kohn (1932) 350–1.

Kohn observed that in the USA '[i]ndividualistic interpretations of liberal principles have thwarted measures of social reform enacted with the strong support of legislature and electorate' and that it was therefore not surprising that the constitutions of new European nations had vested judicial review in special Constitutional Courts 'of semi-political composition'.[73] Strange as it may seem, it is possibly one of these European courts that most influenced the introduction of constitutional review in the Irish Free State. The Constitution of Austria, agreed in 1920, expressly provided for judicial review of legislation and created a Constitutional Court (*Verfassungsgerichtshof*) with the remit of adjudicating on applications for such review.[74] Ireland's 1922 Constitution was the next European constitution to provide for such review. As to whether the US Constitution was indirectly influential remains controversial. While the Irish Constitution was being drafted a letter was apparently written to a British administrator, Lionel Curtis, by Professor Felix Frankfurter, later a US Supreme Court Justice from 1939 to 1962, inquiring whether the provision on judicial review was derived from the USA's experience. Unfortunately there is no record of any reply to this letter.[75]

At the time Kohn was writing (1932) the power of constitutional review had been used only once to limit the applicability of an Act of the Oireachtas. This was in the Court of Appeal's decision in *R (O'Brien) v Military Governor of the North Down Union Internment Camp*.[76] Mrs O'Brien had been interned by the army and she claimed this was unlawful, firstly because there was no state of war or rebellion in Ireland at the time and secondly because the detention could not be justified under the Public Safety (Emergency Powers) Act 1923 because that Act had been passed just a day before the Court's hearing and was still liable to be suspended if enough members of the Oireachtas took advantage of the provisions of Article 47 of the 1922 Constitution.[77] Molony CJ and Ronan LJ agreed with these arguments and ordered Mrs O'Brien's release. They did not accept that the 1923 Act was exempt from Article 47, because no evidence had been produced that both Houses of the Oireachtas had deemed it to be an Act necessary for the immediate preservation of the public peace, health or safety. The State's legal team in this case included Hugh Kennedy and Timothy Sullivan, but Ronan LJ rejected their interpretation of the legislation as 'ridiculous and absurd'.[78] The State, however, had the last word because a day after the Court's decision it secured the enactment of the Public Safety (Emergency Powers) (No 2) Act 1923, which set out the text of the earlier Act in a Schedule and declared in section 2(1) that the second Act was 'necessary for the immediate preservation of the public peace and safety and accordingly the provisions of Article 47 of the Constitution of Saorstát Eireann shall not apply to this Act'.

Leo Kohn rightly predicted that the power of constitutional review would not be frequently used as long as the Free State's Constitution permitted amendments to be made

[73] Ibid, 351–2.

[74] Cahillane (2011b) 9, citing Grant (1934). Cahillane points out (at 3–4) that copies of post-War constitutions were made available to members of the committee set up to draft Ireland's 1922 Constitution and she suggests (at 9) that the Czechoslovakian model may also have been an inspiration to that committee. For a modern assessment of Austria's Constitutional Court see Gamper and Palermo (2009).

[75] See Cahillane (2011b) 9, n 39, citing an extract from a 2001 thesis by Gerard Hogan, later a Court of Appeal judge in Ireland.

[76] [1924] 1 IR 32.

[77] This allowed any Bill to be suspended for 90 days if this was demanded from the President of the Executive Council by 40 per cent of the members of the Dáil or a majority of the members of the Seanad not more than seven days after the Bill was passed. The Bill could then be submitted to a referendum if certain conditions were fulfilled. But Art 47 did not apply to Money Bills or Bills which were declared by both Houses to be necessary for the immediate preservation of the public peace, health or safety.

[78] [1924] 1 IR 32, 51.

to it by ordinary legislation[79] but that thereafter the judges' interpretation of fundamental declarations in the Constitution 'may indeed be fraught with profound import'.[80]

The Courts of Justice Act 1924

Less than three weeks after receiving a copy of the Judiciary Committee's report in May 1923 William Cosgrave wrote to Lord Glenavy to express the Executive Council's thanks for the quality and swiftness of the Committee's work.[81] He announced that a Bill would be introduced in the Dáil at an early date 'on the lines of your report'. The Courts of Justice Bill was indeed given a first reading in the Dáil on 31 July 1923, but its passage could not be completed prior to the general election on 27 August and so it had to receive another first reading in the new Dáil on 20 September.[82] Unfortunately the Dáil and Seanad debates on the legislation, which eventually emerged some seven months later, reveal no greater consciousness of other countries' court systems than the Judiciary Committee itself had displayed. Nor was anything said about the way in which the new Supreme Court might use its power to declare legislation unconstitutional.

The most interesting intervention in the debates was by Lord Glenavy himself, one of whose roles at the time was that of Deputy Speaker (Leas-Chathaoirleach) in the Seanad. In January 1924 he said that members of the Dáil did not yet realise the tremendous constitutional change that had been made as a result of the Treaty and the Constitution:

> It is one that tends to the permanent liberty and security of the subject. It is a protection that no member of the Dáil or no member of the Seanad should allow to be lightly tampered with or interfered with, because it contains within itself the greatest charter of liberty that any country or any nation could wish or hope to have. I refer to the fact that the Constitution has adopted the great theory, call it what you like, of the United States and Canada, and of most modern Governments, that is to say, they have reduced the Constitution of the Irish Free State into writing, and they have, in addition to that, created by statute, and by the Constitution, the principle that our judges in the future are to be 'independent in the exercise of their functions'.[83]

These exaggerated claims for the benefits of a written Constitution and an independent judiciary had little to do with the architecture of the court system or the actual powers of the Supreme Court as provided for in the Bill which was under debate. They also left out of account the outstanding feature of the US Supreme Court, which is that it can strike down legislation that is deemed to be contrary to the federal Constitution, a power which the US Supreme Court claimed for itself in *Marbury v Madison*,[84] there being no provision to that effect in the 1789 Constitution.

Lord Glenavy did add that in his view 'the permanent guarantee and the basis of all personal freedom and of liberty in the USA is to be found in the courage and the conscience of the Courts and their perfect freedom from all Government control'. While he conceded that in theory this was what the Irish Free State's Constitution also provided for, he did not cite the Court of Appeal's decision in *O'Brien*,[85] or any other decision, as an example of the judicial conscience operating in Ireland. Instead he merely railed against the

[79] On which see Chap 3 below, 32-4. [80] Kohn (1932) 353.

[81] Report of Judiciary Committee (1923) 8.

[82] Its final stage in the Dáil took place on 11 December. The Seanad considered the Bill principally on 16 January 1924 (second stage) and 5 and 20 March (report stage). The Dáil approved 42 of the 44 Seanad amendments on 2 April, and the Seanad accepted that position on 3 April.

[83] See Seanad Debs, vol 2, no 11, cols 410–11, 16 January 1924. [84] 5 US 137 (1803).

[85] Note 76 above.

government's proposal to allow the Minister for Home Affairs, in conjunction with the Minister for Finance and with the concurrence of certain members of the courts, to make Rules of Court (including for the Supreme Court) through which supposedly independent judges were to exercise their jurisdiction as regards pleading, practice and procedure. He thought such humiliation of the judiciary was unprecedented,[86] and was especially upset at the prospect of the government telling the judges what kind of costume they should wear in court,[87] there having been a recent press report that the Attorney General (Hugh Kennedy) wanted to dispense with judges' wigs and gowns.

Despite being supported in part by at least two other senators,[88] Lord Glenavy's concern about judicial independence was dismissed by William Cosgrave, who was attending the Seanad debate as President of the Executive Council. Cosgrave pointed out that the Minister for Home Affairs would still be unable to make Rules of Court without the concurrence of the Rules Committees and that under clause 97 of the Bill Rules of Court would in any event have to be laid before each House of the Oireachtas. In March 1924 there was a long debate in the Seanad on an amendment proposed by Samuel Brown which would have deleted the clause authorising Rules of Court to be made but after fraught exchanges involving Seanad personalities such as William Butler Yeats and Oliver St John Gogarty,[89] the amendment was defeated by one vote and the clause was allowed to stand.[90] Shortly afterwards the Attorney General appeared before the Seanad and won approval for an amendment to clause 97 requiring each House of the Oireachtas to approve draft Rules of Court before they could come into operation.[91]

The Courts of Justice Act 1924 very much reflected more generally the proposals in the 1923 report. Considerable thought was given to reform of the lower courts, but remarkably little attention was paid to the higher courts. It does not seem to have occurred to the politicians, or to their legal advisers, that the Supreme Court would be acquiring powers which could make it at least as significant a player in the building of the new nation as the government and the legislature. The spirit of the times, steeped as it was in the Diceyan glorification of the sovereignty of Parliament, simply did not envisage a Supreme Court which would actively develop a peculiarly Irish approach to constitutional review.[92] It is interesting, too, that no mention was made in the parliamentary debates of the role which the Judicial Committee of the Privy Council would continue to play in Ireland's legal system. Of course the Irish Supreme Court has never become anything like as powerful an institution as the US Supreme Court: the Oireachtas did not want it to develop into a body which might restrict the right of elected representatives to shape the country as they thought best. Contrary to what might have been in the minds of the members of the Judiciary Committee in 1923, any presumption that the doctrine of parliamentary sovereignty was being put to death in Ireland was very wide of the mark.

The first three judges of the Supreme Court were appointed on 5 June 1924[93] and the Court began operating immediately. The first of its decisions to be reported in the *Irish Reports* was *Keelan v Garvey*,[94] where the Court overturned Molony LCJ's decision and confirmed

[86] Note 83 above, col 412. [87] Ibid, cols 413–17.

[88] Sir Thomas Esmonde at cols 422–4 and Mr Bagwell at cols 428–9.

[89] Seanad Debs, vol 2, no 19, cols 854–84, 5 March 1924. [90] It became s 36 of the 1924 Act.

[91] Seanad Debs, vol 2, no 55, cols 1154–55, 20 March 1924. This became s 101 of the 1924 Act.

[92] Mac Cormaic (2016), at 32, sums up the situation thus: 'the rhetoric of rupture belied the relative modesty of the changes, at least at the apex of the courts system'.

[93] See Chap 5 below, 90–1.

[94] [1925] IR 1, heard on 3–4 November 1924 and decided on 9 December 1924.

a man's title to a farm in County Monaghan which he had abandoned in 1897 but to which he had returned in 1923 after his wife's death. A decision taken a few months earlier was reported shortly after *Keelan v Garvey*. This was *In re the Estate of Sir E C Nugent*,[95] which was about whether particular land was excluded from the Land Commission's vesting powers conferred by the Land Act 1923. In the early years of the life of the Supreme Court most of the cases considered were as humdrum as those two.

[95] [1925] IR 15, heard on 13 and 16 June 1924 and decided on 3 July 1924.

3

The Supreme Court and the Irish Free State

The Irish Free State existed from 1922 until 1937, when a new Constitution was enacted stripping the country of any lingering ties to the United Kingdom and changing its name to Ireland. The transformation can be traced back to the decision by a majority of anti-Treaty politicians to abandon their support for armed struggle and engage only in democratic processes. The trigger for their *volte-face* was the failure of the Irish government to wring any concessions from the British government concerning the delineation of the border in Ireland. That issue had been assigned to a Boundary Commission, in line with a provision in the Anglo-Irish Treaty of 1921,[1] but in 1925 the Commission's report was suppressed and instead the governments of the Irish Free State, Northern Ireland and the United Kingdom agreed to keep the border exactly where it was. The provisional conclusions of the Commission's report had not been as favourable to the Irish Free State government as it had hoped, so rather than accepting accusations of failure, it agreed in December 1925 to park the matter indefinitely in return for a waiver by the British government of the Free State's obligation under the Treaty to pay a sum of money equating to Ireland's share of the United Kingdom's public debt when Ireland became a dominion.[2] The agreement was given legal force in the Irish Free State by the Treaty (Confirmation of Amending Agreement) Act 1925.

Following an extraordinary meeting of Sinn Féin in March 1926, where delegates could not agree on a way forward, Éamon de Valera resigned as leader and set about creating a new party. It took the name Fianna Fáil, which is Irish for 'soldiers of destiny' or, on another view 'warriors of Ireland', Fál being an ancient word for Ireland synonymous with Éire.[3] In the election to the fifth Dáil in June 1927 Fianna Fáil won 44 of the 153 seats, almost defeating the pro-Treaty party, Cumann na nGaedheal, which won 47.[4] Sinn Féin won only five. Like Sinn Féin, Fianna Fáil representatives had stood for election on the basis that if they were successful they would not take their seats. But on 10 July 1927 the assassination took place of Kevin O'Higgins, Vice-President of the Executive Council—in effect the Deputy Prime Minister. When previously serving as Minister for Justice, O'Higgins had authorised the execution of dozens of republican prisoners and was therefore a hate figure in many republicans' eyes.[5] In response to the murder the Dáil passed the Electoral (Amendment) (No 2) Act 1927, which required every candidate in future elections to swear that, if elected, he or she would take their seat in the Dáil. Knowing this legislation was in the pipeline, and contrary to Sinn Féin's stance, Fianna Fáil's elected members decided in August to sign the Oath of Allegiance and take their seats.[6] Less than four months after the previous election, voters were asked to return to the polling stations in September 1927.

[1] Art 12. [2] Art 5. The Boundary Commission's report was eventually published only in1969.

[3] The party's official title today is 'Fianna Fáil, The Republican Party'.

[4] Two seats were won by independent republicans who did not agree with either Fianna Fáil or Sinn Féin.

[5] One estimate is that he signed 77 death warrants: see http://comeheretome.com/2010/11/24/the-assassination-of-kevin-ohiggins-1927; one related to Rory O'Connor, who had been best man at O'Higgins' wedding in 1921.

[6] The 1927 Act meant that Sinn Féin could no longer put people up for election at all, since its candidates were all unwilling to forswear the use of violence. The party did not abandon abstentionism in Ireland until 1986 and did not win a seat in the Dáil until 1997; in 2016 it won 23 of the 158 seats.

On this occasion Cumann na nGaedheal won 62 seats and Fianna Fáil won 57. Cosgrave continued as President of the Executive Council, with the support of a small number of Farmers Party representatives. During the following four years Fianna Fáil consolidated its position as a plausible government and when the next general election took place in 1932 the tables were turned: Fianna Fáil won 72 seats as opposed to Cumann na nGaedheal's 57 and the former was able to form a government with the support of seven Labour deputies. A year later Fianna Fáil capitalised on its success in an early fresh election, winning 77 of the 153 seats. This was a remarkable turnaround in Irish politics: from their 'defeat' in the debate over the Anglo-Irish Treaty of 1921 it had taken just 11 years for the largest section of the anti-Treaty faction to gain power in the country. Sinn Féin remained outside of government and in favour of abstentionism. As Feeney put it, de Valera 'had quite simply stolen republicans' clothing ... Sinn Féin went into rapid decline, then became lost in the political wilderness'.[7]

Immediately after becoming the head of government in February 1932 Éamon de Valera set about completing the struggle for Ireland's complete separation from the United Kingdom. This culminated in the adoption of a new Constitution in 1937 but even before then he did all he could to consolidate republicanism. One of his bugbears was the fact that the Irish Supreme Court was still not the absolute final court for deciding matters of Irish law: some issues could still be taken to the Privy Council in London. At the same time, de Valera did not want the Supreme Court to acquire too much power in case the judges used it to thwart his plans for a more republican constitution.

Appeals to the Privy Council

As noted in Chapter 2,[8] Article 66 of the Irish Free State Constitution said that the Supreme Court was to be given appellate jurisdiction over all decisions of the High Court and its decisions in those appeals were to be 'final and conclusive'. Nevertheless, this categorical prohibition on any further appeal was immediately undermined by the very next sentence of Article 66, which read:

> Provided that nothing in this Constitution shall impair the right of any person to petition His Majesty for special leave to appeal from the Supreme Court to His Majesty in Council or the right of His Majesty to grant such leave.

The oddness of this provision is all the more stark given the statement in Article 75 of the Constitution that until the Supreme Court was established the provisions of Article 66 concerning the finality of decisions were to be applied to decisions of the Court of Appeal, which was *pro tem* the top court in Ireland. As far as the British were concerned, however, the Judicial Committee of the Privy Council was a natural final destination for disputes about the common law in countries other than Britain itself: the first 'foreign' location from which such appeals were accepted, in the fourteenth century, was the Channel Islands, but as Britain's overseas possessions expanded more and more places became eligible to submit appeals. The online catalogue of cases heard by the Privy Council between 1798 and 1998 reveals that there were 111 locations from which appeals emanated, including 26 in

[7] Feeney (2002) 159 and 161. The new government repealed the Electoral (Amendment) (No 2) Act 1927 by the Electoral (Amendment) Act 1933.

[8] At 10 and 13.

Africa and 39 in South and South-East Asia.[9] The Privy Council's own website claims that in the 1930s the Judicial Committee was the final court of appeal for more than a quarter of the world. The Judicial Committee did sometimes include senior judges working in the territories from which appeals were being brought, but the perception persisted that the Committee was essentially a group of British judges continuing to have the final say over legal matters in former colonies.

One of the causes of the apparent contradiction in the 1922 Constitution was the continuing uncertainty surrounding the meaning of the Irish Free State's status as a 'dominion'. As Mansergh points out,[10] even the British government did not know what this term meant at the very time it was negotiating the Anglo-Irish Treaty in 1921. In modern terms we might say that there was a 'constructive ambiguity' about the word which was convenient for all concerned at that period. From Britain's point of view it was additionally useful that the five existing dominions disagreed about what the status entailed. Mansergh shows how, at the Imperial Conference in 1921, the Prime Minister of Australia differed from his Canadian and South African counterparts in wanting to leave the term undefined.[11]

When Canada became the first area to be granted dominion status by the British North America Act 1867 the pre-existing right to appeal to the Privy Council from the former colonies within Canada was not interfered with. This continued to be the case even after Canada created its own Supreme Court in 1875, meaning that appeals could be taken to the Privy Council from any of the top provincial courts without having to go first to the Supreme Court of Canada. The Criminal Procedure Amendment Act 1888 purported to remove the right of appeal to the Privy Council in all criminal cases, but in 1926 the Privy Council itself held, in *Nadan v The King*,[12] that the provision in the 1888 Act was inoperative because under the Colonial Laws Validity Act 1865 the Canadian Parliament did not have the authority to enact it. This decision was obviously of great interest to the five other dominions which by then had been created. It resonated particularly with the Executive Council of the Irish Free State because, as noted in Chapter 2, the 1921 Treaty and the 1922 Constitution stated that the relationship between the Irish Free State on the one hand and the Imperial Parliament, government and Crown on the other should be the same as that between Canada and those institutions.[13]

As Harkness puts it, the existence of a right of appeal to the Privy Council was 'one of the more regular taunts which the Irish Opposition could fling at their government', and the government itself felt that it was 'the chief slur on its claim to sovereignty'.[14] To some extent the change to making the Privy Council the final court of appeal for the Irish Free State, rather than the House of Lords, which had played that role prior to partition, was a symbolic one, since for the most part the judges sitting in the Privy Council were precisely the same individuals who sat as Lords of Appeal in the House of Lords. Furthermore, several Lords of Appeal had comprehensive knowledge of Irish law.[15] But to many in the Irish Free State the mere possibility of an appeal from that jurisdiction being heard by a court outside Ireland constituted an unwelcome reminder that they were still not complete masters of their own legal system andsomehow remained tied, albeit indirectly, to the British Crown and its titled judges. Kevin O'Higgins, who was the Minister for Justice and External Affairs in the Provisional Government after the Anglo-Irish Treaty was signed in 1921 and then

[9] The database, compiled at the University of Exeter, contains details of 9,368 cases. On the Privy Council's work more generally see Mohr (2011), and for comments on appeals from the Irish Free State and on the Colonial Laws Validity Act see Mohr (2002) and (2008). See too Gwynn (1928) Chap 6.

[10] Mansergh (1991) 200–2.

[11] Ibid.

[12] [1926] AC 482.

[13] Chap 2 above, 15.

[14] Harkness (1969) 113.

[15] See 9 above.

Minister for Justice in the Executive Council when the new Constitution took effect in 1922, made no secret of his antipathy to the idea that appeals could go to the Privy Council. Mohr reveals that in 1922 Irish representatives also tried to use the cost of taking an appeal to the Privy Council as a reason for doing away with the appeal.[16]

The decision in *Nadan v The King*, referred to above, prompted the Canadian government to raise the issue of appeals to the Privy Council at the next meeting of Britain's six dominions at the Imperial Conference, held in London in 1926. The major outcome of that event was the Balfour Declaration,[17] which confirmed that each dominion was an 'autonomous community within the British Empire', that each had equal status with the others, and that no dominion was subordinate to the United Kingdom. Moreover, for the first time the dominions were stated to be 'freely associated as members of the British Commonwealth of Nations'.[18] To an extent this wording was borrowed from Article 1 of the Irish Free State's 1922 Constitution, where the Irish Free State was declared to be 'a co-equal member of the Community of Nations forming the British Commonwealth of Nations'. In his detailed exegesis of that Constitution, published in 1925, MacNeill describes the conversion of the British Empire into 'the Community of Nations forming the British Commonwealth of Nations' as 'a striking illustration of the powers of constitutional development by which momentous political changes have been effected without any legislative enactments whatever producing a startling divergence of law and custom, of theory and practice'.[19]

MacNeill goes on to explain the contrast between the legal position of dominions as mere dependencies of Great Britain to be administered for the convenience of the latter and the actual position of dominions in accordance with the conventions of the British Empire's unwritten constitution.[20] In the course of doing so he cites William Cosgrave's comments to the Empire Parliamentary Association on the very day, 6 December 1922, when the Irish Free State Constitution took effect: Cosgrave relied upon a piece in *The Times* by the then leader of the opposition in Britain, Arthur Balfour, where he asserted that dominion parliaments were 'absolutely independent'[21] and also an address in 1919 by the Prime Minister of South Africa, General Jan Smuts, in which he said: 'We have received the position of absolute equality and freedom, not only among other States of the Empire, but among other nations of the world.'[22] Clearly the Privy Council's decision in *Nadan v The King* did not sit comfortably alongside that stance.

The Report of the 1926 Imperial Conference disclosed that it was no part of British government policy 'that questions affecting judicial appeals should be determined otherwise than in accordance with the wishes of the part of the Empire primarily affected'.[23] The same document explicitly stated that '[t]he question of some immediate change in the present conditions governing appeals from the Irish Free State was not pressed in relation to the present Conference, though it was made clear that the right was reserved to bring up the matter again at the next Imperial Conference for discussion in relation to the facts of this particular case'. William Cosgrave attended the conference as President of the Executive Council of the Irish Free State and he endorsed the Declaration, his position on appeals to the Privy

[16] Mohr (2011) 9, citing a memo from Arthur Griffith to David Lloyd-George dated 2 June 1922.

[17] A copy of the Declaration is available at https://www.foundingdocs.gov.au/scan-sid-13.html. It is also at Cmd 2768. At that time Balfour was Lord President of the (Privy) Council. In 1917 an earlier Balfour Declaration set down British government support for the creation of a Jewish state in Palestine.

[18] Ibid, Report, 2.

[19] MacNeill (1925) 8. MacNeill, a Protestant from Donegal, sat as an Irish Nationalist MP in the UK Parliament from 1887 until 1918; he was also a barrister and a professor of law at the National University of Ireland.

[20] Ibid, 8–25. [21] *The Times*, 7 November 1911, 11. [22] MacNeill (1925) 21.

[23] Note 17 above, 6.

Council having apparently been softened by the urging of Lord Birkenhead and the refusal of support at that time from the Canadian Prime Minister, Mackenzie King.[24]

Appeals in practice

The climb-down by Cosgrave was all the more surprising given that a year earlier, despite having previously dismissed applications for leave to appeal in three cases,[25] the Privy Council had granted special leave to appeal in two Irish cases. The first, *Lynham v Butler*,[26] concerned the interpretation of the Land Act 1923, a matter which the government of the Irish Free State understandably considered to be solely one for the State's own courts to determine. To thwart the hearing of the appeal in the Privy Council the Oireachtas enacted the Land Act 1926, which simply declared, in effect, that the interpretation of the 1923 Act favoured by the Irish High Court, and confirmed by the Supreme Court, was and always had been the correct interpretation of the Act. Since there was no gainsaying the authoritativeness of that enactment, even by the Privy Council, the appeal had to be withdrawn and a constitutional crisis was averted.[27]

The temperature was significantly raised by the second case, *Wigg and Cochrane v Attorney General for the Irish Free State*,[28] in which two Crown civil servants who had retired from their posts when the Irish Free State was established sued the Attorney General of the Irish Free State (at that time John O'Byrne[29]) because in their eyes they had not received an adequate retirement allowance as promised by Article 10 of the Anglo-Irish Treaty of 1921 and Article 78 of the Irish Free State Constitution. Article 10 said that the government of the Irish Free State agreed to pay 'fair compensation on terms not less favourable than those accorded by [the Government of Ireland Act 1920] to officials who retire in consequence of the change of government', while Article 78 provided that civil servants should be entitled to the benefit of Article 10. At first instance Meredith J allowed the claim[30] but on appeal the recently established Supreme Court of Ireland reversed that decision.[31] O'Connor J reached the not unreasonable conclusion that as civil servants did not have any legal *right* to a retirement allowance prior to the partition of Ireland, they could not have acquired such a right merely because the Irish Free State had been carved out of the United Kingdom. He pointed out that the Government of Ireland Act 1920 had intended to continue the former statutory system for awarding retirement allowances, under which the determination of a Civil Service Committee would be 'final and conclusive'.[32] He then stated:

> I can find nothing whatever in the body of the Act of 1920 which suggests an intent on the part of the Legislature to convert a claim which gave no legal right capable of enforcement in a Court of law into a claim giving a right of action.[33]

There was a strong dissent in the Supreme Court by Johnston J, whose judgment is couched in language close to that of natural law. Having lauded the Anglo-Irish Treaty as an 'epoch-making charter' which had brought about a 'great peaceful revolution',[34] the learned judge

[24] Harkness (1969) 114–15.

[25] *Hull v McKenna; The Freeman's Journal v Fernstrom; The Freeman's Journal v Traesliberi* [1926] IR 402.

[26] [1925] 2 IR 231.

[27] Kohn (1932) 358; Lyons (1973) 515–17.

[28] [1927] AC 674, [1927] 1 IR 285 (Viscount Cave LC, Viscount Haldane, Viscount Dunedin and Viscount Finlay).

[29] O'Byrne had succeeded Hugh Kennedy as Attorney General when the latter became the first Chief Justice of Ireland in May 1924. He later served as a Supreme Court judge from 1940 to 1954.

[30] [1924] 58 ILTR 131, reprinted at [1927] 1 IR 293.

[31] [1925] 1 IR 149 (O'Connor and FitzGibbon JJ, Johnston J dissenting).

[32] Government of Ireland Act 1920, ss 55 and 56.

[33] [1925] 1 IR 149, 160.

[34] Ibid, 164.

stressed that the plaintiffs were not seeking superannuation allowances from their own governmental employers but rather were 'seeking compensation from an entirely new governmental authority, who have bound themselves by Act of Parliament to pay it'.[35] He therefore saw Article 10 as giving the plaintiffs 'a definite legal right' and he prayed in aid the early English cases on administrative law[36] to bolster his view that when they are carrying out their statutory duties ministerial departments are subject to the general control of the courts:

> The principal matter involved in this action goes far beyond the mere question of the exercise of discretion by the Ministry. The defendant claims that the Minister has the power to withhold compensation entirely from the plaintiffs. That is a basic matter, in respect of which, in my opinion, the plaintiffs are entitled to a declaration form the High Court of the Free State; and I cannot help thinking that my view is very much more in consonance with the dignity, the prestige and the honour of the Free State than the view put forward on behalf of the defendant, namely, that questions in dispute as to the interpretation and scope of Article 10 should be left to be settled by diplomatic action.[37]

For reasons that are unclear, unless they were motivated by a certain sympathy for former servants of the Crown, the Privy Council granted the two claimants special leave to appeal against the Supreme Court's split decision. The four judges selected to deal with the case held unanimously that the Supreme Court had been incorrect and they restored the judgment of Meredith J, although they did not award the appellants their full costs since their argument that a sliding scale should be applied to the calculation of their pensions had been rejected.[38] But the Privy Council's reasoning is neither as logical nor as literary as Meredith J's, since it rests on the fact that Article 78 of the Constitution said that transferred civil servants 'shall be entitled to the benefit of Article 10 of the Scheduled Treaty'. The Privy Council disingenuously took this to mean that civil servants were thereby conferred a legal *right*.

It is surprising that, although the Privy Council's judgment, delivered by Viscount Cave LC, acknowledged that the questions raised in the case were 'of considerable public importance' because they related to the effect to be given by Irish courts to domestic laws passed in 1922 and because the appellants were representative of a large number of former civil servants, no mention at all was made of how controversial it was for the Privy Council to deal with the case at all. It is also curious that the judges did not examine the content of the Government of Ireland Act 1920 when characterising the nature of a civil servant's retirement allowance. That the Privy Council's position was legally and morally dubious is clear from the fact that, most unusually, two years later the case was re-heard before the Privy Council and a contrary decision was reached.[39] By this time the civil servants in question (and those they represented) had still not received a higher allowance, as was admitted by the Secretary of State for Dominion Affairs when answering questions on the issue in the House of Commons.[40] According to Lyons the dispute was eventually settled by agreement between the two governments.[41]

[35] Ibid, 165.

[36] *The King v Board of Education* [1910] 2 KB 165; *Dyson v Attorney General* [1911] 1 KB 410; *Hodge v Attorney General* (1839) 160 ER 734.

[37] [1925] 1 IR 149, 167.

[38] [1927] AC 674, [1927] 1 IR 285.

[39] *In re Payment of Compensation to Civil Servants under Article 10 of the Treaty between Great Britain and Ireland* [1929] AC 242.

[40] HC Debs, vol 216, cols 1318–19 (30 April 1928) and vol 218, cols 613–14 (11 June 1928).

[41] Lyons (1973) 515.

The Performing Right Society case

In 1930 a further twist occurred in the saga over appeals to the Privy Council. The Performing Right Society brought an action against Bray Urban District Council for authorising the performance of two musical works by a band playing on the esplanade in the town of Bray in County Wicklow. The Society argued that its rights under the Copyright Act 1911 had been infringed since the sole performing right in each of the two works had been assigned to it. At first instance Johnston J held in favour of the Society,[42] but on appeal the Supreme Court reversed this decision.[43] When the Privy Council granted the Society special leave to appeal, the first issue at the substantive hearing was whether the Privy Council had any jurisdiction to hear the matter.[44] Lord Sankey LC, speaking for the Privy Council, upheld the Council's jurisdiction, relying heavily on the proviso in Article 66 of the 1922 Constitution.[45] He thought those words were 'plain and beyond dispute'[46] and that they should not be read as subject to there having been a right to appeal to the Privy Council before the Treaty was agreed. Bray Council had argued that before the Treaty the right to appeal to the Privy Council had never been expressly extended to Ireland. Lord Sankey answered this by relying on Article 2 of the Anglo-Irish Treaty, which required the law governing the relationship of the Crown to the Irish Free State to be the same as that governing the relationship of the Crown to Canada, a country where the right to appeal to the Privy Council still existed.[47] He also cited an *obiter dictum* by O'Connor MR in *R v County Court Judge of Wicklow*, where he said '[t]rue, there is a right to petition His Majesty for special leave to appeal to His Majesty in Council'.[48]

The second issue for the Privy Council in the *Performing Right Society* case was whether the Copyright Act 1911 ceased to be in force in Ireland once the 1922 Constitution came into effect on 6 December 1922. This turned on the interpretation of section 25(1) of the 1911 Act, which stated that 'the Act shall extend throughout His Majesty's dominions provided that it shall not extend to a self-governing dominion unless declared by the legislature of that dominion to be in force therein'. Section 35 of the 1911 Act defined 'self-governing dominion' to mean Canada, Australia, New Zealand, South Africa and Newfoundland, those being the only dominions in existence at the time. When the case was before the Supreme Court it held that the fact that the Irish Free State had become a dominion in 1922 meant that section 25(1) of the 1911 Act had to be read as excluding the Act's application to that territory too, unless the Oireachtas had explicitly extended it (which it had not).

In reaching this conclusion FitzGibbon J, for the Court, argued that the Copyright Act 1911 had not been continued in force in the Irish Free State by virtue of Article 73 of the Constitution[49] because by the time that Constitution came into effect the 1911 Act had already ceased to extend to the Irish Free State. This he deduced from section 3 of the Irish Free State (Constitution) Act 1922, a Westminster statute, which read:

> If the Parliament of the Irish Free State make provision to that effect, any Act passed before the passing of this Act which applies to or may be applied to self-governing Dominions … shall apply or may be applied to the Irish Free State in like manner as it applies or may be applied to self-governing Dominions.

[42] *Performing Right Society v Bray UDC* [1928] IR 506.
[43] [1928] IR 512 (Kennedy CJ, FitzGibbon and Murnaghan JJ).
[44] *Performing Right Society v Bray UDC* [1930] AC 377 (Lord Sankey LC, Lord Blanesburgh, Lord Hanworth MR, Lord Thankerton and Lord Russell).
[45] Cited above, 23. [46] [1930] AC 377, 395. [47] Ibid, 396.
[48] [1924] 2 IR 139, 147, cited ibid at 397. [49] See further at 64-5 below.

FitzGibbon J himself described this section as 'curious', yet he confidently asserted that in enacting it Westminster had in mind provisions such as section 25(1) of the Copyright Act 1911 and that the effect was to add the Irish Free State to the list of self-governing dominions set out in section 35(1) of that Act. It is so difficult to follow the logic of this reasoning that one can only conclude that the Supreme Court wanted to emit a message that, in situations where there was the slightest of doubts, the content of Irish law was to be determined solely by Irish authorities rather than by what the UK Parliament had previously enacted. However the weakness of the Supreme Court's reasoning made it easier for the Privy Council to overturn it: while the latter court might have been prepared to interpret the term 'self-governing dominion' as including Ireland if the term had not been specifically defined in the 1911 Act, the fact that it was so defined made it virtually impossible for the Privy Council to read the word Ireland into the list of dominions in section 35(1).

To complete the story, by the time of the Privy Council's decision in the *Performing Right Society* case the government of Ireland had already taken the initiative in this field. Either because it did not like the decision of the Irish Supreme Court or because it did not approve of the Privy Council's granting the Society special leave to appeal, the government secured enactment by the Oireachtas of the Copyright (Protection) Act 1929. This established that any copyright existing within the United Kingdom on 5 December 1921 (when the Anglo-Irish Treaty was given effect in UK law) was to be deemed always to have existed just as fully within the Irish Free State from that date onwards.[50] In addition, so far as was necessary to enable such a copyright to be transferred or otherwise dealt with, the Copyright Act 2011 was to be deemed always to have had full force and effect in the Irish Free State,[51] but no remedy or relief was to be granted in respect of an infringement of a copyright in that State prior to the passing of the 1929 Act.[52] In this way the Irish Free State 'domesticated' copyright law. In view of this development, when the Privy Council was considering what remedy to grant in the *Performing Right Society* case it restricted itself to overturning the Supreme Court's ruling on costs; if it had overturned the substance of the Supreme Court's ruling this might have had the effect of restoring Johnston J's initial decision to grant the Society's claim for an injunction, thereby contravening the 1929 Act. As in *Lynham v Butler*,[53] therefore, the problems caused by the preservation of the right to appeal to the Privy Council were solved by the Oireachtas enacting specific legislation to make the issue before the Privy Council moot, that is, one which no longer needed to be resolved because an alternative solution had been found.

The Statute of Westminster 1931

Discussions at the Imperial Conference which took place in 1930 focused on the residual power of the Westminster Parliament to enact laws for the dominions. The conclusions led to the Statute of Westminster 1931, an Act of Parliament giving effect to certain resolutions passed by the Imperial Conferences held in 1926 and 1930. It stated that the Colonial Laws Validity Act 1865, which gave full effect to legislation passed by a colony except to the extent that it was repugnant to a UK Act containing powers extending to that colony, was no longer to apply to any law made by the Parliament of a dominion[54] and it added for good measure that no provision of any law subsequently made by the Parliament of a dominion was to be inoperative on the ground that it was repugnant to the law of England or to provisions in any Act of the UK Parliament.[55] The Statute also declared that no later Act of the

[50] s 1. [51] s 3. [52] s 4. [53] Note 26 above. [54] s 2(1). [55] s 2(2).

UK Parliament would extend to a dominion unless the Act expressly declared that that dominion had requested and consented to the Act.[56] Nothing specific was said in the Statute of Westminster about appeals to the Privy Council, but its enactment appears to have been the catalyst for abolition of the right to appeal from both Irish and Canadian courts to the Privy Council.

In November 1933 the then President of the Executive Council, Éamon de Valera, secured the passing by the Oireachtas of the Constitution (Amendment No 22) Act. This removed the proviso from Article 66 of the 1922 Constitution[57] and replaced it with an unequivocal statement that 'no appeal shall lie from a decision of the Supreme Court or of any other Court in the Irish Free State (Saorstát Eireann) to His Majesty in Council, and it shall not be lawful for any person to petition His Majesty for leave to bring any such appeal'.[58] The abolition affected even those appeals which had already been initiated but not yet completed.[59] Fitzpatrick cites the abolition of appeals to the Privy Council as an example of de Valera's 'surreal logic' in refusing 'to take rhetorical advantage of the abnegation of British authority in the Statute of Westminster, on the grounds that it was a British statute and therefore without authority',[60] but an Act of the Oireachtas, albeit one which amended the Constitution, was surely the most authoritative way in which to make the change in *Irish* law.

In *Moore v Attorney-General of the Irish Free State*[61] the validity of the 1933 amendment was challenged on the basis that it was a violation of the 1921 Anglo-Irish Treaty. The Attorney General for England and Wales, Sir Thomas Inskip,[62] was of the view that the Oireachtas could not amend the Treaty, but the Attorney General of the Irish Free State, Conor Maguire, was of the opposite view. The matter came before the Privy Council itself, where the judges ruled unanimously that before the passing of the Statute of Westminster in 1931 the Parliament of the Irish Free State would not have been competent to pass an Act abrogating the Anglo-Irish Treaty, but Statute removed the fetter on the Irish Free State's Parliament. That meant, first, that the Irish Free State's Constitution (Removal of Oath) Act 1933, which deleted from Article 50 of the Constitution the statement that there could be no amendment of the 1922 Constitution unless it was within the terms of the 1921 Treaty, was valid, as was the Constitution (Amendment No 22) Act 1933 dealing with appeals to the Privy Council, even though it otherwise contradicted what was said in Article 2 of the 1921 Treaty about Ireland's relationship with the Crown being the same as Canada's.

Appeals from other dominions

In a contemporaneous move, Canada amended its Criminal Code in 1933 to remove the appeal route to the Privy Council in criminal cases and the legality of this measure was confirmed by the Privy Council itself in *British Coal Corporation v The King*,[63] thereby laying the ghost of the earlier decision in *Nadan v The King*.[64] Abolition of appeals in new civil cases did not occur until 1949.[65] This followed an Advisory Opinion issued by the Supreme Court of Canada in 1939,[66] which was then endorsed by the Privy Council in

[56] s 4. [57] See above, 23. [58] Constitution (Amendment No 22) Act 1933, s 1.

[59] Ibid, s 2. [60] Fitzpatrick (1998) 151. [61] [1935] IR 484.

[62] He later became Viscount Caldecote and served as Lord Chancellor from 1939 to 1940 and Lord Chief Justice of England from 1940 to 1946.

[63] [1935] AC 500. [64] [1926] AC 482. See above, 24-5.

[65] Supreme Court Act Amendment of 1949. For further details see Iacobucci (2002) 28–30; McCormick (2000) Chap 2; Laskin (1964) 125–6 and 143–4.

[66] *Reference re Privy Council Appeals* [1940] SCR 49.

1947.[67] According to Farr, by 1949 the Privy Council had delivered no fewer than 173 major judgments interpreting the British North America Act 1867, in many of which it favoured greater powers being conferred on Canada's provincial governments rather than on the federal government, an attitude which obviously antagonised the latter.[68]

The Australian governments in the first half of the twentieth century did not object as strongly as Canada did to appeals being taken to the Privy Council. Article 74 of the Commonwealth of Australia Constitution Act 1900 contained a provision comparable to Article 66 of the Irish Free State Constitution. Any laws proposing to limit the issues for which special leave could be asked had to be 'reserved by the Governor-General for Her Majesty's pleasure', that is, approved by the British government. It was not until 1968 that the Australian Parliament passed a further law on the issue. This was the Privy Council (Limitation of Appeals) Act 1968, which prohibited appeals from federal courts other than the High Court (the latter being the highest national court) and also from the supreme courts of Australian territories.[69] In addition the Act said that special leave to appeal to the Privy Council from a decision of the High Court could be asked for only where the decision being appealed was itself an appeal from a decision of a State's Supreme Court on a non-federal issue and provided that it did not involve the interpretation of the Constitution or of a law made by Parliament or under its authority.[70] Any remaining possibility of appealing to the Privy Council in cases not covered by the 1968 Act was subsequently removed by section 3 of the Privy Council (Appeals from the High Court) Act 1975.

In South Africa the right to appeal to the Privy Council had been partially retained in the South Africa Act 1909,[71] in ways similar to those used in the Irish Free State and Australia. In other words, the Supreme Court of South Africa could not itself grant leave to appeal but the Privy Council could do so.[72] It was in 1950 that a replacement for section 106 was inserted into the South Africa Act 1909 to make it clear that no future case could under any circumstances be appealed from a court in South Africa to the Privy Council.[73]

It can be seen, therefore, that Ireland's withdrawal from the Privy Council appeal system in 1933 was the first of many: Canada and India finally removed any vestige of the right to appeal in 1949, South Africa in 1950, Australia in 1975 and New Zealand in 2003. Today only a number of small jurisdictions, particularly in the Caribbean, continue to send appeals to the Privy Council.[74] Nevertheless, the Justices of the Supreme Court of the United Kingdom still spend between 20 and 30 per cent of their time dealing with Privy Council appeals. This represents a considerable contribution to the foreign legal systems involved and there does not appear to be any campaign in favour of abolishing the jurisdiction. Courts in Ireland remain free to consider decisions by the Privy Council which are relevant to legal questions coming before them, but the decisions are not in any sense binding precedents. As the years go by there is less and less occasion for decisions by the Privy Council to be cited to the Irish Supreme Court; when they are, they are open to be treated as persuasive precedents, much like decisions of the House of Lords issued after 1924.[75]

[67] *Attorney General of Ontario v Attorney General of Canada* [1947] AC 127.

[68] DML Farr's article on the Privy Council is online at *The Canadian Encyclopaedia*. See too Hogg (2006).

[69] s 4. [70] s 3(1). [71] s 106.

[72] cf Kohn (1932) 355, though he concluded that that there was no parallel for 'such formal self-contradiction' as was found in Art 66 of the Irish Free State Constitution.

[73] Privy Council Appeals Act 1950, s 1.

[74] For details see the website of the Judicial Committee of the Privy Council. Amongst the most prominent jurisdictions which still allow appeals are the Bahamas, Bermuda and Trinidad and Tobago.

[75] For three recent examples where Privy Council cases were cited see *HAH v SAA* [2017] IESC 40, [2017] 1 IR 372 (on the validity of polygamous marriages); *DPP v JC* [2015] IESC 31, [2017] 1 IR 417 (on the inadmissibility of illegally obtained evidence); and *Leech v Independent Newspapers (Ireland) Ltd* [2014] IESC 79, [2015] 2 IR 214 (on the award of damages for defamation).

Parliamentary Sovereignty

Throughout the period 1924 to 1937 the Irish Supreme Court adopted a very traditional approach to judicial law-making. It was a small body, comprised of individuals who were steeped in the British constitutional convention—well-established since the end of the seventeenth century—whereby supreme power is deemed to lie with elected representatives, not with the Head of State, the government or the judges. What is more, in the aftermath of the creation of a new State prompted by the actions of an armed secessionist movement, it is perhaps natural that judges in the new State should be more willing to defer to individuals whom the people have elected as law-makers, since many of those individuals will have risked much more than the judges during the course of the armed struggle. It is true that the Irish Free State differed from the United Kingdom in that it had a written Constitution, but this did not mean that the judges were keen to abandon their preference for restraint when developing the law. In any event, Article 2 of the 1922 Constitution expressly stated that:

> All powers of government and all authority, legislative, executive, and judicial, are derived from the people and the same shall be exercised in the Irish Free State (Saorstát Éireann) through the organisations established by or under, and in accord with this Constitution.

The principal 'organisation' envisaged by Article 2 was the Oireachtas, and Article 12 of the Constitution emphasised the importance of that body by asserting that '[t]he sole and exclusive power of making laws for the peace, order and good government of the Irish Free State (Saorstát Éireann) is vested in the Oireachtas'.[76] Although it is possible to list a number of respects in which this sole and exclusive power was subjected to restraints imposed by other provisions of the Constitution,[77] the fact remains that the Oireachtas was front and centre in the framework of the new State.

Some would point to the fact that Articles 65 and 66 conferred on the High Court and Supreme Court respectively the power to decide on the validity of any law 'having regard to the provisions of the Constitution', but earlier, in Article 50, we read that the Oireachtas in turn was given the power to amend the Constitution, thereby enabling the Oireachtas to subvert a judicial decision invalidating a law if it chose to do so. There were only two limitations to the power conferred by Article 50. The first was that the Oireachtas could make amendments only if the proposed changes did not contradict the provisions of the Anglo-Irish Treaty of 1921. The second was that the power was to endure only for eight years—until 1930—because thereafter its proposed amendments could become law only if they were approved in a referendum of the people, either by a simple majority of those registered to vote or, provided a simple majority had voted, by a two-thirds majority of those who did so.

The decision to suspend the referendum requirement for eight years seems to have been taken in order to allow the Oireachtas to bed down for a period. MacNeill does not discuss the matter,[78] but Kohn draws attention to the fact that, in the course of the deliberations in the Constituent Assembly which considered the draft of the Constitution:

[76] On the expression 'laws for the peace, order and good government' see, generally, Yusuf (2014). For a summary of the whole 1922 Constitution see Donaldson (1957) 136-54.

[77] eg Art 35, which excluded the Seanad from considering Money Bills, and Art 43, which prohibited the Oireachtas from declaring actions to be infringements of the law if they were not so when taken; see generally MacNeill (1925) 103–4.

[78] He mentions it only in passing: MacNeill (1925) 186.

> It was generally felt that in view of the short time available for the drafting of the Constitution and the experimental nature of many of its provisions the need for amendments would inevitably arise at an early stage, and that it was imperative that the latter should be capable of being effected without having to be submitted to the cumbrous process of the referendum.[79]

The period of eight years was chosen because it equated to the duration of two full Dáil terms. To placate those who might object to such a provision, the Constitution made it clear that Bills which proposed amendments to the Constitution could still be subjected to the 'ordinary' referendum procedure provided for by Article 47 of the Constitution. As noted earlier,[80] this provision allowed *any Bill* passed by the Oireachtas to be suspended for 90 days if two-fifths of the members of the Dáil, or a majority of the members of the Seanad, presented a written demand to the President of the Executive Council within seven days of the Bill's passing. The Bill would then have to be submitted to a referendum if this was demanded during the 90-day suspension period either by a resolution agreed to by three-fifths of the Senators or by a petition signed by one-twentieth of all people on the register of voters in Ireland. But even this brake on the principle of parliamentary sovereignty was qualified: it did not apply to Money Bills or to Bills which both Houses of the Oireachtas declared to be 'necessary for the immediate preservation of the public peace, health or safety'. In fact only once was there an attempt to trigger an Article 47 referendum: in 1927 a group of TDs (members of the Dáil) sought to put to the people the Electoral (Amendment No 2) Bill, the Bill which proposed to deny to abstentionists the right to stand for election to the Dáil. But the promoters of this campaign could not garner enough support from other TDs to meet the required two-fifths threshold.

The government was in any case very sceptical of the Article 47 referendum mechanism. Accordingly, following a recommendation made by a sub-committee of the Executive Council, it pushed through the Constitution (Amendment No 10) Act 1928 to repeal Article 47, while leaving intact the possibility of a 'constitutional' referendum under Article 50. A measure of the facility with which the Irish Free State Constitution could be amended is that this was one of six Acts passed in 1928 which had that effect. Between 1922 and 1937 there were no fewer than 27 amending Acts. The debate on Amendment No 10 was, in Mansergh's words, 'one of the most bitter and prolonged which the Dáil has experienced',[81] partly because the legislation also proposed the abolition of a sister provision in the Constitution, Article 48, which conferred on ordinary people a conditional power to initiate legislation. The power was conditional because its conferral depended on either the Oireachtas itself making further provision for it or on the people voting in favour of it after a petition had been lodged with the support of at least 75,000 electors. Mansergh describes Article 48 as 'a further and notable example of a widespread desire that the right of minorities should be fully safeguarded'[82] but in fact neither of the two conditions was ever satisfied and so the power of initiation was never conferred. A Fianna Fáil-inspired petition signed by 96,000 electors was brought to the Dáil in May 1928 in an attempt to trigger conferment of the power, but before the Dáil could consider how to process it the Constitution (Amendment No 10) Act was enacted and the petition became irrelevant.

In a further display of parliamentary sovereignty the next year, the Oireachtas passed the Constitution (Amendment No 16) Act 1929, the effect of which was to alter Article 50 so that the period during which the Constitution could be amended by the Oireachtas alone, without seeking confirmation from the people in a referendum, was extended from eight years to 16 years.

[79] Kohn (1932) 252. [80] See Chap 2 above, 18. [81] Mansergh (1934) 143. [82] Ibid, 142.

From its creation in 1924 until the end of the 1920s the Supreme Court seemed to be an irrelevance as far as these constitutional amendments were concerned because there appeared to be no mechanism for engaging it on the validity of the amending Acts. The Court's passivity was also a function of its own reluctance to assert whatever control it did have or might have created for itself. In that regard it simply took up where the short-lived Court of Appeal of Southern Ireland had left off: a few months before the creation of the Supreme Court in 1924 the Court of Appeal decided in *R (Cooney) v Clinton*[83] that the Oireachtas could even *implicitly* amend the Constitution. The issue in that case was whether the Indemnity Act 1923 should be considered valid despite its seeming inconsistency with the 1922 Constitution: the 1923 Act recognised the validity of decisions by military courts even though those courts had sat at a time when the country was not in a state of war or armed rebellion, the pre-condition for military courts according to Article 70 of the 1922 Constitution.

The Supreme Court did not disassociate itself from this unimaginative approach to law-making, even though it was out of step with that of other common law systems operating under a written constitution. We can contrast its stance with the subtly activist approach adopted by the US Supreme Court shortly after its establishment in 1789. In *Marbury v Madison*, decided in 1803, that Court ruled that, despite the US Constitution being silent on whether any court could adjudicate upon the constitutionality of an Act of Congress, the Supreme Court itself should assume that power. The irony was that the Court reached this conclusion in a case where it declared unconstitutional an Act of Congress purporting to confer more power on the Court through the appointment of additional judges over and above the number provided for in the Constitution.[84] The Irish Supreme Court's opportunity to emulate *Marbury v Madison* arose in the landmark case of *The State (Ryan) v Lennon* in 1934.[85] Before looking in detail at that case we need to set the scene for it by considering the civil unrest in Ireland during the early years of the Free State.

Civil Unrest and Emergency Legislation

As one High Court judge said just two years after the coming into force of the 1922 Constitution: 'What was supposed to herald an era of settled government turned out to be the harbinger of unrest and rebellion'.[86] Leading academic commentators, writing much later, echoed this sentiment: 'this Constitution was not designed to withstand the strains which the Civil War period and the continuing political violence were to place upon it'.[87] The Civil War, which broke out between pro-Treaty and anti-Treaty factions just six months after the Treaty was signed in December 1921, and continued until August 1923, has been estimated to have cost about 4,000 lives. This is more than three times the number lost during the War of Independence between 1919 and 1921, and 300 or so more than the number lost in the 30 years of 'troubles' in Northern Ireland between 1969 and 1998.[88] Ferriter considers it to be a greatly exaggerated figure, suggesting that there may have been 400 republican deaths, 800 within the official Irish army and 1,150 other homicides, executions and deaths resulting from gunshot—a total of 2,350.[89] Even this lower figure means that, on average, at least five people were killed every day while the Civil War lasted.

[83] Decided on 23 May 1924, but not reported until [1935] IR 245. See too Kelly (1967) 5.
[84] *Marbury v Madison* 5 US 137 (1803).
[85] [1935] IR 170.
[86] Dodd J in *R (O'Connell) v Military Governor of Hare Park Internment Camp* [1924] 2 IR 104, 115.
[87] Hogan and Walker (1989) 175.
[88] Fanning (1983) 39; Corcoran (2013) 95; McKittrick et al (2006).
[89] Ferriter (2005) 258, citing Fitzpatrick (1998) 133–4.

The Free State government was conscious of the fact that there was more lawlessness after the creation of the Free State than there had been during the preceding period of British rule. It therefore decided to adopt a hardline position towards the 'new' rebels.[90] On 1 August 1923 the Oireachtas passed the Public Safety (Emergency Powers) Act. This was supposed to remain in force for six months but, as we have seen, the very next day it was struck down by the Court of Appeal as unconstitutional, only to be restored the day after that by the Public Safety (Emergency Powers) (No 2) Act 1923.[91] The 1923 legislation expired on 31 January 1924 and was replaced by the Public Safety (Powers of Arrest and Detention) Temporary Act 1924 and the Public Safety (Punishment of Offences) Temporary Act 1924, both of which were time-limited to one year. They were not re-enacted in 1925 but two other pieces of legislation were passed on 6 June to develop the ordinary criminal law relating to the use of firearms and the crime of treason.[92]

The following year a new approach was adopted, one which had no parallel in the British legal system. The Public Safety (Emergency Powers) Act 1926 allowed the Executive Council to proclaim that a state of national emergency existed 'of such character that it is expedient in the public interest that the provisions listed in Part II of this Act should be put into force'.[93] Those provisions created very extensive powers to arrest, to detain for a limited or unlimited period, to search and to release suspects on bail. A government Minister, for example, was empowered to intern people indefinitely if he or she was satisfied that there was reasonable ground for suspecting such people of being or having been concerned in the commission of one or more of the many offences listed in the Schedule to the Act. A proclamation of emergency was to remain in force for only three months but it could be repeatedly continued in force for periods of three months through further proclamations issued by the Executive Council.

After the assassination of Kevin O'Higgins in July 1927 the Oireachtas passed another Public Safety Act to increase the regulation of associations and provide for the establishment of special courts if the Executive Council proclaimed that these were 'necessary in order to secure the due administration of justice and the sure punishment of crime'.[94] The special courts, also referred to as tribunals, were to consist of three or more members, only one of whom one had to be certified by the Attorney General as having legal knowledge and experience. That person could be, but did not have to be, an officer in the State's Defence Forces, but all the other members of the special courts did have to be such officers, and not below the rank of commandant. The special courts could try people for scheduled offences, though the list of offences scheduled to the 1927 Act did not exactly coincide with the list scheduled to the 1926 Act. The whole Act was viewed by many as a draconian over-reaction to O'Higgins' murder.

The 1927 Act was to have endured for five years[95] but almost as soon as it was enacted the leader of Fianna Fáil, Éamon de Valera, moved for it to be prematurely repealed.[96] Even the government was by then accepting that circumstances in the country had changed and it therefore proposed to limit the Act's life to just two years[97] but there was a sufficient majority to terminate it even earlier, on 26 December 1928.[98] This put an end to the proscribing of unlawful associations and the possible use of special courts. However, in order to counter the practice of defendants not recognising the court (a long-standing tradition

[90] For a further summary of the legislative steps taken see Hogan and Walker (1989) 16–18.
[91] See Chap 2 above, 18. [92] Firearms Act 1925 and Treasonable Offences Act 1925.
[93] Public Safety (Emergency Powers) Act 1926, s 1(1). [94] Public Safety Act 1927, s 20(1).
[95] Ibid, s 1(2). [96] Dáil Debs, vol 21(12), p 36 of online version, 10 November 1927.
[97] Ibid, per the Minister for Finance, Ernest Blythe. [98] Public Safety Act 1928, s 1.

within Irish republicanism) the Juries (Protection) Act 1929 made that practice an offence punishable 'forthwith' with up to six months in prison.[99] The same Act allowed for the identity of jurors to be kept secret in order to protect them from intimidation[100] and it permitted majority verdicts if at least nine of the 12 jurors were agreed on what the outcome of a trial should be.[101]

The Cumann na nGaedheal government remained worried about the level of lawlessness in the country and feared that the 1922 Constitution might stand in the way of measures needed to counter it. That is why, as we have seen, it secured the passage of both the Constitution (Amendment No 10) Act 1928, section 2 of which simply deleted Article 47 from the Constitution,[102] and the Constitution (Amendment No 16) Act 1929, which extended the Oireachtas's amending power for a further eight years. It soon took advantage of its new position to secure the enactment of the Constitution (Amendment No 17) Act 1931.

The 1931 Act inserted a new Article 2A into the Constitution, giving unprecedented powers to the government. It allowed, for example, for the resurrection of a Special Powers Tribunal to try persons suspected of involvement in serious offences.[103] Again a list of the offences in question was added as an Appendix to Article 2A, but it embraced many more offences than were included in the schedules to the Public Safety Acts 1926 and 1927. Today the offences would be referred to as terrorist offences but in 1931 the following wording was used:

> [a]ny offence whatsoever (whether committed before or after this Article was inserted in this Constitution ...) in respect of which an Executive Minister certifies in writing under his hand that to the best of his belief the act constituting such offence was done with the object of impairing or impeding the machinery of government or the administration of justice.[104]

If it thought it necessary or expedient, the Special Powers Tribunal was to be allowed to sentence a person convicted of one of those offences to a greater punishment than that already provided for by law, including even the death penalty.[105] Other provisions in Article 2A conferred special powers on the police in relation to questioning, search, arrest and detention, and imposed new penalties for membership of unlawful associations.[106] It added, for safe measure, that every subsequent Article in the Constitution was to be construed subject to the provisions of Article 2A, 'which was to prevail in the case of any inconsistency'.[107]

It is, frankly, hard to identify a more authoritarian provision than Article 2A in any other constitution in the common law world, and it is likely that even Albert Venn Dicey would have turned in his grave at the thought that a parliament could get away with such extremism. Interestingly, the provision went significantly further than those contained in the Civil Authorities (Special Powers) Acts which were enacted by the Parliament of Northern Ireland each year between 1922 and 1928, when they were extended for a further five years before being made indefinite in 1933 and added to again in 1944.[108]

When Fianna Fáil came to power in 1932 it quickly dismantled some of the existing legislation[109] and released 20 IRA prisoners.[110] Supposedly in response to counter-threats by IRA sympathisers, supporters of the defeated Cumann na nGaedheal party established the Army Comrades Association, largely comprising former members of the Irish Free

[99] Juries (Protection) Act 1929, s 6(3). [100] Ibid, ss 3 and 9. [101] Ibid, s 5.

[102] Section 3 of the Act deleted Art 48 of the Constitution, which had allowed the Oireachtas to provide for the people to initiate proposals for laws or constitutional amendments. See above, 33.

[103] Art 2A, Pt II. [104] Art 2A, App, para 7. [105] Art 2A, s 7(1).

[106] Art 2A, Pts II and III, and Pt V, s 30. [107] Art 2A, s 2. [108] Donohue (2001) Chap 1.

[109] Constitution (Suspension of Article 2A) Order 1932, SR&O No 11 (18 March 1932).

[110] *Irish Times*, 11 March 1932, 7.

State's Defence Forces. This association gradually became more right-wing and militant, adopting practices and symbols favoured by fascist organisations in Italy and Germany. On account of their uniform they became known as the Blueshirts.[111] In July 1933 they chose as their leader Eoin O'Duffy, who had been the head of the Irish Free State's police service (the Garda Síochána) since its formation in 1922 until his dismissal by de Valera in February 1933. There were increasingly frequent clashes between IRA sympathisers and the Blueshirts, thereby confronting de Valera with a challenge to peace and security, issues for which he had not previously held national responsibility. His government felt compelled to take steps to counter the growing violence on 11 August 1933, when it issued the Constitution (Operation of Article 2A) Order 1933,[112] bringing into force Parts II, III, IV and V of Article 2A of the Constitution and on 22 August the government used its power under Part IV to proscribe the Blueshirts.[113] As Hugh Geoghegan and many others have pointed out, there is considerable irony in the fact that a measure dreamed up by a Cumann na nGaedheal government to help combat violence perpetrated by anti-Treaty republicans was first brought into effect by a Fianna Fáil government led by Éamon de Valera.[114]

The State (Ryan) v Lennon

It is remarkable that throughout the first decade of the Supreme Court's existence, from 1924 to 1934, it was not asked on any occasion to adjudicate upon the constitutionality or legality of measures taken under the various emergency laws enacted during that period.[115] Unfortunately, when it did get such an opportunity it can hardly be said to have covered itself in glory.

Four men were arrested in Thurles, County Tipperary, on 22 April 1934. They were charged with a number of offences, including conspiracy to shoot with intent to murder, and were detained in Arbour Hill Detention Barracks in Dublin awaiting trial by military judges sitting without a jury. In seeking to get their clients released their lawyers made a variety of arguments. For a start, they claimed that the 10th and 16th amendments to the Constitution, referred to above, were not valid. The case came first to the High Court, where it was heard by the President, Tim Sullivan, and two Justices, James Creed Meredith and John O'Byrne. Today, the last of these would probably be seen as having a conflict of interest in the case, since he sat on the committee which drafted the 1922 Constitution, but that point was not made in 1934. All three judges had little hesitation in concluding that the Constitution itself had given clear authorisation to the Oireachtas to amend any part of the Constitution through a simple Act, at least for a set period. Sullivan P applied the general principle that 'the words of the statute should be given their ordinary and natural meaning unless that would lead to an absurdity or inconsistency'.[116] He admitted, however, relying on a previous decision by the Judicial Committee of the Privy Council in *Edwards v Attorney General of Canada*,[117] where the interpretation of the British North America Act 1867 had been in question, that 'there is authority for the proposition that an Act such as the Constitution should be liberally interpreted'.[118] It is interesting that neither Meredith J nor

[111] Manning (1970). [112] SR&O No 91.
[113] Constitution (Declaration of Unlawful Association) Order 1933, SI 95, relying upon s 19(2) of Art 2A.
[114] Geoghegan (2013) 46–7.
[115] [1935] IR 170. See too Hogan (2000b); Geoghegan (2013) 46–52; Mac Cormaic (2016) 36–43.
[116] [1935] IR 170, 176. This exemplifies the 'golden rule' approach to statutory interpretation.
[117] [1930] AC 124. [118] [1935] IR 170, 177.

O'Byrne J cited *Edwards*, or any other alleged precedent. Meredith J stressed that the 1922 Constitution had to be interpreted in accordance with its own provisions:

> [I]t is true to say that there are no principles of law in relation to which the validity of any law is to be tested except those enshrined in the Constitution. Our Common Law does not contain any principles of constitutional law, and Article 73 of the Constitution did not enact by reference any principles of constitutional law, in relation to which any law could be held by this Court to be valid or invalid.[119]

The case was then appealed to the Supreme Court, where it was heard over six days at a time which should have been the Court's summer vacation. An indication was given on the last day of the hearing that a majority was in favour of rejecting the appeal, but judgments were not delivered for a further four months, in December 1934, and it seems that the four men remained detained until that date. Counsel for the detainees, who included John Costello KC, specifically argued that the British theory of parliamentary sovereignty was inconsistent with the principle of popular sovereignty as set out in the Preamble to the 1922 Constitution, a document which restrained parliamentary absolutism by safeguarding the people's overriding authority through the referendum procedure in Article 47 and the initiation procedure in Article 48. In this light, the 'sole and exclusive power' of legislation conferred on the Oireachtas by Article 12 merely referred to external authority and international status and did not extend the constitutional powers of the Oireachtas or diminish the internal limitations on such powers. Counsel for the government, on the other hand, Conor Maguire KC (the Attorney General) and George Gavan Duffy SC, argued that the Constitution was based as much on the theory of parliamentary as of popular sovereignty, and that 'considerations imported from theories evolved to suit British history and conditions are misleading in the interpretation of a document enacted by the supreme legislative authority of the Third Dáil Éireann sitting as a Constituent Assembly'; the referendum and initiative procedures were experimental checks or expedients, but otherwise control was not reserved to the people; the Irish Constitution, moreover, unlike the American, French and Norwegian Constitutions, gave no intimation that some of its provisions were so much more fundamental than others that they could not be amended.[120] None of the lawyers relied upon the Privy Council's decision in *Edwards v Attorney General of Canada*.

That the three Supreme Court justices took four months to issue their decision is some indication of how divided they were in this case, the first significant test of the Court's unity of purpose. FitzGibbon J began his judgment by saying: '[i]t is impossible to overestimate the importance of the questions which we have to decide on this appeal'.[121] Like many judges, however, he then delivered a judgment which made it seem as if his preferred result was the inevitable one. He interpreted the amending power in Article 50 of the Constitution to be an extremely wide-ranging one, although he stopped short of endorsing the principle of absolute parliamentary sovereignty by admitting that the Oireachtas could not amend the Constitution in a way which conflicted with the Anglo-Irish Treaty of 1921. This was because to do so would have been a breach not of the Constitution but of the Act of Dáil Éireann, sitting as a Constituent Assembly, which enacted the Constitution and which specified, in section 2, that if any provision of the Constitution, or of any amendment of it, or of any law made under it was in any respect repugnant to any of the Treaty, it shall, to the extent of such repugnancy, 'be absolutely void and inoperative'.[122] FitzGibbon J referred to

[119] Ibid, 178–9. [120] Counsel's arguments are summarised ibid, 183–9.
[121] [1935] IR 170, 220.
[122] Constitution of the Irish Free State (Saorstát Éireann) Act 1922. This was the only Act the Assembly passed.

the Constitutions of Austria, Czechoslovakia, France, South Africa and the United States, pointing out what was different about the Free State's Constitution. He added that his duty was to apply the law as it stood, even if this meant perpetuating uncertainty:

> The particular method of amendment adopted, by enacting that every Article of the Constitution subsequent to Article 2 shall be subject to the provisions of Amendment 17, and that the provisions of that Amendment shall prevail whenever there is any inconsistency between them and any subsequent Article of the Constitution, is unquestionably very inconvenient, and throws almost insuperable obstacles in the way of any citizen or Judge whose duty it is to ascertain the actual law of the Constitution, but an Act of the Legislature is not *ultra vires* or invalid because it is difficult to construe, and amendments of the Constitution which might be made clearly and one at a time are not invalidated because they have been enacted *en masse* in a manner calculated to create the utmost uncertainty and inconvenience.[123]

FitzGibbon J then dealt with the appellants' broader argument, 'that there are certain rights, inherent in every individual, which are so sacred that no Legislature has authority to deprive him of them'.[124] Having briefly surveyed the American and French approaches to fundamental rights, referred to the Constitutions of the Kingdom of Serbs, Croats and Slovenes and those of Austria, Czechoslovakia, Estonia and Poland, and mentioned theorists such as Paine, Godwin, Burke, Bentham and Rousseau, the judge concluded that the Free State had chosen its own specific path, which also differed from that of Great Britain. He could not presume that rights and privileges which inhabitants of England have always enjoyed, either by virtue of the common law or under statutes, were also 'indigenous to the citizens of this Gaelic and Catholic State'.[125] He even seemed accepting of the idea that Amendment No 17 could be a permanent part of the Irish Constitution:

> [W]e find the Briton's conceptions of liberty and justice set forth in his Magna Charta and his Bill of Rights; those of the American in his Declaration of Independence and his Constitution; while those of the Gael are enshrined in Amendment No 17 (which is to prevail, in case of inconsistency, over everything in the Constitution except Articles 1 and 2), and subsequent amendments ... I can find no justification for a declaration that there was some 'spirit' embodied in our original Constitution which is so sacrosanct and immutable that nothing antagonistic to it may be enacted by the Oireachtas.[126]

The judge found support for his position in the fact that the 1931 Act had been passed almost unanimously in the Oireachtas and that those who then opposed it most vehemently 'as unconstitutional and oppressive' had since 'completely changed their opinions, and now accord it their unqualified approval'.[127]

That FitzGibbon J was keen to emphasise the specificity of the Irish constitutional position, while trying to equate it with other nations' choice of position, is evidenced by the extraordinary rhetorical flourish at the end of his judgment, where he adapts a quotation from John of Gaunt in Shakespeare's Richard II:

> Fortunately it can never again be suggested that the Saorstát has obtained citizens by false pretences, now that the Oireachtas has promulgated *urbi et orbi*, to the Czechoslovak and the Mexican, to our kinsmen in the United States of America and throughout the British Commonwealth of Nations, and, above all, to our fellow-countrymen in Northern Ireland ... Amendment No 17 as an integral part of our Constitution, setting forth in the clearest language, in the forefront of that document, the conditions under which liberty is enjoyed and justice may be administered

[123] [1935] IR 170, 229. [124] Ibid, 230. [125] Ibid, 234. [126] Ibid, 235–6.
[127] Ibid, 235.

> in 'this other Eden demi-Paradise, this precious stone, set in the silver sea, this blessed plot, this earth, this realm, this' Saor Stát.[128]

We see here a quixotic mixture of nostalgia for a bygone British past and of sardonic pride in the newly-minted Irish present. Reading between the lines we can conclude that FitzGibbon J's position was: 'We Irish have chosen to make our bed in a certain way, and we must lie in it.' He seems to have put his duty as a judge—to apply the law before him—ahead of his duty as a protector of basic liberties.[129]

Murnaghan J, whom Geoghegan describes as 'primarily an academic', 'essentially non-political' and 'certainly not a republican in the party political sense',[130] began his judgment by acknowledging that the issues involved 'raise considerations of very grave moment' and that the 'extreme rigour of [Amendment No 17] is such that its provisions pass far beyond anything having the semblance of legal procedure, and the judicial mind is staggered at the very complete departure from legal methods in use in these [military] courts'.[131] Nevertheless, Murnaghan J had no doubt as to what decision he had to reach. In a briefer and less passionate judgment than that of FitzGibbon J, he concurred that the Free State's Constitution did not distinguish between provisions which were fundamental and those which were not, that the only constraint on the law-making powers of the Oireachtas was the Anglo-Irish Treaty of 1921 and that the duty of the Supreme Court was to interpret the Constitution irrespective of the outcome of that interpretation, even if the consequences were 'grave and far reaching'.[132] Murnaghan J did not indulge in any philosophising or seek to differentiate Ireland from other nations.

The two judgments just discussed were delivered after that of Hugh Kennedy who, as Chief Justice, enjoyed the privilege of speaking first. Ironically—given that Kennedy had previously been the most pro-Sinn Féin of the three judges, as well as the most politically active—it is only in his judgment that we find a courageous stand being taken in favour of basic liberties and what today would be called common law constitutionalism. The judge's initial objection to the 1931 Act was that the broad powers it conferred could be brought into effect whenever the Executive Council thought it was 'expedient' for this to occur: no other pre-conditions had to be satisfied. This meant that the provision made by the Constitution for suspending citizens' constitutional rights only in times of war or armed rebellion[133] would have to yield to the '*ipse dixit*' of the Executive Council.[134] He then observed that none of the five members appointed to the Special Powers Tribunal had any legal qualifications and that they could be removed at will by the Governor General acting on the advice of the Executive Council. Having referred to some of the powers conferred on the Tribunal as 'staggering', and noted that there could be no appeal against its decisions, he lampooned the law-makers for conferring on police officers a high constitutional status which they did not think they had in that they could now make statements that could not be controverted in any court and they could keep people in custody for a month and 72 hours, and question them throughout that time, before having to charge them with any offence. Disingenuously, Kennedy CJ says that he is not making any criticism of the position brought about by the 1931 Act: he is merely trying to show the conflicts with the 1922

[128] Ibid, 236–7.

[129] See too Geoghegan (2013) 41. At 52, Geoghegan concludes that FitzGibbon J cannot be blamed for his actual conclusion.

[130] Ibid, 42. He added: 'I am not clear that Murnaghan would have had any particular rapport with Chief Justice Kennedy or any emotional national sentiment as to how the new courts of the Irish Free State should operate.'

[131] [1935] IR 170, 237–8. [132] Ibid, 244.

[133] This must be a reference to Art 70, although that is limited to the right not to be tried in non-military courts.

[134] [1935] IR 170, 196.

Constitution and, consequently, 'the awful gravity of the matters before us for determination in this ... momentous case'.[135]

Kennedy CJ's first argument for declaring the 1931 Act invalid was that it offended against the Preamble to the Constitution of the Irish Free State (Saorstát Éireann) Act 1922, which states that 'all lawful authority comes from God to the people':

> From this it seems clear that, if any legislation of the Oireachtas (including any purported amendment of the Constitution) were to offend against that acknowledged ultimate Source from which the legislative authority has come through the people to the Oireachtas, as, for instance, if it were repugnant to the Natural Law, such legislation would be necessarily unconstitutional and invalid, and it would be, therefore, absolutely null and void and inoperative.[136]

This is the first reference to natural law by any judge in the Irish Supreme Court and unfortunately it sowed a seed which is alive and well in Irish constitutional law even today. Neither FitzGibbon J nor Murnaghan J felt the need to deal with this argument: they were, with respect, correct not to do so because the precise content of natural law is at worst unknowable and at best highly speculative.[137]

Kennedy CJ went on to rely upon a second argument for declaring the 1931 Act invalid, namely that the Constituent Assembly had enunciated 'statements of fundamental principle in the constitutional sphere so expressed as to convey clearly the intention that they are to be accepted for the purposes of the Constitution as immutable and absolute, subject only to the specific qualifications expressed in certain cases'.[138] In his view, any amendment of the Constitution which was inconsistent with any fundamental principle so declared was necessarily outside the scope of any power and therefore 'invalid and void'.[139] The difficulty with this proposition, as Kennedy's two judicial colleagues pointed out, is that there is no clear signifier in the Constitution as to which principles are fundamental and which are not. Kennedy CJ's own citation of supposedly fundamental provisions, such as Article 6 on the right to liberty and Article 8 on the freedom of religion, indicates that the Constitution itself permits exceptions to them made 'in accordance with law' or because of 'public order or morality'. Nevertheless, the Chief Justice went on to find that Amendment No 10 to the Constitution, passed by the Oireachtas in 1928, was invalid to the extent that it removed from the power of amendment itself a pre-requisite imposed on its exercise by the Constituent Assembly, namely the need to seek approval by the people in a referendum, which in the judge's logic must be deemed to be a fundamental principle of the Constitution. Amendment No 16 was invalid for the same reason and here he deployed a vivid analogy:

> As well might it be said that one who lends another a pruning knife and leaves it, for the cultivator's convenience, hanging on the tree for the trimming of which it is lent, therefore authorises him to whom it is lent, by some process of inversion, to turn it upon itself, and use it to prune and amend itself into some other kind of instrument wherewith to hack down the tree.[140]

And the Chief Justice then summed up his overall conclusion as follows:

> In my opinion, on the true interpretation of the power before us, upon a consideration of the express prohibition, limitations and requirements of the clause containing it, the absence of any express authority, the donation of the effective act in the exercise of the power to the people as a whole, the relevant surrounding circumstances to which I have already referred, and the

[135] Ibid, 202. [136] Ibid, 204–5. [137] For more on natural law see Chap 6, 136-7.
[138] [1935] IR 170, 208. [139] Ibid, 209. [140] Ibid, 217.

> documents and their tenor in their entirety, there is not here, either expressly or by necessary implication, any power to amend the power of amendment itself.[141]

Having reviewed the reasoning of the three judges in this foundational case we can see that the majority's view is rooted in literalism and conservatism whereas Kennedy CJ's is more subtle and nuanced. Faced with the unambiguous wording of the Constitution, which he (like O'Byrne J) had helped to draft, and with the clear wishes of the Oireachtas, the Chief Justice worked hard to carve out a justification for declaring Amendments 10, 16 and 17 to be invalid. It is submitted that he ably succeeded, subject to two qualifications. First, his reference to natural law was unnecessary and dangerous. Second, he did not adequately develop criteria for identifying fundamental principles of the Constitution. He tried to lay down a marker in this field, but regrettably his fellow judges, both in this case and subsequently, refused to follow it. The Supreme Court was affected by that refusal until at least the mid-1960s and to some extent still suffers from it today.

The majority's position was that the Oireachtas could pass laws which amended the Constitution in ways which quite clearly breached fundamental human rights. Even though Ireland had fought to be free of British parliamentary sovereignty, the Supreme Court was content to replace it with an equally if not more draconian Irish version of the concept. Michael Crowe noted that '[d]espite appearances to the contrary, the Irish Free State Constitution was in fact hardly better than the British Constitution',[142] while Michael Mansergh drew a comparison with the United States: 'Critics in America claim that the judges are legislating under the guise of enactment; in the Free State that the Executive unduly subordinates judicial control'.[143] Ronan Keane, Chief Justice of Ireland from 2000 to 2004, has said that the decision in *The State (Ryan) v Lennon* 'was really the doom of the 1922 constitution because it not only meant that the human rights provisions were no longer effective but … it also completed the undoing of the treaty settlement which, of course, was very much part of the constitution'.[144]

The Court's Performance 1924–37

As we shall see in Chapter 5, considerable care was taken in 1924 to appoint judges to the Supreme Court who would not be openly pro-British in their outlook. It is clear, however, that in the 13 years which followed there was little display of overt Irish nationalism on the Supreme Court bench. As a general guide to the Supreme Court observes: '[f]or the most part, subsequent Supreme Court decisions of the 1920s and 1930s were not affected by and did not reflect any division along nationalist and unionist lines.'[145] Of the two judges in *The State (Ryan) v Lennon* who voted to uphold repressive legislation, FitzGibbon J was perhaps a predictable supporter: his father had been a senior judge, he himself had been a unionist MP and TD, and he had always opposed the use of violence in the struggle for Irish home rule.[146] Murnaghan J was brought up in Northern Ireland but had not been implicated in any violence in the period leading up to the Anglo-Irish Treaty in 1921.[147] The fact that he sided with FitzGibbon J rather than with the Chief Justice was of immense significance because it helped to mould the Supreme Court of Ireland in a way which put an early halt to any suggestion that independent Ireland was truly founded on the basis of inalienable human rights. It was an attitude towards human rights during times of conflict which was

[141] Ibid, 219. [142] Crowe (1971–72) 285. [143] Mansergh (1934) 57.
[144] Keane (2004–06) 142. [145] Kennedy et al (2003), 36.
[146] See further Geoghegan (2013) 38–41. [147] Ibid, 41–3.

to be reflected in the House of Lords during the years of the Second World War[148] and also during the later troubles in Northern Ireland.[149] It was also apparent in the European Court of Human Rights when in its first ever judgment it considered the legality of indefinite detention without trial in Ireland.[150]

While some regard must be had to the political context at the time, it remains clear that the Supreme Court disappointed most objective observers during this initial period of its existence. Indeed it is no exaggeration to say that the Court played a rather insignificant role during the whole life of the Irish Free State. It did not come into existence until the State was nearly two years old, it was not given significant powers by the Constitution, and the powers which it did possess were not exercised with any enthusiasm. The judges were predominantly conservative and unadventurous, even in comparison with their colleagues in the United Kingdom and other British dominions. Compared with the US Supreme Court,[151] the Irish Supreme Court was positively pusillanimous. The overwhelming judicial attitude seems to have been that the construction of the new State should be the preserve of elected politicians, with the role of judges being limited to the adjudication of disputes in accordance with settled principles of law. Above all, judges must remain subservient to the will of the people as expressed through their representatives in the legislature.

While the Anglo-Irish Treaty of 1921 might have seemed like a grant of virtual independence to the Irish nation, in fact it did little to undermine the principle of parliamentary sovereignty on which Britain's unwritten constitution was, and still is, firmly grounded. Judges in the Free State might have relished the challenges of operating in a new nation but this did not lead them to believe that they should start behaving in ways different from how their predecessors had behaved when Ireland was part of the United Kingdom. As a later Chief Justice pointed out, what lay behind the antipathy to judicial activism 'was the innate reluctance of judges who had been bred in the English constitutional tradition to overstep what they saw as the traditional limitations on the role of the courts'.[152] Moreover, Article 73 of the Free State Constitution provided judges with a convenient excuse for not entering where angels feared to tread. By preserving the laws in force at the date of the coming into operation of the new Constitution until they were altered by the Oireachtas Article 73 seems to have acted as a discouragement to Supreme Court justices to develop the law in ways that they might have preferred. The truth is that, despite the rhetoric of Hugh Kennedy and others to the contrary, the court system set up in 1924, and in particular the replacement of the role of the House of Lords by that of the Irish Supreme Court, did not make the Irish judicial system radically different from the British system which preceded it. In Geoghegan's words, 'the changes in 1924 were to a large extent superficial'.[153] He added a comment which would doubtless have stuck in the throat of Hugh Kennedy: 'It would be churlish not to admit that one good thing we inherited from the English was the common law system'.[154]

Donal Coffey has argued that it is unfair to conclude that the Irish Free State judiciary were not receptive to the potential of the 1922 Constitution.[155] He admits that the Constitution was 'an experiment which ended in failure', and he accepts that the judiciary

[148] *Liversidge v Anderson* [1942] AC 206. [149] Livingstone (1994); Dickson (2006).

[150] *Lawless v Ireland* (1978–80) 1 EHRR 1. See Chap 12 below, 270-2.

[151] eg in *Schechter Poultry Corp v US* 295 US 495 (1935) the Supreme Court declared the National Industrial Recovery Act 1933 to be unconstitutional and in *US v Butler* 297 US 1 (1936) it took the same view of the Agricultural Adjustment Act of the same year. Congress had introduced both Acts to try to counter the effects of the Great Depression.

[152] Keane (2000) 188. [153] Geoghegan (2013) 34. [154] Ibid.

[155] Coffey (2011). See too Coffey (2012), where he explores why de Valera became convinced that the 1922 Constitution needed to be replaced.

were excessively positivistic in their approach to adjudication, but he nevertheless credits the Free State judges with at least ensuring that the concept of judicial review survived, allowing it to blossom in later cases such as *Buckley v Attorney General* (the Sinn Féin funds case).[156] To some this may smack of damning with faint praise but it must be remembered that Irish judges were operating in a young new State and would have been acutely conscious of its fragility. One can understand why they did not want to present too much of a challenge to elected politicians.

[156] [1950] 1 IR 67. See Chap 6 below, 120.

4

The Jurisdiction of the Supreme Court

The Role of the Supreme Court

The jurisdiction of Ireland's Supreme Court is wide. Far from being limited to deciding whether a law or a type of conduct is unconstitutional, its remit extends to all legal matters, whether civil or criminal, public or private. There has never been a serious debate in Ireland as to whether there should be a separate apex court dealing only with constitutional matters, so to that extent the country falls into the same category as most other common law legal systems, such as Australia, Canada, India, New Zealand, the United Kingdom and the USA.[1] On the other hand, civil law countries, such as Germany and Spain, and some mixed legal systems, such as South Africa, maintain both a Constitutional Court and a Supreme Court. There are merits and demerits to both approaches but the consensus amongst common law countries seems to be that avoidance of demarcation disputes between two apex courts is a compelling argument for having just one of them.

Within the common law family of legal systems a further distinction can be drawn between those which are federal systems and those which are not. In the former systems the country's top court has the additional role of deciding whether the federal and state or provincial authorities are performing their duties and exercising their powers in a constitutional manner. Since Ireland is not a federal system the role of its Supreme Court is more akin to that of the top courts in the United Kingdom, where a Supreme Court replaced the Appellate Committee of the House of Lords in 2009, and New Zealand, where a Supreme Court took over the role previously played by the Judicial Committee of the Privy Council in 2004.

This chapter considers how the jurisdiction of the Irish Supreme Court has come to be as it is today and explains how recent reforms to its jurisdiction are likely to enhance the efficiency of the Court.[2]

Ireland's Final Court of Appeal

Prior to the creation of the Irish Free State in 1922 the final court of appeal for legal disputes arising in any part of Ireland was the House of Lords in London. The Supreme Court of Judicature Act (Ireland) 1877, like the equivalent legislation for England and Wales in 1873, created a new High Court of Justice in Ireland and a new Court of Appeal in Ireland.[3] Together they were described as two divisions of the Supreme Court of Judicature in Ireland.[4] The Lord Chancellor of Ireland, the Lord Chief Justice of Ireland, the Master of

[1] See Hogan (2011); Coffey (2012). For discussion of the suggestion that there be a Constitutional Court for Northern Ireland, and of the existing courts in Canada, Spain and Germany, see Le Sueur (2004) Chaps 3, 6, 7 and 8.

[2] For details of the procedural rules applicable in the Supreme Court see Ó Floinn (2008) 528–44.

[3] Supreme Court of Judicature Act (Ireland) 1877, s 5. Further provision for the two courts was made by ss 6, 21–2 and 34–52, and by ss 10, 23–4 and 56–8, respectively. For an account of the history of 'supreme judicature' in Ireland prior to 1800, see the scholarly article by the fourth person to be appointed to the Irish Supreme Court: Murnaghan (1912).

[4] Ibid.

the Rolls of Ireland, the Lord Chief Justice of the Irish Common Pleas[5] and the Lord Chief Baron of the Irish Exchequer[6] were entitled in sit in both divisions, with two 'ordinary judges' appointed to sit only as Lords Justices of Appeal in the Court of Appeal. The 1877 Act confirmed that all decisions of the Court of Appeal in Ireland were subject to appeal to the House of Lords in London, under the same conditions as had previously applied to appeals from the Court of Appeal in Chancery in Ireland or the Court of Exchequer Chamber in Ireland to the House of Lords or to the Privy Council.[7]

As mentioned in Chapter 2, under the Government of Ireland Act 1920 a new Court of Appeal in Southern Ireland was created to take over the work in that part of the island of the Court of Appeal in Ireland and to be the equivalent of the Court of Appeal in Northern Ireland.[8] As regards further appeals, the 1920 Act created a new tier of appeal court with jurisdiction throughout the whole of Ireland—the High Court of Appeal for Ireland.[9] This court could hear appeals from any decision of the two regional Courts of Appeal[10] and could sit in whichever part of the island the appeal came from.[11] It was composed of the Lord Chancellor of Ireland, the Lord Chief Justice of Northern Ireland and the Lord Chief Justice of Southern Ireland, with other judges nominated from the two parts of Ireland if necessary.[12] The High Court of Appeal first sat on 15 December 1921 and continued in place for less than a year, sitting for the final time on 5 December 1922.[13] The *Irish Reports* for 1922 and 1923 include nine decisions by the Court, all in civil cases.[14] In the first of these cases the claimant challenged the jurisdiction of the new Court, pointing to legislation which said that the decision of the Court of Appeal in a case begun in a county court was 'final and conclusive',[15] but the High Court of Appeal rejected this argument by holding that the point of setting up the High Court of Appeal was to ensure uniformity of the law throughout Ireland.[16]

The Government of Ireland Act 1920 preserved the same right to appeal from the High Court of Appeal for Ireland to the House of Lords as had existed for the Court of Appeal.[17] In addition it permitted appeals to the House of Lords in any case where a person was aggrieved by any decision of the High Court of Appeal for Ireland in proceedings taken by way of *certiorari, mandamus, quo warranto* or prohibition[18] and also in any case where a decision of the High Court of Appeal concerned the validity of any law made by or having the effect of an Act of the Parliament of Southern Ireland or Northern Ireland and the

[5] The last person to hold this position was Sir Michael Morris. When he was appointed as Lord Chief Justice of Ireland in 1887 his former post was abolished.

[6] The last person to hold this post was Christopher Palles, from 1874 until 1916. When he retired the post was abolished.

[7] Supreme Court of Judicature Act (Ireland) 1877, s 86.

[8] Government of Ireland Act 1920, s 39(1). Chap 2 above, 9. [9] Ibid, s 38. [10] Ibid, s 43(1).

[11] Ibid, s 43(3). [12] Ibid, s 43(2). [13] See [1922] 2 IR, preliminary page, under 'Memoranda'.

[14] *Leyburn v Armagh County Council* [1922] 2 IR 15 and [1922] 2 IR 58; *Cooper v General Accident Assurance Corp* [1922] 2 IR 38; *James Crean & Son Ltd v J Steen McMillan* [1922] 2 IR 105; *McKnight v Armagh County Council* [1922] 2 IR 137; *Wycherly v Flynn* [1922] 2 IR 169; *Re Mary Keane* [1922] 2 IR 221; *Boggan v Motor Union Insurance Co* [1922] 2 IR 222; *Hughes v McNaull* [1923] 1 IR 78; *Jackson v Stopford* [1923] 2 IR 1. Sir John Ross, the Lord Chancellor of Ireland, sat in all nine of these cases; the Northern judge was usually Andrews LJ or Henry LCJ and the Southern judge was usually Molony CJ or O'Connor MR.

[15] County Court Appeals Act 1889, s 8.

[16] *Leyburn v Armagh County Council* [1922] 2 IR 15, 18 (per Sir John Ross) and 21 (per Andrews LJ).

[17] s49.

[18] *Certiorari* was a writ whereby the decision of a lower court was ordered to be delivered to a higher court so that it could be reviewed; *mandamus* was an order from a higher court ordering a public authority to do something; *quo warranto* was a writ requiring the recipient to explain by what authority he or she had exercised a specified power; a writ of prohibition was a court order requiring someone to stop doing something which the court had decided he or she had no power to do. No appeals lay in cases involving these writs unless legislation specifically provided for them, because decisions in such cases were technically 'orders', not 'judgments'.

decision was not otherwise subject to appeal. Existing provisions as to the need to seek leave to appeal were preserved too.[19] Incredibly, at least two of the nine decisions of the High Court of Appeal referred to above were further appealed to the House of Lords, thereby providing a *fourth* appeal for the initially disappointed litigant.[20] In the second of the two cases (*Boggan*) the House of Lords overturned the decision of the High Court of Appeal and in the process followed its own decision in the first of the two cases (*Cooper*).

From December 1922 until June 1924 the highest court in the Irish Free State was the Court of Appeal, although as we have seen in Chapter 3 an appeal could be taken in some instances to the Judicial Committee of the Privy Council in London. The Supreme Court took over the role of top court in Ireland in June 1924 and, because of a transitory provision,[21] continued in being even after the 1937 Constitution made provision for a new Supreme Court.[22] The new Supreme Court was not formally established until 29 September 1961, the commencement date for the Courts (Establishment and Constitution) Act 1961.[23] By the Courts (Supplemental Provisions) Act 1961 the Supreme Court was declared to be 'a superior court of record with such appellate and other jurisdiction as is prescribed by the Constitution',[24] and it went on to specifically confer on the new Court (a) all jurisdiction which was previously vested in the Court of Appeal in Southern Ireland before 1924 and which had later been vested in the existing Supreme Court and (b) all other jurisdiction which was exercisable by the existing Supreme Court.[25]

The Court of Criminal Appeal

Article 66 of the 1922 Constitution said that the Supreme Court 'shall, with such exceptions (not including cases which involve questions as to the validity of any law) and subject to such regulations as may be prescribed by law, have appellate jurisdiction from all decisions of the High Court'. Article 34.4.3 of the 1937 Constitution was worded in essentially the same way but added that the Supreme Court 'shall also have appellate jurisdiction from such decisions of other courts as may be prescribed by law'. Notwithstanding these provisions, from the very start of the Supreme Court's existence there was a major exception, or qualification, to the Supreme Court's jurisdiction in criminal cases. Decisions taken in such cases by the High Court (when it was to be referred to, for no obvious reason, as the Central Criminal Court[26]) could be appealed instead to the Court of Criminal Appeal, although there was still the possibility of a further appeal from the Court of Criminal Appeal to the Supreme Court.

The Court of Criminal Appeal, while not foreseen in the 1922 Constitution, was created at the same time as the High Court and Supreme Court. Its establishment is a consequence of the view that criminal cases deserve to be treated differently for at least three reasons. First, criminal cases are extremely numerous in lower courts and if appeals against their decisions could too easily be brought to the Supreme Court it might be overwhelmed. Second,

[19] Government of Ireland Act 1920, s 49(c)(i).

[20] *Cooper v General Accident Assurance Corp* [1922] 2 IR 214; *Boggan v Motor Union Insurance Co* [1923] 2 IR 136.

[21] Art 58 of the 1937 Constitution.

[22] Art 34.2 said: 'The Courts shall comprise Courts of First Instance and a Court of Final Appeal'. Art 34.4.1 said: 'The Court of Final Appeal shall be called the Supreme Court.'

[23] s1(1) reads: 'On the commencement of this Act, the Court of Final Appeal, which in pursuance of Article 34 of the Constitution is to be called An Chúirt Uachtarach (The Supreme Court), shall stand established.' By s 7 the existing courts 'ceased to exercise any jurisdiction'.

[24] s7(1).

[25] s7(2), referring also to some exceptions mentioned in s 48 of the Act.

[26] Courts (Establishment and Constitution) Act 1961, s 11.

criminal appeals often turn on disputes about facts, the credibility of witnesses, or the appropriate sentence to impose on a person who has been convicted, all of which are matters which do not usually entail the application of great legal acuity and are inappropriate for detailed consideration by the sharpest judicial minds in the country. Third, criminal convictions can have huge consequences for accused persons and it is therefore sensible to make available more than just one opportunity to appeal against those convictions.

The Courts of Justice Act 1924, in section 8, provided that the Chief Justice could, from time to time, request any two ordinary judges of the High Court to sit with him- or herself, or with another judge of the Supreme Court, as the Court of Criminal Appeal of the Irish Free State. Any other available judge of the High Court or Supreme Court could, at the request of the Chief Justice, attend as members of the Court of Criminal Appeal for the occasion in question. The Court was formally *re-established* some 24 years after the 1937 Constitution (where again it was not mentioned), but its jurisdiction remained unaltered.[27] It still had to be comprised of at least three judges: one had to be the Chief Justice or an ordinary judge of the Supreme Court nominated by the Chief Justice, while the other two had to be the President of the High Court and another judge from the High Court nominated by the Chief Justice.[28] In addition, any other available judge of the Supreme Court or High Court could attend at the request of the Chief Justice.[29]

The Court of Criminal Appeal was always a bit of an anomaly in the Irish legal system. It may in part have been established because a court with the same name had been created in England and Wales by the Criminal Appeal Act 1907 and seemed to be working well. But the latter could hear appeals on points of law, points of fact, and sentencing,[30] while in Ireland the Court of Criminal Appeal was limited to hearing appeals on points of law and sentencing. In neither court could there be an appeal by the prosecution against a defendant's acquittal.[31] In Ireland appeals could be brought not only from the High Court but also from the Circuit Court. A peculiarity of both Courts of Criminal Appeal was that from their inception the judgment of the court had to be pronounced by the judge presiding in the court or such other member of the court as that judge directed, with no other member of the court being permitted to issue a separate judgment, whether concurring or dissenting.[32] Presumably this was intended to increase the likelihood that the law stated by the court would be clear and certain.

In *People (AG) v Conmey*[33] a challenge was raised in the Supreme Court against the constitutionality of the appeal path created to the Court of Criminal Appeal, on the basis that it violated the constitutional right to appeal to the Supreme Court.[34] The challenge was unsuccessful because O'Higgins CJ, for the Supreme Court, pointed out that there was nothing in either the 1922 or 1937 Constitutions to prevent the Oireachtas from establishing new courts to hear appeals and that the Courts of Justice Act 1924 expressly allowed for an appeal from the Court of Criminal Appeal to the Supreme Court. According to section 29 of that Act, while a decision by the Court of Criminal Appeal was final, an appeal could lie to the Supreme Court if the Court of Criminal Appeal or the Attorney General certified

[27] Ibid, s 3(1). For a review of the Court's first 30 years see Delany (1952). For collections of unreported judgments of the Court see Frewen (1979), (1984) and Casey (1990); see too McCutcheon and Hanlon (2005).

[28] Ibid, s 3(2). [29] Ibid.

[30] Criminal Appeal Act 1907, s 3. Prior to this the Court of Crown Cases Reserved could deal with criminal appeals only where there was a question of law at stake.

[31] For later developments on this topic see 61-2 below.

[32] Courts of Justice Act 1924, s 28 (Ireland); Court of Criminal Appeal Act 1907, s 1(5) (England and Wales).

[33] [1975] 1 IR 341. See Casey (1975) and (1981).

[34] Art 66 of the 1922 Constitution; Art 34.4.3 of the 1937 Constitution.

that the decision involved a point of law of exceptional public importance and that it was desirable in the public interest that an appeal should be taken to the Supreme Court.[35] In 2006 the certifying power was extended to the Director of Public Prosecutions.[36]

In *People v Lynch*, the Supreme Court asserted that any legal prescriptions depriving the Supreme Court of its appellate jurisdiction needed to be 'clear and unambiguous',[37] but it did not cast any doubt on the interpretation of the provision in the Courts of Justice Act 1924 adopted in *People (AG) v Conmey*. Research conducted for a later Working Group found a lack of uniformity of practice within the Court of Criminal Appeal and Supreme Court as regards whether to hold an oral hearing to deal with applications for leave to appeal and whether to give reasons for granting or refusing leave, but such inconsistency was also apparent in other common law jurisdictions.[38]

Given that a Supreme Court judge was involved in every decision made by the Court of Criminal Appeal during its 90-year history, a case could be made for including the output of that Court within this book's consideration of the Supreme Court's law-making. But as all of the Court of Criminal Appeal's decisions consisted of just one judgment it is impossible to be specific as to which Supreme Court judges were responsible for particular views expressed in those judgments. The Court remains a largely under-researched institution and unfortunately there is no space to say more about it here. As we shall see, the Court of Criminal Appeal was eventually abolished in 2014, almost 50 years after the same step had been taken in England and Wales.[39] It was replaced by a Court of Appeal empowered to deal with both civil and criminal appeals. The creation of the Court of Appeal was the final chapter in the development of appeal routes to the highest courts in Ireland. To aid clarity the stages in that development are set out diagrammatically in Figure 4.1 below.

The Growing Caseload of the Supreme Court

According to section 18 of the Courts of Justice Act 1924:

> The Supreme Court shall be a superior court of record with such appellate jurisdiction as is prescribed by the Constitution, and, subject as in this Act is provided, there shall be transferred to the Supreme Court the jurisdiction which at the commencement of this Act was vested in or capable of being exercised by the existing Court of Appeal of the Supreme Court of Judicature in Ireland or any judges or judge thereof.

This provision meant that the Supreme Court of Ireland took over the entire role of the former Court of Appeal of Ireland, without any further limitation on its jurisdiction. No legal subject-matter was outside its remit and no leave had to be obtained before a litigant could seek the court's attention to his or her case. Right from the start, therefore, the potential workload of the Supreme Court was extraordinarily heavy. Initially, however, the worst fears were not fulfilled. Doubtless because of the costs involved and the limited number of people who were willing to risk so much money in going to law, the judges who were first appointed to the Supreme Court were hardly rushed off their feet during their first few years in office. In 1929 the Minister for Justice was asked in the Dáil for the number of Supreme Court judgments which on that date had been reserved for three months or longer, and the

[35] A further appeal (to the House of Lords) was also permitted in England and Wales under the Court of Criminal Appeal Act 1907, s 1(6).

[36] Criminal Justice Act 2006, s 22, inserting a new s 29(2) into the Courts of Justice Act 1924.

[37] [1982] 1 IR 64. See generally Forde and Leonard (2013) paras 7.13 and 17.63.

[38] Working Group (2009) 79, 178 (Australia), 182 (Canada).

[39] Criminal Appeal Act 1966.

1877 to 1921	1921 to 1922	1922 to 1924
High Court of Ireland	High Court of Ireland	High Court of Ireland
↓	↓	↓
Court of Appeal of Ireland	Court of Appeal of Southern Ireland	Court of Appeal of Ireland
↓	↓	↓
House of Lords	High Court of Appeal of Ireland	Privy Council
	↓	
	House of Lords	

1924 to 1933	1933 to 2014	2014–2018
High Court	High Court	High Court
↓	↓	↓
Court of Criminal Appeal	Court of Criminal Appeal	Court of Appeal
↓	↓	↓
Supreme Court	Supreme Court	Supreme Court
↓		
Privy Council		

Fig. 4.1 The history of appeal routes in Ireland, 1877–2018

answer was just three.[40] In 1935, however, the Minister reported that in one case judgment had been delayed for more than two years.[41]

In 1930 a report on the operation of the Irish court system was issued by a Joint Committee of the Oireachtas on the Courts of Justice Act 1924, but it recommended no changes to the system for bringing appeals to the Supreme Court other than suggesting an unspecified increase in the number of judges sitting on the Court, which at that time was still only three.[42] This led to the Courts of Justice Act 1936, which increased the number of Supreme Court judges to five,[43] partly because, as admitted by a later Minister for Justice, valid objections could be raised against a final appellate court consisting of just three judges.[44] No further reforms were seriously considered during the ensuing 30 years. In 1966 the Committee on Court Practice and Procedure, which had been established in 1962, suggested that the Supreme Court should take over the work of the Court of Criminal Appeal, since a Supreme Court judge was already required to sit in every Court of Criminal Appeal case and in practice it was very rare for a further appeal to be taken from that court to the Supreme Court.[45] Perhaps because of push-back from the Supreme Court itself, this reform was not provided for at the time. A further report from the same Committee six years later made a number of additional suggestions for widening the jurisdiction of the Supreme Court.[46] These would

[40] Dáil Debs, vol 28, no 4 (p 58 online), 27 February 1929.

[41] Dáil Debs, vol 59, no 12 (p 9 online), 4 December 1935.

[42] *Report of the Joint Committee on the Courts of Justice Act 1924* (Stationery Office, 1930).

[43] s 4(1). This number included the Chief Justice, but not the President of the High Court, who was entitled to sit in Supreme Court *ex officio*.

[44] Dáil Debs, vol 118, no 9 (p 18 online), 23 November 1949 (per General MacEoin).

[45] *Seventh Interim Report: Appeals from Convictions on Indictment* (Stationery Office, Pr 9196, 1966). John Kelly suggested that the Constitution should stipulate the permitted number of Supreme Court judges so that the government could not pack the Court with new appointees if this was politically opportune: Kelly (1966a) 7.

[46] Committee on Court Practice (1972); Osborough (1973a).

have allowed the Court to deal directly with cases stated by the District Court (as it could already could do with cases stated by the Circuit Court and the High Court),[47] to hear appeals against a High Court's decision not to grant leave to appeal to the Supreme Court in cases stated to the High Court from the District Court,[48] and to allow constitutional issues brought to the High Court on uncontested facts to be transferred to the Supreme Court with the parties' consent. There was also a proposal to allow Supreme Court judges to give separate opinions in Article 26 references made to that Court by the President of Ireland.[49] As with the proposal in the 1966 report, all the recommendations made in 1972 fell on deaf ears. The report is nevertheless useful for the statistics it revealed about the work of the Court. The average number of cases entered on the Court's list between 1949 and 1959 was 99 and between 1959 and 1969 it was 146; in 1959 there were 48 reserved written judgments while in 1969 there were 62; in 1948–49 there were just 83 sitting days, while in 1968–69 there were 157.[50]

Again there was then another long period—24 years—during which little attention was paid to reforming the jurisdiction of the Supreme Court. We know from questions asked in the Dáil that in the later 1960s and early 1970s the Supreme Court was busy, though this does not seem to have hindered the Court from issuing some of its most imaginative and ground-breaking judgments.[51] In the five legal years from 1965 to 1971 the average number of appeals from the High Court to the Supreme Court which resulted in a variation or reversal of the High Court decision was 43.[52] By way of contrast, in 1968 the Appellate Committee of the House of Lords, operating for the whole of the United Kingdom, was presented with just 52 appeals and heard just 33.[53]

The Constitution Review Group

It was only in 1995, when action was taken to create a Judicial Appointments Advisory Board,[54] that the opportunity was used to increase the membership of the Supreme Court from five judges to eight[55] and to vest in the Supreme Court all the jurisdiction of the Court of Criminal Appeal.[56] The latter was a sensible move that was supported by senior judges, for it ensured that appeals in civil and criminal matters would henceforth be processed in the same way. However, while the increase in the number of judges took effect as soon as the Act was signed by the President (15 December 1995) the transfer of jurisdiction from the Court of Criminal Appeal was never triggered. No clear justification for this omission seems ever to have been officially issued.

[47] The power to state a case was first granted to the High Court by the Courts of Justice Act 1936, s 38(3). It was extended to the Circuit Court by the Courts of Justice Act 1947, s 16, and finally to the District Court by the Courts (Supplemental Provisions) Act 1961, s 52. But the 1961 Act did not expressly permit the referring court to adjourn a decision in the case pending the determination of the case stated by the higher court.

[48] s 52(2) of the Courts (Supplemental Provisions) Act 1961 provided that: 'An appeal shall lie by leave of the High Court to the Supreme Court from every determination of the High Court on a question of law referred to the High Court under subsection (1) of this section', but this did not mean that the refusal of leave could be appealed against. Art 34.4.3 of the Constitution, as already noted, conferred on the Supreme Court the right to hear appeals from the High Court 'with such exceptions and subject to such regulations as may be prescribed by law'.

[49] Art 26 and the 'one opinion rule' are discussed in Chap 6 below.

[50] See too Osborough (1973a).

[51] See Chap 6 below, 125-8.

[52] Dáil Debs, vol 260, no 2 (p 71 online), 13 April 1972 (per Desmond O'Malley, Minister for Justice). In *The State (Browne) v Feran* [1967] IR 147, the Supreme Court confirmed that it had jurisdiction to hear appeals against decisions of the High Court on *habeas corpus* applications.

[53] Blom-Cooper and Drewry (1972) Tables 2A and 2B (pp 42–3).

[54] This body is dealt with in detail in Chap 5 below, 74-6.

[55] Courts and Courts Officers Act 1995, s 6. Again, this figure includes the Chief Justice.

[56] Ibid, s 4.

It was also at this time that the Constitution Review Group looked at what the 1937 Constitution said about the country's court system. The Group noted that the system had come under strain from 'the huge increase in litigation which has occurred over the last twenty years or so'.[57] Unfortunately it provided no statistics to substantiate this claim and it seems that none were officially published until a few years later.[58] The Group recommended that, in order to make it clearly constitutional for the Oireachtas to create additional levels of courts, Article 34.2 of the Constitution should be amended so as to authorise not just courts of first instance and a final court of appeal but also 'such other courts as may be prescribed by law'.[59] This reflected the fact that pressure had already resulted in the inclusion of relevant provisions in the Courts and Courts Officers Act 1995. The Review Group went on to ask itself whether the Supreme Court should be given any *additional* jurisdiction, in particular the jurisdiction to hear constitutional cases brought directly to it without first being considered by a lower court, as proposed by the Committee on Court Practice and Procedure in 1972. However, rather than answer that question directly the Group focused on whether *any* attempt by the Oireachtas to confer additional jurisdiction on the Supreme Court would be constitutional. It concluded that there was 'considerable doubt' whether it would be, and a majority of the Group was unconvinced that the Constitution should be amended to allow for it: '[t]he potential for very exceptional cases which are urgent and of major public importance and where facts are not in issue does not appear to warrant the conferring of an originating jurisdiction on the Supreme Court'.[60]

The Review Group additionally noted that Article 34.4.4 of the 1937 Constitution specifically prohibits any enactment from removing from the Supreme Court's jurisdiction cases involving the constitutional validity of any law. The fact that such a provision was included in the Constitution at all is a clear sign that the framers of that document wanted to preserve the Supreme Court's pre-eminence in the Irish legal system (subject to the will of the people as expressed in a referendum to change the Constitution). In the USA the old case of *Ex parte McCardle*[61] is still good law in so far as it suggests that Congress *can* limit the Supreme Court's jurisdiction to adjudicate upon the constitutionality of laws, although later case law suggests that the Supreme Court would not tolerate the complete displacement of its jurisdiction in a particular field.[62] The Constitution Review Group, again by a majority, favoured consideration being given to amending the 1937 Constitution so as to make it clearer that the Oireachtas could, without fear of violating the Constitution, enact a law denying the prosecution a right of appeal to the Supreme Court against the acquittal of a defendant at the High Court (sitting as the Central Criminal Court).[63] No such amendment was subsequently put before the people for their consideration.

Chief Justice Keane's lecture

In 2001 Chief Justice Ronan Keane delivered a seminal lecture on the court system of Ireland, published as the first article in a new journal designed to assist judicial studies in the country.[64] As far as the jurisdiction of the Supreme Court is concerned Keane CJ regretted

[57] CRG (1996) 158.

[58] The Department of Justice issued Annual Accounts relating to the operation of the courts, but these did not set out detailed figures for the workload of each court.

[59] CRG (1996) 158. [60] Ibid, 174. [61] 74 US 506 (1869).

[62] See Hall (2005) *sub verbo McCardle*. [63] CRG (1996) 177.

[64] Keane (2001a). The lecture was delivered for the UCC Law Society on 23 March 2001 and is available at www.ijsj.ie/assets/uploads/documents/pdfs/2001-Edition-01/article/the-irish-courts-system-in-the-21st—century-planning-for-the-future.pdf. This Journal should not be confused with the new Irish Judicial Studies Journal launched in 2017: see www.ijsj.ie. See too Byrne and McCutcheon (2014) 369–71.

that decisions taken in civil cases by Circuit Courts could not reach the Supreme Court: the decision of the High Court on appeal is final, whatever the importance of the points of law at issue.[65] On the other hand he noted the anomaly that there was an automatic right of appeal from the original jurisdiction of the High Court to the Supreme Court, meaning that 'the Supreme Court regularly hears appeals in cases which are of no general public importance leading to inevitable delays in the hearing of those cases which are'.[66] The Chief Justice concluded that it would be far more satisfactory if there was a Court of Appeal which could hear appeals from the High Court in both civil and serious criminal cases and which could then grant leave to appeal to the Supreme Court where there was a point of law of public importance involved.[67] He did not think the Constitution would need to be amended to bring about the reform, citing the Supreme Court's decision in *Conmey*,[68] which had upheld the establishment of the Court of Criminal Appeal in 1924 even though it was not mentioned in the 1922 Constitution. The lecture ended with a request that a Working Group be established to consider possible reforms. Keane CJ pointed to the example of the Working Group chaired by Judge Susan Denham, whose reports 'led to the greatest revolution in the administration of justice in this country since independence with the establishment of the Court Service'.[69]

A Working Group on the Jurisdiction of the Courts was indeed established in the wake of the Chief Justice's plea, this time under the chairmanship of Fennelly J, another Judge of the Supreme Court. The Group issued a report on the criminal jurisdiction of the courts in 2003.[70] Surprisingly, it did not recommend the abolition of the Court of Criminal Appeal.[71] In fact, to avoid any lingering confusion concerning the status of that court, it proposed that the uncommenced legislative provisions concerning the Court's abolition should be repealed.[72] Three reasons given for this were, first, that the great majority of appeals dealt with by the Court of Criminal Appeal are fairly routine appeals against sentence; second, that allocating all criminal appeals to the Supreme Court would have serious implications for the workload of that Court; and third, the appeals would be dealt with by judges who lack regular trial experience.

The Law Reform Commission

It was at this point that the baton on reform of the court system was taken up by the Law Reform Commission, chaired at the time by Catherine McGuinness, a recently retired judge of the Supreme Court. In its report on prosecution appeals published in November 2006 the Commission recommended the introduction of 'without prejudice' but not 'with prejudice' prosecution appeals, the latter being appeals which, if successful, could lead to the defendant being re-tried. This was notwithstanding the fact that some other common law jurisdictions, including England and Wales and Northern Ireland, had already provided for 'with prejudice' prosecution appeals.[73] Eight months later the Commission issued a well-researched consultation paper on more general reform of the Irish court system,[74]

[65] Ibid, 17. [66] Ibid, 18. [67] Ibid, 19. [68] Note 33 above. [69] Note 64 above, 21–2.

[70] Working Group (2003), also available through the website of the Courts Service (www.courts.ie), under 'Publications' and then 'Policy, Reports and Strategic Plans'. The report relied upon a study of the criminal courts in Ireland conducted by two legal academics from Northern Ireland: Jackson and Doran (2003). This was included as Appendix V to the report.

[71] Ibid, paras 627–30. [72] Courts and Court Officers Act 1995, ss 3(2) and 4.

[73] *Prosecution Appeals and Pre-Trial Hearings* (LRC 81-2006). For the law in England and Wales see the Criminal Justice Act 2003, ss 57–74; for the law in Northern Ireland see the Criminal Justice (NI) Order 2004, arts 16–33.

[74] *Consolidation and Reform of the Courts Acts* (LRC CP 46-2007).

the product of deliberations by a Working Group set up by the Commission in 2005, one of whose members was Hugh Geoghegan, another Judge of the Supreme Court. The Working Group's main aim was to bring about a consolidation of not only the 56 statutes on courts' jurisdiction which had been enacted by the Dáil since 1922 but also the many pre-partition Acts on the subject which were still partly in force.[75] Such a consolidation was seen as a way of improving access to the law for ordinary citizens.

While this was a noble goal, it meant that the recommendations of the Commission had little impact on the caseload of the Supreme Court. Thus, while the report proposed that all appeals in civil cases should be by leave of the court of first instance (not the appeal court),[76] it also suggested that Circuit and High Court judges should be allowed to state a consultative case for the Supreme Court whether or not this had been requested by any of the parties to the litigation[77] and that there should be an automatic right of appeal from the High Court to the Supreme Court in cases where the High Court had determined a question of law referred to it by the District Court.[78] The Commission believed that not imposing a leave requirement would not lead to the Supreme Court having to deal with an undue number of additional cases[79] but it made no comment on the potential effect on the Supreme Court's caseload of the recommendation on consultative cases stated by the Circuit Court or High Court. The consultative case stated procedure—whereby the proceedings in a case in a lower court are suspended while a relevant point of law is ruled upon by a higher court—is not one which is used in England and Wales or Northern Ireland, mainly because of the delays it can cause, but the Law Reform Commission was very much in favour of its retention in Ireland.[80] It balanced this by recommending the abolition of the case stated *appeal* procedure, to which jurisdictions in England and Wales and Northern Ireland have long been wedded.

Statistics on the Supreme Court's workload

Whatever the jurisdiction of the Supreme Court should have been, there was little doubt that by the early years of the 21st century the institution was running very hard just to ensure that it did not fall catastrophically behind with its caseload. Table 4.1 sets out some relevant annual figures since 2001. They are taken from the Annual Reports of the Courts Service, which was established in 1999 as a result of the Courts Service Act 1998, enacted to implement a recommendation in the first Report of the Working Group on a Courts Commission published in 1996.[81] Figures for previous years do not seem to have been published. Unfortunately it is not possible to deduce from the recent statistics how many appeals were still pending at the end of each year, but it is clear that the backlog was steadily rising throughout this period.

The startling conclusions we can draw from these statistics are, first, that in the years leading up to the reform of the Supreme Court in 2014 the number of appeals increased significantly while the number of appeals disposed of increased at a much slower rate and, second, that the waiting time between an appeal being certified as ready to be heard and

[75] Chaps 1 and 2 provide useful summaries of the history of the court system from the late 19th century onwards.

[76] Note 74 above, para 3.177. [77] Ibid, para 3.33. [78] Ibid, para 3.24. [79] Ibid, para 3.23.

[80] Ibid, paras 3.42–3.58.

[81] *Management and Financing of the Courts* (1996, Pn 2690). The Working Group was chaired by Denham J. The Courts Service's first Annual Report covers a 17-month period (August 1999 to December 2000), so its statistics cannot be compared with those in subsequent Annual Reports. All the Annual Reports are available on the Courts Service's website, www.courts.ie.

Table 4.1 Caseload of the Irish Supreme Court, 2001–17[a]

Year	Appeals received	Appeals disposed of or withdrawn	Appeals allowed	Written judgments delivered	Average waiting time after date fixed for hearing
2001	361	243	76	104	< 4 months
2002	415	321	48	89	< 4 months
2003	440	311	76	93	4 months
2004	531	801[b]	76	72	10 months
2005	446	244	67	71	14 months
2006	484	237[c]	45	67	20–22 months
2007	373	276	73	94	26 months
2008	443	334	55	104	31 months
2009	499	341	62	98	33 months
2010	466	309	40	76	37 months
2011	499	258	41	73	39 months
2012	605	255	n/a[d]	114	48 months
2013	558	295	n/a	76	48 months
2014	464[e]	710[f]	n/a	106	54 months
2015	109[g]	481[h]	n/a	155	41 months
2016	212[i]	207[j]	n/a	99	41 months
2017	183	115	n/a	120	48 months

[a] Source: *Annual Reports of the Courts Service*. Some figures have been adjusted in light of explanations given in later reports; 'n/a' means 'not available'.

[b] 432 of these appeals were disposed of in a review of the list of appeals not yet certified for a hearing.

[c] Uniquely the 2006 Annual *Report* reveals that three judges sat in 153 appeals, five judges sat in 41 appeals and seven judges sat in one appeal.

[d] From 2012 the Courts Service's Annual Reports have ceased to provide information on success rates for appeals heard.

[e] 459 of these were appeals lodged before the creation of the Court of Appeal on 28 October 2014; two were appeals from the High Court lodged between then and the end of the year and three were cases stated from the Circuit Court: *2014 Annual Report*, 40.

[f] This high figure is for 'resolved' cases and reflects the fact that in 2014 the Supreme Court transferred 1,355 civil matters to the new Court of Appeal and retained over 800 so-called 'legacy' appeals for itself: *2014 Annual Report*, 35–6.

[g] This seems to comprise 96 appeals and 13 cases in which the Supreme Court granted leave to appeal.

[h] This comprises 447 'legacy appeals', 28 transitional appeals and six cases stated.

[i] This seems to comprise 154 appeals and 58 cases in which the Supreme Court granted leave to appeal.

[j] This comprises 189 legacy appeals, 14 'new' appeals and four transitional appeals: *2016 Annual Report*, 70–1.

the actual hearing lengthened dramatically—from four months to four years. The number of written judgments did not increase, suggesting that the judges were spending a lot more time handling the paperwork connected with appeals but not on writing judgments applying and developing the law.

As a Supreme Court Judge had to sit in every case dealt with by the Court of Criminal Appeal (before its jurisdiction was taken over by the new Court of Appeal in 2014), Table 4.2 presents some statistics on that Court's caseload too.[82] We can see that until 2006 the Court of Criminal Appeal was able to cope with its workload quite efficiently: the number of pending cases at the end of each year was reduced to 194. But during the ensuing seven years that number rose by 248 per cent to 646. The year 2012 seems to have been particularly difficult, with the backlog increasing by 39.5 per cent.

The figures for Ireland's Supreme Court can be put into context by comparing them with figures for supreme courts in other common law countries. Table 4.3 highlights how

[82] For early assessments of the CCA see Delany (1952) and, covering 1959 to 1968, Knight (1969).

Table 4.2 Appeals in the Court of Criminal Appeal, 2001–14

Year	Appeals lodged[a]	Appeals from Circuit Criminal Court	Appeals from Central Criminal Court	Appeals from Special Criminal Court	Appeals by the DPP against unduly lenient sentences[b]	Appeals disposed of	Cases on hand at end of year
2001	287	205	45	13	23	216	437
2002	237	180	30	4	23	273	401
2003	257	165	50	9	27	347	313
2004	257	169	55	9	21	266	304
2005	257	158	36	21	37	290	273
2006	244	155	42	6	41	329	194
2007	267	184	37	4	42	232	229
2008	305	205	39	2	58	279	255
2009	324	221	35	8	57	229	355
2010	326	215	47	4	54	267	414
2011	314	199	44	13	55	290	438
2012	346	262	45	10	21	173	611
2013	279	233	10	1	32	244	646
2014[c]	206	n/a	n/a	n/a	n/a	166	n/a[d]

[a] Apart from the four sources for appeals in columns 3–6 in Table 4.2, there were occasional appeals from the Courts-Martial Appeal Court and, under the Criminal Procedure Act 1993, s 2, second appeals by defendants on the basis of a newly discovered fact.

[b] This jurisdiction was conferred by the Criminal Justice Act 1992, s 2.

[c] The statistics for 2014 cover only the period up to 28 October; on that day 660 appeals still pending in the Court of Criminal Appeal were transferred to the new Court of Appeal.

[d] The Court of Criminal Appeal continued in existence to determine the 26 appeals which had been fully or partly heard before 28 October.

overloaded the Irish Supreme Court became, not just when set alongside the Supreme Court of a country roughly the same size as Ireland (New Zealand) but especially when compared with much more populous nations such as the UK and the USA. Ireland became out of step largely because until 2014 it allowed appeals to be taken to the Supreme Court without the leave either of that Court or of the Court whose decision was being appealed against.[83] The Court was mostly dealing with alleged mistakes by lower courts rather than with challenges to the content of existing law.

There is a remarkable similarity in the number of appeals disposed of each year by the Supreme Courts of Australia, Canada, the UK and the USA. This suggests that there is a limit to the work that a small group of judges can reasonably undertake on important issues of law brought to them within a 12-month period, even though only the US Supreme Court insists upon sitting *en banc* in every case (i.e. with all of its judges present).[84]

The Working Group on the Court of Appeal

The fact that Ireland's Supreme Court was becoming grossly overburdened was the main reason why the eight-member Working Group on the Court of Appeal, established by the

[83] To take just one comparator, 21 per cent of the appeals heard by the Supreme Court of Canada between 2006 and 2016 were 'as of right' rather than by the leave of the Court: *Statistics 2006–2016* (Supreme Court of Canada), available on the website of the Court.

[84] The Supreme Court of New Zealand often sits *en banc*, but by no means always.

Table 4.3 Appeals in common law supreme courts, 2005–17[a]

Country	**Ireland**	**New Zealand**	**Australia**	**Canada**	**United Kingdom**[b]	**United States**
Population[c]	**4.6m**	**4.4m**	**22.5m**	**35.0m**	**63.3m**	**311.7m**
Number of judges	10	5	7	9	12	9
Appeals measured	Appeals disposed of[d]	Appeals disposed of	Appeals disposed of after a hearing[e]	Appeals heard	Appeals disposed of after a hearing	Appeals disposed of[f]
2005	211	13	71	93	102	85
2006	202	27	104	80	94	82
2007	229	33	74	53	82	75
2008	229	n/a	73	82	n/a	n/a
2009	228	n/a	65	72	64	83
2010	233	n/a	72	65	59	77
2011	190	44[g]	54	70	81	83
2012	202	24	68	78	77	73
2013	249	18	68	75	96	76
2014	584[h]	27	58	80	82	77
2015	460	29	62	63	81	75
2016	207	23	58	63	70	70
2017	115[i]	34	65	66	103	68

[a] Source: Working Group (2009) 80–1 and annual judicial statistics for the various national supreme courts.

[b] This column refers to decisions on separate appeals taken by the Appellate Committee of the House of Lords until October 2009 and thereafter by the UK Supreme Court. They are gleaned from the annual Judicial Statistics published by the Department for Constitutional Affairs (until 2006), the Ministry of Justice (from 2007 to 2011) and from the author's own calculations based on judgments issued in calendar years (from 2012).

[c] All population figures are estimates as of 2011, a mid-way point in the period in question.

[d] The figures given exclude appeals that were withdrawn.

[e] These include constitutional matters referred directly to the High Court of Australia. The figures are for the 12-month period ending on 30 June in each year.

[f] The figures in this column are for the 12-month period ending on 30 September in each year. They are taken from the *Year-End Reports on the Federal Judiciary* issued by the Chief Justice of the US Supreme Court.

[g] There was an excess of criminal appeals in this year because of challenges to convictions arising out of armed police raids on a camp in the Urewera mountain range in the north-east of New Zealand in 2007.

[h] This figure is for appeals 'determined in court' (see *2014 Annual Report*, 53). The way in which statistics were presented differed in the 2014 Annual Report from that used in previous years.

[i] The decrease in appeals disposed of reflects the fact that most legacy appeals were dealt with by the start of 2017.

Irish government in December 2006 and chaired by Supreme Court judge Susan Denham, decided to recommend some far-reaching reforms. In its report published in 2009 the Working Group went out of its way to state that the court structure which was established for Ireland in 1922, as reformed in 1937 and 1961, was an 'entirely appropriate and adequate structure for the Ireland of the 20th century',[85] but its central recommendations were that more capacity was needed at the appellate level in the court system and that the establishment of a Court of Appeal was a necessary reform which would transform the efficiency and effectiveness of that system. The proposed Court of Appeal would bring together the current responsibilities of the Court of Criminal Appeal and some of the current responsibilities of the High Court for dealing with civil appeals. This was seen as a preferable reform

[85] Working Group (2009), 11. No supporting evidence was cited to substantiate this assertion.

to simply increasing the number of judges in the Supreme Court because it would allow that court to deal with the really important matters which befitted its status as the country's top judicial body. The Working Group therefore proposed that the Irish Constitution should be amended to clarify the role of the Court of Appeal, the High Court and the Supreme Court in a way which ensured that the public could easily understand the relationship between these superior courts. It specifically stated that:

> The primary role of the Supreme Court is not to engage in error correction. It is primarily to engage in explaining the Constitution to the People... If we really believe in a Constitution where the People gave the law to themselves then we must allow the Court in which the Constitution is interpreted to function as well as it possibly can.[86]

An inevitable consequence of creating an intermediary appellate court is that a mechanism needs to be introduced for determining which appeals heard by that court can be the subject of a further appeal to the Supreme Court. The Working Group's report suggested that litigants who wish to appeal to the Supreme Court, whether from the Court of Appeal itself or by way of a leapfrog procedure from the High Court similar to that which is available in the United Kingdom whenever there is not much point in appealing first to the Court of Appeal,[87] would need to obtain leave to do so. It looked at the practice adopted in other common law jurisdictions[88] and concluded that a common factor seemed to be a focus on questions of 'public importance', sometimes qualified by terms such as 'exceptional'. As already mentioned, within Ireland itself there was already a leave procedure to be satisfied before appeals could be brought from the Court of Criminal Appeal to the Supreme Court: leave was granted only if either Court was satisfied that the appeal raises a point of law of exceptional public importance *and* that it is in the public interest that the appeal be allowed to proceed.[89] On the other hand, research showed that across the common law world there was no uniformity of practice as regards holding an oral hearing for a leave application or giving reasons for granting or refusing a leave application.[90]

Basing itself on an admittedly subjective survey conducted by a serving Supreme Court judge, Hugh Geoghegan, of all the cases prepared for a hearing in the Supreme Court during the legal year 1 October 2005 to 31 July 2006, where he suggested which of them might instead have been dealt with by a Court of Appeal, the Working Group seemed to endorse the following categories of cases as ones which were of sufficient 'public importance' to deserve being heard by the Supreme Court:

- cases raising a legal issue (whether a private or constitutional law issue) which the Supreme Court has not previously ruled upon
- cases involving the application of established principles to changing social or scientific circumstances
- cases concerning the review of the power of branches of government, where justiciable

[86] Ibid, 7. Elsewhere (e.g. at 90) the Report states the main function of the reformed Supreme Court would be 'advancing the principled development of the law', a broader remit that one linked to the Constitution.

[87] Under the Administration of Justice Act 1969, ss 12–16.

[88] Namely England and Wales, Canada, Australia and New Zealand. It did not consider the USA.

[89] Courts of Justice Act 1924, s 29. In England and Wales and Northern Ireland no appeal in a criminal matter can proceed from the Court of Appeal to the Supreme Court unless the Court of Appeal first certifies that there is a point of public importance at stake: Criminal Appeal Act 1968, s 33(2) and Criminal Appeal (NI) Act 1980, s 31(2).

[90] As far as giving reasons are concerned, it appears that none of the other prominent Supreme Courts in the common law world routinely provides details which go beyond a recitation that the statutory criteria for granting leave have or have not been satisfied.

- cases requiring a ruling on the jurisdiction of another court, and
- cases of major commercial significance.[91]

On Geoghegan J's reckoning, only 38 of the 109 cases prepared for hearing by the Supreme Court during the year in question should really have been dealt with by a Supreme Court—just 35 per cent.

The Working Group also suggested that a consequence of creating a Court of Appeal should be that the President of that Court, like the President of the High Court, should be an *ex officio* member of the Supreme Court. In addition, the Chief Justice should be empowered to request ordinary judges in the Court of Appeal to sit in the Supreme Court when needed. More surprisingly, the Working Group was of the view that after the establishment of the Court of Appeal the Supreme Court should always sit *en banc* and not in panels. It observed that this was the usual practice in common law countries (though of course it is not the case in the United Kingdom) because it 'helps to ensure that the decisions of the highest court in the land are consistent and predictable'.[92]

The Jurisdiction of the Supreme Court Today

Following the people's approval of the creation of a Court of Appeal in a referendum held on 4 October 2013,[93] Ireland's Constitution was duly amended.[94] Article 34 now provides that '[j]ustice shall be administered in courts established by law by judges appointed in the manner provided by this Constitution'[95] and those courts shall comprise (i) courts of first instance, (ii) a Court of Appeal and (iii) a Court of Final Appeal.[96] It is not until three sections further on that we are told that '[t]he Court of Final Appeal shall be called the Supreme Court'.[97] The Court of Appeal came into existence on 28 October 2014.

Article 34.4 sets out the jurisdiction of the Court of Appeal and in doing so removes a large chunk from the Supreme Court's previous jurisdiction. It confers on the Court of Appeal—subject to exceptions[98]—all of the jurisdiction previously vested in the Supreme Court, the Court of Criminal Appeal and the Courts-Martial Appeal Court. A new Article 34.5.3 of the Constitution (replacing the former Article 34.4.3) sets out what the new jurisdiction of the Supreme Court is to be:

> The Supreme Court shall, subject to such regulations as may be prescribed by law, have appellate jurisdiction from a decision of the Court of Appeal if the Supreme Court is satisfied that (i) the decision involves a matter of general public importance or (ii) in the interests of justice it is necessary that there be an appeal to the Supreme Court.

So it is now necessary for only one of the two pre-2014 conditions to be satisfied before an appeal can be heard by the Supreme Court in a criminal case, and the term 'general

[91] Working Group (2009), 94. The last criterion was added in emulation of the practice in New Zealand, where matters of 'general commercial significance' can be appealed; some consultees had expressed concerns that the 'public importance' criterion in other jurisdictions allowed disproportionate attention to be paid to constitutional issues at the expense of commercial ones.

[92] Ibid, 135.

[93] The turnout in the referendum was 39.15 per cent, of whom 65.1 per cent voted in favour of the creation of the new court. A separate referendum on the same day suggesting the abolition of the Seanad was defeated by 51.7 per cent to 48.3 per cent of the voters.

[94] By the Thirty-third Amendment of the Constitution Act 2013, signed by President Higgins on 1 November 2013.

[95] Art 34.1. [96] Art 34.2. [97] Art 34.5.1.

[98] As set out in Art 64 of the Constitution and s 78(1)–(3) of the 2014 Act.

public importance' has replaced 'exceptional public importance', but in truth it is difficult to envisage any situation where those changes will make an appeal more likely to occur in a criminal case today than it would have done previously. Moreover, the slightly new wording suggests that the Supreme Court will maintain its earlier position whereby a certificate granting permission to appeal in a criminal case will not be awarded where, even if the appeal were to turn out to be successful, it would not benefit the appellant in any way.[99]

Nevertheless, the introduction of these 'leave', or permission, requirements for appeals to the Supreme Court is perhaps the single most significant procedural reform to have occurred in the whole history of the Court to date. The solicitors' firm Arthur Cox has called the institutional changes 'the most important reform to the organisation and structure of the Irish court system since the foundation of the State'.[100] The consequence is that to a much greater extent than in the past the Supreme Court is now in control of its own 'docket', that is, the list of appeals it is due to hear, whether civil or criminal. It is no longer obliged to deal with appeals that are of relatively minor legal interest, leaving it a lot more time to consider matters of real legal significance. The Supreme Court will have to develop criteria regarding what qualifies as 'a matter of general public importance' and what is 'in the interests of justice', as an appeal can be heard only if the issues raised fall within at least one of those categories. But if it follows the model of top courts in other countries it will not undertake this task systematically. The UK Supreme Court, for example, gives no specific reasons for granting or rejecting permission to appeal: it simply repeats the statutory test and states whether or not it has been satisfied. The Supreme Courts of Canada and the USA, and the High Court of Australia, behave in a similar fashion. Even the European Court of Human Rights, when deciding whether to allow a decision by a Chamber of the Court to be reviewed by the Grand Chamber, does not express the reasons for its decision; nor does it see the refusal to give reasons at the national level as a violation of a state's duty under Article 6 of the ECHR to provide litigants with a fair trial. The extra time available to Supreme Court Justices to write their judgments might lead to an enhanced quality of law-making, since there will be greater opportunity to locate the issues in a comparative setting and to take into account the views of third party interveners. It should also lead to reserved judgments being issued more quickly than in the past.

Leapfrog Appeals to the Supreme Court

Notwithstanding the constitutional right to appeal from the High Court to the Court of Appeal conferred by Article 34.4.1 of the 1937 Constitution, Article 34.5.4 goes on to say that the Supreme Court, subject to such regulations as may be prescribed by law, still has appellate jurisdiction from a decision of the High Court if the Supreme Court is satisfied that there are exceptional circumstances warranting a direct appeal to it, given that the decision involves a matter of general public importance or that a direct appeal would be in the interests of justice. A power has been conferred on the Court of Appeal to stay an appeal before it from a decision of the High Court in order to enable the applicant to apply to the Supreme Court for leave to make one of these direct appeals.[101]

This alternative route to the Supreme Court is comparable to the so-called 'leapfrog' appeal in England and Wales (and Northern Ireland), where an appeal from the High Court

[99] The question is posed by Walsh (2016) 1939.

[100] www.arthurcox.com/publications/irelands-new-court-appeal-september-2014.

[101] s 7B(1) of the Courts (Supplemental Provisions) Act 1961 Act, as inserted by s 9 of the Court of Appeal Act 2014.

can bypass the Court of Appeal and go directly to the Supreme Court if the High Court (or a Divisional Court within the High Court) grants a certificate allowing it and the Supreme Court grants permission to appeal applying its usual criteria.[102] The certificate can be granted by the lower court only if there is a point of law of general public importance involved in the case and (a) it relates mainly to the construction of legislation, (b) it is one in respect of which the judge is bound by a previous decision of the Court of Appeal or Supreme Court, (c) it relates to a matter of national importance, (d) it is so significant that a hearing by the Supreme Court is justified, or (e) the benefits of earlier consideration by the Supreme Court outweigh the benefits of consideration by the Court of Appeal.[103]

Leapfrog appeals are rare in England and Wales (and Northern Ireland), with perhaps two or three a year at most, so it will be interesting to see if the Supreme Court of Ireland will be equally selective in accepting direct appeals under Article 34.5.4. In general it is likely to be keen to deflect appellants to the Court of Appeal, from which, as we have seen, there can in any event be a further appeal to the Supreme Court, but in situations where such a further appeal is almost inevitable, given the controversial nature of the issues at stake, the Supreme Court may think that it would be more efficient in terms of time and costs to allow the appeal to go directly to it from the High Court. The downside would be that the Supreme Court would be deprived of the detailed legal analysis of a group of Court of Appeal judges. Even if Irish law does not specify in as much detail as English law the circumstances in which a direct appeal to the top court would be appropriate, it is clear from the use of the adjective 'exceptional' in Article 34.5.4 that it ought to be a rare occurrence.

It should be noted that because the Constitution allows the Supreme Court to consider the constitutionality of legislation only when it is exercising its appellate jurisdiction, if such an issue arises during an appeal from the High Court but has not previously been considered by the High Court it has to be remitted to that Court before the Supreme Court can deal with it. This occurred in *Dunnes Stores Ireland Co v Ryan*, where Murray J, with whom Denham and Murphy JJ concurred, expressed the view (endorsing a suggestion made in 1967[104]) that where a constitutional issue concerning the validity of a provision in an Act arises in proceedings and no decision on any disputed question of fact is required in order to deal with it, the Supreme Court should be given the power, at least with the parties' consent, to determine the issue.[105] To date, however, such a reform has not occurred.

Referrals to the Supreme Court

To deal with situations where an accused person is acquitted but there is some unease that the state of the current law has permitted such an acquittal, a mechanism was introduced in 1967 whereby the Attorney General could refer a question of law arising from the trial for determination by the Supreme Court.[106] As in the context of certificates permitting an appeal from the Court of Criminal Appeal, this provision was re-worded in 2006 to allow the Director of Public Prosecutions to make the referral if he or she was the prosecuting authority in the trial.[107] At the same time the opportunity was taken to confirm that the

[102] Administration of Justice Act 1969, ss 12–16. [103] Ibid, s 12(3) and (3A).

[104] Committee on Court Practice (1972). [105] [2002] 2 IR 60, 98.

[106] Criminal Procedure Act 1967, s 34. The section did not limit its scope to trials on indictment. The provision was five years in advance of a comparable provision introduced for England and Wales by the Criminal Justice Act 1972, s 36, but that was limited to trials on indictment. This in turn was replicated in Northern Ireland by the Criminal Appeal (NI) Act 1980, ss 15 and 34. In each of these two jurisdictions the ruling of the Court of Appeal on the reference can be appealed to the UK Supreme Court, but only if it appears to the Court of Appeal that this ought to happen.

[107] Criminal Justice Act 2006, s 21.

mechanism is available even for trials in the Special Criminal Court and to specify that when dealing with referrals the Supreme Court must do all that is reasonably practicable to withhold the identity of the acquitted person unless he or she agrees that it can be revealed. 'With prejudice' appeals against an acquittal (ie, appeals which may overturn the acquittal) were not permitted in Ireland until the enactment of the Criminal Procedure Act 2010.[108]

When the Court of Appeal was established in 2014 the 1967 Act was further amended to provide for referrals to be made to that Court in all criminal cases. The option of directing referrals to the Supreme Court was retained only for cases where the accused has been tried on indictment in the Central Criminal Court.[109] The Supreme Court can accept the reference if it is satisfied that there are exceptional circumstances warranting it and that the decision in question involves a matter of general public importance and/or accepting the reference would be in the interests of justice.[110]

If the referral is dealt with by the Court of Appeal there can be an appeal against that Court's decision to the Supreme Court because, as mentioned above, Article 34.5.3 of the Constitution confers appellate jurisdiction on the Supreme Court from any decision of the Court of Appeal as long as the Supreme Court is satisfied that a matter of general public importance is involved or that an appeal is necessary in the interests of justice.

Cases Stated and Original Jurisdiction

The Supreme Court can also deal with appeals that come to it via the 'case stated' procedure, but with the creation of the Court of Appeal in 2014 this is likely to be extremely rare. A 'case stated' is where a lower court poses specific legal questions to a higher court, either during the course of the lower court's hearing (when the process is called a consultative case stated) or after the lower court has already reached its decision in the proceedings.[111] District Courts and Circuit Courts can state cases to the High Court and until 2014 there could have been an appeal against the High Court's ruling direct to the Supreme Court. This needed the permission of the High Court only where the case stated was a consultative one[112] and at no point was the permission of the Supreme Court required. Similarly, under the Courts of Justice Act 1936[113] a judge of the High Court, when hearing an appeal from the Circuit Court, could state a case on a point of law to the Supreme Court and under Article 40.4.3 of the Constitution cases could also be stated to the Supreme Court whenever a detained person made an application for *habeas corpus* to the High Court and the High Court was satisfied that he or she was being detained under a law which was unconstitutional.

Now that there is a Court of Appeal in place for both civil and criminal appeals, rulings by the High Court on cases stated from lower courts, and cases stated by the High Court itself, are to be dealt with by the Court of Appeal rather than the Supreme Court. In theory there could be a further appeal to the Supreme Court against the Court of Appeal's ruling but again any such further appeal is subject to the fulfilment of one of the two conditions set out in Article 34.5.3 of the Constitution, cited above. This further strengthens the Supreme

[108] ss 23–30. For a detailed exposition of these provisions see Walsh (2016) 1881–1906.

[109] Court of Appeal Act 2014, s 47. Note that the Special Criminal Court is not included in this exception.

[110] Art 34.5.4 of the Constitution.

[111] For more details about the appeal systems in general, and the case stated procedure in particular, see Byrne and McCutcheon (2014) 341–69.

[112] In a consultative case stated from a District Court to the High Court, an appeal to the Supreme Court requires the permission of the High Court: Courts (Supplemental Provisions) Act 1961, s 52.

[113] s 38(3).

Court's control over its own docket and brings the Court into closer alignment with apex courts in most other common law jurisdictions.

In addition to its appellate jurisdiction the Supreme Court has 'original' jurisdiction in two situations. The first is under Article 12.3.1 of the Constitution, which gives the Court a role to play in determining whether the country's President should be removed from office on account of permanent incapacity, an issue which has not arisen to date. The second is under Article 26 of the Constitution, which allows the country's President to refer a Bill or part of a Bill to the Supreme Court for an assessment as to its constitutionality. To date Article 26 has been invoked by the President on 15 occasions and the way the Supreme Court has responded to these references is explored in detail in Chapter 6 of this book.

The Impact of the New Court of Appeal

Section 1A(4) of the Courts (Establishment and Constitution) Act 1961, inserted by section 6 of the Court of Appeal Act 2014, provides that the President of the Court of Appeal (the first person appointed to that role was Mr Justice Seán Ryan, but he retired in 2018 and was replaced by Mr Justice George Birmingham) shall be *ex officio* an additional judge of the Supreme Court (and of the High Court), which brings the total number of judges eligible to sit in the Supreme Court to 12.[114] But the Supreme Court is still not required to sit *en banc* in any case. Likewise, under section 1A(5) of the 1961 Act the Chief Justice, at the request of the President of the Court of Appeal, may request any ordinary judge of the Supreme Court, to sit in the Court of Appeal as an additional judge thereof, and every such judge must then sit as requested. To date it does not seem that either of these situations has arisen, certainly not frequently. This may be a function of the fact that the Court of Appeal has been extremely busy since it was established and the Chief Justice has been content to let it get on with its task alone. On his first day in office Mr Justice Birmingham regrettably had to announce the cancellation of some hearings because his court did not have enough judges available to deal with them. He warned that waiting times of at least 20 months for appeal hearings will get worse unless new judges are appointed quickly to replace those who have retired or moved to other positions.[115] In 2017 the number of new appeals lodged in the Court of Appeal (611) far exceeded the number of new appeals disposed of (470); in addition, of the 1,355 appeals transferred from the Supreme Court to the Court of Appeal in 2014, 706 were still pending before the Court of Appeal by the end of 2017.[116]

According to the Courts Service's Annual Reports, the Supreme Court significantly reduced its backlog of 'legacy' appeals during 2015 and 2016, disposing of 447 and 189 such appeals respectively. By the beginning of 2017 the vast majority of legacy appeals had been disposed of, although the average length of the legacy proceedings disposed of in that year was just short of six years (2,175 days). It achieved this by allocating the task to a separate panel of the Court. Meanwhile it has made a fairly good start on the 'new' system of appeals: in 2016 these were being disposed of on average within 38 weeks of being lodged, but in 2017 this period had crept up to 54 weeks. In 2017 there was a 16 per cent increase in new appeals as well as a doubling of new appeals resolved. Applications for leave to appeal are flowing in too, but not at the rate of appeals lodged prior to the creation of the Court of Appeal. In the years 2015, 2016 and 2017 the Supreme Court received, respectively, 96, 152 and 176

[114] The Chief Justice, the nine 'ordinary' judges and the Presidents of the High Court and Court of Appeal.

[115] Mary Carolan, 'Court of Appeal urgently needs more judges, court president says', *Irish Times*, 31 May 2018.

[116] *2017 Annual Report of the Courts Service*, 87.

applications for leave to appeal, which can now be submitted on-line. The percentage of applications granted in 2015 and 2016 was, respectively, 30 per cent and 38 per cent; the figure for 2017 is not clear from the Courts Service's Annual Report.[117] Interestingly, there are still a relatively high number of applications for leave to appeal directly from the High Court to the Supreme Court—22 in 2015, 28 in 2016 and as many as 61 in 2017 (this last figure represents 35 per cent of all leave applications received by the Supreme Court that year). The Chief Justice allocates leave applications to panels of three judges and, as with actual appeals, applications for leave are subjected to new case management procedures conducted by individual judges to ensure that they are disposed of both justly and efficiently. In 2015 the average waiting time for an application for leave to be decided after the papers for it were complete was 28 days; in 2016 it was just 20 days but in 2017 it doubled to 41 days.[118]

The Presumed Continuance of Pre-1922 Laws

Unlike on some other occasions when parts of the British Empire broke away and became self-governing,[119] the Irish Free State decided to retain many of the laws which had applied in Ireland prior to partition of the island. In this regard the Canadian model was once again followed, for when the union was first formed there in 1867 the founding Act provided that '[e]xcept as otherwise provided by this Act, all laws in force in Canada, Nova Scotia, or New Brunswick at the union … shall continue in Ontario, Quebec, Nova Scotia, and New Brunswick respectively, as if the union had not been made', subject to their being repealed or altered by the Parliament of Canada or by the legislature of the respective province.[120] A similar provision had been included in the Act which guaranteed independence to South Africa.[121] According to Article 73 of the 1922 Constitution of the Irish Free State the laws already in force for the territory to be known as the Irish Free State 'shall continue to be of full force and effect until the same or any of them shall have been repealed or amended by enactment of the Oireachtas'. The use of the words 'repealed or amended' suggests that Article 73 was intended to apply only to pre-1922 *legislation*, but in fact the courts of the Irish Free State treated the pre-1922 common law as also continuing in force. That is why in 1936 a majority in the Supreme Court (2 v 1) was able to treat the right of a suspect not to incriminate him- or herself as a well-established common law right but not a constitutional right.[122] The willingness to treat decisions by pre-1922 courts as evidence of the exiting state of the law did not, however, mean that any of those decisions, even if taken by the House of Lords, had to be treated as binding on the courts of the new state. This was made clear by McCarthy J in 1983, when the Supreme Court considered a previous decision by the House of Lords but did not say that they had to follow it.[123] McCarthy J stressed that: 'In no sense are our courts a continuation of or successors to the British courts.'[124]

[117] Unfortunately the 2017 Report sets out some of its statistics in a way which makes direct comparisons with earlier years difficult if not impossible.

[118] The statistics in this paragraph were taken largely from the *2016 Annual Report*, 7, 21, 41, 70, 72, 78 (at 78 some of the information seems to contradict that at 72) and from the *2017 Annual Report*, 7, 92, 95 and 104.

[119] See eg Stoebuck (1968–69).

[120] British North America Act 1867, s 129.

[121] Union of South Africa Act 1909, s 135: 'Subject to the provisions of this Act, all laws in force in the several Colonies at the establishment of the Union shall continue in force in the respective provinces until repealed or amended by Parliament, or by the provincial councils in matters in respect of which the power to make ordinances is reserved or delegated to them.' See too the Constitution of Australia 1900, s 108 (on the saving of state laws).

[122] *The State (McCarthy) v Lennon* [1936] IR 485; McInerney (2010).

[123] *Irish Shell Ltd v Elm Motors Ltd* [1984] IR 200.

[124] Ibid, 227. However O'Higgins CJ and Griffin J said they neither agreed nor disagreed with McCarthy J's views because there had been no argument about them during the appeal. See generally Byrne and McCutcheon (2014) 511–18.

Pre-1922 legislation *was* deemed to be binding unless changed by the Irish Free State, but the Court of Appeal of Ireland, which ceased to function when the Supreme Court began operating in 1924, held that such a change did not have to be made expressly: it was enough if the change could be inferred from the new legislation, provided only that the new legislation was otherwise consistent with the terms of the Anglo-Irish Treaty of 1921.[125] In the case in question the result of the Court of Appeal's conclusion was that the Indemnity Act 1923 was allowed to trump the 1922 Constitution: the latter had suggested that military courts could sit only when there was a state of war or armed rebellion (as defined in Article 6 of the Constitution) but the former provided that the decisions of military courts were valid even if the definition in Article 6 was not complied with. The Supreme Court did not disassociate itself from this imaginative approach to law-making, one that was out of step with that of other common law systems operating under a written constitution. The clearest example of the Supreme Court's apostasy is its infamous split decision in *The State (Ryan) v Lennon* in December 1934,[126] which was discussed in Chapter 3 above.[127]

In the context of the Supreme Court's jurisdiction this rather carefree attitude to constitutionalism might have meant that the Supreme Court would arrogate to itself judicial powers which had not been explicitly conferred upon it by the Constitution. In fact the judges have consistently maintained a more literal and rigorous approach to their own powers, mainly because the 1937 Constitution has a lot more to say about the topic than its 1922 predecessor. It is worth noting, however, that Article 50.1 of the 1937 Constitution mirrors Article 73 of the 1922 Constitution in that it provides that the laws in force immediately prior to the 1937 Constitution coming into operation 'shall continue to be of full force and effect until the same or any of them shall have been repealed or amended by enactment of the Oireachtas'. This extends to pre-1922 laws which were continued in force by the 1922 Constitution. A few years later a similar provision was to be inserted in the Constitution of India 1949, stating that 'all the law in force in the territory of India immediately before the commencement of this Constitution shall continue in force therein until altered or repealed or amended by a competent legislature or other competent authority'.[128]

The Meaning of 'Limited Functions and Powers of a Judicial Nature'

It is one thing to know which courts are to administer justice under the Constitution, but it is a different thing to know what 'the administration of justice' means in this context. The question is important because Article 34.1 of the Irish Constitution appears to ascribe to the lawfully established courts the exclusive competence to perform that function. Within the Constitution Articles 34 to 37 are located in a group of articles headed 'The Courts'; earlier groups of articles are headed 'The National Parliament' (Articles 15 to 27) and 'The Government' (Article 28). Without expressly stating it,[129] the Constitution is making the point that Ireland is a nation organised in accordance with the rule of law, which is the

[125] *R (Cooney) v Clinton* (1924) but not reported until [1935] IR 245. See Chap 3 above, 34.

[126] [1935] IR 170. [127] See 37-42.

[128] Art 372(1). For comparable provisions on the retention of EU law in the UK after Brexit, see ss 2–7 of the UK's European Union (Withdrawal) Act 2018. For more on the position in Ireland see Hogan et al (2018) 2589-2603.

[129] Unlike other countries, including the UK (see the Constitutional Reform Act 2005, s 1), Ireland's Constitution makes no explicit reference to the rule of law. The nearest it comes to doing so is arguably in the Preamble, which states that the people of Ireland are 'seeking to promote the common good, with due observance of Prudence, Justice and Charity, so that the freedom and dignity of the individual may be assured, true social order attained, the unity of our country restored and concord established with other nations'. On the meaning of 'administration of justice' see Hogan et al (2018) 694-726.

traditional way of describing a country where those in power are nevertheless subject to the law of the land and where the law of the land has to be applied by individuals who are entirely separate from the Parliament and the government. But Article 37.1 of the Constitution concedes that in some situations persons other than judges sitting in courts can administer justice. It reads:

> Nothing in this Constitution shall operate to invalidate the exercise of limited functions and powers of a judicial nature, in matters other than criminal matters, by any person or body of persons duly authorised by law to exercise such functions and powers, notwithstanding that any such person or such body of persons is not a judge or a court appointed or established as such under this Constitution.

One can immediately see that the creation of this exception to Article 34.1 raises two important questions: what amounts to functions and powers 'of a judicial nature' and when are those functions and powers 'limited'?

The Supreme Court has had to grapple with these two questions on several occasions.[130] In doing so it has developed an approach to the judicial function which provides an insight into how the Supreme Court perceives its own role within the Irish legal system. Many of the cases have required it to rule on whether a body set up by statute and given power to take decisions affecting individuals should be allowed to continue to do so or whether the arrangements should be deemed unconstitutional and replaced. By and large the Supreme Court has been generous in allowing such bodies to continue exercising their powers because it has categorised them as being either non-judicial or judicial but limited.

The Supreme Court's decisions based on the Free State Constitution of 1922 are not wholly germane to the position today because the provision on judicial power in that Constitution was more restrictively worded than in the 1937 Constitution. Article 64 provided that: 'The judicial power of the Irish Free State (Saorstát Éireann) shall be exercised and justice administered in the public Courts established by the Oireachtas by judges appointed in manner hereinafter provided . . .'. In one early case, *Lynham v Butler (No 2)* the Supreme Court gave a comprehensive definition of 'judicial power', stressing that it can be exercised either in criminal cases or civil cases. Kennedy CJ summed up the position thus:

> The exercise of the Judicial Power, which is coercive and must frequently act against the will of one of the parties to enforce its decision adverse to that party, requires of necessity that the Judicial Department of Government have compulsive authority over persons as, for instance, it must have authority to compel appearance of a party before it, to compel the attendance of witnesses, to order the execution of its judgments against persons and property.[131]

Notwithstanding this definition, the Supreme Court held just a few years later, in *In re Article 26 and the Offences Against the State (Amendment) Bill 1940*, that a Minister's power to order the detention of people without trial was *not* an exercise of the power to administer justice and so was not repugnant to the Constitution.[132] This was a most unfortunate, indeed almost incredible, conclusion to reach. It is explicable only in terms of the perception of the existential threat to the State which prevailed at the time.

In the Supreme Court's leading decision on the 1937 provision, *McDonald v Bord na gCon (No 2)*,[133] the issue was whether the Bord na gCon (the Greyhound Board) was exercising a limited judicial power when it exercised its statutory power[134] to discipline a

[130] See, generally, Morgan (2004b) esp 147–54; Hogan et al (2018) 1216-29.
[131] [1933] IR 74, 100, per Kennedy CJ (capitals in original).
[132] [1940] IR 470; see further Chap 6 below, 109-10. [133] [1965] IR 217.
[134] Conferred by the Greyhound Industry Act 1958.

greyhound trainer by excluding him from racing tracks and greyhound sales. In holding that the Board was *not* exercising a judicial power, the Supreme Court explained that the consequences of the exclusion order in question did not prevent Mr McDonald from continuing to exercise his greyhound business, not least because owners of racing tracks or organisers of greyhound sales did not have to implement the exclusion order if they did not wish to. The Supreme Court suggested that there are five 'characteristic features' of the administration of justice, namely:

- a dispute as to the existence of legal rights or a violation of the law
- ascertainment of the rights of parties, imposition of liabilities or infliction of a penalty
- final determination (subject to appeal) of legal rights, liabilities or penalties
- enforcement of those rights, liabilities or penalties and
- the making of an order 'which as a matter of history is an order characteristic of courts in this country'.

In subsequent cases the Supreme Court has held that Bord na Móna (the Turf Development Board) was not acting judicially when deciding whether to purchase land compulsorily,[135] that tribunals of inquiry set up under the Tribunals of Inquiry (Evidence) Acts 1921 and 1979 are not acting judicially,[136] that the Minister for Justice is not acting judicially when reducing fines imposed by a District Court judge,[137] and that the Institute of Chartered Accountants is not acting judicially when it disciplines its members by expelling them from the Institute.[138] But in none of these cases did the Court come up with a clearer set of criteria to characterise judicial power. The saving grace, perhaps, is that the heightened standards for what is now required in terms of fair procedures whenever bodies are exercising *administrative* power have diminished the consequences of holding that that power isnot judicial in nature.[139]

In at least two cases the Supreme Court has held that a body wasindeed exercising judicial power and that this was not a *limited* power, the result being that the power was being exercised in violation of the Constitution. This occurred first in *Re the Solicitors Act 1954*,[140] where the Law Society's power to strike a solicitor off the roll was invalidated. Legislation was subsequently enacted to ensure that members of professions could be prevented from working as such only if the High Court ordered this.[141] It occurred again in *The State (Clarke) v Roche*,[142] when the Supreme Court declared unconstitutional the practice whereby District Court Clerks decided if District Court summonses were properly drawn up. This was remedied by removing that power from the Clerks and transferring it to the District Judges.[143] Interestingly, no further action was taken to retrospectively validate the thousands of court summonses which had been issued prior to the *Clarke* case in an unconstitutional manner and no further litigation seems to have ensued on that point. By way of contrast, when it was suggested by lawyers in one case[144] that An Bord Uchtála (the Adoption Board) might be exercising judicial powers without express authorisation, the government of the day held a referendum to amend the Constitution to put beyond doubt

[135] *O'Brien v Bord na Móna* [1983] IR 277.
[136] *Goodman International v Hamilton* [1992] 2 IR 542.
[137] *Brennan v Minister for Justice* [1995] 1 IR 612.
[138] *Geoghegan v Institute of Chartered Accountants in Ireland* [1995] 3 IR 86.
[139] For details of what the Supreme Court has said about fairness in administrative law see Chap 8 below, 176-7.
[140] [1960] IR 239.
[141] eg Solicitors (Amendment) Act 1960, s 8; Dentists Act 1985, ss 38–40; Medical Practitioners Act 2007, s 74.
[142] [1986] IR 619. [143] Courts (No 3) Act 1986. [144] *M v An Bord Uchtála* [1977] IR 287.

that no adoption made since the 1937 Constitution had come into effect was invalid merely because it did not result from an order made by a judge or a court.[145]

Non-justiciable Questions

Just as Article 34.1 of the 1937 Constitution states that justice shall be administered by judges, and impliedly not by others, so it implies that judges must not get involved in matters others than those to do with the administration of justice. In other words, the Irish Constitution seems to suggest that some issues are non-justiciable and are better left to either the Oireachtas or the government to deal with. Liberal democracies around the world face the same problem: to what extent should they juridify their polity? Surprisingly, perhaps the most juridified state is that of Israel, where the Supreme Court will even adjudicate upon decisions taken by army generals during war time.[146] South Africa, too, requires its Constitutional Court to express opinions on matters which in most other countries would be regarded as beyond the competence of judges to deal with.[147] In the United Kingdom there is no body of settled case law, let alone any statutory provision, outlining what issues are non-justiciable, but there are countless examples of the House of Lords and Supreme Court declining to express a view on a matter because it is deemed to be the responsibility of Parliament or government.[148] In the USA, by way of contrast, there is a clearly articulated doctrine whereby 'political questions' cannot be dealt with by the courts, even by the Supreme Court—though that did not prevent the Supreme Court from issuing crucially important judgments on the constitutionality of President Franklin D Roosevelt's New Deal legislation in the 1930s,[149] on whether President Nixon's secret tape-recordings of conversations in the White House should be disclosed[150] and on whether the way votes were counted in Florida during the presidential election of 2000 was legal (giving victory to George W Bush rather than to Al Gore).[151]

In Ireland the Supreme Court has tended to behave in a way similar to the top court in the United Kingdom. It has been prepared to interpret the meaning of legislation even though the consequences of adopting a particular interpretation might have significant social, economic or political consequences, but it has stopped short of issuing direct orders to the Oireachtas or government to behave in particular ways in those fields unless there is clear legal backing for such an order. So, just as the UK Supreme Court was prepared to consider whether Members of the House of Commons could rely upon the Bill of Rights of 1689 to avoid being prosecuted for alleged false accounting in relation to their expenses claims,[152] so the Irish Supreme Court was prepared in *Maguire v Ardagh*[153] to rule that, although committees of the Oireachtas could of course hold inquiries, they had no power to conduct an inquiry which could lead 'to adverse findings of fact and conclusions (including a finding of unlawful killing) as to the personal culpability of an individual not a member of

[145] Art 37.2 of the 1937 Constitution, inserted by the Sixth Amendment of the Constitution (Adoption) Act 1979.

[146] Salzberger (2007). [147] Corder (2007).

[148] eg *A v Secretary of State for the Home Dept* [2004] UKHL 56, [2005] 2 AC 68, where eight of the nine Law Lords refused to decide whether the government was right in believing that the State was experiencing an emergency threatening the life of the nation; Lord Hoffmann dissented on this point.

[149] eg *Schechter Poultry Corp v US* 295 US 495 (1935). [150] *United States v Nixon* 418 US 683 (1974).

[151] *Bush v Gore* 531 US 98 (2000).

[152] *R v Chaytor* [2010] UKSC 52, [2011] 1 AC 684 (a unanimous decision by nine Justices). At issue was Art 9 of the Bill of Rights 1689, which reads (in modern spelling): 'That the freedom of speech and debates or proceedings in Parliament ought not to be impeached or questioned in any court or place out of Parliament.'

[153] [2002] IESC 21, [2002] 1 IR 385; see too O'Dowd (2003), Murphy (2002).

the Oireachtas so as to impugn their good name'.[154] This decision is sometimes referred to as the *Abbeylara* case since it involved the investigation of a fatal police shooting of Mr John Carthy in the town of Abbeylara in County Longford in 2000. Referred to by John O'Dowd as 'one of the most controversial that the court has given in the last forty years',[155] the ruling seemed to fundamentally undermine previous understandings of how Ireland was governed. Nevertheless, it chimed with the views of the majority of the population as, nine years later, in a referendum to amend the Constitution to confer greater inquiry powers on the Oireachtas, the people voted by 53 per cent to 47 per cent to reject the amendment.[156] An academic report which later analysed voter behaviour in the referendum concluded that the proposed change was perceived to be too great a step to take and that a widespread distrust of politicians made the people reluctant to grant them greater powers.[157]

In recent times the Irish Supreme Court has also shown itself to be particularly unwilling to command the Oireachtas or government to adopt particular social policies. Contrary to its activism in the 1960s, which is discussed in more detail in Chapter 6, it has adopted a more conservative stance in the past 25 years. Thus, in *TD v Minister for Education*[158] the Supreme Court, by four judges to one, upbraided a High Court judge for ordering a government Minister to provide resources for secure care facilities for troubled young people. The dissenter, it is worth noting, was Denham J, who later became the country's Chief Justice. For the majority the strongest judgment was issued by Hardiman J, who in his extra-judicial writings made no secret of his antipathy to judicial interference in what are essentially political matters.[159] The degree to which the Supreme Court has developed its willingness to protect social and economic rights is explored further in Chapter 6 below.

Conclusion

It is clear that for most of its history the Supreme Court of Ireland has been dogged by the handicap that it could not choose for itself which cases to hear. From 1924 to 2014 it could be accessed as of right by all manner of appellants, the result being that its workload eventually became unbearable and the time available for the production of detailed and well-crafted judgments on important legal issues insufficient. As it dealt with so few appeals in criminal cases its jurisprudence in that field suffered drastically. It also sheltered behind constitutional provisions which allowed it to presume that the common law position prevailing before partition could remain unaltered. It did not construct for itself the role which a dedicated Constitutional Court might have assumed, being too willing to confirm the Anglo-Saxon principle of parliamentary sovereignty and too timid to express opinions on questions which it deemed political. The problems became particularly apparent at the dawn of the twenty-first century, when the backlog of cases began to grow disproportionately. That the required reforms took so long to introduce is both sad and hard to explain, given that many other aspects of Irish society were radically altered during that period.

It is strongly to be hoped that the 2014 reforms will allow the Supreme Court to have a more impressive future. The new Court seems to have started well, having almost entirely disposed of the legacy appeals it inherited and being efficient in applying new case management procedures. The new Chief Justice, Frank Clarke, seems just as keen as his

[154] [2002] 1 IR 385, 573 (per Denham J).
[155] O'Dowd (2003).
[156] Thirtieth Amendment of the Constitution Bill 2011.
[157] Marsh, Suiter and Reidy (2012).
[158] [2001] 4 IR 259.
[159] Hardiman (2004), and the response by Whyte (2006); Hardiman (2017), and the response by O'Mahony (2017).

distinguished predecessor, Susan Denham, to make the Irish court system in general and the Supreme Court in particular one of the most respected in the common law world. It may be that some of the problems which previously beset it have merely been transferred to the new Court of Appeal,[160] but if so there is no reason to believe that they cannot be dealt with effectively at that level too, provided the Court of Appeal is supplied with adequate resources.

[160] Mary Carolan, 'Top judge warns Irish appeal court is close to being "overwhelmed"', *Irish Times*, 26 October 2017. She was commenting on a statement made that day by the President of the Court of Appeal, Seán Ryan. In 2014 that Court inherited 1,650 appeals from the Supreme Court, a figure which had been reduced to about 650 by 2017. But it also receives about 600 new appeals per year, meaning that most of those appellants have to wait at least a year for a hearing. Judge Ryan estimated that about 60 per cent of the remaining legacy appeals would eventually go ahead but that with just ten judges his court could process only about 320 appeals per year.

5

The Judges of the Supreme Court

This chapter explains the development of the Supreme Court in terms of the individuals who have served as its judges. When established on 6 June 1924 the Court comprised a President (known as the Chief Justice) and two other judges, with the President of the High Court being an *ex officio* member. In 1936 the number of other judges was increased from two to four. The Court was re-established in 1961 but the judges remained unchanged. To mark the transition a ceremony was held on Friday, 29 September: all the Supreme and High Court judges were driven in official cars from the Four Courts building to Áras an Uachtaráin in Phoenix Park, where President de Valera issued them with new warrants of appointment. The new courts sat for the first time on Monday, 2 October.[1]

In 1975 a Law Reform Commission was established for Ireland and it was expected that its Chair—or at least one of its members—would be a Supreme Court judge, so it was deemed appropriate to make provision for the appointment of a fifth ordinary Supreme Court judge to replace whichever judge was appointed to the Law Reform Commission. Then, on account of the relentless rise in the number of appeals brought to the Supreme Court, and because it was anticipated that the jurisdiction of the Court of Criminal Appeal would soon be transferred to the Supreme Court, a further, permanent, extension to the maximum number of ordinary Supreme Court judges was made in 1995, raising the number from four to seven.

In 2013, on the back of further complaints concerning delays, and even though the jurisdiction of the Court of Criminal Appeal had *not* yet been transferred to the Supreme Court, the maximum number of ordinary judges was again raised, this time from seven to nine. In 2014, with the creation of a Court of Appeal, the President of that Court was made an additional *ex officio* member of the Supreme Court. All of this means that today the authorised number of judges available to staff the Supreme Court is ten (the Chief Justice plus nine ordinary judges). The Presidents of the Court of Appeal and High Court are available to sit *ex officio*, but rarely do so. According to Mac Cormaic[2] the plan in 2014 was that the next few judges who retired or died would not be replaced, allowing the normal size of the Court to return to the Chief Justice and just four ordinary judges. But this is not what has occurred. In 2015 and 2017 two new Supreme Court judges were appointed, replacing one who retired and one who died. As of November 2018, therefore, the Supreme Court consisted of a Chief Justice, seven ordinary judges and two *ex officio* judges. Two positions as ordinary judges remained vacant. None of the judges currently in post needs to retire until 2021.

Eligibility for Appointment

The eligibility criteria for appointment to the Supreme Court have changed hardly at all since its creation. The Courts of Justice Act 1924[3] stipulated that a person must have practised as a barrister for at least 12 years[4] or served as a judge of the Supreme Court of Judicature in

[1] 'Courts formally established—unique ceremony in Dublin', *Irish Times*, 30 September 1961, 7.
[2] 'Yes vote in "the other referendum" brings relief for court's champions', *Irish Times*, 5 October 2013.
[3] s 16.
[4] Service as a judge of the Circuit Court in the Irish Free State was deemed to be practice at the Bar.

Ireland, a Recorder or County Court Judge in Ireland, a Judge of the Dáil Supreme Court,[5] or a Judicial Commissioner.[6] For the avoidance of doubt, in 1931 it was 'enacted and declared' that a judge of the High Court shall be deemed eligible too.[7] The rules did not materially change when the new Supreme Court was set up in 1961 and it was not until 2002 that solicitors of 12 years' standing could apply to become a judge of the Court (or High Court).[8] In 2014 the same qualification requirements were imposed for persons wishing to be appointed to the Court of Appeal.[9]

Interestingly, the 1924 Act also provided that in terms of precedence amongst judges, the Chief Justice should rank first, the President of the High Court second, and then the other judges of the Supreme Court according to the date of their appointment.[10] With the creation of the Court of Appeal in 2014 the President of that Court was given the second rank and all the others moved down the ladder.[11] This is one reason why so many judges have been appointed to the role of Chief Justice after having served as President of the High Court. Of the 11 Chief Justices appointed since Hugh Kennedy's death in 1936, five previously served as President of the High Court.[12] The four most recent appointees, however, have all been selected from within the existing Supreme Court.[13]

Eligibility for the Supreme Court is still governed by the Courts (Supplemental Provisions) Act 1961, as amended.[14] A person is qualified if he or she is a judge of the Court of Appeal, a judge of the High Court, a Circuit Court judge who has served in that role for at least two years,[15] or a practising barrister or solicitor of not less than 12 years standing who has practised for a continuous period of not less than two years immediately before appointment. A person is also qualified if at any time during the two-year period prior to appointment he or she was a judge or Advocate General at the Court of Justice of the EU, a judge of the Court of First Instance of the EU, a judge of the European Court of Human Rights, a judge of the International Court of Justice, or a judge of the International Criminal Court or of another tribunal as defined by the International War Crimes Tribunals Act 1998. In these situations the person must have been a practising barrister or solicitor before taking up one of those roles, although no minimum period of such practice is specified.

Every person appointed to be a judge of the Supreme Court has to have substantial experience of legal practice. No legal academic who has not practised law can be appointed, let alone anyone who is in no sense legally qualified. Such restrictions are understandable given that the Supreme Court can hear such a wide variety of legal disputes. For courts which are more specialised—such as the Constitutional Court of South Africa—it is reasonable to allow persons who have not been legal practitioners to be part of the judicial panel. As we shall see, the norm as far as appointments to the Irish Supreme Court are concerned is for persons to be appointed who not only have years of legal practice behind

[5] For more on this see Chap 2 above, 10–12.

[6] These last two offices were defined in the Dáil Eireann Courts (Winding-Up) Act 1923.

[7] Courts of Justice Act 1931, s 6.

[8] Courts and Court Officers Act 2002, s 4, inserting a new s 5(2) into the Courts (Supplemental Provisions) Act 1961.

[9] Court of Appeal Act 2014, s 11, further amending s 5 of the Courts (Supplemental Provisions) Act 1961.

[10] Ibid, s 9.

[11] At the time of writing the order of precedence amongst the ordinary judges was O'Donnell J (appointed 2010), McKechnie J (2010), Mac Menamin J (2012), Dunne (2013), Charleton J (2014), O'Malley J (2015) and Finlay Geoghegan (2017).

[12] Timothy Sullivan, Conor Maguire, Cearbhall Ó Dálaigh, Tom Finlay and Liam Hamilton.

[13] Ronan Keane, John Murray, Susan Denham and Frank Clarke.

[14] See too the information about eligibility on the Supreme Court's website.

[15] To become a Circuit or District Judge one must have practised as a barrister or solicitor for at least ten years: Courts (Supplemental Provisions) Act 1961, as amended by the Courts and Court Officers Act 2002, s 5.

them but also years of judicial experience. Of the 36 appointments to the Supreme Court since 1970, 33 (92 per cent) already had judicial experience in lower courts. Only three were appointed directly from the Bar,[16] and none directly from the solicitors' profession. Indeed no-one who was at the time working as a practising solicitor has ever been appointed to the Supreme Court.[17] The Law Society of Ireland has frequently complained about this.[18]

Method of Appointment

Article 35.1 of the Constitution provides that all judges shall be appointed by the President, but the appointment power is exercised, according to Article 13.9, 'only on the advice of the Government'. It is therefore the government which in practice makes the appointments, as was also the case under the Irish Free State Constitution.[19] Many individuals appointed to the Supreme Court in the 70-year period after 1924 were men (*sic*) who had previously made clear where their political allegiances lay, often through having stood for election as a member of a particular party. In 1952 Barrington (himself a future judge) commented that '[t]he Government nearly always appoints one of its own supporters ... It seems strange that a system which we regard as an indefensible method of selecting a sub-postmistress should be regarded as a perfectly natural method of selecting a Supreme Court judge'.[20]

In 1969 Paul Bartholomew conducted an extensive survey not only of judges who were then sitting in the Supreme Court, High Court or Circuit Court but also those who had retired from such posts.[21] Two remarkable findings were that 88 per cent of these judges admitted to having had some party political allegiance when they were appointed to the bench, and only 41 per cent believed they had been appointed because of their legal expertise. Not surprisingly, Bartholomew concluded that all Irish governments were 'to a greater or lesser degree' politically motivated when appointing judges, although less so at the Supreme Court level than at lower levels.[22] What Bartholomew did not find, however, was any evidence that the persons appointed had later demonstrated political bias in the way they decided cases. Indeed in his ground-breaking article on Supreme Court judges in 1985, Colm Tóibin observed that two of the most influential judges to have plied their trade on the Supreme Court, Cearbhall Ó Dálaigh from 1953 to 1973 and Brian Walsh from 1961 to 1990, both of whom were strong supporters of Fianna Fáil when appointed,[23] did not in any way curtail their activism on the Court even though their judicial behaviour flew in

[16] Hugh O'Flaherty, Adrian Hardiman and Donal O'Donnell. Earlier judges appointed to the Supreme Court directly from the Bar were Hugh Kennedy (1924), Gerald FitzGibbon (1924), James Geoghegan (1936), Cecil Lavery (1950), Cearbhall Ó Dálaigh (1953), and William FitzGerald (1966).

[17] James Geoghegan (who served on the Supreme Court from 1936 to 1950) practised as a solicitor for eight years before becoming a barrister in 1915; Conor Maguire (Chief Justice from 1946 to 1961) practised as a solicitor for seven years before becoming a barrister in 1922; Joseph Finnegan (who served from 2006 to 2012) practised as a solicitor for 12 years before switching to the Bar in 1978.

[18] Submission on the Scheme of the Judicial Appointments Commission Bill 2016 (22 March 2017), available on the website of the Law Society, para 5.3.

[19] Art 68: 'The judges ... shall be appointed by the Representative of the Crown on the advice of the Executive Council.'

[20] Barrington (1952) 181. His preference was to allow a committee of existing judges to submit the names of three or four outstanding lawyers to the government, from which an appointee could be chosen (ibid, 182).

[21] There were two such judges who were not interviewed but 17 of the 35 judges of the District Court supplied information.

[22] Bartholomew (1971) 35–6.

[23] Ó Dálaigh served two terms as Attorney General in Fianna Fáil governments (1946–48 and 1951–53) and stood unsuccessfully as a Fianna Fáil candidate in elections in 1948 and 1951. Walsh was a legal adviser to Éamon de Valera during the latter's successful candidacy for the Presidency in 1959 and was a close friend of Charles Haughey, who was Taoiseach on three occasions (1979–81, 1982 and 1987–92).

the face of Fianna Fáil's wishes during those years.[24] Mac Cormaic comments, not unfairly, that Ó Dálaigh and Walsh engaged in 'an essentially nationalist project to de-Anglicize Irish law and create a thriving, indigenous legal system that had the Constitution at its heart'.[25] The most recently published research on the partisanship of Irish Supreme Court judges—based on a review of all the cases heard in the Supreme Court between 1963 and the end of 2006[26]—shows that whether a judge was appointed by a Fianna Fáil government or a Fine Gael government had no discernible impact on how he or she decided cases: 'the evidence for systematic partisanship in areas where the two parties often disagreed over policies is very weak'.[27] Moreover, while there is a low rate of dissent in the Irish Supreme Court, whenever it does occur there is 'no evidence to suggest that it is motivated by partisan heritage'.[28]

Additional work on judicial appointments in Ireland was conducted in 2004 by Jennifer Carroll.[29] In an attempt to draw comparisons with the results of Bartholomew's findings, she conducted interviews with all the then serving Supreme and High Court judges and published her results in the Bar Review.[30] What made the comparison all the more interesting was that in the period which had elapsed since Bartholomew's 1969 study a significant change to the appointment system had been put in place in 1996, so Carroll was also able to compare her pre- and post-1996 findings. The change in question was the creation of the Judicial Appointments Advisory Board. The same author, as Jennifer Carroll MacNeill, later deepened her study in book-length form.[31]

The Judicial Appointments Advisory Board

The impetus for establishing this Board was a political crisis in 1994.[32] Chief Justice Tom Finlay was due to retire and the most qualified person to replace him was seen by many as Liam Hamilton, a High Court judge since 1974 and its President since 1985. The difficulty was that Hamilton had spent the previous three years chairing the Beef Tribunal which, amongst other things, had inquired into links between Fianna Fáil Ministers and key players in the beef industry.[33] When his report was published in July 1994 it was not as condemnatory of Fianna Fáil Ministers as many had expected. Fianna Fáil was in a coalition government with the Labour Party and the latter was especially displeased that Albert Reynolds, the Fianna Fáil Taoiseach, was, in its eyes, let off so lightly by Hamilton's report. Labour was all the more reluctant to let Hamilton become Chief Justice because during the course of the Beef Tribunal the Supreme Court had decided, by three to two, that the Tribunal could not ask Ministers or former Ministers about what had been said at Cabinet

[24] Tóibin (1985). The non-partisan approach of Irish judges was confirmed in the unpublished doctoral thesis of Ruane (1994).

[25] Mac Cormaic (2016) 134; but Mac Cormaic admits at (68) that from 1953 to the early 1960s Ó Dálaigh 'made scant impression' on the Court.

[26] Amounting to 1,511 cases, with 5,055 judicial opinions.

[27] Elgie, McAuley and O'Malley (2018) 100.

[28] Ibid, 105. In the 501 cases where there were at least two justices who had been appointed by Fianna Fáil or Fine Gael, dissent by even one judge occurred in only 59 (11.8 per cent) of the cases: ibid, 99.

[29] See too the valuable comparative report by Feenan (2008), which considers appointment systems in England and Wales, Scotland, Northern Ireland, Canada and South Africa.

[30] Carroll (2005). [31] Carroll MacNeill (2016).

[32] Ibid, 65–9; see too Mac Cormaic (2016) 354–9.

[33] For accounts of this saga see Hussey (1993) 313–6; Kenny (2005) 95–100.

meetings because such meetings enjoyed absolute confidentiality.[34] The assumption was that Hamilton would support that line in any future case.

Labour was also worried that if Hamilton became Chief Justice his own post as President of the High Court would go to the Attorney General, Harry Whelehan, another Fianna Fáil supporter and the man who had successfully persuaded the Supreme Court to keep cabinet discussions completely confidential. There was a British tradition, which Ireland had continued to follow, that Attorneys General could expect to be elevated in due course to the High Court bench.[35] Additionally, Labour was opposed to Whelehan because during the controversy over the *X* case, concerning whether a 14-year-old girl was entitled to leave the country to obtain an abortion in England,[36] he had displayed very conservative Catholic views. In the end Fianna Fáil got its way in relation to both appointments, but the price it had to pay was acceptance of reform of the judicial appointments system. As it happens, Harry Whelehan remained in post for just two days because it transpired that he had given incorrect information when explaining why the government had delayed so long in extraditing a suspected paedophile priest, Brendan Smyth, to Northern Ireland.[37] Moreover the Supreme Court's decision on cabinet confidentiality was effectively reversed by a constitutional amendment approved in a referendum in 1999.[38]

It has been implied that in the immediate wake of the Whelehan affair the government appointed judges who had no political connections,[39] but a more systemic change was also required. This eventually came with the Courts and Court Officers Act 1995,[40] much of which was devoted to the creation of the Judicial Appointments Advisory Board.[41] As its name implies, the Board's main function was to identify possible appointees to judicial office and inform the government of their suitability for appointment. It continues in place today. It has 12 members and is dominated by significant office-holders, including the Chief Justice (in the Chair), the Presidents of the Court of Appeal, the High Court, the Circuit Court and the District Court, and the Attorney General. If requested by the Minister for Justice to do so, the Board advertises vacancies for judicial positions, invites persons to apply and consults persons about the suitability of potential applicants. It has the power to arrange interviews with applicants[42] but apparently has never used it.[43] Under section 16 of the 1995 Act the Board must inform the Minister of the names of all those who apply for appointment to a vacant post and submit the names of at least seven applicants whom the Board recommends for appointment, unless fewer than seven apply or the Board is unable to recommend at least seven. Before advising the President whom to appoint, the government must consider the applicants recommended by the Board. So far as can be

[34] *Attorney General v Hamilton (No 1)* [1993] 2 IR 250. In the majority were Finlay CJ and Hederman and O'Flaherty JJ; McCarthy and Egan dissented.

[35] As one commentator put it: 'the Taoiseach in selecting the Attorney General is usually also selecting a future judge', Anon (1950) 37.

[36] See further Chap 10 below, 235–8.

[37] Mac Cormaic (2016) Chap 15 ('The Whelehan Affair').

[38] See Art 28.4.3, which allows the High Court to order disclosure of discussion at government meetings if this is in the interests of the administration of justice or, if an application is made by an official tribunal of inquiry, 'by virtue of an overriding public interest'.

[39] Carroll MacNeill (2016) 140. Peter Kelly, the current President of the High Court, has admitted that he was a beneficiary of this preference for non-politically aligned candidates: *The Parchment* (magazine of the Dublin Solicitors Bar Association), Autumn 2012, 30. He added that he had no desire to be a Supreme Court judge because he did not find the life of such a judge 'in the slightest bit attractive' and, in any event, appointments to the Supreme Court are 'purely political'.

[40] The genesis of this Act is explained in Carroll MacNeill (2016) 69–80.

[41] Pt IV (ss 12–23). See www.jaab.ie.

[42] Ibid, s 14(2)(e).

[43] Carroll MacNeill (2016) 113 and 119–22.

ascertained, since 1995 no-one has been appointed to a judicial post after having been excluded from a list of names submitted by the Board to the Minister.[44]

Crucially, the Board becomes involved in the selection process only if the Minister for Justice requests this. Under section 17 of the Act the Minister can instead decide to proceed without the Board's advice. This is possible if the government intends to ask the President to appoint someone who is already a serving judge or is otherwise eligible for appointment. As Carroll MacNeill reveals, between 2002 and 2014 there were 100 vacancies in the Circuit Court, High Court or Supreme Court and 27 of these were filled through this 'elevation' method.[45] Of the 11 vacancies which arose in the Supreme Court, no fewer than ten were filled in this way, the exception appearing to be the appointment of Donal O'Donnell straight from the Bar in 2010.[46] The annual reports of the Board provide statistics on the various competitions for judicial posts. The report for 2015, which was published too late to be considered by Carroll MacNeill, reveals that the Board considered only one applicant for the vacancy which arose on the Supreme Court after the retirement of John Murray.[47] This was presumably Iseult O'Malley, who was duly appointed. The same report provides cumulative figures as to the numbers of applicants for Supreme Court vacancies in which the Board *was* in some way involved: between 1996 and 2015 there were only 27 applicants for the 14 vacancies, some of whom could well have been repeat players.[48] Also, people are entitled to submit unsolicited applications at any time, whether or not a vacancy has been advertised.

Beyond the Advisory Board

Carroll MacNeill's conclusions on the work of the Judicial Appointments Advisory Board are that it has brought about 'very little change to the political patronage system of appointments that existed in Ireland, even though there is now a public perception that all judges are appointed by an independent Board'.[49] She discovered that the legal members of the Board set great store by knowing the candidates who have applied (applications are not anonymised),[50] that the Board has never exercised its power to invite particular individuals to apply,[51] that unsuccessful applicants do not receive any feedback on why they were not appointed,[52] and that since 2000 the Board has tended not to limit itself to recommending seven suitable candidates for every vacancy but instead has sent the government the full list of applicants for the vacancy minus the few who have been deemed by the Board to be unappointable.[53] In short, the Board has become a screening mechanism rather than a selecting mechanism. Moreover, interviews with former members of the cabinet revealed that the Minister for Justice usually relies on the advice of the Attorney General as to which of the names forwarded by the Board to select. In respect of senior judicial appointments 'the overwhelming consensus was that the decision was made by the Taoiseach and Attorney General',[54] discussions at cabinet meetings being very rare.[55] It is particularly unsettling that there was agreement amongst Carroll MacNeill's political interviewees that

[44] Ibid, 122–3. See too Morgan (2004a). [45] Ibid, 100.

[46] Ibid, 99 (Table 3.2), 101 and 149 n 23. In an answer to a question from Charlie Flanagan TD, the Minister for Justice (Brian Lenihan Jr) confirmed to the Dáil on 4 March 2008 that since 1995 only two Supreme Court judges had *not* been appointed directly by the government without a recommendation from the JAAB. These were Adrian Hardiman and Nial Fennelly in 2000.

[47] JAAB (2016) 6. [48] Ibid, 20.

[49] Carroll MacNeill (2016) 109–10, citing her own earlier study (2005). See too Moran (2007), who argues for a wholly competence-based appointments system.

[50] Ibid, 111–3. See too 145–7. [51] Ibid, 119. [52] Ibid, 113. [53] Ibid, 126–31.

[54] Ibid, 135. [55] Ibid, 132.

in situations where there are a number of candidates of equal stature and one of them is 'politically sympathetic to the party in power, that person would get the nomination'.[56] Even though party political connections were seen to be much more important for appointments to lower courts, it remains remarkable that in a modern liberal democracy the political leanings of candidates for judicial preferment can play any role at all. Even if there is no evidence that party politics play any role in the way judges behave once appointed, perceptions alone can impact significantly on public confidence.[57]

In 2013 the then Minister for Justice, Alan Shatter, told the Law Society Annual Conference that the time had come to put in place a 'much more transparent and accountable system' for appointing judges.[58] Later that year the Minister announced that he was opening consultations on how the appointments system should be reformed[59] and in 2014 a formal submission on the issue was sent to the government on behalf of the judiciary.[60] It came from the Judicial Appointments Review Committee, a group set up by the judges themselves to produce a collective view.[61] It comprised the presidents of the four tiers of courts, together with five other judges including Donal O'Donnell from the Supreme Court. The submission described the present appointment system as 'demonstrably deficient',[62] 'unsatisfactory' and in need of 'radical improvement'.[63] To its credit, before making any recommendations the Committee looked at the way judicial appointments are handled in other common law jurisdictions, such as England and Wales, Northern Ireland, Scotland, Australia, Canada and New Zealand. It stressed that '[a]s a matter of principle, political allegiance should have no bearing on appointments to judicial office',[64] pointing out that in the United Kingdom the 1945–51 government ended the practice of appointing judges on the basis of their support for the governing party of the day.[65] The Committee recommended that the Judicial Appointments Advisory Board should be reformed (not replaced) and that in future it should send only three names to the government for each judicial vacancy, but in rank order and singling out any candidate regarded as 'outstanding'.[66] In its discussion of judicial 'merit' in this context the Committee emphasised the importance of appointees having long experience in conducting litigation and advocacy; it therefore proposed that the minimum period of legal practice required for appointments to all courts should be extended to 15 years.[67]

Contemporaneously with the government's consultation process, three Private Members' Bills on judicial appointments were tabled during 2013–14.[68] None of these was enacted, but nor did the government proceed with its own legislation, despite promising to do so in 2015.[69] By the time of the general election in 2016 the Bill had still not been published.

[56] Ibid, 137.

[57] See eg 'Five out of six judges appointed have connections to Fine Gael or Labour' *Irish Times*, 14 November 2011.

[58] 'A Time of Change', 11 May 2013, available at: www.justice.ie/en/JELR/Pages/SP13000187.

[59] See www.justice.ie/en/JELR/Pages/PR13000413.

[60] This is available on the website of the Supreme Court. For a summary of a range of submissions see Carroll MacNeill (2016) 180–93. The *Irish Times* described it as 'a remarkably cogent and blunt document', 1 February 2014, 15.

[61] The Association of Judges in Ireland issued a statement fully endorsing the JARC's submission: see http://aji.ie/news/view/preliminary-submission-of-the-judicial-appointments-review-committee.

[62] Note 60 above, para 20. [63] Ibid, para 32. [64] Ibid, para 135.

[65] Ibid, citing a piece by Donal O'Donnell (2004). Carroll MacNeill (2016), at 183, observes that giving politicians some influence over the appointment of judges does not necessarily compromise the subsequent independence of those judges.

[66] Ibid, paras 147–8.

[67] Ibid, para 150. For a fascinating attempt to deduce judicial qualities from judicial obituaries, see Bell (2008).

[68] They are usefully summarised at Carroll MacNeill (2016) 194–204.

[69] See the reply to questions from an independent TD in the Dáil by then Minister for Justice, Frances Fitzgerald, on 2 April 2015, available on the website of the Oireachtas.

During the long subsequent negotiations over the formation of a government, independent TDs were able to use their demand for various reforms as bargaining chips when established parties were seeking their support. Shane Ross TD, in particular, insisted that he would support the proposed minority Fine Gael government only if it agreed to reform the system for appointing judges. He had been behind one of the Private Members' Bills in 2013, where he tried to ensure that judges would be selected by a Joint Committee of the Oireachtas in which a majority of the members would be from parties not in the current government.[70] The Joint Oireachtas Committee on Justice, Defence and Equality heard evidence about, and debated, judicial selection systems during 2014,[71] but it did not issue any report on the matter or make any recommendations to the government.

The Judicial Appointments Commission Bill

In December 2016 the Minister for Justice and Equality, Frances Fitzgerald, finally published the General Scheme of the Judicial Appointments Commission Bill.[72] It provides for a Commission to replace the existing Board and for its members to be mostly lay people, including a lay chair, all of whom are to be selected by the Public Appointments Service. The Commission will deal with all judicial appointments, including promotions from one court to another, and will submit only three names to the government for each judicial vacancy, together with two names for each additional vacancy at the same level. In certain circumstances distinguished academics will be eligible for appointment. In addition, a wholly new system is to be introduced for appointing the Chief Justice, the President of the Court of Appeal and the President of the High Court. They are to be selected by a Committee comprising the lay chair of the Commission, the Chief Justice (or the President of the Court of Appeal if the vacancy in question is the Chief Justice's office), the Attorney General and the Minister for Justice; this Committee will receive from the Commission the names of persons wishing to be considered for appointment and will recommend three names to the government.

To the annoyance of many, especially in the judiciary, the government agreed that no further judicial appointments should be made until the new legislation was in force.[73] However tensions were heightened when, in April 2017, the outgoing Taoiseach Enda Kenny announced that Maire Whelan, the Attorney General, was to be appointed a judge of the Court of Appeal to fill a vacancy created by a retirement. Apart from breaching the commitment not to make further appointments, this decision was controversial for four reasons. First, in January 2017 the Judicial Appointments Advisory Board had invited applications from those who wished to be considered for appointment to the Court of Appeal but no-one who applied had been appointed. Second, in her capacity as Attorney General Ms Whelan was herself a member of the Advisory Board and may have participated in the Board's decision not to recommend any of the persons who had applied. Third, Ms Whelan had no prior judicial experience and the common expectation had been that no-one would be appointed to the Court of Appeal unless he or she had first served as a judge in a lower court. Fourth, Ms Whelan had recently been criticised by a Commission, chaired by former Supreme Court

[70] This would have required a change to the Constitution, so Ross entitled his Bill 'the Thirty-Fourth Amendment to the Constitution (Judicial Appointments) Bill'.

[71] See eg the Committee's session on 26 November 2014, available on the website of the Oireachtas.

[72] Press release from the Department of Justice and Equality, 6 December 2016.

[73] Fiona Gartland, 'No new judges until law on appointments passes, says Ross', *Irish Times*, 27 September 2016; Colm Keena and Pat Leahy, 'Ban on new judges could be "disastrous" for court system', *Irish Times*, 29 September 2016.

judge Nial Fennelly, which expressed concerns about inconsistencies in evidence she had given relating to the recording of phone calls at Garda stations.[74] Not surprisingly, there was a lot of negative reaction to the way this appointment was made. Micheál Martin, the leader of Fianna Fáil, described it as 'directly political' and 'squalid'.[75] The controversy seemed to threaten the succession of Leo Varadkar as Taoiseach, since he had not objected to the way Ms Whelan had been appointed. But both Varadkar and Whelan weathered the storm and the judge has settled down in her new role. The episode vividly highlighted the potential for political patronage to still play a part in judicial appointments. However, when Mary Finlay Geoghegan was appointed to the Supreme Court later in 2017 there were no suggestions at all of any improper political interference.

Returning to the Judicial Appointments Commission Bill, the Law Society has suggested that the new Commission should be required to draw up a list of personal qualities constituting 'merit' and then assess candidates against those qualities. They should include 'common sense, independence, balance, an even temper, humanity, humility, courtesy, compassion and social awareness'.[76] The Chair of the Bar Council, however, thinks that setting up a new Commission is a waste of money, given that in some years only a handful of judicial appointments are made.[77] A former Minister for Justice has stated that appointing a lay person to chair the Commission is a mistake.[78] The Joint Committee of the Oireachtas on Justice, Defence and Equality engaged in pre-legislative scrutiny of the government's Bill in early 2017, alongside yet another Private Members' Bill, this time introduced by Jim O'Callaghan, a Fianna Fáil TD.[79] During the Committee's discussions Minister Fitzgerald staunchly defended the government's prerogative to select judges:

> The role of the Government, in the principle of it but maybe not the detail, under the Constitution in this matter requires a level of discretion. All of the legal advice says that. I would say that is not consistent with a statutory body providing only three names in order of choice. Similarly, even without an order, having only six names be recommended for four vacancies is inadequate for a real choice. As I say, there is a very important point, which is the Government exercising its constitutional prerogative. That may be unconstitutional if one is not giving that level of choice of candidates, by fine-tuning it down to that degree.

Interestingly, the Minister's position seems to be consistent with internationally agreed standards in this domain. The Mount Scopus International Standards on Judicial Independence (first agreed in 2008 and consolidated in 2015) state in Principle 4(2)(a) that: 'The principle of democratic accountability should be respected and therefore it is legitimate for the Executive and the Legislature to play a role in judicial appointments provided that due consideration is given to the principle of judicial independence.'[80] The Mount Scopus Principles, however, are the work of a private international association[81] and not an agreement between States. The UN's Basic Principles on the Independence of the

[74] The 724-page Fennelly Commission Report was published on 6 April 2017. See too Michael O'Regan, 'Taoiseach defends Attorney General's role in Callinan controversy', *Irish Times*, 11 April 2017.

[75] *Irish Times*, 14 June 2017.

[76] The submission, dated 22 March 2017, is available on the website of the Law Society.

[77] Paul McGarry, 'Protecting high quality of judiciary crucial to Irish democracy', *Irish Times*, 5 April 2017. See too the Bar Council's submission on the Scheme, dated 23 January 2017, available on its website, p 4.

[78] Michael O'Regan, 'Michael McDowell criticises judicial reform plans', *Irish Times*, 1 February 2017. Diarmaid Ferriter agreed that this was a flaw in the Bill: *Irish Times*, 1 July 2017.

[79] See www.kildarestreet.com/committees/?id=2017-01-25a.603 (25 January 2017).

[80] See www.jiwp.org/mt-scopus-standards.

[81] The International Association of Judicial Independence and World Peace. Its President is the renowned academic Professor Shimon Shetreet.

Judiciary simply say that: 'Any method of judicial selection shall safeguard against judicial appointments for improper motives'.[82]

When moving the second stage of the Judicial Appointments Commission Bill on 27 June 2017 Charles Flanagan, the Minister for Justice, stated that the Bill brought the appointments system 'to a new level of openness and effectiveness'. It requires the new Commission either to hold interviews or other tests during a selection process, or to state clearly why such methods have not been used.[83] In its Annual Report for 2015 the existing Board had confirmed that the Board was still not availing of its power to interview candidates because: '[t]here are serious practical obstacles to the Board conducting such a process routinely and generally the Board has sufficient information in particular which is provided by the applicants themselves to carry out its function in each instance'.[84] While such a position might be defensible when the Board is faced with a large number of applicants, it is surely not valid when there are just two or three candidates for a seat on the Supreme Court. By October 2018 the Judicial Appointments Commission Bill had still not completed its stages in the Oireachtas, having been through the Dáil and reached its third stage in the Seanad. Worryingly, even the government's own Attorney General, Séamus Woulfe, was at one point describing the Bill as 'a dog's dinner'.[85]

In all of the discussions about reforming the judicial appointments system in Ireland there has been no suggestion that appointments to the Supreme Court should be singled out for different treatment. Yet in practice they have been, as most of the appointments made to the Supreme Court in the past 20 years have not resulted from the Board's involvement. When Frank Clarke was appointed Chief Justice to replace Susan Denham in 2017 it was simply announced by the government with no explanation as to how the selection had been made.[86] In the United Kingdom appointments to the Supreme Court are also treated differently from other judicial appointments, as a report by the House of Lords' Constitution Committee in 2012 made clear,[87] but they still require an application and an interview.[88] The Constitution Committee recommended that the selection commission should comprise seven members, including a lay chair and at least three judges, namely two serving members of the Supreme Court and the Lord Chief Justice of England and Wales.[89] In 2013 the selection system was amended to allow preference to be given to a candidate whose appointment would increase diversity on the Court, but only where he or she was of equal merit with at least one other candidate.[90] When the selection of three new Justices took place in 2016–17 the Constitution Committee's recommendations were not implemented but some tweaking did occur as a result of a report produced by the former Chief Executive of the Court in 2015.[91] Ireland could, with respect, learn something from these developments in the United Kingdom.

[82] Principle 10. [83] General Scheme, 25–6 and Head 11(4). See too Cahillane (2017).

[84] *Annual Report for 2015*, 15. The *Annual Report for 2016*, 6, notes that in 2016 the Board did not meet to consider any appointments to the Supreme Court. The *Annual Report for 2017*, 8, notes that the Board met once in 2017 to consider applications to fill a vacancy on the Supreme Court: there was only one such applicant, a woman with more than 20 years' experience. Presumably this was Mary Finlay Geoghegan, who was appointed to the Court in December 2017.

[85] Fiach Kelly and Rachel Flaherty, 'Pressure mounts on Government to scrap Shane Ross's judicial Bill', *Irish Times*, 24 March 2018.

[86] Government press release, 26 July 2017. The *Irish Examiner* announced the news with the headline 'Frank Clarke named Chief Justice but Government cannot say how he was picked'.

[87] *Judicial Appointments*, 25th Report of 2011–12, Chap 5.

[88] Constitutional Reform Act 2005, ss 26–31. [89] Note 87 above, paras 147–55.

[90] Crime and Courts Act 2013, s 20 and Sch 13, para 9, inserting s 27(5A) into the Constitutional Reform Act 2005.

[91] See *The Supreme Court Annual Report and Accounts 2016–17*, HC 31, 18.

Salaries and Pensions

Under the Courts of Justice Act 1924 judges of the Supreme Court were to be paid £3,000 per annum, with the Chief Justice receiving an additional £1,000.[92] Upon retiring after at least 15 years' service, a Supreme Court judge was entitled to a life-time pension amounting to two-thirds of the salary at the date of retirement, a smaller pension being payable if the judge retired after completing less than 15 but more than five years' service.[93]

Down the years there have been several controversies over the terms and conditions of judicial appointments.[94] One of the earliest involved John O'Byrne, a barrister who succeeded Hugh Kennedy as Attorney General when the latter became Chief Justice in 1924 and who was appointed a High Court judge in 1926 and a Supreme Court judge in 1940. He died in office in 1954 and his widow commenced litigation concerning her husband's pension. She claimed that under the 1922 and 1937 Constitutions a judge's pension could not be taxed because that would amount to a reduction in remuneration.[95] She lost before Dixon J in the High Court and then appealed to the Supreme Court.

In *O'Byrne v Minister for Finance*[96] Maguire CJ, who was supported in his reasoning by Kingsmill Moore and Haugh JJ, found that requiring a judge to pay taxes on his or her income could not be said to be an attack on judicial independence. He relied heavily on jurisprudence from the USA, Australia and South Africa, because the Irish constitutional provisions on judicial salaries were similar to those enacted there. He admitted that he himself, on behalf of his fellow judges, had suggested to the Taoiseach in 1950 that taxation of judicial salaries was unconstitutional, but he was now satisfied, on the basis of the arguments raised in the case before him, that this position was incorrect. While Kingsmill Moore J did not find the comparative jurisprudence as unequivocal as the Chief Justice had done, he made his personal view very clear:

> There are certain general vicissitudes which every man must face—inflation of currency, wars with their consequent increase in taxation, complications of exchange, and so on. These strike at all classes. They are indiscriminate. They are part of the hazard of life. Even a judge cannot claim to live in a financial ivory tower, immune from the common lot of humanity. What he can claim is that there should be no discrimination against him as a judge which will worsen his position vis-à-vis the rest of the citizens of the State.[97]

Remarkably, two Supreme Court judges dissented. Lavery and Maguire JJ (the latter being no relation to the Chief Justice) were of the view that judicial salaries should not be taxed. Lavery J observed that judges appointed under the 1922 Constitution were not successors of the judges of the British regime and that Ireland's courts 'represent a new departure constituted under different ideas'.[98] He thought the Irish Free State Constitution was based on the US Constitution and his analysis of US precedents led him to conclude that in Ireland income tax is not a non-discriminatory general tax and so its application to judicial salaries was unconstitutional. Oddly, no-one seems to have objected to judges who obviously had a vested interest in the outcome of this case being allowed to decide it. But if not they, who?

[92] Courts of Justice Act 1924, s 13. [93] Ibid, s 14. [94] Mac Cormaic (2016) 106–10, 360–70.

[95] Art 68 of the 1922 Constitution provided that the remuneration of all judges should not be diminished during their continuance in office; Art 35.5 of the 1937 Constitution stated: 'The remuneration of a judge shall not be reduced during his continuance in office'.

[96] [1959] IR 1. For a relevant letter by Professor David Gwynn Morgan see the *Irish Times*, 18 March 2009.

[97] Ibid, 71. [98] Ibid, 43.

When the 'new' Supreme Court was established in 1961 the salary of an ordinary judge was set at IR£4,070 and that of the Chief Justice at IR£5,335.[99] In 1964 these sums rose to IR£4,950 and IR£6,360 respectively[100] and in 1968 to IR£7,000 and IR£8,000.[101] From then on the government was permitted to raise judicial salaries by an order laid before the Dáil rather than having to enact primary legislation.[102] After five such orders were issued in the 1970s, by 1979 the salary of an ordinary Supreme Court judge was IR£22,050 and that of the Chief Justice IR£26,520.[103] Around this time federal judges in the US engaged in litigation to avoid their salaries being eroded by inflation and in *United States v Will* the US Supreme Court ruled that it was unconstitutional for Congress to freeze cost-of-living increases which had previously been authorised.[104] In Ireland the salaries were to have risen again in 1980 but the government held back on the proposal.[105] In 1981 they shot up to IR£30,497 and IR£37,297.[106]

When State papers from 30 years earlier were released at the end of 2013 they revealed that in the 1980s senior judges argued strongly with the government over their pay and expenses.[107] In 1982 Tom O'Higgins CJ complained to Taoiseach Charles Haughey about the delay in paying sums to judges to cover a study, library, heating, lighting, laundry, fees to the King's Inns, telephone, motoring, and other expenses. Apparently the sum due had been fixed in 1980 at IR£2,500 per judge. At the end of the same year O'Higgins CJ wrote to the new Taoiseach, Fine Gael's Garret FitzGerald, to complain about the 'undue and extraordinary delay' in applying the public service pay agreement of 1981 to judges. A month later High Court judge Liam Hamilton argued that the failure to pay the salary increases was discriminatory and unconstitutional, and in June 1983 O'Higgins CJ reiterated his complaint about the delay. The result of all this pressure was the Oireachtas (Allowances to Members) and Ministerial, Parliamentary and Judicial Offices (Amendment) Act 1983.[108] This increased the salaries of judges quite considerably: from 1 December 1981 there was to be a 2 per cent rise, from 1 March 1982 a 6 per cent rise, from 1 October 1982 a 5 per cent rise and from 1 September 1983 a 4.75 per cent rise. At the end of 1983 this left the annual salary of a Supreme Court judge at IR£36,268 and that of the Chief Justice at IR£44,355.[109]

In 1979 the Review Body on Higher Remuneration in the Public Sector recommended that reappraisals of pay levels should take place every four years, but the next one was not in fact triggered until 1986.[110] The following year the government announced that it would not immediately implement the Review Body's recommendations, which had called for an average 35 per cent increase (*sic*).[111] Changes were not made until June 1988, when an ordinary judge's salary rose to IR£50,005 and the Chief Justice's to IR£61,140.[112] This was followed by further increases in 1989: a Supreme Court judge's salary was raised by 19 per cent over the course of 16 months to IR£55,032 and the Chief Justice's by 13.5 per cent to IR£65,798.[113] These were years of significant wage inflation in all sectors in Ireland.

In 1997 the government accepted the recommendation of the Review Body on Higher Remuneration in the Public Sector that the salary of a Supreme Court judge should rise by 3

[99] Courts (Supplemental Provisions) Act 1961, s 46. The salary of the President of the High Court was set at the same level as that of a judge of the Supreme Court.

[100] Courts (Supplemental Provisions) (Amendment) Act 1964, s 1.

[101] Courts (Supplemental Provisions) (Amendment) (No 2) Act 1968, s 1(a).

[102] Ibid, s 1(b), inserting a new s 46(9) into the Courts (Supplemental Provisions) Act 1961.

[103] See *Irish Times*, 1 July 1971, 11 March 1975, 9 March 1977, 3 May 1978, 15 August 1979, 6 December 1979.

[104] 449 US 200 (1980).

[105] *Irish Times*, 21 June 1980.

[106] *Irish Times*, 7 November 1981.

[107] Seán McCárthaigh, *Irish Examiner*, 28 December 1983.

[108] s 2(6).

[109] *Irish Times*, 2 November 1983.

[110] *Irish Times*, 15 July 1986.

[111] *Irish Times*, 14 March 1987 and 3 December 1987.

[112] *Irish Times*, 25 June 1988.

[113] *Irish Times*, 29 July 1989.

per cent to IR£89,700, and the Chief Justice's by 2.7 per cent to IR£103,500.[114] Ireland's currency switched to euros on 1 January 2002 and by 2003 a Supreme Court's salary had risen to €182,901, but this was still not enough to attract more than two applicants for a vacancy that had recently arisen.[115] A year later the Minister for Finance announced that judges would not receive any special pay increases (over and above general increases awarded to public sector workers) until 2007, despite the Review Body warning in its 2001 report that top public sector pay was 'substantially out of line with' (ie, lower than) top private sector pay. In its report in 2007 the Review Body recommended that the salary of Supreme Court judges should rise by 15.5 per cent from €233,757 to €270,000 and suggested that the salary of the Chief Justice should continue to be pegged to that of the Taoiseach, as it had been since 1968;[116] his salary was therefore to rise by 15.6 per cent from €268,243 to €316,000.[117]

When Ireland suffered a severe financial crisis in 2008, due largely to some of its banks indulging in risky investments and the Irish government stepping in to bail them out, the government decided it was necessary to reduce public sector pay. The Financial Emergency Measures in the Public Interest Act 2009 provided for deductions of 3 per cent on the first €15,000 of remuneration, 6 per cent on the next €5,000 and 10 per cent on the rest.[118] But no deductions could be made from judges' salaries because of the prohibition on this in the Constitution.[119] Instead judges were invited to make voluntary contributions comparable to the amounts being taken away from other public sector workers. In September 2009 the Revenue Commissioners announced that, pursuant to a deal struck with the judiciary in May 2009, 72 of the country's 144 judges had paid the voluntary pension levy, the average payment being €4,580.[120] By January 2010 the number of judges making the contribution had risen to 111[121] and it eventually reached 125.[122] Mac Cormaic assures us that all of the Supreme Court judges contributed.[123] In 2011 the government's suggestion that the Constitution should be changed to allow reductions in judicial salaries led to a predictable spat with senior judges,[124] a group of whom submitted a document arguing that such a move would be a threat to their independence.[125]

When a referendum on reductions to judicial salaries was eventually held in 2011 the salary of a Supreme Court judge was €257,872 and that of the Chief Justice was €295,916. Predictably, almost 80 per cent of those who voted in the referendum were in favour of allowing judges' salaries to be reduced and the government wasted little time in implementing this proposal. The provisions which were added to the Constitution, where Articles 35.5.2 and 35.5.3 now read as follows:

> 2 The remuneration of judges is subject to the imposition of taxes, levies or other charges that are imposed by law on persons generally or persons belonging to a particular class.

[114] 'Cabinet accepts report on pay for higher public sector levels', *Irish Times*, 5 March 1997.

[115] 'Who'd be a judge? Not, it appears, learned counsel', *Irish Times*, 1 July 2003. Neither applicant was successful; instead the government recommended McCracken J for elevation from the High Court.

[116] This was a result of the Oireachtas (Allowances to Members) and Ministerial and Parliamentary Offices (Amendment) Act 1968 and the Courts (Supplemental Provisions) (Amendment) (No 2) Act 1968. Prior to then the Chief Justice's salary had been higher than that of the Taoiseach.

[117] http://www.reviewbody.gov.ie/Documents/Report_No_42.pdf, 105.

[118] s 2 of the 2009 Act.

[119] See n 95.

[120] 'Half of State's 144 judges have paid voluntary pension levy', *Irish Times*, 29 September 2009.

[121] 'One in five judges yet to pay voluntary pension levy', *Irish Times*, 19 January 2010.

[122] Michael Clifford, 'Power of Attorney', *Irish Examiner*, 8 July 2011. Clifford argued that Ireland's Chief Justice Murray, given his entitlement to various pensions as well as his current salary, was the highest paid judge in the world.

[123] Mac Cormaic (2016) 371.

[124] For a good account see Mac Cormaic (2016) 365–86.

[125] Paul Cullen, 'Government rejects judiciary's call for independent pay review', *Irish Times*, 4 July 2011.

> 3 Where, before or after the enactment of this section, reductions have been or are made by law to the remuneration of persons belonging to classes of persons whose remuneration is paid out of public money and such law states that those reductions are in the public interest, provision may also be made by law to make proportionate reductions to the remuneration of judges.[126]

Article 35.5.2 is clearly intended to give constitutional endorsement to the decision of the Supreme Court in *O'Byrne v Minister for Finance*.[127] Article 35.5.3 is intended to underline the reality that judges are workers in the public sector. The path chosen was not to *require* such reductions merely because other public sector workers were having their pay reduced but to *permit* the reductions if legislation was passed to that effect and reductions were proportionate (presumably this means proportionate to reductions imposed on other public sector workers). This was still a bold move, one which lessens the financial security of Irish judges in a way which their counterparts in other common law jurisdictions do not have to endure. But Ireland's financial crisis after 2008 was extremely serious and in such circumstances it can hardly be argued that the independence of judges is being tampered with if all they are being asked to do is shoulder their share of the burden of sacrifices which all other public sector workers (and countless private sector workers too) are required to bear.

Pursuant to the amended Constitution, the Oireachtas passed the Financial Emergency Measures in the Public Interest (Amendment) Act 2011, section 10 of which reduced the pay and pensions of judges.[128] Taking into account pension related reductions, the salary of an ordinary Supreme Court judge then in office was reduced on 1 January 2012 from €257,872 to €198,226, while that of the Chief Justice went down from €295,916 to €227,168.[129] A judge appointed to the Supreme Court on or after that date was entitled to €178,608 and a Chief Justice to €204,657, both figures being about 10 per cent less than those for judges appointed earlier.[130] Notwithstanding these substantial reductions, a report published by the European Commission for the Efficiency of Justice (an agency within the Council of Europe) showed that in 2012 the salary paid to a Supreme Court judge in Ireland was still more than twice as high as the average salary awarded to judges in comparable positions elsewhere in Europe (€90,188). However Supreme Court judges in the United Kingdom were paid substantially more (€256,506).[131]

A month after the 2011 referendum the Association of Judges of Ireland was established to help the judiciary defend its interests.[132] Until then there had been no representative body with such a role and its creation was not universally welcomed.[133] In 2013 the Association issued a statement criticising the government for cutting judges' pay and pensions without

[126] Twenty-Ninth Amendment of the Constitution (Judges' Remuneration) Act 2011. The new Art 35.5.1 reads: 'The remuneration of judges shall not be reduced during their continuance in office save in accordance with this section.'

[127] See the discussion at n 96 above.

[128] On 28 November 2011 it was revealed that 12 former Supreme Court judges were in receipt of pensions worth more than €83,000. This included Hugh O'Flaherty, who had resigned in 1999. John Murray, the retired Chief Justice who was still serving on the Court at the time, supposedly had a combined salary and pension income of €432,000: Paul Cullen, '13 former judges receive pensions of over EUR 100,000', *Irish Times*, 4.

[129] Figures taken from the website of the Association of Judges of Ireland. It claims that reductions were around 31 per cent, but does not say how this was calculated. Around 21 per cent may be more accurate.

[130] Ibid.

[131] *Report on European Judicial Systems: Efficiency and Quality of Justice* (2014), Table 11.23, 309. The salaries in France and Germany were €110,082 and €104,711 respectively. A report on 2014 data was published by the same organisation in 2016 but unfortunately the comparable Table 3.21 (p 110) does not include data for either Ireland or the UK. In the 37 countries for which data is supplied the average salary of a Supreme Court judge is stated to be €65,760 and the highest salary (paid in Cyprus) was €136,756. In Canada the salary of a Supreme Court judge (as of April 2017) was CAN$375,300 while in the USA (as of January 2017) it was US$251,800.

[132] For further details see the Association's website at: http://aji.ie; also O'Dowd (2012).

[133] David Gwynn Morgan, 'Trade union for judges in no one's interest', *Irish Times*, 6 December 2012.

introducing appropriate safeguards to ensure their continued independence.[134] Few judges of the Supreme Court publically voiced their personal concerns, but a prominent exception was Adrian Hardiman, who said on RTE that:

> The notion that judicial appointments should continue to be entirely political while there is a zero protection, from a financial point of view, for the judges, against the executive, is one not consistent with the maintenance of an independent judiciary as it's understood in the common law world … It is plainly unacceptable and interferes with the perception as well as the reality of judicial independence that government or parliament be in a position directly to control the judges' remuneration and appointment.[135]

The country's Minister for Justice at the time, Alan Shatter, responded to this by denying that there was any political interference in Irish courts and pointing to the views of the overwhelming majority who had voted in the referendum.[136]

The Association of Judges of Ireland continued to point out that in 2013 the take-home pay of judges had fallen by one-third since 2009.[137] Apart from lower salaries for new judges appointed after 1 January 2012, their pension entitlements were also less generous. They have to contribute 13 per cent of their salary towards their pension, as opposed to the 4 per cent paid by judges appointed earlier, and new judges must serve for 20 rather than 15 years before being able to collect their maximum pension, although, as before, this will be 50 per cent of their final salary.[138] At the Supreme Court level a judge's pension accrues at the rate of 2.5 per cent of his or her salary during each of the judge's first five years in office and then at the rate of 3.75 per cent during subsequent years. This is a faster accrual rate than applies to other public sector workers. Besides, most sensible judges will have made provision for a private pension while practising as a lawyer before accepting appointment to the bench.

Under the Financial Emergency Measures in the Public Interest Act 2015,[139] the government now issues orders setting out the rates of pay for judges depending on whether they were appointed before or after 1 January 2012.[140] For judges appointed before that date the amount specified in the government order 'shall not be less than the amount that stood, immediately before [1 January 2017]'.[141] In other words, for those judges, there is a legislative but not a constitutional prohibition on a reduction in their salaries. Judges appointed on or after 1 January 2017 also benefit from a legislative guarantee that their pay will not fall below that which was payable on that date.[142] Moreover for those judges pay scales have been introduced for each level of court. This means that Supreme Court judges may be on different pay depending on the length of time they have served on the Court, a wholly new approach and one which may have a bearing on when judges choose to retire from their position.[143] The 2015 Act also ensures that, if a judge is promoted from one court to a higher court and the first point on the pay scale for the higher court is lower than the amount then being earned by the judge in the lower court, the judge will be entitled to be paid in accordance with the point on the pay scale immediately above his or her current earnings. One consequence of the new arrangements is that a person who has served

[134] Ruadhan Mac Cormaic 'Judges concerned at erosion of autonomy', *Irish Times*, 16 April 2013.

[135] As reported by Jamie Smyth of the *Financial Times*, 16 April 2013.

[136] Ibid.

[137] Ruadhán Mac Cormaic, *Irish Times*, 17 April 2013.

[138] See the Public Service Pensions (Single Scheme and Other Provisions) Act 2012.

[139] s 11, amending the Courts (Supplemental Provisions) Act 1961, s 46.

[140] SI 683/2011. This was the commencement date for s 10 of the FEMPI (Amendment) Act 2011, see 85 above.

[141] Courts (Supplemental Provisions) Act 1961, s 11(9)(c), inserted by the 2015 Act, s 11(1)(b). The first day of January 2017 was the commencement date for the FEMPI Act 2015, s 11.

[142] Ibid, 1961 Act, s 11(9A)(e), inserted by the 2015 Act, s 11(1)(c).

[143] Ibid, 1961 Act, s 11(9A)(d).

for many years on the High Court may earn more than a judge who is appointed to the Supreme Court without first having spent much time as a judge in a lower court.

Eventually, after a meeting with the Attorney General, the Association of Judges of Ireland issued a statement in 2016 expressing satisfaction that its concerns over salaries and pensions were now understood within government, but tensions between the two sectors continue to simmer over the issue. The government announced in the same year that, like police officers, nurses, and teachers, judges appointed since 1 January 2012 would be entitled to substantial pay increases over the coming years to ensure that their salaries are more in line with those of their colleagues who were already in office on that date.[144]

Ensuring Standards of Excellence

In addition to difficulties over appointment methods and salaries, Ireland's Supreme Court still lacks any system whereby members of the Court can benefit from the services of a Judicial Council, that is, a body which can promote high standards of conduct and ensure that public confidence in judicial work is maintained at a high level. There has been talk about forming such a Council for many years but it is yet to come to fruition.

The Constitution Review Group, which reported in 1996, noted that at that time only District Court judges could be subjected to any statutory disciplinary procedures. It did not think that those procedures were inconsistent with the Constitution but it recommended that Article 35.2 should be amended so as to permit judges to regulate their own conduct.[145] In 1999 the Oireachtas's All-Party Committee on the Constitution, in its Fourth Progress Report, also recommended the creation of such a regulatory body[146] and in a report published in 2001 by the Committee on Judicial Conduct and Ethics, set up in the wake of the resignation of Hugh O'Flaherty and others in 1999 and chaired by then Chief Justice Ronan Keane, the same conclusion was reached.[147] The latter report envisaged a Council comprising all judges in the State, as in the case of the Judicial Commission of New South Wales, and it would have a Judicial Conduct and Ethics Committee which would set up an inquiry panel consisting of two judges and a lay person to consider complaints against a judge. If misconduct were established, the judge could be privately or publicly reprimanded and in extreme cases (as envisaged by Article 35.4 of the Constitution) a motion could go before both Houses of the Oireachtas calling for his or her removal.

A preliminary draft Bill was published in 2004 but not much was done about it over the next five years. In 2009 the Minister for Justice, Dermot Ahern, was still saying that he was treating it 'as a matter of high priority'.[148] A General Scheme for a Bill was published in 2010,[149] according to which the Council's functions were to maintain and promote (a) excellence in the exercise by judges of their judicial functions, (b) high standards of conduct among judges, (c) the efficient and effective use of judicial resources, (d) continuing education among judges and (e) respect for the independence of the judiciary. Things then went quiet again because power passed from Fianna Fáil to Fine Gael in the election of 2011.

Clearly losing patience with the politicians, in November 2011 Denham CJ announced the establishment of an Interim Judicial Council[150] and a sub-committee of the Board of

[144] Fiachra Ó Cionnaith, 'Cabinet agrees €20k pay rises for judges', *Irish Examiner*, 10 July 2016.

[145] CRG (1966) 181–2.

[146] See http://archive.constitution.ie/reports/4th-Report-Courts.pdf, 23–5.

[147] Eugene Moloney, 'Watchdog "needed to oversee judiciary"', *Irish Independent*, 26 January 2001. Denham J was also a member of this Committee. For the O'Flaherty affair see 100 below.

[148] Questions in the Dáil, 25 February 2009, 11.

[149] Available on the website of the Department of Justice.

[150] See www.aji.ie/supports/the-interim-judicial-council.

that body was asked to consider a General Scheme for another Judicial Council Bill. The sub-committee passed its views to Minister Alan Shatter in 2012 and later that year he issued drafting instructions to the Attorney General. When addressing the Law Society's Annual Conference in 2013 Mr Shatter anticipated that the Bill would be published later that year,[151] but it was not.[152] In 2014 the issue was returned to by the Judicial Appointments Review Committee which, in its earlier submission to government, had recommended that a Judicial Council be 'established forthwith, with responsibility for representation of the judiciary, an independent disciplinary process, judicial education, and the judicial involvement in the appointment process', although it conceded that this last function could instead be exercised by a separate body, as at present.[153] The Committee noted that both the Chief Justice and Clarke J had already made speeches calling for this reform and that the Council of Europe's Venice Commission and the UN's Special Rapporteur on the Independence of Judges were very supportive of it. In 2015 Denham CJ went so far as to say that Ireland's reputation was being damaged by the absence of such a Council[154] and she repeated this in her speech at the start of the legal year in 2016.[155] The Free Legal Advice Centres (FLAC) also called for the Judicial Council Bill of 2010 to be re-drafted as soon as possible 'to provide for the regulation of judicial conduct, the establishment of an effective complaints mechanism and mechanisms for ensuring judicial accountability'.[156] On 30 May 2017 a Judicial Council Bill was introduced in the Seanad, the same day on which the Judicial Appointments Commission Bill was introduced in the Dáil. It went through its second stage in the Seanad in November but by October 2018 it had not progressed any further. If it is eventually enacted as it currently stands the Bill should provide a valuable additional layer of reassurance to the public that judges in Ireland are, to some extent at least, accountable.

Retirement

Under the Courts of Justice Act 1924 the retirement age for Supreme Court (and High Court) judges was set at 72,[157] although judges appointed to a post when they were at an age greater than the retirement age set for that post by the Act could serve for an additional three years.[158] In 1995 the age was reduced to 70 for those first appointed to the bench after 15 December 1995,[159] but individuals already occupying the role of Supreme Court (or High Court) judge were permitted to continue until 72 if they wished to, as were judges of the Circuit and District Courts.[160] Susan Denham and Mary Laffoy were first appointed as High Court judges in 1991 and 1995 respectively, so they were each able to remain on the Supreme Court until reaching the age of 72 in 2017. Of the eight judges on the Court at the start of 2018 none is obliged to retire until 2021, when both Frank Clarke and Liam McKechnie

[151] See n 58 above.

[152] During this period an investigation was conducted by the Presidents of the High Court and Circuit Court into the appropriateness of a conversation between a High Court judge and a Circuit Judge about a family case which the former was hearing. It concluded that the conversation had no influence on the outcome of the case. See 'Judgment on the Judges', Irish Times, 6 November 2013.

[153] See n 60 above, paras 53–61.

[154] Mary Carolan, 'Judicial council "imperative", says Chief Justice', *Irish Times* 5 October 2015. See too Cahillane (2015).

[155] Daniel McConnell, 'Chief Justice Susan Denham calls for judicial council', *Irish Examiner*, 26 September 2016.

[156] 'Preliminary Submission on the Review of Procedures for Appointment as a Judge' (January 2014), available on the website of FLAC.

[157] s 12. [158] Ibid, s 100. [159] Courts and Court Officers Act 1995, s 47(1).

[160] Ibid, s 47(2) and (3).

will reach the age of 70. Given her relative youthfulness, the second most recent appointee, Iseult O'Malley, could potentially remain on the Court until 2034.

Seventy is also the age at which judges of the UK Supreme Court must retire,[161] although Lord Neuberger, a former President of the Court, has suggested that the age should be returned to what it was before 1993, namely 75.[162] His argument is that if Supreme Court judges must retire at 70 they may not have much of an opportunity to develop substantial experience while in that role, since they are unlikely to have been appointed to it until their mid-60s, especially if the main pool from which appointees are drawn is the Court of Appeal, which in turn will have recruited from the High Court.

At the start of 2018 the average age of the Chief Justice and the seven ordinary Supreme Court judges in Ireland then in post was respectably low, at 63, the same figure as in Canada. The average age of Supreme Court judges in the USA, and also in the United Kingdom was 68.[163] In Australia it was as low as 59.

Those Who Have Served[164]

The top judges before 1924

When the Supreme Court began operating in 1924 it had just three judges,[165] all of whom were appointed on 5 June. This also marked the day when several individuals who had served for several years on the senior bench in Ireland were required to retire.[166] Amongst them were Lord Chief Justice Thomas Molony and Lords Justices Stephen Ronan and Sir James O'Connor. Only one of the three Lords Justices in post in 1924 was appointed to the Supreme Court, Charles O'Connor (no relation to James). Since its creation in 1878,[167] eight other men had served as Lords Justices in the Court of Appeal of Ireland.[168]

Thomas Molony had been a brilliant scholar at Trinity College Dublin and a Queen's Counsel since 1899. In 1910 he unsuccessfully stood for election as a Liberal MP in Liverpool but in 1912 was appointed as Solicitor General for Ireland. A year later he served as Attorney General for just two months before being elevated to the High Court bench. He took over as Lord Chief Justice in 1918 when the holder of that office, James Campbell, was made Lord Chancellor of Ireland. After the partition of Ireland in 1921 Molony took legal action to ensure that he could continue to call himself the Lord Chief Justice of Ireland, not just of Southern Ireland.[169] Although he was a proud Catholic, he was openly royalist in his leanings and during the war of independence of 1919–21 he upheld the authorities' right, under martial law, to carry out reprisals against their enemies.[170] When the post of Lord Chancellor of Ireland was abolished with the coming into force of the Irish Free State

[161] This is also the retirement age for judges of the High Court of Australia. The retirement age for Supreme Court judges in Canada is 75, while in the US there is no retirement age.

[162] Evidence to the House of Lords' Constitution Committee, 29 March 2017, 14, available on the website of the Committee.

[163] This takes account of the appointment of Neil Gorsuch in April 2017, at the age of 49. The youngest judge on the Supreme Courts of Australia, Canada, Ireland, the UK or the US is James Edelman of the High Court of Australia, appointed in 2017 at the age of 43.

[164] The appointments are listed in App 2 below and brief biographical details of each appointee are supplied in App 3.

[165] Courts of Justice Act 1924, s 5.

[166] For an account of what befell these judges see Ruane (2015).

[167] Supreme Court of Judicature (Ireland) Act 1877.

[168] Jonathan Christian (1878), Rickard Deasy (1878–83), Gerald FitzGibbon (1878–97), Charles Berry (1883–97), Samuel Walker (1895–1905), Hugh Holmes (1897–1914), Richard Cherry (1909–16, serving as LCJ from 1913) and John Moriarty (1913–15); see too Ball (1927) vol 2, 327; Osborough (1999a) 267–9.

[169] Osborough (1974); see also Bridget Hourican's entry for Molony in the *DIB*, vol 6, 562, and Daire Hogan in the *ODNB*, vol 38, 550.

[170] See *R v Allen* [1921]; *R v Strickland* [1921]; Heuston (1964).

Constitution in 1922, Thomas Molony, as Lord Chief Justice, became the head of the judiciary in the new state. In that capacity he did his best to keep the court system going in the face of opposition from anti-treaty activists,[171] but he was not the man whom the provisional government wanted to head up its new court system from 1924. He had not been enthusiastic about the refusal of Irish politicians to accept the status of Southern Ireland within the United Kingdom.

Molony had also antagonised Hugh Kennedy in an important case which came before the Court of Appeal in 1923, *R (O'Brien) v Military Governor of the North Dublin Union Internment Camp*.[172] As explained earlier,[173] this was a test case on whether thousands of prisoners were entitled to be released from military detention at the end of the civil war. Kennedy, as Attorney General of the Irish Free State, argued that the releases should not take place because there was still a state of war or armed rebellion in the country and, even if there was not, the detentions were authorised under the Public Safety (Emergency Powers) Act 1923. In the High Court he convinced O'Connor MR of his position but on appeal Molony CJ and Ronan LJ held against the government. They thought that the 1923 Act, passed by the Dáil just a day earlier, was invalid because there was no evidence to show that the right to *habeas corpus*, as guaranteed by Article 6 of the 1922 Constitution, should be suspended due to 'the existence of a state of war or armed rebellion'.[174] In the wake of the judgment further legislation had to be validly enacted to authorise the internees' continued detention.[175] When the new court system was inaugurated in 1924 Molony retired to England and was rewarded with a baronetcy.[176]

Lord Justice Stephen Ronan was a Cork man, graduating from Queen's College in that city in 1864. Working mainly as a prosecutor, he became Queen's Counsel in 1889, a decade before Molony and, like Molony, despite being a Catholic he was politically a unionist. He was appointed to the Court of Appeal of Ireland in 1915 but was already 75 when the Supreme Court was established in 1924 and so beyond the normal retirement age of 72.[177] James O'Connor, the other Lord Justice of Appeal not to survive the transition to the Supreme Court, had practised as a solicitor for five years before being called to the Bar in 1900 and rising to be King's Counsel at the age of 36. A nationalist, he nevertheless served as Solicitor General for Ireland from 1914–17 and as Attorney General from 1917–18. In 1918 he was appointed as a Chancery judge in the High Court and a few months later was promoted to the Court of Appeal when his colleague Thomas Molony was appointed Lord Chief Justice. James O'Connor openly opposed the war of independence, which is no doubt why, although he was only 52 when the new courts were established in 1924, no place was found for him on the bench. Apparently resenting this snub, he accepted a knighthood, moved to London and began practising at the English Bar, although in 1929 he sought disbarment from that profession so that he could again apply to practise as a solicitor in Ireland. The application ended up in the High Court and was dealt with by the Chief Justice, Hugh Kennedy.[178]

[171] See *Johnstone v O'Sullivan* [1923] 2 IR 13 and Gwynn (1928) 168-9.

[172] [1924] 1 IR 32.

[173] Chap 2 above, 18.

[174] There was a long Preamble to the Act detailing the nature of the rebellion in the country, but this was not enough to convince the Court of Appeal.

[175] Public Safety (Emergency Powers) Act (No 2) Act 1923.

[176] In 1931 he became the first Catholic since the 16th century to become President of Trinity College Dublin. His chain of office as the last Lord Chief Justice of Ireland still rests there.

[177] Courts of Justice Act 1924, s 12; but he could still have served for three years under s 100: see n 158 above.

[178] Kennedy CJ secured an undertaking from him that, as a former senior judge, he would not claim the right of audience in any court: *Re Solicitors Acts and Sir James O'Connor* [1930] IR 1. See Hogan (1988) and Robert Marshall's entry on O'Connor in the *DIB*, vol 7, 252.

O'Connor achieved his goal but died in London just two years later. He was also a prolific writer, being best known for his idiosyncratic *History of Ireland, 1798–1924*.[179]

The original judges[180]

Hugh Kennedy, 1924–36
Charles O'Connor, 1924–25
Gerald FitzGibbon, 1924–38

Hugh Kennedy, the serving Attorney General for the Irish Free State, was the person appointed as the first President of the new Supreme Court in 1924. This meant that, according to the Courts of Justice Act 1924, he could now also be referred to as the Chief Justice of the Irish Free State. Promoting the Attorney General to a position on the bench was in line with English legal tradition at the time, and was the first of several subsequent such elevations in Ireland. Many might have thought that there were serving judges better qualified than Kennedy to hold the position of Chief Justice, especially as he was aged just 44, but the predominant view in the Executive Council was that the position of Chief Justice was so symbolically important that it needed to be occupied by a person who represented a clean break with the British past and was a strong advocate of Irish independence. As one of the few practising lawyers to lend public support to the rebel cause, Kennedy was a natural choice to hold the top position,[181] and he did so with distinction. He was educated privately at home (his father was a surgeon, from Donegal) and then at University College Dublin, where one of his contemporaries was James Joyce. Being an enthusiastic supporter of the Irish language (in which his name appears as Aodh Ua Cinneidigh) he became honorary secretary of the central committee of the Gaelic League (Conradh na Gaelige), along with Patrick Pearse and Eoin MacNeill. Although he was not personally active in the armed struggles between 1919 and 1923, he served as legal adviser to the Department of Local Government in the first Dáil and was a prominent member of the committee which drafted the 1922 Constitution. When the Irish Free State came into being in December 1922 he was appointed as Attorney General and in that capacity sat on the Judiciary Committee which recommended reforms to the court system in 1923.

Despite Hugh Kennedy's obvious suitability for the top judicial position, it is said that the first of the three judges to be offered a seat on the Supreme Court was actually Charles O'Connor, the Master of the Rolls since 1912 (ie, head of the Court of Appeal). He was not a relative of James O'Connor, who as we have seen was passed over for appointment to the new Supreme Court. Charles O'Connor's elevation was significant because it lent to the Supreme Court immediate credibility, besides ensuring an element of continuity in the court system. Born in 1854, Charles O'Connor was an advocate of Home Rule even while studying at Trinity College Dublin in the era of Edward Carson. As a successful Chancery barrister he reached the senior bench by way of executive service: he was Solicitor General for Ireland from 1909–11 and Attorney General from 1911–12. He was then elevated directly to the position of Master of the Rolls, retaining it through the rising of 1916, the war of independence of 1919–21 and the civil war of 1922–23. He was the judge who refused to grant *habeas corpus* to Erskine Childers in 1922.[182] Before Childers could appeal against this refusal he was executed, allegedly on advice from Hugh Kennedy that such action

[179] Hardy (1927). [180] See Mac Cormaic (2016) Chap 1, esp 27–31.

[181] See too Mac Cormaic (2016) 19–31, the entry on Kennedy by Ronan Keane in the *DIB*, vol 5, 111 and Keane's appreciation of him at: http://centenaries.ucd.ie/wp-content/uploads/2015/04/Kennedy-Hugh.pdf.

[182] *R (Childers) v Adjutant-General of the Provincial Forces* [1923] 1 IR 5. O'Connor MR ruled that, because a state of war had been sufficiently proved to exist, the military were the sole judges of how force should be used to

would be lawful.[183] O'Connor's handling of the Childers case may have endeared him to the two principal lawyers representing the provisional government of the Irish Free State at the time, Hugh Kennedy and Timothy Sullivan.

Like Kennedy, Charles O'Connor served on the 12-member Judiciary Committee which in 1923 recommended a new court system for the Irish Free State.[184] When the Supreme Court and High Court were established in 1924 O'Connor was allegedly offered the Presidency of the High Court, but turned it down in favour of a position as an ordinary judge on the Supreme Court. At the age of 70, he was perhaps in no frame of mind to shoulder the responsibility of administering a whole tier of the court system. Timothy Sullivan became President of the High Court instead. Charles O'Connor could have remained on the Supreme Court until the end of 1926,[185] but he chose to retire after serving for just ten months. Robert Marshall tells us that this was 'for undisclosed urgent domestic considerations',[186] but he lived on until 1928. His early resignation is perhaps a sign that he was a reluctant appointee to the Supreme Court in the first place and that there had been some secret agreement that he would quickly move on.

The second of the two 'ordinary'[187] judges appointed to the Supreme Court was Gerald FitzGibbon KC, a former Unionist MP in both the House of Commons of Southern Ireland (which had just one session, in June 1921, where he presided as Speaker in an assembly of just four unionists, the Sinn Féin MPs having refused to appear) and in the Third Dáil in 1922. He was the son of one of the Lord Justices of the Court of Appeal of Ireland, who sat there from 1878–97.[188] Elevating him to the Supreme Court sent a signal that the Supreme Court would not be a cold house for individuals who had been opposed to the independence of Ireland. It also began an unwritten convention which has been adhered to almost continuously ever since—that at least one member of the Supreme Court should come from a Protestant background.[189] Mac Cormaic claims that there were underlying tensions between FitzGibbon and Kennedy throughout their time on the Court together[190] but, with the exception of their disagreement in *The State (Ryan) v Lennon*,[191] it is not easy to find evidence of these tensions within their reported judgments.

The Report of the Judiciary Committee in 1923 recommended that the Supreme Court should comprise just three judges, with the President of the High Court and/or another High Court judge being asked to sit when required. Kennedy himself had wanted there to be five Supreme Court judges from the start, but others would not agree 'from motives of economy'.[192] Given the difficulties which the Supreme Court encountered in forging a significant constitutional role for itself over the subsequent two decades it is perhaps a pity that Kennedy's view was not preferred.

repel force. He distinguished *Egan v Macready* [1921] 1 IR 265, where he had ruled that the defendant ought to have been tried by a court-martial

[183] See Hogan (1996). [184] See Chap 2 above, 12-13.

[185] He could not benefit from the additional three years allowed by s 100 of the 1924 Act (see n 158 above), because he was only 69 when appointed to the Supreme Court.

[186] *DIB*, vol 7, 235.

[187] This term was not used in relation to Supreme Court judges in the Courts of Justice Act 1924, but it was used in relation to High Court judges other than the President (see eg ss 8 and 13). It was first used for judges of the Supreme Court in the Courts of Justice Act 1928, s 2.

[188] See n 168 above. In the seventh episode, Aeolus, of *Ulysses* (1922) James Joyce imagines the older FitzGibbon speaking at a debate on the revival of the Irish language.

[189] Barrington (1952) 183, who notes that the convention also applies to the High Court.

[190] Mac Cormaic (2016) 31 and 42. [191] [1935] IR 170; see Chap 3 above, 37-42.

[192] Hugh Kennedy Archive, UCD, P4/1247. He queried whether any other country had so small a court of final appeal and even suggested that four judges would be better than three. A three-judge court, he pointed out, left little margin for sicknesses, reduced the weight attributable to the court's decisions, and diminished access to a greater variety of knowledge and outlook.

Judges appointed between 1925 and 1936[193]

James Murnaghan, 1925–53
James Geoghegan, 1936–50
James Creed Meredith, 1936–42
Timothy Sullivan, 1936–46

When Charles O'Connor resigned in 1925 he was succeeded by James Murnaghan, who was destined to serve in the role for no less than 28 years, the second-longest tenure of any of the judges appointed.[194] Born in the USA but brought up in Omagh, County Tyrone, where his father was an MP for 15 years, Murnaghan studied at the Royal University (now the National University of Ireland) and won a gold medal for oratory. He became a barrister but developed a parallel academic career, becoming a part-time professor of jurisprudence, Roman law and international law at University College Dublin in 1910. He was not active in politics but such was his reputation as a lawyer that he too was invited to join the Committee which drafted the Constitution of the Irish Free State. When the new court system was put in place in 1924 he was one of the six persons appointed to the High Court even though he had not yet taken silk as a barrister. He was a keen Irish nationalist but he was also known for his conservative approach to legal developments.[195]

Between 1925 and 1936 there were no further changes to the composition of the Court, the longest such period in its history to date. It was already becoming apparent, however, that a three-judge Supreme Court could not cope with the amount of business coming its way, so in 1936 the maximum number of judges who could be appointed (including the Chief Justice) was increased from three to five.[196] It was made clear at the same time that, notwithstanding this increase, the Supreme Court could still deal with cases with just three judges sitting.[197]

The two additional judges appointed were James Geoghegan (1936–50) and James Creed Meredith (1936–42). Geoghegan had practised as a solicitor for eight years and as a barrister for 21 years. He had not participated either politically or militarily in the war of independence or the civil war, but he then joined the political party Cumann na nGaedheal, which formed the government of the Irish Free State from 1923 to 1932. In 1930 he crossed the floor and joined Fianna Fáil, being elected TD for Longford-Westmeath.[198] When Fianna Fáil won the election in 1932 Geoghegan was appointed Minister of Justice, serving for a year. During that time he advocated restrictions on the sale of contraceptives and, famously, the introduction of greater controls over dance halls.[199] In 1936 he returned to government as Attorney General but after less than two months he was elevated straight to the Supreme Court without having formerly sat in any judicial capacity. Almost 50 years after his death, which occurred in 1951, his son Hugh was himself appointed to the Supreme Court, still the only example of a parent-and-child duo to have served in that capacity.

James Creed Meredith, a Protestant, had been a brilliant scholar and sprinter at Trinity College Dublin. In 1913 he joined the Irish Volunteers and was involved in gun-running

[193] Mac Cormaic (2016) 47–9.
[194] The longest-serving was Brian Walsh: see 96-7 below; see too Osborough (2011) 4–7.
[195] Murnaghan's grand-niece, Sheelagh Murnaghan, was an Ulster Liberal Party MP for Queen's University in Belfast from 1961 to 1969. For her work on human rights see Rynder (2006).
[196] Courts of Justice Act 1936, s 4(1). [197] Ibid, s 4(3).
[198] Some see this as a deliberate ploy to enhance his chances of judicial preferment: Anon (1950) 35. See too Mac Cormaic (2016) 47–8.
[199] The Public Dance Halls Act 1935 required dancing to take place in licensed halls which could be supervised. This allowed priests and others to report unofficial dancing venues which they believed were morally improper.

the following year, when he also opposed the idea that Irish Volunteers should fight as members of the British forces in the Great War. From 1919 to 1922 he was President of the unofficial Dáil Supreme Court,[200] in which capacity he sometimes applied principles of Brehon law if he deemed them to be more just than English common law. He also served as the Chief Judicial Commissioner when the decision was made to wind up the Dáil Éireann courts[201] and in 1924 was an obvious candidate for appointment to the High Court. His transfer to the Supreme Court in 1936 occurred just a few months before the death of Hugh Kennedy and his replacement as Chief Justice by Tim Sullivan, who had already worked with Meredith for 12 years on the High Court.

It was in December 1936 that Kennedy suddenly died, aged just 57. The tributes paid to him showed that he was a much respected individual who can be credited with playing a very significant role in ensuring that the transition to Irish independence did not lead to any diminution in the quality of the country's legal system.[202] Tim Sullivan, his successor, had served as President of the High Court since its formation in 1924. He was therefore already an *ex officio* member of the Supreme Court[203] but had very rarely sat there. He came from a nationalist family, his father having been a journalist and MP who represented the Irish Parliamentary Party at Westminster from 1880 to 1900 and served as Lord Mayor of Dublin in 1886–87. The judge's younger cousin, Tim Healy, was the first governor-general of the Irish Free State. Tim Sullivan himself had been a legal adviser to the provisional government in 1921–22 and, like Hugh Kennedy and Charles O'Connor, served on the Judiciary Committee in 1923. As President of the High Court he was well used to trying to ensure that legal outcomes did not depend upon personal political preferences. Lawrence White notes that Sullivan P gave the judgment in the first reported case to come before the new courts on the emergency legislation enacted to counter the politically motivated violence which was still occurring,[204] a judgment which 'signalled that judicial scrutiny of emergency powers within the new Irish state would follow much the same loose pattern as under British rule'.[205] White also considers Sullivan's tenure of the position of Chief Justice to have been less dynamic than that of Kennedy:

> Despite their similar nationalist backgrounds, Sullivan proved more cautious and traditional as chief justice than Kennedy, his record more typical of the prevalent conservatism of the Irish bench throughout the first quarter century of the new state. Lacking his predecessor's zeal for an indigenously Irish system of law, and his adventurous approach to constitutional law and judicial review, Sullivan remained immersed in the British positivist tradition of his training and early experience, suspicious of concepts of fundamental law, and devoted to the principle of sovereignty of parliament.[206]

So the make-up of the Supreme Court when the new Constitution came into force on 29 December 1937 was Tim Sullivan as Chief Justice and FitzGibbon, Murnaghan, Geoghegan and Meredith as ordinary judges. During the 16-year life of the Irish Free State only six individuals—all of them men of course—served as judges of the Supreme Court, and three of these (O'Connor, Geoghegan and Meredith) each served for just about a year. By far the

[200] See Chap 2 above, 10-12. [201] See Kotsonouris (1994) and (2004).

[202] Towey (1977); Keane (1996); Hogan (1986) 528. [203] Under the Courts of Justice Act 1924, s 6.

[204] *DIB*, vol 9, 162, referring to *R (Burke) v Governor of Mountjoy Prison* (7 July 1924, unreported). This approach to individual rights was consolidated in Sullivan CJ's infamous judgment in *In re Article 26 and the Offences Against the State (Amendment) Bill 1940* [1940] IR 470 (see Chap 6 below, 109-10), which White describes as 'the culmination of a series of juridical decisions that effectively placed the liberty of the citizen at the mercy of the Oireachtas'.

[205] Ibid. See too *Irish Weekly Times*, 13 December 1924; obituary, *Irish Times*, 30 March 1949.

[206] Ibid, 162.

leading lights were Kennedy, FitzGibbon and Murnaghan.[207] There was provision for the Chief Justice to call upon the services of any High Court judge if for some unavoidable reason there were not enough judges of the Supreme Court available to transact the Court's business,[208] and this power was exercised on many occasions during the life of the Irish Free State. In *Leyden v Attorney General*, for example, *two* additional judges sat alongside Murnaghan J when the Supreme Court partly allowed an appeal against a High Court decision by Meredith J in a case where a teacher complained about a reduction in his salary.[209] As noted in Chapter 4, from the establishment of the Supreme Court one of its judges was required to sit as a member of the Court of Criminal Appeal alongside judges of the High Court.[210] Kennedy CJ himself frequently presided in the Court of Criminal Appeal. Moreover in 1936 the Chief Justice acquired the power to ask a Supreme Court judge to sit as an additional judge in the High Court.[211]

Judges appointed between 1939 and 1954

William Johnston, 1939–40
John O'Byrne, 1940–54
William Black, 1942–51
Conor Maguire, 1946–61
Cecil Lavery, 1950–66
Theodore Kingsmill Moore, 1951–65
Cearbhall Ó Dálaigh, 1953–73
Martin Maguire, 1954–61

The Supreme Court continued with five judges for the next 24 years—until 1961. Gerald FitzGibbon's seat passed to William Johnston in 1939, a man born and educated in Belfast who became a barrister in 1892 and was one of three Protestant judges appointed to the original six-member High Court in 1924.[212] Unfortunately he sat on the Supreme Court for less than two years before dying in office.[213] His place was taken by John O'Byrne, who had already served as a High Court judge for 14 years and was to serve for a further 14 years in the Supreme Court before he too died in office in 1954[214] and was replaced by Martin Maguire, another High Court judge who had served for 14 years but without any obvious political affiliation. In 1946 Chief Justice Tim Sullivan reached the retirement age of 72 and was replaced by Conor Maguire (no relation to Martin) who had also replaced him ten years earlier as President of the High Court. Conor Maguire had been a Fianna Fáil TD and Attorney General before being appointed President of the High Court by de Valera in 1936.

In 1942 James Creed Meredith died in office and was succeeded by William Black, a fellow Protestant who had served on the High Court for just three years and (perhaps because of his religion) was chosen ahead of the President of the High Court, Conor Maguire, who by then had already served for six years. Black remained on the Court until 1951 when he was replaced by Theodore Kingsmill-Moore, another High Court judge.[215] James

[207] As emphasised by Geoghegan (2013).
[208] Courts of Justice Act 1924, s 7.
[209] [1926] IR 334. Another such example is *Fogarty v O'Donoghue* [1926] IR 531.
[210] Courts of Justice Act 1924, s 8. In the death penalty case of *Attorney General v O'Leary and O'Leary* [1926] IR 445, both Kennedy CJ and FitzGibbon J sat, alongside two High Court judges.
[211] Courts of Justice Act 1936, s 5.
[212] See www.newulsterbiography.co.uk/index.php/home/printPerson/753.
[213] His son Denis (1901–84) also trained in the law but became a well-known playwright, while Denis's daughter Jennifer (b 1930) became an even better known novelist.
[214] As noted in the text at n 96 above, O'Byrne's widow litigated to try to protect her pension from being taxed.
[215] Mac Cormaic (2016) 96–7.

Geoghegan retired early from the Supreme Court in 1949, at the age of 63, dying just two years later. He was replaced by Cecil Lavery, a former Fine Gael TD and Senator who was a high-earning barrister and Attorney General in the government led by John Costello when he was appointed directly to the Supreme Court without any previous judicial experience. Mac Cormaic tells the story of how in 1951 Lavery was apparently rejected as a candidate for the Presidency of the High Court because the Department of Justice thought (wrongly of course) that existing Supreme Court judges were ineligible for the post.[216]

After his long stint of 28 years on the Court James Murnaghan finally reached retirement age in 1953[217] and that was when Cearbhall Ó Dálaigh was first appointed to the Court. He would turn out to be the judge who has probably had the greatest influence on the development of the Irish Supreme Court since its creation. Ó Dálaigh was a strong Fianna Fáil supporter who, although never elected as a TD, served as Attorney General in two governments headed by Éamon de Valera, from 1946 to 1948 and from 1951 to 1953. At the start of 1961, therefore, the five Supreme Court judges in post were Conor Maguire as Chief Justice and Lavery, Kingsmill Moore, Ó Dálaigh and Martin Maguire as 'ordinary' judges. Their average age was 66 but Ó Dálaigh, aged 50, was the youngest by a full 17 years. Moreover the two Maguires were on the brink of retirement.

As explained in Chapter 4, the Courts (Establishment and Constitution) Act 1961 formally established the Supreme Court which had been promised by Article 34 of the 1937 Constitution.[218] The Courts (Supplemental Provisions) Act 1961 stipulated that in cases involving the validity of any law under the 1937 Constitution there would need to be a bench of five judges, the Chief Justice being authorised in all other cases to order that they should be heard by a bench of just three judges.

Judges appointed between 1961 and 1976

Kevin Haugh, 1961–69
Brian Walsh, 1961–90
Aindrias Ó Caoimhe 1965–66
Gardner Budd, 1966–75
William FitzGerald, 1966–74
Richard McLoughlin, 1969–72
Seamus Henchy, 1972–88
Frank Griffin, 1973–91
Tom O'Higgins, 1974–85
John Kenny, 1975–82
Weldon Parke, 1976–81

In February 1961 Martin Maguire retired after reaching the age of 72.[219] He was replaced by Kevin Haugh, who had been Attorney General from 1940 to 1942 and a High Court judge since then.[220] On his death he was succeeded by Richard McLoughlin, who himself survived for just three years before being replaced by Seamus Henchy in 1972. Henchy played a

[216] Ibid, (2016) 73–4.

[217] He lived for a further 20 years, continuing to build a considerable art collection, part of which was stolen long after his death: *Irish Times*, 17 July 1999.

[218] Courts (Establishment and Constitution) Act 1961, s 1(1).

[219] *Irish Times*, 1 February 1961.

[220] His son also served as a High Court judge, from 2005 to 2009.

huge role in enhancing the reputation of the Supreme Court during his 17 years in office.[221] Together with Cearbhall Ó Dálaigh and Brian Walsh he is one of the three most significant of the 57 Supreme Court appointments to date. He was not immediately replaced when he retired in 1988: instead there was a period during which the complement of judges dropped by one. Susan Denham eventually took Henchy's seat in 1992.

Conor Maguire also retired in 1961 (but then served as Ireland's judge at the European Court of Human Rights from 1965 to 1971) and to some surprise was replaced as Chief Justice by his colleague Cearbhall Ó Dálaigh.[222] The favourite to succeed had been Cecil Lavery, but he had previously been a Fine Gael TD and Attorney General while the Taioseach at this time was Seán Lemass of Fianna Fáil. What is most likely to have swung the post in favour of Ó Dálaigh, however, is not so much his previous Fianna Fáil connections as his humbler, working-class background and above all his relative youthfulness. Lemass himself was 62 and had been Taoiseach for three years: he may have seen the 50-year-old Ó Dálaigh as a longer-term investment, someone who in a judicial capacity could help to modernise Ireland in the way that Lemass himself was attempting to do as a politician.[223]

Ó Dálaigh's own seat as an ordinary judge on the Supreme Court was given to Brian Walsh, who eventually became the longest-serving and in some people's eyes the most outstanding judge ever appointed to the Court.[224] In 1961 he had been a High Court judge for just two years, and there were several judges with longer experience who might have expected to be elevated ahead of him. Amongst them were Gardner Budd, a judge since 1951, and Richard McLoughlin, a judge since 1952, but each would have to wait several more years before being promoted. Thomas Teevan, a former Attorney General, served on the High Court from 1954 until 1971 without ever being promoted. His colleague George Murnaghan, a relative of James Murnaghan who was a Supreme Court judge from 1925 to 1953, served even longer as a High Court judge without promotion, from 1954 until 1979. One can only speculate either that these two judges were considered to be not very effective or that they did not have the requisite political connections to attract the attention of the Taioseach and Minister of Justice when vacancies on the Supreme Court arose.

During the remainder of the 1960s three further changes were made to the composition of the Supreme Court. In 1965 Aindrias Ó Caoimhe (or Andreas O'Keeffe) was appointed in place of Kingsmill Moore, who retired; Ó Caoimhe had been the Attorney General for five months in 1954 and then for eight years from 1957 to 1965. Within a few months of his appointment to the Supreme Court he agreed to move to the High Court as its President and remained in that post until 1974, when he was appointed Ireland's judge at the European Court of Justice, serving until 1985. His son, of the same name, also served on the High Court (from 1999 to 2004) and from 2004 to 2015 he too was Ireland's judge at the Luxembourg Court. In 1966 Gardner Budd, who had been in the High Court for 14 years, succeeded Ó Caoimhe on the Supreme Court and William FitzGerald replaced Cecil Lavery. Budd came from a Protestant background, so the tradition of reserving a seat for such a person on the Supreme Court was restored after a year's gap. FitzGerald was appointed directly from the

[221] Casey (1978); Hogan (2011) and (2008), where he describes Henchy J as 'assuredly the most elegant and profound judicial writer this country has ever produced'. See too Hogan (2014), which focuses on Henchy J's judgments in *McGee v Attorney General* [1974] IR 284 and *Norris v Attorney General* [1984] IR 36.

[222] Mac Cormaic (2016) 74–5, where it is stressed that Lavery continued to harbour resentment against Ó Dálaigh for quite some time; see too Tóibin (1985).

[223] See, generally, Girvin and Murphy (2005), although, as is common in books on politics and society in Ireland, none of the contributors refers to the significance of Lemass's appointment of Ó Dálaigh.

[224] Though Binchy (2016), at 217, points to 'a rare, but serious, failure of judgment by Walsh J' in a case on vicarious liability in tort law: *Moynihan v Moynihan* [1975] IR 192.

Bar and quickly demonstrated that he was opposed to the judicial activism in which some of his colleagues on the Court—notably the Chief Justice and Brian Walsh—had recently been engaging.

In 1973 Cearbhall Ó Dálaigh resigned after nearly 20 years as Chief Justice in order to take up Ireland's new seat on the European Court of Justice.[225] Many thought that the natural successor would be Brian Walsh, who for 12 years had worked hand in glove with Ó Dálaigh to turn the Irish Constitution into a vehicle for progressive social reform.[226] But that reforming zeal was not to the liking of the politicians of the day because it trespassed on their own territory, whatever their political allegiances happened to be. Hence a Fianna Fáil Taoiseach, Jack Lynch, saw it appropriate to appoint as Chief Justice Billy FitzGerald, a supporter of Fine Gael, rather than Brian Walsh. Although Walsh might have been expecting to be overlooked,[227] he must still have been very disappointed. Mac Cormaic makes the additional point that Walsh was a friend of Charles Haughey, Lynch's Minister for Finance, who in 1970 had been tried for plotting to import arms for use by republicans in Northern Ireland.[228] Although Haughey was acquitted, any association with him was rather toxic, especially for a judge.[229]

As things turned out, FitzGerald remained Chief Justice for just 22 months, as he died suddenly in October 1974. His position as an ordinary judge had been taken by Frank Griffin, who had been on the High Court for just two years, and his role as Chief Justice was now taken by Tom O'Higgins, who was at the time the shortest serving High Court judge and before then had been a barrister and a Fine Gael TD for 25 years. He had even been the Fine Gael candidate for the Presidency of Ireland in both 1966 and 1973.[230] Mac Cormaic comments that the most striking aspect of O'Higgins' ten-year period as Chief Justice was 'the continuity of the work the Ó Dálaigh court had commenced'.[231] In 1975 John Kenny replaced Gardner Budd, and after a few months Weldon Parke (a Protestant) was appointed to take the seat of Brian Walsh, who had agreed to chair the new Law Reform Commission and retained that role until 1985 before returning to the Supreme Court to spend five more years as a full-time judge. The Act which created the Commission stipulated that if a person were an ordinary judge of the Supreme Court when appointed to be a Commissioner, the number of ordinary judges of the Supreme Court could be increased to five.[232]

Judges appointed between 1981 and 1992

Anthony Hederman, 1981–93
Niall McCarthy, 1982–92
Thomas Finlay, 1985–94

[225] Ronan Keane, himself a former CJ, recounts in the *DIB* that Ó Dálaigh's correspondence shows that he would have preferred the post to go to Brian Walsh. In 1974, a month after the sudden death of President Erskine Childers, Ó Dálaigh was nominated without opposition as the fifth President of Ireland.

[226] This period is examined in more detail in Chapters 6, 9 and 10 below; see too Mac Cormaic (2016) 146–54 and also Tóibin (1985), who divides the leading judgments by Ó Dálaigh and Walsh into three loose groups: those curbing the tendency of bodies to give themselves arbitrary powers, those protecting individuals within the criminal law, and those expanding the rights of individuals under the Constitution. See too Hogan (1986) 532.

[227] Mac Cormaic (2016) 149.

[228] Ibid, 149–53; Ferriter (2013) 141–152; Patterson (2006) 170–9. See too Chap 7 below, 141-2

[229] The guilt of Haughey and his co-accused was never examined by the Supreme Court or the Court of Criminal Appeal because at that time the prosecution had no right of appeal against acquittals.

[230] He lost narrowly on both occasions, to Éamon de Valera and Erskine Childers respectively. For O'Higgins' contribution to constitutional law see Casey (1986), and for his views on the distinctiveness of the Irish legal system see O'Higgins (1996), where he thanks England for bringing the common law to Ireland.

[231] Mac Cormaic (2016) 181–2.

[232] Law Reform Commission Act 1975, s 14(1)(a).

Hugh O'Flaherty, 1990–99
Seamus Egan, 1991–95
John Blayney, 1992–1997
Susan Denham, 1992–2017

After 1976 no changes were made to the composition of the Supreme Court for five years. In 1981 Weldon Parke died suddenly and was replaced by Anthony Hederman, who had been the Attorney General in the Fianna Fáil government since 1977. In 1982 Niall McCarthy replaced John Kenny and in 1985 Thomas Finlay, the President of the High Court since 1974, took over as Chief Justice from Tom O'Higgins.[233] Finlay's daughter, Mary, would later be appointed to the Supreme Court herself, in 2017. Seamus Henchy retired in 1988 and almost immediately became the Chairman of the new Independent Radio and Television Commission.[234] His seat on the Court was not filled until 1992 because during those four years there was no Supreme Court judge serving on the Law Reform Commission and so the maximum permitted number of ordinary Supreme Court judges had reverted to four.

The 1990s opened with the retirement of Brian Walsh, who had been a member of the Court since 1961 although, besides being chair of the Law Reform Commission from 1975 to 1985, he had also served as the part-time Irish judge at the European Court of Human Rights since 1980, a role which he held until dying from a stroke in 1998. In 1992 Walsh became the first Irish judge to have a *Festschrift* published in his honour.[235] One of his four daughters, Gabrielle, married John Murray, who some years later was himself to become a long-serving member and Chief Justice of the Supreme Court. There can be little doubt that Brian Walsh stands out as one of the judges who did a huge amount to put the Irish Supreme Court on the legal map. His departure from the bench less than 18 months after that of Seamus Henchy was a severe, if temporary, blow to the institutional memory and intellectual capacity of the institution.

The person appointed to succeed Brian Walsh in 1990 was Hugh O'Flaherty, who came directly from the Bar. In 1991 Frank Griffin retired (although he lived on for a further 25 years)[236] and was replaced by Seamus Egan, while in 1992 Niall McCarthy was replaced by John Blayney;[237] Egan and Blayney had served in the High Court for, respectively, seven and six years. Also in 1992, Susan Denham, the first woman ever to be appointed to the Supreme Court, filled the fifth position as an ordinary judge because Anthony Hederman was by then serving as Chair of the Law Reform Commission. Mrs Denham had been a High Court judge for just a year at the time of her promotion. As she was from a Protestant background, the tradition of having someone from that community on the Court was restored after an 11-year hiatus since the death of Weldon Parke in 1981.

Judges appointed between 1994 and 2006

Liam Hamilton, 1994–2000
Donal Barrington, 1996–2000

[233] Mac Cormaic (2016) Chap 12. He died in 2003; amidst all the praise Fintan O'Toole penned a piece describing his judgment in the *Norris* case as 'theocratic' and 'pitifully shallow': *Irish Times*, 4 March 2003, 16.

[234] Ibid, 268–70.

[235] O'Reilly (1992); it includes contributions from seven former, current or future Supreme Court judges. For Walsh's own views on the Constitution see Walsh (1988a) and (1988b). See too Hogan (2017).

[236] For an obituary see the *Irish Times*, 11 June 2016, 13.

[237] See the tribute to McCarthy J at GH (1992).

Ronan Keane, 1996–2004
Francis Murphy, 1996–2002
Kevin Lynch, 1996–99
Henry Barron, 1997–2000
John Murray 1999–2015
Nial Fennelly, 2000–14
Catherine McGuinness, 2000–06
Adrian Hardiman, 2000–16
Hugh Geoghegan, 2000–10
Brian McCracken, 2002–06
Nicholas Kearns, 2004–09
Fidelma Macken, 2005–12
Joseph Finnegan, 2006–12

The retirement of Anthony Hederman from the bench in 1993[238] (he remained as Chair of the Law Reform Commission for a few more years) meant that the number of ordinary Supreme Court judges returned to four. Liam Hamilton, who had been a judge in the High Court since 1974 and President since 1985, succeeded Tom Finlay as Chief Justice on the latter's retirement in 1994,[239] but the most significant change of the 1990s—and indeed of any period in the history of the Supreme Court to date—took place in 1996, when, following the retirement of Seamus Egan at the end of 1995, the government appointed no fewer than four new judges, bringing the total composition of the Supreme Court (including the Chief Justice but excluding the President of the High Court) to eight.

The new judges were all very highly experienced: Donal Barrington, fresh from his seven-year stint as Ireland's judge at the Court of First Instance in Luxembourg,[240] prior to which he had served as a High Court judge for ten years; Ronan Keane, a High Court judge for the previous 17 years; Francis Murphy, a High Court judge for 14 years; and Kevin Lynch, a High Court judge for 12 years. The appointment of three of these four judges was a result of the Courts and Court Officers Act 1995, which raised the permitted number of ordinary Supreme Court judges from four to seven (or eight if one of them was serving as a member of the Law Reform Commission).[241] The motivation for such a dramatic change was not just the rise in the number of appeals being taken to the Supreme Court and the consequent delays in dealing with them (estimated in early 1996 at between two and three years[242]) but also the prospect of the functions then carried out by the Court of Criminal Appeal being transferred to the Supreme Court. As explained in Chapter 4,[243] this transfer was provided for by the same Act but the provisions were never commenced. Instead, the

[238] Like Frank Griffin, Anthony Hederman enjoyed a long retirement, dying in 2014: *Irish Times*, 18 January 2014, 12. He was a deeply conservative Catholic, very committed to helping the underprivileged. In the *X* case on abortion he was the sole member of the Supreme Court who felt it right to ban a teenager from travelling to England to have an abortion (see Chap 10 below, 235–8).

[239] For a *Festschrift* in honour of Tom O'Higgins see Curtin and O'Keeffe (1992).

[240] His appointment was possible only because the Courts and Court Officers Act 1995, s 28, had amended the Courts (Supplemental Provisions) Act 1961, s 5(2), to allow time spent as a judge or Advocate General in Luxembourg to count as 'practice' for the purpose of calculating eligibility for a judicial post. Carroll MacNeill (2016), at 67, reports that the Labour Party wanted Barrington to be appointed CJ in succession to Tom Finlay in 1994, but it was not then possible as he was not at the time a national judge or serving practitioner. See too Mac Cormaic (2016) 114–8.

[241] s 6(1), amending the Courts (Establishment and Constitution) Act 1961, s 1(2).

[242] *First Report of the Working Group on a Courts Commission* (Pn 2690, 1966), 37.

[243] See 51; also O'Hanlon (1967).

Court of Criminal Appeal was eventually folded into the new Court of Appeal in 2014, from which an appeal can lie to the Supreme Court on a point of law, if leave is granted.

The 1995 Act also allowed the Supreme Court, for the first time, to sit in two or more divisions simultaneously,[244] thereby potentially doubling the Court's 'productivity' but meaning that additional courtroom accommodation had to be made available in Dublin's Four Courts building. The Act added that the Chief Justice could determine that any matter being dealt with by the Supreme Court could be heard by a division of either three or five judges,[245] the only qualification being that matters under Articles 12 and 26 of the 1937 Constitution had to be heard by not less than five judges.[246] Article 12 allows the Supreme Court to decide if the President of the country has become permanently incapacitated, while Article 26 requires the Supreme Court to consider Bills referred to it by the President for a check on whether any of their provisions are 'repugnant' to the Constitution.[247] There is no express constitutional or statutory authorisation for the Supreme Court to sit as a bench of more than five judges, but it did this for the first time in 2001 and has done so on several subsequent occasions.[248] The 1995 Act made it clear, too, that notwithstanding any intimations to the contrary in the Courts Act 1981,[249] 'it shall be the function of the Chief Justice or in his or her absence the senior ordinary judge of the Supreme Court to arrange the distribution and allocation of the business of the Supreme Court'.[250]

Of the eight judges entitled to sit in the Supreme Court at the end of 1996, only one, Susan Denham, was still in place eight years later, at the end of 2004. John Blayney retired in 1997 and was replaced by Henry Barron; he had been a member of the High Court for 15 years and was the first Jew to be appointed to the Supreme Court. In turn Barron was replaced by Nial Fennelly in 2000, a man who had served as an Advocate General at the European Court of Justice since 1995 but had no domestic judicial experience. In 1999 the Supreme Court experienced the embarrassing resignation of Hugh O'Flaherty after he was deemed to have acted inappropriately in relation to the appeal of a litigant who was known to him[251] and his seat was taken by John Murray, then Ireland's judge at the European Court of Justice and before that Attorney General in the Fianna Fáil government from 1987 to 1991. At the end of the same year Kevin Lynch stepped down and his place was taken in January 2000 by Catherine McGuinness, a High Court judge for four years, a former activist in the Labour Party and the second woman to be appointed to the Supreme Court. Like Susan Denham she was also a Protestant, having been reared as the daughter of a Church of Ireland rector in Belfast. In the same month Liam Hamilton was succeeded as Chief Justice by Ronan Keane,[252] already a Supreme Court judge, with the latter's place as an ordinary judge being given to Adrian Hardiman, a very successful barrister who was one of the first

[244] s 7, inserting a new s 7(3) into the Courts (Supplemental Provisions) Act 1961.

[245] Ibid, inserting a new s 7(4) into the 1961 Act. [246] Ibid, inserting a new s 7(5) into the 1961 Act.

[247] This jurisdiction is examined in detail in Chap 6 below, 106-119.

[248] The first such case was *Sinnott v Minister for Education* [2001] 2 IR 545. Subsequent seven-judge decisions include *Maguire v Ardagh* [2002] 1 IR 385 (the Abbeylara case); *In re Article 26 and the Health (Amendment) (No 2) Bill 2004* [2005] IESC 7, [2005] 1 IR 105; *Curtin v Clerk of Dáil Éireann* [2006] IESC 14, [2006] 2 IR 556; *Pringle v Government of Ireland* [2012] IESC 47, [2013] 3 IR 1; *Fleming v Ireland* [2013] IESC 19, [2013] 2 IR 417; and *DPP v JC (No 2)* [2015] IESC 50, [2017] 1 IR 417.

[249] This provision suggested that in the event of the CJ's unavailability, eg through illness, his or her administrative functions should be exercised by the President of the High Court.

[250] s 8.

[251] For the full story see Mac Cormaic (2016) 310–25; Mac Cormaic claims (at 331) that O'Flaherty would have been assured of the Chief Justiceship had he still been serving when Hamilton retired in 2000; see too Vincent Browne, 'I was not wrong on O'Flaherty', *Irish Times*, 4 October 2000.

[252] The other main contenders were John Murray and Catherine McGuinness. Mac Cormaic alleges that Keane was given the post on the understanding that Murray would succeed him when he retired: ibid 333.

members of the Progressive Democrats, a political party founded in 1985. Each of these last three appointments was widely welcomed.[253] Donal Barrington retired in 2000, being replaced by Hugh Geoghegan, a High Court judge for eight years and the first Supreme Court judge to be the child of an earlier Supreme Court judge, though his father James had been dead for almost 50 years. Hugh Geoghegan retired in 2010 but in 2017 his wife, Mary Finlay Geoghegan, was appointed to the Court.[254] After retirement Donal Barrington was appointed the first chairperson of Ireland's newly-formed Human Rights Commission, a post he held for two years. He died in the first week of 2018.[255]

In 2002 Francis Murphy was replaced by Brian McCracken, a High Court judge for seven years, and in 2004 Ronan Keane retired as Chief Justice and gave way, as many had anticipated, to John Murray,[256] whose ordinary seat was in turn occupied by Nicholas Kearns, a member of the High Court for six years. In 2005 an additional judge had to be appointed—Fidelma Macken—because Catherine McGuinness was appointed as Chair of the Law Reform Commission. Judge Macken had spent two years on the High Court but had also been Ireland's judge at the European Court of Justice from 1999 to 2004 (and was the first female judge from any country on that Court). In 2006 Brian McCracken and Catherine McGuinness each retired from the bench but only one replacement was appointed because Catherine McGuinness continued to serve as Chair of the Law Reform Commission until 2011 even though she was no longer an active judge. The new appointee was Joseph Finnegan, who had been on the High Court for seven years, the last five as President.

Judges appointed since 2010

Donal O'Donnell, 2010–
Liam McKechnie, 2010–
John McMenamin, 2012–
Frank Clarke, 2012–
Elizabeth Dunne, 2013–
Mary Laffoy, 2013–17
Peter Charleton, 2014–
Iseult O'Malley, 2015–
Mary Finlay Geoghegan 2017–

After November 2006 there was no new appointment to the Supreme Court until January 2010, when Nicholas Kearns resigned to take up the role of President of the High Court, the first time an ordinary judge of the Supreme Court had moved in that direction since Aindrias Ó Caoimhe did so in 1966. It was still a promotion because the President of the High Court ranked second in judicial precedence to the Chief Justice (and earned the same as an ordinary judge of the Supreme Court). Kearns was replaced on the Supreme Court by Donal O'Donnell, who, like his colleague Adrian Hardiman, was appointed straight from the Bar. Born and brought up in Belfast, O'Donnell was the son of a former Lord Justice of Appeal in Northern Ireland,[257] the first time a child of a top judge in one of the two Irish jurisdictions had taken office as a top judge in the other jurisdiction. In the same year Hugh Geoghegan retired and his seat was taken by Liam McKechnie, who had already served for

[253] *Irish Times*, 26 January 2000, 7.

[254] Her own father, Tom Finlay, was Chief Justice from 1985 to 1994.

[255] Keane (2018).

[256] Mac Cormaic (2016) 332–3. Vol 33 of the *Dublin University Law Journal* is a *Festschrift* of articles in honour of Ronan Keane, edited by Donal Coffey, Gerard Hogan, and David Prendergast.

[257] Turlough O'Donnell was a High Court judge from 1971 to 1979 and a Lord Justice from 1979 to 1990.

ten years in the High Court. In 2011 John Murray had to retire as Chief Justice because he had sat in that role for the maximum permitted period of seven years,[258] but as he had not yet reached the compulsory retirement age for an ordinary judge he reverted to that status and the position of Chief Justice was offered to Susan Denham, who by then had already served on the Court for 19 years. Mrs Denham therefore became the first woman in these islands to lead a top court. It is widely acknowledged that she was an excellent administrator as well as a good judge.[259] She certainly amply demonstrated her abilities in the role of Chief Justice during the subsequent six years: she reached her compulsory retirement age of 72 in 2017.

In 2012 John Mac Menamin and Frank Clarke were appointed to fill the vacancies left by the retirements of Joseph Finnegan and Fidelma Macken; each of the new appointees had been judges of the High Court for eight years. In 2013 the pressure put on the government by senior judges for additional appointments to the Supreme Court to help deal with the backlog of cases was finally successful when provision was made by the Courts and Civil Law (Miscellaneous Provisions) Act 2013[260] for the creation of two new posts. Two women, Elizabeth Dunne and Mary Laffoy, both already High Court judges, the former for nine years and the latter for 18 years, were duly elevated. In 2014 Nial Fennelly retired and was replaced by Peter Charleton, a judge of the High Court for eight years, and in 2015 the long-serving former Chief Justice, John Murray, also retired, being replaced by Iseult O'Malley, again a judge of the High Court, though only for three years. Aged just 51 at the time, and a supporter of the Labour Party, she was the youngest person to be appointed to the Supreme Court since Adrian Hardiman, who was 48 when he was appointed in 2000. Rather shockingly, Adrian Hardiman himself died very suddenly in March 2016, aged just 64. The first Supreme Court judge to die or retire since the formation of the Court of Appeal in 2014, his fellow judges paid him warn tributes[261] and his seat on the Court was not immediately filled. Neither was that of Mary Laffoy, who retired in 2017, nor of Frank Clarke who in October 2017 replaced Susan Denham as Chief Justice upon her retirement after 25 years on the Court. Clarke is the twelfth person to hold the role of Chief Justice.[262] RTE reported that there had been 15 applicants for the post, of whom three were shortlisted for consideration by the cabinet, but only Clarke's name was actually discussed.[263] He is primarily a commercial lawyer, having graduated from UCD in 1972 with a degree in mathematics and economics rather than law.

At the end of 2017, just when we thought the government was allowing the size of the Supreme Court to diminish given that the Court of Appeal had been created to help relieve the pressure on the former, Mary Finlay Geoghegan was appointed as a Supreme Court judge, having spent more than 12 years as a High Court judge and three as a Court of Appeal judge. She is the first judge to be promoted from the Court of Appeal to the Supreme Court, and that may well set the pattern for future career trajectories. As already mentioned, Mary Finlay Geoghegan is someone with significant family connections to the work of the Supreme Court going back many years.[264]

[258] This limit was introduced by the Courts (No 2) Act 1997, s 4; a similar, non-renewable, time limit was applied to the presidencies of the High Court, Circuit Court and District Court.

[259] Mac Cormaic (2016) 378–9.

[260] s 22 amended s 1(2)(b) of the Courts (Establishment and Constitution) Act 1961 by substituting 'nine' for 'seven'.

[261] eg Fennelly (2017); see too Mac Cormaic (2016) 394–5; Walsh (2016) xiv; *Irish Times* 8 March 2016 (p 2) and 12 March 2016 (obituary).

[262] For some details about the 11 Chief Justices who preceded Clarke CJ, see the Supreme Court's website.

[263] See www.rte.ie/news/2017/0726/893003-cabinet.

[264] See above, 98 and 101.

Table 5.1 Female judges on common law Supreme Courts in 2018[a]

	Australia	Canada	Ireland	New Zealand	United Kingdom	United States
Number of current judges	7	9	8	5	12	9
Number of current female judges	3 (including CJ)	4	3	3 (including CJ)	2 (including the President)	3
Number of former female judges	2	6 (including 1 CJ)	4 (including 1 CJ)	0	0	1
Year when a female judge was first appointed	1987	1982	1992	1999	2004	1981

[a] In Northern Ireland no woman was appointed even at the High Court level until 2015.

At the time of writing, therefore (October 2018), there are ten individuals who are authorised to sit in the Supreme Court. Apart from the President of the Court of Appeal (George Birmingham[265]) and the President of the High Court (Peter Kelly), neither of whom sits *ex officio* in the Supreme Court very often, the full-time judges are the Chief Justice (Frank Clarke) and the seven ordinary judges, namely (in order of their length of service) Donal O'Donnell, Liam McKechnie, John McMenamin, Elizabeth Dunne, Peter Charleton, Iseult O'Malley and Mary Finlay Geoghegan. No serving Supreme Court judge has been a member of the Law Reform Commission since 2006, so no 'substitute' judge has had to be appointed to replace that person on the Court.

The Representativeness of the Supreme Court Judges

A Supreme Court which has been served by 57 judges to date, only seven of whom have been women, can hardly be said to have been fully representative of Irish society down the years, though the current situation, where three of the eight judges are female, compares reasonably well with that in other common law jurisdictions, particularly the United Kingdom, as Table 5.1 above indicates.[266]

To date there has been no judge appointed from a black or minority ethnic background, though in the census of 2016 only 3.4 per cent of the population of Ireland identified themselves as having a black or Asian background. Nor has anyone been appointed with a notable disability or who is openly gay or lesbian.[267] The tradition of having at least one judge from a Protestant background has been almost continuously observed, but few other judges have been non-Catholic.

[265] George Birmingham, already a judge of the Court of Appeal and a former Fine Gael TD and Minister of State, was appointed in April 2018 to replace Seán Ryan, who retired.

[266] In relation to the US, it should be recalled that the turnover of Supreme Court judges is much less frequent because they are appointed for life, with no fixed retirement age.

[267] It was only in 2015 that a judge at the High Court level came out as gay: *Irish Independent*, 21 January 2015.

The attribute which every one of the 57 persons appointed has been able to display is competence in legal practice, as the eligibility requirements dictate.[268] While in theory there is no barrier to a member of any socio-economic group acquiring that competence, which usually means obtaining a law degree and holding a significant position in a firm of solicitors or developing a good reputation as a self-employed barrister, in reality it is people from better off backgrounds who tend to attain those positions. But no solicitor has been appointed directly to the Supreme Court and of the 28 people appointed since 1985 only three have been appointed directly from the Bar.[269] The vast majority of those appointed have first served as a judge in the High Court: that was the case for 25 of the 28 appointees since 1985, with the length of service in the High Court varying from one to 20 years,[270] the average being between eight and nine years. For women appointees the average period of previous experience at High Court level or above is five years. Two of the 25 judges who served in the High Court also had several years' experience in Luxembourg,[271] while two further individuals were appointed to the Supreme Court having only served in Luxembourg.[272]

Just as in the United Kingdom, people who have been to fee-paying schools feature disproportionately amongst those who have risen to the top rank of the judiciary in Ireland. Information about the school background of each of the 28 Supreme Court Justices appointed since 1985 does not seem to be in the public domain, but from what is available it is possible to state confidently that at least one-half and perhaps as many as three-quarters of those appointed attended fee-paying secondary schools. Even more dominant is the role of University College Dublin (UCD) as the institution where appointees pursued their tertiary education: no fewer than 21 of the last 28 appointees (75 per cent) attended UCD, although not all of them studied law there. All the others seem to have studied at Trinity College Dublin, the only exception being William McKechnie, who attended University College Cork. The preponderance of UCD graduates in Ireland's Supreme Court is almost as pronounced as that of Oxbridge graduates in the United Kingdom's Supreme Court.

In October 2018 the average age of the judges on the Irish Supreme Court was 63, the range being 54 to 67.

[268] See 71-3 above. The figure of 57 excludes individuals who have sat in the Supreme Court while serving as judges of the High Court or Court of Appeal. Seven former Presidents of the High Court were never appointed specifically to the Supreme Court.

[269] Hugh O'Flaherty, Adrian Hardiman and Donal O'Donnell.

[270] Susan Denham and Liam Hamilton respectively.

[271] Donal Barrington (seven years at the Court of First Instance) and Fidelma Macken (five years at the ECJ).

[272] John Murray (eight years at the ECJ) and Nial Fennelly (five years as Advocate General). For the latter's reflections on the role of Advocate-General see Fennelly (1996).

6

The Supreme Court and the Constitution

As we saw in Chapter 3, given the power of the Oireachtas during the life of the Irish Free State to pass laws notwithstanding the provisions of the 1922 Constitution, the Supreme Court of that era was inevitably trammeled in what it could achieve in the constitutional field.[1] The 1937 Constitution presented an opportunity for a new approach,[2] especially as the Oireachtas had no overriding legislative power after 25 June 1941,[3] but for the next 25 years or so the Court failed to grasp that opportunity. As Francis Beytagh puts it: 'even after the 1937 Constitution became effective, the Irish courts remained, for the most part, conservative in outlook and quite tentative about utilising the interpretive authority clearly conferred on them by that document'.[4] However, if we compare the judgments of the Irish Supreme Court with those of other supreme courts in common law countries at that time, the shortfall in inventiveness is by no means unique.[5] It was only in the 1960s that supreme courts in general began to realise and utilise their power to transform societies. In Ireland the three main stimuli for this florescence were, it is submitted, the creation of a 'new' Supreme Court in 1961, the influence of judgments of the US Supreme Court (particularly on Ó Dálaigh CJ and Walsh J) and the 'spirit of liberty' which was the hallmark of Western democracies throughout the 1960s.[6] It can be no coincidence, for example, that in the 1960s the UK's House of Lords came up with a series of seminal judgments in the area of administrative law which signaled that from then on the courts would be keeping a closer eye on whether public authorities were acting in accordance with the principle of legality and the rule of law.[7] A fourth factor in Ireland, as Beytagh points out, was that by the 1960s 'a new generation of jurists, educated in Irish universities and less enamored of the British legal tradition than their predecessors' came to the fore.[8]

In two later chapters in this book close attention is paid to landmark judgments by the Irish Supreme Court in the 1960s protecting the rights of persons accused of crimes.[9] These include *The State (Quinn) v Ryan* (on when a person can be extradited),[10] *The People (AG) v O'Brien* (on the right to have evidence that has been obtained unconstitutionally declared inadmissible in a trial)[11] and *The People (Attorney General) v O'Callaghan* (on the right to be presumed innocent until proven guilty).[12] Likewise, amidst numerous conservative judgments in the realms of family and personal life, including on adoption and abortion,[13] there were two significant decisions in the 1960s and 1970s emphasising the right to bodily

[1] Delany (1957–58).

[2] For a collection of documents connected with the drafting of the 1937 Constitution see Hogan (2012). For a useful presentation of the Constitution as it stood in 1995, see Foley and Lawlor (1995).

[3] Art 51(1) of the Constitution brought the overriding power to an end three years after Douglas Hyde took up office as the first President of Ireland, which was on 25 June 1938.

[4] Beytagh (1997) 43. In Chap 3 (43–111) Beytagh summarises 15 Supreme Court decisions issued prior to 1960 and 70 post-1960 decisions. See too Donaldson (1957) 172-80, where he notes that by then only three statutory provisions had been found repugnant to the Constitution.

[5] Donaldson (1957) Chaps 2 and 4; a review of constitutional developments from 1921 to 1951 mentions the Supreme Court just once, *en passant*: Grogan (1951) 389.

[6] Though this spirit was more muted in Ireland than elsewhere: Gray (1994); Daly (2016).

[7] See too Chap 8 below, 173.

[8] Beytagh (1997) 57.

[9] See Chaps 7 and 9.

[10] [1965] IR 70; see Chap 7 below152-3.

[11] [1965] IR 142; see Chap 9 below, 209-10.

[12] [1966] IR 501; see Chap 9 below, 207-8.

[13] See Chap 10.

integrity in *Ryan v Attorney General*[14] (on the fluoridation of water) and the right to a private life in *McGee v Attorney General* (on access to contraceptives).[15]

In this chapter attention will be focused on a few particular aspects of the Supreme Court's involvement with the Irish Constitution.[16] First, there will be a review of the constitutional principles it has espoused when dealing with requests from the country's President, under Article 26 of the Constitution, to preview the constitutionality of proposed legislation. This prompts a discussion of two rules attendant upon that preview process, the so-called 'one judgment' and 'immutability' rules. There will then be a consideration of the Court's concept of 'unenumerated' constitutional rights and a review of recent cases in which this concept has, unfortunately, not been applied in the context of social and economic claims. This in turn begs a discussion of 'natural law' theory, which some believe might still be a useful concept in the struggle for judicial recognition of the importance of a rights-based approach to the attainment of social justice.

The President's Power to Refer Legislation to the Supreme Court

One of the innovations of the 1937 Constitution was the creation of the office of President of Ireland, a matter dealt with in Articles 12 to 14.[17] Until then the Head of State had been the King of England, in line with the idea that the conferment of Home Rule in 1922 did not affect the position of Ireland as a constitutional monarchy. Ireland was in the same position as Canada and Australia, with a Governor appointed to represent the monarch on a day-to-day basis. Without explicitly abolishing the role of the monarch, Article 12.1 of the 1937 Constitution said that the President of Ireland (*Uachtarán na hÉireann*) 'shall take precedence over all other persons in the State'. Directly elected by the people on the basis of proportional representation by means of the single transferable vote system,[18] the President must be at least 35 years of age[19] and can serve for a maximum of two terms, each of seven years.[20] Before taking up office he or she must make a declaration in the presence of judges of the Supreme Court and High Court (as well as members of the Dáil and Seanad) that, amongst other things, he or she 'will maintain the Constitution of Ireland and uphold its laws'.[21]

The role of the President of Ireland is titular rather than executive. He or she acts more like the Presidents of Germany or Italy than the Presidents of France or the USA. The President must appoint as head of government (ie, as *Taoiseach* or Prime Minister) the person who is nominated to that role by the Dáil (the lower House of Parliament, the *Oireachtas*)[22] and, likewise, the President must appoint the other members of the government on the nomination of the *Taoiseach*.[23] Indeed the Constitution makes it clear that, in the absence of any provision in the Constitution saying that he or she must act in his or her absolute discretion or after consultation with the Council of State[24] or advice from any

[14] [1965] IR 294; see 125-6 below. [15] [1974] IR 284; see Chap 9 below, 232-4.

[16] For more detailed surveys see Byrne and McCutcheon (2014), Chap 15; Doyle (2008); Hogan et al (2018); Forde and Leonard (2003); Casey (2000). For how the Constitution evolved between 1937 and 1997 see Murphy and Twomey (1998); Ward (1994) Chaps 11 and 12; Litton (1988); and Farrell (1988); for a 70th anniversary collection see Carolan and Doyle (2008). For quasi-political and theoretical accounts see, respectively, Cahillane, Gallen and Hickey (2017) and Daly and Hickey (2015).

[17] See, generally, Casey (2003) 332–38; Hogan et al (2018)241-78. [18] Arts 12.2.1 and 12.2.3.

[19] Art 12.4.1. [20] Arts 12.3.1 and 12.3.2. [21] Art 12.8. [22] Art 13.1.1.

[23] Art 13.1.2

[24] This is an advisory body provided for by Arts 31 and 32 of the Constitution. It comprises senior serving politicians, judges and the Attorney General, together with former Presidents, Taoisigh and Chief Justices and up to seven other members nominated by the President.

other body, the President must exercise and perform the powers and functions conferred by the Constitution 'only on the advice of the Government'.[25] That is why the President has no discretion to refuse to appoint individuals to the Supreme Court whom the government has nominated for that role. For the avoidance of doubt (although the provisions are clumsily worded) the Constitution goes on to say that, while additional powers and functions may be conferred on the President by law, no law can make these additional powers or functions exercisable or performable other than on the advice of the government.[26]

Bills deemed to have been passed by the Dáil and the Seanad are not enacted into law until they have been signed by the President,[27] and he or she must officially 'promulgate' those laws,[28] but there is no constitutional obligation on the President to sign every Bill presented to him or her. In another break with the Irish Free State Constitution,[29] Article 26 of the 1937 Constitution allows the President, after consultation with the Council of State,[30] to refer any Bill, with some exceptions,[31] to the Supreme Court 'for a decision on the question as to whether such Bill or any specified provision or provisions of such Bill is or are repugnant to this Constitution or to any provision thereof'.[32] Any such reference must be made no later than the seventh day after the date on which the Bill is presented by the *Taoiseach* to the President for signature[33] (so a consultative meeting of the Council of State will be called at short notice) and the President must not sign any such Bill while the Supreme Court's decision on its constitutionality is pending.[34]

Articles 26.2.1 and 26.2.2 of the Constitution give specific directions as to how the Supreme Court must deal with a reference made to it under Article 26.1.1:

1. The Supreme Court, consisting of not less than five judges shall consider every question referred to it by the President under this Article for a decision, and, having heard arguments by or on behalf of the Attorney General[35] and by counsel assigned by the

[25] Art 13.9. [26] Arts 13.10 and 13.11. [27] Art 13.3.1.

[28] Art 13.3.2. Promulgation occurs through the publication at the President's direction of a notice in the Official Journal (*Iris Oifigiúil*) stating that the Bill has become law: Art 25.4.2 (inserted by the Second Amendment of the Constitution Act 1941).

[29] The absence of a referral power in the 1922 Constitution may be attributable to the desire not to mirror what the UK Parliament had enacted in the Government of Ireland Act 1920, s 51 of which permitted the Lord Lieutenants to refer to the Judicial Committee of the Privy Council any Bill introduced in the Parliament of Southern Ireland or the Parliament of Northern Ireland (or any Act made by either of those Parliaments). This provision remained in force for Northern Ireland until 1973. It was used on just one occasion, in relation to Stormont's imposition of a duty on ratepayers to contribute to the cost of education services, but the Privy Council found no breach of the Parliament's powers: *Re Section 3 of the Finance Act (NI) 1934* [1936] AC 352. It was replaced by s 18 of the Northern Ireland Constitution Act 1973, which was restricted to references concerning legislation that had been made; it did not apply to Bills and was never used. Under the Northern Ireland Act 1998, s 11(1), the Attorney General for Northern Ireland has the power to refer to the UK Supreme Court the question of whether a provision in a Bill of the Assembly is within the legislative competence of the Assembly, but this power too has not been exercised to date.

[30] See n 24 above.

[31] These are 'a Money Bill, or a Bill expressed to be a Bill containing a proposal to amend the Constitution, or a Bill the time for the consideration of which by the Seanad Éireann shall have been abridged under Article 24 of this Constitution'. A Money Bill is defined in Art 22.1.1. Abridgements of consideration of Bills by the Seanad (except Bills proposing to amend the Constitution) can occur if the *Taoiseach* certifies (and the President concurs and the Dáil so resolves) that in the government's opinion the Bill is 'urgent and immediately necessary for the preservation of the public peace and security, or by reason of the existence of a public emergency, whether domestic or international' (Art 24.1). Once a Bill has become law after an abridgement of discussion in the Seanad, it will lapse after 90 days unless before then both Houses of the Oireachtas pass resolutions stating that it should remain in force for a specified longer period (Art 24.3).

[32] Art 26.1.1. [33] Art 26.1.2, as amended by the Second Amendment of the Constitution Act 1941.

[34] Art 26.1.3. On Article generally see Hogan et al (2018) 477-93.

[35] It is odd that the Attorney General has a role here as well as being a member of the Council of State. It is also odd that serving judges can discuss a Bill in the Council of State even though they may later find themselves considering it in the Supreme Court.

Court, shall pronounce its decision on such question in open court as soon as may be, and in any case not later than sixty days after the date of such reference.

2. The decision of the majority of the judges of the Supreme Court shall, for the purposes of this Article, be the decision of the Court and shall be pronounced by such one of those judges as the Court shall direct, and no other opinion, whether assenting or dissenting, shall be pronounced nor shall the existence of any such other opinion be disclosed.

If the Supreme Court decides that any provision in a referred Bill is repugnant to the Constitution, the President must decline to sign the Bill.[36] If the Supreme Court decides that the Bill is not repugnant to the Constitution, and there has meanwhile been no petition sent to the President by parliamentarians, the President must sign the Bill into law 'as soon as may be after the date on which the decision of the Supreme Court shall have been pronounced'.[37] If the Bill is one in relation to which a petition has been made to the President by a stipulated number of parliamentarians to the effect that it contains a proposal of such national importance that the will of the people on the Bill should be ascertained,[38] the President can then wait for at least six days after the pronouncement of the Supreme Court's decision before pronouncing a decision on the petition.[39] This means that, even if the Supreme Court rules that the Bill is not repugnant to the Constitution, the President can still accede to the petition that the will of the people on the matter should be ascertained. This can be done within the following 18 months in one of two ways, as the government so desires: either through a referendum or, after the Dáil has been dissolved and reassembled, through a resolution of the Dáil.[40] If the Bill is approved in one of these ways the President then has no option but to sign and promulgate it.[41]

Emergency Laws: An Early Test and Its Aftermath

In the late 1930s the IRA ratcheted up its campaign of violence to try to persuade the British government to give up its claim to Northern Ireland. [42] While most of the attacks occurred in England there were some in Ireland too, enough to persuade de Valera's government to push an Offences Against the State Act through the Oireachtas in June 1939.[43] Part V of this Bill allowed for the creation of special criminal courts if the government proclaimed that it was satisfied that ordinary courts were inadequate to secure the effective administration of justice and the preservation of public peace and order.[44] Such a proclamation was also required before internment without trial could be authorised,[45] an additional condition being that a Minister had to be 'satisfied that [the person interned] is engaged in activities calculated to prejudice the preservation of the peace, order, or security of the State'.[46] A proclamation under the 1939 Act was duly made on 22 August 1939 and a Special Criminal Court was established on 24 August. On 2 September, a day after Germany invaded Poland and

[36] Art 26.3.1. [37] Art 26.3.3.

[38] This is provided for by Art 27.1. The number of parliamentarians required for the petition is a majority of the members of the Seanad and not less than one-third of the members of the Dáil.

[39] Art 27.4.2, as inserted by the Second Amendment to the Constitution Act 1941. [40] Art 27.5.1.

[41] Art 27.5.2.

[42] See, generally, Hogan and Walker (1989) 177–83; Ó Longaigh (2006) Chap 6. Lyons (1973), at 534, notes that in the first six months of 1939 there were more than 120 incidents in Britain, killing one person and wounding 55. In July a bomb in Coventry killed five.

[43] The Oireachtas also passed the Treason Act 1939.

[44] Offences Against the State Act 1939, s 35(2).

[45] Ibid, s 54(2). On internment 1939–45 see Maguire (2008) Chap 2. [46] s 55(1).

a day before Britain and France declared war on Germany, the Oireachtas passed the First Amendment of the Constitution Act 1939 to make it clear that when Article 28.3.3 of the 1937 Constitution says that the Constitution cannot be invoked to invalidate any law enacted by the Oireachtas 'for the purpose of securing the public safety and the preservation of the State in time or war or armed rebellion', the phrase 'time of war' is to be taken to include a time when there is an armed conflict in which the State is not participating but in respect of which the Oireachtas has resolved that 'a national emergency exists affecting the vital interests of the State'. A national emergency motion was approved by the Oireachtas later the same day and on 3 September the Emergency Powers Act 1939 was enacted to bolster the Offences Against the State Act passed a few months earlier.[47] In 1941 Article 28.3.3 was further amended to make it clear that a declaration of national emergency could be ended only if both Houses of the Oireachtas so resolved.[48]

The internment power conferred by the Offences Against the State Act 1939 was challenged before Gavan Duffy J by a detainee named Seamus Burke. To the government's surprise, on 1 December 1939 the judge granted a writ of *habeas corpus* because he thought the Minister had exceeded his powers by 'administering justice', contrary to Article 34.1 of the Constitution.[49] The government appealed to the Supreme Court but by four to one the judges ruled two weeks later that they had no power to deal with an appeal against an order awarding *habeas corpus*.[50] Fifty-three other detainees were released on the back of this litigation.[51] In an attempt to overcome such judicial opposition to internment the government then secured the passing of the Offences Against the State (Amendment) Bill. Under section 4, a person could be interned '[w]henever a Minister of State is of opinion that [that] person is engaged in activities which, in his opinion, are prejudicial to the preservation of public peace and order or to the security of the State'. Just as under the 1939 Act, such detention would be without trial and could potentially last until the emergency ended. Section 5 allowed the police to search, photograph and fingerprint detainees. Section 8 provided for the creation of a Commission to which a detainee could apply for release if no reasonable grounds existed for continuing the detention. On 8 January 1940 President Hyde referred the Bill to the Supreme Court under Article 26.

These internment provisions were nothing like as severe as the provisions examined by the Supreme Court a few years earlier—and approved—in *The State (Ryan) v Lennon*,[52] but unfortunately the Court in 1940 maintained a similarly deferential attitude. Three of the five judges who sat in the Article 26 case had also sat in the *Ryan* case and upheld the government's position there – Timothy Sullivan and John O'Byrne in the High Court and James Murnaghan in the Supreme Court. *By a majority* the Court in 1940 held that the Minister's power to intern did not amount to the administration of justice by the government rather than the courts (and so was not contrary to Article 34 of the Constitution), that the indefinite detention of persons was not a punishment but an exercise in 'preventive justice' (and so not contrary to Article 38 of the Constitution[53]), and that there was nothing else in the Bill which contravened either Article 40.3 of the Constitution (requiring the State

[47] Ó Longaigh (2006) 186–93. Ireland, of course, remained neutral during the Second World War.

[48] Second Amendment of the Constitution Act 1941, Sch, para 22; Ó Longaigh (2006) 193–207.

[49] *The State (Burke) v Lennon* [1940] IR 136 (Sullivan CJ, Murnaghan, Meredith and Geoghegan JJ; Johnston J dissenting); Ó Longaigh (2006) 239–41. For more on 'administering justice' see Chap 4 above, 65-8.

[50] Ibid, 161, relying on the House of Lords' decision in *Cox v Hakes* (1890) 15 App Cas 506.

[51] Ó Longaigh (2006) 241. Later that month the IRA seized 100 million rounds of ammunition from a State arsenal in Phoenix Park, Dublin.

[52] [1935] IR 170; see Chap 3 above, 37-42.

[53] Art 38(1) reads: 'No person shall be tried on any criminal charge save in due course of law.' On this point the Supreme Court relied on the House of Lords' decision in *The King (Zadig) v. Halliday* [1917] AC 260.

to defend and vindicate the personal rights of the citizen) or any other provision in that document.[54] Due to the 'one judgment' rule we do not know which judge or judges were in the minority in 1940,[55] but looking back it is difficult to comprehend how such a decision could have been arrived at by the majority. Perhaps the underlying reason is simply the point made towards the start of the collective judgment, namely that the framers of the 1937 Constitution would have been aware of similar Acts passed by the Oireachtas of the Irish Free State and yet chose not to prohibit them in the new Constitution. This led the Court to conclude, illogically, that if a law is not expressly prohibited by the Constitution any repugnancy to that document 'must be clearly established'.[56] The Court also chose to interpret the Constitution first and foremost in accordance with 'the common good', which it said was the main object of the Constitution as set out in the Preamble. It added, rather worryingly, that: 'There is nothing in this clause of the Preamble which could be invoked to necessitate the sacrifice of the common good in the interests of the freedom of the individual.'[57]

Allowing internment without trial is bad enough, but worse was to come. In 1940 an alleged member of the IRA, Thomas MacCurtain, was tried and convicted of murdering a police officer, one of three who had attempted to arrest him.[58] He was sentenced to death, the compulsory punishment for murder. When he sought an order of *habeas corpus* on the grounds that he had been tried by a military court, contrary to Article 38.4 of the Constitution (since he was not a member of the State's armed forces), both Gavan Duffy J and, in July 1940, a three-judge Supreme Court held against him,[59] as they were all of the view that the trial court had been lawfully constituted. MacCurtain's sentence was later commuted to life imprisonment and he was released after seven years but, as O'Hanlon convincingly argues, it is remarkable that such an apparent flouting of the rule of law can have been tolerated by the Supreme Court.[60] Although not otherwise a great supporter of the Article 26 procedure he is firmly of the view that the Offences Against the State Act 1939, like the Amendment Bill the following year, ought to have been referred to the Supreme Court under Article 26 for a preview of its constitutionality. There is no guarantee, of course, that the Supreme Court would have been any readier to find it unconstitutional than they were the Amendment Bill a year later.

Meanwhile the law enforcement bodies were also making use of the Emergency Powers Act 1939. Two of the exemptions provided for in that Act were that it did not allow the internment of 'natural-born Irish citizens' nor the trial by courts-martial of civilians.[61] Within a year, however, both of these exemptions had been removed by the Oireachtas,[62] meaning that from then on any person could be interned indefinitely or tried summarily for a range of specified offences, even if committed prior to the coming into force of the 1939 Act. If found guilty such a person could be sentenced to death and had no right of appeal.[63] In a case similar to *MacCurtain*, pursuant to these new provisions two men were tried for the murder of a police officer, found guilty and sentenced to death. They applied

[54] *In re Article 26 and the Offences Against the State (Amendment) Bill 1940* [1940] IR 470 (Sullivan CJ, Maguire P, Murnaghan, Geoghegan and O'Byrne JJ); Ó Longaigh (2006) 243–4.

[55] See too 119-21, below. [56] [1940] IR 470, 478. [57] Ibid, 479.

[58] MacCurtain's own father had been shot by the police in 1920.

[59] *In re MacCurtain* [1941] IR 83 (Sullivan CJ, Maguire P and Murnaghan J); Ó Longaigh (2006) 252–4.

[60] O'Hanlon (1965). Roderick O'Hanlon later served as a High Court judge from 1981 to 1995. In 1992 he was briefly the President of the Law Reform Commission but was sacked from that position for allegedly stepping beyond his remit by giving vent to strongly held personal views.

[61] ss 2(2)(*k*) and (*l*), and 2(5).

[62] By, respectively, the Emergency Powers (Amendment) Act 1940 and the Emergency Powers (Amendment) (No 2) Act 1940.

[63] Ibid, (No 2) Act, s 3.

unsuccessfully to Gavan Duffy J for a writ of *habeas corpus* and equally unsuccessfully to the Supreme Court (because it *is* possible to appeal to the Supreme Court against *refusals* of habeas corpus).[64] O'Hanlon is again critical of these decisions because the military court in question should not have been regarded as a 'special criminal court' as there had been no determination that the ordinary courts were inadequate to secure the effective administration of justice and the preservation of peace and order, as required by Article 38.3 of the Constitution. McGrath and Harte were duly executed by firing squad, as were three other men out a total of 13 who were tried under the 1940 provisions.[65]

Some might argue that the decisions of the Supreme Court in the Article 26 case, *MacCurtain* and *McGrath and Harte*, should not be judged by the standards of today. They might say that, given the wording of the 1937 Constitution and the Acts passed by the Oireachtas in 1939 and 1940, the Supreme Court had no option but to decide these cases as it did.[66] But if Kennedy CJ was able to dissent in *The State (Ryan) v Lennon* in 1934 it does not seem unreasonable to suppose that at least one of the judges might have dissented in *MacCurtain* or in *McGrath and Harte*, just as at least one such judge did in the Article 26 case, albeit anonymously. It is certainly true that the decisions, especially the Article 26 decision, cast a long shadow, one that was darkening the atmosphere even 36 years later. Donal Barrington recalled that the decision created a general feeling that the 1937 Constitution was 'a broken reed' or 'all sail and no anchor'.[67] The Emergency Powers Act 1939 was continued in force during each of the next six years, until it was allowed to lapse in 1946. The proclamation of an emergency, however, endured. The Committee on the Constitution recommended in 1967 that declarations of emergency should lapse after three years unless specifically renewed, but that proposal has never been implemented.[68]

Unbelievable though it may be, the emergency was not officially ended until 1 September 1976, but on that same day a new proclamation was issued at the behest of Liam Cosgrave's Fine Gael government. The troubles in Northern Ireland were at their height (nearly 1,600 people were killed there between 1972 and 1976) and on 21 July 1976 the British Ambassador to Ireland and a senior British civil servant were killed when a landmine exploded in Dublin. Two weeks later a new Emergency Powers Bill was passed by the Oireachtas and on 26 September it was referred to the Supreme Court by President Ó Dálaigh.[69] Amongst other things, section 2 of the Bill allowed a member of the Garda Síochána, without a warrant, to stop, search, question and arrest any person if he or she suspected with reasonable cause that that person had committed, was committing or was about to commit an offence under the Offences Against the State Act 1939 or a 'scheduled' offence, or if he or she suspected with reasonable cause that that person was carrying any document or item, or was in possession of information, relating to the commission or intended commission of such an offence. A person so arrested could be kept in custody initially for 48 hours but then for up to five further days if a member of the Garda Síochána not below the rank of chief superintendent so directed.[70]

[64] *In re McGrath and Harte* [1941] IR 68.

[65] For details see Ó Longaigh (2006) 254–8.

[66] Heuston (1976), at 208, said of the Art 26 judgment that 'if the men of violence win, there will be no Constitution and no court'.

[67] Barrington (1987) 110. He added (at 111) that when he was a student at UCD in the 1940s the standard textbook on constitutional law was still Dicey's *Law and the Constitution*.

[68] For comments on the Committee's recommendations see Foley and Lawlor (1995) App 2.

[69] His decision to do so was heavily criticised by the Minister for Defence. The President felt so undermined by this, and by Taoiseach Liam Cosgrave's refusal to accept the Minister's resignation, that he decided to resign himself in order to protect the dignity of his office.

[70] Von Prondzynski (1976).

The Supreme Court responded to the reference on 15 October.[71] It held that, while the President had the power to refer the Bill, once it had been established that the procedural requirements affecting a Bill to which Article 28.3.3 of the Constitution applies were satisfied, no part of the Constitution could be invoked to invalidate it. To its credit the Court refused to accept the Attorney General's even broader submission that whether there is a national emergency satisfying the terms of Article 28.3.3 is not a justiciable issue.[72] The judgment stated:

> The Court expressly reserves for future consideration the question whether the Courts have jurisdiction to review such resolutions ... The Bill's stated expression of its purpose accords with the requirements of the sub-section; and there is a presumption which has not been displaced that the facts stated in the resolutions are correct.[73]

Despite this reservation, the decision gave the distinct impression that the Supreme Court would not be particularly keen in any future case to second-guess the assertion by parliamentarians that an emergency existed.[74] To do so, of course, might well damage the legitimacy of the Court in the eyes of the public. Clarke, on the other hand, convincingly argues that the Court could and should have interpreted Article 28.3.3 of the Constitution as subordinate to the fundamental rights provisions in the Constitution, where they are referred to as 'antecedent' and 'superior' to positive law.[75]

Section 2 of what became the Emergency Powers Act 1976 was intended to remain in force for just one year, unless continued for further one-year periods with the approval of the Oireachtas. A Fianna Fáil government allowed it to lapse in 1977 but the executive power to bring it into force again without the Oireachtas's approval was preserved. That power was still in place in 1993, when the United Nations' Human Rights Committee strongly urged the government to critically examine whether it (and the Special Criminal Court) were still needed.[76] The national emergency was not brought to an end until 1995 when, as part of its response to the ceasefires announced by paramilitary organisations in Northern Ireland in the previous year, John Bruton's Fine Gael government persuaded the Oireachtas to withdraw it.[77] Its demise also meant that the Defence Forces lost their powers of arrest and search which they had held since 1976.[78] However the decision had no impact on the Offences Against the State Acts 1939–1985, under which the Special Criminal Court was established. A review of those acts was undertaken by the Hederman Commission, which reported in 2002.[79]

How Have Article 26 References Worked in Practice?

Altogether there have so far been 15 references to the Supreme Court under Article 26. For ease of reference, the bare details of the cases are set out in Appendix 4 to this book and the judgments are helpfully listed together on the Supreme Court's website.[80] In seven of the 15

[71] *In re Article 26 and the Emergency Powers Bill 1976* [1977] IR 159 (O'Higgins CJ, Walsh, Henchy, Griffin and Kenny JJ). See Morgan (1978–79).

[72] On non-justiciability more generally, see Chap 4 above, 68-9. [73] [1977] IR 159, 176.

[74] But it can be claimed that the emergency powers were effective during the 1940s. Feeney (2002) 175 says that as a result of the draconian emergency legislation 'the IRA virtually ceased to exist as an organisation outside jail'.

[75] Clarke (1977).

[76] Comments on Ireland's first periodic report under the International Covenant on Civil and Political Rights, CCPR/C/79/Add.21, 3 August 1993, paras 11 and 19.

[77] Dáil Debs, vol 448, no 6, cols 1538–87, 7 February 1995; Seanad Debs, 16 February 1995.

[78] Criminal Law Act 1976, s 15. [79] For more details see Chap 9 below, 205-6.

[80] See, generally, Collins and O'Reilly (2003), Chap 8; O'Hanlon (1965) 5 saw Art 26 as 'of very doubtful benefit'.

cases the Supreme Court held that at least one proposed legislative provision was repugnant to the Constitution, but only one such case has occurred in the last 20 years.[81] Given that in Ireland the only person who can make a reference is the President (unlike, say, in France, where a much wider range of persons can do so[82]), 15 references within an 80-year period is not a negligible number. In a further 13 instances the Council of State has been asked to consider Bills but the President has decided not to refer them to the Supreme Court.[83] In fact only one of the last eight Bills considered by the Council of State has been referred to the Supreme Court by the President. Notwithstanding this, it is too early to conclude that the appetite for referrals has truly waned.

In recent cases the Supreme Court has baulked at the practice of referring whole Bills to it,[84] because Bills can be long and complex and the Court is allowed only 60 days to go through the process of commissioning counsel's opinion, holding a hearing, deliberating on its conclusions and issuing a collective judgment. In its judgment relating to the Employment Equality Bill in 1996, the Supreme Court, through Hamilton CJ, pointed out that 'When one considers that the Bill consists of 74 sections and either amends or refers to 33 other statutes one can see that the task confronting the Court is a formidable one'.[85] As James Casey observes, in that case the provision which had been very contentious during Oireachtas debates was found by the Supreme Court to be constitutional, while another provision which had raised no controversy at all in the Oireachtas was found to be unconstitutional.[86] Of course the correlative difficulty is that, if the President refers only the most controversial provisions in a Bill and the Supreme Court upholds their constitutionality, the Bill may then become an Act but contain other possibly unconstitutional provisions which will remain valid unless and until a future litigant finds the money and energy to challenge them through normal posterior constitutional review. If one or more of those provisions is found to be unconstitutional this may have serious consequences for actions already taken based on the assumption that they were constitutional. This danger was alluded to, but ignored, in the Supreme Court's ruling in the Article 26 reference concerning the Housing (Private Rented Dwellings) Bill in 1982: having found provisions in the Bill to be in breach of landlords' property rights, the Court briefly mentioned the possibility that some tenants may also suffer hardship and that their equality and personal rights (including property rights) may therefore be affected.[87] However it refused to adjudicate on that point, saying only that:

> ... having regard to the obligation imposed on the State by the Constitution to act in accordance with the principles of social justice, the Court recognizes the presumption that any such hardship will be provided for adequately by the State.[88]

[81] *In re Article 26 of the Constitution and the Health (Amendment) (No 2) Bill 2004* [2005] 1 IR 105.

[82] Art 61 of the Constitution of the French Republic 1958 permits references of draft Acts to be made to the Constitutional Council by the President, the Prime Minister, the President of the National Assembly, the President of the Senate, 60 Members of the National Assembly or 60 Senators. For France's position on posterior review see 124 below.

[83] The Bills in question were: the Health Bill 1947, the Income Tax (Consolidation) Bill 1966, the Criminal Law Bill 1976, the Criminal Justice Bill 1984, the Fisheries (Amendment) Bill 1990, the Criminal Justice (Public Order) Bill 1993, the Housing (Miscellaneous Provisions) (No 2) Bill 2001, the Defamation Bill 2006, the Criminal Justice Bill 2007, the Criminal Justice (Amendment) Bill 2009, the Credit Institutions (Stabilisation) Bill 2010, the Protection of Life During Pregnancy Bill 2013, and the International Protection Bill 2015.

[84] The three exceptions are *In re Article 26 and the School Attendance Bill 1942* [1943] IR 334 (which looked only at s 4 of the Bill), *In re Article 26 and Part V of the Planning and Development Bill 1999* [2000] 2 IR 321, and *In re Article 26 and Sections 5 and 10 of the Illegal Immigrants (Trafficking) Bill* [2000] 2 IR 360.

[85] *In re Article 26 and the Employment Equality Bill 1996* [1997] 2 IR 321, 331.

[86] Casey (2000) 338.

[87] These are the rights protected by Arts 40.1 and 40.3 of the Constitution.

[88] [1983] IR 181, 192.

Generally speaking, it is efficient to clarify the constitutional position of legislative provisions as early as possible after they have been enacted but, given the unforeseeability of possible future challenges, this is a counsel of perfection. What is required is some mechanism to ensure that, while the Supreme Court is empowered to continue to provide valuable reassurance concerning the constitutionality of particular proposed provisions, it is also able to exert some influence over the number and nature of questions that are expressly put to it for consideration. Under Article 13.8.1 of the Constitution the President is not answerable to any court (or to either House of the Oireachtas) for the way he or she exercises presidential powers and functions, but this would not preclude the Supreme Court from indicating more resolutely in its judgments what kinds of factors it would like to see the President taking into account when deciding what issues to refer to it under Article 26. It is to be hoped that the President would interpret the power of referral with those factors firmly in mind.

Developments in the 1990s

The first nine rulings in Article 26 cases, up to that in the Matrimonial Home Bill in early 1994,[89] were dealt with in relatively short judgments, averaging less than nine pages of law reports per judgment, and they will not be revisited here. In the six subsequent rulings the Supreme Court has appeared to take its role much more seriously, issuing judgments which average 61 pages of law reports. There has been a rise in judgment length in all types of cases, but in Article 26 referrals the Supreme Court now goes out of its way to examine the issues from a multitude of angles. Counsel, too, are spending longer in developing their arguments for or against constitutionality. The change in approach may be attributable to the appointment of Liam Hamilton as Chief Justice in 1994 or to the growing national regard for the Constitution given the fact that the Northern Ireland peace process swung into action in that year through the announcement of republican and loyalist ceasefires. But the likeliest trigger for the deeper Supreme Court engagement is that for the first time the issue of the constitutionality of laws concerned with abortion was made the subject of an Article 26 reference.

In its judgment on the constitutionality of the Regulation of Information (Services outside the State for Termination of Pregnancies) Bill[90] the Supreme Court had to decide whether any of its provisions concerning the giving of information about abortion services outside Ireland were unconstitutional. The judges were required to assess whether the balance struck by the Oireachtas between the rights of the unborn child, the rights of the mother, the right to information and the right to freedom of expression was fully compatible with the Constitution.[91] They were confronted by two amendments to the Constitution which, on their face, appeared to conflict with each other but which had each been inserted following votes in referenda. The Eighth Amendment of the Constitution Act 1983 inserted sub-section Article 40.3.3, which read: 'The State acknowledges the right to life of the unborn and, with due regard to the equal right to life of the mother, guarantees in its laws to respect, and, as far as practicable, by its laws to defend and vindicate that right'. The

[89] *In re Article 26 and the Matrimonial Home Bill 1993* [1994] 1 IR 305. The six references made before 1983 are considered in Jaconelli (1983).

[90] *In re Article 26 and the Regulation of Information (Services outside the State for Termination of Pregnancies) Bill 1995* [1995] 1 IR 1 (Hamilton CJ, O'Flaherty, Egan, Blayney and Denham JJ).

[91] See too Doyle (2003), who uses this case as a starting-point for an analysis of where the legal validity for Ireland's legal system ultimately lies.

Fourteenth Amendment of the Constitution Act 1992 added this paragraph to that subsection: 'This subsection shall not limit freedom to obtain or make available, in the State, subject to such conditions as may be laid down by law, information relating to services lawfully available in another State.'

Faced with this apparent conflict the Supreme Court relied upon the approach it had adopted less than a year earlier in *Tuohy v Courtney*.[92] There the Court had considered the constitutionality of a provision in the Statute of Limitations 1957 which said that actions in tort could not be brought more than six years after the date on which the cause of action accrued.[93] Finlay CJ, for the Court, accepted that in so legislating the Oireachtas was essentially balancing a claimant's right to litigate on the one hand against a defendant's property right to be protected against burdensome claims and the public's interest in the avoidance of stale claims on the other.[94] When assessing the constitutionality of that balance the role of the courts 'is not to impose their view of the correct or desirable balance in substitution for the view of the legislature' but rather 'to determine from an objective stance whether the balance contained in the impugned legislation is so contrary to reason and fairness as to constitute an unjust attack on some individual's constitutional rights'.[95] In the case before it at that time the Court held the balance to be acceptable and in the Article 26 case it did likewise.[96] In particular, it could see nothing in the Bill which constituted an unjust attack on the rights of a pregnant woman, or indeed the rights of the parents of a child who was seeking abortion information or the rights of the husband of a woman who was doing so.[97] The approach adopted by the Supreme Court was clearly one of deference to the will of the national Parliament. The test applied was not dissimilar to that used in judicial reviews of administrative action.[98]

The next two Article 26 references displayed the same approach to the balancing issue, the rights at issue being the right to equality, the right to earn a livelihood and the right to property. As regards the Employment Equality Bill 1996,[99] the Court held that not protecting people under the age of 18 or over the age of 65 from age discrimination in the employment field was not irrational or arbitrary, given that these are the ages at which significant numbers of people enter or leave the workforce. Nor were the measures taken to facilitate the integration into employment of persons over the age of 50 irrelevant, unfair or irrational, given the justifiable objective of reducing the problem of people being unemployed for long periods. Moreover it was acceptable to exclude from the Bill people employed in the defence forces, the police or the prisons and to make special provision for people of particular religious denominations. On the other hand, the Bill's provisions which allowed for positive discrimination on the ground of disability improperly limited the right of employers to carry on a business and earn a livelihood (under Articles 40.3 and 43 of the Constitution) because they imposed on one group the whole cost of promoting equality in the workplace, without even making an exception for small firms. This, said the Court, constituted an unjust attack on the property rights of employers. Moreover to make employers vicariously liable for criminal activities of their employees—even though the offences in question were not connected with health and safety, the work environment or the protection of a consumer—was disproportionate to the mischief being targeted and meant that a trial for such offences would not be held 'in due course of law' as required by Articles 38.1

[92] [1994] 3 IR 1 (Finlay CJ, O'Flaherty, Egan, Blayney and Denham JJ). [93] s 11(2)(a) and (b).

[94] [1994] 3 IR 1, 47. [95] Ibid. [96] [1995] 1 IR 1, 45. [97] Ibid, 45–50 and 51–2.

[98] See Chap 8 below, 177-83.

[99] *In re Article 26 and the Employment Equality Bill 1996* [1997] 2 IR 321 (Hamilton CJ, O'Flaherty, Denham, Barrington and Keane JJ).

and 40.1 of the Constitution.[100] There was a further breach of Article 38.1 as regards the provision which allowed a certificate that a person had obstructed or impeded the Court, the Director of Equality Investigations or an equality officer in the exercise of their powers to constitute full proof of that person's guilt, without any need for an oral hearing.[101]

The judgment in this case was, of necessity, a bold foray on the part of the Court into the constitutionality of a range of important measures allegedly promoting equality.[102] That it was so meticulous in considering a variety of issues, and in providing a rationale for its contrasting conclusions while maintaining a credible overall framework of relevant criteria, is much to its credit, even if the protective approach it took towards employers as regards the employment of people with disabilities appears in retrospect to be somewhat generous. We must remember, however, that when the United Kingdom enacted its Disability Discrimination Act a year earlier it did include a provision which exempted a large part of the Act from applying to employers of less than 20 people. Likewise, in the USA the Americans with Disabilities Act of 1990 did not apply to employers of less than 15 people. When the Irish Bill was eventually enacted as the Employment Equality Act 1998 a provision was included which stated that discrimination on the disability (or age) ground is not unlawful 'where it is shown that there is clear actuarial or other evidence that significantly increased costs would result if the discrimination were not permitted'.[103] No further constitutional challenge has been raised against that provision.

A month later the same five Supreme Court judges delivered a joint judgment in an Article 26 reference relating to the Equal Status Bill.[104] This was a less complex piece of legislation than the Employment Equality Bill but one can understand why the appetite of the Supreme Court judges for engaging in another detailed analysis of every section of the Bill was not great. Rather daringly, they latched on to the point that there were two provisions in the Bill[105] which were very similar to those in the Employment Equality Bill that had been declared unconstitutional because they anticipated trials not 'in due course of law'. This, they decided, was enough to excuse the Court from having to consider the constitutionality of any other provision in the Equal Status Bill, despite the wording of Article 26.2.1 of the Constitution, which requires the Court to 'consider every question referred to it by the President under this Article for a decision'. Their reasoning was that, because of the indisputable unconstitutionality of two provisions of the Bill at the time it was referred to the Court, the Bill no longer enjoyed the benefit of the presumption of constitutionality and so there was no justiciable issue for the Court to try. By adopting this stance the judges effectively returned to the position they had taken in two earlier Article 26 references,[106] without convincingly explaining why they had adopted a different position vis-à-vis the Employment Equality Bill. Although that Bill would have had the presumption of constitutionality when it was referred it surely lost it as soon as the Court found certain of its provisions not to be constitutional, yet the Court proceeded to pronounce upon the constitutionality of several other provisions in the Bill. It is tempting to accuse the Supreme Court of abrogating its constitutional duty in the way that it considered the Equal Status Bill.

[100] The Court, at 374, expressly contrasted the position in the UK where, because of the doctrine of parliamentary sovereignty, courts have to give effect to such legislation even if it means criminalising individuals who are in no way blameworthy (citing Lord Reid in *Sweet v Parsley* [1970] AC 132, 150).

[101] On this point, at 383, the Court relied upon two decisions of the Canadian Supreme Court, *Chaulk v R* [1990] 3 SCR 1303 and *R v Oakes* [1986] 1 SCR 103.

[102] For earlier thorough expositions of case law on equality see Beytagh (1983) and Forde (1982).

[103] s 34 (2).

[104] *In re Article 26 and the Equal Status Bill 1997* [1997] 2 IR 387.

[105] ss 40(3) and 71.

[106] *In re the Housing (Private Rented Dwellings) Bill 1981* [1983] IR 181 and *In re the Matrimonial Home Bill 1993* [1994] 1 IR 305.

Developments in the 2000s

In *In re Article 26 and Part V of the Planning and Development Bill 1999*[107] the Court found no unconstitutionality in a Bill which interfered with the property rights of developers. The Bill required planning authorities to have a housing strategy containing a general policy that a percentage of land developed for residential use must be reserved for affordable housing; they had also to ensure that sufficient and suitable land was zoned for residential use to meet the needs of the housing strategy; and they were allowed to make planning permission conditional on the applicant's agreement to transfer ownership of land required for housing to the planning authority, subject to the payment of compensation.[108] Counsel attacking the Bill relied on the Court's decision on the Employment Equality Bill to argue that, even if a Bill's purpose was intended to serve the common good, it was unconstitutional if it unfairly transferred the burden of achieving that goal to a particular section of the community, in this case developers.[109] In response the Court found that the presumption of the Bill's constitutionality had not been rebutted and that, in line with 'the double construction rule', its provisions could be reasonably interpreted as constitutional.[110] Having asserted that 'every person who acquires or inherits land takes it subject to any restrictions which the general law of planning imposes on the use of the property in the public interest',[111] the Court stressed that:

> It is peculiarly the province of the Oireachtas to seek to reconcile in this area the conflicting rights of different sections of society and that clearly places a heavy onus on those who assert that the manner in which they have sought to reconcile those conflicting rights is in breach of the guarantee of equality.[112]

The Supreme Court found support for its stance in *James v UK*,[113] where the European Court of Human Rights had accepted that interfering with one entity's property rights (in this case those of the estate of the Duke of Westminster) could be justified if it was pursuant to a 'public interest' such as the achievement of greater social justice and if some compensation was paid. Council of Europe States have a wide margin of appreciation in this regard. The Supreme Court was also applying the law in a way which was reminiscent of the approach taken by the United Kingdom's top court towards the right to property.[114]

In *In re Article 26 and Sections 5 and 10 of the Illegal Immigrants (Trafficking) Bill 1999*,[115] in which judgment was delivered on the same day as in the previous case, the question was about fairness in the context of immigration controls, but again the Court found no unconstitutionality in the Bill. The main issue was whether it was contrary to the Constitution to limit non-nationals who wished to challenge decisions regarding their refugee or immigration status to applications for judicial review brought within 14 days, a period which could be extended if the High Court thought there was 'good and sufficient' reason for doing so. No appeal to the Supreme Court was to be possible in such cases unless the High Court gave leave, certifying that its decision involved a point of law of exceptional public importance and that it was desirable in the public interest that an appeal should be taken.

[107] [2000] 2 IR 321 (Keane CJ, Murphy, Murray, McGuinness and Geoghegan JJ). Only Keane CJ had previously sat in an Art 26 case.

[108] ss 94–96 of the Bill.

[109] [2000] 2 IR 321, 340.

[110] Ibid, 346, citing its decision in *McDonald v Bord na gCon (No 2)* [1965] IR 217. For more on the double construction rule see Chap 8 below, 175.

[111] Ibid, 353.

[112] Ibid, 358.

[113] (1986) 8 EHRR 123.

[114] Dickson (2013) 339–66.

[115] [2000] 2 IR 360 (Keane CJ, Murphy, Murray, McGuinness and Geoghegan JJ).

The Supreme Court held that non-nationals were entitled to the same natural justice and procedural fairness as citizens of the State, but that the Bill's provisions did not amount to a denial of the right of access to the courts under Article 40.2 of the Constitution. Imposing a tight deadline on challenges to refugee and immigration decisions pursued the legitimate objective of achieving legal certainty and better administration and so there was no violation of the constitutional right to equal treatment in applying rules just to non-nationals. The High Court's power to extend the 14-day time period was reasonable and complied with the need to avoid injustice. A restriction on the right to appeal from the High Court to the Supreme Court did not have to be justified or proportionate because the Oireachtas had an express statutory power to impose such a restriction. A secondary issue was whether the Minister's powers to detain and deport non-nationals who failed to challenge decisions going against them were unconstitutional or contrary to the right to liberty as guaranteed by the European Convention on Human Rights,[116] but here too the Supreme Court saw no violation of the Constitution. The Supreme Court has been criticised for failing to express a more inclusive interpretation of the term 'citizen' in this case.[117]

Finally, the Supreme Court's judgment in *In re Article 26 and the Health (Amendment) (No 2) Bill 2004*[118] is the most detailed yet in an Article 26 case and was the first to be delivered by a bench of seven rather than five judges. The context for the reference was a decision by the Irish government in 2004, following advice from the Attorney General, Rory Brady, that there was no legal basis under any legislation for charging patients who had medical cards for services received in hospital, including long-stay care.[119] The Health (Amendment) Bill 2005 was drafted to allow the government to keep payments made by patients in the past and to impose them on patients in the future, but in its judgment on the Article 26 reference the Supreme Court ruled that, while the imposition of future charges was not a violation of the rights to life and bodily integrity protected by Article 40.3 of the Constitution, the retrospective validating of charges imposed illegally was a violation of Articles 40.3.2 and 43. This was partly because the right to ownership of property 'had a moral quality which was intimately related to the humanity of each individual' and 'was one of the pillars of the free and democratic society established under the Constitution'.[120] Bearing in mind that most of the people who had initially paid the unlawfully levied charges were people of low income, the Court added that '[t]he property of persons of modest means must necessarily, in accordance with those principles [of social justice], be deserving of particular protection, since any abridgement of the rights of such persons will normally be proportionately more severe in its effects'.[121]

The Court distinguished its decision on the Planning and Development Bill 1999[122] on the basis that here the proposed Bill was not just interfering with a right but running directly against it, given that the Health Act 1970[123] had expressly conferred on persons with medical cards the right to in-patient services *without charge*.[124] Most remarkably, the Court was not perturbed by the suggestion that the cost to the State of not being able to prevent recovery of charges paid could be as much as €500 million.[125] In the Court's view, abrogating

[116] Ibid, 413, citing *Amuur v France* (1996) 22 EHRR 533. [117] Dewhurst (2013) 108.

[118] [2005] IESC 7, [2005] 1 IR 105 (Murray CJ, Denham, McGuinness, Hardiman, Geoghegan, Fennelly and McCracken JJ); the judgment runs to 55 pages. See O'Dell and Whyte (2005).

[119] The Office of the Ombudsman had long been arguing that the charges were unlawful: see www.ombudsman.ie/publications/reports/failure-to-refund-illegal/.

[120] [2005] 1 IR 105, 201–2.

[121] Ibid, 202. 'Principles of social justice' is a phrase found in Art 43.2.1. See too 128-36 below.

[122] See above 117. [123] s 53(1). [124] [2005] 1 IR 105, 204. [125] Ibid, 205.

the rights was not 'an imperative for the avoidance of an extreme financial crisis or a fundamental disequilibrium in public finances'.[126] This suggests that if the question had come before the Supreme Court just three years later, when a severe banking crisis hit the country, it might not have been so willing to uphold the patients' rights. In the wake of this significant judgment, one which ably demonstrates that the Supreme Court can at times display a deep commitment to social justice, the Health (Repayment Scheme) Act 2006 was enacted to ensure that charges which had already been unlawfully collected from patients would be reimbursed.

The 'One Judgment' Rule

It will not have escaped readers' notice that in each of the Article 26 cases analysed above there was one single judgment.[127] While it was delivered by the Chief Justice in each instance, the judgment was 'of the Court', being the outcome of discussions amongst several if not all of the sitting judges. There were no concurring or dissenting judgments. This is because of the wording of Article 26.2.2, cited above,[128] which explicitly states that in Article 26 cases the judgment given must be the decision of the Court and that even the very existence of any other opinion must not be disclosed.

This 'one judgment' rule was written into the Constitution by the Second Amendment of the Constitution Act 1941,[129] which was enacted within the three-year period after the first President of Ireland took office on 25 June 1938, during which constitutional amendments could be made by ordinary legislation. The 1941 Act made the same amendment to Article 34 of the Constitution,[130] meaning that even in *posterior* reviews of the constitutionality of post-1937 legislation there could be just one judgment. The Dáil debates on the 1941 Act reveal that the amendments were made in reaction to the Supreme Court's judgment in the first of the Article 26 references, on the Offences Against the State (Amendment) Bill 1940,[131] where Sullivan CJ admitted that it was 'the decision of the majority of the judges'. The country's five most senior judges sat in the case[132] but at least one of them must have disagreed with the judgment, which was that the preventative detention provisions in the 1940 Bill did not violate the Constitution. Less than two weeks after the judgment was pronounced a claim was made in the Dáil by James Dillon TD, a future leader of Fine Gael, that Murnaghan and Geoghegan JJ had dissented in the case,[133] but de Valera, the Taoiseach at the time, denied all knowledge of this. Sixty years later, in his detailed exegesis of the legal and political context within which the case was decided, Gerard Hogan was unable to point to convincing reasons why Murnaghan and Geoghegan JJ would have been inclined to dissent; he thought a more likely candidate was the Court's newly appointed judge, John O'Byrne.[134]

[126] Ibid, 206–7. [127] See, generally, Keane (2006) and Barrington (1987) 120–2. [128] See 108.

[129] Sch, para 15, enacted pursuant to Art 51(1) of the Constitution.

[130] Sch, para 25, inserting a new Art 34.5.

[131] [1940] IR 470; see 109-10 above; Mac Cormaic (2016) 49–57, where he explains the political tensions surrounding this decision, one in which 'the Supreme Court was finding its feet, taking the measure of its new powers, marking out its place in the new constitutional landscape' (57).

[132] Sullivan CJ, Maguire P and Murnaghan, Geoghegan and O'Byrne JJ. The President of the High Court, who ranked second in precedence to the CJ, sat in place of Meredith J, who was reportedly indisposed at the time. O'Byrne J had been appointed to the Supreme Court less than a week before the hearing commenced, replacing Johnston J, who had reached the retirement age. Compared to Meredith J's almost 16 years' experience as a senior judge, Maguire P had less than four.

[133] Dáil Debs, vol 78, no 12, cols 1724–26 (21 February 1940). [134] Hogan (2000a) 271–3.

In the Seanad debate on the Second Amendment of the Constitution Act 1941 the Taoiseach suggested that the one judgment rule was required (at least in Article 26 cases) in order to avoid attempts being made to speculate on which judges may have dissented: 'There would be counting of heads, and people saying that the matter was not settled at all.'[135] By way of contrast, during the debate in the Dáil's Committee of Finance, John Costello TD, a former Attorney General and a future Taoiseach, argued that allowing for dissenting judgments would be healthy for the Constitution:

> Certainly the dissentient judgments in various branches of the law have been the bones on which students, so to speak, metaphorically sharpened their legal teeth. A dissentient judgment on constitutional matters may be as valuable from the point of view of constitutional theory and the stimulation of constitutional thought as the judgment of the majority; in fact, sometimes it may be very much more valuable.[136]

De Valera acknowledged Costello's 'very excellent case' but still preferred what he called 'finality' in decision-making.[137] This is the approach which is often taken in criminal courts, presumably to promote the importance of certainty in an area of law which can lead to people being deprived of their liberty for long periods. When Ireland's Court of Criminal Appeal was established in 1924 it was mandated to deliver single judgments as a general rule,[138] and when the Special Criminal Court was created in 1939 it was required to issue a single judgment in every case.[139] In England and Wales decisions by the Court of Appeal (Criminal Division) are also always in the form of a single judgment, with no dissents indicated.[140] But to require single judgments in cases other than criminal cases is very unusual indeed.

Following its introduction for Article 26 cases, the one judgment rule was applied almost immediately in a reference concerning the School Attendance Bill 1942, where the Supreme Court held that a section in the Bill was repugnant to the Constitution because it allowed the Minister to require private schools (and people educating their children at home) to provide more than the minimum standard of education required in other schools.[141] The rule was first applied in a case involving posterior constitutional review in *Buckley v Attorney General*,[142] where the Supreme Court, in a judgment delivered by O'Byrne J,[143] held that the Sinn Féin Funds Act 1947 was beyond the powers of the Oireachtas to make because it unduly interfered with the right to private property. This was a significant decision in the Supreme Court's history because it demonstrated the Court's commitment to the separation of powers doctrine: rather than allow the Oireachtas, at the behest of a Fianna Fáil government led by de Valera, to pass an Act which purported to confiscate the assets of

[135] Seanad Debs, vol 25, no 13, cols 1218–19 (21 May 1941).

[136] Dáil Debs, vol 82, no 13, col 1862 (24 April 1941). [137] Ibid, col 1864.

[138] Courts of Justice Act 1924, s 28, which reads: '... *unless the court direct to the contrary*, the judgment of the court shall be pronounced by the President of the court, or by such other member of the court as the President directs, and no judgment with respect to the determination of any question shall be separately pronounced by any other member of the court' (emphasis added).

[139] Offences Against the State Act 1939, s 40.

[140] Judicial Office, *The Judicial System of England and Wales: A Visitor's Guide*, 8. There appears to be no statutory requirement for this approach.

[141] *In re Article 26 and the School Attendance Bill 1942* [1943] 1 IR 334.

[142] [1950] IR 67 (Murnaghan, Geoghegan, O'Byrne, Black and Martin Maguire JJ). Conor Maguire CJ recused himself because he had already been consulted by the Attorney General on the Act in question. See too Mac Cormaic (2016) 60–7; Feeney (2002) 178–81; Hogan (1997b). On posterior review more generally see 123-5 below.

[143] Interestingly he was only the third most senior judge sitting in the Court, perhaps suggesting that Murnaghan and Geoghegan JJ, his seniors, did not agree with the judgment of their three colleagues. See too Mac Cormaic (2016) 61–7.

a political party (of which de Valera used to be a member) and transfer them to a new organisation chaired by the Chief Justice, the Court insisted that the court proceedings which had already been commenced in relation to the ownership of the assets should be allowed to continue. It ultimately held that the assets did not belong to the party now headed by Mrs Buckley, and most of the money was eaten up in legal costs, but the central point was made that the jurisdiction of the courts cannot be arbitrarily subverted in the way that de Valera had attempted.

Under Article 34.4.5 the single judgment rule was limited to reviews of legislation passed after the 1937 Constitution came into force,[144] and some statutory instruments made under powers conferred by post-1937 Acts were also reviewable laws for this purpose.[145] Over time, however, the one judgment rule came to be seen as a hindrance rather than a help to the development of the Supreme Court's jurisprudence. De Valera's worries about a lack of definitiveness in the Court's jurisprudence can now be viewed as political rhetoric rather than as an objective assessment of the rule's merits. It was criticised in the 11th Interim Report of the Committee on Court Practice and Procedure in 1970 and also, after a thorough review of arguments for and against the rule, by the Constitution Review Group in 1996.[146] But the latter Group recommended its abolition only in relation to *posterior* constitutional reviews under Article 34.4, not for anterior reviews under Article 26. The leading text on Ireland's constitutional law agreed with that proposal.[147] Forde and Leonard are amongst the many who have observed that the rule runs counter to the common law tradition in constitutional and human rights cases, whereby if a court comprises more than one judge each judge is free to contribute a separate judgment.[148] This is now the approach of the Federal Constitutional Court of Germany and the European Court of Human Rights in Strasbourg,[149] though a major outlier continues to be the Court of Justice of the EU (where neither concurrent not dissenting judgments are permitted). At last, when a referendum was held in 2013 on the establishment of a Court of Appeal in Ireland,[150] the opportunity was taken to ask the people to remove the one judgment rule from Article 34.4, and they voted in favour of that proposition.[151] It was duly removed from 28 October 2014.[152] The rule still applies in Article 26 cases and to that extent continues to inhibit the development of the Court's constitutional jurisprudence. Unfortunately further reform does not seem to be on the horizon.

[144] That was the meaning given to the word 'law' in the immediately preceding paragraph of the Constitution, Art 34.4.4: see *State (Sheerin) v Kennedy* [1966] 1 IR 379.

[145] *State (Gilliland) v Governor of Mountjoy Prison* [1987] 1 IR 201; see too Forde and Leonard (2013) 161. The statutory instrument in question was one which applied the provisions of the Extradition Act 1965 to a particular country; Finlay CJ, at 229, said it was therefore 'the machinery expressly created in that Act for the application of Part II of it'. A different view was taken of the statutory instrument considered by the Supreme Court in *Meagher v Minister for Agriculture* [1994] 1 IR 329, though without any reference being made to the Supreme Court's earlier decision in *Gilliland*: see Chap 11 below, 256-8.

[146] CRG (1996), 80–5. On this report more generally see Butler and O'Connell (1998), a largely negative assessment.

[147] This was the case in the fourth edition in 2003 (p 350) but the fifth edition does not take a clear position on the matter: Hogan er al (2018), 485-6; see too Whyte (1983).

[148] Forde and Leonard (2013) 57.

[149] See, generally, Kirby (2007).

[150] As provided for in the Thirty-third Amendment of the Constitution (Court of Appeal) Act 2013, s 5(2)(f) and (g).

[151] This was contrary to the expectation of Supreme Court judge Niall McCarthy, who wrote in 1992 that 'unless a wholly new Constitution is adopted, it is unlikely that [Article 34.4] will be changed': McCarthy (1992) 165. He thought the multiple judgment system was '[a]t the centre of the common law, the genius of its dynamism' (ibid, 168).

[152] Court of Appeal Act 2014 (Establishment Day) Order 2014 (SI 477/2014).

The 'Immutability' Rule

In Article 34.3.3 the Constitution provides that if a provision in a Bill, or a whole Bill, has been referred by the President to the Supreme Court under Article 26, and has been found not to be repugnant to the Constitution, 'no court whatever' shall subsequently have jurisdiction to question the validity of that provision, or of the resulting Act, as the case may be. The effect of this provision is broad, especially as, in all but three of the references so far made under Article 26, a whole Bill has been referred to the Supreme Court. If, when looking at a whole Bill, the Supreme Court finds no fault with its provisions, no later court is able to entertain a challenge to the constitutionality of those provisions. On the other hand, if the President refers only one or more provisions of a Bill, the Supreme Court's decision that the provisions are not repugnant to the Constitution will not preclude a subsequent court from examining the constitutionality of other provisions in the same Bill which were not referred.

Like the one judgment rule in this context, the 'immutability' rule has been the subject of considerable criticism, but it remains in place. As regards a Bill's provisions which are not expressly considered by the Supreme Court in a case where the whole Bill is referred and some of them are found to be unconstitutional, the Article 26 judgment amounts to an advisory opinion to the effect that those other provisions are constitutional. In Canada, where questions can be referred to the Supreme Court for an advisory opinion, great weight is given to such opinions. According to Hogg, 'there do not seem to be any recorded instances where a reference opinion was disregarded by the parties, or where it was not followed by a subsequent court on the ground of its advisory character'.[153] Jaconelli is one commentator who has argued that in Ireland it is inappropriate to take too rigid a view of the binding nature of Article 26 judgments for future cases.[154] Forde and Leonard suggest that the ban applies only to decisions pronounced by the Supreme Court after the 'new' Supreme Court was established in 1961, but that is not much of a limitation on the rule.[155] A complete removal of the ban was recommended by the Report of the Constitution Review Group in 1996,[156] mainly on the ground that it was in any event unlikely that the Supreme Court would want to depart from an earlier decision to uphold the constitutionality of a particular Bill. A year later the Review Group's recommendation was endorsed by the All-Party Oireachtas Committee on the Constitution[157] but to date no Irish government has made a formal proposal to put the proposed change to the people in a referendum. The Article 26 reference procedure is possibly considered too arcane a matter to justify such a procedure.

An interesting side-question is whether the reasoning on which the ruling in an Article 26 case is based can be held not to apply when the Supreme Court is considering its applicability in a later case. Hogan et al now say that 'the dominant view is that such a decision is binding in the ordinary way'[158] which presumably also means that 'Article 34.3.3 does not prevent the Supreme Court overruling part of the reasoning contained in an earlier Article 26 reference'.[159] For the latter proposition they cite not only *McGimpsey v Ireland*,[160] where part of the reasoning in *In re Article 26 and the Criminal Law (Jurisdiction) Bill 1975* was overruled,[161] but also *DPP v Best*,[162] where aspects of the Supreme Court's earlier decision

[153] Hogg (2012) 8–18. [154] Jaconelli (1983) 337. [155] Forde and Leonard (2013) 35.
[156] CRG (1996) 76–80. [157] *First Progress Report* (Pn 3795) 63. [158] Hogan et al (2018) 484.
[159] This was stated in the fourth edition of *Kelly: The Irish Constitution* (2003) 913.
[160] [1990] 1 IR 110.
[161] [1977] IR 129. The statement overruled was the suggestion that the previous versions of Arts 2 and 3 of the Constitution did not constitute a claim of legal right concerning the territory of Northern Ireland. See Chap 7 below, 146-9.
[162] [2000] 2 IR 17. See Hogan et al (2018) 484, nn 239 and 240.

on home schooling in the *School Attendance Bill*[163] were departed from. Two years before *DPP v Best*, in *SPUC v Grogan (No 5)*,[164] two future Chief Justices—Keane and Denham JJ—suggested that on constitutional issues the Supreme Court should not adopt as conservative an approach to the doctrine of precedent as it should on other issues. The remaining judges in that case did not agree with Keane and Denham JJ that on the facts before them an earlier decision of the Supreme Court should be overruled,[165] but they did not expressly disagree with their colleagues' suggestion that in principle there is a need for a different approach to precedent in constitutional cases. Commenting on what might appear a contradiction between Keane J's two approaches in *DPP v Best* and *SPUC v Grogan*, Byrne and McCutcheon suggest that 'the difference might be more apparent than real',[166] but a more fundamental point is surely that there is nothing in the wording of Article 34.3.3 to require the Supreme Court to slavishly follow its reasoning in a previous case if by doing so it risks perpetuating an approach to a constitutional matter which is *per se* undesirable. In the very first reference made to the Supreme Court under Article 26 the judges held (by a majority) that indefinite detention without trial did not violate Articles 34, 38 or 40.3 of the Constitution, that is, that it did not permit the Minister to administer justice, to punish someone or to violate the personal rights of the citizen. It would be strange indeed, as Forde and Leonard have observed,[167] if such reasoning were to be binding on the Supreme Court today.[168]

Given that the Court has conceded that part of the reasoning in an earlier Article 26 case *can* be departed from and that, more generally, the Court has been prepared since 1965 to refuse to follow one of its own earlier decisions if it was 'clearly wrong',[169] there seems little justification for maintaining a rigid approach to the principle of *stare decisis* in Article 26 cases. On the contrary, there is a lot to be said for implementing the recommendation of the Constitutional Review Group, made more than 20 years ago, that Article 34.3.3 should be repealed. A mature legal system should have confidence that its Supreme Court judges will not play fast and loose with fundamental constitutional principles but will change established practice only if there are very good reasons for doing so. They do not need or want to be shackled in such a way as prevents them from putting even a toe on to new ground.

Posterior constitutional review

The argument in favour of changing the immutability rule begs the question as to the value of posterior review whenever it is available. *A priori* review is obviously a much less common occurrence than *a posteriori* review under Article 34.3.2 of the 1937 Constitution:

> Save as otherwise provided by this Article, the jurisdiction of the High Court shall extend to the question of the validity of any law having regard to the provisions of this Constitution, and no such question shall be raised (whether by pleading, argument or otherwise) in any Court

[163] *In re Article 26 and the School Attendance Bill 1942* [1943] IR 334.
[164] [1998] 4 IR 343.
[165] ie the decision in *Attorney General (SPUC) v Open Door Counselling* [1998] IR 593.
[166] Byrne and McCutcheon (2014) 498.
[167] Forde and Leonard (2013) 857.
[168] *In re Article 26 and the Offences Against the State (Amendment) Bill 1940* [1940] 1 IR 470 (see 109-10 above). The reference was made by President Douglas Hyde. This is the decision which led to the insertion of the 'one judgement' rule into the Constitution: see 119-21 above.
[169] See *The State (Quinn) v Ryan* [1965] IR 70 (on which see Mac Cormaic (2016) 91–3) and *Attorney General v Ryan's Car Hire Ltd* [1965] IR 642. In the former case Walsh J preferred to follow the approach to precedent adopted by the US Supreme Court over that adopted by the UK's House of Lords. Just a year later the House of Lords itself issued a Practice Statement making it clear that it would be willing to depart from earlier decisions 'when it appears right to do so': *Practice Statement (Judicial Precedent)* [1966] 1 WLR 1234.

established under this or any other article of this Constitution other than the High Court, the Court of Appeal or the Supreme Court.[170]

Posterior review arises in situations where the constitutionality of a legislative provision is called into question during the course of court proceedings. The context within which the constitutionality is considered will be taken into account by the reviewing judges in their reasoning and conclusions, implicitly if not explicitly.

Some countries, noticeably Germany since 1949 and South Africa since 1996, have established special constitutional courts to focus only on constitutional questions which arise in 'ordinary' litigation or which are specifically referred to them. Ireland deliberately rejected this route.[171] In France the main body to which the right to rule on the constitutionality of laws is allocated is the *Conseil constitutionnel*, but this is not an exclusive jurisdiction and many judgments have also been issued on constitutional matters by the country's top administrative law court (the *Conseil d'État*) and its top civil and criminal court (the *Cour de cassation*).[172] Since 2008, however, the position of the *Conseil constitutionnel* as France's main arbiter of constitutional issues has been further entrenched since it was then empowered to conduct not just prior but also posterior reviews: a litigant in any court proceedings can ask the judge for a review of the constitutionality of a law involved in the case and if certain conditions are met this request will be referred by the judge to the *Conseil d'État* or *Cour de cassation* for additional consideration of whether it should be further referred to the *Conseil constitutionnel*. Between 2008 and 2016 there were no fewer than 506 decisions issued by the *Conseil constitutionnel* on these so-called '*questions prioritaires de constitutionalité*', whereas between 1958 and 2008 there had been just 727 *a priori* claims.[173] Even allowing for France's proportionally larger population, this is a remarkable rate of posterior constitutional challenge.[174] In Ireland, unfortunately, no official statistics appear to be kept on the number of times a request is made in court for review of the constitutionality of an Act of the Oireachtas, let alone on the number of reviews which actually occur.[175]

More common than having a specialised court to deal with constitutional matters, especially in common law countries, is the allocation of judicial review to the ordinary courts, which must deal with them alongside all sorts of other legal matters. This is the model followed not just by Ireland but also by Australia, Canada, India, New Zealand, the United Kingdom and the USA. There are arguments to be made for and against the various ways in which legal systems distribute judicial responsibilities within the State.[176] The most persuasive in favour of a fully integrated approach is that it eliminates the possibility of difficult demarcation disputes arising between different top courts, while the most persuasive argument against such a system is that it can lead to long delays in obtaining a definitive decision on the constitutional point at issue. Delay can be a particular problem if any court in the land can vouchsafe an opinion on a law's constitutionality, as in the USA. It is to avoid such a plethora of opinions, and to speed up decision-making, that in Ireland only the High

[170] This is the successor to Art 65 of the 1922 Constitution. It needs to be read in conjunction with Arts 34.4.3, 34.4.4 and 34.4.5, which make further provision for the Supreme Court's jurisdiction to deal with questions about the validity of any law having regard to the provisions of the 1937 Constitution.

[171] Hogan (2011b); Coffey (2012).

[172] As the titles of these bodies indicate, two of them are not 'courts' at all, but 'councils'. But to all intents and purposes they operate as courts, in the same way that the Judicial Committee of the Privy Council functions as a court in the UK.

[173] *Conseil constitutionnel, Rapport d'activité 2016*, 23.

[174] See, especially on developments in 2016, Luquiens et al (2017).

[175] Byrne and McCutcheon (2014) 741 use the number of cases listed in successive editions of Kelly's *The Irish Constitution* as a proxy indicator of the popularity of constitutional review. See too Hogan, Kenny and Walsh (2015), referred to at 125 below.

[176] Dickson (2004). See too Chap 4 above, 45.

Court, the Court of Appeal and the Supreme Court are permitted to issue judicial opinions on a law's constitutionality.[177] In Article 26 reviews the Supreme Court has to issue its judgment within 60 days of the reference first being made. While there is no such time limit in cases of posterior reviews, the Supreme Court does tend to expedite its judgments in those cases as it is understandably conscious of their significance.

In 2015 research was published on the extent to which courts in Ireland had issued declarations of unconstitutionality under the 1937 Constitution. It revealed that up to August 2015 there had been 93 declarations, 58 of which had been issued by the Supreme Court.[178] Seven of the 58 Supreme Court declarations were in Article 26 cases, leaving 51 which were in the course of posterior reviews, beginning with *National Union Railwaymen v Sullivan* in 1946[179] and concluding with *McGowan v Labour Court* in 2013.[180] The researchers note that probably the greatest period of activity in this context was 1970 to 1975, but that the 1980s also 'witnessed a good deal of judicial activism'. There are few declarations based on violations of unenumerated rights, with more being based on the *ultra vires* doctrine and on the rights to equality and property.[181] Overall, the list is said to 'demonstrate a continued and resilient vibrancy in contemporary constitutional law'.[182] One can only agree with that, though it does not of course mean that human rights more generally are as well protected as they might be in Irish law.

Unenumerated Rights

It was in the fluoridation case of *Ryan v Attorney General*[183] that the concept of unenumerated rights was first accepted by the Irish Supreme Court, although that particular descriptor was not used in the judgment.[184] The Supreme Court famously upheld the personal right of a woman whowas complaining about the fluoridation of water. Speaking for the Court, Ó Dálaigh CJ accepted the view of Kenny J in the High Court that that the 'personal rights' mentioned in Article 40.3.1 of the Constitution are not exhausted by the enumeration of 'life, person, good name, and property rights' in Article 40.3.2 nor by the more detached treatment of specific rights later in the Article.[185] Understandably the Supreme Court refused to list all the rights which might properly fall within the category of 'personal rights', but it did accept the contention by Gladys Ryan's counsel, Seán MacBride, that the category should include the right to 'bodily integrity', something which the Attorney General also conceded by acknowledging the term 'a right to the integrity of the person'.[186] On the facts of the case the Court rejected Mrs Ryan's challenge to the law authorising fluoridation because any interference with bodily integrity was negligible (and beneficial to boot). Nor did it think that the law violated her family's rights which, under Article 41.1.1,

[177] Art 34.3.2. Cf the position under the UK's Human Rights Act 1998, where under s 4 only certain courts such as the High Court and the Supreme Court can issue declarations that a piece of primary legislation is incompatible with 'Convention rights'.

[178] Hogan, Kelly and Walsh (2015) 3. Of the remaining 35 declarations, 33 were issued by the High Court, one by the Court of Criminal Appeal and one by the Court of Appeal. There were also 14 declarations issued by the High Court which were later overturned by the Supreme Court: ibid, 30.

[179] [1947] IR 77.

[180] [2013] IESC 21, [2013] 2 ILRM 276.

[181] See Arts 15.2.1, 40.1 and 40.3.2/43 of the Constitution respectively.

[182] Hogan, Kelly and Walsh (2015) 29.

[183] [1965] IR 294; Mac Cormaic (2016) 84–90.

[184] The term 'unspecified rights' is also used: Hogan et al (2018); Forde and Leonard (2013). See too Clarke (2011a). Some use 'personal rights', which is the heading for Art 40 in the Constitution: Heuston (1976).

[185] [1965] IR 294 (decided 3 July 1964).

[186] [1965] IR 294, 335.

are supposedly 'inalienable and imprescriptible' and 'antecedent and superior to all positive law'.[187]

The term 'unenumerated' rights derives from the USA, where Article 9 of the Bill of Rights 1791 states: 'The enumeration in the Constitution, of certain rights, shall not be construed to deny or disparage others retained by the people.' A modern-day equivalent is section 11 of the UK's Human Rights Act 1998, which reads: 'A person's reliance on a Convention right does not restrict ... any other right or freedom conferred on him (*sic*) by or under any law having effect in any part of the United Kingdom.' In the USA the Supreme Court has used Article 9 to help justify its support for a wide number of rights not explicitly mentioned in the US Constitution. One of the first examples was the right not to have the State interfere with a married couple's right to plan how many children they would like to have. This was in *Griswold v Connecticut*,[188] in 1965. When the issue of bans on contraceptives arose before the Irish Supreme Court in 1973 both Henchy and Griffin JJ relied upon *Griswold v Connecticut* to justify their decision in favour of the claimant;[189] Walsh J noted that the case had been cited by counsel but he chose not to rely upon it because he felt that the reasons he had already given for holding in favour of the claimant did not need such external support.[190] FitzGerald CJ, who dissented, distinguished *Griswold v Connecticut* on the somewhat specious basis that the Connecticut statute criminalised the use of contraceptives whereas the Irish statute criminalised only their importation.[191]

Books on Irish constitutional law or the Irish legal system usually list the unenumerated rights that have so far been recognised by the High Court or the Supreme Court.[192] Those explicitly accepted by the Supreme Court, either directly or through confirming in a later case the position adopted by the High Court in an earlier case, are the following, listed in chronological order of recognition: the right to bodily integrity, the right to travel within the State and the right to marry (1965),[193] the right to access the courts (1966),[194] the right of an unmarried mother in relation to her child (1966),[195] the right to fairness in criminal procedures (1971),[196] the right to earn a livelihood (1973),[197] the right to marital privacy (1974),[198] the right to legal representation if charged with a criminal offence (1976),[199] the right to beget children (1985),[200] the rights of children (1989),[201] the right to dignity in the

[187] It also rejected Mrs Ryan's claim that the fluoridation law violated her right as a parent, under Art 42 of the Constitution, to provide for the physical education of her children.

[188] 381 US 479 (1965).

[189] *McGee v Attorney General* [1974] 1 IR 284, 328 and 335.

[190] Ibid, 319.

[191] Ibid, 304.

[192] See eg Byrne and McCutcheon (2014) 728–9; Hogan et al (2018) 1683-1729 1413–46; Casey (2000) 394–433. See too CRG (1996) 246.

[193] *Ryan v Attorney General*, n 183 above.

[194] *Macauley v Minister for Posts and Telegraphs* [1966] IR 345, where Kenny J held in the High Court that it was unconstitutional to require legal proceedings brought against State bodies to be based on the consent of the Attorney General. This position was approved by the Supreme Court in *Byrne v Ireland* [1972] 1 IR 241. Walsh J described this as 'the fundamental political right of the citizen': Walsh (1988a) 88.

[195] *The State (Nicolaou) v An Bord Uchtála* [1966] IR 567; see too *G v An Bord Uchtála* [1980] IR 32 and Chap 10 below, 220-1 and 223.

[196] *In re Haughey* [1971] IR 217; see Chap 7 below, 141-2. See too *Garvey v Ireland* [1980] IR 75, where the Supreme Court held that the government's removal of Edmund Garvey from the post of Commissioner of the Garda Síochána was void because he had not been informed of the reason for his removal or given an opportunity to make representations on the matter.

[197] *Murphy v Stewart* [1973] IR 97, where Walsh J, with whom Ó Dálaigh CJ, Budd, FitzGerald and Butler JJ agreed, held that Mr Murphy had a constitutional right to join a trade union of his choice but that on the facts this right had not been breached because the reason he could not join the ITGWU was that his current union would not allow him to give up his membership of that union. With respect, this reasoning seems bizarre.

[198] *McGee v Attorney General* [1974] 1 IR 284; see Chap 10 below, 232-4.

[199] *The State (Healy) v Donoghue* [1976] IR 325; see 129-30 below.

[200] *Murray v Ireland* [1991] ILRM 465. Costello J's High Court decision in 1985 was not affirmed by the Supreme Court until 1991 but no reason was supplied as to why such a delay occurred. Both courts recognised the right of a prisoner to beget children but held that it would be too disruptive in this case to permit a conjugal visit.

[201] *In re Article 26 and the Adoption (No 2) Bill 1987* [1989] IR 656; see Chap 10 below, 221-2.

context of refusing medical treatment (1995)[202] and the right to know the identity of one's natural mother (1998).[203] Instances of unenumerated rights which the Supreme Court has refused to recognise include the right not to be criminalised for exercising one's homosexuality,[204] the right not to have to prove that one has suffered harm when there has been an environmental nuisance,[205] the right not to be secretly observed while moving around public streets[206] and the right not to have the source of one's private finances investigated.[207] Moreover, the Court has been keen to point out that, like most of the specified constitutional rights, unspecified ones cannot be considered to be absolute.

The High Court has also recognised some unenumerated rights which the Supreme Court has not yet explicitly confirmed or denied. These are: the right not to be ill-treated or to have one's health endangered (1976),[208] the right to travel outside the State (1979),[209] the right to communicate with others (1984),[210] the right to individual privacy (1987),[211] the rights to an independent domicile and to maintenance (1988 and 1989)[212] and, most recently, the right to environmental protection (2017).[213]

As only two unenumerated rights have been expressly endorsed by the Supreme Court since 1989, and none since 1998, it may be tempting to deduce that the concept is past its sell-by date. But that would be premature. While distinguished authors have intimated extra-judicially that considerable caution should be exercised by courts before they create any additional unenumerated rights,[214] and Keane CJ said as much on two occasions, in *O'T v B*[215] and *TD v Minister for Education*,[216] no-one has suggested that the era of judicial activism in this context is, or should be, over. At the same time, no Supreme Court judge has yet delineated the appropriate criteria to be applied when trying to identify an unenumerated constitutional right in the future, and nor has any non-judicial constitutional expert for that matter. Keane CJ probably represented the majority judicial view (as

[202] *Re a Ward of Court (No 2)* [1996] 2 IR 79. Assuring the dignity of the individual is one of the goals mentioned in the Preamble to the 1937 Constitution.

[203] *O'T v B* [1998] 2 IR 321; Keane J dissented; see Chap 10 below, 225.

[204] *Norris v Attorney General* [1984] IR 36; see Chap 12 below, 275-8.

[205] *Hanrahan v Merck Sharp and Dohme* [1988] ILRM 629.

[206] *Kane v Governor of Mountjoy Prison* [1988] IR 757.

[207] *Haughey v Moriarty* [1999] 3 IR 1, a case taken by Charles Haughey and members of his family challenging resolutions by the Oireachtas to set up a public inquiry into his affairs; the Supreme Court distinguished the High Court case of *Kennedy v Ireland*, n 211 below, and Hamilton CJ cited (at para 192) the words of Lynch J in the Supreme Court case of *National Irish Bank Ltd v RTE* (unreported, 20 March 1988): 'there is also a public interest in defeating wrong doing and where the publication of confidential information may be of assistance in defeating wrong doing then the public interest in such publication may outweigh the public interest in the maintenance of confidentiality'.

[208] *The State (C) v Frawley* [1976] IR 365 (Finlay P). The case was brought by a prisoner who had a sociopathic personality disorder and was restrained while in prison for his own protection; he lost on the facts and although an appeal was brought to the Supreme Court it was later struck out with his consent.

[209] *The State (M) v Attorney General* [1979] IR 73 (Finlay P).

[210] *Attorney General v Paperlink Ltd* [1984] ILRM 343. Here Costello J held that individuals have the personal constitutional right under Art 40.3.1 to communicate with others, but on the facts of the case this right had not been violated by provisions of the Post Office Act 1908 conferring a monopoly on the Postmaster General to run postal services.

[211] *Kennedy v Ireland* [1987] IR 587 (Hamilton P). IR£50,000 was awarded to three political journalists whose phones had been illegally tapped, an incident leading to the resignation of Charles Haughey as Taoiseach. Geraldine Kennedy later became a Progressive Democrat TD (1987–89) and the first female editor of the *Irish Times* (2002–11).

[212] *CM v TM (No 2)* [1990] 2 IR 52 and [1991] ILRM 268. Barr J held that Mrs Murray's right to maintenance under an Irish court order made before her husband obtained a decree absolute of divorce in England was not dependent on the subsistence of the marriage.

[213] Per Barrett J in *Merriman v Fingal County Council* [2017] IEHC 695.

[214] eg Hogan (1990–92); McCarthy (1992) 179–82.

[215] n 203 above.

[216] [2001] 4 IR 259, paras 64–6. See too his extra-judicial thoughts at Keane (2004) 15–18. Also O'Mahony (2005).

we shall see in the next section) when he said in 2001 that 'I would have the gravest doubts as to whether the courts at any stage should assume the function of declaring what are today frequently described as "socio-economic rights" to be unenumerated rights guaranteed by Article 40'.[217] In 1996 the Constitutional Review Group proposed that Article 40.3.1 of the Constitution should be amended so as to provide a comprehensive list of fundamental rights which 'should confine further recognition of fundamental rights by the courts to those necessarily implicit in the rights expressly listed',[218] but this idea has been resisted and is unlikely to be implemented today.[219]

Compared with other common law supreme courts the Irish court has performed moderately in the field of constitutional law.[220] It has rightly eschewed the exceptional, and to some extent counter-productive, activism of the Supreme Courts of India[221] and Israel,[222] but it has been more inventive than either the High Court of Australia[223] or the apex courts in New Zealand.[224] For a while, in the 1960s and 1970s, it was ahead of the constitutionalism displayed by the Supreme Court of Canada, but since those decades the latter has overtaken the Irish Supreme Court as far as its dynamism and internationalism are concerned.[225] The enactment of the national Charter of Rights and Freedoms in 1982 was the trigger which allowed the Canadian Court to spread its wings and aspire to the heights of the US Supreme Court, which, for all its antipathy to positions adopted by supreme courts in other countries or by international courts, must still rank as the world's foremost national court promoting constitutionalism as a concept. In the United Kingdom, where there is no single constitutional document to interpret, the House of Lords and its successor the Supreme Court have developed their constitutional jurisprudence only spasmodically, most noticeably in the recent decision that only Parliament and not the government had the power to trigger the process by which the United Kingdom is leaving the European Union.[226] While those courts have been very prolific in the field of human rights law, following the enactment of the Human Rights Act 1998,[227] there are no real signs that a human rights culture has yet been deeply embedded into the common law. This means that if the Human Rights Act were to be repealed and not replaced by something as comprehensive in its protection, the common law may not be adequate to meet the challenge of protecting fundamental rights in the years thereafter.

Expenditure of Public Money and Socio-Economic Rights

Not infrequently it comes to light during a case, as it did in *In re Article 26 and the Health (Amendment) (No 2) Bill 2004*,[228] that one consequence of the court deciding it a certain way will be that large sums of money will need to be spent (or not recovered). When the money in question is public money, questions are often asked about the legitimacy of judges taking financial decisions, given that it is generally the function of *elected* representatives to decide how public funds should be distributed.[229] Not all demands on the public purse can be met and part of the difficult job of politicians, especially those in government, is to take the hard decisions as to what should be funded and what should not. If people do not like those decisions they can seek further public dialogue with the politicians and express

[217] Ibid, 166. [218] CRG (1996) 259. [219] Kelly (1966a); Parker (1997).
[220] For a comparison with a civil law country (Germany) see Von Prondzynski (1978–80).
[221] Iyer (2007). [222] Salzberger (2007). [223] Wheeler and Williams (2007).
[224] Harris (2007). [225] Roach (2007); Schertzer (2016).
[226] *R (Miller) v Secretary of State for Exiting the EU* [2017] UKSC 5, [2018] AC 61.
[227] Dickson (2013). [228] [2005] IESC 7, [2005] 1 IR 105. [229] Phelan (1994).

their disapproval by voting for alternative candidates at the next election. If judges take distributive decisions there is no easy way for people to hold them to account. Judges do not engage in public dialogues and if they were to do so there could well be a diminution of public respect for their office.

One context in which public expenditure often comes before the courts is that of legal aid. Compared to other common law jurisdictions Ireland was relatively slow to establish any kind of legal aid system: it was only when the Oireachtas passed the Criminal Justice (Legal Aid) Act 1962 that it became available even in the criminal sphere.[230] In *The State (Healy) v Donoghue* the question arose as to what kind of 'right', if any, was bestowed by this legislation.[231] The case involved two young men, one aged 16 and the other 18, who had been convicted of offences such as breaking and entering, stealing and causing malicious damage. One of the 18-year-old's offences was dealt with without him having any legal representation whatsoever; for the other offences the offenders were granted legal aid at the sentencing stage but no solicitor turned up and they were each given 12 months' detention. Confirming in part the decision of Gannon J in the High Court, the Supreme Court held that none of the convictions could stand. O'Higgins CJ cited the words of Walsh J in *McGee v Attorney General*,[232] where he had drawn upon the reference in the Constitution's Preamble to 'seeking to promote the common good, with due observation of prudence, justice and charity'. The Chief Justice then said that when Article 38.1 of the Constitution provides that '[n]o person shall be tried on any criminal charge save in due course of law' it meant that it was:

> mandatory that every criminal trial shall be conducted in accordance with the concept of justice, that the procedures applied shall be fair, and that the person accused will be afforded every opportunity to defend himself. If this were not so, the dignity of the individual would be ignored and the State would have failed to vindicate his personal rights.[233]

To support his conclusion that if a person cannot afford to pay for his or her defence the State should provide it, O'Higgins CJ cited not just the decision of the US Supreme Court in *Gideon v Wainwright*[234] but also Article 6(3)(c) of the European Convention on Human Rights, one of the earliest references to that Convention by a judge of the Irish Supreme Court.[235] When ratifying that Convention the Irish government had entered a reservation relating to this paragraph in Article 6, saying that it did not interpret it 'as requiring the provision of free legal assistance to any wider extent than is now provided in Ireland'. But the Chief Justice effectively held that domestic Irish law had moved on since then because the Criminal Justice (Legal Aid) Act 1962 recognised the fundamental right guaranteed by Article 6(3)(c). The Chief's colleagues on the Court adopted his reasoning,[236] agreeing in particular that a right to apply for legal aid was worthless unless the court trying an individual was not also under a positive obligation to make sure that the accused knew that he or she had that right.[237]

[230] Prior to then, under the common law, only persons charged with capital murder were assigned legal representation if none existed.

[231] [1976] IR 325; Mac Cormaic (2016) 194–6.

[232] [1974] IR 284, 319.

[233] [1976] IR 325, 349.

[234] 372 US 335 (1963).

[235] For the potential role of the ECHR in protecting socio-economic rights see Thornton (2014).

[236] Henchy, Griffin and Kenny JJ wrote supportive judgments; Parke J merely concurred with his brethren.

[237] The Supreme Court has subsequently held that it is not a breach of constitutional rights for a police officer to ask questions of a detained person before a legal adviser arrives at the place of detention or after the adviser's visit is over: *The People (DPP) v Buck* [2002] 2 IR 268; Ryan (2003). But the trial judge retains a discretion to exclude from the evidence any answers given to such questions.

While nothing was said in *Healy* about the cost of making legal aid available in such cases, it must have been obvious to the judges that the cost would be substantial. The Supreme Court felt confident in mandating such expenditure because it thought it had no option but to do so. As O'Higgins CJ put it: 'No court under the Constitution has jurisdiction to act contrary to justice.'[238] Sadly, this resort to 'justice' as a justification for the protection of rights incurring public expenditure has not been made in many other contexts. In *Cox v Ireland*,[239] where the Supreme Court upheld a decision by Barr J in the High Court that section 34 of the Offences Against the State Act 1939 was unconstitutional in that it disqualified any person convicted by the Special Criminal Court of a scheduled offence from occupying any public sector job for a period of seven years, it did not refer to the values mentioned in the Constitution's Preamble. Instead it focused on the fact that the ban imposed was 'impermissibly wide and indiscriminate' in its failure to protect constitutional rights, namely the unenumerated right to earn a living and the property rights protected by Article 43 of the Constitution. The Supreme Court was particularly unhappy at the fact that the ban applied regardless of the seriousness of the offence of which the person affected had been convicted. The fact that allocation of public money was involved was not alluded to, perhaps because if the money in question was not going to be spent on this particular claimant it would have been spent on someone else who had not been convicted of a scheduled offence, but the case is still important for the way it highlights the determination of the Supreme Court to protect an important socio-economic right.

The expenditure point was much more evident in the slightly earlier case of *O'Reilly v Limerick Corporation*,[240] where a claim was made by members of the Traveller community that the housing conditions which they had to endure, especially the lack of water and sanitary services, amounted to a breach of their constitutional rights for which they should be compensated. In the High Court, Costello J rejected this claim, his primary reason being that he could not agree that there was a constitutional right of the kind suggested, but he went on to address the appropriateness of a claim for damages if the claim was valid. The questions he framed for himself were these:

> [C]an the courts with constitutional propriety adjudicate on an allegation that the organs of Government responsible for the distribution of the nation's wealth have improperly exercised their powers? Or would such an adjudication be an infringement by the courts of the role which the Constitution has conferred on them?[241]

The unequivocal answer he supplied to these two questions were 'no' and 'yes' respectively. He relied specifically on the traditional distinction between distributive justice (a matter for elected politicians) and commutative justice (a matter for judges). But one could argue that the learned judge was too ready to adopt a binary approach to this issue. He might have acknowledged, for example, that when exercising their judicial review jurisdiction judges do regularly 'supervise' government decisions which have public expenditure implications, even if the reviews are supposedly based on alleged procedural defects rather than on substantive wrongdoing.[242] He might also have noted that judges regularly assess what amount of damages should be awarded to someone who succeeds in convincing a court that his or her constitutional rights have been violated. To Costello J's concern that awarding compensation to members of the Traveller community would mean that other categories of claimants, such as homeless or deprived young people, could also claim

[238] [1976] IR 325, 348.
[239] [1992] 2 IR 503 (Finlay CJ, Hederman, McCarthy, O'Flaherty and Egan JJ).
[240] [1989] ILRM 181.
[241] Ibid, 193.
[242] See, eg, Chap 8 below, 176-9.

compensation,[243] the answer could have been given that limits can lawfully be imposed on the extent of all retrospective claims and that in each kind of claim the issue of causation would still need to be satisfied.

No appeal was taken to the Supreme Court against Costello J's decision, but his approach was, unfortunately, approved by that Court in *MhicMathúna v Attorney General*,[244] a case on the fairness of the taxation system. The appellants argued that the withdrawal from married couples of a tax free allowance relating to dependent children amounted to discriminatory treatment: people were not being dealt with equally before the law, in breach of Article 40.1 of the Constitution, and the State was failing to abide by its duty under Article 41 to ensure that mothers 'shall not be obliged by economic necessity to engage in labour to the neglect of their duties in the home'. Upholding the judgment of Costello J in the court below, the Supreme Court said that judges could consider whether a piece of legislation or the collection or expenditure of money adversely affected any constitutional rights, obligations or guarantees, but they could not assess the effectiveness or fairness of the policy choices represented by such legislation.[245] More particularly, it said that as there were 'abundant grounds for distinguishing between the needs and requirements of single parents and those of married parents living together and rearing a family together' the courts could not interfere 'by seeking to assess what the extent of the disparity should be'.[246]

Again, this could be seen as a dereliction of duty on the part of the Supreme Court: it should surely have asked itself whether the discrimination in question was necessary and proportionate? In his alternative feminist judgment for this case,[247] Liam Thornton suggests that in some situations it would be appropriate for judges to recognise a right to a minimal level of social support, but he accepts that judges should not fly in the face of the clear wording of the Constitution. Commenting on Thornton's hypothetical judgment Colm O'Cinneide points out that he could have gone further in applying a feminist approach to the need for a constitutional right to an adequate standard of income, though he himself does not explain how this would have been possible within the current approach to the separation of powers doctrine in Ireland (or, one might add, in most other common law jurisdictions).[248] Doing so would require a deeper questioning of the gendered nature of some of the foundations of constitutional interpretation, such as the assumption that a legislature, composed overwhelmingly of men, should not be second-guessed or even challenged by a court, where the gender balance may be better and/or where the mandate to find just and fair solutions to problems is more obvious.

Constitutional provisions and the *Sinnott* and *TD* cases

The Irish Constitution does expressly protect some rights which could be classified as social or economic rights, traditionally the category of rights which require positive action on the part of the State and therefore the expenditure of public money, although the guaranteeing of a fair criminal justice system, for example, also costs considerable sums. As just noted, Article 41.2.2 provides to this day that 'the State shall endeavour ... to ensure that mothers shall not be obliged by economic necessity to engage in labour to the neglect of their duties

[243] [1989] ILRM 181, 193. [244] [1995] 1 IR 484.

[245] Ibid, 496 (per Finlay CJ, for the Court, citing O'Higgins CJ in *Madigan v Attorney General* [1986] ILRM 136, 159).

[246] Ibid, 499.

[247] 'Commentary on *MhicMathúna v Attorney General*' in Enright, McCandless and O'Donoghue (2017), Chap 7, 147–56.

[248] Ibid, 146.

in the home'.[249] Article 42.4 adds that '[t]he State shall provide for free primary education and shall endeavour to supplement and give reasonable aid to private and corporate educational initiative and, when the public good requires it, provide other educational facilities or institutions'. And by Article 43.1.2 the State 'guarantees to pass no law attempting to abolish the right of private ownership or the general right to transfer, bequeath, and inherit property'. Then, in Article 45, the Constitution sets out 'principles of social policy … intended for the general guidance of the Oireachtas … [and not] cognisable by any Court under any of the provisions of this Constitution'. In its elaboration of those principles the Article refers to the values mentioned in the Preamble: the State must 'strive to promote the welfare of the whole people by securing and protecting as effectively as it may a social order in which *justice and charity* shall inform all the institutions of the national life' and it must also direct its policy towards securing that 'the ownership and control of the material resources of the community may be so distributed amongst private individuals and the various classes as best to subserve the *common good*'.[250]

The Supreme Court has been very restrained in its interpretation of all of these Articles.[251] In particular it has failed to develop the right to education mentioned in Article 42.4 and has steered clear of taking any cognisance of the directive principles in Article 45. The Court's main justification for its stance is that it is no part of the judicial function to allocate public expenditure. The main exponent of this philosophy was Adrian Hardiman, who served on the Supreme Court from 2000 until his sudden death in 2016. In two particular cases, *Sinnott v Minister for Education*[252] and *TD v Minister for Education*,[253] Hardiman J indicated quite stridently his staunch opposition to judicial interventionism of this sort. In *Sinnott*, where the claim concerned the right to education of a 23-year-old man who had autism, the Supreme Court overturned the decision of Barr J[254] and held (by five to two[255]) that the right to education guaranteed by Article 42.4 of the Constitution could be claimed only by those under the age of 18. Jamie Sinnott was therefore entitled only to a declaration that he had been deprived of that right while he was under 18 and no mandatory injunction was issued directing the State to provide a certain form of education thereafter. However, because the State did not appeal the award of damages to Jamie Sinnott, he was allowed to keep the sum already awarded to him. It is important to recall, also, that there was no appeal from the decision of Kelly J in the *TD* case that children in need of secure accommodation had a constitutional right to such accommodation. Only Keane CJ, *obiter*, expressly agreed with the views expressed by Hardiman J on the role of courts in this field[256] and those views were focused on the proposed mandatory injunction which in an earlier case O'Hanlon J had suggested was available to be issued.[257] Hardiman J took a swipe at the theory of justice proposed by the political philosopher John Rawls, whereby judges should develop and apply a body of principles 'to the virtual exclusion or marginalisation of the political process': the judge thought that if judges became involved in designing the details

[249] In July 2018 the Irish government announced that there would be a referendum on whether Art 41.2 should be deleted from the Constitution.This was to have occurred in the autumn of 2018 but it was postponed because the government had not decided whether to replace the section with some other provision: Colin Gleeson, 'Referendum on "sexist" reference to women's place in the home postponed', *Irish Times*, 5 September 2018.

[250] Arts 45.1 and 45.2(ii) (emphasis added).

[251] For an excellent review of the case law see Thornton (2015).

[252] [2001] 2 IR 545. The case also involved a claim by Jamie Sinnott's mother, but that is not discussed here. See too Quinlivan and Keys (2002); Ryan (2002); Mac Cormaic (2016) 337–43.

[253] [2001] 4 IR 259.

[254] Barr J had awarded Mr Sinnott £222,500 in compensation.

[255] Denham, Murray, Hardiman, Geoghegan and Fennelly JJ; Keane CJ and Murphy J dissenting in part. The judgments extend to 54,000 words.

[256] [2001] 2 IR 545, 640.

[257] In *O'Donoghue v Minister for Health* [1996] 2 IR 20 (High Court).

of policy or in ranking some areas of policy as more important than others, this would take them 'beyond their appointed role'.[258] Of the seven judges involved in the *Sinnott* case, only Denham J suggested that in 'a rare and exceptional case' the courts might feel obliged to make a mandatory order against the State in order to protect constitutional rights.[259] This was prophetic, for within six months she was faced with the very kind of case where she thought such an injunction should be issued.

This was *TD v Minister for Education*[260] and Denham J was the sole dissenting judge. In the High Court, Kelly J had issued an injunction requiring the State to provide disadvantaged children with appropriate accommodation and treatment in special care units. This time only five judges sat to hear the appeal but the majority was as opposed to intervening on expenditure issues as the Court had been in *Sinnott*. Keane CJ again objected to the issuing of an injunction, arguing that it would breach the separation of powers mandated by the Constitution.[261] He stressed that this was not a case where there was a lack of resources available to the State: the question was how those resources should be best allocated, and that was a matter for the government, not the courts.[262] Murphy J agreed with the Chief Justice, confirming that the Constitution had not conferred any socio-economic rights except the right to education (he did not mention the right to property); in this case he did not think that the right to education should be interpreted so broadly as to justify the injunction issued by the High Court.[263] Murray J followed suit in that he thought the power of judicial review was just that—a power to review rather than to exercise executive or legislative power.[264] Hardiman J expanded on what he had said in *Sinnott*, his judgment extending to almost 17,000 words. He again praised what Costello J had said in *O'Reilly v Limerick Corporation* and he cited several US Supreme Court decisions on the importance of the separation of powers doctrine.[265] It was left to Denham J to put a spanner in the works. For her, the *O'Reilly* case was distinguishable on the ground that no breach of any constitutional right had been identified there whereas in the case before her it had been.[266] Likewise, *Sinnott* was not binding because in that case '[n]o decision fell to be made on the issue of a mandatory order'.[267]

Alternative approaches[268]

On the basis of stark assertions by so many senior judges that if the Supreme Court were to order the government to spend moneys in certain ways it would be a breach of the separation of powers principle enshrined in the Constitution, it is daunting to raise counter-arguments. And yet, the assertions may seem unassailable only because the question being answered is not the one that needs to be asked. As posed, it sets up a false duality. It suggests that a pot of money needs to be spent and that either the executive or the courts should decide how to spend it. There is, of course, an easily conceivable *via media* which would allow the executive to take the spending decisions but permit the courts some reviewing power as to the reasonableness, equitableness and/or proportionality of those decisions. That, in essence, was the approach adopted by the Supreme Court in the most recent of the Article 26 references analysed above, *In re Article 26 and the Health (Amendment) (No 2) Bill 2004*.[269] There, it will be recalled, the Court was well aware that the cost to the public

[258] [2001] 2 IR 545, 710–1. [259] Ibid, 656.
[260] [2001] 4 IR 259; Kieran (2004); Mac Cormaic (2016) 343–6. [261] Ibid, 287. [262] Ibid, 288.
[263] Ibid, 316–22. [264] Ibid, 333. [265] Ibid, 357–64 and 373–4. [266] Ibid, 304–6.
[267] Ibid, 306. [268] See too McDermott (2000a); O'Mahony (2002), (2005) and (2006).
[269] [2005] IESC 7, [2005] 1 IR 105 (Murray CJ, Denham, McGuinness, Hardiman, Geoghegan, Fennelly and McCracken JJ).

purse of deciding the case the way it did would be an estimated €500 million. Ironically the Court reached this conclusion by distinguishing *Sinnott*, apparently on the basis that the right being interpreted in that case was a constitutional right while in the Article 26 case it was a statutory right.[270] It seems strange that the latter variety of right is deemed worthy of greater protection, at least in terms of judicial preparedness to see expenditure incurred on helping the victims of its breach. Unfortunately, due to the one judgment rule, we do not know whether any of the seven judges who sat in the *Health (Amendment) Bill* case disagreed with the outcome: Murray CJ and Hardiman J, like Denham J, sat in both that case and *Sinnott* (and *TD*).

With respect, this *via media* seems to be what the UK Supreme Court now adopts when faced with difficulties over spending decisions. It too has avoided placing itself in the shoes of elected politicians serving in government, but it has not shied away from measuring the legality of spending decisions made by those politicians against a variety of review criteria which allow it to reassure the public that fundamental principles of (to cite the Irish Constitution's Preamble), 'justice, charity and the common good' are being adhered to. By way of illustration as to how the law on equality has been applied by the UK Supreme Court in this context, four recent examples can be cited.

First, in *Patmalniece v Secretary of State for Work and Pensions*[271] the Court considered whether national rules on entitlement to State pension credit were compatible with EU law, which prohibits discrimination between nationals of different Member States; by four to one the Court held that the discrimination was justified because it was a proportionate response to the legitimate aim of protecting the UK public purse, a justification that was independent of the claimant's nationality. Second, in *Humphreys v Commissioners for Her Majesty's Revenue and Customs*[272] a challenge was raised against the rules on allocation of child tax credit on the basis that they were discriminatory because the credit was always payable to the child's mother; again, although this time unanimously, the UK Court found that there was discrimination but it was justifiable. Third, in *R (Rotherham Metropolitan Borough Council) v Secretary of State for Business, Innovation and Skills*[273] the UK Court held, by four to three, that there was no improper discrimination in the way EU Structural Funds were allocated by the UK government as between regions in England and the regions of Scotland and Northern Ireland. Fourth, in *R (SG) v Secretary of State for Work and Pensions*[274] the UK Supreme Court examined the limit to benefits introduced by the Benefit Cap (Housing Benefit) Regulations 2012, made under the Welfare Reform Act 2012; the issue was whether the cap was unlawfully discriminatory against women because of its greater impact on lone parents; once more, this time by three to two, the Court held the differential impact was justifiable under both domestic law and European Convention law.

These UK cases illustrate how the Irish Supreme Court might have chosen to develop its analysis of the expenditure of public money in cases raising putative socio-economic rights. While it is true that in all four cases the challenge to the government decision was rejected, in three of them the Court was split, and on two occasions very narrowly. The point is that the UK Supreme Court felt able to adjudicate on the rights in question precisely because it was being asked to consider whether the way they were being protected was unlawfully discriminatory. As O'Connell has validly observed, this is how the Irish Supreme Court might profitably proceed in this field.[275] It is an option which the Irish Human Rights

[270] [2005] 1 IR 105, 166. [271] [2011] UKSC 11, [2011] 1 WLR 783.

[272] [2012] UKSC 18, [2012] 1 WLR 1545. [273] [2015] UKSC 6, [2015] 3 All ER 1.

[274] [2015] UKSC 16, [2016] 1 WLR 1449.

[275] O'Connell (2008) esp 336–46, where he draws upon case-law from South Africa, Canada and the European Court of Human Rights.

Commission considered in a valuable discussion document published in 2005.[276] An alternative and depressing view, propounded by Murray, is that the forces ranged against a more judge-friendly approach to the protection of collective socio-economic rights in Ireland are global in nature and are so powerful that it is unlikely that Irish institutions will ever be able to bring about greater social justice.[277] That is a counsel of despair.

The UK Supreme Court, and its predecessor the Appellate Committee of the House of Lords, has also made much more use of its traditional judicial review powers in this context than its Irish counterpart. In *R v Gloucestershire County Council, ex parte Barry*[278] the House of Lords ruled that a local authority, in assessing whether to make arrangements to meet the need of a disabled person, could take into account the resources available to it. This decision was approved (though distinguished) in *R v East Sussex County Council, ex parte Tandy*,[279] where a local education authority was held to be entitled to take account of available resources when deciding in what way 'suitable education' should be provided to a girl suffering from chronic fatigue syndrome; the judges admitted that the availability of resources should not be taken into account when defining 'suitable education' in the first place. And in *R (KM) v Cambridgeshire County Council*[280] the UK Supreme Court held that the way a local authority had allocated resources to a severely disabled man was not unlawful on the ground of irrationality. Finally, in *R (N) v London Borough of Newham*[281] the UK Court rejected appeals brought by two homeless persons who had been allocated temporary housing: their right to a 'home' under Article 8 of the ECHR had not been violated because recovery of possession of the homes by the Councils was proportionate, as housing authorities had limited resources to provide accommodation to those who claimed to be homeless and in priority need.

As with the discrimination cases mentioned earlier, these four decisions all resulted in the lack of available public money being viewed as a relevant factor to be taken into account by judges when justifying the alleged denial of a socio-economic right, but at least they recognise that socio-economic rights are to that extent justiciable. If judges were to accord such rights the status of 'fundamental rights', which UK judges have done when considering the impact of excessive court fees on the right of access to justice in both *R v Lord Chancellor, ex parte Witham*[282] and *R (Unison) v Lord Chancellor*,[283] there is every possibility that the cost to the public purse could be overridden by the importance of guaranteeing the right in question.[284] Such was the outcome in *In re Article 26 and the Health (Amendment) (No 2) Bill 2004*: the fact that Ireland's economy was apparently strong enough at that time to take a €500 million hit contributed to the Supreme Court's willingness to uphold the patients' rights to reimbursement of the fees they had paid.[285] Even if the Supreme Court does not follow the UK line there is still room for a more expansive approach to be adopted

[276] IHRC (2005) 105–7.

[277] Murray (2016) Chap 4. He says (at 185): 'the emergent socio-economic rights discourses represented a politically determined, ideological containment of shared values. Globally, there remains a strong coherence between the emergence of neoliberalism and the globalisation of human rights discourse'.

[278] [1997] AC 584. [279] [1998] AC 714. [280] [2012] UKSC 23, [2012] 3 All ER 1218.

[281] [2014] UKSC 62, [2015] AC 1259.

[282] [1998] QB 575. Here the Divisional Court declared *ultra vires* a regulation on legal aid which had the effect of denying access to justice to people on income support.

[283] [2017] UKSC 51, [2017] 3 WLR 409. Here the UK Supreme Court declared that fees imposed on applicants who bring claims to employment tribunals were unlawful under the common law, under the Equality Act 2010 and under EU law.

[284] See too the dicta in *R (Limbuela) v Secretary of State for the Home Dept* [2005] UKHL 66, [2006] 1 AC 396, [8] in connection with the right of destitute people not to be subjected to inhuman or degrading treatment; Dickson (2013) 156–8.

[285] See 118-9 above.

regarding socio-economic rights. As Gerry Whyte has convincingly argued, 'judicial enforcement of [socio-economic] rights is both constitutionally and democratically legitimate'; he maintains that an activist role for the courts would 'fit with the constitutional text' and 'would promote the development of deliberative democracy in our society requiring the political system to take account of the needs of marginalised groups who otherwise tend to be ignored.'[286] This is also the view of David Langwallner, who shows that a refusal even to recognise that social and economic rights are justiciable is a failure to fully vindicate the rights to life and to freedom from inhumane and degrading treatment.[287] It seems, however, that the prevailing judicial view in Ireland is to the contrary.[288] The Supreme Court is more likely to adopt the conclusion reached by Gerard Hogan when he examined this thorny issue in 2001: 'judicial prudence (if nothing else) dictates that the role of the courts in protecting these new emerging socio-economic rights (ranging from education to health care) must be a strictly limited one, confined to the most exceptional of cases and circumstances'.[289]

The Influence of 'Natural Law'

No discussion of the way in which the Irish Supreme Court has developed its constitutional jurisprudence would be complete without some reference to the use it has made, at times, of the theory of natural law.[290] Put crudely, this is the idea that the main source of law should be morality, or what is good for humanity. It posits that every person has natural rights which exist prior to, and take precedence over, the positive rights conferred on every person by law. Some supporters of this approach go on to locate the authority for this morality in a divinity or, in the case of utilitarians, in the concept of 'the common good'. The hold that this approach has had on law-making in Ireland since the days of independence in 1922 has been surprisingly strong and there seem to be several law teachers who are still wedded to it.[291] In the Supreme Court it first surfaced in the otherwise highly commendable judgment of Kennedy CJ in *The State (Ryan) v Lennon*,[292] but it has reappeared in many subsequent judgments. This is partly because the word 'natural' appears in five different Articles of the 1937 Constitution, in the phrases 'natural resources',[293] 'natural ... unit group of society' (referring to the family),[294] 'natural educator of the child' (referring again to the family),[295] 'natural ... rights of all children'[296] and 'the natural right ... to the private ownership of external goods'.[297] It is also because, once the concept of unenumerated rights was accepted by the Supreme Court in the fluoridation case of *Ryan v Attorney General*,[298] some commentators assumed that unenumerated rights were necessarily a manifestation of natural rights and not just rights that could be inferred from the text of the Constitution.

[286] Whyte (2006) 25; he was responding to Adrian Hardiman's extra-judicial defence of his approach to socio-economic rights (2004). See too Whyte (2012), where he focuses on the concept of 'disability rights'.
[287] Langwallner (2008) 262–70.
[288] See eg *NHV v Minister for Justice and Equality* [2017] IESC 35; Chap 10 below, 228-9.
[289] Hogan (2001b) 198.
[290] See generally Hogan et al (2018) 1461-72; Kavanagh (2012); O'Connor, Kelly and McSwiney (2012); Doyle (2009); De Blácam (1997); Whyte (1996); Humphreys (1993) and (1993–95); O'Hanlon (1993); Hogan (1984) and (1979); Clarke (1982); Casey (1979–80); Redmond (1979–80a); Von Prondzynski (1977b); Costello (1962) and (1956).
[291] eg O'Connor et al (2012). [292] [1935] 1 IR 170; see Chap 3 above, 37-42. [293] Art 10.1.
[294] Art 41.1. [295] Art 42.1.
[296] Art 42A.1. This was inserted into the Constitution after a referendum in 2012: Thirty-First Amendment of the Constitution (Children) Act 2012; it did not come into force until 2015, after the Supreme Court had rejected a challenge to the way the referendum had been conducted: *Jordan v Minister for Children and Youth Affairs* [2015] IESC 33, [2015] 4 IR 232.
[297] Art 43.1.1. [298] [1965] IR 294; see above, 125-6.

It was in the contraception case of *McGee v Attorney General*[299] that Walsh J expounded his own (theologically based) approach to natural law, although this was after he had already found in favour of the claimant on the basis that the right to marital privacy was implicit in Article 41 of the Constitution, and the four other judges in the case did not feel any need to resort to natural law reasoning. Reliance on the theory re-emerged in *Norris v Attorney General*,[300] where the Supreme Court held by 3 v 2 that criminalising homosexuality between consenting adults was not a violation of any constitutional right in Ireland, despite a ruling from the European Court of Human Rights a few years earlier that in an almost identical case emanating from Northern Ireland there had been a breach of the right to a private life. O'Higgins CJ, for example, stressed that according to the teaching of all Christian churches homosexual acts are wrong, that people who are homosexual tend to be sad, lonely and suicidal, and that the practice is a threat to public health and a danger to the institution of marriage.[301] He asserted that homosexual conduct 'is, of course, morally wrong, and has been so regarded by mankind through the centuries'.[302]

Today, such theologically-based moralising by Supreme Court Justices is a thing of the past, the fatal blow having been struck in one of the Article 26 references examined earlier concerning the Regulation of Information (Services outside the State for Termination of Pregnancies) Bill.[303] There the Supreme Court explicitly rejected the idea that in Ireland natural law is a source of law superior to the Constitution. Nevertheless, it went on to stress that Irish courts should interpret the Constitution bearing in mind the paragraph in its Preamble which states that the people of Ireland adopted the Constitution in order 'to promote the common good, with due observance of Prudence, Justice and Charity'.[304] In this way natural law thinking may still enter judicial reasoning by the back door. For Kavanagh this is not a concern, provided that natural law 'means simply working out what justice requires in the instant case'.[305] That is true, but the danger remains, given the number of references to religious concepts elsewhere in the Preamble and in the Constitution itself and the still considerable preponderance of Catholicism within Ireland, that individual judges will tend to interpret 'justice' in a way which accords with their religious beliefs rather than with evidence derived from sociological or economic research.

Conclusion

Writing in 1983, by which time only six references had been made to the Supreme Court under Article 26, Joseph Jaconelli weighed up the pros and cons of retaining this 'advisory' procedure and concluded that, on balance, it should remain in place.[306] James Casey points out, rightly, that the procedure is not actually 'advisory', because the President is obliged to sign a referred Bill if it is found by the Supreme Court to be constitutional and not to sign it if the Court finds it to be unconstitutional,[307] but he also stresses that the Supreme Court itself has intimated that in some instances it may be better for the President not to refer a Bill and instead wait for its constitutionality to be considered by the courts under Article 34.4 after it has become an Act. In cases of posterior review it may be easier to adduce strong evidence of the Act's allegedly unconstitutional effects, whereas in Article 26 cases any such evidence has to be hypothetical, with argumentation and discussion proceeding on an entirely abstract basis. It seems, however, that there is nothing in the Constitution or in any

[299] [1974] IR 284; see too Chap 10 below, 232-4. [300] [1984] IR 36; see too Chap 12 below, 275-8.
[301] Ibid, 61–3. [302] Ibid, 64. [303] See 114-5 above. [304] [1995] 1 IR 1, 42.
[305] Kavanagh (2012) 99. [306] Jaconelli (1983). [307] Casey (2000) 89, n 36.

other legislation which explicitly precludes the Supreme Court from allowing third party interventions in Article 26 cases, a process which would provide an opportunity for a range of organisations to give the Court the benefit of their views as to the consequences of the ruling going one way or the other. This is already permissible not just in Canada (where *a priori* review has been widely resorted to[308]), but also in the United Kingdom whenever the competence of a devolved legislature is being examined in relation to a proposed Bill[309] or when the protection of fundamental rights is at stake.[310] Both Australia and the USA have eschewed purely advisory opinions, primarily because they are viewed as incompatible with the judicial function,[311] but when the Supreme Court of Canada's power to issue advisory opinions was challenged in the Privy Council, it was found not to be in breach of the separation of powers doctrine.[312] In a much later case the Supreme Court of Canada itself upheld its power to issue advisory opinions even though its governing statute requires the Supreme Court to be 'a general court of *appeal* for Canada'.[313]

Apart from its work on Article 26 references the Supreme Court's record on constitutional issues is a reasonable one, though it has fluctuated over time. In his 1954 assessment of the impact made by the Court in conducting constitutional reviews, the US lawyer and scholar Edward McWhinney found that, in view of the break with the past which the 1937 Constitution represented, 'the Supreme Court's work to date has been rather less than daring and innovatory than one might have expected'.[314] He noted that the Court's contact with US constitutional cases and trends was 'rather casual and general at best'[315] and suggested that the Irish Supreme Court was most influenced by English practices, meaning that it had 'moved rather cautiously in translating the policy norms set out in the guarantees and directives of the Constitution of 1937 into law-in-action'.[316] McWhinney seemed disappointed that the Court had not adopted a more Catholic approach to issues. A decade later Max Abrahamson also noted how willing the Supreme Court seemed to be to rely on United Kingdom precedents but he seemed to think it was dangerous for the Court to trespass into issues (such as industrial relations) which in his view are better left to other organs of the State to deal with.[317]

In 1971 a further survey was undertaken by a professor of ethics in Dublin, Michael Crowe.[318] He focused exclusively on the extent to which the Supreme Court and other

[308] Under s 53 of the Supreme Court Act 1985; s 54 allows the Senate or House of Commons to make rules or orders allowing for references to the Supreme Court of any private bill or petition for a private bill presented to the Senate or House of Commons. See too Hogg (2012) 8.15 to 8.21. He points out that in practice it is the federal and the ten provincial governments who have the right to secure a ruling from the Supreme Court under s 53.

[309] There have been six such cases to date, three relating to Acts of the Scottish Parliament and three to Acts of the Welsh Assembly: *Whaley v Lord Advocate* [2007] UKHL 53, 2008 SC (HL) 107; *Martin v HM Advocate* [2010] UKSC 10, 2010 SLT 412; *Christian Institute v Lord Advocate* [2016] UKSC 51, 2016 SLT 805; *Attorney General v National Assembly for Wales Commission* [2012] UKSC 53, [2013] 1 AC 792; *In re Agricultural Sector (Wales) Bill* [2014] UKSC 43, [2014] 1 WLR 2622; and *In re Recovery of Medical Costs for Asbestos Diseases (Wales) Bill* [2015] UKSC 3, [2015] AC 1016. Only in the last case did the UK Supreme Court hold that the Welsh Assembly did not have legislative competence, under the Government of Wales Act 2006.

[310] eg *Belhaj v Straw* [2017] UKSC 3, [2017] AC 964, a case on the application of the foreign act of State doctrine in the context of extraordinary rendition, where interventions were permitted from four NGOs: the International Commission of Jurists, Justice, Amnesty International and Redress.

[311] See *In re Judiciary and Navigation Acts* (1921) 29 CLR 257 (HCA). In the US the disinclination to allow advisory opinions is based mainly on Art 3(2) of the Constitution, which limits judicial power to 'cases' and to 'controversies'. However some states within the US do allow advisory opinions, eg the advisory opinion of the Supreme Judicial Court of Massachusetts on a proposed Bill which would have given 'spouses in civil unions' the same rights as spouses in marriages: *Opinions of the Justices to the Senate* (Mass 2004) 802 NE 2d 565.

[312] *Attorney General of Ontario v Attorney General of Canada* [1912] AC 571.

[313] *Re Secession of Quebec* [1998] 2 SCR 217; the quotation (emphasis added) comes from s 101 of the Constitution Act 1867.

[314] McWhinney (1954–5) 71. [315] Ibid, 75. [316] Ibid, 85. [317] Abrahamson (1963).

[318] Crowe (1971–72).

courts had developed the protection of human rights under the two Constitutions of 1922 and 1937. He observed that 'a certain boldness or even a maximising tendency in interpretation seems to have become much more prevalent since 1937', ascribing this partly to two liberally minded High Court judges, Gavan Duffy and John Kenny, and citing the Supreme Court's approval of the latter's discovery of unenumerated personal rights in the fluoridation case of *Ryan v Attorney General*.[319] Crowe described that case as 'a pregnant one' because it greatly enlarged the possible field for future activity by the courts when reviewing legislation.[320] This view of the *status quo* was largely reflected by Barrington in his brief conspectus published in 1987. He concluded that the the Irish Supreme Court 'can more properly be compared nowadays with the American Federal Supreme Court than with the English Court of Appeal or the House of Lords'.[321]

Looking back from the vantage point of 2018 it has to be admitted that in the field of constitutional law the Supreme Court deserves considerable credit on three fronts. First, it has accepted the existence of constitutional rights which are not explicitly listed in the Constitution. While at times these have been confused with the concept of natural rights, they can today be viewed as textually implicit. Second, as we will see in later chapters of this book, the Court has frequently applied the explicit words of the Constitution in ways which ensure that individual rights and freedoms have been protected as comprehensively as in most other Western European and common law legal systems. Third, the Supreme Court has not allowed itself to get mired in disputes over interpretative approaches to the Constitution. John Kelly is amongst the critics who have regretted some excessive literalism on the part of the Supreme Court when interpreting the Constitution,[322] but there has not been a school of thought which advocates an 'originalist' attitude to the exegesis of that text.[323] Rather, as Desmond Clarke has put it, the Supreme Court seems to have accepted that 'the occurrence of essentially contested concepts in the Constitution is symptomatic of its normative character' and that 'such concepts need to be interpreted anew, in each generation, with due fidelity to the principles that they were meant to articulate'.[324] Such open-mindedness might, in turn, call into question the wisdom of maintaining the presumption of constitutionality, a doctrine which the Supreme Court has espoused since 1940[325] but which some now think could usefully be dropped.[326]

On the other hand, there are perhaps three ways in which the Supreme Court could be said to have under-performed in the field of constitutional law. First, it has not sufficiently developed its concept of unenumerated rights because it has neglected to develop a theory for the identification of those rights. It might have fallen back on international human rights treaties in that regard, or at least on those treaties which Ireland has ratified, but it has not done so. This has meant that the Court has shied away from accepting social and economic claims as unenumerated rights. Citing the non-justiciability of the directive principles of social policy in Article 45 of the Constitution is not an adequate justification for such shyness. Second, the Court has been too inward-looking when deciding how to

319 Ibid, 293–4. *Ryan v AG* [1965] IR 294 is dealt with at 125-6 above.

320 Ibid, 294.

321 Barrington (1987) 126.

322 Kelly (1988b) 170–1, where he cites *The State (Ennis) v Farrell* [1966] IR 107. In memorable phrases he reminds us (at 171) that 'the Constitution, back in 1937, was not intended by anyone to become a sort of machine lathe, engineered to minute tolerances, which could shear away whole strips of legal timber on the strength of a linguistic usage which, at that time, no-one thought it necessary to scrutinise closely or indeed at all'.

323 *Pace* Brittain (2010).

324 Clarke (2008) 113. See too Clarke (2011b); Kavanagh (1997); Morgan (1988).

325 *Re Article 26 and the Offences Against the State (Amendment) Bill 1940* [1940] IR 470 and see 109-10; Hogan et al (2018) 982-1009.

326 eg Foley (2007).

develop the Irish Constitution. By definition a Constitution is tailor-made for the country in question, and should reflect the values of that country, but this does not mean that the judges who interpret it, or the lawyers who plead their cases before those judges, should confine themselves only to Irish precedents. Fortunately the Court has in recent years been less reluctant than in the past to consider the constitutional jurisprudence of other common law supreme courts,[327] and it has recently accepted more *amicus curiae* briefs,[328] but more could be done on these fronts.[329] In the field of socio-economic rights such constitutional comparativism could be particularly rewarding.[330] Third, the Supreme Court has not been quick enough to adapt its approach to remedies. In particular it was very slow to accept the idea that it could declare a law or policy to be unconstitutional but then suspend the effect of that declaration for a set period to allow another organ of the State to rectify the problem. A plea for that reform was made by Eoin Carolan in 2011,[331] and in 2017 it was at last heeded when, in *NHV v Minister for Justice and Equality*, the Supreme Court suspended for six months the issuing of a declaration concerning the inconsistency between the ban on asylum-seekers obtaining employment in Ireland and the constitutional right of people in Ireland to look for employment.[332]

[327] Carolan (2005), who concludes that the Supreme Court is more likely to be influenced by 'horizontal' foreign courts, whether national or international (including the Court of Justice of the EU), than by 'vertical' courts, such as the European Court of Human Rights. A more modern survey comparable to this one is overdue.

[328] O'Brien (2004), on *Iwala v Minister for Justice, Equality and Law Reform* [2003] IESC 38, [2004] 1 ILRM 27.

[329] Gallagher (2010) esp 33–43. But see the note of caution expressed by O'Connell (1999), who compares judicial activism in this field in Germany, Ireland and India.

[330] The most commonly cited comparator jurisdiction is South Africa, but it should be noted that, while the jurisprudence of the Constitutional Court of that country has benefited greatly from the liberal wording of the 1996 Constitution, the socio-economic consequences flowing from the Court's decisions have not been as significant as some may have hoped. See Belinskij, Kotze and Fuo (2017); Cameron and Taylor (2017); Stafford (2017); Dugard (2016); Le Roux-Kemp (2016).

[331] Carolan (2011).

[332] [2017] IESC 35 (Denham CJ, O'Donnell, Clarke, MacMenamin, Laffoy, Charleton and O'Malley JJ). See too Chap 10 below, 228-9.

7

The Supreme Court and Northern Ireland

On several occasions the Supreme Court has had to deal with cases involving the relationship between the Republic of Ireland and Northern Ireland, the six counties of Ireland which opted to remain part of the United Kingdom in 1922.[1] The cases have usually raised constitutional issues but often political and criminal justice questions have been involved as well. Collectively the cases reflect the views of Ireland's Supreme Court judges on how the relationship between the two jurisdictions should be managed from a legal point of view. Tempting though it may be to ascribe political motivations to what was said by some of the judges from time to time, it has to be admitted that finding solid evidence for political bias is difficult, even in the controversial field of extradition law. The judges have maintained the line that their function is wholly separate from that of the government and the Oireachtas and, to the extent that they have had discretion as to how to interpret certain phrases in the Constitution or legislation, they have exercised it in a manner which betrays no obvious prejudice. They have adhered firmly to the rule of law, even if at times they have differed amongst themselves as to what that entails. The chapter examines the cases more or less in chronological order, but it delays discussion of the Law Enforcement Commission's 1974 report and of a relevant Article 26 reference in 1976 until the part of the chapter where discussion of extradition begins.

Arms Smuggling and *R v Haughey*

In the realm of criminal justice the Irish Supreme Court became indirectly involved in the troubles of Northern Ireland when allegations of arms smuggling arose in the early 1970s. In 1969 the Irish government had created a fund of £100,000 out of which sums could be paid to alleviate the distress experienced by nationalists in Northern Ireland as a result of the civil unrest there. A cabinet sub-committee was established to administer the fund and Charles Haughey (Minister for Finance) and Neil Blaney (Minister for Agriculture and Fisheries) effectively gained control of it. In May 1970 it transpired that money from the fund was being earmarked for the purchase of weapons to be used by nationalists in the North and the then Taoiseach, Jack Lynch, felt obliged to sack both Ministers. Almost immediately the Ministers, along with three others, were put on trial for illegal arms smuggling. The charges against Blaney ended when the District Court decided that he had no case to answer. Haughey went through the trial but, along with the three others, was acquitted in October 1970.[2] At the time no appeal was possible against an acquittal, so the Supreme Court did not become involved.

[1] See, generally, Forde and Leonard (2013) paras 3.35–3.36. Technically the six counties were part of the Irish Free State for one day because the Free State's Constitution of 1922 was ratified by an Act of the UK Parliament on 5 December 1922 and on 6 December 1922 the King issued the proclamation required by Art 83 of that Constitution. Only on 7 December 1922 did the Northern Ireland's Parliament present an address to the King under Art 12 of the Anglo-Irish Treaty of 1921 stating that the powers of the Parliament and government of the Free State would no longer extend to Northern Ireland and the provisions of the Government of Ireland Act 1920 would continue to be of full force and effect so far as they related to Northern Ireland.

[2] For the full story see O'Brien (2000).

In the wake of the trial, however, the Dáil's Committee of Public Accounts was tasked in December 1970 with investigating the way in which the fund set up by the government had been administered. Later the same month the Oireachtas passed an Act which specifically provided that, if a witness refused to answer any question to which the Committee might legally require an answer, the Committee could 'certify' that witness and the High Court, after conducting such an inquiry as it thought proper, could then punish that witness 'as if he [or she] had been guilty of contempt of the High Court'.[3] One such witness was so certified, this being Pádraic Haughey, the brother of Charles. An experienced High Court comprising the President of that Court (Andreas O'Keeffe)[4] and Murnaghan and Henchy JJ—sitting without a jury—found in March 1971 that Pádraic Haughey was guilty of contempt and should be sent to prison for six months.[5] He immediately appealed to the Supreme Court and his imprisonment was suspended while the appeal lasted. In June 1971 the Supreme Court unanimously allowed the appeal, holding that the offence in question was not actually contempt but rather an ordinary serious criminal offence the trial of which, under Article 38.5 of the Constitution, had to occur before a jury.[6] As drafted, section 4(3) of the 1970 Act could not be read as requiring a trial by jury, so it was unconstitutional. These conclusions were set out in a single judgment of the Court but other issues were dealt with separately by each of the five judges.[7] In addition, four of the five judges[8] stated that, because Pádraic Haughey had given his evidence to the High Court by way of affidavit rather than orally and had not been given the opportunity to cross-examine witnesses who gave evidence against him, there were further grounds for concluding that his conviction was unsafe. The conviction was therefore quashed. Haughey spent no time in prison and could not be re-tried in relation to the same behaviour.

The situation in Northern Ireland was peripheral to the trials of both Charles and Pádraic Haughey, but the legal processes involved were keenly observed by unionists in Northern Ireland for traces of any political bias. However no objective observer could have any complaints on that front.[9] While many may have thought the evidence against the defendants in the arms trial was convincing, the jury clearly did not feel that guilt had been proved beyond reasonable doubt. It took just 48 minutes to reach its conclusion. Pádraic Haughey's case highlighted the idiosyncrasies of Ireland's system for ensuring that the national Parliament is not misled, but in the United Kingdom this can also be a controversial issue.[10] Whether the Irish judges were just as impartial when it came to applying the law on extradition between the Republic and Northern Ireland is a different matter, to which we will return later in this chapter.

The Sunningdale Agreement

The new Constitution which was approved in Ireland in 1937 made no specific reference to Northern Ireland. Indeed its wording suggested that Ireland had not been partitioned in 1921 for, under the heading 'The Nation', Article 2 provided that 'The national territory consists of the whole island of Ireland, its islands and the territorial seas'. Moreover Article 3 stated that:

[3] Committee of Public Accounts of Dáil Éireann (Privilege and Procedure) Act 1970, s 4(3).
[4] Who had also presided over the arms trial defendants a year before.
[5] *In re Haughey* [1971] IR 217.
[6] Ibid, 231 (Ó Dálaigh CJ, Walsh, Budd, FitzGerald and McLoughlin JJ); see too Tóibin (1985) 14-16.
[7] Though Walsh and Budd JJ simply agreed with Ó Dálaigh CJ on these matters too.
[8] The exception was McLoughlin J.
[9] See eg Ferriter (2012) Chap 12 (141–52); Patterson (2006) 172–6.
[10] Street and Gordon (2012).

> Pending the re-integration of the national territory, and without prejudice to the right of the Parliament and Government established by this Constitution to exercise jurisdiction over the whole of that territory, the laws enacted by that Parliament shall have the like area and extent of application as the laws of Saorstát Éireann and like extra-territorial effect.

To many in the Republic these two provisions were articles of faith. It was difficult for them to accept that, if the serious civil unrest which broke out in Northern Ireland in 1969 was to be brought to an end through political compromise, it would be necessary to reassure the majority population of Northern Ireland that their status within the United Kingdom was in the meantime guaranteed. After the suspension of Northern Ireland's Parliament in March 1972, and the consequential transfer of powers to the Secretary of State for Northern Ireland within the British government under 'direct rule',[11] new proposals for restoring devolution were put forward by the British government in a White Paper in March 1973.[12] These suggested that a Northern Ireland Assembly should be elected, with committees whose members would reflect the balance of political parties represented in the Assembly. The committees would be associated with each Northern Ireland Department and their chairs would be the heads of those Departments and together form the Northern Ireland Executive. Pending agreement on the devolution of powers the committees would have only advisory functions. Most of these proposals were put into law through the Northern Ireland Assembly Act 1973[13] and the Northern Ireland Constitution Act 1973.

Section 1 of the latter declared that:

> Northern Ireland remains part of Her Majesty's dominions and of the United Kingdom, and it is hereby affirmed that in no event will Northern Ireland or any part of it cease to be part of Her Majesty's dominions and of the United Kingdom without the consent of the majority of the people of Northern Ireland voting in a poll held for the purposes of this section in accordance with Schedule 1 to this Act.[14]

The Irish government fully accepted that principle and went along with the plan to sign a formal agreement to that effect and register it as a treaty at the United Nations. Elections to the Northern Ireland Assembly took place on 28 June 1973. The Assembly met for the first time a few days later but attempts to set up an Executive failed. Eventually further talks involving all the local political parties and the British and Irish governments were arranged for a four-day period in December in the small town of Sunningdale in Berkshire.

Under the resulting Sunningdale Agreement—though in fact only a communiqué was issued, not a formal agreement[15]—a power-sharing Executive was established on 1 January 1974. But there was also to be a Council of Ireland. This was to comprise a Council of Ministers with executive and harmonising functions and a consultative role; it would have at least seven members drawn from the Irish government and seven from the Northern Ireland Executive. There would also be a Consultative Assembly with advisory and review

[11] Northern Ireland (Temporary Provisions) Act 1972. This 'temporary' Act was not repealed until a new Executive was put in place in Northern Ireland on 2 December 1999. It was supplemented by a further Northern Ireland Act in 1974.

[12] See http://cain.ulst.ac.uk/hmso/cmd5259.htm. The White Paper had been preceded in October 1972 by a discussion paper entitled *The Future of Northern Ireland: A Paper for Discussion*.

[13] This too was not repealed until 2 December 1999: see n 11 above.

[14] Sch 1 provided that such a poll could not occur before 9 March 1983 or within 10 years of an earlier poll. This date was chosen because there had been a poll on 8 March 1973 under the Northern Ireland (Border Poll) Act 1972. It was largely boycotted by nationalists but of those who voted 591,820 favoured Northern Ireland remaining part of the UK and only 6,463 favoured Northern Ireland joining the Republic of Ireland.

[15] For the communiqué issued after the Agreement was reached see http://cain.ulst.ac.uk/events/sunningdale/agreement.htm.

functions, with 30 members from the Dáil and 30 from the Assembly. The Council of Ireland would have a Secretariat and areas would be identified in relation to which the Council would take executive decisions, such as the exploitation and conservation of natural resources, agricultural matters, trade and industry, electricity generation, tourism, transport, public health, sport, culture and the arts. The Oireachtas and the Assembly would have to enact legislation setting out the precise functions to be devolved to the Council.

As regards the specific topic of law and order, the British government promised to discuss the devolution of responsibility for policing to the Northern Ireland Executive as soon as the existing security problems were resolved and the new institutions were working effectively. The Irish government undertook to set up a Police Authority while the British government would review the membership of the already existing Police Authority in Northern Ireland and create a system for allowing complaints against the police to be dealt with not by the police themselves but by an independent body. In addition the British government reaffirmed its commitment to releasing some internees within the following three weeks and to ending internment altogether as soon as the security situation allowed for it. All parties also agreed that consideration should be given to how the principles of the European Convention on Human Rights could be expressed in domestic legislation in each part of Ireland and to whether further legislation or institutions were required to protect human rights.[16]

The Executive set up in January 1974 lasted only until May. It was suspended and then abolished by the UK government due to extensive disruption caused by a strike promoted by the Ulster Workers Council, a loyalist organisation strongly opposed to the idea of Irish ministers having a say through the Council of Ireland over matters relating to Northern Ireland. The Sunningdale Agreement was never turned into a formal treaty. The only aspect of it which had lasting impact was the one relating to the enforcement of the criminal law. Unionists were of the view that the Republic of Ireland needed to do more to bring to justice perpetrators of violent crime in Northern Ireland who then moved to the Republic. A way of dealing with this could not be agreed during the talks at Sunningdale but shortly thereafter the two governments set up a Commission to consider possible solutions 'as a matter of extreme urgency'. As we shall see, this led to the Supreme Court having to assess whether the arrangements made for this purpose were consistent with the Irish Constitution.

Boland v An Taoiseach

While the Sunningdale Agreement was not to the liking of extreme unionists in Northern Ireland, it was also unsatisfactory in the eyes of extreme republicans, whether in Northern Ireland or the Republic. One such was Kevin Boland, a Fianna Fáil supporter who had always taken a hard line against the partition of Ireland and favoured a more interventionist approach by the Irish government to events in Northern Ireland. In 1970 he resigned as the Minister for Local Government when both Charles Haughey and Neil Blaney were sacked from the government prior to being charged with conspiring to import arms for use in Northern Ireland. Later that year he was expelled altogether form Fianna Fáil.

Boland reacted to the Sunningdale Agreement by initiating legal proceedings arguing that what the Irish government had agreed to was in breach of the 1937 Constitution. He sought an injunction stopping the government from entering into any international agreement which would limit the exercise of Irish sovereignty over any portion of the national

[16] For details see paras 10–18 of the communiqué, n 15 above.

territory. His leading counsel was initially Sean McBride SC, but he lost in both the High Court[17] and the Supreme Court[18] on the basis that what the Irish government had agreed at Sunningdale was an exercise of executive power and that the Courts had no power to review its legality. In his short *ex tempore* judgment in the High Court Murnaghan J (a nephew of James Murnaghan who had served on the Supreme Court from 1925 to 1953) said he could not accept that the Sunningdale Agreement had affected the rights of Irish citizens living in either part of Ireland, though he conceded that if it were translated into legislation those rights *might* be affected.[19] Relying upon a phrase used by O'Byrne J in the Sinn Féin funds case,[20] Murnaghan J said 'this Court must assume, until it is clearly established to the contrary, that any declaration of policy by the government is within the constitutional powers conferred on the government'.[21] Presumably he intended to base this proposition on Article 28.2 of the Constitution, which reads: 'The executive power of the State shall, subject to the provisions of this Constitution, be exercised by or on the authority of the government.' In any event he added that under Article 28.4.1 the government is responsible to Dáil Éireann and not to the courts:

> In my opinion, it would not be consonant with what has been described as the 'checks and balances' contained in the Constitution, in relation to the three organs of State mentioned in Article 6.1 of the Constitution, that this Court should purport to usurp the functions of Dáil Éireann; I am far from convinced that this Court should concern itself with a declaration of policy by the Government which, in itself, cannot affect the legal rights of any citizen.[22]

For good measure Murnaghan J relied as well on Article 29.4.1, which is more specific than Article 28.2 in stating: 'The executive power of the State in or in connection with its external relations shall in accordance with Article 28 of this Constitution be exercised by or on the authority of the government'. He admitted, however, that courts could supervise the government's exercise of its functions if 'the circumstances are such as to amount to a clear disregard by the government of the powers and duties conferred on it by the Constitution'.[23]

Having heard Boland's appeal a month later, the Supreme Court announced on 22 February 1974 that it was dismissing it, but it waited a further week before publishing its reasons. FitzGerald CJ held that none of the three clauses in the communiqué relating to the Sunningdale conference relied upon by Mr Boland contained a present agreement,[24] but merely intentions as to what might happen in the future, so none of the clauses were capable of 'being construed as any action by the government which would bring it within the jurisdiction of the Courts to supervise or restrain'.[25] O'Keeffe P[26] agreed with FitzGerald CJ and with the other judgments delivered later. The one concession he made to Boland's position was that in his opinion it would clearly not be within the constitutional competence of the government to acknowledge that the State is not entitled *de iure* to jurisdiction over Northern Ireland. Budd J likewise held that the Sunningdale deal amounted to no more than declarations of policy and not an agreement as to the future of Northern Ireland.[27] The

[17] [1974] 1 IR 338 (Murnaghan J). [18] Ibid. McBride did not appear in the Supreme Court.

[19] Ibid, 353. [20] *Buckley v Attorney General* [1950] IR 67, 80. See too Chap 6 above, 121-2.

[21] [1974] 1 IR 338, 353. As von Prondzynski (1978–80) observes, at 18 n 22, this is comparable to the accepted principle that post-1937 legislation is presumed to be constitutional. For more on 'political questions' see Chap 4 above, 68-9.

[22] [1974] 1 IR 338, 353-4. [23] Ibid, 363.

[24] These were paras 5, 6 and 20. Boland argued they were repugnant to Arts 1–6 and 34 of the Constitution.

[25] [1974] 1 IR 338, 362–3. Henchy and Walsh JJ did not sit in the appeal because they were members of the Law Enforcement Commission, established under the Agreement being challenged in the case: Casey (1979) 33–4. See too 155-7 below.

[26] As President of the High Court Andreas O'Keeffe (Aindrias Ó Caoimh) was the second most senior judge in Ireland and an *ex officio* member of the Supreme Court, although he rarely sat there.

[27] [1974] 1 IR 338, 367.

courts could not be called upon to pronounce on what the government proposed to do on any matter of policy which it was in the process of formulating.[28] Griffin J agreed that the courts had no authority to review government policies but he mentioned as well Article 29.6 of the Constitution, which stipulates that '[n]o international agreement shall be part of the domestic law of the State save as may be determined by the Oireachtas'. Like Murnaghan J in the court below, he was not prepared to accept the government's claim that the Courts could never interfere with the exercise of its executive functions: he stated that if the government were to act in a way which contravened the Constitution it would be the duty of the courts to intervene when called upon to do so. Pringle J (a member of the High Court) agreed with all four of the preceding judgments.

It is obvious from this decision that each of the five judges in the Supreme Court thought it was premature for them to be asked to rule that the government had acted unconstitutionally at Sunningdale. They would all have been aware of the opprobrium to which such a ruling would have exposed the judiciary from politicians both north and south of the border. Nevertheless, it is arguable that the Supreme Court did not sufficiently fulfil its duty to review policies adopted by government to see if they violated principles of administrative justice or fundamental rights. It was left to Henchy J more than a decade later, in *Crotty v An Taoiseach*,[29] where the Supreme Court held that it would be unconstitutional for the government to ratify a particular treaty unless the Constitution was first amended, to assert that 'in the conduct of the State's external relations, as in the exercise of the executive power in other respects, the government is not immune from judicial control if it acts in a manner or for a purpose which is inconsistent with the Constitution'.[30]

The Anglo-Irish Agreement and *McGimpsey v Ireland*

The next occasion on which Northern Ireland featured in a discussion of the Republic's Constitution was *McGimpsey v Ireland*[31] where, in a mirror image of the *Boland* case, two brothers who were members of the Ulster Unionist Party took proceedings arguing that the Anglo-Irish Agreement of 1985 was a violation of the Republic's Constitution. The Anglo-Irish Agreement was struck between the British and Irish Governments at a time when the latest attempt to set up a power-sharing Executive and Assembly in Northern Ireland had failed. The attempt had followed the publication of a White Paper by the British government in 1982.[32] The intention was that an Assembly elected in 1982 would initially debate matters and give its views on legislation proposed by the Secretary of State, with legislative powers then being devolved to it on a rolling basis if at least 70 per cent of the Assembly agreed or if a majority agreed and the Secretary of State was satisfied that the proposed devolution would 'command widespread acceptance throughout the community'.[33] Unfortunately the Assembly was boycotted by nationalist parties and at times by the Ulster Unionist Party and in June 1986 the British government dissolved it.[34] The Anglo-Irish Agreement was an inter-governmental effort to produce an alternative to rolling devolution. It provided for the establishment of an Anglo-Irish Inter-Governmental Conference and Secretariat through which Irish Ministers would be able to express views on a range of matters relating to the

[28] Ibid, 366.
[29] [1987] 1 IR 713; see Chap 11 below, 252-5.
[30] Ibid, 786. See, generally, Forde and Leonard (2013), para 10.10.
[31] [1990] 1 IR 110.
[32] *Northern Ireland: A Framework for Devolution*, Cmnd 8541, available at http://cain.ulst.ac.uk/hmso/cmd8541.htm.
[33] Northern Ireland Act 1982, s 1(4).
[34] Northern Ireland Assembly (Dissolution) Order 1986, SI 1036.

governance of Northern Ireland. In some respects it could be perceived as 'Sunningdale-lite', but unlike the Sunningdale Agreement it was formally struck as a treaty and registered as such at the United Nations.[35] It was also overwhelmingly approved by a vote in the UK House of Commons and, much more narrowly, by a vote in the Dáil.[36]

Unionists, however, were vehemently opposed to the Agreement. The leader of the Ulster Unionist Party went to the High Court in London to argue that it was illegal under UK law, but the judge quickly dismissed the claim by ruling that the court had no power to inquire into how the government exercises its prerogative power to enter into international agreements.[37] Even Mary Robinson, the future President of Ireland, felt that unionists were right to be opposed to the Agreement and she resigned from the Labour Party in Ireland when it lent its support to the document. Fianna Fáil was also opposed to the Agreement, but for the converse reason, namely that it formally recognized the *de iure* right of the United Kingdom to govern Northern Ireland.[38]

The two McGimpsey brothers cleverly took advantage of Fianna Fáil's position to bring a case to the Irish High Court arguing that in recognising the legitimacy of the present status of Northern Ireland the Agreement was repugnant to Articles 2 and 3 of the Irish Constitution and that the bodies established by the Agreement restricted the Irish government's discretion concerning the State's external relations, contrary to Articles 28 and 29 of the Constitution.[39] They also argued that in entering the Agreement the Irish government had neglected its duty to the majority (unionist) community in Northern Ireland. Barrington J accepted that the brothers had standing to bring the claim and that the government was not totally exempt from judicial review of the way it exercised its powers in the area of international relations,[40] but he stressed that a court would need to exercise appropriate judicial restraint in this field.[41] He added that there is a presumption that treaties entered into by the government are compatible with the Constitution and that here the presumption had not been rebutted.

As regards Article 1 of the Agreement and whether it was inconsistent with Articles 2 and 3 of the Constitution in that it recognised the current status of Northern Ireland, Barrington J explored the argument put forward by counsel for the plaintiffs that there were two ways of interpreting Articles 2 and 3. The first was that those Articles asserted only a political right to Irish unity, while the second was that they asserted a legal right. The former approach appeared to be favoured by O'Higgins CJ in the Article 26 reference relating to the Criminal Law (Jurisdiction) Bill 1975[42] and by Hederman J in the extradition case of *Russell v Fanning*.[43] The latter view appeared to be favoured by O'Keeffe P in the Supreme Court in *Boland v An Taoiseach*.[44] Barrington J said that his own preference was for the first of

[35] It came into force on 29 November 1985, when the two governments exchanged notifications of their acceptance of it (see Art 13). It was registered at the UN on 20 December 1985 as Treaty No 23668.

[36] For legal annotations on the Agreement see Hadden and Boyle (1989) and for its political consequences see Aughey and Gormley-Heenan (2013).

[37] *Ex parte Molyneaux* [1986] 1 WLR 331.

[38] In the words of Charles Haughey, the Fianna Fáil leader: 'We are deeply concerned that by signing this Agreement the Irish Government are acting in a manner repugnant to the Constitution of Ireland by fully accepting British sovereignty over a part of the national territory and by purporting to give legitimacy to a British administration in Ireland.' Dáil Debs, 19 November 1985, vol 361(11), para 2581.

[39] See, in particular, Art 29.4.1, cited above at 145. The plaintiffs were represented by two future judges of the Supreme Court, Hugh O'Flaherty SC and Frank Clarke SC. Gerard Hogan assisted them in the Supreme Court.

[40] [1988] IR 567, 578–81.

[41] Ibid, 582. For an extra-judicial statement of the judge's views see Barrington (1988).

[42] [1977] IR 129, 145. See 157-9 below.

[43] [1988] IR 505, 537. See 164-6 below.

[44] [1974] IR 338, 363; see 144-6 above. This may also have been the view of John Kelly, who suggested that the language of Articles 2 and 3 was 'too polemical', adding that 'matters which, to any outsider, would seem highly intricate and doubtful, are presented as legalistic claims of right': Kelly (1966a) 14.

the two approaches but he was clear than on either approach Article 1 of the Anglo-Irish Agreement was not repugnant to either Article 2 or 3 of the Constitution.[45] He added that the proposed Inter-Governmental Conference did not mean that the Irish government was transferring its power to conduct foreign policy to a supranational authority. In that regard the case was 'totally different'[46] from *Crotty v An Taioseach*,[47] where the Supreme Court had overruled the High Court and held that Ireland could not ratify the Single European Act without there being a change to the Constitution. In that case what was at stake was indeed the transfer of power to a supranational authority, namely the European Communities. Finally the judge did not accept that the Agreement reflected a breach of the government's duty to protect unionists in Northern Ireland: the balance struck between different community interests there was a matter within the political judgment of the government and it could not be challenged by a court unless the balance was a clear violation of a provision in the Constitution.[48]

An appeal against Barrington J's decision was not heard by the Supreme Court until more than a year-and-a-half later, in March 1990.[49] Finlay CJ gave the lead judgment and rejected the appeal. Three of his colleagues[50] simply agreed with him and McCarthy J added a short judgment in which he agreed with the Chief Justice but made it clear that because the McGimpsey brothers had not proved their citizenship of Ireland he felt they could not challenge the government's making of a treaty. As he succinctly put it, they cannot 'approbate *and* reprobate'.[51] The Chief Justice had also expressed 'considerable doubt' over whether even a citizen of the State had standing to challenge the constitutionality of government action if their sole purpose in doing so was to achieve an objective directly contrary to the purpose of the constitutional provision invoked.[52] The five judges unanimously rejected the preference expressed by Barrington J that the national claim to unity was a political rather than a legal right.[53] In short, they reaffirmed the view expressed by Hederman J in *Russell v Fanning*[54] that the re-integration of the national territory is 'a constitutional imperative'.[55] The Chief Justice then set out the official judicial position on the partition of Ireland:

> Article 3 of the Constitution ... is an express denial and disclaimer made to the community of nations of acquiescence to any claim that, pending the re-integration of the national territory, the frontier at present existing between the State and Northern Ireland is or can be accepted as conclusive of the matter or that there can be any prescriptive title thereby created and an assertion that there can be no estoppel created by the restriction in Article 3 on the application of the laws of the State in Northern Ireland.[56]

However Finlay CJ, like Barrington J,[57] also referred to the fact that in Article 29.1 and 29.2 of the Constitution Ireland 'affirms its devotion to the ideal of peace and friendly co-operation amongst nations' and 'its adherence to the principle of the pacific settlement of international disputes'.[58] Cleverly, the Supreme Court managed to square the circle: it

[45] [1988] IR 567, 586–7. [46] Ibid, 590. [47] [1987] IR 713; see Chap 11 below, 252-5.
[48] [1988] IR 567, 590–2.
[49] [1990] 1 IR 110. For an interesting alternative feminist judgment in this case see O'Donoghue (2017) and the commentary by Houghton (2017).
[50] Walsh, Griffin and Hederman JJ. [51] [1990] 1 IR 110, 123 (emphasis added).
[52] Ibid, 114–5. He might also have cited Art 17 of the ECHR, which prohibits people from claiming rights in order to destroy or unduly limit other people's rights. In civil law countries this is called the abuse of rights principle.
[53] Ibid, 119. [54] [1988] IR 505, 537. This case is discussed below at 164-6 below.
[55] [1990] 1 IR 110, 119. [56] Ibid. [57] [1988] 1 IR 567, 587–8.
[58] [1990] 1 IR 110, 121. Art 29.2 actually speaks of the pacific settlement of international disputes 'by international arbitration or judicial determination'.

upheld the Constitution's aspiration for a united Ireland while at the same time endorsing an agreement which seemed to reinforce partition.

The Anglo-Irish Agreement 1985 ceased to have effect with the entering into force of the British-Irish Treaty which was agreed alongside the Multi-Party Agreement to form the Belfast (Good Friday) Agreement on 10 April 1998. One of the pre-conditions for that entry into force was that amendments to the Irish Constitution set out in the Multi-Party Agreement[59] would first have to be approved by a referendum. This was planned for Friday, 22 May 1998.

The Good Friday Agreement and *Riordan v An Taoiseach (No 2)*

At this point there was an intervention by Denis Riordan, a marine communications lecturer in Limerick and serial litigant of constitutional points.[60] He had already brought a case as far as the Supreme Court in which he unsuccessfully challenged a number of government decisions, such as the appointment of judges to positions on commissions or tribunals of inquiry and the appointment of a Minister of State to the office of Tánaiste (deputy Prime Minister), which was not a department of State.[61] He now brought a further case in which he argued on three grounds that the referendum planned for 22 May was unconstitutional. First, he claimed that the Bill which the referendum sought approval for—the Nineteenth Amendment to the Constitution Bill—was in violation of Article 46 of the Constitution because it left it to the government to decide when the new Articles 2 and 3 should come into force (namely, when it was satisfied that other aspects of the Good Friday Agreement had been implemented).[62] Second, he suggested that the proposed new Article 3 was inconsistent with the State's right to exercise extra-territorial jurisdiction. Third, he professed that it would be unconstitutional to release prisoners under the terms of the Good Friday Agreement because the Constitution allocates to the President the right to commute a sentence.

Representing himself, Mr Riordan lost before Kelly J in the High Court just two days before the referendum was due to occur, whereupon he announced that he did not intend to lodge an appeal.[63] Voting went ahead but two months later Mr Riordan changed his mind and did appeal to the Supreme Court. In October 1998 he brought a further motion to the Supreme Court requesting additional remedies, including an order that a second referendum be held to validly amend Articles 2 and 3. The Supreme Court issued its decision on this motion in November, Barrington J issuing the lead judgment with which the other four judges concurred.[64] The Court rejected the relief sought and explained to Mr Riordan that there was no reason why the people of Ireland could not approve an amendment to

[59] Under 'Constitutional Issues, Annex B'.

[60] Later claims lodged by Mr Riordan were categorised as wholly unreasonable and he was eventually issued with an 'Isaac Wunder' order requiring him to seek the leave of the court before bringing any further proceedings (*Wunder v Hospitals Trust (1940) Ltd*, unreported decision of the Supreme Court, 24 January 1967); Moore (2001). In at least one further case where he sought such leave, it was refused: *Riordan v Ireland (No 5)* [2001] 4 IR 463 (O'Caoimh J). See too *Riordan v An Tánaiste* [1997] 3 IR 502 and *Riordan v Ireland* [2000] 4 IR 537, both Supreme Court decisions.

[61] *Riordan v An Taoiseach (No 1)* [1999] 4 IR 321 (Hamilton CJ, O'Flaherty, Barrington, Lynch and Barron JJ). In the same case he unsuccessfully challenged the Family Law (Divorce) Act 1996 on the ground that it contravened the Constitution's pledge to guard the institution of marriage and protect the family.

[62] Nineteenth Amendment to the Constitution Bill 1998, s 7(3). Art 46, on amending the Constitution, does not expressly confer a delaying power on the government in relation to an amending Act that has been approved by the people in a referendum, signed by the President and 'duly promulgated by the President as law' (Art 46.5).

[63] *Riordan v An Taoiseach (No 2)* [1999] 4 IR 343 (Kelly J).

[64] Ibid, 350 (Hamilton CJ, O'Flaherty, Barrington, Lynch and Barron JJ).

the Constitution subject to the happening of a particular future event; by doing so here the people were not delegating to the government the right to amend the Constitution.[65]

Despite this decision Mr Riordan continued his appeal against Kelly J's decision. A single judgment was delivered for the Supreme Court by Barrington J on 20 May 1999. This reiterated some of what was said in the judgment on the appellant's motion six months earlier but two points were added. The first was one that the Court had already made in Mr Riordan's previous case challenging various government decisions.[66] It was that there could be no question of a law enacted by the Oireachtas being unconstitutional if it had first been approved by the people in a referendum: 'That is why the President has no power to refer to the Supreme Court a bill containing a proposal to amend the Constitution for an opinion on its constitutionality'.[67] The second additional point clarified a matter which may have been left unclear in another earlier decision of the Supreme Court, *Finn v Attorney General*.[68] There the plaintiff unsuccessfully sought an injunction to stop the holding of a referendum on the Eighth Amendment to the Constitution Bill on the basis that the amendment was unnecessary since the right to life of the unborn child was already protected by the Constitution.[69] In the High Court Barrington J had suggested that the President might be able to refuse to sign a Bill which had been approved by the people in a referendum if the Bill included some other proposal (which, under Article 46.4 of the Constitution, it is not meant to do).[70] In *Riordan v An Taoiseach (No 2)* Barrington J, now in the Supreme Court, strongly implied that in 'a situation which is even worse' than that contemplated in *Finn*, the validity of the Act amending the Constitution could still not be questioned.[71]

The referendum held on 22 May 1998 resulted in a 'yes' vote of 94.4 per cent. The Nineteenth Amendment to the Constitution Act 1998 duly altered Article 29 of the Constitution so as to expressly allow the State to consent to be bound by the British-Irish Agreement of 1998, thereby making it impossible for a future constitutional challenge to be made to that Agreement. Articles 2 and 3 were not actually altered until 2 December 1999, when the Irish government declared (being satisfied that other aspects of the Good Friday Agreement had by then been implemented) that the re-worded Articles were now in force. Not coincidentally, this was also the date on which full powers were devolved to the Northern Ireland Executive by the British government and the cross-border bodies were formally established. The new Articles 2 and 3 read as follows:

Article 2

It is the entitlement and birthright of every person born in the island of Ireland, which includes its islands and seas, to be part of the Irish nation. That is also the entitlement of all persons otherwise qualified in accordance with law to be citizens of Ireland. Furthermore, the Irish nation cherishes its special affinity with people of Irish ancestry living abroad who share its cultural identity and heritage.

Article 3

(1) It is the firm will of the Irish nation, in harmony and friendship, to unite all the people who share the territory of the island of Ireland, in all the diversity of their identities and traditions, recognising that a united Ireland shall be brought about only by peaceful means with the consent of a majority of the people, democratically expressed, in both jurisdictions in the island. Until then, the laws enacted by the Parliament established by

[65] Ibid, 354. [66] *Riordan v An Taoiseach (No 1)* [1999] 4 IR 321. [67] Ibid, 335.
[68] [1983] IR 154 (O'Higgins CJ, Walsh, Henchy, Griffin and Hederman JJ).
[69] See too Chap 10 below, 235 and 239. [70] [1983] IR 154, 161–2.
[71] *Riordan v An Taoiseach (No 2)* [1999] 4 IR 343, 361–3.

this Constitution shall have the like area and extent of application as the laws enacted by the Parliament that existed immediately before the coming into operation of this Constitution.

(2) Institutions with executive powers and functions that are shared between those jurisdictions may be established by their respective responsible authorities for stated purposes and may exercise powers and functions in respect of all or any part of the island.

The interpretation of these Articles does not appear to have since troubled the Irish Supreme Court. As will be explained in Chapter 10, however, the flow of migrants into Ireland during the 1990s and early 2000s led the Oireachtas to qualify the *ius soli* principle in Irish nationality law, whereby anyone born in Ireland was automatically entitled to Irish citizenship. The Irish Nationality and Citizenship Act 2004[72] amended the existing law by providing that a person can acquire nationality through being born in Ireland (North or South) only if one of his or her parents has, during the four-year period preceding the birth, been resident in either part of Ireland for not less than a period aggregating three years. This amendment to citizenship law was possible without any change being made to Article 2 of the Constitution because at no point does that Article expressly confer citizenship on all people born in Ireland: it merely states that every such person is entitled 'to be part of the Irish nation'. A further anomaly exists in so far as British citizens living in Ireland do not enjoy the same degree of equality there as Irish citizens do who live in Northern Ireland; Richard Humphreys, now a High Court judge, has suggested a further constitutional amendment to correct this.[73]

Prisoner releases under the Belfast (Good Friday) Agreement were at issue before the Supreme Court in *O'Neill and Quinn v Governor of Castlerea Prison*.[74] The Criminal Justice (Release of Prisoners) Act 1998 was enacted by the Oireachtas in implementation of the Agreement but the two applicants were not considered to be 'qualifying prisoners' because they had been tried and convicted before the Agreement was reached (for, amongst other things, the manslaughter in 1996 of Garda Jerry McCabe in Adair, County Limerick). The five judges unanimously held that this did not amount to unequal treatment under Article 40.1 of the Constitution, even though other prisoners who had been tried and convicted before the Agreement *were* released. The two men then took their case to the Human Rights Committee of the United Nations (as Ireland, unlike the UK, has allowed the right of individual petition to that Committee since 1989), but they lost there too, the Committee ruling by a majority in 2006 that there had been no arbitrariness or improper discrimination in the men's continuing imprisonment. In her comment on this ruling Joseph rightly points out that using 'political necessities'—in this case support for the peace process in Northern Ireland—as a reason for limiting human rights could in other circumstances be a dangerous precedent.[75] Quinn was released in 2003 but O'Neill continued to be incarcerated until 2007.

Extradition

At the time Ireland was partitioned in 1922 arrangements for extradition between the United Kingdom and the Irish Free State[76] were governed by the Petty Sessions (Ireland) Act 1851.[77] This provided for warrants of arrest issued in one jurisdiction to be 'backed' (i.e. endorsed) in the other jurisdiction. In Ireland the backing could be done by police officers,

[72] s 4, inserting a new s 6A into the Irish Nationality and Citizenship Act 1956.
[73] Humphreys (2008) 117–20.
[74] [2004] IESC 7 and 73, [2004] 1 IR 298 (Keane CJ, Denham, Murray, McGuinness and McCracken JJ).
[75] Joseph (2007) 574–5.
[76] See, generally, Hogan et al (2018) 1930-32; there was longer coverage in the fourth edition of *Kelly: The Irish Constitution* (2003) 1644–75.
[77] s 29.

while in the United Kingdom it had to be done by a judicial officer, usually a Justice of the Peace. In 1929, following partition, the High Court of Ireland effectively ruled in *O'Boyle and Rodgers v Attorney General* that this backing of warrants system could not apply between the two jurisdiction in Ireland because it was only ever envisaged as operating between Great Britain and Ireland.[78] In 1921 two men had been tried by a General Court Martial sitting in Belfast under the Restoration of Order in Ireland Act 1920 and were convicted of the murder of a Mr McDowell. Their death sentence had been commuted to life imprisonment but after spending about six years in prison they escaped and fled to the Irish Free State. When they learned that the Irish police were seeking to arrest them on the basis of a warrant issued in Northern Ireland and backed in the Irish Free State, the men successfully applied for an injunction from Meredith J preventing any such arrest, the inevitable implication being that if such an arrest were to occur it would be unlawful.

For the next 35 years or so, as Kelly puts it, 'extradition across the Irish border in both directions appears to have been carried on reciprocally and informally by the respective police authorities without any lawful authority, or even ostensible authority, at all'.[79] However the nineteenth century system continued to operate between the Irish Free State and Great Britain and in 1937 the Supreme Court confirmed its constitutionality in *The State (Dowling) v Brennan and Kingston*.[80] The judges held that the 1851 arrangements remained in place under Article 73 of the 1922 Constitution because they had not since been changed by the Oireachtas. This was despite a finding by Gavan Duffy J in the High Court (albeit dissenting) that preservation of the pre-partition arrangements was incompatible with 'the emergence of an Irish state, bound to protect its citizens'.[81] After the enactment of the 1937 Constitution, that particular judge became reconciled to the majority view, which was reaffirmed by the Supreme Court in *The State (Duggan) v Tapley* in 1950.[82]

Curiously, the Supreme Court changed its mind on this issue in 1963. In *The State (Quinn) v Ryan*[83] Philip Quinn was arrested in Dublin on the basis of an English warrant endorsed by the Irish police. He was ordered by a judge to be released but while he was waiting in the court's precincts to talk to his legal representative he was apparently rearrested by the police and taken back into custody. He was then whisked to the border with Northern Ireland and later that evening placed on a boat to England. This shocking behaviour by the Garda Síochána, whether deliberate or simply mistaken, seems to have so enraged the Supreme Court judges that they felt prompted not just to reassert the inapplicability of the 1851 arrangements to the transfer of accused persons within Ireland but also to re-examine the constitutionality of the arrangements regarding transfers to Great Britain. Ó Dálaigh CJ agreed that the 1851 Act purported to authorise a person's removal from the jurisdiction immediately, without the person being given an opportunity to invoke the courts;[84] this was because '[h]owever unreal, the theory was that an Irishman, as a subject of the Queen, should have been as happy, safe and as much at home in Britain as in Ireland'.[85] But rather than just decide that the 1851 Act should be read subject to the implicit proviso that no such removal should take place until the person in question has been given the opportunity to challenge their removal in a court of law (as the accused in *Brennan and Kingston* and *Tapley* had been allowed to do), Ó Dálaigh CJ concluded that '[t]he claim made on behalf of the police to be entitled to arrest a citizen and forthwith bundle him out of the jurisdiction

[78] [1929] IR 558.

[79] This was in the fourth edition of *Kelly: The Irish Constitution* (2003) 1646. For the position up to the late 1950s see O'Higgins (1958).

[80] [1937] IR 699.

[81] Ibid, 716.

[82] [1952] IR 62 (Maguire CJ, Murnaghan, O'Byrne, Black and Lavery JJ).

[83] [1965] IR 70.

[84] Ibid, 118.

[85] Ibid, 119.

before he has an opportunity of considering his rights is the negation of law and a denial of justice'.[86] The two earlier Supreme Court decisions were distinguished on the basis that they had not dealt with the specific point at issue in *The State (Quinn) v Ryan*; moreover the *Brennan and Kingston* case had been decided by the 'former' Supreme Court of the Irish Free State on a provision in the Irish Free State's Constitution, the implication being that decisions of that Court were not binding on the 'new' (post-1961) Supreme Court even when interpreting similar provisions in the 1937 Constitution.[87]

The other four judges agreed with Ó Dálaigh CJ's judgment, but Walsh J added two important points of substance.[88] The first was that the protection given by Article 40.4 of the 1937 Constitution to the right to challenge one's deprivation of liberty is, effectively, absolute:

> [A] right to apply to the High Court or any Judge thereof is conferred on every person who wishes to challenge the legality of his detention. It must follow that any law which makes it possible to frustrate that right must necessarily be invalid having regard to that provision of the Constitution.[89]

Walsh J's second point related to the operation of the doctrine of precedent. Aware that at that time the House of Lords still doggedly adhered to the principle that it could not go against its own previous decisions on any matter, Walsh J stressed that the Irish Supreme Court:

> ... is the creation of the Constitution and is not in any sense the successor in Ireland of the House of Lords ... I reject the submission that because upon the foundation of the State our Courts took over an English legal system and the common law that the Courts must be deemed to have adopted and should now an adopt an approach to Constitutional questions conditioned by English judicial methods and English legal training which despite their undoubted excellence were not fashioned for interpreting written constitutions or reviewing the constitutionality of legislation. In this State one would have expected that if the approach of any Court of final appeal of another State was to have been held up as an example for this Court to follow it would more appropriately have been the Supreme Court of the United States rather than the House of Lords.

Mac Cormaic has traced how at this time Brian Walsh was in regular correspondence with Justice William Brennan of the US Supreme Court,[90] and clearly this dictum was influenced by Walsh's growing awareness of the accomplishments of that Court. In 1963 the US Supreme Court's seminal decision in *Brown v Board of Education*[91] was still a fairly recent memory.

Some five months after declaring the 1851 legislation to be incompatible with the Constitution, the Supreme Court considered charges of criminal contempt against two members of the Garda Síochána and two members of the London Metropolitan Police who had been involved in the *Quinn* case. Each of them was found guilty but, in light of their fulsome apologies, and of their supposed ignorance of the correct legal position in Ireland, they were spared any punishment.[92]

The Extradition Act 1965, *Bourke* and *Magee*

The main impact of the decision in *The State (Quinn) v Ryan* was that it prompted new legislation in Ireland—the Extradition Act 1965. The government was already planning such

[86] Ibid, 121. [87] For the establishment of the 'new' Supreme Court see Chap 4 above, 47.
[88] The other three judges were Lavery, Kingsmill Moore, and Haugh JJ. [89] [1965] IR 70, 124.
[90] Mac Cormaic (2016) 82–4, 138–9, 192–3. [91] 347 US 483 (1954). [92] [1965] IR 70, 136–41.

legislation to enable it to ratify the Council of Europe's treaty on extradition, which had been agreed in 1957. Part II of the Act duly covered extradition based on treaties while Part III dealt with extradition arrangements with Northern Ireland, England and Wales, Scotland, the Isle of Man and the Channel Islands. By way of reciprocation the UK Parliament enacted the Backing of Warrants (Republic of Ireland) Act 1965. The arrangements were similar to the 1851 system in that they depended on a warrant issued in one jurisdiction being 'backed' in the other, but they differed in that they recognised for the first time the so-called 'political offence defence'.[93] This was because Article 3 of the Council of Europe's 1957 Convention allowed for such a defence. In Ireland's Act provision was made for the release of a person whose extradition had been requested if the offence was a 'political offence or an offence connected with a political offence',[94] which mirrors the wording of Article 3. Despite the IRA's border campaign of 1956–62, which had prompted the Republic to introduce internment,[95] the government of the day did not choose to qualify its acceptance of Article 3 to take account of how the political offence exception might operate vis-à-vis offences committed in Northern Ireland relating to the campaign to reunify Ireland.[96] Ireland duly ratified the Convention in 1966. The United Kingdom remained opposed to any general political offence defence so it chose not to ratify the Council of Europe Convention and in its Act allowing extradition from and to Ireland it limited the defence to where the offence was 'of a political character'.[97] However in the United Kingdom's legislation this bar was mandatory, meaning that if the offence was of a political character the person could not be extradited. In the Irish legislation the wording was discretionary: it said that if the offence was political or connected with a political offence the court 'may' direct that a warrant not be endorsed or that an accused person be released.

It was not long before the Irish Supreme Court was confronted with the argument that this apparently discretionary wording should be interpreted as if it were mandatory. This was in *Bourke v Attorney General*,[98] where police in England had requested the extradition of Mr Bourke for his alleged involvement in the escape from Wormwood Scrubs Prison in London of George Blake, a convicted Russian spy.[99] In the High Court O'Keeffe P ruled that George Blake's offences were clearly political and that Mr Bourke's offence in assisting him to escape was 'connected with' those offences even though it was not itself a political offence. He went on to hold, surprisingly, that although the legislation said that he 'may direct' Mr Bourke's release he should interpret it as reading 'shall direct'. The only justifications he gave for this conclusion were that the Attorney General, against whom the action was being taken, had conceded the point and that he did not have 'very much choice as to what course to adopt'.[100] On appeal the Supreme Court came to the same conclusion, holding that the wording of section 50(2) of the Extradition Act 1965 was mandatory and not discretionary. Ó Dálaigh CJ pointed out that under section 11 in Part II of the 1965 Act (dealing with extradition generally) extradition *must* not be granted for offences which are political or connected with political offences; he then simply asserted that under section 50 in Part III of the 1965 Act (dealing with extradition between Ireland and the UK), despite its saying that a direction not to extradite *may* be given in those circumstances, 'there can

[93] See, generally, Hogan et al (2018) 11932-58; Gilbert (1992); Delany and Hogan (1993).

[94] Extradition Act 1965, ss 44(2) and 50(2), both within Part III of the Act. The equivalent provision in Part II was s 11(1).

[95] Maguire (2008) Chap 5 (esp 130–42).

[96] A point made by Walsh J in a later Supreme Court case on extradition, *Finucane v McMahon* [1990] 1 IR 165, 215 (see 166-8 below).

[97] Backing of Warrants (Republic of Ireland) Act 1965, s 2(2).

[98] [1972] IR 36. See Mac Cormaic (2016) 217-220.

[99] The escape occurred on 22 October 1966.

[100] [1972] IR 36, 47.

be no room for doubt that section 50 of the same Act is also a mandatory provision'.[101] With respect, it is hard to see how the Chief Justice could have been so categorical on the matter. FitzGerald J did not dissent on that point but he did say that the words in section 50 'are quite plain and their meaning is quite clear' and he did not think that Bourke's offence was itself either a political offence or connected with Blake's political offences.[102]

In another case decided on the same day, *The State (Magee) v O'Rourke*,[103] the same five Supreme Court Justices, by 3 v 2, refused to extradite a man to Northern Ireland where an arrest warrant had been issued for his alleged involvement in housebreaking, driving without insurance, malicious damage and assaulting a police officer.[104] While the man in question, George Magee, did not argue that any of these offences were political in nature, he did claim that if he were returned to Northern Ireland he feared being prosecuted for his alleged involvement in a raid on military barracks in Holywood, County Down in 1963, seven years earlier. He swore an affidavit in connection with those fears and, because the police in Ireland were unable to rebut that evidence, it was believed. Thus, at a time when the troubles in Northern Ireland were becoming extremely serious the Irish Supreme Court was doing its best, as it saw it, to uphold the rule of law by refusing to take a course of action which was not wholly evidence-based. In the course of his judgment, with whom Walsh and Budd JJ agreed, Ó Dálaigh CJ said that:

> In as clear language as perhaps one could expect in the circumstances, Magee has confessed to being concerned in the preparation of an armed IRA raid on Holywood military barracks. There can be little room for doubt that his action falls either within the category of 'political offence' or of 'offence connected with a political offence'. Counsel for the respondent has offered no argument to the contrary and, in any event, in my judgment Magee has clearly brought himself within the terms of paragraph (*b*) of s 50(2) of the Extradition Act 1965.[105]

FitzGerald J, on the other hand, with whom Teevan J agreed,[106] was of the view that Magee had failed to establish substantial reasons for believing that he would be detained or prosecuted for any political offence in the North. For him it was not the applicant's fears or belief that mattered so much as the probability of a prosecution occurring. He also had regard to the purpose of the Extradition Act 1965 and the corresponding Act in the United Kingdom and added:

> Unless and until statutes are abused by a requesting country, I consider that it should be assumed that it will be properly used. On extradition subsequent to a decision of the High Court or the Supreme Court in this country, I am not prepared to hold that the requesting country is likely to be guilty of a breach of faith by prosecuting or detaining the alleged offender for a political offence.

With this dissenting judgment, and the one in *Bourke*, we see fissures opening up within the Supreme Court on this highly sensitive issue. FitzGerald J, of course, was to become Chief Justice in 1973.

The Law Enforcement Commission Report

I have set out elsewhere the difficulties which the Irish Supreme Court's approach to extradition created for the legal system of Northern Ireland in the 1970s and 1980s.[107] They were

[101] Ibid, 50. [102] Ibid, 67. [103] [1971] IR 205. See Mac Cormaic (2016) 220-1.
[104] FitzGerald and Teevan JJ dissented. [105] [1971] IR 205, 211.
[106] Teevan J was a judge of the High Court who had been asked to sit in the Supreme Court for this case.
[107] Dickson (2010) 217–21. See too Connelly (1982).

perhaps most starkly reflected in the schism which developed within the intra-jurisdictional Commission established as a result of the Sunningdale Agreement in 1973. The four members of that Commission from the Republic of Ireland (led by Walsh J and including Henchy J) supported the view that extradition was not the way to solve the problems in bringing to justice people living in one of the jurisdictions but suspected of having perpetrated serious crimes in the other.[108] Their view was that it was not possible to change Irish and UK law in that way because of prohibitions existing under Irish constitutional law and Ireland's international obligations. The four members from the United Kingdom, including the current and a future Lord Chief Justice of Northern Ireland (both of whom eventually became Lords of Appeal in Ordinary),[109] staunchly supported the view that extradition *was* the best option.[110] They did not accept that international law necessarily stood in the way of such a reform. The view of the UK Commissioners was that a list of offences could be included in both the Irish and the UK Acts 'in respect of which it would no longer be possible for a fugitive in one jurisdiction to claim protection on political grounds against extradition to the other'.[111] They carefully analysed the judgment of the Supreme Court delivered by Maguire CJ in *The State (Duggan) v Tapley*,[112] concluding that he firmly established that under international law there was no absolute rule that States could not extradite persons accused of political offences; they added that 'the international climate is arguably more favourable to extradition for political offences than in 1950',[113] the date of the decision in *Tapley*. Amazingly, *Tapley* does not appear to have been cited to or by the Supreme Court judges in either *Bourke v Attorney General*[114] or *Re Article 26 and the Criminal Law (Jurisdiction) Bill 1975*.[115]

The UK Commissioners also relied on two earlier Supreme Court decisions, *The State (Sumers Jennings) v Furlong*[116] and *In re Ó Laighléis*,[117] to show that the Irish Constitution was also no barrier to the proposed changes to extradition law. While Article 29.3 of the Constitution states that 'Ireland accepts the generally recognised principles of international law as its rules of conduct in its relations with other States', this did not mean (even if it is assumed that there is a generally recognised principle against extradition of political offenders) that it prevailed over domestic Irish law. As Davitt P put it in *In re Ó Laighléis*:

> Where there is an irreconcilable conflict between a domestic statute and the principles of international law or the provisions of an international convention, Courts administering the domestic law must give effect to the statute.[118]

Finally, in a rare example of resort to the authority of public opinion, the UK Commissioners noted that 'only a very small minority in any part of Ireland has in fact voiced disapproval of the declared joint intention to bring to trial those who have committed crimes of violence, however motivated, in any part of Ireland'.[119]

The riposte of the Irish members of the Commission to the points raised by the UK Commissioners was focused on three matters. First, they stressed that the refusal to extradite persons accused of 'political offences' (even though countries may differ as to how to

[108] *Report of the Law Enforcement Commission* (1974), Cmnd 5627 and Prl 3832, paras 41–74.

[109] These were, respectively, Sir Robert Lowry and Brian Hutton QC; Scarman LJ was also a member.

[110] Note 108 above, paras 75–110.

[111] Ibid, para 13.

[112] [1952] IR 62. The other judges were Murnaghan, O'Byrne, Black and Lavery JJ. The Supreme Court affirmed the decision of Gavan Duffy P in the High Court.

[113] Note 108 above, para 89. At paras 101–04 the UK members of the Commission found further support for this view in the Resolution on International Terrorism agreed by the Committee of Ministers of the Council of Europe on 24 January 1974.

[114] Note 98 above.

[115] See 147 above and 157-9 below.

[116] [1966] IR 183.

[117] [1960] IR 93. See too Chap 12 below, 270-2.

[118] Ibid, 103.

[119] Note 108 above, para 105(b).

define that term) *was* a well recognised principle of international law. Second, they observed that the UK government had itself adhered to that view when faced with the UN's Convention on Genocide of 1948: it delayed ratifying that treaty until 1969 because of its preference for retaining the option of trying alleged genocidists within the United Kingdom rather than being obliged to send them abroad. Third, although there may be a trend towards allowing the extradition of political offenders in the context of 'international terrorism', that was not the context within which the current debate was taking place. The Irish Commissioners cited some of the same academic experts as the UK Commissioners (Wheaton, Oppenheim and O'Connell, all well-known international law scholars) but they focused on different aspects of what was written by those experts. They also suggested that because extradition is not permitted under the common law of either Ireland or England, the statutes which derogate from that position must be strictly construed.[120] As regards the *Tapley* case, they suggested it was 'to say the least, open to doubt for several reasons that this case would now be accepted as authoritative'[121] because in the 23 years which had elapsed since it was decided all of the multilateral extradition treaties had excluded political offenders from being extradited.[122] Similar doubts were cast on the UK Commissioners' interpretation of *The State (Sumers Jennings) v Furlong*[123] and *In re Ó Laighléis*:[124] the relevant judicial statements were *obiter dicta* and should not be applied in different contexts. The Irish contingent also disputed the suggestion that Ireland and the UK were at liberty, notwithstanding the European Convention on Extradition of 1957, which Ireland had ratified but the UK had not, to make their own bilateral arrangements for the extradition of political offenders. That would amount, it was said, to a proposal from the Law Enforcement Commission that the Irish government should denounce the Convention.[125] It would also be anomalous and impractical since it would lead to people being extradited from Ireland to Northern Ireland for offences for which they could not be extradited to Great Britain.

Re Article 26 and the Criminal Law (Jurisdiction) Bill 1975

The dispute between the representatives of the two jurisdictions was eventually resolved in favour of the option of 'extra-territorial jurisdiction'. The UK Parliament enacted the Criminal Jurisdiction Act 1975 and the Oireachtas approved the Criminal Law (Jurisdiction) Bill 1976. But a week after the latter Bill was agreed President Ó Dálaigh referred it to the Supreme Court, as was his right under Article 26 of the Constitution,[126] for an opinion on whether it was compatible with the Constitution. His decision was doubtless prompted by some of the dicta in the *Boland* case. The Supreme Court assigned solicitors and counsel to argue that the Bill was unconstitutional while the government's own lawyers argued for its validity.[127]

The provisions which came under close scrutiny were sections 2, 3 and 11. Section 2 stated that where a person had done an act in Northern Ireland which, if done in the Republic, would constitute an offence specified in the Schedule to the Act, he or she would be guilty of an offence in the Republic and if convicted would be liable to suffer the penalty he or she would have been liable to if the act had been done in the Republic.[128] This applied also to persons accused of aiding, abetting, counselling or procuring one of the scheduled offences, and to persons impeding the apprehension or prosecution of such accused

[120] Ibid, para 55. [121] Ibid, para 56. [122] Ibid, para 61. [123] [1966] IR 183.
[124] [1960] IR 93. [125] For a contrary view see Symmons (1973) and (1978).
[126] For more comprehensive treatment of this provision see Chap 6 above, 106–19.
[127] The appointed counsel included Donal Barrington SC and Hugh O'Flaherty. [128] s 2(1).

persons, whether in Northern Ireland or the Republic.[129] Section 3 made it an offence in the Republic, punishable with up to seven years in prison, to have escaped from custody in Northern Ireland after having been charged with or convicted of one of the scheduled offences. Section 11 provided that for the purposes of the trial of an offence under section 2 or 3,[130] or of any appeal from such a trial, the trial court must, if requested to do so by the prosecution or the accused and unless satisfied that it was not in the interests of justice to do so,[131] ask the Lord Chief Justice of Northern Ireland to arrange for evidence to be taken by a High Court judge, in the presence of the members of the Republic's court, from a specified witness.[132] The scheduled offences included murder, manslaughter, arson, kidnapping, false imprisonment, malicious damage, causing grievous bodily harm, causing explosions, robbery, aggravated burglary and possession of firearms.[133]

In responding to the President's reference, O'Higgins CJ delivered the single judgment of the Court.[134] His initial point was that the presumption of constitutionality should apply to Article 26 references in the same way as it applies in cases where the constitutionality of Acts is in question.[135] He then considered the argument that sections 2 and 3 of the Bill were repugnant to Articles 2 and 3 of the Constitution because the latter provisions purported to prohibit the Oireachtas from legislating in relation to matters occurring in Northern Ireland. The Court's answer to this was twofold. First, Article 3 of the Constitution ties the extra-territorial effect of the jurisdiction of the Oireachtas to 'the like area and extent of application as the laws of Saorstát Éireann', and there was no doubt that Saorstát Éireann did have jurisdiction to pass laws with extra-territorial effect. This jurisdiction was acquired when the Dáil passed an Act approving the 1922 Constitution of the Irish Free State,[136] even if other dominions did not acquire that right until it was conferred by the Statute of Westminster 1931. Second, international law recognised that every sovereign State has 'power to legislate with extra-territorial effect in the sense that it may enact that acts or omissions done outside its borders are criminal offences which may be successfully prosecuted within its borders ... provided that the events, acts or persons to which its enactment applies bear upon the peace, order and good government of the legislating State'.[137] This is a rare example of the Supreme Court accepting the binding effect within Irish domestic law of a principle of international law, though whether the authorities cited would have been enough to persuade the Court to reach the conclusion it did in the absence of some relevant case law is a moot point.

As regards the compatibility of section 11 of the Bill with the Constitution, the Court again had two answers. First, it did not think the Bill was unconstitutional simply on the basis that it envisaged special courts dealing with the offences in question: the Court could not accept that the effective administration of justice or the preservation of public peace and

[129] ss 2(2)–(6),

[130] Strangely, s 11(1) limits this to trials before the Special Criminal Court (established under Art 38.3.1 of the Constitution), the implied assumption being that all such trials would take place there.

[131] It also allowed the Republic's court to make a request of its own motion.

[132] s 12 provided for evidence to be taken in the Republic in relation to a trial in Northern Ireland.

[133] To accommodate the Act some amendments were made by ss 4–9 to Ireland's Explosive Substances Act 1883, Larceny Act 1916 and Firearms Act 1964, bringing the law into line with laws applying in Northern Ireland.

[134] *Re Article 26 and the Criminal Law (Jurisdiction) Bill 1975* [1977] IR 129. The other judges were Finlay, Griffin, Kenny and Parke JJ; Redmond (1978).

[135] He cited, eg, *Re Article 26 of the Constitution and the Offences against the State (Amendment) Bill 1940* [1940] IR 470, 478 (per Sullivan CJ).

[136] Constitution of the Irish Free State (Saorstát Éireann) Act 1922. O'Higgins CJ cited in support the view expressed by FitzGibbon J in *R (Alexander) v Circuit Judge for Cork* [1925] 2 IR 165.

[137] [1977] IR 129, 149. O'Higgins CJ cited the decision of the Permanent Court of International Justice in *The Lotus Case* (1927) PCIJ Ser A, No 10 and *O'Connell on International Law* (2nd ed, Vol 2, 602).

order within the State, which are the prerequisites set out in the Constitution for the creation of special courts,[138] could not be affected by an offence the constituent acts of which are committed outside the State. Second, section 11 did not conflict with the Constitution because it did not permit the operation of unfair trial procedures, fail to provide for trial in due course of law, or in any other way fail to defend or vindicate the personal rights of the citizen as required by Article 40.3.1 of the Constitution. In reaching these conclusions it could be argued that the Supreme Court adopted a laxer approach to some procedures under the Bill than it would have done if the Bill had not been the result of an international agreement struck between the Irish and British governments. For a start, it saw nothing wrong with the accused person having to be in police custody while in Northern Ireland if a witness's evidence was to be taken in that jurisdiction: the implication was that such custody was necessary to prevent the accused absconding. In addition, the Court saw no contradiction between the accused having to be in police custody while in Northern Ireland and his or her right under the Republic's law not to be refused bail just because he or she might later commit another offence:[139]

> the requirements as to custody are obviously necessary, and no more than necessary, to secure that the accused while in Northern Ireland will receive proper protection and will be returned at the conclusion of the evidence to the jurisdiction of the State, there to be returned into such custody as had existed or to be released on bail, as the court may decide.[140]

The Court did concede, however, that when an accused was present to hear a witness's evidence in Northern Ireland he or she should be supplied in advance, as would be the case in the Republic, with a copy of what the witness intends to say.[141]

In holding the Bill to be compatible with the Constitution the Supreme Court was clearly endorsing the Irish government's efforts to comply with the agreement it had entered into with the British. Had the Court found an incompatibility such compliance would at the very least have been delayed, but the impression would also have been given that the Republic was not serious about helping to bring to justice people accused of appalling crimes in Northern Ireland. Tellingly, O'Higgins CJ referred to this context at the very beginning of the Court's judgment[142] and it no doubt influenced the Court in its assessment of whether the Bill struck 'a fair and just balance between the exercise of individual freedoms and the requirements of an ordered society'.[143]

A Change of Heart

The Criminal Law (Jurisdiction) Bill thus became an Act, but the practice of United Kingdom authorities asking for suspects to be extradited from Ireland to Great Britain continued, and in turn the suspects tried to use Irish law to resist such requests. The first of these cases to reach the Supreme Court was *Hanlon v Fleming* in 1981,[144] where Maurice

[138] Art 38.3.1.

[139] A right affirmed by the Supreme Court in *The State (Attorney General) v O'Callaghan* [1966] IR 501; see too Chap 10 below, 207-8.

[140] [1977] IR 129, 154.

[141] Ibid, 155–6. But the Court specifically did not decide whether there is a constitutional right to have prior notice of evidence to be given in a criminal trial.

[142] Ibid, 142–3.

[143] Ibid, 152. This was with reference to the phase 'due course of law' in Art 38.1 of the Constitution.

[144] [1981] IR 489; see too Chap 12 below, 273. In the later cases of *McMahon v Leahy* and *Shannon v Fanning* (see nn 158 and 163 below) reference is made to the unreported High Court decision of Finlay J, as he then was, in *Burns v Attorney General* (4 February 1974): he refused to extradite to England a man who was accused of the unlawful possession of explosives for use by the IRA. There were several other unreported High Court decisions

Hanlon fought extradition to England by arguing that the offences for which he was charged there—dishonestly receiving nine electric detonators and four ounces of gelatine, knowing them to be stolen goods—were political offences. Henchy J (one of the Irish judges who had sat on the Law Enforcement Commission, where he had been opposed to extradition) held that they were not political offences, and O'Higgins CJ and Griffin J agreed with him. The reason for so concluding was the finding of fact by the High Court judge in the court below that there was no acceptable evidence that any of the proceeds of the accused's alleged crimes were used for the purposes of the IRA 'in such a way as to lend political colour to the offences'.[145] Intriguingly, Henchy J went on to say that even if there had been such evidence it did not necessarily follow that the accused would have been exempt from extradition because of the political offence defence: 'There has been no decision of this Court on such a point. It must be left open for an appropriate case.'[146] In the subsequent case of *Maguire v Keane*[147] the Supreme Court seemed to agree that such evidence would not necessarily lead to a different result. In the High Court Egan J believed that a man who had allegedly committed a robbery in England had given his share of the stolen money to the IRA on whose behalf he said he had been acting at the time, but Walsh J, supported by his four brethren in the Supreme Court,[148] perhaps all of them suspecting that this was a clever ruse by an 'ordinary' criminal to escape justice, held that Maguire had not adduced sufficient evidence to show that he had in fact been acting on behalf of the IRA. He too was therefore extradited to England.

The *McGlinchey* litigation

Just over a year later, in 1982, the extradition issue arose before the same judges in another case, but this time the requesting jurisdiction was not England and Wales but Northern Ireland. The use of juryless Diplock courts in that jurisdiction made the matter all the more controversial, even though the juryless Special Criminal Court was also operating in Dublin. In *McGlinchey v Wren*[149] the wanted person, Dominic McGlinchey, was accused of shooting dead a grandmother in the course of an attack on her house in Northern Ireland committed by him and three other men in 1977. In the High Court McGlinchey argued that the alleged offence was 'a political offence or an offence connected with a political offence', under section 50(2)(a) of the Extradition Act 1965, and that he had engaged in it as a member of the Provisional IRA. Gannon J rejected that claim, but as his decision is not officially reported we do not know his reasoning. McGlinchey had submitted excerpts from the *Ballymena Guardian*, a copy of a 'wanted' poster referring to him by name and a charge sheet relating to another man who was accused of withholding information about McGlinchey's involvement in terrorist activities, but all of this did not amount to sufficient evidence to persuade Gannon J that McGlinchey was a politically motivated offender. On appeal to the Supreme Court McGlinchey abandoned his claim under section 50(2)(a) and instead relied on section 50(2)(b), which prohibits extradition where 'there are substantial reasons for believing that the person named or described in the warrant will, if removed

between 1874 and 1976; they are listed in McCarthy J's judgment in *Finucane v McMahon* [1990] 1 IR 165, 223 and in Hogan and Walker (1989) 303.

[145] Ibid, 495. The fact that the High Court judge is unnamed may not be unconnected to the fact that it came to light that he or she had delayed for five-and-a-half years between the hearing of the case in April 1975 and the delivery of a judgment in October 1980!

[146] Ibid. [147] [1986] IR 154. [148] Finlay CJ, Henchy, Griffin and McCarthy JJ.

[149] [1982] IR 154 (O'Higgins CJ, Henchy, and Griffin JJ).

from the State under this Part [of the 1965 Act], be prosecuted or detained for a political offence or an offence connected with a political offence'. O'Higgins CJ strongly hinted that even if McGlinchey had not conceded that the murder of Hester McMullan could not be regarded as a political offence he would have held that to be the case; he said that 'modern terrorist violence, whether undertaken by military or para-military organisations, or by an individual or groups of individuals, is often the antithesis of what could reasonably be regarded as political, either in itself or in its connections'.[150]

As regards the argument that McGlinchey might still be prosecuted or detained in Northern Ireland for a political offence the Chief Justice held that no evidence had been adduced to support that possibility. Significantly he added:

> This Court is invited to assume that, because of the existence of widespread violence organised by para-military groups in Northern Ireland, any charge which is associated with terrorist activity should be regarded as a charge in respect of a political offence or an offence connected with a political offence. I am not prepared to make any such assumption.
>
> The excusing *per se* of murder and of offences involving violence, and the infliction of human suffering by, or at the behest of, self-ordained arbiters, are the very antithesis of the ordinances of Christianity and civilisation and of the basic requirements of political activity.[151]

These very strong words seem a mile away from the arguments put forward by Walsh and Henchy JJ when they were sitting as two of the four Irish members of the Law Enforcement Commission eight years earlier. Yet in *McGlinchey*, Henchy J was one of the two judges who concurred with everything O'Higgins CJ said.[152] Perhaps the fact that more than 1,400 people had been killed in Northern Ireland's troubles between 1974 and 1982 had a sobering effect on the judges. It has been observed that to substantiate their change of heart the judges could have pointed to the Preamble to the Constitution, which promotes ideals hardly in line with those pursued by those in Ireland who use violence for political ends.[153]

During the course of the proceedings in his claim for political exemption McGlinchey absconded while on bail. He was on the run for over a year before being re-arrested after a shoot-out with the Garda Síochána in County Clare in March 1984. There was then a further challenge to his extradition order, based on the alleged unconstitutionality of the Extradition Act 1965, and this led to an unreported *ex tempore* judgment of the Supreme Court on 17 March 1984 summarily dismissing the challenge.[154] After being extradited he was convicted of the murder of Hester McMullan but was acquitted on appeal, whereupon he was extradited back to Ireland at that country's request to face charges arising out of the shoot-out in County Clare. He was convicted in the Special Criminal Court and sentenced to 10 years in prison, a challenge against that decision again failing in the Supreme Court[155] and also in the European Commission of Human Rights.[156] Undeterred, while he was in prison McGlinchey issued yet another challenge, this time arguing that the initial warrant for his arrest issued in Belfast in 1981 was invalid. Costello J actually agreed that McGlinchey was correct on this point, because amongst other reasons the police officer who swore the complaint leading to the issue of the warrant had not signed the complaint

150 Ibid, 159. 151 Ibid, 160.

152 The other was Griffin J. Humphreys thinks that if there had been five judges in this case 'there would have been far greater continuity in judicial decision-making in this most sensitive of areas': Humphreys (1990) 127, 130.

153 Hogan et al (2018) 1938.

154 *Irish Times*, 19 March 1984 (O'Higgins CJ, Henchy and Griffin JJ); Humphreys (1990) 129–30. The story of this hearing and the context within which it took place is grippingly told by Tóibin (1985).

155 *McGlinchey v Governor of Portlaoise Prison* [1988] IR 671.

156 *McGlinchey v Ireland* App No 16751/90 (5 March 1991). See too App 5 below, 334.

as required by law, but the judge then held that there were sufficient other safeguards in the extradition legislation to allow McGlinchey to have relied on the warrant's invalidity at earlier stages in various court proceedings.[157] Costello J also rejected an argument that the Extradition Act 1965 was unconstitutional because it deprived McGlinchey of the right to protection of his constitutional right to liberty: McGlinchey could still claim that right to protection if he had evidence to support a breach of his right to liberty, but he did not. This decision was not appealed to the Supreme Court. McGlinchey was released from prison in March 1993 but within a year he had been murdered. To date no-one has been prosecuted in relation to his killing.

McMahon v Leahy, *Shannon v Fanning* and *Quinn v Wren*

In June 1984 the three judges who had sat in *McGlinchey v Wren* were joined by two additional judges, Hederman and McCarthy JJ, to hear an appeal to the Supreme Court by Philip McMahon.[158] He had fled to the Republic after having escaped from custody in Northern Ireland where he was serving an eight-year sentence for robbery and unlawful possession of a firearm. When challenging his extradition he admitted that he had carried out the offences as a member of the IRA. In the High Court, Keane J (a future Chief Justice), followed the approach taken by O'Higgins CJ in *McGlinchey*, namely, that before a person could evade extradition on the basis of the political offence exception he or she would have to adduce evidence that the offence arose, directly or indirectly, out of political activity: it could not be presumed from the existence of widespread violence organised by paramilitary groups in Northern Ireland.[159] Applying that test, Keane J said the evidence before him 'falls far short of the clear and cogent evidence which would be required to elevate such a crime into the genus of political crime in respect of which the State must afford asylum to the fugitive criminal'.[160] Surprisingly, this decision was overturned on appeal. What persuaded all five Supreme Court judges to adopt such a generous attitude was the fact that seven years earlier, in two High Court applications, four men who had escaped from custody in Northern Ireland at the same time as McMahon had successfully pleaded the political offence exception before Butler J and Finlay P; the State, moreover, had not sought to appeal those decisions to the Supreme Court. The Supreme Court therefore felt it would breach the right of all citizens of Ireland to be held equal before the law[161] if McMahon were not also allowed to evade extradition (as if the High Court can never be mistaken). McCarthy J agreed with this conclusion but added that he would in any event have refused extradition because there were flaws in the documentation produced by the police and the magistrate in Northern Ireland, flaws which he described as slipshod and careless.[162]

A month later the same five Supreme Court Justices applied *McGlinchey v Wren* to allow the extradition of Séamus Shannon to Northern Ireland for his alleged involvement in the 1981 murders of Sir Norman Stronge and his son James, both former members of the House of Commons of Northern Ireland, at their home in Tynan Abbey, County Armagh.[163] Once more the case reduced itself to the criteria which should be used for deciding what constitutes a political offence. O'Higgins CJ (with whom again Henchy and Griffin JJ concurred without adding anything) held that it depended on 'the particular facts and circumstances

[157] *McGlinchey v Ireland (No 2)* [1990] 2 IR 220. [158] *McMahon v Leahy* [1984] IR 525.

[159] Keane J also cited the words of Finlay J in *Burns v Attorney General* (High Court, 4 February 1974), on which see n 144 above.

[160] [1984] IR 525, 533. [161] Art 40.1 of the Constitution. [162] [1984] IR 525, 546–7.

[163] *Shannon v Fanning* [1984] IR 569. The Stronges' home was also burnt down.

of each case, viewed in the light of the standards and values which obtain in this country at the particular time'.[164] After citing his own words from the *McGlinchey* case, O'Higgins CJ added that:

> Apart from the fact that, as appeared from other cases coming before this Court, the Provisional IRA has abjured normal political activity in favour of violence and terrorism, the circumstances (as so disclosed) of the murders in question here were so brutal, cowardly and callous that it would be a distortion of language if they were to be accorded the status of political offences or offences connected with political offences.[165]

Hederman J's criterion for marking out political offences, on the other hand, was simply whether the person accused had acted with a political motive or for a political purpose. There must be evidence that this person did the act alleged and did so for political reasons. The nature of the offence itself, under this test, seems to be irrelevant. As the burden of proving such motive or purpose lies on the person accused, and as no such evidence had been forthcoming in this case, the offences charged could not be labelled as political or as connected with political offences. The judge could not agree with the test applied by O'Higgins CJ and Henchy and Griffin JJ: he thought it 'could only create uncertainty'[166] and he cited the example of the murder of a despotic ruler: this would be repugnant to people who regard any violence as unreasonable and uncivilised, but it would still be regarded by many others as political activity. McCarthy J, the fifth judge in the case, agreed with Hederman J that assessing the true motivation of the person who committed the offence was key to determining whether it was a political offence but he thought that the nature of the offence, the identity of the victim and the 'proximity' of these factors to the alleged political aim were important too. In rejecting Shannon's argument that if the aim of a criminal is truly political it does not matter how revolting the circumstances of the crime committed may be, McCarthy J alluded to the case where a young woman might be shot dead on a public street in order to deter her father, a Belfast magistrate, from carrying out his duties in that role. This was probably a thinly veiled reference to the murder of Mary Travers in Belfast on 8 April 1984, just three months before the Supreme Court's hearing of the appeal in *Shannon*.[167]

Quinn v Wren,[168] decided in 1985, is another Supreme Court decision which undermines the reasoning adopted by the Irish members of the Law Enforcement Commission in 1974. John Quinn admitted that he had dishonestly obtained £600 from a branch of Barclay's Bank in London by deceitfully trying to cash forged travellers' cheques, but he argued that he should not be extradited from Ireland to England to face trial for that offence because he had committed it as a member of the Irish National Liberation Army (INLA), an illegal organisation which was seeking to establish an all-Ireland Republic by force of arms. By now Finlay CJ had assumed the role of Chief Justice in place of Tom O'Higgins, but he and his four colleagues[169] could all see how perverse it would be to allow such a person to claim the protection of the political offence defence whenever he himself wanted to overthrow the State from whose legal system he was seeking protection. The word used by McCarthy J to describe such an argument was 'ludicrous'.[170] None of the judges thought

[164] Ibid, 580. It should be noted that the headnote to this case (at 570) slightly distorts what O'Higgins CJ said by suggesting that his test for deciding whether an offence was political was whether 'reasonable, civilised people would regard [it] as political activity'. That language occurs in the *McGlinchey* case, not *Shannon*.

[165] Ibid, 581.

[166] Ibid, 588.

[167] See Deborah McAleese, 'Judge Travers agony over daughter Mary's murder revealed in book', *Belfast Telegraph*, 2 November 2015.

[168] [1985] IR 322.

[169] Henchy, Griffin, Hederman and McCarthy JJ.

[170] [1985] IR 322, 340.

it was possible to set out a comprehensive definition of political offence; they preferred to adopt O'Higgins CJ's approach in *Shannon v Fanning*, which was to assess each case on its own particular facts.

The Extradition (Convention on the Suppression of Terrorism) Act 1987

In 1977 the Council of Europe agreed a Convention on the Suppression of Terrorism, the main purpose of which, by way of supplementing its 1957 forerunner,[171] was to make it easier for countries to extradite people who were suspected of committing acts of terrorism. It did this by indicating some offences which should not be regarded as political or as connected with political offences and these included 'acts of particular gravity', kidnapping and taking of hostages, and the use of bombs and rockets. The Convention also allowed states to exclude from the 'political offence' category any act of violence against the life, physical integrity or liberty of a person. The United Kingdom ratified the Convention just a few months after it was agreed and in the Suppression of Terrorism Act 1978 it included a list of offences not qualifying as political which was much longer than that required by the Convention.[172] Ireland did not react positively to the Convention until 1987, when it passed the Extradition (Convention on the Suppression of Terrorism) Act 1987.[173] This came into force domestically on 1 December 1987 although Ireland did not actually ratify the Convention until 1989 after a list of designated countries was issued in secondary legislation.[174] However the range of offences excluded from the political offence category in Ireland's legislation remained much narrower than in the United Kingdom's. Both the British and the Irish Act amended existing national law so as to allow an extradition request to be refused when there were substantial grounds for believing that the warrant was issued for the purpose of prosecuting, punishing or prejudicing the position of the person concerned on account of his or her race, religion, nationality, or political opinion.[175]

Russell v Fanning

It is perhaps the Supreme Court's decision in the fifth extradition case post-dating the Law Enforcement Commission report that most starkly represents the *volte-face* which Irish judges began to make in this context, even though the decision itself resulted in extradition. In *Russell v Fanning*[176] Robert Russell was fighting his extradition to Northern Ireland where he would be returned to the Maze prison from which he had escaped in 1983 along with many others, after having served just one year of a 20-year sentence for attempting to murder a police officer. He admitted to being a member of the IRA and to having escaped in order to carry on that organisation's violent campaign to end British rule in Northern Ireland. Finlay CJ and Henchy and Griffin JJ upheld the decision by O'Hanlon J in the High Court that the presumption of the constitutionality of the Extradition Act 1965 required the term 'political offence' in that Act to be interpreted in a way which prevented a person

[171] See 153-4 above. [172] Suppression of Terrorism Act 1978, Sch 1.

[173] The Act was slightly altered later in the year by the Extradition (Amendment) Act 1987. It was also in 1987 that the Extradition Act 1965 was extended to extradition arrangements with the USA: Extradition Act 1965 (Part II) (No 22) Order 1987 (SI 33). See too Gageby (1991) and, for an account of the political tension at the time, Peter Murtagh, 'Haughey's foot-dragging on extradition angered British government', *Irish Times*, 30 December 2017, 6.

[174] Extradition (European Convention on the Suppression of Terrorism) Act 1987 (Designation of Convention Countries) Order 1989 (SI 115).

[175] Suppression of Terrorism Act 1978, s 2(1); Extradition (Convention on the Suppression of Terrorism) Act 1987 (Ir), ss 8 and 9.

[176] [1988] IR 505 (decided by the same five judges as in *Quinn v Wren*).

from relying on the concept when the purpose of the offence in question was to subvert the country's Constitution or usurp the functions of the state. O'Hanlon J explicitly stated that what the IRA was seeking to do was 'not merely to end British rule in Northern Ireland but to impose its will on the people of Ireland in a manner which subverts the Constitution', citing Article 6.[177] This was a straightforward application of the Supreme Court's ruling in *Quinn v Wren*, decided less than three years earlier.

Hederman and McCarthy JJ, who had also sat in *Quinn v Wren*, were not prepared to go that far, notwithstanding McCarthy J's use of the epithet 'ludicrous' in that earlier case. Their position in *Russell v Fanning* was that acting as a member of the IRA should be distinguished from acting as a member of the INLA, even though both were subversive organisations which were illegal in both Ireland and the United Kingdom and were fundamentally opposed to the existence of separate states on the island of Ireland. Hederman J characterised the conflict in Northern Ireland as follows:

> What is happening in Northern Ireland is that a small fraction of the population there has raised a political revolt against the administration with a view to overthrowing that administration. This type of revolt or insurrectional activity is the classic form of political offence.[178]

The learned judge did not see any inconsistency between that description of what the IRA were seeking to do and his words in *Quinn v Wren* about the INLA, where he said: 'The admitted objective of the organisation referred to in the present case is by force of arms or other violent means to over-throw the Government established by the Constitution.' One would have to conclude that in this judge's mind John Quinn's deceitful acquisition of £600 in London somehow threatened the stability of the Irish state much more than Robert Russell's attempted murder of a police officer in Northern Ireland. This conclusion is only confirmed by what the judge added: 'I am not aware of any law in this State which prohibits anybody publicly urging the raising of an armed revolt in another State, aimed at the overthrow of the government of that State or urging Irish support for any such revolt, even though such policy is contrary to the stated policy of the organs of government of this State'.[179]

McCarthy J endorsed Hederman J's view that just because a person disagrees, even to the extent of using violence, with a policy of the government of the day, this does not prevent that person from seeking to rely upon the political offence exception. He described the majority's position as amounting to 'judicial repeal' of parts of section 50(2) of the Extradition Act 1965.[180] He alluded to the Extradition (Amendment) Act 1987, which had inserted provisions into the Extradition Act 1965 allowing extradition to be refused if it would be unjust, oppressive or invidious and requiring the Attorney General to be satisfied, before endorsing a warrant for extradition, that there was a clear evidence-based intention on the part of the requesting jurisdiction to prosecute the person named in the warrant.[181]

[177] Ibid, 516. Art 6.1 reads: 'All powers of government, legislative, executive and judicial derive, under God, from the people, whose right it is to designate the rulers of the State and, in final appeal, to decide all questions of national policy, according to the requirements of the common good.'

[178] Ibid, 539.

[179] Ibid, 539–40. Hederman J was influenced by the Supreme Court's decision in *McMahon v Leahy*, n 158 above.

[180] Ibid, 546–7.

[181] It was supposedly on the basis of this provision that in December 1988 the Attorney General John Murray (later a Chief Justice of Ireland) decided that a warrant for Fr Patrick Ryan's extradition to England would not be executed. He was wanted in England on suspicion of involvement in IRA activities in the Netherlands, where earlier in 1988 three off-duty British servicemen had been murdered. The Attorney General said the chances of Ryan receiving a fair trial in England had been 'irredeemably prejudiced' by reports in the British press and by statements in Parliament, including by Prime Minister Margaret Thatcher.

McCarthy J implied that the Oireachtas cannot be assumed to have accepted that from 1987 any IRA person asking not to be extradited should fail in that plea. Perhaps unwisely, given that judges should not pre-judge issues that might come before them later, he stated that if the Oireachtas intended to leave it to the courts to reduce further the application of the political offence exception, 'it will gain no support from me' as it would amount to 'judicial legislation'.[182] He did not think that the objectives of the IRA amounted to subversion of Article 6 of the Constitution[183] and he did not consider the attempted murder of a police officer in Northern Ireland as having the nature of an act that removes it from the category of being political.[184] He went on to mention two other reasons for refusing extradition in Russell's case: the risk that he might be ill-treated by prison officers if returned to Northern Ireland and the risk that he might be interrogated by police officers before being brought before a magistrate (he cited the experiences of McGlinchey and Shannon with regard to the latter risk).[185]

In accordance with the majority's decision Robert Russell was indeed extradited. This occurred a week after eight British soldiers were killed by an IRA bomb in Ballygawley, County Tyrone, and three days before three members of the IRA were shot dead by British soldiers elsewhere in the same county. In Belfast republicans reacted to Russell's extradition by planting bombs and invoking riots. In April 1989 another Maze escapee, Paul Kane, was extradited from Dublin to Belfast on the order of the Irish High Court. Perhaps because of the outcome in *Russell v Fanning* he decided not to appeal to the Supreme Court, as explained in the Dáil by Gerry Collins, the Fianna Fáil Minister for Justice.[186]

A Further U-turn: *Finucane v McMahon* and Its Aftermath

In 1990 the minority position adopted by Hederman and McCarthy JJ in *Russell v Fanning* became the new official orthodoxy of the Court in *Finucane v McMahon*.[187] It was the judgment of Walsh J which swung the matter, with Hederman and McCarthy JJ repeating the views they expressed in *Russell* and with Finlay CJ and Griffin J willing to go along with their colleagues' application of the agreed principle to what had occurred in this particular case. The fact that it was the first occasion on which the Chief Justice sat with all four of the ordinary judges in the Supreme Court in an extradition case is, suggests Humphreys, one reason why the Court was willing not to follow the decision in *Russell*.[188] The applicant, Dermot Finucane, another escapee from the Maze in 1983, had lost in the High Court[189] because the judges there applied what they thought was the *ratio* in *Russell*; they also held that Finucane had not sufficiently proved the risk that he would be ill-treated by prison staff in Northern Ireland if he were returned there. It was this latter point that Finlay CJ dealt with first in the Supreme Court.

Basing himself on facts found by the High Court, and in particular on uncontested evidence showing that many prisoners in the North had been paid *ex gratia* sums by the Northern Ireland Office for injuries they had sustained through mistreatment by prison officers and yet there had been 'a total absence of any repercussions on the staff' as a result of such ill-treatment, the Chief Justice found that it was 'a probable risk' that Finucane

[182] [1988] IR 505, 548. [183] Ibid, 552. [184] Ibid, 554. [185] Ibid, 554–8.

[186] See https://web.archive.org/web/20071127133659/http://historical-debates.oireachtas.ie/D/0388/D.0388.198904130075.html.

[187] [1990] 1 IR 165. [188] Humphreys (1990) 128–9.

[189] [1990] 1 LR 165. The judges were Hamilton P, Gannon and Costello JJ.

would be ill-treated if he were to be returned to the North.[190] This own-goal by the prison officers may well have made it easier for Finlay CJ to then hold that Finucane should also escape extradition on the basis that what he was accused of having done was a political offence even though it was done in the name of the IRA. The Chief Justice clearly came to that conclusion reluctantly, but he felt reassured that the constitutional principle he had stated in *Quinn v Wren* was to be retained,[191] even if its application in *Russell v Fanning* was now being questioned. Griffin J's judgment is in similar terms to that of Finlay CJ as regards the risk of Finucane being ill-treated if returned to Northern Ireland, but he differed from three of his colleagues in thinking that *Russell v Fanning* was correctly decided and in holding that Finucane's conviction for possessing firearms and ammunition with intent to endanger life or property was not properly classifiable as a political offence. Given that the ultimate decision as to whether an action is a political offence is one of mixed law and fact, it seems reasonable that individual judges can disagree on that point provided they state plausible reasons for their conclusion.

Walsh J's judgment in *Finucane v McMahon* is one of the most lucid in this whole field of extradition, but it is clearly underpinned by his continuing adherence to the view he advocated while serving on the Law Enforcement Commission in 1974, namely that as regards fugitive offenders from Northern Ireland an extra-territorial jurisdiction solution was much to be preferred to an extradition solution. He does not mention his membership of that Commission but he cites Colm Campbell's work as showing that the former approach had been much more effective than the latter in securing convictions.[192] He also explains how Ireland had taken account of the Council of Europe's 1977 Convention on the Suppression of Terrorism without thereby equating all politically motivated violence with terrorism. In sum, his view was, however unpalatable to many outside Ireland, that the Oireachtas 'intentionally refrained from characterising as matters directed to the overthrow of this State or as activities designed to usurp the functions of our government, the political violence in Northern Ireland which had as its objective the re-integration of the national territory'.[193] He stressed, perhaps disingenuusly, that Irish courts cannot treat extradition as a question of foreign policy: '[t]hey must remain completely impartial and detached and free from all political or diplomatic pressure in their objective determination of the issues involved'.[194] He concluded that the offence for which Finucane was convicted in Northern Ireland—having guns and ammunition with intent to endanger life, for which he was sentenced to 18 years' imprisonment—was one which qualified for the political exemption and he agreed with Finlay CJ that extradition should also be barred because of the risk of ill-treatment in Northern Ireland's prisons. Walsh J also pointed out that the sort of actions in which Finucane was alleged to have been participating *could have been* but had not yet been made justiciable in Ireland even though they were conducted outside the territory of Ireland.[195] Hederman J agreed with Finlay CJ on the ill-treatment point and with Walsh J on the political offence point; McCarthy J did likewise, but he also affirmed the views he expressed, and the reasons he gave for them, when dissenting in *Russell v Fanning*.

There was, of course, vocal opposition to the decision in *Finucane v McMahon*, in Ireland, in Northern Ireland and in Great Britain. Humphreys points out, in agreement with Walsh J, that the task of a court, especially a Supreme Court, is to apply the law in a politically

[190] Ibid, 206. Finlay CJ referred to *Pettigrew v Northern Ireland Office* [1989] 3 BNIL 83, where Hutton J, as he then was, found there had been a widespread conspiracy amongst prison officers to falsely and absolutely deny all accusations of assault and to refuse requests for medical assistance made by prisoners.

[191] This was that the political offence exception could not be applied to any person charged with an offence 'the admitted purpose of which is to further or facilitate the over-throw, by violence, of the Constitution and of the organs of State established thereby': *Quinn v Wren* [1985] IR 322, 337.

[192] [1990] 1 IR 165, 212; Campbell (1989).

[193] Ibid, 215. [194] Ibid, 216. [195] Ibid, 215. Humphreys (1990) agrees with this point (at 136).

impartial manner and he sees the decision as 'a reassuring sign of [the Supreme Court's] vigour and independence'.[196] After all, if the Oireachtas wanted to change the law it was within its power to do so. But some would think it strange that a Supreme Court believes it is being politically neutral when it characterises the kind of violence supported by Dermot Finucane as qualifying for the political offence exemption. It is also difficult to reconcile the ruling with that in *Russell v Fanning*. It may just be that Finucane's legal team were more assiduous than Russell's in unearthing evidence of the nature of the offences their clients had committed and in examining the likelihood of ill-treatment occurring in a Northern prison. Yet Finucane's offences had still merited a sentence in Northern Ireland of 18 years, just two years shorter than Russell's, and by 1990 greater safeguards were in place to combat physical abuse of those in custody in Northern Ireland than had existed in 1988.[197]

Nevertheless the Supreme Court confirmed its position just four weeks later in *Carron v McMahon*,[198] where Blayney J sat in place of Walsh J. Owen Carron, later to be elected a Sinn Féin MP in Northern Ireland as successor to the hunger-striker Bobby Sands, was sought by the police in Northern Ireland for possession of an assault rifle and ammunition with intent to endanger life. He had given a lift in his car to another man who was convicted of the possession offences. Carron had skipped bail in Northern Ireland and fled to the Republic. As in the *Finucane* case the High Court ordered his extradition but the Supreme Court overturned that decision. This time, strangely, they did not refuse extradition on the basis that the applicant risked ill-treatment at the hands of police or prison officers in Northern Ireland. The High Court's conclusion as to the weight of the evidence on that point was not doubted. It is also worth noting that pending the consideration of his ultimately successful challenge to the extradition process, Carron had been kept in custody in the Republic for more than two years.

In *Ellis v O'Dea*[199] the Supreme Court affirmed the decision of Hamilton P that Dessie Ellis, a prisoner in Ireland who was serving a sentence for crimes committed in Ireland after having been extradited from the USA, could then be extradited to England to face trial for his alleged involvement in explosions there. For some reason Ellis did not argue that his alleged offences could be described as political offences or connected with political offences and he failed to convince the Court that if he was extradited to England he would risk being dealt with in breach of the reasonable standards of fair trial required by the Irish Constitution. The bench was the same as in *Finucane v McMahon*[200] but the outcome was different. Other than that the jurisdiction requesting extradition was England and Wales rather than Northern Ireland, it is difficult to see what justifies deciding the two cases differently. Today Dessie Ellis is a Sinn Féin TD (ie MP) for a constituency in Dublin. Prior to becoming a TD he was a Dublin City Councillor for 12 years.

In *Magee v Culligan*[201] the Supreme Court was again confronted with three appeals by men who were facing extradition having escaped from prison in Northern Ireland in 1981 (this time from Belfast's Crumlin Road prison). A bench which comprised both Finlay CJ and Hamilton P, together with Hederman, McCarthy and Egan JJ, unanimously upheld the appeals by Anthony Sloan and Michael McKee, principally because they had been convicted only of possession of a machine gun and ammunition, not of their use, and so they

[196] Humphreys (1990), 137.

[197] The Criminal Injuries (Compensation) (NI) Order 1988 improved the law on recovery of compensation from April 1988 and the Police and Criminal Evidence (NI) Order 1989 gave greater rights to persons in police custody from 1 January 1990.

[198] [1990] 1 IR 239; Thompson (1991) 33–40.

[199] [1991] 1 IR 251.

[200] [1990] 1 IR 165.

[201] [1992] 1 IR 223.

qualified for the political offence defence under section 50(2)(a) of the Extradition Act 1985 as interpreted by the Supreme Court in *Finucane v McMahon*.[202] In the same case the Supreme Court rejected the appeal by Paul Magee, who had been convicted of the murder of British army captain Richard Westmacott in 1980, for which he could not claim the political offence defence. However Magee fled before the judgment was issued in November 1991. In 1993 he was convicted of murdering a part-time police officer in England and was given an 18-year sentence there. Shortly after the Good Friday Agreement in 1998 he was returned to Ireland to serve the remainder of his sentence but was released the following year in compliance with the terms of the Agreement. In 2000 the authorities in Northern Ireland sought his extradition on the back of the Supreme Court's judgment in 1991, but the British and Irish governments agreed that there was little point in pursuing that line and Magee was issued with an official royal pardon.

An interesting side-note to this litany of case law concerning extradition in cases relating to Northern Ireland's troubles is that in 1986 it came to light that the 1957 Convention on which Part II of the Extradition Act 1965 was based had never been properly ratified by Ireland. The realisation was made in *The State (Gilliland) v Governor of Mountjoy Prison*,[203] where an American citizen successfully challenged the attempt to extradite him to the USA because the relevant treaty between Ireland and the USA, the terms of which imposed a charge on public funds because it required Ireland to pay for some of the USA's expenses arising out of a person's extradition to that country,[204] had not been approved by the Dáil as required by Article 29.5.2 of the Irish Constitution.[205] As in some other extradition cases, Hederman and McCarthy JJ dissented, this time because they thought that the government's 1984 Order which extended the 1965 Act to cases involving extradition to the USA[206] was not itself a 'law' the constitutional validity of which could be referred by the High Court to the Supreme Court under Article 40.4.3 of the Constitution, but once that point was settled by the majority a single judgment of the whole Court was issued confirming the unconstitutionality of the Order on the separate ground that the treaty had not been approved by the Dáil.[207] The consequences of this decision for the validity of the 1965 Act itself were not adverted to by the Supreme Court either in *Gilliland* itself or any later case,[208] but on 12 July 1988 the Irish government informed the Council of Europe that a decision of the Supreme Court had made it impossible for Ireland to comply with its international obligations under the 1957 European Convention on Extradition because Dáil approval of its terms had not been obtained prior to its ratification by Ireland in 1966. The government rectified the matter by obtaining such approval on 29 June 1988 and deposited a new instrument of ratification with the Council of Europe.[209] For 22 years, therefore, Ireland had been extraditing people in breach of its own Constitution but no-one had noticed. No-one who was so extradited seems to have later sought a remedy for this breach of the rule of law.

[202] Note 187 above. [203] [1987] IR 201.

[204] Art 17 of the Treaty, scheduled to the Order mentioned in n 206 below.

[205] This provision reads: 'The State shall not be bound by any international agreement involving a charge upon public funds unless the terms of the agreement shall have been approved by Dáil Éireann'.

[206] Extradition Act 1965 (Part II) (No 20) Order 1984, SI No 300/1984.

[207] [1987] IR 201, 235–8.

[208] It is not mentioned in Hogan et al (2018), where the constitutionality of the 1965 Act is dealt with at 1934-5.

[209] See www.coe.int/en/web/conventions/full-list/-/conventions/treaty/024/declarations?p_auth=EEeUcjX8.

Extradition Today

Extradition between the United Kingdom and Ireland is today governed by the procedures put in place as a result of the EU's adoption of the Framework Decision on the European Arrest Warrant (EAW) in 2002.[210] These replaced the extradition arrangements in the 1965 Acts and also those between Ireland or the United Kingdom on the one hand and any other EU Member State on the other. In Ireland the Framework Decision was given effect through the European Arrest Warrant Act 2003 and in the United Kingdom through the Extradition Act 2003. Under the new procedures an EAW is issued, usually electronically, through an 'alert' being placed on a database known as the Schengen Information System. If the person named is found in one of the EU member states a certificate can be issued there justifying his or her arrest. Once an arrest has been made there must be a court hearing within 48 hours to check the identity of the individual and then a formal hearing within three weeks of the arrest to decide if the person should be extradited to the requesting state. The Framework Decision which created the EAW did not specify a 'political offence exemption' as such, but its preliminary Preamble states that:

> Nothing in this Framework Decision may be interpreted as prohibiting refusal to surrender a person for whom a European arrest warrant has been issued when there are reasons to believe, on the basis of objective elements, that the said arrest warrant has been issued for the purpose of prosecuting or punishing a person on the grounds of his or her sex, race, religion, ethnic origin, nationality, language, political opinions or sexual orientation, or that that person's position may be prejudiced for any of these reasons.[211]

The wording of this part of the Preamble is faithfully reflected in Ireland's domestic legislation,[212] which also prohibits extradition if it would be incompatible with the European Convention on Human Rights (ECHR) or in contravention of the Irish Constitution.[213] But to the latter two 'defences' there is the major exception, provided for by Article 2(2) of the Framework Decision, that extradition cannot be denied if the offence of which the person is accused is (for example) participation in a criminal organisation, terrorism, murder, grievous bodily injury, kidnapping, illegal restraint, hostage-taking, racketeering or extortion. The only prerequisite which must be satisfied in such cases is that the offence must be one which is punishable by at least three years of detention in the requesting state. It is not even necessary for the 'double criminality' of the behaviour in question to be verified, that is, no check needs to be made that the behaviour is also an offence in the requested state. In the United Kingdom's domestic legislation the wording of the Framework Decision has not been quite so faithfully reproduced. While it adheres to the rules that extradition cannot be denied if the offence in question falls within Article 2(2),[214] or if it is incompatible with the ECHR,[215] it limits the defence based on the accused's personal characteristics, or on the risk of prejudice on such a basis at his or trial, to the characteristics of gender,

[210] Council Framework Decision of 13 June 2002 on the European Arrest Warrant and the Surrender Procedure between Member States (2002/584/JHA).

[211] Preamble to the EU Framework Decision, para 12. The paragraph adds that 'This Framework Decision does not prevent a Member State from applying its constitutional rules relating to due process, freedom of association, freedom of the press and freedom of expression in other media.'

[212] European Arrest Warrant Act 2003, s 37(1)(c)(i) and (ii). See too Hogan et al (2018) 1959-67.

[213] Ibid, s 37(1)(a) and (b).

[214] Extradition Act 2003, s 11(4); it follows that from the omission from the list of 'bars to extradition' in s 11 of any mention of a bar based on the nature of the alleged crime that the UK judge *must* order the person's extradition if none of the other defences exists on the facts.

[215] Ibid, s 21(2).

race, religion, nationality, political opinion and sexual orientation. It omits 'ethnic origin' and 'language'.[216] And of course the United Kingdom's Act has no exception based on protections guaranteed by the national Constitution. In neither country, it should be noted, is there any defence that the person whose extradition is being sought is a national of that country. Both Ireland and the United Kingdom have always been prepared to extradite their own nationals, unlike many civil law countries around the world, prominent examples being Brazil, China, France, Germany, Japan, Russia and Switzerland.

To date there have been no Supreme Court cases in which the operation of the EAW system in relation to offences allegedly connected with the troubles in Northern Ireland has been examined. There have been challenges to the return of suspects to Northern Ireland on the basis that they might be ill-treated while in custody there, but these have been rejected by the lower Irish courts.[217] The concern at present is what arrangements will be put in place when the UK leaves the EU, for such an exit may mean that the UK can no longer be part of the EAW system and there is no default extradition agreement between the UK and Ireland to fall back on. Either an arrangement will need to be made to allow a non-EU State to participate in the EAW system or a new bilateral extradition treaty will have to be negotiated between the two countries.[218]

Conclusion

It is clear from the Supreme Court decisions surveyed in this chapter that on many occasions the judges have found it uncomfortable to have to deal with issues pertaining to Northern Ireland. In effect, they have had to juggle their commitment to the Irish Constitution with their commitment to non-violence and justice. Normally there should be no difficulty in that regard, because there should rarely be a clash between the two sets of values. But it is only to be expected that some judges are more willing than others to promote the view, indirectly, that reunification of the island of Ireland is a goal which deserves high priority. Thankfully the amendments made to the Irish Constitution as a result of the Belfast (Good Friday) Agreement seem to have greatly reduced the likelihood that Supreme Court judges will again be required to adjudicate on the constitutionality of the relationship between the Republic of Ireland and Northern Ireland.

During the long saga of the extradition cases Hederman, McCarthy and Walsh JJ clearly stuck their necks out by arguing for an approach to republican violence that was more understanding of the phenomenon than was the approach preferred by their judicial colleagues, especially O'Higgins CJ and Henchy J. But it is difficult if not impossible to demonstrate that there was any direct political prejudice applied during any of the decision-making in these cases, certainly no more than could be identified in decisions by the judiciaries of Northern Ireland or of England and Wales during the same period. Numerous instances of miscarriages of justice occurred in the latter jurisdiction in troubles-related cases;[219] decades later miscarriages are still being unearthed and acknowledged in Northern Ireland.[220] The flip-flopping of the

[216] Ibid, s 13.

[217] On 12 December 2017, after having been arrested in the Republic pursuant to an EAW issued in Northern Ireland, Damien McLaughlin was extradited to Northern Ireland to be tried in relation to the murder of prison officer David Black in 2012.

[218] See ECAS (2017).

[219] eg the Guildford Four (convicted 1975, convictions overturned 1989); the Birmingham Six (convicted 1975, convictions overturned 1991); the Maguire Seven (convicted 1976, convictions overturned 1991).

[220] See eg *R v Fitzpatrick and Shiels* [2009] NICA 60 and the successful appeal by Terry Laverty in 2015 against his imprisonment for rioting in 1971: www.bbc.co.uk/news/uk-northern-ireland-31373774. See too Requa (2015).

Supreme Court in the extradition cases was certainly frustrating for those in the North who experienced the violence of the troubles in a much more direct fashion than the judiciary in the Republic ever did, but it has to be accepted that occasionally the rule of law requires uncomfortable decisions to be made which can easily give the wrong impression that the decision-makers' motivation was politically-based rather than justice-oriented.

8

Administrative Law

One of the hallmarks of a democratic State is its willingness to subject its public authorities to judicial review, that is, to a process by which the courts can hold these authorities to account for the way in which they exercise their functions. Under English common law, which applied in Ireland prior to the partition in 1921, there were limited opportunities to take legal proceedings of this nature. With the advent of the Irish Free State Constitution of 1922 judicial review took on the additional challenge of checking whether legislation and actions were in breach of constitutional provisions, but after the 1937 Constitution replaced the former document[1] the courts began to develop non-constitutional review as well.[2] In England, as is well documented, the 1960s was the period during which seminal decisions were issued by the House of Lords laying the foundations for what has since become known as administrative law.[3] In Ireland there was a similar florescence of constitutional review around that time but in subsequent years many non-constitutional review principles have been developed too.[4] In this chapter we look at the most significant decisions by the Supreme Court in which these latter principles have been discussed.

State Side Orders, Applications for Judicial Review, and Public Law

Once the Crown all but disappeared from Ireland's legal architecture it became the practice to refer to applications for judicial review as 'State side' actions. The courts were taken to have retained the power to issue what in England were referred to as 'prerogative' orders, but in Ireland were called 'State side' orders even though the terms '*certiorari*', 'prohibition', 'mandamus' and '*quo warranto*' were still used, alongside 'declaration' and 'injunction'.[5] In 1962 provision was made for State side orders in the Rules of the Superior Courts[6] and in 1979 a Working Paper published by the Law Reform Commission recommended a number of changes to those rules. Revisions were not made, however, until 1986, when new Rules of the Superior Courts were issued.[7] Reflecting in part the position in England and Wales,[8] and in Northern Ireland,[9] these Rules require applications for leave to bring judicial review proceedings to be made 'promptly and in any event within three months from the date when grounds for the application first arose, or six months where the relief sought is *certiorari*, unless the Court considers that there is good reason for extending the period within which the application is made'.[10] In addition the 1986 Rules unified all the previous

[1] Art 34.3.2 of the 1937 Constitution, as amended by the Second Amendment of the Constitution Act 1941, allows the High Court or the Supreme Court (and only those courts) to adjudicate upon 'the validity of any law having regard to the provisions of this Constitution'.

[2] See the useful history by Beth (1967); also Donaldson (1957) 200-10, where he compares the scrutiny exercised by courts in Northern Ireland and Ireland.

[3] Tomkins (2003) 170–82; Blom-Cooper and Drewry (1972) 255–70.

[4] The most respected text is Hogan and Morgan (2010). A shorter, student version was published in 2012. See too, on principles of judicial review, Hogan et al (2018) 726-80.

[5] For explanations of these terms see Chap 4 above, 46, n 18.

[6] SI 72/1962, RSC, Ord 84.

[7] SI 15/1986, RSC, Ord 84.

[8] Rules of the Supreme Court (Amendment No 3) 1977 (SI 1955), r 5, substituting a new Ord 53 in the Rules of the Supreme Court 1965.

[9] Anthony (2014) 76–8. The term 'promptly' was removed from Northern Ireland's Rules in 2018.

[10] RSC, Ord 84, r 21(1).

remedies, so that an applicant for judicial review can now ask for any of them, including damages if these 'would have been awarded had the applicant made his (*sic*) claim in a civil action'.[11] Outside of the constitutional context judicial review has not been placed on a statutory footing in Ireland,[12] unlike in both England and Wales[13] and Northern Ireland.[14] In all of the jurisdictions, however, the judicial review process takes place over two stages. The applicant must first seek leave (ie, permission) to challenge the decision in question and this can be granted in the absence of any views being expressed by the public body whose decision is being challenged.[15] If leave is granted the applicant then brings the judicial application itself.

The changes in England and Wales and Northern Ireland hastened adoption of the term 'public law' to describe those legal rules which were applicable only to public bodies. This mirrors the practice in civil law countries, such as France and Germany, where special rules have existed for public bodies ever since the promulgation of the Code Napoléon in 1804 (*droit administratif* and *Verwaltungsrecht* respectively). It also flies in the face of Dicey's thesis, part of which was that everyone in the country should be bound by the same set of laws. In England and Wales and Northern Ireland the tendency to segregate public and private law was exacerbated when the House of Lords, in *O'Reilly v Mackman*,[16] ruled that, in general, applications for judicial review should be considered as inconsistent with possible private law actions, that is, that both types of proceedings could not be brought in relation to the same complaint. In Ireland, however, this segregation is not as marked. In *O'Donnell v Dun Laoghaire Corporation*[17] Costello J allowed the plaintiffs to pursue their request for a declaration that the demand made by the Corporation for water rates was *ultra vires* and void, even though they had not brought judicial review proceedings to that end. The judge specifically refused to follow *O'Reilly v Mackman*. No appeal was brought by the Corporation to the Supreme Court on this point and in no subsequent case has the Supreme Court voiced any outright support for the attitude struck by the House of Lords in *O'Reilly v Mackman*. In any event that attitude is now less widely accepted even in England and Wales, where new procedural rules and court discretion provide some flexibility.

The *Ultra Vires* Doctrine and Beyond

The *ultra vires* doctrine is the rule that a person or body given statutory powers cannot exercise those powers in a way which goes further than is permitted by the statute in question.[18] It is the classic example of a situation where courts will review the exercise of powers and declare it unlawful. In the late 1960s the Supreme Court (as well as the High Court) began to go beyond this doctrine and allow judicial review on other grounds. Writing in 1966 the great constitutional expert John Kelly asserted that in Ireland the exercise of an administrative discretion, if *intra vires* and not contrary to natural justice, could not be successfully challenged on the ground that it was unreasonable.[19] In suggesting that a short statute should be enacted 'conferring power on the High Court to review administrative acts on a new and wider criterion',[20] he proposed that models for reform might lie in the longstanding principle of both Irish and English law that bye-laws can be invalidated by the

[11] Ibid, r 24(1).
[12] Hogan and Morgan (2010) 32, where it is observed that a good deal of statutory interpretation is involved in administrative law.
[13] Supreme Court Act 1981, s 31.
[14] Judicature (NI) Act 1978, ss 18–25.
[15] RSC, Ord 84, r 20.
[16] [1983] 2 AC 237.
[17] [1991] ILRM 301. See Hogan and Morgan (2010) 947–9.
[18] Hogan and Morgan (2010) 440–49.
[19] Kelly (1966b).
[20] Ibid, 218.

courts if they are unreasonable[21] or in the German rule that administrative policies can be invalidated if they are 'entirely inappropriate'. By 1971, however, Kelly was eating his words, describing how the courts had 'within the last three years, explicitly marked out bridgeheads from which the exercise of statutory discretion can be controlled on more penetrating criteria than mere *vires* (as traditionally understood) or natural justice'.[22]

He points to two Supreme Court cases to support his thesis. In the first, *Listowel Urban District Council v McDonagh*,[23] Ó Dálaigh CJ, with whom Walsh and FitzGerald JJ agreed, held that an order made by the Council under the Local Government (Sanitary Services) Act 1948 was invalid because it was made in bad faith, the ulterior motive being the Council's desire to prevent itinerants from setting up temporary dwellings in the area. In the second case, *East Donegal Co-operative Livestock Mart Ltd v Attorney General*,[24] various co-operative societies and farmers challenged the constitutionality of the Livestock Marts Act 1967 because it conferred what seemed like unduly wide discretionary licensing powers on the Minister for Agriculture and Fisheries. On the facts the Supreme Court rejected all but one of the plaintiffs' arguments[25] but the single judgment of the Court, pronounced by Walsh J, has become one of the seminal elaborations of the foundations of the Irish Constitution. Besides confirming its own previous ruling in *McDonald v Bord na gCon*[26] that persons directly affected by an Act can bring an action to test its constitutionality and that Acts passed after the 1937 Constitution benefit from a presumption that they are compliant with that Constitution, the Supreme Court set out three basic principles. First, that when it is possible to interpret an Act in two ways, one that makes it constitutional and the other unconstitutional, 'an interpretation favouring the validity of an Act should be given in cases of doubt'.[27] Known as the 'double construction principle'[28] this is an approach to statutory interpretation which has been imitated in, for example, the European Convention on Human Rights Act 2003.[29] Second, powers conferred by an Act have to be exercised within the boundaries set by the objectives of the Act and what those objectives are will depend on the long title of the Act, its general scope and the wording of the whole Act. Third, and perhaps most importantly, 'proceedings, procedures, discretions and adjudications which are permitted ... by an Act of the Oireachtas are to be conducted in accordance with the principles of constitutional justice',[30] meaning that when exercising discretionary powers a Minister 'is required to consider every case upon its own merits, to hear what the applicant or the licensee (as the case may be) has to say, and to give the latter an opportunity to deal with whatever case may be thought to exist against the granting of a licence or for the refusal of a licence or for the attaching of conditions ... as the case may be'.[31]

Kelly rightly suggests that the Supreme Court's decision in the *East Donegal* case is as important to Irish administrative law as the House of Lords' decision in *Padfield v Minister of Agriculture, Fisheries and Food*[32] is to English administrative law.[33] Decided more than two years earlier, *Padfield* was cited by the government in its arguments to the Court in *East Donegal* but, strangely, the plaintiffs do not seem to have relied upon it and the Court itself did not refer to it in its judgment. *Padfield* could be read as going one step beyond *East*

[21] Kelly cites the High Court case of *Corporation of Limerick v Sheridan* (1952) 90 ILTR 59 as an example.

[22] Kelly (1971).

[23] [1968] IR 312. The facts are similar to those in the *Sheridan* case, n 21 above.

[24] [1970] IR 317.

[25] It held that the part of s 4 of the Act which purported to allow the Minister to exempt an individual from the operation of the Act was repugnant to Art 40.1 of the Constitution (the guarantee of equality). For more on 'dispensing powers' see Forde and Leonard (2014) 324–5 and 400.

[26] [1965] IR 217. See too Chap 4 above, 66–7.

[27] [1970] IR 317, 341.

[28] Forde and Leonard (2014) 43–5.

[29] s 2(1). See too the UK's Human Rights Act 1998, s 3(1).

[30] [1970] IR 317, 341.

[31] Ibid, 344.

[32] [1968] AC 997.

[33] Kelly (1971) 49.

Donegal in that the House of Lords actually ordered the Minister in question to exercise his powers in a certain way (to refer a grievance to a particular committee).[34] *Padfield* is one of several seminal decisions of the House of Lords around this time which form the bedrock of English administrative law. Irish law has by and large followed suit but has done so by developing its own precedents and with reference to its own Constitution. On account of the latter document, there has been little need for Ireland's Supreme Court to take a stand on whether common law constitutionalism provides a set of values against which judges may assess the legality of a public body's actions. Thus, as Hogan and Morgan observe, there has been little debate in Ireland about the 'revisionist' approach to the *ultra vires* doctrine which some commentators in England see as the basis for common law constitutionalism.[35]

Principles of Natural Justice

While we saw in Chapter 4 that the Supreme Court has been keen to ensure that bodies other than those upon which judicial functions have been imposed by the Constitution do not in fact exercise such functions, the corollary is not that bodies which do not have judicial functions can therefore act arbitrarily. Legal mechanisms have been developed to seek to ensure that such bodies, if they are deemed to be exercising a function concerning the general public (as opposed to conducting some entirely private business), adhere to basic principles of natural justice. The most obvious of these are, first, that there should be some way in which a party who is dissatisfied with the decision made by a body exercising a public function can challenge its correctness; second, that the body taking the decision should not be biased either in its own favour or in favour of one of the parties to a dispute it is resolving; third, that if the body is resolving a dispute it should give all sides to that dispute an equal opportunity to state their case; and fourth, the decisions issued by the body should be backed up with good reasons. In Ireland, as in other common law jurisdictions, these principles have been developed by the common law or by reference to the Constitution, but at times they are supplemented by legislative provisions applying to the body in question. The first of the principles may be satisfied by giving the disappointed party a statutory right to appeal against the decision, which will usually mean that the merits of the decision as well as the way in which it was taken will be re-examined. The common law has not developed a right to appeal as such. Instead it has hit upon judicial review as the next best thing. The crucial difference is that judicial review is meant to look only at the way a challenged decision was arrived at, not at whether it was the correct decision as far as the competing merits are concerned. The distinction can be a fine one, but the underlying rationale for it is that according to the separation of powers doctrine unelected judges should not be substituting their views on how the country should be run for those of elected politicians in the government and Parliament.

The State (Healy) v Donoghue is the Supreme Court's leading decision regarding the need for procedural fairness.[36] That, however, was a criminal case, one where the Supreme Court ensured that if a person is charged with a serious offence and needs the help of a lawyer to defend him- or herself, as well as payment for that help, the person has a right to obtain the help at the State's expense under the statutory legal aid scheme,[37] even if he or she has not explicitly applied for it. But in a later civil case, *Carmody v Minister for Justice, Equality*

[34] See generally Supperstone et al (2014) 149–50. [35] Hogan and Morgan (2010) 449–53, esp 452.

[36] [1976] IR 325 (O'Higgins CJ, Henchy, Griffin, Kenny, and Parke JJ). See too Chap 6 above, 129-30.

[37] The governing statute at the time was the Criminal Justice (Legal Aid) Act 1962.

and Law Reform, the Supreme Court saw no constitutional inequality in granting an indigent person the help of only a solicitor even though the opposing side was represented by both a solicitor and a barrister.[38] As regards procedural fairness in administrative law the Supreme Court has developed most of its jurisprudence in situations where a challenge has been made to the exercise by a public authority of a discretionary power. Thus, in *Breen v Minister for Defence* it ruled that the exercise of a discretionary power had been abused because it had not been founded on adequate evidence-based reasons.[39] In *The State (Cussen) v Brennan* it held that a public body taking a decision on who should get a particular job must not take into account criteria which are irrelevant to that job.[40] And in *Glencar Exploration plc v Mayo County Council (No 2)*[41] the Court endorsed the principle that a decision could be quashed if it went against the legitimate expectations of the applicant for judicial review, though it set out stringent conditions for this principle to apply and on the facts of the case before it the Court held that it did not.[42] Hogan and Morgan note that the terminology in this field is confusing at times, especially in cases decided since 2000; they make a plea for the judiciary to express themselves with more clarity, precision and consistency.[43]

Reasonableness

The *locus classicus* in English law regarding challenges to administrative decisions on the basis of their unreasonableness[44] is the Court of Appeal's decision in *Associated Provincial Picture Houses Ltd v Wednesbury Corporation*,[45] which has given rise to the term '*Wednesbury* unreasonableness'. This refers to 'a conclusion so unreasonable that no reasonable … authority could ever have come to it'.[46] Despite its continuing centrality in English law the *Wednesbury* case has been largely ignored by the Irish Supreme Court even if the basic principle it enshrines has been adhered to. The Court's first reference to it seems to have occurred as late as 1986, in *The State (Keegan) v Stardust Victims' Compensation Tribunal*.[47] At issue was whether the Compensation Tribunal, in refusing to award damages for nervous shock to the father of two girls who had been killed in the Stardust dancehall fire in 1981, had acted unlawfully. The father relied on the *Wednesbury* case, and also on the gloss

[38] [2010] 1 IR 635; on the facts of this case, though, the Supreme Court held that the applicant should be allowed to apply for a barrister's help as well. See too Whyte (2010), who complains that in *Magee v Farrell* [2009] 2 ILRM 453 the Supreme Court 'closed the door on the argument that the Constitution might protect a right to legal aid in civil cases' and yet in *Carmody* 'it strengthened the constitutional right to legal aid in criminal cases'. He comments (at 365) that: 'These contrasting results offer an interesting insight into the philosophical values that may implicitly inform judicial reasoning in the current Supreme Court and also calls into question the cogency of the Court's reasoning that underpins its rejection of the notion of justiciable implied socio-economic rights' (on which see Chap 5 above, 128-36).

[39] [1994] 2 IR 34. See too *Mallak v Minister for Justice, Equality and Law Reform* [2012] IESC 59, [2012] 3 IR 297, which held that a Minister has to supply reasons if an application for naturalisation is rejected. In *Connelly v An Bord Pleanála* [2018] IESC 31 and 36 (Clarke CJ and O'Donnell, Dunne, O'Malley and Finlay Geoghegan JJ) the Supreme Court accepted that when EU environmental law is involved the duty to give reasons may be more demanding than in some other contexts.

[40] [1981] 1 IR 181. [41] [2002] 1 IR 84.

[42] Nor did it support a claim for damages, holding that it was not just or reasonable to impose a duty of care on the facts. It distinguished its earlier decision in *Webb v Ireland* [1988] IR 353, see 188 below, where it first recognized the principle.

[43] Hogan and Morgan (2010) 586.

[44] See generally De Blácam (2009) 335–50; Bradley (2000) 477–506. [45] [1948] 1 KB 223.

[46] Ibid, 233–4, per Lord Greene MR.

[47] [1986] IR 642; O'Connell (2008–09). Another English Court of Appeal decision from the 1940s, *Carltona Ltd v Commissioners of Work* [1943] 2 All ER 560, which allows officials to do things on behalf of Ministers even if there has been no express act of delegation to that effect, was not endorsed by the Irish Supreme Court until *WT v Minister for Justice and Equality* [2015] IESC 73.

put on it by Lord Diplock in *Council of Civil Service Unions v Minister for the Civil Service* (known as the *GCHQ* case).[48] Lord Diplock had said that the *Wednesbury* test 'applies to a decision which is so outrageous in its defiance of logic or of accepted moral standards that no sensible person who had applied his mind to the question to be decided could have arrived at it'.[49] In *Keegan* the Supreme Court rejected the father's appeal and refused to adopt Lord Diplock's interpretation of *Wednesbury*, with Henchy J holding that neither logic nor morality was a reliable guide in this context. Henchy J preferred to sum up the Irish law on unreasonableness in this way:

> I would myself consider that the test of unreasonableness or irrationality in judicial review lies in considering whether the impugned decision plainly and unambiguously flies in the face of fundamental reason and common sense. If it does, then the decision-maker should be held to have acted *ultra vires*, for the necessarily implied constitutional limitation of jurisdiction in all decision-making which affects rights or duties requires, *inter alia*, that the decision-maker must not flagrantly reject or disregard fundamental reason or common sense in reaching his decision.[50]

The other four judges agreed with Henchy J's approach.[51] Whether it is identical to that intended by Lord Greene in the *Wednesbury* case is a moot point: Henchy J chose his own phrasing ('fundamental reason and common sense') but commentators have not identified how such a test might lead to a different outcome from that which would result from a direct application of Lord Greene's wording.[52] For example, when the Supreme Court invalidated a statutory instrument on grounds of unreasonableness in *Doyle v An Taoiseach*,[53] there is every likelihood that an English court would have arrived at the same conclusion; likewise as regards *Stroker v Doherty*, where the Supreme Court ruled that an Appeal Board had not acted unreasonably in dismissing an officer from the Garda Síochána because of statements he had made about his wife in his local public house one evening when he was off-duty.[54] The Supreme Court frequently cites the *Wednesbury* test without suggesting that it is of a different strength from that in *Keegan*.

Keegan may seem a harsh decision, but the particular facts reveal that the harshness derives more from the state of the law on nervous shock than from any inconsistency on the part of the Compensation Tribunal (Mr Keegan's wife, the mother of the dead girls, had been awarded IR£50,000 in compensation). Just over a year later the Supreme Court held in another case that a decision by the Criminal Injuries Compensation Tribunal to refuse compensation to a widow *was* unreasonable within the *Keegan* test because the law made it clear that compensation was payable if someone died honestly believing that another person's life was in danger even though in fact that may not have been the case.[55] Here the widow's husband had been dragged under a van which he was trying to stop from rolling down a hill towards a busy junction in Cork, with his one-year-old son sitting in the front of the van. The Supreme Court also held that it was inconsistent with the principles of proper administration that the Tribunal had not given any reasons for the decision it had reached.

In 1991 the Supreme Court elaborated further on its approach to unreasonableness. This was in a planning case, *O'Keeffe v An Bord Pleanála*,[56] where a man living 300 metres from

[48] [1985] AC 374. [49] Ibid, 410. [50] [1986] IR 642, 658.

[51] The judges were Finlay CJ, Hamilton P and Griffin and Hederman JJ.

[52] Hogan and Morgan (2010) 734–60 (esp 756–8) appear to see no differences between the two formulations.

[53] [1986] ILRM 693. [54] [1991] 1 IR 23.

[55] *The State (Creedon) v Criminal Injuries Compensation Board* [1988] IR 51 (Finlay CJ and Walsh and McCarthy JJ).

[56] [1993] 1 IR 39.

the proposed site of a 300-metre radio mast challenged the Planning Board's decision to grant permission for the mast's erection. Costello J, in the High Court, had acceded to Mr O'Keeffe's challenge, citing the *Wednesbury* case in support of his conclusion that no reasonable planning authority could have reached a decision that erection of the mast was consistent with the proper development of the area. To many people's surprise the Supreme Court unanimously overturned this decision. Finlay CJ, with whom the other four judges all agreed,[57] strongly endorsed Henchy J's words in *Keegan*, saying that they were 'not only a correct but a comprehensive description of the circumstances under which a court may, according to our law, intervene in such a decision on the basis of unreasonableness or irrationality'.[58] The Chief Justice was anxious to point out as well that judicial review is just that, a review, and not an appeal; if the court was to substitute its own view for that of the administrators it would be usurping power. He agreed with the Planning Board's position on 'the height of the fence against judicial intervention by way of review on grounds of irrationality',[59] namely that a court cannot interfere with an administrative decision just because on the facts as found it would have reached a different conclusion or because it was satisfied that the case against the decision made was much stronger than the case for it. He stressed that the planning authorities and the Board had special skill, competence and experience in planning questions which the courts lacked. In short, he thought that to meet the test of irrationality 'the applicant should establish to the satisfaction of the court that the decision-making authority had before it no relevant material which would support its decision'.[60]

On the face of it the approach adopted in *O'Keeffe* seems to set the bar for judicial review even higher than *Keegan* had done. Arguably the *Keegan* test was already a tougher one to satisfy than the *Wednesbury* test. Bradley explains *O'Keeffe* on the basis that in Irish law the planning code has a special pre-eminence to which the courts traditionally defer, but he regrets that '*O'Keeffe* unreasonableness' has become '*the* definitive interpretation of the test', even for non-statutory administrative acts.[61] He wonders if the *O'Keeffe* formulation was 'a step too far'.[62] Subsequent Supreme Court decisions have continued to endorse *O'Keeffe*, though in one of them, *Radio Limerick One Ltd v Irish Radio and Television Commission*,[63] the Court added that if a decision-maker were to make a mistake of law when arriving at its decision (eg, by considering a broadcast to be, in law, an advertisement, when it was not) then that too would breach the reasonableness test laid down by Henchy J in *Keegan*. This is reminiscent of the Supreme Court's attitude in the *Creedon* case, mentioned above.[64]

As in the United Kingdom, however, courts in Ireland have had to adjust their approach to judicial review to take account of the requirements of the European Convention on Human Rights. The European Court of Human Rights has insisted that when reviewing administrative decisions national courts must pay particular regard to the Convention rights of individuals affected by those decisions.[65] Thus, in *Holland v Governor of Portlaoise Prison*[66] McKechnie J, in the High Court, upheld a claim by a prisoner that he was being improperly denied access to the media to argue his case that his conviction was a miscarriage

[57] Griffin, Hederman, McCarthy and Lynch JJ. [58] [1993] 1 IR 39, 70. [59] Ibid, 71.
[60] Ibid, 72. [61] Bradley (2000) 494. [62] Ibid. [63] [1997] 2 ILRM 1.
[64] See above, 178.
[65] See eg *Smith and Grady v UK* (2000) 29 EHHR 493, where, even though the Court of Appeal of England and Wales had applied a stricter than usual approach to judicial review when considering whether the Ministry of Defence had acted lawfully in refusing to allow gay people to serve in the country's armed forces (*R v Secretary of State for Defence, ex parte Smith* [1996] QB 517), the European Court held that that standard of review was not strict enough.
[66] [2004] 2 IR 573.

of justice. The judge ruled that in situations where the exercise of a fundamental constitutional right such as the right to communicate is at stake it is not enough simply to ask whether the decision-maker had the relevant material before him or her (as in *O'Keeffe*); the decision-maker also has to give consideration to the rights of the specific individuals affected by the decision.

Proportionality

The Supreme Court had a further opportunity to develop its thinking on unreasonableness in 2010, in *Meadows v The Minister for Justice, Equality and Law Reform*,[67] one of many recent decisions dealing with migration rights. The applicant was a Nigerian woman who was challenging a deportation order made against her on the basis that the Minister had not taken proper account of the risk that if the applicant were deported to Nigeria she would be subjected to female genital mutilation there. At the time of the Supreme Court's ruling the applicant was 27 years of age, having first entered Ireland in 1999 when she was 17. The Refugee Act 1996 specifically prohibited the State from retuning any person to the frontier of another country where, 'in the opinion of the Minister, the life or freedom of that person would be threatened', and a person's freedom was to be regarded as threatened if, amongst things, 'in the opinion of the Minister, the person is likely to be subject to a serious assault (including a serious assault of a sexual nature)'.[68] In the High Court Gilligan J rejected the applicant's challenge, applying the *O'Keeffe* test. An appeal to the Supreme Court was possible only because Gilligan J certified, as required under the Illegal Immigrants (Trafficking) Act 2000,[69] that his decision involved a point of law of exceptional public importance and that it was desirable in the public interest that an appeal should be taken to the Supreme Court. Six years later that Court held by 3 v 2 that when determining the reasonableness of an administrative decision affecting constitutional or fundamental rights, the standards set out in *O'Keeffe v An Bord Pleanála* were not the ones to apply.[70] The majority thought that the *O'Keeffe* approach was too restrictive in that context.

While not going so far as to adopt an 'anxious scrutiny' test, which had been favoured in the United Kingdom, the judges in the majority supplemented the *Keegan* and *O'Keeffe* tests by declaring that they could be applied alongside the principle of proportionality. Murray CJ reminded us that the Supreme Court was already willing to apply a proportionality test when examining the compatibility of a statutory provision with the provisions of the Constitution. He said this was done by the Court 'without trespassing on a core constitutional function of the Oireachtas to decide policy and to legislate accordingly'.[71] The Chief Justice then intimated that he saw no reason why the principle of proportionality could not also be used when the Court is examining whether a decision properly flows from the premises on which it is based and whether it is at variance with fundamental reason and common sense, two expressions used by Henchy J in *Keegan*. The Chief Justice did not see anything in *Keegan* or *O'Keeffe* which excluded the Court from applying the principle of

[67] [2010] IESC 3, [2010] 2 IR 701. See Hogan and Morgan (2010) 779–81, read in the light of 772–8. For an excellent account of the pre-*Meadows* position see Buckley (2004) and for an English Law Lord's extra-judicial views on proportionality, expounded for the benefit of an Irish audience, see Hoffmann (1997).

[68] s 5(1) and (2).

[69] s 5(2)(b), which was declared constitutional in the Art 26 reference relating to this legislation: see Chap 6 above, 117-8.

[70] Murray CJ, Denham and Fennelly JJ in the majority; Kearns P and Hardiman J dissenting.

[71] [2010] 2 IR 701, [45], citing *Heaney v Ireland* [1994] 3 IR 593, *In re Article 26 and the Employment Equality Bill* [1997] 2 IR 321 and *In re Article 26 and the Health (Amendment) (No 2) Bill 2004* [2005] 1 IR 105.

proportionality in this context; indeed he noted that the Supreme Court had already alluded to that principle as long ago as 1989 in *Fajujonu v Minister for Justice*[72] when deciding whether to allow immigrants to remain in Ireland. *Fajujonu* was a case where the Supreme Court had to decide if the Minister had properly balanced the interests of the common good in limiting the movement of foreigners unlawfully in Ireland against the family and personal rights of a couple from Africa who had been in Ireland for six years and had had three children of Irish nationality through having been born in Ireland. Walsh J was quite explicit on that occasion:

> In my view, [the Minister] would have to be satisfied, for stated reasons, that the interests of the common good of the people of Ireland and of the protection of the State and its society are so predominant and so overwhelming in the circumstances of the case, that an action which can have the effect of breaking up this family is not so disproportionate to the aims sought to be achieved as to be unsustainable.[73]

In *Fajujonu* the Supreme Court remitted the case to the Minister for re-consideration. Between *Fajujonu* and *Meadows* Murray CJ supported the approach adopted in *Fajujonu* when he gave his judgment in yet another immigration case, *AO and OJO v Minister for Justice, Equality and Law Reform.*[74] He specifically indicated there that the Minister was entitled to take into account whether a refusal to make a deportation order in a particular case 'could call in question the integrity of the immigration and asylum systems including their effective functions'.[75] In *Meadows*, therefore, having clarified the test to be applied, Murray CJ allowed the applicant to proceed with her application for leave to seek judicial review. He rejected the suggestion that it should adopt the recent English terminology (derived in turn from the US) of 'anxious' or 'heightened' scrutiny in cases involving fundamental rights: citing McGuinness J in *VZ v Minister for Justice, Equality and Law Reform*,[76] Murray CJ was of the view that 'the issue raised in this case can be properly and more appropriately resolved in the context of our constitutional framework and the case law of this court'.[77] Once again we see an example of Irish judges studiously avoiding the adoption of terminology coined by English courts.

Two of the Chief Justice's fellow judges in *Meadows* agreed with him. Denham J said 'the issue should be addressed in this State by applying Irish jurisprudence'.[78] She also stressed that, in situations where access to the Supreme Court is limited, as here, the common law should not further restrict access to an effective remedy for fear of violating the constitutional right of access to the courts.[79] She thought that 'while the term "proportionality" is relatively new in this jurisdiction, it is inherent in any analysis of the reasonableness of a decision', and she cited the Canadian Supreme Court's decision in *Chaulk v R*[80]as a comparative precedent.[81] Fennelly J, in the most learned of the judgments, admitted that '[t]he courts are by tradition and instinct very slow to interfere with decisions regarding technical or administrative matters. It is natural, however, for any decision-maker to be the more hesitant, the more deliberate, the more cautious as the decision he or she is considering will the more gravely trench on the rights or interests of those likely to be affected'.[82] He

[72] [1990] 2 IR 151.

[73] Ibid, 172. Finlay CJ's endorsement of the proportionality principle was much more implicit: ibid, 162. Griffin, Hederman and McCarthy JJ agreed with both Finlay CJ and Walsh J.

[74] [2003] 1 IR 1. For more on this case see Chap 10 below, at 227-8. [75] Ibid, 92.

[76] [2002] 2 IR 135, 158, where McGuinness J said it was difficult to define the difference between different levels of scrutiny. She asked, rhetorically: 'Can it mean that in a case where the decision-making process is subject to "anxious scrutiny" the standard of unreasonableness/irrationality is to be lowered?'

[77] [2010] 2 IR 701, [74]. [78] Ibid, [122]. [79] Ibid, [132]. [80] [1990] 3 SCR 1303.

[81] [2010] 2 IR 701, [134] and [139]. [82] Ibid, [443].

maintained that '[t]he courts have always examined decisions in context against their surrounding circumstances'[83] and he impliedly endorsed the government's view that the adoption of an 'anxious scrutiny' test 'would significantly alter the role of the courts in judicial review and would effectively constitute the courts as the ultimate appellate tribunal from a vast range of administrative decisions'.[84]

Regrettably, two of the five Supreme Court judges could not go along with their colleagues. Their reasons for adopting this position, with respect, are not convincing. Kearns P just did not believe that the test of proportionality had a role to play in determining whether the court should intervene to quash a High Court decision after there had already been two merit-based hearings—before an immigration officer and the Refugee Appeals Tribunal—against which no judicial review proceedings had been brought. Referring to the tests laid down in *Keegan* and *O'Keeffe*, he did not favour 'recalibrating the principles in a way which would create uncertainty and confusion as to where the parameters for intervention by a court would now lie'.[85] Hardiman J was much more fulsome (his judgment covers 40 pages[86]) but no more persuasive. He suggested that if Ms Meadows were to succeed in changing the long-accepted criteria for obtaining judicial review in Ireland this would represent 'a major revolution in our immigration arrangements and in administrative law more generally'.[87] He added:

> Specifically it will represent a major transfer of power from the executive to the judicial arm of government by conferring on the latter a general supervisory role over the exercise of a function conferred by law on a member of the government.[88]

This calls to mind the same judge's approach in *Sinnott v Minister for Education*,[89] decided nine years earlier, for he again placed 'a high constitutional value' on the fact that, under the separation of powers doctrine, responsibility for immigration had been allocated to a ministerial rather than a judicial assessment of the requirements of the public good and the public interest.[90] In support of his view he cited two recent unanimous decisions of the Supreme Court. The first was *FP v Minister for Justice*,[91] in which Hardiman J himself gave the only judgment,[92] where the Court rejected appeals against the High Court's refusal of leave to challenge by judicial review decisions that the applicants should not be allowed to remain in Ireland on humanitarian grounds. The second was *Baby O v Minister for Justice*,[93] where the applicant was not claiming that she would be at risk of female genital mutilation if she was returned to Nigeria but rather of homicidal activities carried out by a cult called the 'Ogboni Fraternity'; again the Court held that, in the absence of a breach of the requirement to comply with fair procedures, there was no ground for quashing a decision to refuse refugee status to the applicant.

Hardiman J then went on to deliver a withering critique of developments in the law of England and Wales in this field, referring disparagingly to 'those who feel that many of the ills of humanity are susceptible of a judicial or judicially imposed solution' and singling out the judgments and extra-judicial writings of Sir John Laws, a Court of Appeal judge, for particular opprobrium. He considered the term 'anxious scrutiny' to be a Trojan horse or, if not that, 'the verbal or linguistic equivalent of a Russian doll, concealing layers of meaning

[83] Ibid, [445]. [84] Ibid, [444]. [85] Ibid, [108].
[86] He said that the length of his judgment was proportionate to the importance of the case: ibid, [187].
[87] Ibid, [183]. [88] Ibid.
[89] [2001] 2 IR 545. Hardiman J refers to this case at [2010] 2 IR 701, [201] and [307].
[90] [2010] 2 IR 157, [201]. [91] [2002] 1 IR 164.
[92] With which Keane CJ and Denham, Murphy and Murray JJ all agreed.
[93] [2002] 2 IR 169 (Keane CJ, Denham, Murphy, Murray and McGuinness JJ).

unsuspected even on a detailed scrutiny of the exterior, however intense or "anxious".'[94] He believed that ministerial decisions deserved respect and deference, and that they did not need 'justification': 'the test now proposed to be applied ... looks for explanation and justification from the decision-maker which I believe to be inconsistent with the proper principles of judicial review'[95] and he added that to fault the minister for failing to set out the material which was before him 'is wholly to withhold from him that curial deference ... to which any court from the lowest to the highest and a great many administrative bodies and public sector decision makers are entitled'.[96] Later Hardiman J stated that to require the Minister to come before the court and justify his decision would be 'very significantly to interfere with the separation of powers and to hamper or obstruct the Minister in taking a decision which is clearly within his scope ... [T]he courts must respect the minister's jurisdiction and interfere only upon proper proof by the applicant that the Minister's decision is flawed'.[97] Hardiman J ended by stressing that in such cases the burden of proof does not shift from the applicant to the decision-maker.

It has been necessary to set out the separate judicial views expressed in *Meadows* in some detail in order to substantiate two, apparently contradictory, observations. The first is that on one reading there does not appear to be a significant difference between the wording of the test as formulated by the majority and minority judges. Both fall back on the *Keegan* and *O'Keefe* formula, but they interpret it in different ways. In so far as the difference boils down to who bears the burden of proof, even that may not be a significant distinction, for a lot depends on what *standard* of proof has to be reached, wherever it lies, and on whether the burden can shift once a *prima facie* case has been made by one side or the other on a particular point. The second observation is that the apparent agreement over the wording of the test masks a fundamental disagreement over the function of the courts, and of the Supreme Court in particular, with regard to the powers exercised by the executive branch of government. *Meadows* is a good example of the rift which then existed within the Supreme Court between the liberals and the conservatives. This was a deeper rift than was apparent within the United Kingdom Supreme Court and was more akin to that which existed within the United States Supreme Court between the constructivists and the originalists. It is perhaps going too far to align Hardiman J with the views of Antonin Scalia in the US Supreme Court, but there are similarities as regards their views on how interventionist a top court should be in relation to government decision-making. It is an amazing and very sad coincidence that in 2016 the two judges both suddenly died, within four weeks of each other.[98]

Reaction to *Meadows*

Academic and judicial reaction to the decision in *Meadows* has, on the whole, been less than positive. The view most commonly expressed is that the decision has left the law in a more uncertain state than it was before. Many commentators seem pleased that Irish administrative law has adopted the principle of proportionality, but they do not all agree that this can happen within the confines of the *Keegan* and *O'Keeffe* tests. In other words, while not many support the ultimate position of Kearns P and Hardiman J, they tend to accept the argument of those dissenting judges that proportionality was never meant to be part and parcel of the earlier approach to unreasonableness adumbrated in *Keegan* and *O'Keeffe*.

94 [2010] 2 IR 157, [306]. 95 Ibid, [336]. 96 Ibid, [350]. 97 Ibid, [373].

98 Scalia J died on 13 February 2016 and Hardiman J on 7 March 2016.

Price points out that the three judges in the majority differ among themselves as to the exact formulation of the new test[99] and, along with Donnelly and Delany,[100] he regrets that the majority did not adopt the four-stage analysis of proportionality developed by the Privy Council and the House of Lords.[101] This requires asking (1) whether the legislative objective in question is important enough to justify limiting a fundamental right, (2) whether the measures designed to meet the objective are rationally connected to it, (3) whether the means used to impair the right are no more than necessary to accomplish the objective, and (4) whether the rights of the individual have been fairly balanced with the interests of society.[102] Price is also sceptical of the rejection of the 'anxious scrutiny' approach, concluding that the net effect of *Meadows* is that it leaves the courts in too deferential a position vis-à-vis the government. Biehler and Donnelly go so far as to suggest that the proportionality test adopted in *Meadows* is inconsistent with what is required by the European Court of Human Rights.[103] On the basis of their review of the post-*Meadows* jurisprudence, including that of the Supreme Court,[104] these authors claim that 'in the vast majority of … cases, even where rights protected by Article 8 of the ECHR are at issue [this is the provision guaranteeing the right to a private and family life], there has been a failure to apply a structured proportionality standard of review'.[105] The particular defects which are identified as putting Irish law out of step with the ECHR in this context are, first, that the *Meadows* test does not require Irish courts to consider whether the administrative decision in question has met a social pressing need even though it interfered with a fundamental right and, second, that it does not require consideration of whether the degree of interference with the right is proportionate to the public interest being pursued by the interference.[106] Elsewhere Biehler[107] supports the view that when deferring to an administrative body the Court should focus less on the so-called 'spatial' dimension (ie, on the nature of the subject-matter being reviewed) and more on the overall context within which the administrative body's decision was taken (the 'multi-textured' approach[108]), the fact that fundamental rights might be at stake being a crucial one to bear in mind. Biehler and Donnelly also rightly observe that the restrained approach of the Supreme Court in this area of administrative law is surprising because the Court has 'long applied a structured proportionality analysis when reviewing the constitutionality of legislation'.[109]

At the time of writing the Supreme Court is in a difficult position as regards the standard to be applied in judicial reviews.[110] On the one hand it is well aware of the importance of certainty in the law, on the other it is naturally reluctant to admit so soon after *Meadows* that its attempt to bring greater certainty to the law may have back-fired. In the eight years that have elapsed since *Meadows* not as much has happened within the courts as might have been expected.[111] It is submitted here that a way out for the Court might be to state

[99] Price (2013). [100] Donnelly and Delany (2011).

[101] In *De Freitas v Permanent Secretary of the Ministry of Agriculture, Fisheries, Land and Housing* [1999] 1 AC 69 and *Huang v Secretary of State for the Home Department* [2007] UKHL 11, [2007] 2 AC 167.

[102] *Huang*, ibid, [19]. [103] Biehler and Donnelly (2014).

[104] eg *Donegan v Dublin City Council* [2012] IESC 18.

[105] n 103 above, 278. At 274–6 the authors explain what they mean by a 'structured' standard. For discussion of *Meadows* in an employment law context see Lyne (2011).

[106] Biehler and Donnelly (2014) 282. [107] Biehler (2013a) 39–42. See too Foley (2008) *passim*.

[108] As advocated by, eg, Kavanagh (2008) and Hunt (2003).

[109] Citing *Heaney v Ireland* [1994] 3 IR 593, 607 (per Costello J). See too Daly (2010) 391–2.

[110] In the words of Hogan and Morgan (2010) 789: '[i]n Ireland, at present, there are various levels of difficulty' and 'there is a need to weed the present wilderness of substantially duplicating concepts'. Earlier another commentator wrote that 'Irish standard of review analysis is … "all over the ballpark"' (Margulies (2002) 30.

[111] Cf Brady (2010) 170: 'The *Meadows* decision is an important watershed and it can be expected to lead to significant further developments in the law of judicial review in the coming years.'

openly that judicially reviewing an administrative body's decision which impacts on fundamental rights entails a multi-faceted inquiry into whether the body in question has taken into account all relevant factors, put out of its mind all irrelevant factors and paid due regard to the need to balance individual rights against societal interests. As far as EU law on refugee status is concerned, the Supreme Court has recently confirmed that judicial review qualifies as an 'effective remedy' for someone who has been refused that status in Ireland, with Charleton J saying that how proportionality in decision-making interacts with the duty to act reasonably can await scrutiny in a subsequent case.[112]

A possible model to follow is that adopted by the Canadian Supreme Court. As De Blácam observes, that Court has sub-divided the concept of unreasonableness into three categories, setting the bar a bit lower for applicants whenever it seems clear that Parliament's intention was to give the decision-makers a wider choice as to the decisions available to them. This was in *Baker v Canada (Minister of Citizenship and Immigration)*,[113] where the Minister had refused to allow the appellant an exemption from the requirement that if she wished to apply for permanent residence in Canada she had to do so from outside the country, despite the fact that she had lived there for 11 years during which she had had four children who were all Canadian citizens. Biehler also draws upon a Canadian precedent, *Dunsmuir v New Brunswick*,[114] when advocating a more nuanced and contextual approach to judicial review. It is regrettable that the Irish Supreme Court has not considered the applicability of the more modern Canadian approach in any detail. While one must be careful not to assume that legal principles can easily be transplanted from one legal system to another, even if they are both common law systems, there is still merit in one system weighing up the pros and cons of another system's approach, perhaps taking advice from an *amicus curiae* on the point. England's precedents may not be attractive to the Irish Supreme Court but those from other former dominions may well be.

Deference

The question of deference is best regarded as an aspect of the separation of powers principle: judges must be aware that on some matters they can be the ideal people to assess whether the appropriate processes were used when a decision was being made but that on other matters they do not have the requisite expertise to second-guess decisions taken by experts in the field.[115] As in the law of negligence, where evidence from experts is not treated as conclusive but weighs heavily with the judges, so in administrative law due respect must be accorded to the professionalism of experienced decision-makers. It seems clear that, at present, judicial deference to administrative expertise remains the default position for the Supreme Court.[116] But the Supreme Court should be wary of trying to be too systematic in its formulation of a test for judicial review. The four-stage test used in England, Wales and Northern Ireland[117] is not always easy to apply, since reasonable people can reasonably disagree over how to answer each of the questions involved, particularly whether the rights of individuals have been properly balanced against the interests of society. On occasions even the European Court of Human Rights can be severely split on that issue. In *Animal*

[112] *AAA v Minister for Justice* [2017] IESC 80, para 26. [113] [1999] 2 SCR 817.

[114] [2008] SCC 9.

[115] Cf Brady, n 111 above, who argues that the issue of deference should be integrated within the proportionality test. See too Foley (2006).

[116] Hogan and Walker (2010) 767 ('the *Keegan-O'Keeffe* line of judicial deference remains the normal law').

[117] See 184 above.

Defenders International v United Kingdom,[118] for instance, the Court was divided nine to eight on whether England's laws restricting political advertising on broadcast media were a justifiable limitation on the individual's right to freedom of expression, given the interests of society in maintaining free and fair elections. The restrictions in that case were held to be acceptable, but in the USA the opposite conclusion was reached in a comparable case, *Citizens United v Federal Election Commission*.[119] This demonstrates that even between democratic countries there can be different conceptions of where it is appropriate to draw the line between individual freedom and collective well-being. Coming up with a fixed set of criteria of how to do so in all situations is not easy, perhaps not even possible.

Public Liability

While liability in tort law is often portrayed as an archetypal area of 'private law', it does not have to be so limited. Exactly how far up the public law ladder liability should go is a matter for each country to decide for itself. When Ireland was part of the United Kingdom the courts in Ireland applied the principle that the State as such could not be sued, because it enjoyed 'immunity'. Individuals acting on behalf of the State could in some situations be sued, but the State could not then be held vicariously liable for their actions. This remained the position in the United Kingdom even after the passing of the Crown Proceedings Act 1947, which for the first time imposed civil liability on the Crown for torts committed by any part of the UK government.[120] In Ireland the extension of liability to the State took even longer to establish.

Byrne v Ireland

The question whether the Irish State could be sued for its tortious actions did not arise for consideration by the Supreme Court until the new State was already 50 years old. In *Byrne v Ireland* the plaintiff claimed that she suffered an injury when a public footpath she was walking along in Bray, County Wicklow, subsided beneath her.[121] She argued that the subsidence had been caused by workmen employed by the government's Department of Posts and Telegraphs and that therefore the State was required to compensate her for her injuries. In the High Court Murnaghan J held that the State of Ireland was not liable because under Article 5 of the Constitution Ireland is sovereign. He added:

> The simple statement [in Article 5] that 'Ireland is a sovereign . . . State' is completely inconsistent with the propositions that the State is subject to one of the organs of the State, the judicial organ, and can be sued as such in its own courts.[122]

Yet on appeal the Supreme Court unanimously held that the immunity from suit enjoyed by the British State prior to the creation of the Irish Free State in 1922 was not carried forward to the new State. Four of the five judges held that the Irish State is a juristic person who can be held vicariously liable for the tortious acts of its servants, even in the absence of any express statutory statement of that liability. The two main judgments were by Walsh and Budd JJ, and they are important indicators of how the then Supreme Court conceptualised

[118] (2013) 57 EHRR 21. [119] 558 US 310 (2010). [120] s 2

[121] [1972] IR 241. Counsel for the plaintiff included Niall McCarthy SC and Donal Barrington, two future Supreme Court judges. See Hogan and Morgan (2010) 1085–87; Osborough (1973) and (1976).

[122] Ibid, 254–5.

the Irish State.[123] Walsh J's judgment is surely one of the best crafted of his or of any other Supreme Court judge's career.

Walsh J began by saying it was 'abundantly clear' from the Irish Constitution that in Ireland the sovereign authority is the people, whereas in the USA it is the States and the people of the States and in Great Britain (he avoided saying 'United Kingdom') it is the monarch. He then noted that the question before the Supreme Court was 'whether the judicial power of government which is exercised by the judiciary through the Courts is exercisable so as to bind the State itself, one of whose organs is the judiciary'.[124] This was almost as fundamental a question for the Irish Supreme Court as the question posed to the US Supreme Court in *Marbury v Madison* in 1803.[125] In *Byrne v Ireland* the Irish Supreme Court derived its power to hold the State liable in civil actions from the Constitution itself. In doing so it set aside a basic principle of the common law, that the sovereign is immune from being sued. Even the US Supreme Court, as Walsh J himself points out,[126] had not gone that far: as late as 1882 the US Supreme Court was still asserting that 'the supreme power in every State, wherever it may reside, shall not be compelled, by process of courts of its own creation, to defend itself from assaults in those courts'.[127]

By way of contrast Walsh J checklisted many other countries which had explicitly allowed the State to be sued—France, Germany, Australia, Canada, New Zealand, South Africa and India. He believed that the true origin of the idea that the State was immune from suit lay in the assumption that, as the King was the personification of the State, it would be illogical for the King to issue a writ against himself. But the Constitution of the Irish Free State, in Walsh J's eyes, 'rejected the concept that any of the powers of government … derived from the Crown'.[128] He said:

> In Saorstát Éireann [the King] was not the personification of the State and, therefore, the common-law immunities or prerogatives of the King which were personal to him did not exist in Saorstát Éireann.[129]

The judgment ended in a stirring fashion. He concluded that there was no basis, in theory or otherwise, for a claim that the State can do no wrong or that it cannot be made vicariously liable for a wrong committed by its servants.[130] Moreover, if the Constitution imposes obligations on the State and confers rights on the citizens as against the State then in principle a wrong which arises from the failure to honour the obligations must be capable of a remedy in the courts unless the Constitution expressly excludes this.[131] In short, '[i]t is as much the duty of the State to render justice against itself in favour of citizens as it is to administer the same between private individuals'.[132]

Budd J's judgment endorsed most of what Walsh J said. FitzGerald J agreed that sovereign immunity from suit had not survived the creation of the Free State but, crucially, he felt that to assert that the State was a juristic person liable under the law of tort 'involves such a radical change in the accepted view both of the Courts and of the Legislature that this Court should decline to undertake such a step',[133] suggesting that if anyone should make the change it should be the Oireachtas. This is a further example of FitzGerald J's excessively conservative stance towards judicial activism. We see it elsewhere in cases such as *McGee v Attorney General*, on access to contraceptives.[134]

[123] Ó Dálaigh CJ agreed with both judgments, O'Keeffe P agreed with the judgment of Walsh J. FitzGerald J, as we shall see, dissented.
[124] [1972] IR 241, 262–3.
[125] 5 US 137 (1803). See Chap 3 above, 34.
[126] [1972] IR 241, 266–7.
[127] *United States v Lee* 106 US 196 (1882). 206.
[128] [1972] IR 241, 273.
[129] Ibid, 274.
[130] Ibid, 279.
[131] Ibid 279–80.
[132] Ibid, 281.
[133] Ibid, 301–11.
[134] [1974] 1 IR 284. See also Chap 7 above, 154 and Chap 10 below, 232-4.

Webb v Ireland

As a result of the decision in *Byrne v Ireland* any legal action taken against a State body is considered to have been taken against 'Ireland', whereas in the United Kingdom the name of the State body itself is recorded as the defendant. Prosecutions in Ireland are brought in the name of 'The State' or 'The People', whereas in the United Kingdom they are brought in the name of the Crown ('*R*', for '*Rex*' or '*Regina*'). The decision in *Byrne* has been the object of much academic commentary, most of it complimentary.[135] Subsequent courts have cited it frequently and deferentially, but on at least one occasion they have impliedly qualified it. This was when the Supreme Court was asked to determine who should be declared the owner of the 'Derrynaflan Hoard', a collection of eighth and ninth century Celtic liturgical vessels found in County Tipperary in 1980. The father and son who found the hoard claimed that it belonged to them or, if not, that they should be awarded IR£5 million in compensation for unearthing it. In law, whether they could claim ownership depended in part on whether the common law of treasure trove had been carried over from the United Kingdom when the Irish Free State was created in 1922. That law, like the principle of sovereign immunity, derived from the royal prerogative, so if *Byrne v Ireland* were followed then ownership of the hoard would not pass to the State but stay with the finders. In *Webb v Ireland* that is exactly what was decided by Blayney J in the High Court, but he was overturned on appeal by the Supreme Court.[136]

All five judges agreed that the prerogative right to treasure trove had not been carried over into Irish law in 1922 and that the Irish State owned the treasure for another reason, but they differed amongst themselves as to what that reason was. The majority (Finlay CJ, Henchy, and Griffin JJ) held that it was because of Article 10.1 of the 1937 Constitution, under which '[a]ll natural resources … and all royalties within the jurisdiction belong to the State subject to all estates and interests therein for the time being lawfully vested in any person or body'. The minority (Walsh and McCarthy JJ) held that it was because Article 5 declared Ireland to be a sovereign State, ownership of treasure being a facet of sovereignty.[137] The difference in opinion between the two sets of judges is not that significant because the majority agreed that a necessary ingredient of sovereignty in Ireland, having regard to the Constitution's emphasis on its historical origins and a concern for the common good, is 'ownership by the State of objects which constitute antiquities of importance which are discovered and which have no known owner'.[138] All the judges agreed, moreover, that it would be inequitable and unjust if the State were not to abide by the assurance given to the finders of this hoard by the Director of the National Museum that they would be 'honourably treated'. To support that conclusion Finlay CJ even cited the doctrine of promissory estoppel, familiar to contract and property lawyers.[139] The net result of this decision, even though it seems contradictory to that in *Byrne v Ireland*, was that Ireland's cultural heritage was more securely preserved for posterity; if this required a clever manipulation of legal doctrine it was a price worth paying.

[135] See Binchy (2011) 339–40; Von Prondzynski (1978–80); Osborough (1976) and(1973b).
[136] [1988] IR 353. See Costello (1997); Lenihan (1989); Kelly (1988a); Morgan (1988).
[137] Ibid, 393 (per Walsh J) and 398 (per McCarthy J).
[138] Ibid, 383 (per Finlay CJ).
[139] Ibid, 384–5.

Duties of Care, Economic Loss and Nervous Shock

In most areas of tort law the Supreme Court has tended to make statements which are at one with the law of torts in England and Wales, although priority is naturally given to domestic precedents. In the past 50 years or so the Court has hugely extended liability for negligence, even when the defendant is a public body.[140] The first reported instance of *Donoghue v Stevenson*[141] being considered in an Irish court is when High Court judge Gavan Duffy J commented on it in *Kirby v Burke and Holloway* in 1944.[142] He pointed out that the three-to-two decision was won by 'a Celtic majority'[143] but he nevertheless refused to assume 'as a matter of course, that the view which prevailed must of necessity be the true view of the common law in Ireland'.[144] *Donoghue v Stevenson* was cited to the Supreme Court in 1951[145] but was not discussed in any *reported* Supreme Court judgment until 1959, almost 30 years after its emergence. In that case, *Power v Bedford Motor Co,*[146] a man was killed in 1955 when the steering failed in the car he was driving. The steering had supposedly been repaired by the defendant garage six months earlier, but since then the car had been sold to another owner and a second garage had checked the steering and found nothing wrong with it. The Supreme Court held that the first garage should still be held liable for negligently causing the driver's death.[147] Lavery J said that the principle in *Donoghue v Stevenson* was now 'well established' and 'has been followed and applied in this Court in several cases – notably in *Robinson v Technico Ltd* (unreported)'.[148]

In subsequent years, however, the Supreme Court has tended not to adopt the more restrictive approach to the duty of care principle laid out by the House of Lords in the early 1990s in *Caparo Industries plc v Dickman*[149] and *Murphy v Brentwood District Council.*[150] Healy calls this an 'incremental' approach and says that by 2006 it had not been formally endorsed in Ireland.[151] By and large, Irish judges seemed content to let liability fall on the party who could more easily have prevented or insured against the damage or injury occurring, while denying remedies to plaintiffs who themselves acted very incautiously. That said, there do not appear to be any types of conduct which are tortious in Ireland but not in England and Wales, even in fields such as employers' liability, economic torts and defamation. As far back as 1973 the Supreme Court suggested, in *Meskell v Coras Iompair Eireann*[152] (Ireland's public bus company), that if a commercial organisation violates a person's constitutional rights that of itself can justify a claim in tort for damages.[153] It looked as if this might become a distinctive feature of the Irish legal system, 'a groundbreaking and, by international standards, precocious recognition of the importance of protecting constitutional rights against violations of those rights by private bodies'[154] but, as O'Cinneide has demonstrated, the principle was 'inadequately developed', 'tamed' and 'rendered partially

[140] See the excellent survey by Binchy (2016), esp 208–10. [141] [1932] AC 562.

[142] [1944] IR 207.

[143] A reference to the fact that the three judges in the majority were Lords Atkin (raised in Wales), Thankerton (a Scot) and Macmillan (another Scot): the case was an appeal from Scotland. Lords Buckmaster and Tomlin, in the minority, were both English.

[144] [1944] IR 207, 215. [145] *Keegan v Owens* [1953] IR 267, 269. [146] [1959] IR 391.

[147] Kingsmill Moore J dissented on the basis that it was 'the purest conjecture' (ibid, 420) that it was the first rather than the second garage which had reversed the track rod ends on the Ford Zephyr in question.

[148] [1959] IR 391, 407. [149] [1990] 2 AC 605. [150] [1991] 1 AC 398.

[151] Healy (2006) 83–4. [152] [1973] 1 IR 121.

[153] But Binchy (1992) pointed out some of the difficulties with that proposition. The same author later observed that *Meskell* (together with *Byrne*) indicated 'a view of the State as the agent of the People rather than the People's master': Binchy (2011) 340. See too Hogan (1986) 533.

[154] O'Cinneide (2007) 251; see too O'Cinneide (2003).

toothless' by the Supreme Court's decision in *Hanrahan v Merck Sharp and Dohme (Ireland) Ltd*,[155] where it refused to supplement the existing tort of nuisance by shifting the burden of proof on to the defendant whenever constitutional rights are at stake. That will occur, said the Court, only if the tortious remedy is 'ineffective' in protecting the constitutional rights. We shall see in Chapter 12, moreover, that the Supreme Court seems to favour a more limited approach to vicarious state liability for some torts.[156]

In the field of liability for economic loss, the Supreme Court has moved more firmly on to the ground occupied by the House of Lords in *Caparo*. This is clear from *Glencar Exploration plc v Mayo County Council*,[157] where a company was suing the Council to recover financial losses suffered as a result of the Council's decision to renew a ban on mining. In an earlier application for judicial review the company had succeeded in getting the ban quashed because the council had acted *ultra vires*,[158] but the Supreme Court did not think that that meant damages should be awarded to the company for the resultant losses. While it might have been foreseeable by the Council that such losses would be suffered, there was no 'relationship of proximity' between the parties to make it 'just and reasonable' to impose liability on the Council. After reviewing both English and Irish case law Keane CJ opted for an approach that was 'consistent with the reluctance of the law to impose liability for negligence arising out of an omission to act'.[159] The Council's statutory powers in relation to development were ones which were exercisable for the benefit of the whole community rather than for a defined category of persons and so the applicant was entitled to rely on 'no more than a general expectation that the respondents would act in accordance with the law',[160] which was not a sufficient ground on which to base the existence of a duty of care on their part.

Keane CJ distinguished the Supreme Court's decision in *Ward v McMaster*,[161] where Louth County Council had been held liable in negligence to purchasers of a home who had borrowed money from the Council on the basis of what turned out to be an inexpert valuation which the Council had obtained of the home. The facts of *Ward v McMaster* were similar to those in the House of Lords' case of *Anns v London Borough of Merton*[162] (where liability was imposed) whereas the *Glencar* case was more akin to the House of Lords' decision in *Caparo* (where no duty of care was found). As is well known, the House of Lords later overruled the *Anns* case in *Murphy v Brentwood District Council*,[163] but those two cases were about the recoverability of economic loss suffered as a result of a negligent misstatement rather than an act or omission and in *Glencar* the Irish Supreme Court saw no need to take a position on exactly how far liability should extend. It specifically declined to overrule *Ward v McMaster* or another of its earlier decisions in the field, *Siney v Dublin Corporation*.[164] Fennelly J, who also gave a judgment in *Glencar*, completely agreed with Keane CJ but added a significant comparative law dimension to his analysis in order to illustrate how courts often need to distinguish between private interests and public interests. He relied on a decision of the Privy Council in an appeal from New Zealand,[165] as well as on a decision by the Supreme Court of Canada,[166] when considering whether a

155 [1988] ILRM 629.

156 See 298-301. Also Hogan and Morgan (2010) 1088–90.

157 [2002] 1 ILRM 481.

158 *Glencar Exploration plc v Mayo County Council* [1993] 2 IR 237 (Blayney J).

159 [2002] 1 ILRM 481, 511–12.

160 Ibid, 512.

161 [1988] IR 337.

162 [1978] AC 728.

163 [1991] 1 AC 398.

164 [1980] IR 400. Here the local authority was held liable to pay damages to a homeless family who had been housed in accommodation unfit for human habitation.

165 *Rowling v Takaro Properties Ltd* [1988] AC 473.

166 *Welbridge Holdings Ltd v Metropolitan Corporation of Greater Winnipeg* (1970) 22 DLR (3d) 470.

public authority should owe a duty of care when exercising its statutory powers and he cited decisions of the European Court of Human Rights and the European Court of Justice to demonstrate that the problem is one which confronts European jurisdictions too. This shows a laudable commitment to situate issues coming before the Irish Supreme Court in their proper international context. It also provides evidence to support Binchy's comment that the *Glencar* decision 'has cast a shadow over the subsequent judicial development of the duty of care'.[167] The judgments in *Glencar* also recognize that whenever an individual or private company suffers losses as a result of an *ultra vires* action on the part of a public authority, there is a potential remedy through seeking damages in an application for judicial review. As we have noted earlier in this chapter,[168] however, that route can be just as difficult to travel down as the duty of care route.

The Irish Supreme Court has to date emulated the English courts when it comes to awarding damages for 'nervous shock' that is, trauma suffered as a result of a tortious act. In *The State (Keegan) v Stardust Compensation Tribunal* it was accepted by the Tribunal[169] that the nervous shock claims brought by the parents of two siblings who had been killed in the Stardust dancehall fire in Artane, County Dublin, in 1981, should be dealt with in accordance with the principles set out by the House of Lords in *McLoughlin v O'Brian*.[170] That was a case where a woman recovered damages for the psychiatric injury she suffered upon being told that her husband and children had been involved in a serious car crash. The court said recovery should be restricted to situations where the claimant was a close relative of the victim and had been in close proximity to the event as regards both time and place. In *Keegan* the Irish Supreme Court reserved for a future occasion any decision on whether *McLoughlin v O'Brian* should be expressly followed in Ireland. That approval came a decade or so later, in a case where the facts were similar to those in the English case. In *Kelly v Hennessy*[171] the Supreme Court reduced the damages awarded to Mrs Kelly by the High Court judge but affirmed the principles applied. It found support as well in a decision of the High Court of Australia.[172]

A few years later, in *Fletcher v Commissioner of Public Works*,[173] the Supreme Court denied damages to a plaintiff who complained of the nervous shock he had suffered as a result of his fear that he might contract a serious disease due to being negligently exposed by his employers to asbestos. His fear was characterised as irrational because according to medical experts the risk of any such disease occurring was remote. In the course of his judgment Keane CJ recognized the law's apparent illogicality in compensating recognisable psychiatric conditions but refusing to compensate for grief or mental anguish. Consistent with these earlier decisions the Supreme Court refused damages in *Devlin v The National Maternity Hospital*,[174] where the plaintiff suffered psychiatric injury when she learned that after a *post mortem* examination of her stillborn baby the hospital had removed and retained some of the baby's organs without the knowledge of the plaintiff. She lost because no physical injury to herself had been reasonably foreseeable at the time she suffered her trauma (the baby having already died).

[167] Binchy (2016) 208. See too Ryan and Ryan (2004) 134, where they describe *Glencar* as 'a clear statement of judicial unease with the relentless rolling of the negligence bandwagon'.

[168] See 174 and 177.

[169] [1986] IR 642; see above 177-9; the parents lost their claim.

[170] [1983] 1 AC 410.

[171] [1995] 3 IR 253 (Hamilton CJ, Egan and Denham JJ).

[172] *Jaensch v Coffey* (1984) 155 CLR 549.

[173] [2003] 1 IR 465 (Keane CJ, Denham, Murray, Hardiman and Geoghegan JJ).

[174] [2008] 2 IR 222.

Police and Army Cases

Suing the police in negligence can be every bit as difficult in Ireland as in England because in both jurisdictions the preferred view is that requiring police officers to exercise a duty of care might divert them from pursuing their central goal of detecting and solving crimes.[175] Of course it ought to be possible for the police to satisfy that goal as well as doing more to protect potential victims of crime, without any loss of overall efficiency or effectiveness. An outstanding example of the Supreme Court's preparedness to impose tortious liability even on the police is *Lynch v Fitzgerald*,[176] where in 1934 three men had been killed by undercover police officers in Cork when they fired at protestors who had broken through a police cordon and entered a yard where a controversial cattle sale was to take place. The officers were former members of the IRA who were skilled in the use of firearms long before joining the police, but in the execution of their duties 'they were uncontrolled and left to their own undisciplined judgment in the use of firearms'.[177] The father of one of the victims sued the police for damages under the Fatal Accidents Act 1846 and in the High Court Hanna J awarded him £300 compensation. The Supreme Court affirmed that decision, holding that on the evidence presented it had not been necessary for the officers to fire at the men, even as a last resort. The case is a remarkable instance of the Supreme Court firmly upholding the rule of law in the Irish Free State at a time when it would have been all too easy to take the side of the State forces. Sadly, the Court's judgments contrast starkly with those delivered years later by courts in Belfast and the House of Lords in cases arising out of the troubles in Northern Ireland.[178]

The Irish Supreme Court was also well ahead of other common law supreme courts in holding that the State can be liable in negligence if it breaches its duty of care to serving soldiers. This occurred in *Ryan v Ireland*,[179] where an Irish soldier who was serving with the UN's peace-keeping force in Lebanon was injured by shrapnel while obeying an order to take some rest from his sentry duty at an exposed billet. In the High Court Keane J withdrew the case from the jury because the plaintiff had not demonstrated that the Irish Army rather than the UN was responsible for his safety. On appeal that point was conceded by the State, so attention focused on whether Irish law imposed a duty of care on the Irish Army in relation to its soldiers while on active service and, if so, whether the Army could rely on the defence of *volenti non fit iniuria*, that is, that the plaintiff had assumed the risk of being injured when he joined the Army. In relation to the first question Finlay CJ, with whom the other four judges agreed,[180] began by surveying comparable common law jurisdictions, citing cases from England,[181] Scotland,[182] Australia[183] and the USA,[184] all of which suggested that the State was indeed immune from being sued in negligence by soldiers injured

[175] See, generally, Hogan and Morgan (2010) 1093–6; Walsh (2013). In *Commissioner of Police of the Metropolis v DSD* (the Derek Warboys case) [2018] UKSC 11 the UK Supreme Court softened its stance on this point by holding that the police could be sued under the Human Rights Act 1998 if they breached the positive obligation imposed by Art 3 of the ECHR to investigate effectively reported crimes perpetrated by private individuals.

[176] [1938] IR 382 (Sullivan CJ and Fitzgibbon, Murnaghan and Meredith JJ).

[177] Ibid, 391.

[178] The House of Lords' decision in *Attorney General for Northern Ireland's Reference* (the McElhone case) [1977] AC 105 springs immediately to mind. See Dickson (2010) 250–4.

[179] [1989] IR 177.

[180] Hamilton P, Walsh, Griffin and Hederman JJ.

[181] *Dawkins v Lord Paulet* (1869) LR 5 QB 94.

[182] *Wilson v First Edinburgh City Royal Garrison Artillery Volunteers* (1904) 7 F 168. Some would categorise Scotland as a mixed rather than a purely common law jurisdiction.

[183] *Shaw, Savill & Albion Co Ltd v The Commonwealth* (1940) 66 CLR 344; *Parker v The Commonwealth* (1965) 112 CLR 295.

[184] *Feres v United States* 340 US 135 (1950).

while on active service. But the Chief Justice was not overawed by these precedents. Instead he returned to first principles and asked whether the common law applicable in Ireland created an immunity for the State in such cases and, if so, whether this would be consistent with the Constitution.

In just a few short paragraphs he answered both questions in the negative, although he was careful to point out that he was stating the law only in relation to a soldier serving with a UN peacekeeping force, not a soldier fighting in a war or in defence of the State. He noted that Articles 40.3.1 and 40.3.2 of the Constitution guarantee that the State will respect, defend and vindicate the personal rights of the citizen. On this basis he concluded that it was impossible to accept the application of a *common law* doctrine of immunity for the State. He was fortified in this conclusion by the fact that the Defence Act 1954 allows for legal proceedings to be brought in respect of alleged neglect in the execution of the Act.[185] On the question of whether the State could raise the *volenti* defence Finlay CJ cited the Supreme Court's decision in *O'Hanlon v Electricity Supply Board*,[186] where it stipulated that a prerequisite for the defence was the existence of a contract under which the plaintiff had agreed to waive his or her right to sue if injured by the negligence of the other party, and no such contract existed here.

Aggravated Damages

A further noteworthy example of the Supreme Court's willingness to provide compensation for wrongdoing by the State is its decision in *Shortt v Commissioner of An Garda Síochána*.[187] Counsel for the police conceded that the oppression suffered by the plaintiff was the worst that was known to have occurred. On the basis of perjured evidence submitted by the police the plaintiff had been convicted in 1995 of knowingly allowing drugs to be sold in his public house in County Donegal.[188] As a result he spent 27 months in prison, lost his business, became estranged from his family and endured physical and mental ill-health. Even when he applied to have his conviction declared a miscarriage of justice the police continued to proffer perjured evidence.[189] When he brought an action for compensation in the High Court Finnegan J awarded him compensation of €1.9 million, including €500,000 as general damages[190] and €50,000 as exemplary damages.[191] If matters had been left at that the case would still have been a significant precedent. But the plaintiff felt that justice had not yet been fully done so he appealed to the Supreme Court, claiming not just exemplary damages but aggravated damages. To many people's surprise the Supreme Court increased the plaintiff's compensation to €4.6 million.[192] The two substantive judgments are replete with pejorative comments about the corruption at the centre of the case: Murray CJ called it 'a stain of the darkest dye on the otherwise generally fine tradition of the institution of An Garda Síochána'[193] while Hardiman J labelled it 'nothing less than an obscenity'.[194]

[185] Though after the Crown Proceedings Act 1947 in the UK the doctrine of immunity from suit remained in being, albeit reduced in scope. See *Halsbury's Laws of England* (4th ed, Reissue), vol 12(1), 'Crown Proceedings and Crown Practice'.

[186] [1969] IR 75.

[187] [2007] IESC 9, [2007] 4 IR 587.

[188] Corruption by police officers in Donegal more generally was the subject of a public inquiry by the Morris Tribunal, which issued reports in 2005, 2006, and 2008.

[189] *The People (DPP) v Shortt (No 2)* [2002] 2 IR 696.

[190] This was awarded under s 9(2) of the Criminal Procedure Act 1993.

[191] *Shortt v Commissioner of An Garda Síochána* [2005] IEHC 311.

[192] For an account of the Irish law on aggravated and exemplary damages in tort law just before the decision in *Shortt*, see Healy (2006) 448–53.

[193] [2007] 4 IR 587, [11]. Denham J agreed with the judgment of Murray CJ.

[194] Ibid, [246]. Geoghegan and Fennelly JJ agreed with the judgments of both Murray CJ and Hardiman J.

From a legal point of view the decision is important because it stressed that if a case involves circumstances where there are clearly aggravating factors then aggravated damages *must* be awarded; here the Supreme Court raised the High Court's award by €1.75 million, reversing Finnegan J's view that this would amount to duplicate compensation for the same losses. The decision also confirmed that exemplary damages are different from aggravated damages in that they are intended to compensate the plaintiff not for any particular loss but for the outrageousness of the defendant's conduct. Here the abuse of power was so outrageous that the Supreme Court increased the exemplary damages twentyfold, from €50,000 to €1 million.

When considering the award of aggravated damages the Supreme Court applied its own earlier ruling in *Conway v Irish National Teachers Organisation*,[195] a case arising out of the fact that a nine-year-old girl had been deprived of school education for almost six months in 1976–77 because of a circular issued by a teachers' trade union directing neighbouring schools not to provide teaching to this or any other pupil from three particular schools with which the union was in dispute. In separate litigation the union was held liable in the High Court for interfering with a child's constitutional right to be provided with free education,[196] and was ordered to pay IR£4,000 in compensation.[197] In *Conway* the High Court awarded the plaintiff the higher sum of IR£11,500, to include a sum of IR£1,500 as exemplary damages, and on appeal the Supreme Court approved that amount. It chose not to follow the UK's House of Lords, which in *Rookes v Barnard* had suggested that exemplary damages should be awarded only where there had been oppressive conduct by an agent of the government or where the defendant proceeded with his or her conduct because of a calculation that a greater advantage would thereby be gained than the amount of damages which might have to be paid to the plaintiff.[198] The Supreme Court recognized that no aggravated damages were being claimed in this case but Finlay CJ nevertheless set out when such damages would be available, namely, to reflect (a) the manner in which the wrong was committed, (b) the conduct of the wrongdoer after the commission of the wrong or (c) the conduct of the wrongdoer or his representatives when defending legal proceedings arising out of the wrong. It was this catalogue which the Supreme Court later approved, and applied, in *Shortt v Commissioner of An Garda Síochána*.

Conclusion

The extent to which national judges are prepared to interfere with decisions made by executive or administrative bodies is obviously an important factor in determining the character of the nation's legal system. Yet, because the language used by judges in such cases tends to be technical and obscure, the average journalist, let alone an ordinary member of the public, does not pay much attention to the phenomenon or view it in terms of power balances, the protection of rights or the application of justice. As far as Ireland is concerned, even writers who have sought to identify the critical junctures in the development of Irish identity or to sum up the impact of the legal system on the values lying at the heart of society have not devoted much ink to the subject of judicial review *per se*[199] or to the concept of public authority liability. Yet the relationship between the courts (particularly the Supreme Court) and the other organs of government is crucial to the maintenance of confidence in national

[195] [1991] 2 IR 305. [196] *Hayes v Ireland* [1987] ILRM 651.
[197] *Crowley v Ireland* [1980] IR 102. [198] [1964] AC 1129.
[199] eg Fanning (2008); Kenny (2005); Hussey (1993); Tobin (1984).

institutions, belief in the availability of justice and trust in the *bona fides* of all persons who wield power. There remains a need for the Irish Supreme Court to bring more clarity to this area of Irish law, not least because it relates directly to the question of how power should be distributed within Irish society. While it has taken some bold steps as far as holding public authorities liable for torts is concerned, the Supreme Court has not been noted to date for its adventurous stance towards judicial review of administrative action, particularly when constitutional rights are not at stake.

9

Criminal Justice

Introduction

One of the most challenging tasks facing any Supreme Court is to ensure that its country's criminal justice system operates in a way that commands high levels of public confidence. In most countries, however, the opportunities which the Supreme Court has to make or suggest improvements to the criminal justice system occur infrequently. This is because it is usually a matter of happenstance whether a case comes before the Court which brings to light a defect that needs to be addressed. Until very recently Ireland's Supreme Court could not dictate what issues it would consider and in any event the types of defects the Court can address are mostly limited to those which are inherent in the substance of the law rather than in the workings of bureaucracies. Even when the defect is substantive the Court may be able to identify the defect but still remain powerless to make any changes because they require detailed legislation. This powerlessness often risks bringing the credibility of the Court into disrepute, for many members of the public may not be fully aware of the intricacies of the separation of powers doctrine: all they see is a group of well-paid senior judges wringing their hands. That said, the Court can sometimes make an immediate practical difference by declaring a piece of legislation to be unconstitutional.

In Ireland the position is made more complex than in the United Kingdom because of the existence of the 1937 Constitution, even though that document is not often explicit about criminal justice. O'Malley's tentative view is that Ireland's Constitution places Ireland ahead of the United Kingdom 'in respect of due process values in criminal justice'.[1] Article 38 of the Constitution provides that: (1) no person shall be tried on any criminal charge 'save in due course of law', (2) minor offences may be tried by courts of summary jurisdiction, (3) special courts may be established by law for the trial of offences in cases where 'the ordinary courts are inadequate to secure the effective administration of justice, and the preservation of public peace and order', (4) military tribunals may be established for the trial of offences against military law, (5) 'no person shall be tried on any criminal charge without a jury', except for offences dealt with by courts of summary jurisdiction, special courts or military tribunals, and (6) special courts and military tribunals do not need to comply with the provisions in Articles 34 and 35 of the Constitution, which deal, amongst other things, with how judges are appointed, the declaration they must subscribe to when appointed, their independence and their removal from office. Article 39 of the Constitution defines the offence of treason. Article 40.4.1 provides that: 'No citizen shall be deprived of his personal liberty save in accordance with law', with the remainder of the subsection fleshing out the procedures that must be available for allowing claims of *habeas corpus* to be taken to the courts. And Article 40.5 states that: 'The dwelling of every citizen is inviolable and shall not be forcibly entered save in accordance with the law.'[2]

[1] O'Malley (2009) 6.

[2] Other relevant provisions are Art 13.6 (Presidential pardons and commutation etc of sentences); Arts 15.5.1 and 15.5.2 (prohibiting the Oireachtas from enacting retroactive criminal law or laws providing for the death penalty).

The Irish Supreme Court: Historical and Comparative Perspectives. Brice Dickson. © Brice Dickson 2019. Published 2019 by Oxford University Press.

It must be remembered, as observed in Chapter 6, that the Supreme Court has supplemented the Constitution by enunciating a series of constitutional rights which are not expressly specified in the text of the 1937 document. The Court has done so by artful interpretation of Article 40.3 of the Constitution, which provides as follows:

1 The State guarantees in its laws to respect, and, as far as practicable, by its laws to defend and vindicate the personal rights of the citizen.

2 The State shall, in particular, by its laws protect as best it may from unjust attack and, in the case of injustice done, vindicate the life, person, good name, and property rights of every citizen.

While many of Ireland's unspecified (or 'unenumerated') constitutional rights are not directly related to the operation of the criminal justice system (eg, the rights to marry and to seek a livelihood), the Supreme Court has also created such rights in that area. They are listed by Walsh as including the right to legal representation paid for by the State (if the accused is facing a serious charge and cannot afford to pay for a lawyer), the right to be presumed innocent, the right to silence, the right not to incriminate oneself, the right of access to a solicitor if in police custody and not to be questioned until a solicitor has had a reasonable opportunity to attend, the right to be heard, the right to be tried in public, the right to a trial free from bias, the right to a reasonably expeditious trial and the right to proportionality in sentencing.[3]

For reasons of space, this chapter cannot analyse each of the innumerable judgments issued by Supreme Court on rights relating to criminal justice. Instead it focuses on five issues which have been particularly controversial, with no claim that they represent a wholly balanced view of the Supreme Court's impact in this field. The relevant cases are examined with a view to illustrating the competing tensions with which the judges have had to contend and assessing the quality of law-making apparent from their judgments. The five issues are: ensuring that a criminal trial proceeds fairly, the holding of trials in the Special Criminal Court, the right to bail, the admissibility of evidence which has been obtained illegally and the retrospectivity of declarations of unconstitutionality in criminal cases.[4]

Ensuring that a Criminal Trial Proceeds Fairly

The separation of powers doctrine requires that, while the government and its agencies can create, support and make use of institutions or processes within the criminal justice system, those bodies should not seek to influence the manner in which the institutions and processes work in practice. Otherwise the independence of the judicial arm of the State risks being compromised. The Irish Constitution encapsulates this principle in Article 34.1:

> Justice shall be administered in courts established by law by judges appointed in the manner provided by this Constitution, and, save in such special and limited cases as may be prescribed by law, shall be administered in public.[5]

[3] Walsh (2016) 25. For recent clarification of the extent of the right to silence see *DPP v M* [2018] IESC 21 (Clarke CJ and O'Donnell, Dunne, Charleton and O'Malley JJ), where the Supreme Court held that if a suspect submits a prepared statement when being interviewed by the police this does not preclude the suspect from exercising his or her right to silence when faced with further questions.

[4] A sixth issue essential to criminal law, the right to remain silent, is touched upon in Chap 12 below, 283-5.

[5] This is the wording as amended by the Second Amendment of the Constitution Act 1941, which was passed just before the end of the three-year period during which amendments could be made by the Oireachtas without requiring a referendum. The original wording of Art 34.1 allowed for no exceptions to the administration of justice in public.

This provision asserts first and foremost that the administration of justice is a matter for judges, not for anyone else. Article 37.1 goes on to allow for 'the exercise of limited functions and powers of a judicial nature' by any person or body other than a judge or court, provided this is duly authorised by law, but the exercise of such functions and powers in criminal matters is specifically excluded from the scope of this provision.[6] The Supreme Court has therefore not found it necessary to invoke Article 34.1 to prevent government interference in the administration of criminal justice.

The second limb of Article 34.1 emphasises the need for justice to be administered in public,[7] not in some private setting, and the Supreme Court has had to reassert the importance of this principle on several occasions. It was described by Walsh J in *In re R Ltd* as 'fundamental' and he added that any exception had to be expressly created by an Act of the Oireachtas.[8] But less than a decade later the Supreme Court felt confident enough to relax that strict position by interpreting[9] the phrase 'save in such special and limited cases as may be prescribed by law' in Article 34.1 as authorising the Supreme Court itself, and not just the Oireachtas, to create exceptions to the rule requiring public trials. The power seems to arise from the inherent jurisdiction of the Court to ensure fairness. The case concerned was *Irish Times Ltd v Ireland*,[10] where a Circuit Court judge had imposed restrictions on what the media could report about the trial of four foreign nationals accused of smuggling drugs. He had done so with the best of intentions in that he was worried lest inaccurate press reports of the trial led to it having to be aborted, thereby leading to further long periods of detention on remand for the four accused. The Supreme Court did not agree that reporting restrictions were necessary on the facts of this case but it did confirm Judge Murphy's view that, in principle, reporting restrictions can be imposed if this is necessary to protect the right of the accused to a fair trial. It added that the risk of an unfair trial can often be averted through the trial judge giving proper directions to the jury. Presumably this would include a direction that jurors should avoid reading newspaper, internet or social media comments or listening to broadcasts about the trial. The Supreme Court referred in this context to the accused's constitutional rights to a fair trial[11] but did not suggest that these alone were determinative of whether the accused was receiving a fair trial. In 1999 Denham J, as she then was, hinted that 'inherent jurisdiction' derives from the Constitution,[12] but O'Malley rightly points out[13] that a few years later the Supreme Court accepted that the inherent power predates and goes beyond whatever power is be found in the interstices of the Constitution.[14]

This self-proclaimed 'inherent' power may be seen as but one example of a wider judicial power—of greatest significance at the Supreme Court level—to take steps to ensure that there is no 'abuse of process'. This doctrine is part and parcel of English common law and has been adopted by the Supreme Court of Ireland as part of Irish law. An instance of its use is the case of *Sun Fat Chan v Osseous Ltd*,[15] where the Supreme Court ruled that it would be an abuse of process to allow the defendant to defend a civil action in a plenary hearing if the facts were clear and it had been shown that the defence was unsustainable. In *Kelly v Ryan* the Supreme Court used the abuse of process doctrine to halt a private prosecution which it thought was prompted by ulterior motives rather than by a genuine desire to see justice done.[16] (The doctrine has also been invoked to prevent a civil action from proceeding if it

[6] For the Supreme Court's case law on Art 37.1 see Chap 4 above, 65-8.
[7] See generally Walsh (2016) 1453–65; O'Malley (2009) 604–38.
[8] [1989] IR 126, 134.
[9] Portier (2006), at 214, describes it a 'significant reinterpretation' of Art 34.1.
[10] [1998] 1 IR 359.
[11] In particular under Arts 34.1 and 40.3 (set out at 197 above).
[12] *De Gortari v Smithwick* [1999] 4 IR 223, 229.
[13] O'Malley (2009) 30.
[14] *People (DPP) v O'C (P)* [2006] 3 IR 238.
[15] [1992] 1 IR 425.
[16] [2015] IESC 69, [2015] 1 IR 360 (Denham CJ, Hardiman, O'Donnell, Clarke and Dunne JJ).

is deemed to be vexatious.[17]) In the criminal law context it is most frequently applied where there has been prejudicial pre-trial publicity or an inordinate delay in the prosecution process,[18] but there is no reason why the Supreme Court should not feel itself empowered to stop a trial and/or release a person from custody if it is convinced on other grounds that there has been such unfairness in the trial to date that the trial should be halted and the accused acquitted. Walsh has shown how the abuse of process idea has been used by the Supreme Court to strike at prosecutorial practices which would not otherwise be caught by the principle against being tried twice for the same behaviour (the double jeopardy, *autrefois acquit* or *ne bis in idem* principles).[19]

In *Eviston v DPP* the Director of Public Prosecutions had written to the applicant telling her that she would not be prosecuted in relation to her part in a fatal road traffic accident, but he later changed his mind and proceeded with a prosecution.[20] Affirming the decision by Kearns J in the High Court, the Supreme Court ruled that continuing with the prosecution would be unfair: even though the DPP had the power to review his initial decision he had not made the applicant aware of that power. In 2010, however, the Supreme Court distinguished *Eviston* in *Carlin v DPP*,[21] where the fact that there was no evidence that the accused had suffered increased anxiety as a result of the DPP's change of mind was enough for the Court to uphold the decision to proceed with a prosecution. In 2014 a famous example of prosecutorial unfairness occurred in England when the prosecution of a resident of Ireland, John Downey, for his alleged involvement in a bomb attack in London in 1982 was stayed after the trial judge ruled that Downey's receipt of a 2007 letter from the UK government telling him that he was not a person of any interest to police forces throughout the United Kingdom meant that it would be an abuse of process to arrest and prosecute him while he was visiting the United Kingdom.[22] Writing in 2008, Rogers suggested that the abuse of process doctrine was the most significant common law development of the previous 40 or so years.[23]

In relation to trials in Ireland's District and Circuit Courts it is also possible for an application for judicial review to be made to the High Court and for the High Court's decision to be appealed to the Supreme Court,[24] but Walsh observes that it is more common for the High Court to refuse such applications if the trial court itself can remedy the alleged unfairness.[25] It would appear that the Irish Supreme Court is well placed to contribute to development of the unfairness principle in this context. It could do so when responding to applications for an order of prohibition to prevent a criminal trial from starting, a procedure which does not seem to occur in England and Wales, where there is a greater aversion to 'satellite' litigation on issues that could just as easily be dealt with by the judge in the criminal trial. In 2005 the Irish Supreme Court confirmed, in *C(D) v DPP*, that:

[17] See *Keaveney v Geraghty* [1965] IR 551. The Supreme Court followed that decision in *Wunder v Irish Hospitals Trust* (unreported, 24 January 1967) and such court orders are now referred to as 'Isaac Wunder orders'. See Moore (2001), commenting on the Supreme Court's ruling in *Riordan v Ireland (No 4)* [2001] 3 IR 365; see too Chap 7 above, 149.

[18] See eg 'Woman's trial for intent to murder halted over delay', *Irish Times*, 13 June 2015, 4.

[19] Walsh (2016) 1201–02.

[20] [2002] 3 IR 260 (Keane CJ, Denham, McGuinness and Geoghegan JJ; Murphy J dissenting in part). On whether it is unfair to pursue a prosecution after an order of *nolle prosequi* has been issued, see *State (O'Callaghan) v O'hUadhaigh* [1977] IR 42 and *O'Callaghan v DPP* [2011] 3 IR 356.

[21] [2010] 3 IR 547; Ring (2010).

[22] *R v Downey*, 21 February 2014, available at www.bailii.org. in November 2018 Mr Downey was arrested on foot of a European arrest warrant relating to the killings of two British soldiers in Northern Ireland in 1972.

[23] Rogers (2008). See too Choo (2008), *passim*.

[24] See eg *State (O'Connell) v Fawsitt* [1986] IR 362 (Finlay CJ, Walsh, Henchy, Griffin and McCarthy JJ).

[25] Walsh (2016) 1871–75.

> In circumstances where there is a real or serious risk of an unfair trial the courts will intervene so that a defendant may not be exposed to the commencement of the process, it being the assumption that should such a trial commence it will be stopped by the direction of the trial judge by reason of the real or serious risk of an unfair trial.[26]

It remains unclear whether the definition of an unfair trial in this judgment can be taken to equate with that in the European Convention on Human Rights. There would be no problem if the Supreme Court's definition were wider, because the Convention itself allows the State to go further than the Convention in protecting human rights,[27] but there would be a problem if the Supreme Court's definition were narrower. This scenario has arisen in England, where the House of Lords confirmed, in a trial connected with alleged dishonest conduct by the appellants in the run-up to the buying of shares in Distillers Co plc by Guinness plc in 1986, that, just because the appellants had obtained a ruling from the European Court of Human Rights that their trial had violated Article 6 of the Convention, this did not in itself entitle the appellants to have their convictions quashed at the national level.[28] With respect, this seems to be a sensible conclusion, because minor breaches of Article 6 can usually be remedied in other ways than through acquittal. A national court is entitled to decide, for example, that although one piece of evidence should not have been admitted at the accused's trial, the accused would have been convicted anyway on the basis of other evidence which was legally admitted. O'Malley cites an unreported decision of the Supreme Court as authority for the proposition that 'the category of cases in which a reviewing court may be persuaded to prohibit a trial is by no means closed',[29] but this does not mean that the Irish courts should necessarily elevate the right of an individual to a fair trial above the interests of society in securing justice. We will return to this theme when discussing evidence that has been obtained illegally.

The Special Criminal Court

One of the most remarkable features of the Irish legal system is the frequent resort to a 'special' court, as allowed by Article 38.3 of the Constitution.[30] The prerequisite laid down by that section is that 'the ordinary courts are inadequate to secure the effective administration of justice, and the preservation of public peace and order'. The Offences Against the State Act 1939 adds to this that a special court can be established only if the government makes and publishes a proclamation that it is satisfied that the prerequisite in Article 38.3 is met,[31] but it does not require the government to specify the evidence it is relying upon to justify its state of satisfaction. Three proclamations have been made to date, in 1939 (withdrawn in 1946), in 1961 (withdrawn in 1962) and in 1972 (still valid),[32] and no successful attempt to challenge any of the proclamations has yet been mounted. These proclamations are of course different from the declarations of national emergency which the Oireachtas can issue under Article 28.3.3 of the Constitution: as we have seen, two such declarations

[26] [2005] 4 IR 281, 283. [27] Art 53.

[28] *R v Lyons* [2003] 1 AC 976. The case was argued on the basis that Convention rights were not part of UK law when the alleged misconduct and the original trials occurred, but its ratio is broader and still applicable even though the Human Rights Act 1998 is now in force.

[29] O'Malley (2009) 36, citing *McLoughlin v DPP* (8 November 2001).

[30] See generally Walsh (2016) Chap 23; Byrne and McCutcheon (2014) 266–70; Davis (2007); Hogan and Walker (1989) Chap 10.

[31] s 35(2). See too Chap 6 above, 108.

[32] The proclamation was issued on 26 May 1972 and the Special Criminal Court was established on 30 May 1972: Offences Against the State (Scheduled Offences) Order 1972 (SI 142).

have been made, the first lasting from 1939 to 1976 and the second from 1976 to 1995.[33] Special courts can operate even when there is no national emergency.

The main differences between the ordinary criminal courts and the Special Criminal Court are, first, that the judges sitting in the latter do not have to be appointed in the same way as is required for other judges under the Constitution and, second, there cannot be a jury in a Special Criminal Court. The special courts established during World War II and in the early 1960s were staffed by military officers, but today's court is staffed by ordinary judges who have been appointed in the normal way and are specifically allocated to the Court on a temporary basis.[34] The absence of a jury, however, remains a crucial difference. The law seeks to mitigate this by requiring the Special Criminal Court to have at least three judges hearing each case,[35] whereas an ordinary Circuit Court would have just one judge (sitting with a jury). Serious crimes such as murder and rape can also be tried in the High Court, which is then known as the Central Criminal Court, and the President of that Court can direct that more than one judge should sit together to conduct the trial, but that rarely happens. As Walsh points out, whatever the make-up of the Special Criminal Court it is still obliged to try defendants 'in due course of law', as stipulated under Article 38.1 of the Constitution.[36] The same rules of evidence apply in both courts.

The Supreme Court has had several opportunities to consider the constitutionality of the special courts established as a result of the proclamations. In the eyes of many it has not displayed much bottle in its handling of those cases. In the first important challenge, mounted against the court created during 'the Emergency' (ie, World War II) to combat activities of the IRA, the Supreme Court held in *In re MacCurtain*[37] that the constitutionality of the courts was effectively beyond the power of judges to question because the government's assessment that such courts were necessary was essentially a political act which could not be judicially reviewed.[38] By today's standards the Court's approach seems excessively timorous, but it matches the prevailing judicial conservatism at that time in other common law jurisdictions. In Britain the House of Lords adopted a similarly deferential attitude in *Liversidge v Anderson*[39] and in the USA the Supreme Court went along with government-imposed internment of Japanese citizens in *Korematsu v USA*.[40] The US Supreme Court applied a 'rigid scrutiny' test to the legality of the treatment of Mr Korematsu, given that it was based on racial grounds, but still a majority of the Justices (6 v 3) upheld the constitutionality of the law and did not examine the government's claim that American security was threatened by Japanese residents of California.[41] The reluctance of the Irish Supreme Court to get involved in what was deemed to be an exclusively governmental responsibility (ie, keeping people safe from subversive activities) was maintained into the 1960s,[42] as we shall see when discussing the Court's relationship with the European Court of Human Rights in Chapter 12.

[33] Chap 6 above, 109 and 112.

[34] The Supreme Court's website states that, as of 7 November 2014, there was a panel of 11 judges appointed to sit in the Special Criminal Court. They were drawn from the High Court, Circuit Courts and District Courts. Usually one judge from each of these levels sits in a case. See too n 88 below.

[35] Offences Against the State Act 1939, s 39(1). The number of judges must be uneven.

[36] Walsh (2016), 1468. Art 38.1 reads in full: 'No person shall be tried on any criminal charge save in due course of law.'

[37] [1941] IR 83. See too Chap 6 above, 110. By the end of April 1940 the Special Criminal Court had convicted 131 people, mostly for alleged IRA activity: Ó Longaigh (2006) 236 and 244. Two prisoners died on hunger strike in April 1940.

[38] For more on non-justiciable issues see Chap 4 above, 68-9.

[39] [1942] AC 206.

[40] 323 US 214 (1944). See too *Hirabayashi v US* 320 US 81 (1943), where the judgment was 9 v 0.

[41] The three dissenters were Roberts, Murphy and Jackson JJ.

[42] *Re O'Laighléis* [1960] IR 93.

In 1974 the then Reid Professor of Criminal Law at Trinity College Dublin, Mary Robinson, a future President of Ireland, published a stinging critique of the Special Criminal Court.[43] In particular she argued that the Attorney General's power to refer non-scheduled offences to the Court[44] was unconstitutional, because it amounted to a determination of the inadequacy of the ordinary courts being made not 'in accordance with … law'[45] but 'in accordance with executive discretion'.[46] Robinson relied particularly on the recent Supreme Court decision in *East Donegal Co-operative Livestock Marts Ltd v Attorney General*,[47] where it affirmed that a Minister's discretion in exercising statutory powers could be used 'only within the boundaries of the stated objects of the Act [conferring the powers]'.[48] However other commentators, such as Nial Osborough, supported the prevailing judicial position, according to which prosecutorial decisions are almost totally immune from judicial review.[49]

Mrs Robinson was already complaining in 1974 that people were being brought before the Special Criminal Court, and thereby denied the constitutional right to a trial by jury, even though they had no known connection with any unlawful organisation such as the IRA.[50] The prosecuting authorities continued to adopt this practice in subsequent years and to use the powers conferred by the Offences Against the State Act 1939 to facilitate the collection of evidence relating to 'ordinary' crime. In *The People v Quilligan (No 1)* the Supreme Court held that there was no constitutional objection to the 1939 Act being applied in cases where arrests occurred under section 30 of that Act even though there was no suspicion that the offences committed had any political or subversive connotations.[51] The two accused in that case had been arrested on suspicion of malicious damage occasioned by their alleged break-in at the victims' home. Malicious damage was a scheduled offence under the 1939 Act. While being questioned about the malicious damage the accused made incriminating statements implicating them in the fatal injuries suffered by one of the victims. The accused were then tried for murder, albeit in the Central Criminal Court, not the Special Criminal Court, but the evidence obtained from the arrests based on the 1939 Act was admitted against them, even though, rather perversely, murder was not a scheduled offence.

In the High Court Barr J thought that this was an unconstitutional way of proceeding, but the Supreme Court expressed no qualms about it: as the arrest for non-subversive malicious damage was lawful, there was no breach of the constitutional right to liberty and so the confession could be admitted in evidence. Walsh J, who gave the leading judgment, justified his conclusion partly on the premise that Dáil Éireann, as well as the government, had authorised the proclamation triggering the establishment of the Special Criminal Court. He did not even think that the special questioning powers conferred by the 1939 Act[52] made the position of a person arrested under that Act any worse than that of a person arrested

[43] Robinson (1974), reviewed by Osborough (1975), who disagrees with Robinson's claim that the Attorney General's power to refer non-scheduled offences direct to the Special Criminal Court is unconstitutional.

[44] Conferred by s 47 of the Offences Against the State Act 1939.

[45] As required by Article 38.3.1 of the Constitution.

[46] Robinson (1974) 12.

[47] [1970] IR 317. See too Chap 8 above, 175-6.

[48] Ibid, 343. Robinson also cited *Macauley v Minister for Posts and Telegraphs* [1966] IR 345, where Kenny J, in the High Court, held that s 2(1) of the Ministers and Secretaries Act 1924 was unconstitutional to the extent that it made the right to bring a claim against a government Minister conditional upon the agreement of the Attorney General.

[49] Osborough (1975), at 371: 'No Irish precedent of which I am aware provides proof that the wind of change blowing through administrative law generally has yet reached the sheltered waters of prosecutorial discretion.'

[50] Robinson (1974) 35–6.

[51] [1986] IR 485.

[52] Section 30 required the arrested person to supply his or her name and address, while s 52 required a full account of the person's movements and actions during a specified period. The latter provision was later declared incompatible with the ECHR: see Chap 12 below, 283-4.

under the ordinary law.[53] The four other Supreme Court judges confined their inquiry to whether the wording of the 1939 Act indicated that the concept of 'scheduled offence' was restricted to offences of a subversive nature, all agreeing that it was not.[54]

Developments since the 1990s

A decade later the Supreme Court refused to change its stance. In *Kavanagh v Ireland*[55] the applicant had been sent for trial in the Special Criminal Court for offences connected with the false imprisonment of a bank manager and the use of threats towards him. The DPP had certified that the conditions set down in the Constitution for such a trial had been met but Mr Kavanagh challenged this on the basis that there was no evidence to show that the offence had been committed on behalf of any subversive organisation and that to try him in a special court meant that he was being denied the equal protection of the law. The Supreme Court dismissed this challenge rather summarily, reasserting that the assessment of the need for a trial in a special court was a political one, even though in this case it had been made by the DPP, an official who is meant to be strictly independent of the government.[56] Mr Kavanagh was duly tried and convicted, receiving two concurrent 12-year prison sentences. His lawyers then took advantage of Ireland's decision to allow petitions to be brought to the United Nations' Human Rights Committee, the body which considers complaints that a State's obligations under the International Covenant on Civil and Political Rights have not been met.[57]

In 2001 the Committee upheld the complaint and ruled that Ireland had violated Mr Kavanagh's right to equal protection of the law, as guaranteed by Articles 14 and 26 of the Covenant.[58] Ireland had failed to provide any reasonable and objective grounds for prosecuting the applicant in a special court.[59] However, when Mr Kavanagh sought recognition of this conclusion in the Irish courts he failed to obtain it. The Supreme Court affirmed that a provision in a treaty which has not been incorporated into Irish law cannot trump the verdict of a court that was lawfully constituted under Irish law.[60] This is probably the conclusion which any common law supreme court would have reached, but with a little ingenuity the Supreme Court could have turned a more critical eye on the expansion of the Special Criminal Court's remit. As Kilcommins et al have justifiably observed:

> The unfettered and arbitrary nature of this arrangement—which requires no reasons or justification to be given by the DPP for circumventing the ordinary criminal process and the right to trial by jury—seems inherently unjust, particularly so in relation to offences that do not involve subversive activities.[61]

[53] [1986] IR 495, 512.

[54] Three of the judges delivered judgments (Henchy, Griffin and McCarthy JJ) and Hederman J agreed with them.

[55] [1996] IR 321 (Barrington and Keane JJ, with whom Hamilton CJ and O'Flaherty and Blayney JJ agreed).

[56] In the High Court Laffoy J distinguished the English case of *R v Secretary of State for the Home Dept, ex parte Fire Brigades Union* [1995] 2 AC 513, which some see as evidence that judges will, when pushed, curtail governmental power if it is exercised in a manner that frustrates legitimate expectations.

[57] Ireland allowed such petitions from the date when its ratification of the Covenant took effect, 8 December 1989.

[58] Art 14(1) begins: 'All persons shall be equal before the courts and tribunals.' Art 14(3) confers guarantees in criminal cases on everyone 'in full equality'. Art 26 reads: 'All persons are equal before the law and are entitled without any discrimination to the equal protection of the law. In this respect, the law shall prohibit any discrimination and guarantee to all persons equal and effective protection against discrimination on any ground such as race, colour, sex, language, religion, political or other opinion, national or social origin, property, birth *or other status*' (emphasis added).

[59] CCPR/C/7D/819/1998 (4 April 2001).

[60] *Kavanagh v Governor of Mountjoy Prison* (unreported, 1 March 2002).

[61] Kilcommins et al (2004) 158.

Attempts have also been made to challenge the constitutionality of the Special Criminal Court on the basis that its independence is compromised by the fact that the tenure and salary of judges appointed to the Court are in the hands of the government. But these too have been unsuccessful. In *Eccles v Ireland*[62] the Supreme Court rejected the argument on the weak ground that any suggestion that judges were influenced by their personal vulnerability could be tested through a challenge in the ordinary courts brought by a defendant who felt that his or her trial had been unfair. That reasoning presupposes that political influence brought to bear on judges comes to the attention of the defendant: it does not stop the influence being exerted in the first place. Nevertheless, when Eccles took his complaint to Strasbourg the European Commission of Human Rights rejected it because in practice no undue influence seems to occur.[63] The Commission also noted that the Special Criminal Court was subject to the supervisory jurisdiction of the High Court and that its decisions could be appealed to the ordinary courts.

There is a parallel to be drawn here with the use of juryless courts to try people for scheduled offences in Northern Ireland. They were first established in 1973 on the recommendation of a commission chaired by Lord Diplock[64] because of concerns that jurors might be intimidated if they were trying alleged members of paramilitary organisations or that they might be unduly influenced in their verdicts by their own political views.[65] Until 2007 persons charged with scheduled offences[66] could avoid a juryless trial if the Attorney General certified that the offences in question should not be treated as scheduled,[67] but some offences were excluded from this 'certifying out' power, such as robbery[68] and aggravated burglary. This exclusion inevitably led to many people being tried in Diplock Courts even though they were 'ordinary decent criminals' with no connection to a paramilitary organisation.[69] From 2007 the system was changed to one where, unless the DPP for Northern Ireland positively certifies that a trial should take place without a jury, all persons accused of serious offences must be given the option of being tried by a jury.[70] The DPP can so certify only if one or more conditions are fulfilled, all of which require that the alleged offence was committed on behalf of a proscribed organisation or in connection with religious or political hostility towards another person or group of persons.[71] In addition the DPP must be satisfied that there is a risk that the administration of justice might be impaired if the trial were to be conducted with a jury, a test which is reminiscent of the first limb of Article 38.3 of the Irish Constitution.[72]

Under both the pre- and post-2007 systems it has been very difficult to challenge decisions by the Attorney General or the DPP in Northern Ireland. Attempts to do so by way of an application for judicial review are possible, but the standard of review is light and the reviewing judge will almost inevitably give the benefit of any doubt to the prosecution. The claimant, in effect, has to demonstrate either bad faith or complete unreasonableness. In

[62] [1985] IR 545.

[63] *Eccles, McPhillips & McShane v Ireland* App No 12839/87, 59 DR 212 (1988). See too Chap 12 below, 274.

[64] *Report of the Commission to Consider Legal Procedures to Deal with Terrorist Activities in Northern Ireland*, London, HMSO, Cmnd 5185 (1972).

[65] Northern Ireland (Emergency Provisions) Act 1973, ss 2 and 27, and Sch 4. These provisions were re-enacted in similar Acts in 1978 (ss 7 and 27, and Sch 3), 1991 (ss 1 and 10, and Sch 1) and 1996 (ss 1 and 11, and Sch 1), and finally in the Terrorism Act 2000 (ss 65 and 75, and Sch 9).

[66] These were set out in Sch 1 to the Northern Ireland (Emergency Provisions) Acts 1973–96 (Sch 4 in the 1978 Act).

[67] Ibid, 1973 Act, Notes 1 and 2 to Sch 1, Pt 1.

[68] This was limited to robbery where it was charged that an explosive, firearm, imitation firearm or weapon of offence was used to commit the offence: ibid, Note 4 to Sch 1, Pt 1.

[69] Jackson and Doran (1995) 19–23.

[70] Justice and Security (NI) Act 2007, ss 1–9.

[71] Ibid, s 1(3)–(6).

[72] See 200 above.

2017 a former British soldier who was accused of attempting to murder a man during disturbances in County Armagh in 1974 was denied the right to be tried by jury.[73] In England, Wales and Northern Ireland juryless trials can also take place in situations unrelated to Northern Ireland's troubles.[74] Any attempt to challenge such procedures under the ECHR are almost bound to fail because the European Court of Human Rights does not see juryless trials as in themselves incompatible with the right to a fair trial guaranteed by Article 6 of the ECHR.

In the wake of the Belfast (Good Friday) Agreement in 1998 the Irish government set up a Committee to Review the Offences Against the State Acts 1939–98, under the chairmanship of Anthony Hederman, a former judge of the Supreme Court.[75] Its terms of reference required it to take into account (a) the view of the participants in the Belfast Agreement that 'the development of a peaceful environment on the basis of the Agreement ... can and should mean a normalisation of security arrangements and practices, (b) the threat posed by international terrorism and organised crime, and (c) Ireland's obligations under international law'. A chapter of the report was devoted to the Special Criminal Court and a section within that chapter considered the various Supreme Court decisions relating to the Special Criminal Court. The Committee stated that the practical effects of those decisions were that it was 'all but impossible' to challenge a decision of the government to retain the Special Criminal Court or a decision of the DPP to direct that an accused face trial in that Court.[76] Walsh's characteristically comprehensive treatment of the latter issue demonstrates that, as in Northern Ireland, there is a considerable lack of accountability in this sphere. He sums up the current situation thus: 'since the early 1980s ... the courts have moved from the position of declaring the [DPP's] power unreviewable to accepting that it is amenable to review, albeit in very limited circumstances'.[77] The most recent and authoritative Supreme Court decision is the high-profile case of *Murphy v Ireland*,[78] where the Justices conceded that the DPP's certification power *can* be reviewed on grounds of bad faith, improper motive or in other exceptional circumstances. But on the facts the Court held that power had not been improperly exercised. Nor could Mr Murphy argue that his constitutional right to 'be held equal before the law' had been violated:[79] the Oireachtas had lawfully permitted people to be tried differently if the ordinary courts were inadequate to secure the effective administration of justice and the preservation of the public peace. Provided that assessment had been rational, there was nothing unconstitutionally unequal in having separate trial systems.

In the end a majority of the Hederman Committee held that the security threat from paramilitary organisations in Ireland was still sufficiently high to justify retention of the Special Criminal Court, as was the security threat from organised crime gangs. The whole Committee agreed that section 35 of the Offences Against the State Act 1939 should be amended to ensure that any government resolution establishing the Special Criminal Court would automatically lapse unless it was positively affirmed by resolutions passed by both Houses of the Oireachtas at three-yearly intervals. It also asked for a triennial report from the government on the working of the Special Criminal Court.[80] The Committee thought

[73] *Hutchings' (Dennis) Application* [2017] NIQB 121 (Div Ct).
[74] Criminal Justice Act 2003, ss 44–50.
[75] Hederman (2002). For Hederman J's views on extradition to Northern Ireland see Chap 7 above, 147-69.
[76] Ibid, para 9.23. [77] Walsh (2016) 1500.
[78] [2014] 1 IR 198. Thomas 'Slab' Murphy is an alleged former IRA leader who was put on trial for failing to submit full tax returns. After being convicted and sentenced to 18 months in prison, his appeal to the Court of Appeal was dismissed: *DPP v Murphy* [2017] IECA 6.
[79] Art 40.1. [80] Hederman (2002), para 9.41–9.44.

Table 9.1: Cases dealt with by the Special Criminal Court, 2008–2017

Year	Persons tried	Offences and appeals resolved
2008	22	
2009	31	
2010	21	
2011	32	
2012	30	
2013	23	
2014		26
2015		29
2016		67
2017		50[a]

[a] The *Annual Report of the Courts Services 2017*, at 83, reveals that in 2017 there were 12 trials in the Special Criminal Court involving 27 defendants, while in 2016 there were 8 trials involving 23 defendants.

it unlikely that the European Court of Human Rights would now endorse the European Commission's decision in *Eccles*, cited above,[81] given the more recent emphasis on the need for judges to be secure in their posts.[82] In a ten-paragraph addendum to the relevant chapter of the Committee's Report a minority of three members (the Chairman, William Binchy and Dermot Walsh) explained why they had to dissent.[83] They simply did not think that a case had been made out for the continued existence of the Court. They were particularly unhappy with the power given to the DPP to refer particular cases to the Court and did not feel that the majority's recommendations would satisfy the UN's requirements in *Kavanagh v Ireland* for reasonable and objective criteria to be applied when such referrals occur.[84]

Since the publication of the Hederman Committee's Report there has been little serious debate about discontinuing the Special Criminal Court. Indeed its jurisdiction was extended by the Criminal Justice (Amendment) Act 2009 to require its use for the trial of specified organised crime offences unless the DPP directs that it should *not* be so used.[85] In accordance with section 8(4) the Dáil has renewed this extension for set periods ever since, even though in the 2015 debate on renewal (for a further one-year period) the Justice Minister admitted that 'while there have been arrests under the relevant sections of the Criminal Justice Act 2006, no cases have yet come before the Special Criminal Court in accordance with section 8'.[86] Human rights NGOs have objected to the extension of the Court's jurisdiction,[87] but to no avail.

The Annual Reports of the Courts Service reveal the statistics set out in Table 9.1 above. The method for presenting the Court's workload was changed in 2014, so it is difficult to identify any significant trends over time. It is clear, however, that on average at least two dozen people are processed through the Court every year. The hike in 2016 is because in April of that year a second division of the Court began to sit.[88] The average waiting time between the date when the accused was charged and the date when a final court order

[81] See n 63. [82] Hederman (2002), para 9.49. [83] Ibid, paras 9.88–9.97.
[84] Ibid, para 9.97. [85] ss 8(1) and (2). [86] Seanad Debs, 11 June 2015.
[87] See eg ICCL (2009).
[88] The government appointed an additional seven judges to help run this second court: Stephen Collins, 'Non-jury court to get seven judges', *Irish Times*, 29 October 2015, 7.

was made was 827 days in 2016, up from 585 days in 2015. This sounds atrocious, but the average waiting times for cases in the Central Criminal Court were even longer: 865 days in 2016 and 645 days in 2015. The scourge of such delays is further examined from a human rights point of view in Chapter 12 below.

The Right to Bail

In *The People (Attorney General) v O'Callaghan* the Supreme Court delivered a set of judgments which put clear blue water between Ireland's position on the right to bail (and to some extent the right to be presumed innocent until proven guilty) and the position of other common law jurisdictions on that issue.[89] Roger O'Callaghan had been returned for trial in the Central Criminal Court on charges which included larceny, breaking and entering, malicious damage and assault. The offences were alleged to have been committed at a time when the accused was already on bail for other alleged offences committed two months earlier. The police opposed his application for bail in relation to the more recent offences on the ground that he might interfere with witnesses. Murnaghan J refused bail but on appeal the Supreme Court allowed it. Its conclusion that there was no evidence to support the suggestion that Mr O'Callaghan would interfere with witnesses was relatively uncontroversial, but the Supreme Court, *obiter*, went further than it needed to and stated categorically that bail cannot be denied to an accused person purely on the ground that he or she might be likely to commit further offences during the period of bail: a denial of bail would be a form of preventive detention. No lawyer can take the credit for persuading the Supreme Court to enunciate this principle: Mr O'Callaghan represented himself before both judicial levels. Ó Dálaigh CJ expressed himself strongly when dealing with the Attorney General's suggestion that the likelihood of a person's committing further offences was relevant to whether he or she should be granted bail:

> The reasoning underlying this submission is, in my opinion, a denial of the whole basis of our system of law. It transcends respect for the requirement that a man shall be considered innocent until he is found guilty and seeks to punish him in respect of offences neither completed nor attempted. I say 'punish'. For deprivation of liberty must be considered a punishment unless it can be required to ensure that an accused person will stand his trial when called upon ...The Courts owe more than verbal respect to the principle that punishment begins after conviction, and that every man is deemed to be innocent until tried and duly found guilty.[90]

The Chief Justice added that he did not think it was appropriate for a judge to be made aware of an accused person's previous convictions when considering a bail application. Walsh J agreed that the object of bail is to secure the appearance of the accused at his or her trial by setting bail at a reasonable amount. To support that proposition each judge cited the Supreme Court's decision in *The People v Crosbie*,[91] decided less than four months earlier. Walsh J also agreed that, unlike in some recent English decisions:

> [i]n this country it would be quite contrary to the concept of personal liberty enshrined in the Constitution that any person should be punished in respect of any matter upon which he has not been convicted or that in any circumstances he should be deprived of his liberty upon only the belief that he will commit offences if left at liberty, save in the most extraordinary circumstances carefully spelled out by the Oireachtas and then only to secure the preservation of public peace

[89] [1966] IR 501. [90] [1966] IR 501, 508–9. [91] [1966] IR 426.

> and order or the public safety and the preservation of the State in a time of national emergency or in some situation akin to that.[92]

Walsh J did not wholly agree with the Chief Justice as regards keeping the previous record of the accused out of the sight of the judge. He and Budd J thought that a bad previous record was likely to mean that a greater sentence would be imposed if the accused was eventually convicted and that it might be an incentive to the accused to avoid turning up for trial, a relevant consideration when deciding whether to grant bail.[93]

The decision in *The People (Attorney General) v O'Callaghan* was one of several from the mid-1960s in which the Supreme Court, largely through the two judges who featured prominently in that decision, set about developing the fundamental rights protected by the Irish Constitution, thereby differentiating the Irish approach to such rights from those in the United Kingdom.[94] It is interesting that this was done almost entirely without reference to the European Convention on Human Rights which Ireland, like the United Kingdom, had been one of the first countries to ratify a decade earlier, but which was not formally incorporated into domestic Irish law until the last day of 2013,[95] Ireland being the last Council of Europe State to take that step.

By the 1990s, however, it had become clear that in *O'Callaghan* the Supreme Court had gone too far. Even at the time it was presciently criticised.[96] Restricting bail to situations where there might be a fear that the accused would not turn up for trial or would seek to interfere with potential witnesses at the trial[97] was insufficient to reassure the public. Of course the law should be very cautious before authorising someone's pre-trial detention on the basis of a concern that he or she might commit another offence while on bail, but in certain circumstances the likelihood of further offences being committed might be quite high. The matter was looked at by the Law Reform Commission in a report issued in 1995,[98] a substantial part of which consisted of information about bail provisions in other jurisdictions, notably the USA, Canada, Australia, England and Wales, Scotland and several European countries.[99] It noted that in all these jurisdictions custodial remand was permitted in order to prevent the commission of further offences, although it observed that in Europe (including under the ECHR) custodial remand tended to be permissible even if the release of the accused would merely alarm public opinion, while the Supreme Court of Canada had declared a similar provision to be unconstitutional.[100] The Law Reform Commission was not asked to make specific proposals for reform, but such was the public concern that in 1996 almost every political party supported an amendment to the Constitution on the point.[101]

In the resulting referendum the Sixteenth Amendment to the Constitution Act 1996 was supported by 75 per cent of those who voted. It altered Article 40.4 by inserting subsection 7, which reads: 'Provision may be made by law for the refusal of bail by a court to a person charged with a serious offence where it is reasonably considered necessary to prevent the commission of a serious offence by that person.' The required legislation was enacted a few

[92] [1966] IR 501, 516–7. [93] Ibid, 516. [94] See too Chap 6.

[95] European Convention on Human Rights Act 2003. [96] By a future Chief Justice: Keane (1967).

[97] See the Supreme Court's decisions in *The People (Attorney General) v Gilliland* [1985] IR 643 (an extradition case) and *Ryan v DPP* [1989] IR 399.

[98] *An Examination of the Law on Bail* (LRC 50–1995). As the government was then still considering the LRC's report, the Constitution Review Group did not deal with the issue: CRG (1966) 286–7.

[99] Ibid, Chap 4 (78–162).

[100] Ibid, 160 and *R v Morales* [1992] 3 SCR 711. The Canadian Charter of Rights and Freedoms 1982 confers on all accused persons the right 'not to be denied reasonable bail without just cause' (s 11(e)).

[101] See eg Frank Kilfeather, 'Parties press Owen to take tougher action on crime' *Irish Times*, 12 January 1996.

months later as the Bail Act 1997.[102] To its credit the Supreme Court has since striven not to allow the Act to interfere with the crucial presumption of innocence[103] and has maintained other common law principles relevant to a decision on whether to grant bail.[104] In particular, it has insisted that a prolonged period of custodial remand requires particular justification on the part of the State, one that goes beyond a mere assertion that there is a severe backlog of cases to be dealt with.[105] In 2006, when Michael McDowell, the then Tánaiste and Minister for Justice, Equality and Law Reform, established a Review Group on Balance in the Criminal Law, he did not feel it necessary to include the law on bail within the Group's terms of reference.

Evidence Obtained Unconstitutionally

Generally speaking the Irish Supreme Court has adhered to the rule in English common law which holds that evidence obtained illegally can nevertheless be used by the prosecution in a criminal trial.[106] In England the rule was severely qualified by the Police and Criminal Evidence Act 1984, whereby a court may refuse to admit evidence on which the prosecution proposes to rely 'if it appears to the court that, having regard to all the circumstances, including the circumstances in which the evidence was obtained, the admission of the evidence would have such an adverse effect on the fairness of the proceedings that the court ought not to admit it'.[107] There is an additional qualification regarding the admissibility of a confession, which a court must not admit unless the prosecution proves beyond reasonable doubt that it was not obtained '(a) by oppression of the person who made it or (b) in consequence of anything said or done which was likely, in the circumstances existing at the time, to render unreliable any confession which might be made ... in consequence thereof'.[108]

An opportunity to depart from the common law rule arose before the Irish Supreme Court in *People (AG) v O'Brien*,[109] where two brothers were convicted of housebreaking and of stealing or receiving articles of clothing. The items had been found in the course of a police search of a house where the brothers lived, but by an apparent oversight the address on the search warrant was written as '118 Cashel Road, Crumlin' rather than as '118 Captain's Road, Crumlin' (the two roads converge). In appealing against their convictions the brothers relied on Article 40.5 of the Constitution, which reads: 'The dwelling of every citizen is inviolable and shall not be forcibly entered save in accordance with law.' But the appeal was unsuccessful, both at the Court of Criminal Appeal and at the Supreme Court. In the latter, Walsh J said *obiter* that, whatever the rule should be in respect of general illegality in the obtaining of evidence, courts must refuse to admit evidence if it was obtained 'as a result of a deliberate and conscious violation of the constitutional rights of the accused person where no extraordinary circumstances exist, such as the imminent destruction of vital evidence or the need to rescue a victim in peril'.[110] Kingsmill Moore J, the only one of the four other judges to issue a substantial judgment, agreed with Walsh J's formulation

[102] See s 2(1); s 2(2) sets out the factors which the court must take into account before reaching its decision. For an extensive exegesis of s 2 see Walsh (2016) 1089–106.

[103] *McDonagh v Governor of Cloverhill Prison* [2005] 1 IR 394.

[104] *Maguire v DPP* [2004] 3 IR 241.

[105] *Maguire v DPP (No 2)* [2005] 1 IR 371.

[106] See, generally, Walsh (2016) 740–819; O'Malley (2009) 741–71.

[107] Police and Criminal Evidence Act 1984, s 78. Prior to the enactment of this legislation there was also a discretion at common law to exclude evidence if the strict rules of admissibility would operate unfairly against the accused: *Kuruma v The Queen* [1955] AC 197 (PC), *Harris v DPP* [1952] AC 694 (HL) and *Noor Mohamed v The King* [1949] AC 182 (PC). A similar discretion existed in Scottish law: *Lawrie v Muir* 1950 SC (J) 19.

[108] Ibid, s 76(2).

[109] [1965] IR 142; O'Connor (1982).

[110] Ibid, 170.

of the rule but preferred not to give any examples of its application. He agreed that on the facts before him the violation of constitutional rights had not been deliberate and conscious, only accidental and unintentional. Both Walsh and Kingsmill Moore JJ examined the way the exclusionary rule operated in the USA, citing *Weeks v US*,[111] *Olmstead v US*,[112] *Silverman v US*[113] and *Mapp v Ohio*.[114] They acknowledged that it was applied very strictly but Walsh J stressed that this was mainly because the courts wanted to ensure proper behaviour by the police.

In 1982, in *People (DPP) v Shaw*,[115] the Supreme Court had to consider whether a breach of constitutional rights had been deliberate and conscious when a man who had been arrested because he was suspected of being in possession of a stolen car was then kept in custody for further questioning about the disappearance of two women. During this unauthorised detention the man confessed to the rape and murder of one of the women. The police tried to argue that because they did not know that the man's detention was unauthorised under statute the breach of his constitutional rights was not deliberate and conscious, but unsurprisingly the Supreme Court had little difficulty in holding to the contrary. As Walsh J put it: 'It is the doing of the act which is the essential matter, not the actor's appreciation of the legal consequences or incidents of it.'[116] On that basis, of course, one could easily deduce that the evidence obtained in *O'Brien* should also have been excluded because there too the act in question (the search of a house) was illegal, whether the police were aware of that fact or not. A possible distinguishing factor is that in *Shaw* the evidence in question took the form of the accused's confession, which is a type of evidence to which courts the world over apply particularly strict scrutiny in order to be sure that it was made completely voluntarily. In *People (DPP) v Lynch* the Supreme Court, through O'Higgins CJ, made it clear that it did not want the *O'Brien* ruling to apply to confessions.[117]

This shift in the understanding of the phrase 'deliberate and conscious' was confirmed in 1990, when, in *People (DPP) v Kenny*,[118] the Supreme Court considered a situation where a search warrant had been issued by a peace commissioner even though the police had supplied the commissioner with insufficient information to justify its issuance. The gardaí who then executed the warrant were not aware of this defect but the Supreme Court held, albeit by a narrow majority of three to two,[119] that that ignorance was irrelevant. The search of the accused's home had been 'deliberate and conscious' regardless of the state of mind of the police officers, and nor were there any extraordinary circumstances to excuse the breach of constitutional rights.

This re-interpretation of *O'Brien* persisted even though, a few years after *Kenny*, in *People v Buck*,[120] the Supreme Court applied a slightly different approach to the admissibility of confessions: these were held to be inadmissible unless the prosecution proved beyond reasonable doubt that they were made 'voluntarily', but even then there was said to be a residual judicial discretion to exclude the confession if it was made to the police in a manner which contravened accepted practices. As late as 2002 these accepted practices were stated to be those embodied in England's 'Judges' Rules' (which by then had been replaced in England by the Police and Criminal Evidence Act 1984).

When the issue of unconstitutionally obtained evidence was considered by the Balance in the Criminal Law Review Group in 2006–07[121] all but one member of the Group

[111] 232 US 383 (1914). [112] 277 US 438 (1928). [113] 353 US 505 (1961).
[114] 367 US 643 (1961). [115] [1982] IR 1. [116] Ibid, 23. [117] [1982] IR 64.
[118] [1990] 2 IR 110; McGrath (2004).
[119] Finlay CJ, Walsh and Hederman JJ were in the majority; Griffin and Lynch JJ dissented.
[120] [2002] 2 IR 268. [121] BCLRG (2007), 146–65.

recommended in its Final Report that the stringent rule on the exclusion of such evidence should be replaced by one which allowed the courts a discretion to admit unconstitutionally obtained evidence 'having regard to the totality of the circumstances and in particular the rights of the victim'.[122] But the Group hoped that the new rule would result from a case brought to the Supreme Court[123] rather than from an amendment to the Constitution or ordinary legislation, and it did not propose any legislative wording. Significantly, Gerard Hogan, the chair of the Group (later a judge of the High Court and of the Court of Appeal) dissented from this recommendation,[124] saying that the fundamental rights and freedoms enshrined in the Constitution had to be taken seriously and that if the price of doing so was 'the occasional exclusion of otherwise relevant evidence' it was a price worth paying, 'even if one unfortunate consequence is that a particular victim may feel that "their" case has not been fairly dealt with'.[125] Hogan's view was endorsed by other commentators.[126]

The *Damache* and *JC* cases

In 2012, in *Damache v DPP*,[127] the Supreme Court held to be unconstitutional section 29 of the Offences Against the State Act 1939, which allowed a senior garda officer to issue a warrant for the search of a person's home even if that officer was already directly involved in the investigation of the crime in question. The Justices viewed such warrants as lacking the independence required for their issuance. Denham CJ delivered the judgment of the Court[128] and, having approved a judgment of the Supreme Court of Canada dealing with search warrants,[129] set out the following principles:

> For the process in obtaining a search warrant to be meaningful, it is necessary for the person authorizing the search to be able to assess the conflicting interests of the State and the individual in an impartial manner. Thus, the person should be independent of the issue and act judicially. Also, there should be reasonable grounds established that an offence has been committed and that there may be evidence found at the place of the search.[130]

The Supreme Court deduced from these principles that on the facts before it the search warrant had not been issued by a person who was independent. Its issuance was therefore a breach of Article 40.5 of the Constitution, which as mentioned above provides that a person's dwelling must not be forcibly entered 'save in accordance with law'. Denham CJ said that this meant 'without stooping to methods which ignore the fundamental norms of the legal order postulated by the Constitution',[131] a phrase coined by Henchy J some 30 years earlier in *King v Attorney General*.[132] This resurrection of 'the fundamental norms of the legal order' led one commentator to express his 'dismay', because in his view it purports to subordinate the Oireachtas, which the Constitution says is the State's sole lawmaker,[133] to whatever norms

[122] Ibid, 165.

[123] Under new provisions inserted as s 34 of the Criminal Procedure Act 1967 by s 21 of the Criminal Justice Act 2006. These allowed the Attorney General (or in some cases the DPP) to refer a question of law to the Supreme Court arising out of the acquittal of a person tried on indictment, without prejudice to that person. See too Chap 4 above, 61-2.

[124] Note 121 above, 286–94.

[125] Ibid, 287.

[126] Collins (2009); Daly (2009b).

[127] [2012] IESC 11, [2012] 2 IR 266; Kieran (2012).

[128] The other judges were Murray, Hardiman, Fennelly and Finnegan JJ.

[129] *Hunter v Southam Inc* [1984] 2 SCR 145.

[130] [2012] 2 IR 266, [51].

[131] Ibid, [55].

[132] [1981] IR 233, 257.

[133] Art 15.2.1: 'The sole and exclusive power of making laws for the State is hereby vested in the Oireachtas: no other legislative authority has power to make laws for the State.'

a group of Supreme Court Justices sitting in a particular case decides are assumed although not expressed by the Constitution:[134]

> I argue that it is at best unwise for the judiciary to read into the Constitution provisions that it does not actually contain. And I say that when judges do that, and their interpretation interferes with the ability of other organs of government to function, then both the ability of the government to govern the country and the democratic nature of the State are endangered.[135]

Williams believes that the Supreme Court should restore the balance between different organs of government through acknowledging that judges have over-reached themselves. He concedes that the Supreme Court is respected and admired and is therefore hopeful that it will bow to the will of the people as represented through their Parliament.[136]

As a result of the Supreme Court's decisions in *Damache*, the defendant in *DPP v JC*[137] argued that, at his trial for robbery, evidence obtained through a warrant issued in a similar manner to that in *Damache* should not be admitted against him. The prosecution argued that, even if the warrant was invalid, the gardaí still had the right to enter the house in question because section 6(2) of the Criminal Law Act 1997 allows gardaí to lawfully enter premises without a warrant for the purposes of effecting an arrest and, in doing so, to search those premises. The trial judge preferred the defendant's arguments and ordered the jury to enter a verdict of not guilty. The DPP appealed, taking advantage of a relatively new power to challenge an acquittal.[138] In particular the DPP asked the Supreme Court to overrule its earlier decision in *Kenny*.[139] By a majority of four to three the Supreme Court upheld the DPP's appeal and did overrule *Kenny*.

The Supreme Court's decision in *DPP v JC* is a momentous one for two reasons. It not only marks a shift in the Court's approach to the law on illegally obtained evidence; it also provides a remarkable example of the Supreme Court's current adjudicatory style. In relation to the former, the majority held that the almost absolute rule laid down in *Kenny* should be relaxed. It was prepared to retain the position that if a breach of constitutional rights is deliberate and conscious then any evidence obtained as a result of that breach should, unless there are exceptional circumstances, be excluded. But if the breach of constitutional rights is *not* deliberate and conscious then the majority thought that, while there should still be a presumption in favour of excluding any resulting evidence, the presumption could be rebutted if the breach in question was either inadvertent or (as in *DPP v JC* itself) derived from subsequent legal developments. In effect this amounts to a revision of the meaning given to 'deliberate and conscious' in *Kenny*, because it seems to exclude from the definition breaches of constitutional rights which, although fully intended, are in one sense accidental and therefore understandably forgivable. Walsh thinks the decision is an example of the Supreme Court exceeding its constitutional role: '[i]t has all the appearance of a flagrant exercise in judicial legislation, contrary to the terms of Article 15.2.1 of the Constitution, which confers the Oireachtas with the exclusive right to make legislation.'[140]

Critics of this shift in the law, including the judges who dissented in the Supreme Court, have also condemned it as unprincipled and dangerous[141] but, with respect, such criticisms

[134] Williams (2013), 134–5, 137–9, 140–2, 220–7. [135] Ibid, 139. [136] Ibid, 147.

[137] [2015] IESC 31, [2017] 1 IR 417. For extensive discussion of this decision see Walsh (2016) 784–805.

[138] Conferred by the Criminal Procedure Act 2010, s 23. [139] See n118 above.

[140] Walsh (2016) 805.

[141] Ibid, 803: '[the decision] risks undermining, and even putting into reverse, the distinctive contribution that the Irish judiciary have made to the protection and vindication of the rights of the individual in the criminal process since at least the seminal judgment of O'Higgins CJ in *State (Healy) v O'Donoghue*'. On the *Healy* case ([1976] IR 325) see Chap 6, 129-30.

seem wide of the mark, especially as the first limb of the rule, concerning deliberate and conscious breaches of constitutional rights, already admits of qualifications when there are exceptional circumstances. There is surely more to justice than ensuring that constitutional rights are not breached, very important though the latter might be. If the breach of constitutional rights has not caused the victim any harm, and if in any event compensation can be paid to recognise the breach, it is hard to see why the breach should prevent the application of other constitutional values such as 'the requirements of the common good'.[142] In a different context, William Binchy has usefully downplayed the focus on rights under the Constitution and proposed instead 'that courts engage in the more challenging task of crafting a tapestry composed of a more elaborate and intricate relationship of rights, wrongs and remedies, taking account of social and economic considerations necessary to promote the common good'.[143] There is much to be said for that approach.

As regards the Supreme Court's adjudicatory style, the decision in *DPP v JC* is extraordinary. For a start, it is exceptionally long—more than 158,000 words. Secondly, it contains six separate judgments, ranging from 12,000 words by Murray J to 44,500 words by Hardiman J. At times, inevitably, there are subtle differences in the views expressed, even between judges who are in agreement as to whether the appeal should be upheld or not.[144] Thirdly, the six judges who delivered judgments are sharply divided on the outcome, three against three, with the most senior judge, Denham CJ, simply indicating that she preferred the view of the three judges who thought that the appeal should be allowed. Fourthly, the difference of opinion between the two sets of judges goes deep, with each side firmly entrenched in their positions. The differences relate to three key questions: should the DPP have been allowed to appeal at all (given the wording of the recent legislation which extended appeal rights to the prosecution), how important is it to exclude evidence obtained as a result of a breach of constitutional rights even when that breach was not in any sense a serious one, and when is it appropriate for the Supreme Court to overrule one of its own previous decisions? The judges dealt with those questions in a way which was really a proxy for their attitude to Irish constitutionalism more generally, and at times the language they used brought out significant differences in that attitude. For example, McKechnie J described the majority's change to the existing law as 'unworkable'.

Prior to *DPP v JC* academic commentators were generally supportive of the apparently tough line taken in *Kenny*. Bloom and Dewey compared the Irish law with that in Canada, New Zealand and the USA, concluding that Irish law vindicated constitutional rights more effectively than any of the other systems.[145] They applauded the fact that in Ireland there is no 'balancing test' in situations where there are constitutional violations, asserting that this gives 'power, thrust, and credibility' to the exclusionary rule.[146] Clearly that assessment of Irish law will need to be recalibrated in the light of *DPP v JC*. Early in 2018 the Supreme Court extended the majority's approach in that case to a situation where a challenge was

[142] Art 6.1 of the 1937 Constitution. See too Noonan (2007) 142, where he argues that, rather than courts overruling precedents by describing them as 'wrong', they should openly admit that the earlier decisions are no longer *morally* justifiable.

[143] Binchy (2011) 341.

[144] David Gwynn Morgan, arguing for more precision and less passion, has suggested that one majority judgment and one minority judgment would have sufficed: 'Ruling on admission of evidence lack clarity', *Irish Times*, 18 April 2015. Contrast *Director of Public Prosecutions v O'R* [2016] IESC 64, where a seven-judge Supreme Court ruled succinctly and unanimously (per Charleton J), that a man's belief that a woman 'might' be consenting to sex is not in law a defence to a rape charge.

[145] Bloom and Dewey (2011).

[146] Ibid, 72.

being made to the seizure of property by the Criminal Assets Bureau because the property had been found during the course of an illegally conducted search.[147]

The Retrospectivity of Declarations of Unconstitutionality

It is not just the admissibility of unconstitutionally obtained evidence that raises fundamental questions about the Irish criminal justice system. In the last decade a particularly controversial question has been what should be the consequences if a person has been convicted under a law which has subsequently been ruled unconstitutional?

In *CC v Ireland*[148] the Supreme Court held by 4 v 1 that a person charged with unlawful and carnal knowledge of a girl under the age of 15 could not, under the statutory provision involved, use as a defence his or belief that the girl in question was aged 15 or older: the provision starkly declared that '[a]ny person who unlawfully and carnally knows any girl under the age of fifteen years shall be guilty of a felony'.[149] While the judges in the majority accepted the general principle that a person should not be convicted of a crime unless he or she had a 'guilty mind' (*mens rea*), in this case they felt that the statute had deliberately intended that principle not to apply, because it was expressly mentioned in relation to another offence, that of unlawful and carnal knowledge of a woman or girl who is 'an idiot, an imbecile or feeble-minded'.[150] In addition, the statutory provision which section 1 replaced[151] expressly mentioned the defence, while section 1 did not. Although both of these justifications for the majority's conclusion have been challenged as unreliable,[152] they have a superficial attractiveness, even though they mean that a person may be convicted of a serious offence despite a genuine belief that what he or she was doing was lawful.

Geoghegan J relied on the House of Lords' decision in *R v K*,[153] which interpreted a statutory provision similar to Ireland's.[154] Fennelly J likewise relied on *R v K*, but he pointed out that there the judges recognised that other provisions of the English Act in question *did* create offences of strict liability. Hardiman and McCracken JJ simply concurred with Geoghehan and Fennelly JJ, but Denham J strongly disagreed. In her view *CC* did have the right to argue that he could be convicted of an offence under section 1 only if the prosecution showed that he had the requisite *mens rea*. At first glance this looks like a pro-defendant conclusion (and pro-male, given that most defendants under section 1 are likely to be men), but it actually meant that in Denham J's view *CC* could not raise a constitutional argument but could seek to demonstrate on the facts that he had at least an honest belief that the girl he admitted to having sex with was aged 15 or older.

The consequence of the majority's interpretation was, as Geoghegan and Fennelly JJ freely admitted, that the constitutionality of section 1 could be called into question. That issue therefore formed the subject of further litigation.[155] The composition of the Court was the same, except that Murray CJ sat in place of Denham J. Only one judgment was issued, since it was now a case on the constitutional validity of legislation. The conclusion was that section 1 was indeed unconstitutional, since it 'wholly removes the mental element and criminalises the mentally innocent'.[156] The Court was satisfied with a declaration to that

[147] *Criminal Assets Bureau v Murphy* [2018] IESC 12 (Clarke CJ and McKechnie, MacMenamin, Dunne and O'Malley JJ).

[148] [2005] IESC 48, [2006] 4 IR 1.

[149] Criminal Law Amendment Act 1935, s 1.

[150] Ibid, s 4(1).

[151] This was s 5 of the pre-partition Criminal Law Amendment Act 1885.

[152] Williams (2013) 152–5.

[153] [2002] 1 AC 462.

[154] Sexual Offences Act 1956, s 14, though the offence was indecent assault, not unlawful and carnal knowledge.

[155] See the pulsating account by Mac Cormaic (2016) 1–13.

[156] *CC v Ireland (No 2)* [2006] IESC 33, [2006] 4 IR 1, para 41. The judgment was issued for the Court by Hardiman J.

effect, without suggesting which of the various options for rectifying the unconstitutionality should be adopted. Williams observes that, had the constitutionality of section 1 been considered in the original litigation, the Court might have applied the well-established principle that if legislation can be interpreted in a way which renders it constitutional then it should be presumed to be so unless its incompatibility with the Constitution is clearly demonstrated. It did not matter that the legislation was enacted prior to the 1937 Constitution, because a post-1937 amendment to the 1935 Act re-enacted it, thus converting it into post-1937 legislation.[157]

There is something in this argument, but there is no guarantee that the presumption would have prevailed in the face of the interpretative arguments referred to earlier. Williams is on even shakier ground when he suggests that the Supreme Court's conclusion on the section's constitutionality would have been different if it had taken into account the principles of social policy listed in Article 45 of the Constitution. The principle he calls in aid is that which requires the state to endeavour to ensure that 'the tender age of children shall not be abused', but Williams ignores the fact that this phrase occurs in a sub-section dealing with the health of workers and the need to prevent people from being 'forced by economic necessity to enter avocations unsuited to their sex, age or strength'. Moreover, far from it being 'astonishing' that no judge referred to Article 45 in the two Supreme Court hearings, to do so would have flown in the face of the express instruction within Article 45 that the principles of social policy 'shall not be cognizable by any Court under any of the provisions of this Constitution'.

The conclusion of the Supreme Court was ultimately that section 1 of the 1935 Act was inconsistent with Article 40.3.1 of the Constitution cited at the start of this chapter. This was startling, since no-one had previously noticed the unconstitutionality of the provision during the previous 70 years. Counsel for *CC* also relied on Articles 38, 40.3.2 and 40.4, but the Court did not give those provisions separate attention. Nor, crucially, did the Supreme Court say what the consequences of its decision were for those persons who had previously been convicted of the offence which had now been declared unconstitutional. Within days of the Court's second decision a man who was in the middle of a three-year sentence for the offence brought proceedings in the High Court claiming that his detention was unconstitutional and that he should therefore be released in accordance with Article 40.4.2 of the Constitution, Ireland's version of a *habeas corpus* law. Laffoy J duly released the applicant (Mr A) but within three days the Supreme Court heard an appeal against this ruling, held against Mr A and ordered his return to prison.[158]

The Supreme Court qualified its own previous ruling on the retrospectivity of declarations of constitutional invalidity in *Murphy v Attorney General*, where it had struck down a provision of tax law which disadvantaged married couples because they could not each claim a personal tax allowance, a disadvantage which the Supreme Court found to be in violation of the Constitution's guarantee, under Article 41, that 'the family' would be protected.[159] While it asserted that the invalidity of sections 192–96 of the Income Tax Act 1967 was retrospective, it held in that case that only those people who had already started legal proceedings were entitled to be compensated for the disadvantage they had suffered. In *A v Governor of Arbour Hill Prison* the Supreme Court emphasised that it was dealing with a criminal matter and that in that context the principle of 'finality' was particularly important

[157] Namely, the Criminal Justice (Miscellaneous Provisions) Act 1997, s 10(1) and Sch 1.

[158] *A v Governor of Arbour Hill* [2006] IESC 45, [2006] IR 88. See the trenchant critique by Fanning (2005), who concludes (at 219) that just because the decision was expedient does not mean it was correct; also O'Neill (2007).

[159] [1982] IR 241. See Cleary (2011).

if the prosecution had acted in good faith and the accused had not at any stage during the trial impugned the constitutionality of the legislation he or she is alleged to have violated. It therefore concluded that Mr A could not benefit from the unconstitutionality of section 1 of the Criminal Law Amendment Act 1935, although it recognised that 'for wholly exceptional reasons related to some fundamental unfairness amounting to a denial of justice' verdicts in particular criminal cases should not be allowed to stand. The government's response to the Supreme Court's decisions in *CC v Ireland* was to persuade the Oireachtas to enact the Criminal Law (Sexual Offences) Act 2006, which introduced a defence of honest and reasonable mistake as to whether a child was under the age of 15.[160]

As *A v Governor of Arbour Hill* was not about the constitutionality of a provision but about the consequences of a finding that a provision was unconstitutional, each member of the Court was entitled to issue a separate judgment, and they did so. The decision certainly provoked considerable public debate.[161] Williams is of the view that the Court again got it wrong.[162] He criticises the Court for reversing the previous approach whereby things done pursuant to an unconstitutional provision were deemed to be void unless it was almost impossible to give effect to that voidness: in *A v Governor of Arbour Hill* the Court suggested that things done under an unconstitutional provision should remain valid unless there was a good reason for treating them as void. That is, however, an overly dramatic portrayal of the effect of the Court's decision in *A*, and Williams' additional point—that the Constitution itself invalidates all things done under unconstitutional legislation—is, with respect, a misreading of both Articles 15.4.2 and 50.1, neither of which say anything about the retrospective effect of a declaration of unconstitutionality. Williams continues by asserting that the decision in *A v Governor of Arbour Hill* 'is inadequately reasoned, sets aside established principles, and creates a bizarre precedent. It casts doubt on the reliability of the Supreme Court'.[163] Fanning, too, is disappointed by the decision but suspects that the Supreme Court had public opinion very much in mind.[164] He thinks the Supreme Court found itself under a degree of pressure that was exceeded in modern times only by that experienced in the *X* case on abortion,[165] and he added:

> A different outcome might have had ramifications, in a manner unprecedented in the history of the State, for the institutional respect that the Supreme Court is afforded by the public and the body politic. Put bluntly, it would be difficult to think of a much more unpopular decision than the premature release of a child molester on a legal technicality.[166]

There is an emerging view that the Irish Supreme Court should move to adopt the position of the US Supreme Court regarding declarations of unconstitutionality, namely that they make the relevant legislation void only from the date of the declaration.[167] Murphy points out that the US Court might have decided a case such as *A v Governor of Arbour Hill* in the same way, as might the Canadian Supreme Court.[168] His general thesis, which chimes

[160] s 2(3) and (4).

[161] The debate was re-opened three years later upon the death of High Court judge Seán O'Leary, whose critical views on the *A* case were published posthumously in *The Irish Times* (3 January 2007). He said: 'The lengths to which the Supreme Court went to obfuscate the fact that the continued detention of a prisoner in an Irish jail (in fact the re-arrest of a released prisoner) for an offence that did not exist in law at the date of his conviction, smacks of an attempt to curry favour with a potentially hostile media'.

[162] Williams (2013) 165–82, esp 178–80. [163] Ibid, 178. [164] Fanning (2005).

[165] Ibid, 215. [166] Ibid, 219.

[167] This is favoured by Byrne and McCutcehon (2014) 735, citing O Doyle and E Feldman in R Byrne and W Binchy, *Annual Review of Irish Law 2006* (2007), 184–5.

[168] Murphy (2007). He relies particularly on *R v Sarson* [1996] 2 SCR 223.

with that of Williams already mentioned, is that the Irish Supreme Court could learn much from its North American counterparts in this context:

> ... the tendency in US law is to avoid a crisis akin to that presented in *A* by presuming constitutionality, reaching constitutional issues last and, if necessary, reading into an offending statute the necessary saving measure, e.g. a *scienter* requirement for statutory rape, a step too far for the Irish Supreme Court in *CC*.[169]

The Supreme Court's decisions in *CC* and *A* have also thrown into question other provisions of Irish criminal law which may be interpreted as imposing strict liability. Prendergast[170] argues that in *CC* the Court could be taken as implying that treating a serious offence as one of strict liability is always unconstitutional, yet in at least two subsequent cases it has held that no *mens rea* is required for the offence of possessing a controlled drug with a market value of €13,000 or more for the purposes of sale or supply[171] or for the offence of assault causing harm.[172] He too supports using the Supreme Court's 'double construction' rule, whereby legislation is to be interpreted as constitutional if that is a possible reading of it.[173]

Conclusion

It is clear that the Supreme Court has played a very prominent role in shaping the criminal justice system in Ireland, as such a court inevitably does in any nation operating under a written Constitution. For the most part it has proceeded with considerable care, even if the judges involved have not always been unanimous in their decisions. On account of the 'one judgment rule' we will probably never know whether there was unanimity in the rulings on whether certain legislative provisions were constitutional or not. It would certainly be unfair to blame the Supreme Court judges for phrases in the Constitution which are ambiguous and it cannot be doubted that their insistent protection of the rights not to be subjected to preventive detention or tried on the basis of unconstitutionally obtained evidence was always based on the highest of motives, namely their duty to uphold the Constitution (in the spirit as well as the letter) rather than on any desire to differentiate Ireland's criminal justice system from that of England and Wales purely for appearance's sake. But it remains true that in this domain the Court has got itself into several pickles of its own making. On several key issues it has not been forthright enough in laying down clear principles, thereby leaving the law in considerable confusion. It has also tolerated the continuance and expansion of the Special Criminal Court, an institution which very few other common law jurisdictions would countenance and whose continuing existence is something of a blot on the Irish legal landscape.

[169] Ibid, 105, citing *US v X-Citement Video Inc* 513 US 64 (1994). '*Scienter*' refers to a requirement that a person can be convicted of a crime only if he or she knew that the conduct in question was criminal.

[170] Prendergast (2011a) and (2011b).

[171] Under s 15A of the Misuse of Drugs Act 1977, as interpreted in *People (DPP) v Power* [2007] IESC 31, [2007] 2 IR 509.

[172] Under s 3 of the Non-Fatal Offences Against the Person Act 1997, as interpreted in *Minister for Justice v Dolny* [2009] IESC 48.

[173] See the exposition of this 'rule' in Hogan and Whyte (2003) 853–6, and also Chap 8 above, 175. Foley (2008) argues that the presumption of constitutionality should be abandoned. He would place an onus on the State to justify any legislation which limits rights.

10
Family and Personal Life

Introduction

Article 41 of Ireland's 1937 Constitution famously makes provision for 'the Family',[1] a topic which was not addressed at all by the Constitution of 1922. While by no means unique in doing so, the Constitution pulls no punches in the degree of protection it affords to that institution. Article 41.1.1 recognises the family as not only 'the natural and fundamental unit group of Society' but also as 'a moral institution possessing inalienable and imprescriptible rights, antecedent and superior to all positive law'. Article 41.1.2 proceeds: 'The State, therefore, guarantees to protect the Family in its constitution and authority, as the necessary basis of social order and as indispensable to the welfare of the Nation and the State.' Very few other constitutions or treaties accept the family as a rights-holder at all, let alone to such an overriding extent as Article 41.1.1.[2] The Constitutions of some countries where the population adheres predominantly to the Catholic religion undertake to protect the family[3] and some international human rights treaties do likewise, such as the African Charter of Human and People's Rights and the American Convention on Human Rights.[4] This latter phenomenon is a reflection of the Universal Declaration of Human Rights in 1948, which provides: 'The family is the natural and fundamental group unit of society and is entitled to protection by society and the State.'

Ireland's Constitution goes on to guarantee protection not just to the family but also to mothers and to the institution of marriage. Thus Article 41.2.2 provides: 'The State shall ... endeavour to ensure that mothers shall not be obliged by economic necessity to engage in labour to the neglect of their duties in the home.' The reference to 'mothers', rather than to 'women' or even 'wives', indicates that the drafters of the Constitution wanted to focus on the duties of women to bring up children in the home.[5] In 2018 pressure mounted to have this provision deleted from the Constitution and the government has agreed to hold a referendum on the matter in due course. Article 41.3.1 continues: 'The State pledges itself to guard with special care the institution of Marriage, on which the Family is founded, and to protect it from attack'.[6] This provision was originally followed by a sub-section banning the dissolution of marriage.[7] After botched efforts at bringing about a reform in this area in the mid-1960s,[8] an attempt to remove the ban was heavily defeated in a referendum held in 1986[9] but a further attempt was narrowly successful[10] less than a decade later on 24

[1] The capital is in the original. See too Staines (1976).

[2] Art 11(3) of the Luxembourg Constitution (1868) provides: 'The State guarantees the natural rights of the individual and of the family', while Art 29 of the Constitution of Italy (1948) states: 'The Republic recognises the rights of the family as a natural society founded on matrimony.'

[3] eg the Constitution of Spain (1978), Art 39(1); the Constitution of the Philippines (1987), Art 15(1); the Constitution of Brazil (1988), Art 226; the Constitution of Peru (1993), Art 4; the Constitution of Argentina (1994), Art 14bis; the Constitution of Poland (1997), Art 18. In contrast, 'the family' is not mentioned in the Constitutions of the USA (1789) or France (1958).

[4] Arts 18(1) and (2) of the African Charter and Art 17(1) of the American Convention.

[5] See the critique by the Commission on the Status of Women (1993) and, more generally, Martin (1998) 87–91.

[6] Again the capitals are in the original. For the pre-1968 position concerning marriage law see Davitt (1968).

[7] Art 41.3.20: 'No law shall be enacted providing for the grant of a dissolution of marriage.'

[8] For details see Martin (1998) 80–2.

[9] Only 37 per cent voted to remove the ban.

[10] 50.28 per cent voted to allow divorce.

November 1995: the Fifteenth Amendment of the Constitution Act 1995 took effect from 17 June 1996.[11] The new Article 41.3.2 limits the availability of divorce to situations where a court is satisfied that at the start of the dissolution proceedings the spouses have lived apart from one another for at least four years during the previous five years, that there is no reasonable prospect of a reconciliation between them and that proper provision has been or will be made for the spouses, any children of either or both of them and any other person prescribed by law. There is no requirement to prove fault on the part of one of the spouses, although the subsection does say that further conditions can be prescribed by law.[12] To date the Supreme Court has not had to engage to any significant extent with the operation of the divorce law.

It should be noted that during the period when divorce was banned in Ireland it was still possible for married persons to seek decrees of nullity. These were a creation of the common law and largely remain so.[13] As the years went by the attitude of Irish courts to the granting of decrees of nullity became more generous than that of English courts, perhaps because (although this was never admitted by the judges) there was no divorce option available in Ireland. A glance at the Supreme Court's 1985 decision in *N (otherwise K) v K*[14] shows how willing the judges were (with the exception of Henchy J) to declare a marriage null because the woman who entered into it (at 19 years of age in that case) felt pressured to do so by her parents. Since the introduction of divorce the Supreme Court has intimated that it may not be so easy to obtain a decree of nullity.[15]

The Supreme Court has had to engage with family law more generally on numerous occasions. On the whole it has done so in a conservative manner, though there are occasional instances where it has been progressive. Article 41 itself has been the object of 'a deluge of academic criticism'.[16] On most issues the majority of the people of Ireland appear to have been ahead of the Court's thinking: as in other contexts, the Supreme Court has followed rather than led. There are signs, however, that a more modern mindset is gaining ground. In a 2014 case on surrogacy, discussed below, Clarke J said that the definition of marriage in a constitutional context:

> ... may need to be reconsidered in the light of the fact that the Constitution now recognises that the parties to an original marriage may become divorced and remarry other persons so that they may, in many senses, belong to a number of families. While the constitutional statement that the family is based on marriage remains, the precise definition of 'family' is a matter which may need to be looked at again in an appropriate case.[17]

In 2012 it seemed that the Court might have the opportunity to consider whether same-sex marriage was constitutional or not[18] but the particular case before it had to be remitted to

[11] The Family Law (Divorce) Act 1996 took effect from 27 November 1996; Burley and Regan (2002).

[12] More details are set out in the Family Law (Divorce) Act 1996.

[13] The Family Law (Divorce) Act 1996, s 39(2), allows a court to grant a decree of nullity where proceedings are pending in respect of an application for a decree of divorce; the Civil Partnership and Certain Rights and Obligations of Cohabitants Act 2010, ss 107–8, also allows for decrees of nullity to be issued. The Marriage Act 2015 (allowing same-sex marriages) is silent on the issue. For more on the 2010 and 2015 Acts see nn 18 and 19 below.

[14] [1985] IR 733. Counsel for the petitioner were Mary Robinson SC and Catherine McGuinness.

[15] *PF v GO'M (orse GF)*, 28 November 2000, on which see Ryan (2000b).

[16] Martin (1998) 85.

[17] *MR v An tArd Chláraitheoir* [2014] IESC 60, at para 8.2 (per Clarke J).

[18] 'Gay couple in Supreme Court over right to wed', *Irish Times*, 9 May 2012. The earlier High Court decision, by Dunne J, is reported at [2006] IEHC 404, [2008] 2 IR 417. Although the judge rejected the argument that the definition of marriage used in the Civil Registration Act 2004 was unconstitutional, she hinted heavily that the law should be changed. The Civil Partnership and Certain Rights and Obligations of Cohabitants Act 2010 was then passed to allow same-sex couples to enter into civil partnerships.

the High Court for further argument on certain issues and before it could return to the Supreme Court the matter was moot because in a referendum in 2015 the people of Ireland overwhelmingly voted in favour of making same-sex marriage lawful.[19]

The Family, Illegitimacy and Adoption

There has been no shortage of criticism concerning the overly narrow conceptualisation of 'family' in Ireland's Constitution. Much of it is reflected in the pithy but convincing analysis by Ivana Bacik in her 2004 manifesto for reform to Ireland's legal system.[20] She points out that even in 1937 the kind of family promoted by the new Constitution was far from universal in Ireland: a large proportion of people, whether men or women, never married, and those who did marry tended to do so at an older age than in most other countries.[21] Many children were brought up by aunts and uncles or grandparents,[22] as was the architect of the Constitution himself, Éamon de Valera. Article 41.1 reflected the Catholic ideal of family life, not the reality on the ground. An example from the mid-1960s illustrates well the prevailing narrow-mindedness of senior Irish judges in this context, even some who on other issues were more progressive. In *The State (Nicolaou) v An Bord Uchtála* the Anglo-Cypriot father of an illegitimate child argued that he had a right to be heard by the Adoption Board in Ireland before it decided whether his child should be adopted.[23] He relied upon Article 41.1 but both a three-judge Divisional Court of the High Court and a five-judge Supreme Court rejected his plea on the basis that Article 41 was intended to benefit only families founded on the institution of marriage. They said that even if the mother of an illegitimate child had sought to rely on Article 41, she too would have been refused the right to do so.

Amongst the judges who reached this conclusion were Henchy J in the High Court and Ó Dálaigh CJ and Walsh J in the Supreme Court, judges who are otherwise lauded for their progressiveness. The High Court not only concluded that the father, because he was not an Irish *citizen*, could not rely on the right to be held equal before the law (Article 40.1) or on the right to have his personal rights vindicated (Article 40.3.1), but also that he had no standing to argue that the Adoption Act 1952 was unconstitutional because it deprived any Irish father of an illegitimate child of any right to a hearing prior to the child's adoption. The High Court had heard no argument on the matter from any such actual or hypothetical party,[24] but this did not prevent it from taking a position on the issue. The Supreme Court chose not to base its judgment on the fact that the appellant was not an Irish citizen, but it joined the High Court in ruling that his rights as a father had not been violated because he was not part of a family founded on marriage. The Supreme Court saw nothing wrong in the Adoption Act allowing the Adoption Board to hear from the child's *relatives*, a term defined as the mother's parents, brother, sister, step-brother, step-sister, brother-in-law or

[19] The Constitution was duly amended by the Thirty-fourth Amendment of the Constitution Act 2015, which in turn led to Marriage Act 2015.

[20] Bacik (2004). See too the comments of the CRG (1996) 321–3. For a more legalistic but equally convincing overview see Martin (2005).

[21] Ibid, 61, citing Byrne (1997). See too, O'Mahony (2003) and, more generally, Howlin and Costello (2017), especially on how Irish family law developed differently from English family law.

[22] See generally Lynch (1996).

[23] [1966] 1 IR 567. The mother of the child would not marry the father because he was a member of the Greek Orthodox Church and refused to join the mother as a practising member of the Roman Catholic Church.

[24] On this they followed the US Supreme Court's decision in *Tileston v Ullman* 318 US 44 (1943).

sister-in-law, but excluding the child's father.[25] Walsh J alluded to this anomaly in very loaded language:

> When it is considered that an illegitimate child may be begotten by an act of rape, by a callous seduction or by an act of casual commerce by a man with a woman, as well as by the association of a man with a woman in making a common home without marriage in circumstances approximating to those of married life, and that, except in the latter instance, it is rare for a natural father to take any interest in his offspring, it is not difficult to appreciate the difference in moral capacity and social function between the natural father and the several persons described in the sub-sections in question.[26]

Notwithstanding the reputation of the 1960s as an era of liberation, the breathtaking moralising of this dictum was in tune with the religious orthodoxy of the times, and not just in Ireland. It was not an ultra-feminist attitude but rather an ultra-conservative one. It suggests not only that most unmarried fathers are unworthy to be parents but that the very concept of adoption is one which should be primarily reserved for children whose parents are unmarried. Indeed, because of a concern that some adoption orders issued by the Adoption Board might not have been validly issued due to the Board not being a judicial authority, the government of the day drew up an amendment to the Constitution and sought approval for it in a referendum in 1979. The people voted almost unanimously in favour of the amendment,[27] leading to the insertion of Article 37.2 into the Constitution which says that no adoption taking effect after the coming into force of the Constitution under laws enacted by the Oireachtas shall be invalid just because the person or body who authorised it was not a judge or a court.[28]

While illegitimate children began to achieve more rights throughout the common law world in the 1970s and 1980s, it took much longer for the father of illegitimate children to do so. It was only through the Adoption Act 1998 that Ireland gave a natural father the right to be consulted before an adoption order is made in relation to his child. It was only in 2003 that such fathers in England and Wales could acquire parental responsibility through a court order, an agreement with the child's mother or joint registration of the birth with the child's mother.[29] As we shall see in Chapter 12, in 1994 the European Court of Human Rights found in *Keegan v Ireland*,[30] disapproving of a decision of the Irish Supreme Court in *K v W*,[31] that Ireland's adoption law was in violation of Articles 6 and 8 of the ECHR because it did not fully recognise the rights of the father of an illegitimate child. Later, in *Krušković v Croatia*, the European Court found a violation of Article 8 when a man was prevented from having his name registered as his child's biological father.[32]

Ireland was also long resistant to the idea that a legitimate child could be adopted: this became possible only through the Adoption Act 1988, and then only in limited circumstances, mainly those anticipated by Article 42.5 of the Constitution, 'where the parents for physical or moral reasons fail in their duty towards their children'. The constitutionality of the Bill which became the Adoption Act 1988 was considered by the Supreme Court as a result of a reference made to it by President Hillery under Article 26 of the Constitution.[33]

[25] Adoption Act 1952, s 3. [26] [1966] 1 IR 567, 641.

[27] 99 per cent voted yes, the highest ever percentage vote for or against a proposition in any Irish referendum.

[28] Sixth Amendment of the Constitution (Adoption) Act 1979.

[29] Adoption and Children Act 2002, s 111(2). Northern Ireland's law was similarly altered by the Family Law Act (NI) 2001, s 1(2).

[30] (1994) 18 EHRR 342. [31] [1990] 2 IR 437.

[32] App No 46185/08, judgment of 21 June 2011; on the more general influence of the ECHR on the concept of the family in Irish law see McGuinness (2002) 75–86.

[33] *In re Article 26 and the Adoption (No 2) Bill 1987* [1989] IR 656. On Art 26 references more generally see Chap 6 above, 106-19.

Basing itself on the presumption that the Bill should be considered constitutional if this was a reasonable interpretation of its provisions, the Supreme Court ruled that, even though Article 41.1 of the Constitution recognised that the family possessed 'inalienable and imprescriptible rights, antecedent and superior to all positive law', the State could still vindicate and restore the personal rights of a member of a family by altering the composition of that family if necessary:

> The guarantees afforded to the institution of the family by the Constitution, with their consequent benefit to the children of a family, should not be construed so that upon the failure of that benefit it cannot be replaced where the circumstances demand it, by incorporation of the child into an alternative family.[34]

The Bill, therefore, did not undermine the rights of the family, children, parents or any other concerned person. More particularly, the Court said that when Article 42.5 of the Constitution stated that 'in exceptional cases, where the parents for physical or moral reasons fail in their duty towards their children, the State as guardian of the common good, by appropriate means shall endeavor to supply the place of the parents', this did not limit the State's power of intervention to situations where the parents had failed in their duty to provide education for their children (which is the subject-matter of the remainder of Article 42).

Further Cases on Adoption

The Supreme Court's tolerance of the Constitution's limited concept of 'the family' has been apparent in many decisions subsequent to *The State (Nicolaou) v An Bord Uchtála*, though on occasions it has developed the category of 'unenumerated rights' in ways which have indirectly extended the concept. In *M v An Bord Uchtála* the Court ruled by 4 v 1 that an adoption order made in 1971 should be declared void in proceedings started in 1974 and concluded in 1976.[35] The majority did not think that in 1971 the then unmarried mother had been made adequately aware that her consent to the adoption of her child could be withdrawn at any time prior to the adoption order being made. They held that the voidness of the order meant that the child in question, who was now six-years-old, had never met his father, had last been seen by his mother when he was five weeks old, and had been living virtually all his life in a provincial Irish town, should be taken away from his adoptive parents and given over to his natural, now married, parents to be looked after in an unnamed foreign country. While Article 41 is not expressly mentioned anywhere in the judgments, this looks like a ruling heavily biased in favour of the concept of the family advocated by the Constitution. O'Higgins CJ said that since the natural parents were now married the child had become part of their family.[36] Henchy J, dissenting to this extent, ruled that even if the adoption order was void the Supreme Court had a discretion whether or not to quash it. In his view, given what had happened over the course of recent years and that the majority were acting without hearing representations from the child or his adoptive parents, the order should not be quashed because to do so would be incompatible with the boy's welfare. As the learned judge put it: 'No account would be taken of the possible ill-effects of the sudden and drastic transfer of this six-year-old boy to strange parents in a strange home in a far-away country.'[37]

[34] [1989] IR 656, 663 (Finlay CJ, Walsh, Henchy, Griffin and Hederman JJ). [35] [1977] IR 287.
[36] Under the Legitimacy Act 1931, s 1(1). [37] [1977] IR 287, 301.

G v An Bord Uchtála[38] was a case on the principles to be applied when an unmarried mother withdraws her consent to an adoption order but the putative adoptive parents still wish to proceed with the adoption without the mother's consent. Walsh, Henchy and Kenny JJ gave custody of the child to the mother in this case, while O'Higgins CJ and Parke J would have remitted the case to the High Court for a ruling on what would be in the best interests of the child. O'Higgins CJ, Walsh J and Parke J, all citing the *Nicolaou* case discussed above, said that a mother had 'a natural right' to the custody and care of her child, this being one of the unenumerated personal rights within the meaning of Article 40.3 of the Constitution.[39] Henchy J, on the other hand, pointed out that what was said in *Nicolaou* on this point was not part of the case's *ratio decidendi*,[40] while Kenny J thought that a mother had a statutory right to the custody of her child, under the Guardianship of Infants Act 1964, but not a constitutional right.[41] A few years later, in *KC v An Bord Uchtála*, the Supreme Court reiterated its preference for returning a child from the custody of prospective adoptive parents to its *married* natural parents, there being a constitutional presumption that the welfare of a child is best protected within 'the family'.[42] Finlay CJ stated that a child legitimated through the marriage of his or her parents has the following rights under the Constitution:

(a) to belong to a unit group possessing inalienable and imprescriptible rights antecedent and superior to all positive law (Article 41.1)

(b) to protection by the State of the family to which it belongs (Article 41.2)

(c) to be educated by the family and to be provided by its parents with religious, moral, intellectual, physical and social education (Article 42.1).

This emphasis on the traditional family idealised in Article 41 is also apparent from the Supreme Court's decision in *The Western Health Board v An Bord Uchtála*,[43] where a married father sought the return of his daughter from prospective adoptive parents on the basis that, even if he had failed in his duty towards his daughter in the three years since her birth, and might well continue to do so until she was 18, such failure did not amount to the abandonment of all his parental rights with respect to the child,[44] which is the third of the conditions that needs to be satisfied before the High Court can authorise the Adoption Board to make an adoption order relating to a legitimate child who has at least one parent still living.[45] The Supreme Court unanimously accepted the father's argument, with Hamilton CJ[46] citing the Supreme Court's words in the Article 26 case on the constitutionality of the 1988 Act:

> Failure in any one of these proofs absolutely prohibits the making of an authorising order, no matter how strong might be the evidence available of its desirability from the point of view of the interests of the child . . . The necessity for the proof of abandonment indicates a special regard for the constitutionally protected parental rights.[47]

Finally, in *O'C v Sacred Heart Adoption Society*,[48] Hamilton CJ reviewed the differences of opinion in *G v An Bord Uchtála* as to whether the natural mother's right to custody of her child was constitutional or not; he held that it was, but that for the purposes of the operation of Ireland's adoption law it did not matter whether it was labelled constitutional or merely legal.[49]

[38] [1980] IR 32. [39] Ibid, 55 (per O'Higgins CJ), 66 (per Walsh J) and 99 (per Parke J).
[40] Ibid, 88. [41] Ibid, 97.
[42] [1985] ILRM 302 (sometimes cited as *In re JH (infant)*); Duncan (1986). [43] [1995] 3 IR 178.
[44] On parental rights in the Constitution see Duncan (1996). [45] Adoption Act 1988, s (1)(1).
[46] [1995] 3 IR 178, 190 (O'Flaherty, Egan, Blayney and Denham JJ agreed with Hamilton CJ).
[47] [1989] IR 656, 664. [48] [1996] 1 ILRM 297; Noctor (1996). [49] Ibid, 305–7.

The Court's tendency to favour the unmarried mother's rights over the unmarried father's rights has extended to tug-of-love cases which are regulated by the Hague Convention on Civil Aspects of International Child Abduction 1980, a treaty which was incorporated into Irish domestic law by the Child Abduction and Enforcement of Custody Orders Act 1991. The scheme of the Act is that a child who has been removed from one jurisdiction to another should be returned to the former jurisdiction if the removal was in breach of 'rights of custody'. So, in *HI v MG (Child abduction: Wrongful removal)*,[50] where an Egyptian man who had been living with a British woman and their son in New York sought the return of his five-year-old son from Ireland after the mother had moved there with him, the Supreme Court overturned Laffoy J and held that the father's claim must fail because as an unmarried father he had no 'rights of custody' as such. The majority of the Court[51] chose to define that phrase strictly, disapproving of a contrary decision taken by the English Court of Appeal.[52] Only Barron J held out for a more flexible approach.[53]

One further glaring example of the willingness of the Supreme Court to uphold the concept of 'the marital family' is *N v Health Service Executive*, sometimes referred to as the *Baby Ann* case.[54] Having been born to unmarried parents in July 2004, a baby girl was placed in the care of foster parents in November 2004 with a view to them applying to adopt her. In September 2005 the mother withdrew her consent for the adoption and in January 2006 she married the baby's father. The couple then sought custody of the child as a family recognised under the Irish Constitution. In the High Court MacMenamin J was convinced that the constitutional presumption in favour of returning the child to its parents had been rebutted on the facts, not least because psychological reports suggested that the child had already formed a strong attachment to the prospective adoptive parents and that a return to her parents could cause her emotional damage.[55] But the Supreme Court disagreed,[56] reasserting that there is a constitutional presumption that it is in the best interests of a child to be with its natural parents within a family based on marriage and only in 'very exceptional circumstances' or where there are 'compelling reasons' could the presumption be rebutted, which was not the case here. McGuinness J, who admitted that she had previously been critical of the position of the child under the Irish Constitution,[57] felt some doubt about returning Baby Ann to her natural parents but in the end found herself compelled to require just that because of the unequivocal wording of Articles 41 and 42 of the Constitution.[58] Hardiman J reached the same conclusion and rejected the suggestion that the parents of baby Ann might have decided to get married as a mere stratagem in order to bolster their case for the return of their child.[59] Fennelly J cited a decision of the UK's House of Lords of a few months earlier, *In re G (Children)*,[60] where Lady Hale and Lord Nicholls (two very experienced family lawyers) had stressed the importance of children being reared by their natural parents. The Justices distinguished the case before them from their decision in *Northern Area Health Board v An Bord Uchtála*,[61] where the mother in

[50] [2000] 1 IR 110.
[51] Keane J, with whom Hamilton CJ, Denham and Barrington JJ agreed.
[52] In *Re B (A Minor) (Abduction)* [1994] 2 FLR 249. See too *WPP v SRW (Child Abduction: Wrongful Removal)* [2000] 4 IR 401, a simpler case, where the Supreme Court (Keane CJ, McGuinness and Hardiman JJ) refused to order the return to California of two children aged nine and ten, because the father living there had been granted only visitation rights by a court, while the mother had been granted legal and physical custody.
[53] [2000] 1 IR 110, 143.
[54] [2006] 4 IR 374; Kelly (2007).
[55] MacMenamin J's judgment runs to 90 pages (353 paragraphs).
[56] In five separate judgments running to more than 120 pages (337 paragraphs).
[57] Particularly in the report of the Kilkenny Incest Inquiry in 1973. See [2006] 4 IR 374, [84].
[58] Ibid, [82]. McGuinness J, like all her fellow judges, relied particularly on the Supreme Court's decision in *In re JH (infant)* [1985] ILRM 302, discussed in the text at n 42 above.
[59] Ibid, [190].
[60] [2006] UKHL 43, [2006] 1 WLR 2305.
[61] [2002] 4 IR 252 (McGuinness, Hardiman and Geoghegan JJ).

question was unmarried and suffered from chronic schizo-affective psychosis, while her daughter was aged 13, suffered from cerebral palsy and had been with foster parents for all but six weeks of her life. In authorising the adoption of the child in that case the Supreme Court was motivated by the general purpose of the Adoption Act 1988, which they saw as correcting the 'mischief' that an illegitimate child who had been with foster parents for a long period could not be adopted because its parents had never agreed to place the child for adoption in the first place.[62]

The Position Today

Disputes over the reach of the Constitution in the context of adoption did not rest there. In *O'T v B* the Supreme Court had to consider claims by two women who had been informally adopted in Ireland before legally recognised adoption was introduced by the Adoption Act 1952.[63] They wanted to know the identity of their mothers. When considering those requests the Supreme Court had also to bear in mind the desire of the mothers to have their privacy respected. In weighing up the competing claims the judges did not rely on any part of Article 41 of the Constitution. After commenting on the need to be cautious when developing the category of personal rights other than those expressly specified in the Constitution, the Court held (with Keane J dissenting on this point) that the right of a natural child to know the identity of his or her natural parent (not just his or her mother) is indeed an unenumerated right guaranteed by the Constitution under Article 40.3.1. But the four judges in the majority also held that (at least in the case of mothers) the right they had recognised could be limited by a mother's constitutional right to privacy or to privilege in respect of any confidential communication concerning her motherhood. As the latter rights are not any more absolute than the natural child's rights, the Supreme Court listed a number of factors that needed to be taken into account when balancing the two sets of rights. These included, for example, the present circumstances of the mother and the effect on her of having her identity disclosed to her child.

Hamilton CJ quoted Walsh J in *The State (Nicolaou) v An Bord Uchtála*, as well as the judgment of O'Higgins CJ in the Supreme Court's decision in *G v An Bord Uchtála*,[64] to support his conclusion that '[t]he right to know the identity of one's natural mother is a basic right flowing from the natural and special relationship which exists between a mother and her child'.[65] Keane J, however, was more cautious. He pointed out that the courts' power to recognise the existence of unenumerated rights, first expounded in *Ryan v Attorney General* by Kenny J in the High Court[66] and by Ó Dálaigh CJ in the Supreme Court,[67] had to be exercised in accordance with principles, but he added that the courts had not yet developed 'a coherent, principled jurisprudence in this area' and that therefore 'some degree of

[62] Ibid, 266 (per McGuinness J).

[63] [1998] 2 IR 321. The 1952 Act was widely invoked to enable the adoption of children born outside of marriage. At the time, illegitimacy still carried considerable stigma for both mother and child and the Catholic church established 'mother and baby homes' to allow illegitimate births to take place in private settings. However it is clear that many of the adoptions which occurred after such births were not fully in line with the 1952 Act because the mothers would not have been made wholly aware of their rights in the matter. Many children were sent to the USA for adoption, a situation portrayed in Martin Sixsmith's book *Philomena* (2009). The 1952 Act was passed just a year after the Catholic church expressed its strong opposition to the Mother and Child Service proposed by Dr Noel Browne, the Minister for Health, on the grounds that the State should not be interfering in private lives to that extent. The government duly dropped the Bill. See Whyte (1979).

[64] [1980] IR 32; Redmond (1979–80b). See above, 223.

[65] [1998] 2 IR 321, 348. Denham and Barrington JJ simply agreed with Hamilton CJ's judgment, while Barron J did so in a judgment of his own.

[66] [1965] IR 294, 313.

[67] Ibid, 344. See Chap 6, 125-6.

judicial restraint is called for in identifying any new rights of this nature'.[68] He cited the extra-judicial views of McCarthy J[69] and those of the then practitioner and academic (subsequently a judge of the High Court and Court of Appeal) Gerard Hogan.[70] Keane J also noted that to say that a person who has been denied information about the identity of his or her natural parents has failed to realise 'his or her full personality and dignity as a human being' was 'a grave overstatement'.[71] Having considered the possible bases for deriving the right in question from either the rights expressly guaranteed by the Constitution or from an unenumerated right identified by the courts, Keane J was not satisfied that it had been established that there was a necessity to declare such a right at all.[72]

Despite much debate and many recommendations for reform, Article 41's concept of the family remains unchanged to this date. The Constitution Review Group proposed in 1996 that the Constitution should retain a pledge by the State to protect the family based on marriage but that it should also guarantee to all individuals a right to respect for their family life whether or not that family is based on marriage.[73] The Group added that: 'Giving to the family unit rights which are described as "inalienable or imprescriptible", even if they are interpreted as not being absolute rights, potentially places too much emphasis on the rights of the family as a unit as compared with the rights of individuals within the unit'.[74] The Group's recommendations in this area were not implemented and in 1998 a Commission on the Family reported at some length but was rather inconclusive and again did not stimulate any legislative reforms.[75] However the Oireachtas has since enacted the European Convention on Human Rights Act 2003, which obliges all Irish courts to interpret and apply all statutory provisions and rules of law, 'in so far as is possible, subject to the rules of law relating to such interpretations and application ... in a manner compatible with the State's obligations under the Convention provisions'.[76] This opens the door to the Supreme Court, and other lower courts, using Strasbourg's jurisprudence on the right to a family life under Article 8 of the ECHR in ways which will effectively implement the Constitution Review Group's proposals.[77]

In 2010 a new Adoption Act was enacted, amending and consolidating the existing law, making provision for the recognition of foreign adoptions, and replacing the Adoption Board (An Bord Uchtála) with the Adoption Authority of Ireland (Údarás Uchtála na hÉireann).[78] In 2012 another referendum took place asking the people to approve greater constitutional rights for children,[79] and consent was given by 58 per cent to 42 per cent of those voting. The resulting amendment to the Constitution took effect in 2015. It deletes the old Article 42.5 and replaces it with a new Article 42A, section 1 of which reads: 'The State recognises and affirms the natural and imprescriptible rights of all children and shall, as far as practicable, by its laws protect and vindicate those rights.' Article 42A.2.1 then provides that:

> In exceptional cases, where the parents, regardless of their marital status, fail in their duty towards their children to such an extent that the safety or welfare of any of their children is likely to be prejudicially affected, the State as guardian of the common good shall, by proportionate

[68] [1998] 2 IR 321, 370. [69] McCarthy (1992). [70] Hogan (1990–92).

[71] [1998] 2 IR 321, 370–1. The quotation is from the judgment of O'Higgins CJ in *G v An Bord Uchtála* [1980] IR 32, 55.

[72] Ibid, 374–6. [73] CRG (1996) 323–4 and 336. [74] Ibid, 330–2.

[75] *Strengthening Families for Life* (Dublin, Department of Social, Community and Family Affairs).

[76] s 2(1). [77] See the excellent account by Shannon (2005) 81–100.

[78] Crowley (2013) 317–21.

[79] Under the Thirty-First Amendment of the Constitution (Children) Act 2012.

means as provided by law, endeavour to supply the place of the parents, but always with due regard for the natural and imprescriptible rights of the child.

Articles 42A.2.2 to 42A.4, for the first time, set out constitutional provisions governing the process of adoption, with Article 42A.4.1 making it clear that in the resolution of all adoption proceedings 'the best interests of the child shall be the paramount consideration'.[80] These new constitutional provisions came under close scrutiny in a 2018 decision of the Supreme Court, *In the matter of the Adoption Act, 2010, section 49 (2), and in the matter of JB (a minor) and KB (a minor)*.[81] The Court was split 3 v 2 in favour of allowing the Adoption Authority of Ireland and the Central Authority of the children's birth country to take 'remedial measures' which would allow the children's adoption to be recognised in Ireland;[82] the minority, in contrast, would have disallowed recognition and also adoption of the children within Ireland.[83]

Also in 2010, the Law Reform Commission published detailed proposals for updating the law relating to the rights and responsibilities of unmarried fathers and members of the extended family.[84] Some of the proposals eventually found their way into the Children and Family Relationships Act 2015. For present purposes the main changes to note are that two people who are not married to each other can now jointly adopt a child, a wider range of people can apply to be a child's guardian, unmarried parents can sign a statutory declaration of guardianship when they are registering or re-registering their child's birth, and an unmarried father will automatically become a child's guardian if he has lived with that child's mother for 12 months including at least three months following the child's birth. The Act also confirms that in all decisions affecting a child his or her best interests must be paramount and sets out the factors which courts must consider when reaching their decision.[85]

Immigration

In recent years the right to a family life has been particularly pertinent in situations where an immigrant is seeking the right to stay in the country by arguing that denying that right would violate his or her right to a family life because of family connections in Ireland. As is well known, the European Court of Human Rights has greatly expanded the scope of Article 8 of the ECHR in recent years, so that many more people than before are now able to claim the benefit of the right to a family life.[86]

The controversy famously came to a head in Ireland in the Supreme Court case of *AO and OJO v Minister for Justice, Equality and Law Reform* in 2003.[87] Eight individuals (five were Czechs and three were Nigerians) had come to Ireland having already been refused refugee status in the United Kingdom and while in Ireland two of the women in the group had given birth. By virtue of being born in Ireland those children, at the time, were automatically entitled to Irish citizenship (in accordance with the *ius soli* principle).[88] As regards their

[80] See the useful treatment in Forde and Leonard (2014) 715–22.

[81] [2018] IESC 30. For a helpful summary of this complicated case see Seosamh Gráinséir, 'Supreme Court: "Pragmatic approach" to couple's inter-country adoption favoured by majority', *Irish Legal News* (www.irishlegal.com), 16 July 2018.

[82] MacMenamin, Dunne and O'Malley JJ. [83] O'Donnell and McKechnie JJ.

[84] *Legal Aspects of Family Relationships* (LRC 101-2010).

[85] For further information see the website of the Citizens Information Board; also Tobin (2014).

[86] See eg the Factsheet on 'Parental Rights' published by the European Court of Human Rights (February 2018).

[87] [2003] 1 IR 1 (Keane CJ, Denham, Murray, Hardiman, Geoghegan, McGuinness and Fennelly JJ). The appeal was expedited because so many other cases depended on the Supreme Court's ruling. See too Chap 8 above, 181.

[88] Irish Nationality and Citizenship Act 1956, s 6(1). *Ius soli* means 'a right from the ground'.

parents and siblings, the Supreme Court had already decided, in the earlier case of *Fajujonu v Minister for Justice*,[89] that non-nationals could be deported from Ireland only if there were grave and substantial reasons for this based on the interests of the common good of the people of Ireland or the protection of the State and its society. In *AO and OJO* the only real reason for going ahead with the deportation was the need to protect the integrity of the domestic and EU systems for asylum and immigration. The Supreme Court sat as a bench of seven judges to hear the case and decided by five to two that on the facts before them the non-Irish citizens could be deported. In support of this position two judges cited cases from the USA, where the *ius soli* principle also applies.[90] Fennelly and McGuinness JJ dissented, holding that the Minister's reasons for justifying the deportations could not trump the constitutional rights of the two Irish children (so-called 'anchor children') to the company and care of their parents within the State.

The majority's position is another example of how the Supreme Court, over the years, has had to accept the reality that the wording of the 1937 Constitution cannot be interpreted too literally. In two respects it demonstrated laudable pragmatism. First, it conceded that the constitutional right of children born in Ireland to the company, care and parentage of their parents within the State could not be absolute, for very young children do not have the capacity to decide where they want to live and the best interests principle will sometimes mean that they should be taken out of Ireland to live with their parents elsewhere. Second, it acknowledged that in assessing the common good in the context of deportation it needed to take into account not just the personal factors mentioned in *Fajujonu* but also the broader policy considerations arising from treating some immigrants more favourably than others. Hardiman J was particularly strong on the latter point, citing a paragraph he had written in an earlier judgment.[91]

In the wake of the Supreme Court's decision there were no 'mass deportations'[92] but the Oireachtas wasted little time in amending the legislation on acquisition of Irish nationality. A person can now acquire nationality through being born in Ireland (North or South) only if one of his or her parents has, during the four-year period preceding the birth, been resident in Ireland for not less than a period aggregating three years.[93] Just as the Supreme Court had to adapt its principles in order to prevent abuse of the immigration system, so did the Oireachtas. Despite these changes, the protection afforded to the right to a family life in Ireland is still strong. It was further bolstered, albeit indirectly,[94] by the 2017 decision of seven Supreme Court judges in *NHV v Minister for Justice and Equality*.[95] Here the Court ruled that indefinitely banning all asylum seekers from looking for work was a violation of the unenumerated constitutional right to seek employment. In its single judgment, delivered by O'Donnell J rather than the Chief Justice, the Supreme Court cast further doubt on the justiciability of socio-economic rights,[96] but nevertheless ruled that section 9(4) of the Refugee Act 1996[97] went too far in prohibiting access to work: 'I cannot accept that if a

[89] [1990] 2 IR 151. See Chap 8 above, 181.
[90] eg *Perdido v Immigration and Naturalisation Service* 420 F 2d 1179 (5th Circuit, 1969).
[91] In *FP v Minister for Justice* [2002] 1 IR 164, 174, cited at [2003] 1 IR 1, 162. Geoghegan J agreed with Hardiman J on this point.
[92] The then Minster for Justice, Michael McDowell SC, gave assurances to that effect immediately: *Irish Times*, 24 January 2003, 1.
[93] Irish Nationality and Citizenship Act 1956, s 6A, inserted by the Irish Nationality and Citizenship Act 2004, s 4. See too Chap 7 above, 151.
[94] Having a job helps a person to maintain a family life.
[95] [2017] IESC 35 (Denham CJ, O'Donnell, Clarke, MacMenamin, Laffoy, Charleton and O'Malley JJ).
[96] On socio-economic rights more generally, see Chap 6 above, 128-36.
[97] Which has since been re-enacted as s 16(3)(b) of the International Protection Act 2015.

right is in principle available ... it is an appropriate and permissible differentiation between citizens and non-citizens, and in particular between citizens and asylum seekers, to remove the right for all time from asylum seekers.'[98] However, as reform of the law was 'first and foremost a matter for executive and legislative judgement',[99] the Court put off making a final order in the case for a period of six months and invited the parties to make submissions on the form such an order should take at that time. When the six months were up but no reform had yet been announced the Court indicated that it would be issuing its injunction on 9 February 2018.[100] Even more instructive in this context is *Luximon and Blanchand v Minister for Justice and Equality*,[101] which concerned immigrants who had entered Ireland legally as non-EEA nationals on student visas but had then lost their eligibility to remain in the country because of changes to immigration law. The Supreme Court held that the Minister's decisions to reject their applications for 'stamp four' status, which would have allowed them to stay, needed to be reconsidered because the Minister had not taken into account the immigrants' rights to a private and family life under Article 8 of the ECHR.

The right to a family life was also indirectly engaged in the Court's decision in *M v Minister for Justice and Equality (No 2)*, a case heard and decided just before the 2018 referendum on abortion.[102] At issue was whether a Nigerian man who had been refused asylum in Ireland could be deported without regard to the fact that, at the time when a decision was being taken whether to revoke his deportaion order, his partner was pregnant with his child. In the High Court Humphreys J had held, in 2016,[103] that the unborn child might have rights under the new Article 42A of the Constitution—which requires the State to protect and vindicate the natural and imprescriptible rights of *all* children,[104] including, he implied, the child's right to a future family life. On a leapfrog appeal to the Supreme Court,[105] Humphreys J's judgment was overturned on this point. Clarke CJ, for the Court, said that in deciding whether to deport Mr M the Minister had to take into account that he would soon become a father and that, when born, the child's constitutional rights might be affected by his father's deportation, but that prior to being born the child had no constitutional right to a family life.

It seems clear that the Supreme Court does not want the family rights conferred by Article 8 of the European Convention to become too tight a constraint on Ireland's immigration policies. This is an issue for all Council of Europe countires, especially in this era of the mass migration to Europe of asylum-seekers from North Africa, the Middle East and Afghanistan. The United Kingdom Supreme Court seems equally loathe to allow family right to dictate government policy in this field.[106].

Matrimonial Property

Ireland's law on matrimonial property has not been the object of many decisions by the Supreme Court, but those which have been delivered have been influential. The Succession Act 1965 ensured that when one spouse dies the remaining spouse is entitled to at least

[98] [2017] IESC 35, para 19. [99] Ibid, para 21.

[100] *NHV v Minister for Justice and Equality* [2017] IESC 82 (30 November 2017).

[101] '[2018] IESC 24 (Clarke CJ and O'Donnell, MacMenamin, Dunne and O'Malley JJ)

[102] [2018] IESC 14. But it should be stressed that the Supreme Court did not directly consider the status of 'the family', which the parties agreed was not an explicit part of the High Court's reasoning in the case.

[103] *M v Minister for Justice and Equality (No 2)* [2016] IEHC 478.

[104] See 226-7 above (emphasis added).

[105] [2017] IESCDET 147 (the granting of leave); [2018] IESC 14 (Clarke CJ, O'Donnell, McKechnie, MacMenamin, Dunne, O'Malley and Finlay Geoghegan JJ). A month earlier the Supreme Court had rejected an application from the Pro Life Campaign to be an intervenor in the case: [2018] IESC 7 (O'Donnell, McKechnie and Dunne JJ). See too 239 below, in the section on abortion.

[106] See, eg, *KO (Nigeria) v Secretary of State for the Home Department* [2018] 1 WLR 5273, interpreting s 117B of the Nationality, Immigration and Asylum Act 2002.

one-third of that person's estate if there are children of the marriage or to at least one-half if there are no children. Moreover the Family Home Protection Act 1976 stipulated that a spouse could not dispose of the family home unless first obtaining the written consent of the other spouse. At the time when it was not possible for a spouse to obtain a decree of divorce under legislation, the only option was to seek what was called under the common law 'a decree of divorce *a mensa et thoro*'. That is what the wife applied for in *L v L*,[107] on the basis of her husband's physical and mental cruelty and his adultery. She also asked for a declaration under the Married Women's Status Act 1957 as to what beneficial interest she was entitled to in the family home and farm. In the High Court Barr J awarded the wife a 50 per cent interest in the family home purely on the basis of the work she had done within that home, but the Supreme Court overturned that decision. The Court accepted that the established principles of equity, which required a wife to have directly or indirectly contributed money or money's worth towards the purchase price of the family home in order to become entitled to a beneficial interest in it, were inconsistent with the preferred role granted to a mother in the home by Article 41 of the Constitution. But it went on to rule that awarding a mother a one-half beneficial interest in the family home was the creation of an unenumerated constitutional right which was not unambiguously warranted by the Constitution. Identifying it as such was 'a usurpation of the powers of the legislature'.[108] According to the Court, Article 41 did not create *any* specific rights to individual members of a family.

The Supreme Court's judgments in this case made no reference to a relevant report which had been issued in the period elapsing since Barr J's decision. This was a Charter for Women's Rights, published in 1989 by the Commission on the Status of Women, a body established by the Irish government in 1970 to work on proposals for improving the position of women in Irish society. Shortly afterwards the Commission formally proposed that Irish law should follow the example of many continental jurisdictions by introducing a 'community of property regime' for married couples. The Judicial Separation and Family Law Reform Act 1989 was an attempt by the Oireachtas to assist women by allowing any married person to apply for a court order recognising the couple's formal separation and conferring on the court a discretion to order one spouse to transfer his or her assets to the other, whether as a lump sum or through periodic payments.[109] In 1993 the government dutifully sought to go beyond that provision by implementing the Commission's recommendation concerning community of property. It did so by drafting a Matrimonial Home Bill. This sought to vest an equitable interest in the matrimonial home in the husband and wife as joint tenants, whether the home had been acquired before or after the marriage and regardless of what agreement the spouses may already have come to regarding its ownership. Mary Robinson, the then President, referred the Bill to the Supreme Court for a check on its constitutionality.

In *In re Article 26 and the Matrimonial Home Bill 1993* the Supreme Court again struck a firm blow in favour of maintaining 'the Family' as recognised by Article 41 of the Constitution.[110] Far from seeing the Bill as a mechanism for strengthening marriage in that it would help to ensure that women in particular would gain greater financial equality and security, the Supreme Court saw it as a threat to marriage because it would disrupt the traditional concept of that institution as understood in Ireland. Following the position it had articulated in *L v L*,[111] the Court accepted that encouraging joint ownership of the

[107] [1992] 2 IR 77 (also sometimes listed as *BL v ML*); Jackson (1992).
[108] Ibid, 107 (per Finlay CJ).
[109] Pt II (ss 10–29).
[110] [1994] 1 IR 305 (Finlay CJ, O'Flaherty, Egan, Blayney and Denham JJ); see too Hogan (1994a).
[111] Note 108 above.

matrimonial home was conducive to the stability of marriage and the general protection of the family, and so was an important element of the common good. On the other hand, it viewed the right of a married couple to make a joint decision as to the ownership of their matrimonial home as one of 'the rights of the family' recognised by Article 41.1.1 of the Constitution as superior to all positive law. As the Bill, if enacted, would sometimes automatically cancel such a freely made joint decision and replace it with a wholly different decision unless the spouses agreed to a new joint decision, or unless a court order was made on the matter, the Bill was not a reasonably proportionate interference by the State with the rights of the family. In fact it constituted a failure by the State to protect the authority of the family. What was objectionable to the Supreme Court was not the potentially discriminatory character of the provisions (sex discrimination was not argued in the case) but rather the *indiscriminate* nature of the way the provisions would operate to undermine otherwise sound decisions already made. Taken as a whole, the judgment was cryptic and not thoroughly reasoned.[112] It did not even address the potential effect of the Bill on existing property rights, which are protected under Article 43.1 of the Constitution.

Today the judgment continues to divide opinion, including amongst feminists. In her alternative judgment for the case Lucy-Ann Buckley concludes that the Bill did not disproportionately interfere with spousal property rights under the Constitution,[113] but a commentator on that judgment observes that under the Family Law Act 1995 and the Family Law (Divorce) Act 1996 domestic contributions to a marriage are now given express significance in the context of judicial separations and divorces respectively,[114] the implication being that the solution proposed by the 1993 Bill was comparatively rigid and confiscatory. In *T v T*,[115] where each spouse was well off but the husband was some 15 times richer than the wife, the Supreme Court recognised marriage as a partnership and interpreted the duty to make 'proper provision' for each spouse as entitling it to redistribute some of one spouse's wealth, even if it was gained after the spouses had begun to live separately. Both Murray and Fennelly JJ seemed to approve of what Nicholls LJ, as he then was, had said in the English case of *White v White*,[116] namely: 'If, in their different spheres, each [of the spouses] contributed equally to the family, then in principle it matters not which of them earned the money and built up the assets. There should be no bias in favour of the money-earner and against the home-maker and the child-carer.'[117] With respect, this seems a fairer way of approaching the distribution of matrimonial property upon the breakdown of a marital relationship, and impinges less on established property rights, than does the automatic community of property regime contained in the 1993 Bill.

Given the strong re-assertion of 'the rights of the family' in the Article 26 case, it is little wonder that shortly afterwards the constitutionality of the Judicial Separation and Family Law Reform Act 1989 (allowing judicial separation) was also called into question. This was in *TF v Ireland*,[118] where a husband argued that the Act violated the Constitution's commitment to protect the institution of marriage as well as his own constitutional right to property.[119] But in its single judgment the Supreme Court this time ruled that providing for

[112] It did however confirm that Bills referred to the Court under Art 26 should continue to benefit from the presumption of constitutionality and that once it had found at least one provision of the Bill to be repugnant to the Constitution the Court was not obliged to examine every other provision in the Bill and decide on their constitutionality: ibid, 315–7 and 327. See too Chap 6 above, 116.

[113] Buckley (2017) 163–75. [114] Crowley (2017) 158.

[115] [2002] 3 IR 334; Power (2003); also McGuinness (2002), where the judge-author refused to speculate on the outcome in *T v T*.

[116] [2001] 1 AC 596.

[117] Ibid, 605, cited by Murray J and Fennelly J, n 115 above, at 410 and 418 respectively.

[118] [1995] 1 IR 321 (Hamilton CJ, O'Flaherty, Egan, Blayney and Denham JJ); Crowley (2013) 492–508.

[119] Arts 41.3.1 and 43.1.

judicial separation did not in itself amount to a failure to guard the institution of marriage with special care and protect it from attack. It added that the Constitution's protection of personal rights was not unlimited and that courts should not interfere with the Oireachtas's decision on how to reconcile personal rights with the common good unless the balance struck was oppressive to one group or the benefit conferred on some people was not reasonably proportionate to the interference with other people's personal rights. The Court also endorsed Murphy J's sensible refusal to admit as evidence the views of theologians on the issues involved in the case!

Although the Court in *TF v Ireland* purported to follow its previous judgment in the *Matrimonial Home Bill* case, it is not altogether easy to reconcile the decisions. If the Oireachtas's choice of legislative options was acceptable in the former, it is not entirely clear why it was not acceptable in the latter. The judges who sat in the two cases were the same, except that by the time *TF v Ireland* came to be decided Finlay CJ had given way to Hamilton CJ. It is possible that the new Chief Justice persuaded his colleagues to adjust the attitude they had maintained in the *Matrimonial Home Bill* case. In any event, in the ensuing years the Supreme Court has not had much more to say about matrimonial property law. Today the law in Ireland seems to operate much as it does in England and Wales, with courts retaining a discretion as to how to calculate a spouse's degree of legal interest in a piece of matrimonial property. There does not appear to be much dissatisfaction with the current state of the law from a female perspective.[120] As yet the Irish Supreme Court has not had to consider the validity of pre-nuptial contracts.[121] It will be interesting to see what position it eventually adopts towards them.

Contraception

Having earlier documented the conservatism of the Supreme Court concerning rights in the context of adoption, it is refreshing to be able to turn to an aspect of the Court's jurisprudence which shows a more liberal frame of mind. I am referring to the Court's landmark decision concerning contraception in *McGee v Attorney General* in 1973.[122] The socio-political context in which this decision was taken is very ably recounted by Roy Foster,[123] who reminds us that the sale and importation of contraceptives had been criminalised in 1935,[124] that a young Mary Robinson, then a Senator, introduced a Bill to repeal the prohibition in 1971 but could not get the required six supporters to secure a debate,[125] and that later the same year many women travelled to Northern Ireland on the 'Contraception Train' in order to bring back large quantities of contraceptives. Indeed Foster agrees with Garret Fitzgerald that 'a liberalisation of social law in the Republic of Ireland was a necessary part of a realistic accommodation with Northern Ireland'.[126] The opportunity for the Supreme Court to get involved came when a 27-year-old married woman with four children, who was advised that having more children would put her life at risk, ordered some contraceptive

[120] The topic does not feature in a recent substantial report on women's rights: IHREC (2017). The Fine Gael government has promised to establish a new Commission on the Status of Women to tackle gender pay inequality: see www.thejournal.ie, 12 November 2017. The previous Commission changed its name to the National Women's Council of Ireland in 1995.

[121] For the law in England and Wales on this topic see *Granatino v Radmacher* [2010] UKSC 42, [2011] 1 AC 534, where Lady Hale dissented.

[122] [1974] IR 284. [123] Foster (2007) 42–5.

[124] Criminal Law Amendment Act 1935, s 17(1): 'It shall not be lawful for any person to sell, or expose, offer, advertise, or keep for sale or to import or attempt to import into Saorstát Éireann for sale, any contraceptive.'

[125] Robinson (1976).

[126] Note 123 above, 52. Foster entitles Chap 2 of his book 'How the Catholics became Protestants'.

'Staycept Jelly' from a supplier in England, only to find that the package containing the jelly was seized by Irish customs authorities. She brought proceedings claiming that the ban on the sale of contraceptives in Ireland was unconstitutional, her principal barrister being Sean MacBride. She lost in front of the President of the High Court, O'Keeffe P, but won by 4 v 1 in the Supreme Court. The decision is hugely important in the history of the Irish Supreme Court, although it is a rose amongst many thorns.

Walsh J provided the lead judgment for the majority in *McGee*. It is a well-constructed judgment, beginning with a summary of the plaintiff's claims and continuing with an explanation that, in the section of the Constitution headed 'Fundamental Rights', Articles 41, 42 and 43 'emphatically reject the theory that there are no rights without laws, no rights contrary to the law and no rights anterior to the law'. The learned judge went on:

> They indicate that justice is placed above the law and acknowledge that natural rights, or human rights, are not created by law but that the Constitution confirms their existence and gives them protection. The individual has natural and human rights over which the State has no authority; and the family, as the natural primary and fundamental unit group of society, has rights as such which the State cannot control.[127]

A later Chief Justice characterised this part of Walsh J's judgment as 'an eloquent rejection of Benthamite positivism'.[128] Walsh J then discussed whether section 17 of the 1935 Act was consistent with Article 41 of the Constitution and concluded that, while the 1935 Act did not prohibit the use of contraceptives, it did unreasonably restrict their availability for use within marriage and that that was 'an unjustified invasion of the privacy of husband and wife in their sexual relations with one another'.[129] Interestingly, although the judge was careful to say that this case was about appliances and drugs designed to prevent pregnancy and not about those which take effect after conception,[130] he did state in relation to Articles 40.1 and 40.3 that if the life of a married woman would be endangered by a pregnancy she has 'a right to be assisted in her efforts to avoid putting her life in jeopardy'; indeed he thought that those provisions imposed a positive obligation on the State to make available to such a woman the means whereby a conception might be avoided.[131] Walsh J did not think that the plaintiff could rely on Article 44 of the Constitution (the right to freedom of conscience and religion) and did not return at all to her claims based on Articles 42 and 45. He did however refer to the Constitution's Preamble and confirmed that when interpreting 'the dignity and freedom of the individual' judges had to do so 'as best they can from their training and their experience ... in accordance with their ideas of prudence, justice and charity' and that 'no interpretation of the Constitution is intended to be final for all time'.[132]

Budd, Henchy and Griffin JJ delivered judgments agreeing that section 17 was inconsistent with Articles 40.1 and 40.3. Henchy J said that to qualify as an unspecified personal right guaranteed by Article 40.3.1 'it must be shown that it is a right that inheres in the citizen in question by virtue of his human personality'.[133] He found that the ban on the sale of contraceptives 'will endanger the security and happiness of [the plaintiff's] marriage, ... will imperil her health to the point of hazarding her life, and ... will subject her family to the risk of distress and disruption', all of which 'are intrusions which she is entitled to say are incompatible with the safety of her life, the preservation of her health,

[127] [1974] IR 284, 310. Later, at 318, Walsh J stressed that the structure and content of the Constitution's Articles on fundamental rights 'clearly indicate that justice is not subordinate to the law'. He added, at 319, that judges must be aware 'that from time to time the prevailing ideas of [prudence, justice and charity] ... may be conditioned by the passage of time'.

[128] Keane (1990–92a). [129] [1974] IR 284, 314. [130] Ibid, 305. [131] Ibid, 315.

[132] Ibid, 319; see too his extra-judicial comments in Walsh (1977). [133] Ibid, 325.

her responsibility to her conscience, and the security and well-bring of her marriage and her family'.[134] He expressly applied the reasoning of the US Supreme Court in *Griswold v Connecticut*,[135] even though the statute which was there held to be unconstitutional was one which banned the use, not just the sale, of contraceptives. Griffin J's judgment is very much along the same lines.

But Fitzgerald CJ dissented. He did so primarily on the basis that section 17 of the 1935 Act did not prohibit the *use* of contraceptives and that 'the evidence adduced on behalf of the plaintiff does not establish that she is prohibited from making or obtaining this product'.[136] Quite how she would learn how to make the product, or how she would obtain it without breaching the ban on its importation, is not explained. The Chief Justice dealt fairly summarily with the plaintiff's claims based on Articles 40 and 41[137] and he warned (without saying why) that upholding the plaintiff's claim would 'benefit' every other Irish citizen, whether married or not. He finished by expressing sympathy for the plaintiff's dilemma, which was attributable to her own physical health, but added that this was one of those 'natural hazards which must be faced by married couples with such fortitude as they can summon to their assistance'.[138]

One of the peculiar features of the decision in *McGee* is that none of the judges referred to any of their colleagues' judgments. It is as if they wrote their judgments completely separately and never conferred or shared their drafts. The rift between the Chief Justice and his four colleagues was particularly unfortunate, especially as the former's reasoning was, with respect, jejeune to say the least. Most commentators at the time welcomed the decision, but a prominent academic, William Binchy, did not[139] and more than five years were to pass before the Oireachtas enacted a law allowing easier access to contraception.[140] Previous efforts to put legislative flesh on the judicial bones of the *McGee* decision had failed.[141] Meanwhile the Supreme Court had ruled that the Censorship Board had been wrong to ban a book on family planning published by the Irish Family Planning Association, because it was neither indecent nor obscene.[142] As Foster observes, this was the first challenge to a Censorship Board decision in half-a-century.[143]

Contraception as such has not since been the subject of an appeal to the Supreme Court, but it is worth mentioning one decision which indirectly impacts on pregnancy rates. This is *MD (a minor) v Ireland*,[144] where the Supreme Court upheld the constitutionality of section 3 of the Criminal Law (Sexual Offences) Act 2006, which criminalised engagement in sexual intercourse by boys under the age of 17 even though section 5 went on to exempt girls under that age from any such guilt. The chief justification put forward by the Court for the unequal treatment was the social policy of protecting young girls from becoming pregnant. For the Court, Denham CJ noted that for her the fundamental constitutional question was 'whether it falls to the court or to the Oireachtas to make the judgment as

[134] Ibid, 326. [135] 381 US 479 (1965). [136] [1974] IR 284, 300. [137] Ibid, 301–2.

[138] Ibid, 305.

[139] Binchy (1977). He suggests, at 331, that the Supreme Court's reliance on the concept of marital privacy might lead it in due course 'to accommodate the recognition of the "right" to abortion'.

[140] Health (Family Planning) Act 1979. This made contraceptives available on prescription only, for adequate medical reasons or for *bona fide* family planning purposes. The Taioseach at the time, Charles Haughey, referred to the Act as an 'Irish solution to an Irish problem', which Bacik interprets as meaning 'it allowed enough contraceptive use to keep some of the campaigners happy, but did not offend the Catholic Church's sacred cow that sex should only take place within marriage': Bacik (2004) 101–2.

[141] Von Prondzynski (1977a).

[142] *Irish Family Planning Association v Ryan* [1979] 1 IR 295 (O'Higgins, CJ, Henchy, Griffin, Kenny and Parke JJ, affirming Hamilton J in the High Court).

[143] Foster (2007) 43. [144] [2012] IESC 10, [2012] 1 IR 697. See too App 5 below, 338.

to whether the risk that the female will become pregnant justifies exempting her, but not her male counterpart, from prosecution'.[145] The answer to this, inevitably, was that it falls to the Oireachtas but that the judgment made by the Oireachtas can then be evaluated by the court to see whether it was made on an objective basis and was not arbitrary. Here the Supreme Court found that the Oireachtas's choice—made as recently as 2006—satisfied that test:

> While the legislature could have enacted another social policy, it was an approach the legislature was entitled to take, it was an issue to which the legislature had to respond. The danger of pregnancy for the teenage girl was an objective which the Oireachtas was entitled to regard as relating to 'differences of capacity, physical and moral and of social function', as provided for in Article 40.1 of the Constitution.[146]

The Justices relied to a considerable extent on a five-to-four judgment of the US Supreme Court where a similar conclusion had been reached in relation to a Californian law on statutory rape.[147] This was despite the fact that that decision was more than 30 years old and that California's law had since been changed to make it gender-neutral. The Irish judges were taken with the majority's point in *Michael M* that the US's equal protection clause did not require 'things which are different in fact ... to be treated in law as though they were the same';[148] they used this to support their statement that in sexual intercourse the male and female 'each perform a distinct physiological function ... Thus some natural and inevitable differentiation of treatment is inherent in the statutory scheme'.[149] The Court did not explain how *not* making it a crime for a girl under the age of 17 years to have sexual intercourse would make it less likely that such girls would become pregnant.

Abortion

Of all the topics considered by the Supreme Court in its more than 90-year history there has been none more controversial than that of abortion. Chapter 12 of this book[150] tells the story of how the Supreme Court had decisions in this field challenged in the European Court of Justice (unsuccessfully) and the European Court of Human Rights (successfully), but those cases related to peripheral matters and not directly to whether a particular girl or woman was entitled to obtain an abortion. That first occurred in *Attorney General v X*,[151] where Ireland's top law officer at the time, Harry Whelehan, sought an injunction from the courts to prevent the 14-year-old victim of a rape from travelling to England to obtain an abortion, which Costello J in the High Court duly granted.[152] In reaching that decision the judge was heavily influenced by the Eighth Amendment to the Constitution, which had been inserted in 1983. Bacik suggests that the Supreme Court's decision in *McGee* was one of the developments which prompted the pressure from the Pro-Life Amendment Campaign (PLAC)

[145] Ibid, [49].

[146] Ibid, [56]. The full wording of Art 40.1 is: 'All citizens shall, as human persons, be held equal before the law. This shall not be held to mean that the State shall not in its enactments have due regard to differences of capacity, physical and moral, and of social function.'

[147] *Michael M v Sonoma County Superior Court* 450 US 464 (1981). See Landau (1981–82).

[148] Ibid, 469.

[149] [2012] 1 IR 697, [47].

[150] At 280-82 and 297-8. See too Bacik (2004) 112–16.

[151] [1992] 1 IR 1; for background see Sherlock (1989).

[152] As a much younger man Costello had written in praise of the Constitution's provisions on the family: Costello (1962). Costello J was a former Fine Gael TD and Attorney General who later served as President of the High Court from 1995 to 1998. He was the son of John Costello, a Fine Gael Taoiseach from 1948 to 1951 and from 1954 to 1957.

for such an amendment,[153] but that is rather far-fetched. In so far as PLAC itself stoked the flames of prospective judicial activism in this field it did so in contradiction of the Supreme Court's own words in *McGee*, where all of the judges stressed that they were dealing with a case on contraceptives and not abortifacients. There had been no other decisions in the 1970s which could give people cause to think that the Irish Supreme Court was suddenly going to strike out and make a new law on a topic as problematic as abortion.

The amendment to the Constitution, approved in a referendum on 7 September 1983,[154] added a new Article 40.3.3, which read:

> The State acknowledges the right to life of the unborn and, with due regard to the equal right to life of the mother, guarantees in its laws to respect, and, as far as practicable, by its laws to defend and vindicate that right.

This equating of the rights to life of the unborn child and of the mother suggests that in some situations the life of the mother should be sacrificed for that of the child, which even most pro-life campaigners would probably find difficult to justify on moral or religious grounds. As Bacik observes, '[n]o other country sets up the two rights against each other in this way'.[155] The unworkability of the wording was what lay at the heart of the *X* case in 1992.

In considering the appeal from the decision by Costello J to issue an injunction preventing *X* from travelling to England for an abortion, the Supreme Court fell back on what the law had been before the Constitution was amended in 1983. As regards the Offences Against the Person Act 1861, which is the Victorian legislation that originally criminalised abortion throughout the then United Kingdom,[156] there was a common law exception applicable in England and Wales, laid down by England's Central Criminal Court in *R v Bourne*,[157] to the effect that procuring a miscarriage was not unlawful if it was done in good faith for the purpose only of preserving the life of the mother. Indeed the judge in that case said that it was obvious that where a doctor anticipates that a child cannot be delivered without the death of the mother the doctor is not only entitled but obliged to operate with a view to saving the life of the mother.[158] He added that a 'reasonable' meaning should be given to the words 'preserving the life of the mother', which entailed concluding that it embraced situations where, if the pregnancy continued, the probable consequence would be that the woman is made 'a physical or mental wreck'.[159] While *R v Bourne* is also considered to be part of the law in Northern Ireland[160] there was never any unequivocal decision by an Irish court endorsing the English interpretation of the words 'preserving the life of the mother'. In 1997 Keane J, as he then was, stated that the preponderance of judicial opinion was that *R v Bourne* could not have been followed in Ireland.[161] The 1983 amendment to the Constitution suggested very strongly that, far from the mother's right automatically trumping that of the unborn child, her right was merely equal to that of the child.

One way out for the Supreme Court in the *X* case would have been to focus on the amendment's instruction that 'due regard' had to be given to the equal right of the mother. This phrase allows the judges some discretion in the way that they weigh up the two competing claims to the right to life. But the majority of the Supreme Court chose instead to

[153] Bacik (2004) 111. She also cites the decision of the US Supreme Court in *Roe v Wade* 410 US 113 (1973), but that link is also difficult to sustain.

[154] On a 54 per cent turnout, 67 per cent voted in favour of the amendment and 33 per cent voted against.

[155] Bacik (2004) 112. See too Hogan et al (2018) 1788-1806.

[156] ss 58 and 59. These provisions still apply in Northern Ireland.

[157] [1939] 1 KB 687 (Macnaghten J). [158] Ibid, 693. [159] Ibid, 694.

[160] See eg *Northern Health and Social Services Board v AMNH* [1994] NIJB, 1, 5.

[161] *Society for the Prevention of the Unborn Child (Ireland) Ltd v Grogan (No 5)* [1998] 4 IR 343, 381–2.

focus on what degree of likelihood of the mother's suicide there had to be before it could be considered as outweighing the unborn child's right to life. Finlay CJ, McCarthy, O'Flaherty and Egan JJ all held that the 'true' interpretation of Article 40.3.3 was that a pregnancy could be terminated if it was *probable* that there was a real and substantial risk to the life of the mother: there was no need to show that there was a risk of immediate or inevitable death of the mother. However Hederman J, dissenting on this point, said it was 'obvious' that before a pregnancy could be terminated 'the evidence required to justify the choice being made must be of such a weight and cogency as to leave open no other conclusion but that the consequences of the continuance of the pregnancy will, *to an extremely high degree of probability* cost the mother her life and that any such opinion must be based on the most competent medical opinion available'.[162] The majority therefore thought that an injunction should not be granted restricting the right of the 14-year-old pregnant girl from travelling to England, while Hederman J thought that a more general injunction should be imposed restraining the girl from procuring or arranging a termination of pregnancy or abortion whether within Ireland or outside Ireland.

While it is likely that most people in Ireland approved of the majority's decision—and Morgan, for one, suspects that the judges were influenced by expressions of public concern in the three-week gap between the High Court and Supreme Court judgments[163]—the reasoning on which it is based leaves something to be desired. The reality is that the evidence to suggest the girl was going to commit suicide if she was forced to continue with the pregnancy was very thin, based as it was on just one report from a clinical psychologist. Finlay CJ devoted less than a page to this evidence and McCarthy, O'Flaherty and Egan JJ simply concurred with this assessment. It was left to Hederman J to point out that neither the High Court nor the Supreme Court had heard or seen the girl in question, that there was no evidence of any obstetrical problems and that the clinical psychologist's opinion was influenced by what he had been told about the girl's attitude and behaviour by her parents and police officers. He also pointed out that if the girl was indeed suicidal she should and could be protected until her child was born:

> If this young person without being pregnant had suicidal tendencies due to some other cause then nobody would doubt that the proper course would be to put her in such care and under such supervision as would counteract such tendency and do everything possible to prevent suicide ... The duration of the pregnancy is a matter of months and it should not be impossible to guard the girl against self-destruction and preserve the life of the unborn child at the same time.[164]

There was a second worrying feature of the judgments in that a majority of the judges intimated that if a pregnant mother was not suicidal it would be right for courts to restrain her from leaving the jurisdiction in order to 'defend and vindicate' the right to life of the unborn child.[165] This was the view of Finlay CJ, Egan J and, of course, Hederman J, but McCarthy and O'Flaherty JJ disagreed, on the basis that such a restraint would be an unwarranted interference with the right to freedom of movement and in particular the right to leave the country, even if the purpose of leaving was to do something in another country which was illegal in Ireland. In this regard McCarthy J cited *The State (M) v Attorney General*,[166] commenting that the right to travel recognised by the High Court as an unenumerated right enjoys the same guarantee as those expressly mentioned in Article 40 of the Constitution.[167]

162 [1992] 1 IR 1, 75 (emphasis added).
163 Morgan (2001) 26.
164 [1992] 1 IR 1, 76.
165 As required by Article 40.3.3 of the Constitution (see above, 236).
166 [1979] IR 73 (Finlay P).
167 [1992] 1 IR 1, 84.

In *Attorney General v X* the Supreme Court did not have its finest day. The leading publication on the Irish Constitution accuses Finlay CJ and McCarthy J of sophistry and casuistry,[168] Morgan says 'there seems to have been a lack of thought behind the majority judgments'[169] and Binchy decried the majority's view that when calibrating constitutional values the Supreme Court should reflect 'prevailing views and concepts'.[170] To some extent the Supreme Court's position was made more difficult due to the absence of any legislation putting flesh on the bones of Article 40.3.3 of the Constitution. Indeed McCarthy J lamented the Oireachtas's dereliction of duty in that respect:

> I think it reasonable ... to hold that the People when enacting the Amendment were entitled to believe that legislation would be introduced so as to regulate the manner in which the right to life of the unborn and the right to life of the mother could be reconciled.[171]

Following the Supreme Court's decision, announced on 5 March 1992, pressure was exerted to further amend the Constitution to take account of it. Consequently, on 25 November 1992 the views of the people were sought in a referendum on three questions. The first was whether Article 40.3.3 should be amended to exclude an abortion where there was 'a risk of self-destruction' (ie, of the pregnant mother committing suicide); this proposal was decisively rejected by 65 per cent to 35 per cent of the votes cast, thereby providing an endorsement for the main thrust of the majority's view in the *X* case.[172] The second was whether Article 40.3.3 should be amended to make it clear that the prohibition on abortion did not affect the right of the pregnant mother to travel to another country for an abortion if she so wished; this was accepted by the people, by 62 per cent to 38 per cent, providing further support for the majority's decision in the *X* case.[173] The third question was whether Article 40.3.3 should make it clear that Irish citizens have the freedom to pursue and learn about abortion services in other countries; this too was fairly strongly approved, by 60 per cent to 40 per cent of the votes cast.[174] The net result of the referendum was that Article 40.3.3 of the Constitution, acquired two additional (unnumbered) paragraphs, reading as follows:

> This subsection shall not limit freedom to travel between the State and another State.
>
> This subsection shall not limit freedom to obtain or make available, in the State, subject to such conditions as may be laid down by law, information relating to services lawfully available in another State.

In 2002 one further referendum (the fifth within 20 years) was held on an abortion issue. It was a second attempt to remove the risk of the pregnant mother's suicide as a ground for allowing an abortion. The proposed amendment was again rejected, but by a much narrower majority than when the issue was put to the people less than nine months after the Supreme Court's decision in the *X* case in 1992: 50.4 per cent voted against it and 49.6 per cent voted in favour, a difference of less than 11,000 votes out of more than 1.2 million cast.[175] Doubtless the rise in the number of voters willing to exclude the risk of suicide as a justification for abortion was partly attributable to the fact that the proposed amendment

[168] Hogan et al (2018) 1796-7. [169] Morgan (2001) 27. [170] Binchy (2008) 313.

[171] [1992] 1 IR 1, 81–2. Most other constitutional amendments have been followed by implementing legislation, eg the Family Law (Divorce) Act 1996 which implemented the referendum on divorce in 1995.

[172] The vote was on the proposed Twelfth Amendment to the Constitution Bill 1992.

[173] The vote was on the proposed Thirteenth Amendment to the Constitution Bill 1992.

[174] The vote was on the proposed Fourteenth Amendment to the Constitution Bill 1992.

[175] The vote was on the proposed Twenty-fifth Amendment to the Constitution (Protection of Human Life in Pregnancy) Bill 2001.

referred to a Protection of Human Life in Pregnancy Bill which would, once enacted, effectively provide a legal code stipulating when precisely an abortion would be permissible.[176]

The continuing absence of legislation specifying exactly when the life of the mother is in play under Article 40.3.3 was partly why in 2010 the European Court of Human Rights found Ireland to be in violation of the ECHR in *A, B and C v Ireland*,[177] where one of the applicants, who was suffering from cancer, could not obtain a medical decision as to whether a termination of her pregnancy would be lawful or not. To help it decide how to respond to this judgment from Strasbourg the Irish government set up an expert group to make recommendations.[178] These ultimately led to the enactment of the Protection of Life During Pregnancy Act 2013, which President Higgins, after consulting with his Council of State, chose not to refer to the Supreme Court under Article 26 of the Constitution for *a priori* review.[179] As it is a complex piece of legislation[180] there remains every possibility that challenges to its application will reach the Supreme Court in due course. The Act repealed the provisions in the Offences Against the Person Act 1861 criminalising the procurement of an abortion, replacing them with the offence of 'destruction of unborn human life', punishable by up to 14 years in prison.

As already mentioned,[181] the Supreme Court was more recently involved in a case where the extent of the rights of the unborn child were at issue. This was in *M (Immigration—Rights of Unborn) v Minister for Justice and Equality*,[182] a leapfrog appeal from the High Court where Humphreys J had made a declaration that the Minister was obliged to consider, when deciding whether to revoke a deportation order made against *M*, who was about to become the father of a child in Ireland, the rights of the unborn child.[183] A seven-judge Court unanimously reversed Humphrey J's decision on that point, holding that 'the present constitutional rights of the unborn are confined to the right to life guaranteed by Article 40.3.3', the result of the Eighth Amendment to the Constitution.[184] Yet the Supreme Court confirmed that the Minister still had to consider the fact that *M's* partner was pregnant and that his child will acquire Irish citizenship when born.

Meanwhile, pressure mounted to repeal the Eighth Amendment to the Constitution, which grants equal recognition to the rights to life of the mother and the unborn child. The campaign gained impetus after the death of Savita Halappanavar while giving birth in 2012. In July 2016 a Citizens' Assembly was created to consider this topic amongst several others, chaired by the Supreme Court judge Mary Laffoy. It proposed that another referendum should be held. The government accepted that proposal and in December 2017 a Joint Oireachtas Committee made suggestions as to what new legislation on abortion might say, suggesting that it should allow more or less unrestricted access to abortion during the first 12 weeks of a pregnancy and the government later backed that idea. In a referendum held on 25 May 2018 66 per cent of those who voted approved the repeal of the Eighth Amendment, with only County Donegal returning a majority 'No' vote (by 52 per cent to 48 per cent). The government subsequently introduced the Health (Regulation of Termination of Pregnancy) Bill before the Dáil and at the time of writng this was at its third stage. If enacted it will repeal the Protection of Life During Pregnancy Act 2013.

[176] And the Bill, once enacted, would have been amendable only by referendum. It was not enacted.

[177] (2011) 53 EHRR 13. See too Chap 12 below, 297-8.

[178] The Group's Report is available at http://cdn.thejournal.ie/media/2012/11/judgment_abc.pdf.

[179] For the Art 26 procedure see Chap 6 above, 106-19.

[180] See eg Forde and Leonard (2014) 735.

[181] See above, 229.

[182] [2018] IESC 14.

[183] *M v Minister for Justice and Equality (No 2)* [2016] IEHC 478.

[184] [2018] IESC 14, para 13.3.

Human Assisted Reproduction

In 2009 the Supreme Court had a further opportunity to comment on the scope of Article 40.3.3 of the Constitution in *Roche v Roche*,[185] where a woman claimed that three frozen embryos created *in vitro* through the fertilisation of her eggs by her husband's sperm enjoyed the right to life and should be protected by a court order preventing their destruction. The whole subject of *in vitro* fertilisation had been considered in an official report published in 2005 by a 25-member Commission.[186] Although it made 40 recommendations, the chief of which was that a body should be established by an Act of the Oireachtas to regulate assisted human reproduction services in Ireland, no legislative proposal had since materialised. Unanimously the Supreme Court endorsed the decision by McGovern J in the High Court that the frozen embryos were not 'unborn' within the meaning of that term in Article 40.3.3, since that subsection presupposed that 'unborn' meant a foetus within a woman's womb. More startlingly, the Supreme Court declared that whether the embryos had the right to life under some other legal heading was not a justiciable issue at all. As Murray CJ put it:

> I do not consider that it is for a court of law, faced with the most divergent if most learned views in the discourses available to it from the disciplines referred to [moral, philosophical, theological and scientific], to pronounce on the truth of when human life begins. Absent a broad consensus or understanding on that truth, it is for legislatures in the exercise of their dispositive powers to resolve such issues on the basis of policy choices.[187]

Denham, Hardiman, Geoghegan and Fennelly JJ did not go quite as far as the Chief Justice, but Hardiman and Fennelly JJ commented adversely on the Oireachtas's failure to legislate in the wake of the *X* case.[188] Fennelly J warned that, if the executive and legislature failed to act, 'it may be open to the courts in a future case to consider whether an embryo enjoys constitutional protection under other provisions of the Constitution'.[189]

The rights of a known sperm donor were at issue in *McD v L*,[190] where the donor to a lesbian couple applied to be the guardian of the boy conceived by the donated sperm and also to have access to the child, despite the fact that the donor had initially agreed with the lesbian couple that he would have no parental role in relation to the child and would behave as 'a favourite uncle'. In allowing the donor access to the child, but not conferring on him the role of guardian, the Supreme Court could not resist stressing that the *de facto* family recognised under Article 8 of the ECHR was not an institution recognised in Ireland and that the effect of the European Convention on Human Rights Act 2003 had not been to introduce the European version of that institution into domestic Irish law.[191] Both Murray CJ and Denham J cited with approval[192] the words of Henchy J in *The State (Nicolaou) v An Bord Uchtála*:

185 [2010] 2 IR 321; Mulligan (2010), (2011) and (2012).

186 Available at www.lenus.ie/hse/bitstream/10147/46684/1/1740.pdf .

187 [2010] 2 IR 321, [49]–[50]. See too [51]–[54].

188 Ibid, [190] (per Hardiman J) and [230] (per Fennelly J). Denham J restricted herself to whether embryos were protected by Article 40.3.3, while Geoghegan J said that the question of when life begins was not relevant to the appeal ([194]).

189 Ibid, [230].

190 [2010] 2 IR 199; Hogan (2010); Cahill (2010).

191 Ibid, [59]–[62] (per Murray CJ), [146] and [168] (per Denham J), [191] (per Geoghegan J) and [211] (per Fennelly J).

192 Ibid, [64] (per Murray CJ) and [142] (per Denham J).

> For the State to award equal constitutional protection to the family founded on marriage and the 'family' founded on extra marital union would in effect be a disregard of the pledge which the State gives in Article 41.3.1 to guard with special care the institution of marriage.[193]

At first blush this statement sounds like an unwelcome throwback to attitudes displayed by the Supreme Court in the 1960s, though to be fair both judges were prepared to evade the narrowness of the strict constitutional position by accepting that the most important issue in such cases is often the welfare of the child. Murray CJ stated that: 'In the end these often difficult situations have to be determined by the best interests of the child being considered paramount and, *subject to that*, with due regard to constitutional and other rights in law vested in other parties.'[194] Denham J agreed that '[i]in assessing the welfare of a child all the circumstances require to be analysed'.[195]

In 2014, in *MR v An tArd Chlćraitheoir*, the Supreme Court had to decide whether, in a case where a surrogate mother had borne the twin children of her sister and brother-in-law, the 'mother' of the children for the purposes of the registration of its birth was their genetic mother or their gestational mother. In the High Court Abbott J held that the genetic mother should be registered as the mother,[196] but on appeal the Supreme Court ruled that the gestational mother should play that role.[197] Denham CJ thought there was a lacuna in the law, since neither the Status of Children Act 1987 nor the Civil Registration Act 2004 seemed to allow the genetic mother to take precedence over the gestational mother (although the reasoning employed here seems, with respect, a little question-begging); she therefore called for legislation in this area.[198] O'Connell J treated the issue as essentially one of interpretation of the Civil Registration Act 2004 and on that narrow basis he preferred to register the name of the woman who gave birth to the twins. Clarke J, as he then was,[199] took a more activist approach: in his view it was not possible to say that the common law preferred the genetic mother to the gestational mother because the truth is that it never realised that the two roles could be played by different individuals. He therefore proposed that both women were entitled to be registered in some way; this was 'the least bad solution' and, pending the enactment of legislation, it was a matter for the Chief Registrar to 'put in place such administrative measures as might be necessary to give effect to that type of registration'.[200] Hardiman expressly disagreed with Clarke J in so far as the latter was proposing that the Supreme Court should fill the vacuum left by the Oireachtas. To Hardiman J this was:

> ... an invitation to overrule the established understanding of 'mother' and then to legislate in the area left vacant, and to do so without any evidence-based assessment of the merits of the new dispensation. If the Court were to accede to the respondents' invitation, it would dangerously approach illegitimacy.[201]

MacMenamin J, akin to Clarke J, was motivated by the need to allow the twins in this case to be brought up within a family unit. Without specifying which provision of the Constitution he had in mind, he remarked that 'a number of steps could be taken further to secure the constitutional and legal position' of the twins. He therefore put forward the novel proposition that the father and genetic mother could be appointed as guardians of

[193] [1966] IR 567, 622. 'An tArd Chláraitheoir' means 'the Chief Registrar'.
[194] [2010] 2 IR 199, [65] (emphasis added). [195] Ibid, [146].
[196] [1993] I ILRM 44. See the post by Andrea Mulligan at http://humanrights.ie/children-and-the-law/surrogacy-in-the-courts.
[197] [2014] IESC 60, [2014] 3 IR 533 (Denham CJ, Murray, Hardiman, O'Donnell, McKechnie, Clarke and MacMenamin JJ).
[198] Ibid, [116]. [199] He became Chief Justice in October 2017. [200] [2014] 3 IR 353, [512].
[201] Ibid, [196].

the children under the inherent jurisdiction of the High Court, with a view to them later adopting the children. He added:

> The power of the courts should be sufficiently ample to vindicate the rights of children which arise under the Constitution[202] ... [The twins] do have constitutional rights to be parented, and to be reared and educated where possible, in a family unit. They have, at minimum, a clear interest in having their identities and status established in law.[203]

The Supreme Court's decision in *MR v An tArd Chláraitheoir* was not cited when a similar issue reached the High Court of England and Wales in 2016. But there too the court held that the surrogate mother is the child's mother in the eyes of the law unless and until a parental order is made in favour of the genetic mother.[204]

Almost a decade before surrogacy was considered by the Irish Supreme Court, as alluded to above, a report had been published by the Commission on Assisted Human Reproduction.[205] It recommended that a child born through surrogacy should be presumed to be that of the commissioning couple. It also pointed out that, although Article 40.3.3 of the Constitution provided constitutional protection for the 'unborn', it would require either the Supreme Court or a referendum to clarify whether such protection applies from fertilisation of the egg or from some later point in the process.[206] Such clarity has still not been provided. The Children and Family Relationships Act 2015 allows for the regulation of donor-assisted human reproduction and for the conferment of rights on donor-conceived people to access information about their genetic heritage. It also requires donations not to be anonymous and the establishment of a National Donor-Conceived Person Register. By early 2018 these provisions were not yet in force, but it was anticipated that they would be commenced later in the year. At the end of 2017, after a period of public consultation, the government also approved a General Scheme for an Assisted Human Reproduction Bill. If enacted, this will create a Regulatory Authority and set out the specific conditions under which surrogacy in Ireland will be permitted. There would be a court-based mechanism for transferring the parentage of a child who is born through surrogacy from the surrogate mother to the commissioning parent(s). It seems as if the legislators are on the same page as the senior judges on this issue: they want the genetic mother to retain parental rights but are struggling as to how exactly to achieve that.

The Right to Die

Given the Supreme Court's conservatism in dealing with the topic of abortion, it might have been expected that a similar attitude would be adopted as regards keeping people alive. But that is only partly true. While the Court has not supported the right of a disabled person to choose the moment of his or her passing, it has permitted the withdrawal of treatment from a severely disabled person who lacked personal capacity, thereby ensuring that her death would be hastened.

The latter scenario was before the Court in *In re a Ward of Court (Withholding medical treatment) (No 2)*,[207] where a 45-year-old woman had for 23 years been in a near persistent

[202] Here the judge cited *DG v Eastern Health Board* [1997] 3 IR 611.

[203] [2014] 3 IR 533, [581]. He cited *Mennesson v France* App No 651952/11 and *Labasse v France* App No 65941/11 (judgments of 26 June 2014), where the ECtHR found a violation of Art 8 of the ECHR when French law denied any family ties between surrogate children and their biological parents; see too Nila Baa, 'The hidden costs of the European Court of Human Rights' surrogacy decision' (2014) *Yale Journal of International Law Online*.

[204] *Re AB (Surrogacy Consent)* [2016] EWHC 2643.

[205] See n 187 above.

[206] At 37. The same point was made by the Constitution Review Group 40 years earlier: CRG (1966) 275–6.

[207] [1996] 2 IR 79; Harrington (1995).

vegetative state as a result of suffering brain damage during a minor operation. She had been kept alive by being fed and hydrated through a tube inserted into her stomach. Her mother and siblings sought an order from the High Court that it would be lawful to discontinue the artificial nutrition and hydration and let their loved one die. In the High Court Lynch J granted such an order, and this was confirmed by the Supreme Court. It is important that since 1974 the woman in question had been a ward of court, because she was of unsound mind and incapable of looking after her own affairs. This meant that it was the High Court and not the family which had the responsibility for deciding all matters relating to the woman's future. From a constitutional point of view the issues which the courts faced were, first, that under Article 40.3.2 the State has a duty to 'protect as best it may from unjust attack' the life of every citizen; second, that under Article 41.1.1 the State recognises that the family possesses 'inalienable and imprescriptible rights, antecedent and superior to all positive law'; and third, that under Article 41.1.2 the State guarantees 'to protect the family in its constitution and authority'.

On the first issue the Supreme Court held that the importance of the right to life was such that there was a strong presumption in favour of taking all steps capable of preserving life, but it added that in exceptional circumstances, such as here, life did not have to be preserved. If the patient had been mentally competent she would have been entitled to exercise her right to terminate her life through foregoing medical treatment, although she would not have had the right to have her death accelerated, only the right to die through natural causes. Adopting and applying the test which the House of Lords had used in the case of Tony Bland just a year earlier (he had been left in a permanent vegetative state after being crushed at the Hillsborough football stadium disaster in 1989),[208] the Supreme Court ruled that it was in the ward of court's best interests for her life not to be further prolonged through artificial nourishment and for her to be allowed to slip away through withdrawing her treatment.

The Supreme Court's answer to the second and third issues was, in effect, that the family's rights under Article 41 had to take second place to the High Court's *parens patriae* jurisdiction, which had originally been exercised by the Lord Chancellor of Ireland as a delegate of the British Crown but which had been transferred to the High Court by the combined effects of the Courts of Justice Acts 1924 and 1936.[209] This aspect of High Court jurisdiction had already been confirmed by the Supreme Court in *In re D*,[210] but at no point in that judgment is any reference made to the relationship between the jurisdiction and the rights of the family under Article 41. In *In re a Ward of Court (Withholding medical treatment) (No 2)*,[211] it seems abundantly clear that the Supreme Court approved the carving out of a huge limitation to the rights conferred by Article 41, despite the family's rights being referred to there as 'antecedent and superior to all positive law'. To date the apparent contradiction has not been directly addressed in any subsequent Supreme Court judgment and nor has any constitutional amendment been proposed.

Like many other top courts the Supreme Court of Ireland has recently had to grapple with the argument that the law should protect the right of a disabled person (who has retained his or her full mental capacity) to die with dignity at a time of his or her own choosing. In the United Kingdom the House of Lords decided on two occasions that no such right existed in domestic law and nor could it be inferred from the ECHR.[212] As a result of the House's first decision being reviewed by the European Court of Human Rights[213]

[208] *Airedale NHS Trust v Bland* [1993] AC 789. [209] ss 19 and 9(1) respectively.
[210] [1987] IR 449 (Finlay CJ, Walsh, Henchy, Hederman and McCarthy JJ). [211] Note 208 above.
[212] *R (Pretty) v DPP* [2001] UKHL 61, [2002] 1 AC 800; *R (Purdy) v DPP* [2009] UKHL 45. [2010] 1 AC 345.
[213] *Pretty v UK* (2002) 35 EHRR 1.

the House did at least concede in the second case that the right to a private and family life, as guaranteed by Article 8(1) of the ECHR, was engaged in these situations, even if the State could lawfully deny the right under the exceptions set out in Article 8(2). In that second case the House went further than the European Court had done by ordering the Director of Public Prosecutions to produce clearer guidance on when a person might be prosecuted for assisting a suicide in this kind of situation.

The issue came before the Supreme Court of Ireland in 2013, in *Fleming v Ireland*.[214] The facts were very similar to those in *Pretty* and *Purdy* in that the plaintiff was a woman who was terminally ill with multiple sclerosis and was seeking reassurance that if her partner assisted her to kill herself he would not then be prosecuted and punished.[215] Under section 2(2) of the Criminal Law (Suicide) Act 1993 it is a crime to assist the suicide or attempted suicide of another person and the punishment can be imprisonment for up to 14 years. Ms Fleming argued that section 2(2) was unconstitutional and incompatible with the ECHR. Unsurprisingly, both the High Court (sitting as a bench of three)[216] and the Supreme Court (a bench of seven) rejected the plaintiff's claims and in the course of doing so revealed the prevailing thinking amongst the country's top judges concerning the values protected by the Constitution. Again, because the case was a challenge to the constitutionality of a provision in a post-1937 Act, the Supreme Court's judgment was pronounced by a single member, in this case Denham CJ.[217]

The plaintiff focused on the suggestion that as a person with a disability she was being treated unequally in that a non-disabled person had the freedom to end his or her life at a moment of their own choosing. The Irish Human Rights Commission was allowed to appear as an *amicus curiae* and supported Ms Fleming's position, stressing that section 2(2) of the 1993 Act provided an unnecessary and effectively discriminatory blanket criminalisation of assisted suicide. In its judgment the Supreme Court referred to decisions from Canada,[218] the United Kingdom[219] and the USA,[220] but naturally focused on whether the right being claimed was one available under the Irish Constitution. The Court did not adopt any of the reasoning of the Supreme Court of British Columbia in *Carter v Canada (Attorney General)*,[221] which suggests that it would have come to the same conclusion even after that decision was later affirmed by the Supreme Court of Canada in 2015, striking down the relevant provincial legislation as violating the right to life, liberty and security of the person guaranteed by section 7 of the Canadian Charter of Rights and Freedoms 1982.[222]

The Irish Supreme Court started from the position that the presumption of constitutionality which every Act of the Oireachtas enjoys 'may be regarded as having particular force in cases where the legislature is concerned with the implementation of public policy in respect of sensitive matters of social or moral policy'.[223] It then proceeded to consider whether any of the express provisions of the Constitution could be interpreted as conferring a right to commit suicide and whether it was an unenumerated right. Article 40.3.1 was the likeliest contender in this regard, as it provides that 'The State guarantees in its laws to protect, and, as far as practicable, by its laws to defend and vindicate the personal rights of the citizen'.

[214] [2013] 2 IR 417 (Denham CJ, Murray, Hardiman, Fennelly, O'Donnell, McKechnie and Clarke JJ).

[215] Sadly, Marie Fleming died less than eight months after losing her case in the Supreme Court. She was 59 and had been suffering from multiple sclerosis for 25 years.

[216] [2013] IEHC 2, [2013] 2 ILRM 9 (Kearns P, Carney and Hogan JJ).

[217] For discussion of the single judgment rule required by Art 34.4.5 of the Constitution, see Chap 6 above, 119-21.

[218] eg *Rodriguez v British Columbia (Attorney General)* (1993) 50 BMLR 1 (Sup Ct of Canada); *Carter v Canada (Attorney General)* [2012] BCSC 886 (Sup Ct of British Columbia).

[219] *R (Pretty) v DPP* [2001] UKHL 61, [2002] 1 AC 800; oddly, *R (Purdy)* was not cited at all.

[220] *Washington v Glucksberg* 521 US 702 (1997) (US Sup Ct).

[221] See n 219 above.

[222] *Carter v Canada (AG)* 2015 SCC 5.

[223] [2013] 2 IR 417, [95]; Byrne (2013).

Article 40.3.2 was also a contender: 'The State shall, in particular, by its laws protect as best it may from unjust attack and, in the case of injustice done, vindicate the life, person, good name and property rights of every citizen.' This latter right is obviously a sub-category of the rights conferred by the former provision, and it is unfortunate that when the Supreme Court was considering whether it could derive the unenumerated right in question from an express provision of the Constitution it chose to do so only by reference to the more particular right. With that starting point it was to be expected that the Court would conclude that vindication of the right to life was inconsistent with vindication of the right to terminate that life: '[i]n the social order contemplated by the Constitution, and the values reflected in it, that would be the antithesis of the right rather than the logical consequence of it.'[224] Had the Court asked itself whether vindication of the right to be assisted in one's suicide was inconsistent with vindication of one's personal rights its conclusion might have been different. There would have been no logical contradiction between such a different conclusion and the existence of a right to have one's right to life vindicated by the State. For the Court to say at one point that the Constitution undoubtedly recognises and respects the values of autonomy, self-determination and dignity[225] but then to add shortly afterwards that it is not possible to discern in the Constitution any support for the theory that the State is not entitled to interfere with decisions made by a person in respect of the termination of his or her life is, with respect, contradictory.[226] It is also disappointing that, in its discussion of whether current Irish law discriminates against people with severe disabilities such as Ms Fleming, the Supreme Court did not closely enough consider the plight of people with such disabilities and expressly rejected the invitation to follow the example of the Supreme Court of British Columbia by engaging in an effects-based analysis of the Criminal Law (Suicide) Act 1993. This approach does a disservice to people with severe disabilities and the suggestion that it is too difficult to construct a law which would not create a slippery slope leading to euthanasia is simply not true.[227]

It may be unfair to criticise the Irish Supreme Court for not taking steps that at the time had not been taken by any other national supreme court or indeed any international human rights court. The Court was also to some extent hamstrung by the express wording of the Constitution. But a different outcome was conceivable and more watertight argumentation might have been expected. It is also regrettable that Ms Fleming did not appeal against the High Court's dismissal of her argument that the DPP should be ordered to issue guidelines on prosecutions in this field. The issuing of such guidance in England and Wales and Northern Ireland has made the law more flexible and compassionate in those jurisdictions. The Canadian Supreme Court has since displayed even greater courageous leadership by requiring the legislators in that country to amend the law so that it deals directly with the plight of severely disabled people who wish to exercise the right to end their lives at the moment and in the manner of their own choosing.[228] The Court allowed the law-makers a 12-month period (later extended to 16 months) to come up with appropriate legislation and this was eventually enacted in 2016, though some believe that it does not go as far as the Canadian Supreme Court's judgment requires.[229] It is surely only a matter of time before that more enlightened attitude prevails in all common law countries and indeed within the Strasbourg regime.

[224] Ibid, [113]. [225] Ibid, [110]. [226] Ibid, [113].

[227] This suggestion is implied in at least two places in the Supreme Court's judgment: [107] and [115].

[228] See n 223 above.

[229] An Act to amend the Criminal Code and to make related amendments to other Acts (medical assistance in dying) 2016. This inserts a new s 227 into the Criminal Code and radically amends s 241.

Conclusion

As in other areas of law, Ireland's Supreme Court has not been as dynamic as it might have been in the important field of family and personal life because it has to some extent been constrained by the wording of the 1937 Constitution. The Court took a long time to wake up to the reality that families come in all sorts of forms, that what should determine a child's future is its own best interests and not just its connection to its birth mother, and that leaving the law on abortion in a state of uncertainty helps no-one. It is a matter of some regret that the Oireachtas did not give the Court clearer guidance on what factors to take into account when interpreting the law in this sphere, not only as regards abortion but also matrimonial property, human-assisted reproduction and the right to assisted suicide. To that extent the Irish Supreme Court has performed no less creditably than Supreme Courts in many other common law jurisdictions. As the years have gone by the Irish Court has examined the issues before it more thoroughly and with greater reference to the jurisprudence of other countries. While maintaining deference to the Oireachtas's choice of policies, it has become more willing to ensure that correct processes are adopted and that fundamental human rights are protected. It has upheld constitutional principles but has not been unwilling to resort to a considerable dose of pragmatism when required, particularly in the areas of adoption law and immigration law. We may well see that trend continue, not least because it is an approach which is likely to endear the Court to the general public, if not always to the legislators.

11

The Supreme Court and the European Union

The Reception of European Law by the Supreme Court

Ireland joined the European Economic Community (EEC) on the same day as the United Kingdom, 1 January 1973.[1] This followed a referendum held in Ireland on 10 May 1972, in which 83 per cent of those who voted supported membership. Little were the voters to know that that was to be the first of, to date, nine referenda on European issues.[2] As a result of the initial vote the Third Amendment of the Constitution Act 1972 inserted a new Article 29.4.3 into the Constitution expressly subordinating the Constitution to laws and actions required by membership of the EEC:

> No provision of this Constitution invalidates laws enacted, acts done or measures adopted by the State necessitated by the obligations of membership of the Communities[3] or prevents laws enacted, acts done or measures adopted by the Communities, or institutions thereof, from having the force of law in the State.

This was undoubtedly the biggest single change to the Irish Constitution since its proclamation in 1937. It represented a huge transfer of sovereignty in that it seemed to set at naught Article 15.2.1 of the Constitution, which proclaims that '[t]he sole and exclusive power of making laws for the State is hereby vested in the Oireachtas: no other legislative authority has power to make laws for the State'. Although Article 15.2.2 qualifies this statement by adding that provision may be made by law for the creation or recognition of 'other legislatures', these have to be 'subordinate' in nature. Ronan Keane, a former Chief Justice of Ireland, describes the impact of European law in Ireland, primarily what we now call EU law, as one of two major revolutions in Irish law during his lifetime (he was born in 1932), and one which has been characterised by a 'genuine intellectual excitement' on the part of Irish lawyers.[4] The other revolution, he claims, was 'the development by the judges from the 1960s onwards of a body of principles which gave vitality and relevance to the Constitution'.[5]

[1] European Communities Act 1972, s 2: 'From the 1st day of January, 1973, the treaties governing the European Communities and the existing and future acts adopted by the institutions of those Communities shall be binding on the State and shall be part of the domestic law thereof under the conditions laid down in those treaties.'

[2] As we shall see, the other eight took place in 1987, 1992, 1998, 2001, 2002, 2008, 2009 and 2012. For the influence of the Supreme Court on countering knowledge-deficits prior to referenda see Scott (2010), analysing, amongst others, the Supreme Court decisions in *McKenna v An Taoiseach (No 2)* [1995] 2 IR 210 and *Coughlan v Broadcasting Complaints Commission* [2000] IESC 44, [2000] 3 IR 1; see too Barrett (2009), who says (at 33) that 'if the decision not to ratify the Lisbon Treaty is not ultimately reversed, it may well be that [the Supreme Court's judgments in *Crotty, McKenna* and *Coughlan*] will collectively come to be regarded as the most significant exercises in judicial activism in Irish legal history'. Pressure of space prevents further examination of that line of cases here.

[3] Ireland joined not just the EEC but also the European Coal and Steel Community and the European Atomic Energy Committee (even though Ireland has no nuclear power programme and virtually no coal and steel industries).

[4] Keane (1987) 2. At the time he wrote this article Keane was a judge of the High Court and President of the Law Reform Commission.

[5] Ibid, 1.

When such a fundamental shift is made to the governance of a nation one is entitled to examine the reaction of the nation's top court to see how it has responded to the challenges thrown up by the turn of events. In the case of Ireland's Supreme Court the reaction was, and remains, a compliant, almost deferential one. In the cases where it has had to consider the consequences of EEC, EC or EU membership it has usually adopted a position which is consistent with that expressed by the government of the day. This has helped to maintain stability and certainty but at the same time the Supreme Court has been keen to ensure that Ireland's constitutional architecture is otherwise respected and that the nation's fundamental democratic values are not undermined. The most senior judges have been able to reassure the people of Ireland, albeit indirectly and implicitly, that they do not have to sacrifice any pride in their own national identity in order to be good Europeans. At no point has the Supreme Court engaged in the kind of alarmist rhetoric which Lord Denning used when explaining the impact of EEC membership on the United Kingdom's legal system. He talked of the Treaty of Rome as:

> ... like an incoming tide. It flows into the estuaries and up the rivers. It cannot be held back ... Any rights or obligations created by the Treaty are to be given legal effect in England without more ado. Any remedies or procedures provided by the Treaty are to be made available here without being open to question. In future, in transactions which cross the frontiers, we must no longer speak or think of English law as something on its own. We must speak and think of Community law, of Community rights and obligations, and we must give effect to them.[6]

For a view from a judge on the Irish Supreme Court we can turn to the extra-judicial comments made a few years later by Seamus Henchy, who wrote that:

> It is as if the people of Ireland had adopted Community law as a second but transcendent Constitution, but with the difference that Community law is not to be found in any single document—it is a living growing organism and the right to interpret it and give it conclusive judicial interpretation is reserved to the institutions of the Community and to its Court.[7]

Twenty years later another Supreme Court judge, Hugh O'Flaherty, commented in similar terms on Ireland's experience within Europe up to that point:

> Prior to entry into the European Community, Ireland was formally independent but, in fact, largely under the economic domination of Great Britain. Since joining the European Community, Ireland's freedom of economic and political action has increased immensely, but at the same time the Irish people, by virtue of the constitutional amendment to Article 29, have become subject to a system of Community law which, where applicable, overrules not only the common and statutory law of Ireland but its Constitution as well.[8]

O'Flaherty J went on to cite the High Court decision of Carroll J in *Tate v Minister for Social Welfare*,[9] against which the government did not appeal to the Supreme Court, as offering 'a revealing insight into the relationship between Community law and national law in the Irish legal order generally'.[10] Carroll J awarded damages to women whose social welfare benefits had been lower than they should have been if Ireland had complied in time with the Council Directive 79/7/EEC on equal treatment between men and women in the field of social security.

A quarter of a century after joining the EEC Phelan and Whelan attempted to summarise how Ireland had managed to accommodate the transfer of sovereignty required by

[6] *Bulmer Ltd v Bollinger SA* [1974] Ch 401, 418F–419B.
[7] Henchy (1977) 23.
[8] O'Flaherty (1996–97) 1153.
[9] [1995] 1 ILRM 507.
[10] O'Flaherty (1996–97) 1172.

the European integration project.[11] They did so by considering various 'threats' which EEC membership posed to State sovereignty, to the way the Irish government is internally organised, and to substantive constitutional guarantees. They concluded that to date these threats had been contained. They were less sanguine about the threats posed by the Treaty on European Union (the Maastricht Treaty), which was agreed in 1992 and came into effect for all member states on 1 November 1993.[12]

Campus Oil and *Pesca Valentia*

As it happens, the first court case which required serious consideration of the relationship between Irish law and Community law was one which involved the powers of the Supreme Court itself. Under Article 34.4.3, as we know from Chapter 4, the Supreme Court has appellate jurisdiction 'from all decisions of the High Court', subject to 'such regulations as may be prescribed by law'. At the same time, Article 177 of the Treaty of Rome 1957, the treaty which established the EEC, allowed a national court to request a ruling from the Court of Justice in Luxembourg if it considered that a decision on, amongst other things, the interpretation of the Treaty, was necessary to enable the national court to give a judgment on an issue. In *Campus Oil Ltd v Minister for Industry*[13] the issue was whether the Supreme Court could hear an appeal against a decision by a High Court judge to request a ruling from the Court of Justice in Luxembourg.

After hearing argument on this issue in February 1983 the Supreme Court, comprising O'Higgins CJ, Walsh and Hederman JJ, announced that it had no power to hear such an appeal, but it waited a further four months before setting out its reasons for this decision in a three-page judgment delivered by Walsh J. The reasons were (a) that a decision had been taken within Ireland not to issue any rules of court to regulate such appeals because it was assumed that such rules would be in breach of the Treaty rights conferred upon national judges, (b) that the procedure for requesting a ruling from the Court of Justice was similar to that which is used domestically when a lower court 'states a consultative case' for a higher court asking for a ruling on a point of law, and in Irish law there is no appeal against a judge's decisions to state a consultative case,[14] (c) that Article 177 confers on national judges the right to request a ruling in unqualified terms, and (d) that a High Court judge's decision to request a ruling is not a 'decision' for the purposes of Article 34.4.3 of the Constitution and, even if it is, Article 34.4.3 must yield to Article 177 of the Treaty of Rome because of the effect of the new Article 29.4.3 of the Constitution.[15] In Walsh J's words: '[t]o fetter [the judge's] right, by making it subject to review on appeal, would be contrary to both the spirit and the letter of Article 177 of the Treaty'.[16] Walsh J was aware of decisions in other EEC countries on this point, and also of comments made by the Court of Justice itself, but he declined to comment on these cases because he saw the Supreme Court's duty as being to decide the matter purely as a question of Irish law. In fact the attitude of the Court of Justice was, and is, that the procedures adopted within any particular country for an Article 177 reference are entirely a matter for the national legal system to decide, so if that system allows an appeal to be brought against such a reference then the Court of Justice should await the outcome of that appeal before giving its own ruling.[17]

[11] Phelan and Whelan (1997). [12] Ibid, 54–64. [13] [1983] IR 82; O'Keeffe (1983) and (1984).

[14] 'Stating a consultative case' is where a lower court poses a question to a higher court and meanwhile suspends its consideration of the case until the higher court has answered the question; see too Chap 4 above, 62.

[15] Cited above, 247. [16] [1983] IR 82, 87. [17] As in eg *Chanel v Cepeha* [1970] ECR 403.

Walsh J's judgment has been viewed as leaning too far in favour of the primacy of EEC law over Irish law. In O'Keeffe's memorable phrases it was '*plus catholique que le pape*'[18] and '*plus royaliste que le roi*',[19] while for Hogan and Whyte the reasoning employed 'has the effect of virtually scheduling the European Treaties to the Constitution itself'.[20] Hogan and Whelan point out that Walsh J's position could be seen as 'more *communautaire* than the Community'[21] and that the end result is hard to reconcile with the judge's earlier statement that the Court of Justice is 'the only one having jurisdiction to give … binding interpretations'[22] of the Treaty of Rome.

A bizarre feature of this litigation is that, during the four month wait for the Supreme Court to give its reasons for not hearing an appeal against the High Court judge's decision to request a ruling from Luxembourg, the substantive issue in the dispute between Campus Oil Ltd and the government proceeded to a full hearing before both the High Court and the Supreme Court and the judgments of these courts were issued before the reasons for the preliminary decision were made known. The substantive issue progressed in this way because the government sought a mandatory injunction from the High Court requiring the company to comply with the current law pending the outcome of the company's challenge to that law's constitutionality. The law in question, the Fuels (Control of Supplies) Order 1982 (renewed in 1983), obliged oil importers such as Campus Oil Ltd to buy a fixed proportion of their required supplies directly from the state-owned oil refinery in County Cork. Campus Oil Ltd saw this as a breach of the prohibition in the Treaty of Rome[23] on the placing of quantitative restrictions on imports between member states of the EEC. In the High Court Keane J granted the injunction, ruling that the test for doing so was not whether the applicant government would probably ultimately win the dispute on its merits but whether there was a fair question to be determined about the right sought to be protected by the government and whether the balance of convenience lay on the side of granting the injunction.[24] That double-headed test, incidentally, was the one which the UK House of Lords had enunciated in *American Cyanamid v Ethicon Ltd*.[25] Keane J thought it was already reflected in the Supreme Court's decision in *Educational Company of Ireland Ltd v Fitzpatrick*[26] and the Supreme Court fully endorsed Keane J's decision, including his view that the injunction could be issued notwithstanding that a ruling from the Court of Justice in Luxembourg was still pending. Griffin J added[27] that the *American Cyanamid* test had already been applied by the Supreme Court in a number of recent cases, the latest of which was *TMG Group Ltd v Al Babtain Trading and Contracting Co*.[28]

The European Court of Justice delivered its preliminary ruling in the *Campus Oil* case in July 1984.[29] On the Article 177 point it repeated that it is for each national court to decide at what stage in the national proceedings it is appropriate to refer a question to the European Court for a preliminary ruling. In support of this stance it cited its earlier ruling in *Irish Creamery Milk Suppliers Association v Ireland*,[30] a case where the reference had been made by the High Court of Ireland without troubling the Supreme Court. On the substantive point in *Campus Oil* the ECJ largely accepted the Irish government's position, stating that if a member state was almost totally dependent on imports for its supplies of petroleum products it could, under Article 36 of the Treaty of Rome, rely on grounds of public security

[18] O'Keeffe (1983) 290. [19] O'Keeffe (1984) 97. [20] Hogan et al (2018) 600.
[21] Hogan and Whelan (1995) 19; and see generally 17–24. [22] [1983] IR 82, 86.
[23] Arts 30 and 31. [24] *Campus Oil Ltd v Minister for Industry (No 2)* [1983] IR 88.
[25] [1975] AC 396. [26] [1961] IR 323. [27] [1983] IR 88, 111.
[28] Unreported, 28 March 1980.
[29] *Campus Oil Ltd v Minister for Industry and Energy*, Case 72/83, [1984] 3 CMLR 544.
[30] Case 36/80, [1981] 2 CMLR 455.

in order to require importers to purchase products from a refinery in its own territory at prices fixed by the government if the product could not otherwise be freely disposed of at competitive prices on the market.

In *Pesca Valentia Ltd v Ministry for Fisheries and Forestry*[31] the Supreme Court issued an order restraining the State (pending litigation on the matter) from enforcing an EEC requirement that licences for fishing within Ireland's exclusive fishing limits could be granted only to ships on which at least 75 per cent of the crew were nationals of a member state of the EC. The plaintiff company owned a fishing vessel which had been arrested in Irish waters and was found to have a crew made up entirely of Spanish nationals at a time when Spain was not yet a member of the EC (it joined in 1986). It argued that the Irish legislation in question[32] was discriminatory but also that it was contrary to EEC law because it was made after the expiry in 1982 of the 10-year transitional period following Ireland's accession to the Economic Community. The Supreme Court accepted that the domestic legislation benefited from the presumption of constitutionality but, in accordance with the usual principles governing the issuing of injunctions, it granted an injunction to the company because there was a fair question to be tried and the balance of convenience lay in the company's favour even though it meant that a law introduced to comply with EEC law would be suspended. This made it clear that EEC law did not quite have the overriding force in Irish law which some had imagined it had.

When the case returned to the High Court the government argued that rather than seeking a preliminary ruling the judge, Keane J, should decide the substance of the issue so that there could then be an appeal to the Supreme Court which, if it wanted to, could request a preliminary ruling. But Keane J thought it would save time and money if he himself proceeded with the request for a preliminary ruling.[33] In its response, the ECJ accepted the arguments of the government that it did have the power to enact the legislation in question and that the legislation in question was not improperly discriminatory.[34] Keane J then applied that ruling and considered what damages, if any, could be recovered by the State on the basis of the company's prior undertaking, given at the time the injunction was issued in its favour, to pay such damages should it ultimately lose the case. He concluded, however, that the State had failed to establish that it had suffered any loss, so he could not award compensation. He rightly pointed out that had such a result been anticipated at the time the injunction was requested it might never have been issued.

This whole dispute presaged the *Factortame* litigation in the United Kingdom a few years later, where there was legislation requiring ships that were registered in the United Kingdom to have a majority of British owners. This time a company which owned Spanish-registered fishing vessels was complaining of another State's failure to adhere to EEC law. The European Court of Justice agreed with this contention in a preliminary ruling[35] and the House of Lords held that in consequence a provision in the Merchant Shipping Act 1988 had to be 'disapplied',[36] arguably the first occasion ever on which the doctrine of parliamentary sovereignty had been compromised in the United Kingdom.[37] Indeed in a follow-up

[31] [1985] IR 193.
[32] Fisheries (Consolidation) Act 1959, s 222B, inserted by the Fisheries (Amendment) Act 1983, s 2.
[33] *Pesca Valentia Ltd v Minister for Fisheries and Forestry (No 2)* [1990] 2 IR 305, 307.
[34] *Pesca Valentia Ltd v Minister for Fisheries and Forestry*, Case 223/86, [1988] 1 CMLR 888.
[35] *R v Secretary of State for Transport, ex parte Factortame Ltd* Case C-213/89, [1990] ECR I-2433.
[36] *Factortame Ltd v Secretary of State for Transport (No 2)* [1991] 1 AC 603.
[37] Of course some argued that the Court was only doing what is was obliged to do under the European Communities Act 1972.

case the House of Lords ruled that the Spanish company was entitled to compensation.[38] In the end £55 million was paid over, not including the reimbursement of legal costs.[39]

The *Crotty* Case

From what has been said so far it might appear that in the 1970s the Supreme Court was not as adept at handling matters of EEC law, as they were still then called, as it needed to be. But even greater challenges lay ahead. The next one arose in 1987.

Raymond Crotty, a former farmer who later became a lecturer in agricultural economics and statistics, was a life-long opponent of Ireland's membership of the EEC. He was particularly opposed to the efforts being made in the mid-1980s to create a more effective single market throughout the organisation. The wording of a treaty to that end was agreed by all 12 of the Member States in February 1986 and was given the name of 'the Single European Act' (SEA), although it was not of course a parliamentary Act in the common law sense of that term. The chief changes proposed by the SEA were (a) increased use of voting by qualified majority in the European Council (the body composed of national government ministers), (b) the listing of specific objectives for the EEC, (c) the creation of an additional court of first instance inferior to the Court of Justice in Luxembourg, and (d) a commitment by each Member State to adapt its foreign policy to that of other Member States and to refrain from impeding agreed joint actions within a framework known as European Political Cooperation. The goal was to have the SEA formally ratified by each Member State by the end of 1986. Eleven of the States managed to achieve that, but thanks to Mr Crotty Ireland could not do so and therefore the establishment of the enhanced single market had to be postponed.

Mr Crotty's legal argument was that Ireland could not implement the SEA without amending the 1937 Constitution, which required a referendum. The government had sought to implement the SEA by securing the passage of the European Communities (Amendment) Act 1986, but Mr Crotty believed that Act to be repugnant to the Constitution. It should be remembered that the SEA was also controversial in the United Kingdom, though more so after the event than at the time it was agreed: Mrs Thatcher, the Prime Minister, was very much in favour of the treaty because she saw it as a mechanism for ensuring that Britain's businesses would acquire easier access to customers in Europe (votes to remove trade barriers would require only a qualified majority at European Council meetings, not unanimity), but she failed to see that other parts of the SEA would make it easier for Europhiles to press for greater political co-operation across a range of fields, thereby leading the continent even closer to the formation of a United States of Europe. In Ireland this ambivalence to the expansion of the European project was nowhere near as pervasive.

Mr Crotty first went to the High Court seeking an injunction to restrain Irish ratification of the SEA. On Christmas Eve 1986 he persuaded Barrington J that he had *locus standi* to bring the case and also that the issues were important enough to merit the issue of an interlocutory injunction.[40] The judge applied the test for granting an interlocutory injunction set out by the Supreme Court in *Campus Oil Ltd (No 2)*.[41] But after a nine-day hearing in a Divisional Court of the High Court in January 1987 a three-judge bench discharged (i.e. terminated) the injunction and ruled that the European Communities (Amendment) Act

[38] *R v Secretary of State for Transport, ex parte Factortame Ltd* [2000] 1 AC 524.

[39] HL Debs, vol 621, col WA120 (8 February 2001), per Baroness Hayman, Minister of State.

[40] *Crotty v An Taoiseach* [1987] IR 713.

[41] See text at n 24 above.

1986 *was* within the scope of the 'licence' granted by the first sentence of Article 29.4.3 of the Constitution: 'This is a licence to join a living dynamic Community of the kind described by the defendants'.[42] As regards parts of the SEA not covered by the 1986 Act, Mr Crotty had no standing to challenge their constitutionality because he had not demonstrated that he had suffered any special injury or infringement of his rights. On that latter point the High Court relied on the Supreme Court's views in *Cahill v Sutton*,[43] where it denied standing to a woman who was bringing a disinterested challenge to the statutory three-year limitation period for personal injury actions.[44] The High Court made no specific ruling on Mr Crotty's standing to challenge Title III of the SEA, dealing with European Political Cooperation, saying merely that they had no function in that area.

Mr Crotty, persistent as ever, immediately sought a ruling from the Supreme Court that the High Court's order discharging the injunction should be stayed. This was granted and within a week the Supreme Court was hearing argument on the substantive issues. In April 1987 it issued both a single judgment on the constitutionality of the 1986 Act (as required by Article 34.4.5 of the Constitution) and a set of separate judgments dealing with other matters.[45] The Court held that Mr Crotty had standing to challenge the 1986 Act and that the High Court was correct to hold that the Act was constitutional: 'It is the opinion of the Court that the first sentence of Article 29.4.3 of the Constitution must be construed as an authorisation given to the State not only to join the Communities as they stood in 1973, but also to join in amendments of the Treaties so long as such amendments do not alter the essential scope or objectives of the Communities.'[46] More particularly, the Court thought that, just because more issues would now be dealt with by the European Council under the qualified majority voting scheme, 'it does not follow that all other decisions of the Council which now require unanimity could, without a further amendment of the Constitution, be changed to decisions requiring less than unanimity'.[47] But the Supreme Court then split, three to two, in favour of holding that the part of the SEA which required Ireland to adopt its foreign policy within the European Political Cooperation Framework could not be ratified within the terms of the Constitution because it would mean Ireland conceding part of its sovereignty regarding its relations with other states. A constitutional amendment was required to authorise such a concession, and that in turn would require a referendum. The majority comprised Walsh, Henchy and Hederman JJ, while the minority consisted of Finlay CJ and Griffin J.[48]

Walsh J stressed how the Constitution, in Article 29.4.1,[49] vests in the government the executive power of the State in its external relations but he added that it was not within the government's competence, or even that of the Oireachtas, 'to transfer their powers to other bodies unless expressly empowered so to do by the Constitution'. In answer to the government's argument that the Courts are not empowered to interfere with the government's treaty-making powers unless the treaties are translated into domestic legislation, Walsh J fell back on the rather circular reasoning that '[t]o the judicial organ of

[42] [1987] IR 713, 759 (per Barrington J). Barrington J was delivering the judgment of the Court, which included Hamilton P and Carroll J.

[43] [1980] IR 269 (Higgins CJ, Henchy, Griffin, Kenny and Parke JJ).

[44] Statute of Limitations 1957, s 11(2)(b).

[45] [1987] IR 713; Temple Lang (1987). Of course, because of the single judgment rule (see Chap 6 above, 119-21), we do not know if the Supreme Court's decision on constitutionality was unanimous.

[46] Ibid, 767; Temple Lang (1987). [47] Ibid, 770.

[48] Garrett Fitzgerald, Taoiseach at the time, has said that the government was surprised at the decision: Fitzgerald (1991) 600.

[49] 'The executive power of the State in or in connection with its external relations shall in accordance with Article 28 of this Constitution be exercised by or on the authority of the Government.'

government alone is given the power conclusively to decide if there has been a breach of constitutional restraints'.[50] He also relied on the notion of sovereignty: 'the essential nature of sovereignty is the right to say yes or to say no. In the present Treaty that right is to be materially qualified'.[51] For good measure he added:

> The freedom to formulate foreign policy is just as much a mark of sovereignty as the freedom to form economic policy and the freedom to legislate. The latter two have now been curtailed by the consent of the people to the amendment of the Constitution which is contained within Article 29.4.3 of the Constitution. If it is now desired to qualify, curtail or inhibit the existing sovereign power to formulate and to pursue such foreign policies as from time to time to the Government may seem proper, it is not within the power of the Government to do so.[52]

Henchy J's position was similar to that of Walsh J but he referred as well to the little-cited Article 1 of the 1937 Constitution, whereby the Irish nation 'affirms its inalienable, indefeasible, and sovereign right … to determine its relations with other nations'. More could probably have been made of that provision in the majority's judgments for it appears to categorically rule out any transfer of responsibility for foreign relations away from 'the nation', which in this context presumably means 'the people'. Hederman J delivered a very short judgment in which he agreed with both Walsh and Henchy JJ. These three judges were prepared to uphold Mr Crotty's claim that ratification of the SEA would be unconstitutional even though he was not able show that any of his own rights would be violated by such ratification. The decision is therefore a welcome example of an ordinary person being able to remind the State of its obligations to adhere to the Constitution.

The minority's position, as put by Finlay CJ, was that the provisions in the SEA calling for co-operation in the formation of foreign policy, and consultations and discussions leading thereto, were not inconsistent with the Constitution. He relied upon the Supreme Court's decision in *Boland v An Taoiseach*,[53] concerning the Sunningdale Agreement reached in relation to the governance of Northern Ireland.[54] There both FitzGerald CJ and Budd J had stressed that there were certain matters of State policy which were non-justiciable by the courts. Griffin J also relied on *Boland* but he emphasised as well that Title III of the SEA, dealing with European Political Cooperation, used language which 'would appear to have been chosen with extreme care to ensure that the obligations of the parties under the treaty would permit the utmost freedom of action to each of the parties in the sphere of foreign policy, and is in stark contrast to that used in Title II'.[55] Like Finlay CJ, he did not think Mr Crotty could successfully challenge Title III of the SEA because he was unable to show that it amounted to an actual or threatened breach of any of his constitutional rights. Strangely, that was a point to which none of the judgments in the majority makes reference, which subsequently led Keane CJ, writing extra-judicially many years later, to suggest that the majority judgments were therefore delivered *per incuriam*.[56]

Taken in the round, the decision of the majority of the Supreme Court in *Crotty* was a bold incursion by the judges into Irish political affairs. Gerard Hogan observed that the decision 'will probably rank as one of the most extraordinary ever delivered by the Court … a remarkable display of judicial activism'.[57] It effectively meant that any future attempt on the part of the government to extend the country's commitment to European integration

[50] [1987] IR 713, 778. [51] Ibid, 781.

[52] Ibid, 783. Sherlock believes that the Court as a whole failed properly to address what is meant by sovereignty: Sherlock (1987) 108.

[53] [1974] IR 338. [54] See also Chap 7 above, 144-6. [55] [1987] IR 713, 790.

[56] Keane (2014). Keane clearly considers the decision of the majority on Part III of the SEA to be wrong.

[57] Hogan (1987c) 55. Many of the points in this piece are expanded upon in Hogan and Whelan (1995) 25–49.

would first require a vote in a referendum approving a change to the Irish Constitution. As the judgment of the Court put it:

> To hold that the first sentence of Article 29, section 4, sub-section 3 does not authorise any form of amendment to the Treaties after 1973 without a further amendment of the Constitution would be too narrow a construction; to construe it as an open-ended authority to agree, without further amendment of the Constitution, to any amendment of the Treaties would be too broad.[58]

Of course the Irish government had to react to the decision and the only way of doing so was to seek an amendment to the Constitution through a referendum. No doubt believing that the people probably did not fully appreciate the subtleties of the majority's reasoning in *Crotty*, the government chose to ask them to approve the insertion of an additional sentence into Article 29.4.3, between the first and second sentences which had been approved in the referendum of 1972. The additional sentence simply read: 'The State may ratify the Single European Act (signed on behalf of the Member States of the Communities at Luxembourg on the 17th day of February 1986 and at The Hague on the 29th day of February 1986).'[59] In May 1987 the people voted yes to this by 70 per cent to 30 per cent. The turnout was just 44 per cent, perhaps an indicator of the obscurity of the issue in many people's minds (in 1972 the turnout had been 71 per cent).

While this vote put to bed the immediate issue, it did not resolve the bigger questions arising out of the breadth of the majority's reasoning in *Crotty*. The first of those was, when are laws enacted, acts done or measures adopted 'necessitated by the obligations of membership of the Communities' and therefore immune from constitutional challenge because of the wording of Article 29.4.3? In truth none of the judgments in the Supreme Court provides a clear answer to that question, although they imply that 'necessitated' means legally as opposed to politically required.[60] The second important question was when, if ever, should the Supreme Court (and lower courts) refuse to get involved in policy decisions made by the government? It is ironic that the SEA itself precludes the Court of Justice in Luxembourg from reviewing decisions taken under the European Political Cooperation framework[61] yet the Irish Supreme Court felt it had the power to require that the involvement of Ireland in such decisions should be first approved by the people of Ireland. There is much in Hogan's point that the reasoning of the majority in *Crotty* 'appears to cast doubt on the Government's general treaty-making powers rather than emphasising the unique features of the Single European Act'.[62]

Maastricht and the *Meagher* and *Mallon* Cases

On 18 June 1992 a further referendum in Ireland supported the ratifying of the Treaty on European Union (the TEU, or Maastricht Treaty) by 69 per cent to 31 per cent of the votes cast. This led to the enactment of the Eleventh Amendment to the Constitution Act 1992, which followed the Third and Tenth Amendments by inserting Article 29.4.4 saying that: 'The State may ratify the Treaty on European Union signed at Maastricht on the 7th day of February, 1992, and may become a member of that Union'. What had formerly been the third sentence of Article 29.4.3, already quoted,[63] was repealed and in its place a new Article 29.4.5 was created to take account of the new European Union and, for the avoidance of

[58] [1987] IR 713, 767. [59] See the Tenth Amendment to the Constitution Act 1987.
[60] See, generally, Whelan (1992). [61] Art 31. [62] Hogan (1987c) 69.
[63] See above on this page.

doubt, to ensure that priority could also be given to laws, acts or measures of 'bodies competent under the Treaties establishing the Communities'.

These constitutional amendments put the ratification of the TEU more or less beyond challenge in the Irish courts. France, too, obtained the consent of the people in a referendum, as did Denmark, although there the matter had to be put to a vote for a second time because the first referendum resulted in a narrow 'No' majority. It was in Germany that the major legal battle took place, despite the ground for acceptance of the Treaty having been laid in advance through amendments made to the country's Constitution, the *Grundgesetz*, by the two houses of parliament, the *Bundestag* and the *Bundesrat*. The new Article 23, for example, expressly stated that:

> The Federal Republic of Germany participates in the fulfilment of a united Europe through the development of a European Union that is obligated to respect democratic, legal, state, social, and federal principles as well as the principle of subsidiarity, and to secure basic rights protection essentially similar to those of this Grundgesetz. The Federation may with approval of the Bundesrat transfer sovereign rights through a statute.

The reason why this and other constitutional amendments were not enough to immunise the TEU from further challenge in Germany's courts is that Article 79(3) of the Grundgesetz says that amendments cannot be made to the Constitution if, for example, they affect the core principles laid down in Articles 1 and 20, one of which is that Germany is 'a democratic and social federal state'. In Ireland there is no such limiting provision: Article 46(1) of the 1937 Constitution says that *any* provision of the Constitution may be amended.

Germany's Federal Constitutional Court, the *Bundesverfassungsgericht*, eventually pronounced on the constitutionality of ratification of the TEU in the *Brunner* case.[64] It ruled that ratification of the Treaty still left the *Bundestag* with sufficient control over law-making to maintain the country's status as 'a democratic and social federal state'. It did not see the proposed European Union as a state-like entity, not least because it could take action only in a limited number of fields and had to comply with the doctrines of subsidiarity and proportionality. Moreover the Court said that it retained the right to review the legal instruments produced by European institutions to assess whether they were within the powers of those institutions to make. Overall the *Bundesverfassungsgericht* has carved out for itself a more prominent role in determining the nature of the nation's relationship with the EU than the Irish Supreme Court has been able to do.

The latter's first opportunity to express its views in this field arose in 1993. The case in question focused on the apparent contradiction between, on the one hand, Article 15.2 of the Constitution, which conferred sole and exclusive law-making power on the Oireachtas, and Article 29.4.5, which said that '[n]o provision of this Constitution invalidates laws enacted, acts done or measures adopted by the State which are necessitated by the obligations of membership of the European Union or of the Communities'. It had been obvious for more than 20 years that there was a *prima facie* inconsistency between these two provisions, but during all of that time it had not been addressed by any court, let alone the Supreme Court. In *Meagher v Minister for Agriculture*,[65] the applicant was a farmer who was objecting to the fact that his premises had been searched by police officers and officials from the Department of Agriculture, that some veterinary medical products had been

[64] *Brunner v The European Union Treaty* [1994] 1 CMLR 57; Crossland (1994); Wieland (1994); Makowski (1995).

[65] [1994] 1 IR 329. See generally Whelan (1993); Hogan (1994b); Hogan (1994c); Hogan and Whelan (1995) 51–67.

seized during that search and that he was subsequently charged with breaching regulations governing the possession of proscribed veterinary medicines.[66] The regulations had been issued by the Minister for Agriculture and Food in 1988 and 1990 in implementation of a European Council Directive of 1985[67] and it was common ground between the parties that the regulations amended the pre-existing law in Ireland.

In the High Court, Johnson J held that section 3(2) of the European Communities Act 1972, to the extent that it allowed a Minister, by regulation, to repeal, amend or apply a law other than that laid down in the 1972 Act itself, was unconstitutional, as was section 4 of the same Act to the extent that it allowed regulations to have statutory effect unless nullified by 'the Houses of the Oireachtas'. Obviously this judgment set alarm bells ringing when it was delivered on 1 April 1993, for it seemed to strike at the very heart of Ireland's membership of the European Communities. The judge was clearly swayed by the persuasive advocacy of Gerard Hogan, who acted for the applicant. On appeal, however, the Supreme Court held unanimously that the inconsistency between the 1972 Act and the 1937 Constitution was more apparent than real: there was in fact nothing unconstitutional about the way Ireland was giving effect to EC Directives and therefore no changes needed to be made to correct any anomalies in the Irish legal system in this regard.

As in *Crotty*, the Supreme Court delivered two sets of judgments. The first was the single opinion of the Court delivered under Article 34.4.5 of the Constitution. This confirmed that the number of laws, acts and measures of the EC which had to be incorporated into Irish law was such that in some instances resort to the regulation-making power provided by section 3(2) of the 1972 Act was 'necessitated by the obligations of membership of the Communities' and therefore any challenge to the constitutionality of the regulations so made was precluded by Article 29.4.3 of the Constitution.[68] The second set of judgments (by Blayney and Denham JJ, with both of which Finlay CJ, O'Flaherty and Egan JJ all agreed) dealt with whether the 1988 and 1990 regulations were valid or not: this was not an issue requiring a single judgment of the Supreme Court because Article 34.4.5 applies only to decisions of the Supreme Court 'on a question as to the validity of a law having regard to the provisions of this Constitution' and 'a law' means, according to Article 15.2.1, a law made by the Oireachtas. The arguments put forward by Gerard Hogan for the invalidity of the regulations were that they made provision for searches and imposed a two-year limitation period for the prosecution of offences created by the regulations (in place of the usual six months).[69] Neither Blayney J nor Denham J had much difficulty in demonstrating that these provisions were clearly permissible within the terms of the relevant Directive. They pointed in particular to section 3(2) of the 1972 Act, which provides:

> Regulations under this section may contain such incidental, supplementary and consequential provisions as appear to the Minister making the regulations to be necessary for the purposes of the regulations (including provisions repealing, amending or applying, with or without modification, other law [*sic*], exclusive of this Act).

[66] The European Communities (Control of Oestrogenic, Androgenic, Gestagenic and Thyrostatic Substances) Regulations 1988 and the European Communities (Control of Veterinary Medicinal Products and their Residues) Regulations 1990. There appeared to be a suspicion that certain prohibited substances (so-called 'angel dust') were being sprinkled over animal food.

[67] Council Directive 85/358/EEC, and also Council Directive 86/469/EEC. Other Directives were involved as well: see [1994] 1 IR 329, 361 (per Denham J).

[68] Some years prior to *Meagher* Curtin observed that if directives were required to be transposed by legislation passed by the Oireachtas Ireland would frequently fail to implement them by the stipulated deadline: Curtin (1989). Travers claims that Ireland's slowness in implementing Council Directive 79/7/EEC on equal treatment in the context of social welfare may have cost the State IR£265 million in 'fines': Travers (1998) 166.

[69] This latter was achieved through an amendment to s 10(4) of the Petty Sessions (Ireland) Act 1851.

Denham J observed that the Directive left no choice to the national authority as to matters of principle or policy: had it done so 'then the "choice" of the Minister would require legislation by the Oireachtas. But ... where there is in fact no choice on a policy or principle it is a matter appropriate for delegated legislation'.[70] She actually went so far as to say that if the Oireachtas were to debate the policies and principles determined by a directive it would be 'a sterile debate'.[71] Blayney J made the same point but from a different angle: merely because Article 189 of the Treaty of Rome leaves to the State the choice of the form and methods of implementing a directive, this does not mean that what the State chooses to do by way of implementation is not 'necessitated by the State's obligations of membership'.[72]

Predictably, given his own role in the litigation, Gerard Hogan was subsequently very critical of the Supreme Court's decision in *Meagher*. He considered the decision to be at odds with that in *Crotty* in that it extended what was considered to be 'necessitated' by the obligations of EC membership. But to say that the difference of approach is 'quite marked',[73] in view of how vague the Supreme Court was on the issue in *Crotty*, is surely an exaggeration. He also goes too far when he suggests that Blayney J's characterisation of national implementing measures 'effectively collapses the distinction between a directive and a regulation' for it ignores the reality that, unlike EC Regulations, EC Directives are still not in force in any Member State until some steps have been taken to implement them at the national level. A stronger aspect of Hogan's critique is that the Supreme Court in general, and Denham J in particular, gave no guidance as to when a matter is one of policy or not. He repeats his view that opting for a two-year limitation period for prosecutions was clearly a policy choice, and not one dictated by any directive. To conclude, however, that this was a glaring example of democratic deficit is over-egging the pudding. With respect, there is more to be said for the line taken by Noel Travers in his comments on *Meagher*.[74] While he argues for greater scrutiny of ministerial regulations by committees of the Oireachtas,[75] and laments the absence of any general guidance on when to use primary or secondary legislation to implement directives, he approves of the Supreme Court's realistic approach to implementation:

> ... the Court's non-literal approach to 'necessity', as well as its willingness flexibly to interpret that constitutional notion in the light of the overriding Community objective that directives be implemented on time rather than exclusively by reference to the traditional doctrine of the separation of powers, is correct.[76]

Whatever the verdict on the Supreme Court's handling of *Meagher* there was a surprisingly early opportunity for the Supreme Court to look again at the ministerial regulations in question. This arose in *Mallon v Minister for Agriculture, Food and Forestry*,[77] where the applicant had been charged with offences similar to those alleged against Mr Meagher. He relied on two main arguments: that it was unconstitutional for the regulations to permit a sentence of up to two years in prison for an offence that could be tried summarily, and that Ireland had not properly transposed the relevant Directive into domestic law because

[70] [1994] 1 IR 329, 365–6.
[71] Ibid, 367. She added: 'That is not a role envisaged for the Oireachtas in the Constitution.'
[72] Ibid, 360. [73] Hogan (1994b) 194.
[74] Travers (1994) and (1998). At the time of the 1998 article Mr Travers was the Legal Secretary in the Chambers of Advocate General Fennelly at the Court of Justice in Luxembourg. Fennelly served in that capacity from 1995 to 2000 and then as a judge of the Supreme Court of Ireland from 2000 to 2014.
[75] Travers (1998) 177. He also calls (at 166) for greater use to be made of the preliminary reference procedure, originally in Art 177 of the Rome Treaty. On this see Hogan et al (2018) 621 and also below, 266.
[76] Ibid, 176. [77] [1996] 1 IR 517.

the Minister's regulations did not include provisions dealing with the Ministry's system for testing samples taken from premises. Costello J agreed that the two-year maximum prison sentence was unconstitutional but ruled that the offending words could be severed from the regulation in question without requiring the prosecution of the plaintiff to be terminated. He also ruled that the exclusion of the testing procedures from the regulations did not invalidate them. On appeal the Supreme Court agreed that the two-year maximum prison sentence was unconstitutional but did not think that the offending words could be severed, so the prosecution would have to be halted. It also agreed with Costello J that the omission of the testing procedures from the regulations did not invalidate them: the regulations had to be considered as valid to the extent that they complied with the Directives, provided that they did not contain any material which went beyond what was required by the policies and principles of the Directives. It was open to Ireland to provide for the testing procedures through administrative measures short of regulations.

No doubt Mr Meagher gave a wry smile when he learned of the outcome in *Mallon*. But Mr Mallon was very lucky to escape prosecution: Blayney and Denham JJ, dissenting, would have allowed the regulations to stand in so far as they imposed a fine of up to £1,000, and Barron J, who otherwise agreed with Hamilton CJ, would have substituted a maximum sentence of one year's imprisonment in place of two years if only a submission to that effect had been made. All in all the case illustrates the uncertainty which still attends the Supreme Court's approach to the severability of unconstitutional wording from the rest of the legislation in question. It had looked at that issue in previous cases[78] but the *Mallon* case did little to clarify exactly when some wording would be severable and when it would not.

The *Maher* Case

In 2001 the Supreme Court revisited the way in which Ireland implements what had by then become 'EU law'. This was in *Maher v Minister for Agriculture and Rural Development*,[79] the context being the operation of the EU's milk quota system. At issue was the way in which the Minister of Agriculture and Rural Development had implemented Council Regulation (EC) No 1256/1999 through the European Communities (Milk Quota) Regulations 2000. The three applicants, who were farmers from County Tipperary but not themselves milk producers, argued that Ireland's Regulations were not 'necessitated' by membership of the EU, that they provided for matters that ought to have been provided for by an Act of the Oireachtas, that they expressed policy choices going beyond what the Council Regulation required, and that the fact that the milk quota system forced the holder of lands with a milk quota in certain circumstances to sell the quota to the Minister at a fixed price was a form of compulsory acquisition of their property without adequate compensation. Both Carroll J in the High Court and each of the five judges in the Supreme Court rejected all four of these arguments.

The four Supreme Court judgments[80] extend to 110 pages in the law reports, with three of them deferring to Fennelly J with resepect to the characterisation of the EU's milk quota system (an acknowledgement of his great expertise in EU law).[81] The first of the applicants' four arguments was easily answered because the Council Regulation itself, in Article 7(1), expressly required Member States to make detailed rules concerning the transfer of quotas,

[78] eg *Maher v Attorney General* [1973] IR 140; *Desmond v Glackin (No 2)* [1993] 3 IR 67.

[79] [2001] 2 IR 139; Travers (2003).

[80] Murray J simply concurred with Denham J.

[81] Strangely, Keane CJ and Denham J do not refer at all to each other's judgments, and nor does Fennelly J refer to either of his colleagues' judgments.

although Article 8a(b) allowed States a discretion not to apply Article 7(1) provided they ensured that quotas were solely attributed to milk producers. The second and third arguments were disposed off together, with Keane CJ adopting Fennelly J's analysis in holding that in this case the Council Regulation effectively reduced the policy choices available to Member States to vanishing point and that therefore using a set of regulations rather than an Act of the Oireachtas to implement the Council Regulation was permissible; the Council Regulation was looked upon as if it were an enabling Act of the Oireachtas. Denham J, as she then was, summed up the position succinctly:

> ... if the principles and policies are to be found in the European regulations then it is open to the [Minister for Agriculture] to proceed by way of statutory instrument. If there are choices to be made within a scheme then these choices may not be policy decisions. The exercise of a choice governed fully by a structure established in a policy document (such as a European regulation) is not the determination of a policy.[82]

Denham J also took time to address the applicants' supplementary argument (also made by critics of Ireland's membership of the EU) that there was a democratic deficit in the way EU law was being made for Ireland. She said that any such deficit needed to be addressed prior to the making of Council Regulations. On the farmers' fourth argument, which meant treating a milk quota as a property right, none of the Supreme Court judges could see an analogy with any other well-established property right under the Irish Constitution and in any event the Court of Justice had already made it clear in an earlier case that the right to dispose of a market advantage for profit was not a right to property in the eyes of EC law.[83]

The tone of the judgments in the *Maher* case is again one of pragmatism.[84] On the one hand there was a tacit acceptance that ordinary Irish citizens expected their directly elected politicians to make laws for the country, but on the other there was a realisation that in this increasingly complex and inter-connected world, especially in the economic field, there were advantages in sub-contracting some policy-making functions to EU institutions even if this then limited the Irish government's options when it came to making detailed regulations in that area. There are bigger problems to be confronted about the democratic nature of decision-making in Brussels, but they are not best solved, even in the short term, by heaping ever greater legislative burdens on the law-making authorities in each Member State.

The Amsterdam, Nice and Lisbon Treaties

In a referendum on 22 May 1998 the Irish people voted by 62 per cent to 38 per cent to approve ratification of the Treaty of Amsterdam. This led to the enactment of the Eighteenth Amendment to the Constitution Act 1998, which inserted yet another provision expressly authorising ratification of the Treaty (the new, re-numbered, Article 29.4.5) and a further provision (the new, re-numbered, Article 29.4.6) allowing the State to exercise options or discretions provided by the Treaty and its Protocols, provided that any such exercise was given prior approval by both Houses of the Oireachtas.[85]

[82] [2001] 2 IR 139, 208. Denham J cited her own words from *Meagher v Minister for Agriculture* [1994] 1 IR 329, 366–7.

[83] *R v Ministry of Agriculture, ex parte Bostock* Case C-2/92, [1994] ECR I-955, 984.

[84] Doherty (2004), at 141, thinks the Supreme Court is 'edging towards a stricter approach to "necessitated", quietly changing the law without overtly departing from the previous judgments'.

[85] The former Arts 29.4.5 and 29.4.6 were re-numbered Arts 29.4.7 and 29.4.8. On the Treaty more generally see Fennelly (1998).

However on 7 June 2001, for the first time, the Irish electorate did *not* support the ratification of a treaty connected with European integration. This was the Treaty of Nice, rejected by 54 per cent to 46 per cent of the voters. The Treaty aimed to prepare the European Union for an influx of new Member States from central and Eastern Europe and in Ireland some factions saw this expansion as a threat to smaller States like Ireland which were already members of the Union. There was also a fear that the Treaty might compromise Irish neutrality because it foresaw a common defence policy for the EU. As Ireland was the only one of the then 15 Member States who submitted the ratification of the Treaty to a referendum, it greatly delayed its implementation. After securing some adjustments to the Treaty to set at rest the worries of the sceptics, the matter was again put to the people in a referendum in 2002. This time ratification was approved, by 63 per cent to 37 per cent and the Twenty-Sixth Amendment of the Constitution Act 2002 was enacted. This inserted three more sections into Article 29.4 (as Articles 29.4.7 to 29.4.9), with the former Articles 29.4.7 and 29.4.8 being re-numbered as Articles 29.4.10 and 29.4.11.

A similar change of heart occurred in relation to the Treaty of Lisbon, which was agreed by Member States in 2007.[86] This was the successor to an earlier initiative aimed at agreeing a Treaty establishing a Constitution for Europe, which was abandoned in 2005 after voters in referenda in both France and the Netherlands rejected the idea. The Treaty of Lisbon aimed merely to 'reform' rather to re-constitute the European Union, the goal being to have all Member States ratify it before the end of 2008. Once again the process was delayed thanks to Ireland's failure to get the Treaty approved in time by its people. Approval was initially denied in a referendum on 12 June 2008 (by 53 per cent to 47 per cent) but was then granted in a follow-up referendum on 2 October 2009 (by 67 per cent to 33 per cent). A challenge to the constitutionality of the second referendum was raised by a Mr Rea, but he lost in both the High Court and the Supreme Court because he could not point to any legal irregularities in the holding of the referendum—his objections were political only.[87] The Supreme Court was satisfied that its own role in relation to the interpretation of the Irish Constitution would not be adversely affected by the Treaty. The second referendum led to the Twenty-eighth Amendment of the Constitution (Treaty of Lisbon) Act 2009, which repealed Articles 29.4.4 to 29.4.11 and replaced them with new Articles 29.4.4 to 29.4.9. Article 29.4.9 explicitly stated that Ireland shall not agree to be part of a common European defence pursuant to Article 42 of the TEU.

Pringle and the European Stability Mechanism

The most recent controversy surrounding the European integration project occurred in 2012. A year earlier, by a Council Decision, the EU had decided to set up a 'European Stability Mechanism' (ESM) to help ensure economic stability within the 17 eurozone countries, Ireland having adopted the euro as its currency on 1 January 2002. There was to be an amendment to Article 136 of the Treaty on the Functioning of the European Union (TFEU), which already required the European Council to 'adopt measures specific to those Member States whose currency is the euro: (a) to strengthen the coordination and surveillance of their budgetary discipline; (b) to set out economic policy guidelines for them, while ensuring that they are compatible with those adopted for the whole of the Union and

[86] Denham and Burke (2009).

[87] *Rea v Ireland* [2016] IESC 19 (Denham CJ, O'Donnell and MacMenamin JJ); that the appeal was decided six-and-a-half years after Ryan J's High Court ruling illustrates well the delays affecting the Supreme Court's work around this time. For more on this issue see Chap 4 above, 54-6.

are kept under surveillance'. The amendment made by the Council Decision added a paragraph to Article 136 saying, in part, that '[t]he Member States whose currency is the euro may establish a stability mechanism to be activated if indispensable to safeguard the stability of the euro area as a whole'. To reflect this change the Oireachtas passed the European Communities (Amendment) Act 2012 in order to insert a reference to the Council Decision in the definition of 'treaties governing the European Union' in section 1 of the European Communities Act 1972. Then, in exercise of the power conferred by the Council Decision, the eurozone countries duly entered into the ESM Treaty on 2 February 2012, thereby establishing an international financial institution to be known as the ESM. The Oireachtas duly enacted the European Stability Mechanism Act 2012 to give effect to Ireland's commitments under the ESM Treaty. Importantly, that Treaty was one agreed outside of the EU legal order.

Exactly a month later 25 of the 28 Member States of the EU signed the separate Treaty on Stability, Coordination and Governance in the Economic and Monetary Union (the Fiscal Stability Treaty or the Fiscal Compact), which was to enter into force after 12 eurozone countries had ratified it.[88] The purpose of this agreement was to complement the ESM Treaty by requiring eurozone countries (and other EU countries which agreed with the fiscal provisions in the Treaty) to establish a self-correcting mechanism, guided by an independent advisory council, to guarantee that their national budget would be in balance or surplus within the Treaty's definition.[89] On 31 May 2012 the people of Ireland voted by 60 per cent to 40 per cent to allow ratification of the Fiscal Stability Treaty, thereby approving the Thirtieth Amendment of the Constitution (Treaty on Stability, Coordination and Governance in the Economic and Monetary Union) Act 2012, which inserted a new Article 29.4.10 into the Constitution.[90]

In *Pringle v Government of Ireland*[91] a challenge was raised against the ESM Treaty by Thomas Pringle, a left-wing independent member of the Dáil from Donegal. Mr Pringle wanted the courts to grant an interlocutory injunction restraining Ireland's ratification of the ESM Treaty until the proceedings he had brought were concluded. He argued that the ESM Treaty required such a degree of transfer of sovereignty on Ireland's part as to make ratification incompatible without an amendment to the Constitution, citing *Crotty v An Taoiseach*.[92] In his view, if the State was prepared to hold a referendum on the Fiscal Stability Treaty it ought also to hold one on the ESM Treaty because the latter involved a permanent transfer of sovereignty. It created a binding policy which was not just a funding mechanism or a bank but a promise to provide support to States if this was necessary to protect the euro area as a whole. Moreover the Oireachtas had committed to paying more than €11 billion into the fund and if it did not meet these payments it would lose its voting rights within the ESM, which would be a loss of sovereignty at a time of great peril for the State (the proceedings were started in 2012, when Ireland was still in the midst of a serious financial crisis brought on by the decision to bail out several failing banks). Mr Pringle also wanted the Irish courts to ask the Court of Justice in Luxembourg for a ruling on whether the 2011 Council Decision to create the ESM was compatible with the EU's other Treaties.[93]

[88] Croatia, the Czech Republic and the UK did not sign the Treaty.

[89] A 'balanced budget' is defined as a general budget with a deficit of no more than 3 per cent of the country's GDP and a structural deficit of between 0.5 per cent and 1 per cent of GDP depending on the country's existing debt-to-GDP ratio.

[90] The history of Art 29.4 is also traced in Barrett (2012).

[91] [2012] IESC 47, [2013] 3 IR 1 (Denham CJ, Murray, Hardiman, Fennelly, O'Donnell, McKechnie and Clarke JJ). The judgments run to 173 pages.

[92] [1987] IR 713.

[93] Council Decision 2011/199/EU.

The Supreme Court, sitting as a bench of seven judges and affirming Laffoy J in the High Court,[94] held against the plaintiff on the constitutional issues but did agree to refer the validity of the Council Decision to the Court of Justice. To avoid any further delay in implementing the ESM the Supreme Court announced its decision on 31 July 2012, thereby allowing the government and the Oireachtas to ratify the ESM Treaty the very next day, but it did not issue its reasons until 19 October 2012. At the core of those reasons lay the Court's interpretation of its decision in *Crotty v An Taoiseach* more than a quarter of a century earlier.[95] Both Mr Pringle and the government relied on the majority's judgments in that case, by Walsh, Henchy and Hederman JJ, a sure sign that those judgments could have been clearer. It is indeed surprising that *Crotty* survived such intense scrutiny without being overruled. In essence six of the seven judges in *Pringle* were able to distinguish the case because there the Single European Act was effectively restricting the way in which the government could exercise its constitutional powers to conduct the external relations of the State, powers which had been assigned by the Constitution to the government for the common good of the people of Ireland. Any decision to relinquish the powers of an organ of State must be taken by the people. Here, in *Pringle*, '[n]o such fundamental decision arises in relation to the ESM Treaty'.[96] Likewise, while the ESM Treaty requires Ireland to contribute to the ESM fund and empowers it to apply for financial assistance from the fund, '[n]either of the above functions impinges upon the economic or monetary sovereignty of the State'.[97] Furthermore, 'the decisions from which the State may be excluded or vote against without impact on the result … are decisions concerning the implementation of the policy, and are not decisions that (i) determine policy, (ii) create a mechanism of policy determination, or (iii) increase the State's specified maximum financial contribution'.[98] Denham CJ concluded by showing that whether one uses the version of the *Crotty* test favoured by Walsh J, by Henchy J or by Hederman J, under none of them does the ESM Treaty amount to a transfer of sovereignty which is incompatible with the Constitution.[99] Finally, applying the *Campus Oil* test,[100] the Supreme Court found that the balance of convenience weighed heavily against the granting of an interlocutory injunction, given the expedition with which both the Irish courts and the Court of Justice were dealing with his claims.

O'Connell J was quite satisfied that the plaintiff's arguments 'involve a clear misunderstanding and misinterpretation of *Crotty*, but perhaps more importantly, of the Constitution'.[101] He too distinguished *Crotty*, on the basis that:

> The ESM does not concern Ireland's foreign policy as a whole. Instead it relates solely to a decision by Ireland to invest, alongside other Member States, in an institution which may make those funds available in accordance with the terms and criteria established by the Treaty, to contracting states, including Ireland. The decision to participate in the ESM was in my view an exercise in sovereignty rather than an alienation of it, and was taken by the organ of Government to which such decisions are consigned by the Constitution.[102]

O'Donnell J also explained why it was wrong to reduce the *Crotty* test, as may be implied from Walsh J's judgment in that case, to the question of whether Ireland had deprived itself of the right to say 'yes' or 'no' to some foreign relations issue.[103] McKechnie J also thought that *Crotty* was a very different case from *Pringle*: 'the fundamental difference between both is the fact that the ESM Treaty is essentially policy implementing and not policy making. Therefore, it cannot be said that there is any fundamental transfer of sovereign power to the

[94] [2012] IEHC 296. [95] See 252-5 above. [96] [2013] 3 IR 1, para 98 (Denham CJ).
[97] Ibid, para 103. [98] Ibid, para 105. [99] Ibid, para 109. [100] See 249-51 above.
[101] [2013] 3 IR 1, para 306. [102] Ibid, para 20. [103] Ibid, paras 3–9.

institution or to the other subscribing states'.[104] Likewise Clarke J said that the ESM Treaty 'does not involve a transference of the power to make policy into the future, in any material way, to other countries or institutions … [and it] does not involve a permanent commitment to a set of policies which is so far reaching as to amount to an effective transference of sovereignty'.[105]

Hardiman J, however, dissented from his fellow judges. His judgment is a good example of his conservative, traditionalist and almost nationalistic approach to his judicial role. For him there most certainly was a transfer of sovereignty involved in ratification of the ESM Treaty, and in three respects.[106] First, 'by requiring a substantial sum of Irish public money to be transferred to a new financial institution, outside both Irish and European Union control'.[107] Second, by requiring Ireland to submit to decisions concerning expenditure of the ESM fund and to exercise its own powers in the way laid down by the Treaty. Third, by requiring Ireland to enter into commitments without ensuring the democratic accountability of the government to the Irish people. In short, Hardiman J's view was that if an agreement with other States obliged the Irish government to exercise Ireland's sovereign power (or not) in a particular way this was inconsistent with the Constitution because it shifted the point of reference from the common good of the Irish people to the interests of other nations.[108]

Just a few weeks after the Supreme Court's decision in *Pringle* the Court of Justice issued its judgment on the preliminary reference made to it by that court earlier in the year. Sitting as a plenary court of 27 judges (a very unusual event[109]), and after considering interventions from no fewer than 11 other EU Member States and (for the first time ever) the European Council itself, the Court of Justice ruled in an expedited procedure[110] that the Council Decision of 2011 did validly amend Article 136 of the TFEU because it did not violate any other articles in the TFEU or the TEU.[111] More particularly, the amendment could be made by the 'simplified revision procedure' provided for by Article 48(6) of the TEU and did not require the more onerous 'ordinary revision procedure' provided for by Article 48(4).[112] Only the latter required the proposed amendment to be ratified by each Member State in accordance with its own constitutional requirements before it could come into force. As de Witte and Beukers point out in their exhaustive analysis of the decision, it was the first judgment from the Luxembourg court dealing with the financial consequences of the debt crisis within Europe[113] and it confirms that even when Member States enter into agreements outside of the context of the EU they must do so in a way which complies with EU law. The authors also allude to the fact that, because of the smallness of its financial contribution to the ESM, a failure by Ireland to ratify the ESM Treaty would not have prevented it from coming into force, a reality that also confronted the national supreme courts of Austria, Belgium and Estonia, which were each asked to adjudicate on the Treaty's compatibility with their own Constitutions.[114] The German Constitutional Court's view did, however, matter because as a contributor of more than 10 per cent of the financial contributions a failure by Germany to ratify the ESM Treaty would have stopped it in its tracks.

[104] Ibid, para 362. [105] Ibid, para 472. [106] Ibid, paras 285–90. [107] Ibid, para 286.

[108] Ibid, para 179.

[109] See Art 16 of the Statute of the Court of Justice of the EU. Between 2012 and 2016, for example, a plenary court was convened on only two occasions: *CJEU Annual Report 2016*, 93.

[110] See Art 105 of the Rules of Procedure of the Court of Justice of the EU.

[111] *Pringle v Government of Ireland* Case 370/12, [2013] 2 CMLR 2.

[112] See Forde and Leonard (2013) 233–4. [113] De Witte and Beukers (2013) 806.

[114] Ibid, 815–6.

Fortunately the German Constitutional Court held that domestic ratification of the ESM Treaty would not breach the German Constitution.[115]

Although he lost, Mr Pringle's application did at least give Ireland's top judges the opportunity to analyse fundamental questions about the nature of the country's Constitution and how it has been affected by the country's membership of the EU. The value of Mr Pringle's doggedness was recognised by the fact that at the end of it all the High Court of Ireland held that the exceptional circumstances of the case justified a departure from the basic rule on costs: Laffoy J ordered the State to pay his costs in full.[116]

No really comparable litigation occurred in the United Kingdom until the Supreme Court there was asked to adjudicate on whether the State's constitutional traditions required Parliament and not just government to trigger the process for exiting the EU under Article 50 of the TEU. For the first time ever, a bench of 11 judges heard the case and they decided by eight to three that only Parliament could trigger Article 50.[117] Due to the absence of a written Constitution and the centrality of the doctrine of parliamentary sovereignty in the United Kingdom, the courts there have been spared the agonies of deciding what does or does not fall within the law-making powers of the national Parliament as regards ratifying new EU treaties. In the European Union Act 2011, Parliament tried to restrict its own powers – by enacting provisions which provide that before the United Kingdom can ratify a treaty or decision amending the TFEU or the TEU, or approve of certain other EU decicions, there must first be a referendum on the matter.[118] But of course Parliament could agree to repeal those provisions if it so wished, thereby removing the need for a referendum in such situations. Once the European Union (Withdrawal) Act 2018 comes into effect, on 29 March 2019, there will of course be no need for the United Kingdom to worry about power seeping away to Brussels in any circumstances.

Other Encounters with EU Law

There have, naturally, been many other occasions on which the Irish Supreme Court has had to engage with EU law not at the grand constitutional level but on specific questions which have turned on the interpretation of EU-derived legislation or the application of some principle derived from the case law of the Court of Justice of the EU. Thus, in *Dunnes Stores Ltd v Mandate*[119] the Supreme Court rejected the plaintiff's claim for an injunction to stop a trade union from publishing information relating to a dispute between the plaintiff and its workforce. The plaintiff had relied on the European Communities (Misleading Advertising) Regulations 1988,[120] which transposed into Irish law the Council Directive 84/450/EEC on misleading advertising. But the Court held that the information which the trade union had published did not amount to an 'advertisement' for the purposes of the Regulations: it did not promote any goods or services. Likewise, in *Nathan v Bailey Gibson* the Supreme Court, overturning Murphy J in the High Court, unanimously applied the Court of Justice's *Marleasing* principle[121] when holding that when a woman is complaining about indirect sex discrimination in an employment context she does not have to prove that there was a causal connection between the disadvantage she suffered and her gender.[122]

[115] BVerfG, 2 BvR 1390/12 (decision of 12 September 2012), available in English on the website of the *Bundesverfassungsgericht*. See Wendel (2013).

[116] *Pringle v Government of Ireland* [2014] IEHC 174.

[117] *R (Miller) v Secretary of State for Exiting the EU* [2017] UKSC 5, [2018] AC 61.

[118] ss 2(1), 3(1) and 6(1). [119] [1996] 1 IR 55 (Hamilton CJ, Blayney and Denham JJ).

[120] SI 1998/134.

[121] *Marleasing SA v La Comercial Internacional de Alimentación SA*, Case 106/89, [1992] 1 CMLR 305. See too Hogan et all (2018) 613-4.

[122] [1996] ELR 14, discussed in Flynn (1997).

The Court of Justice's decision in the *Marleasing* case was to the effect that the courts in EU member states should interpret domestic legislation in the light of EU directives, even if those directives have not yet been implemented in the State in question. In *Minister for Justice and Equality v Ostrowksi* the Supreme Court clearly had regard to the same principle when upholding the validity of a European arrest warrant issued in Poland for the arrest of a person in Ireland who was suspected of possessing cannabis.[123] Again, in *Emerald Meats Ltd v Minister for Agriculture* the Supreme Court recognised for the first time that, in line with the Court of Justice's decision in the *Francovich* case,[124] Ireland could be held liable to pay damages to a victim of its failure to implement an EC Regulation, in this case one concerning the importing of frozen beef and veal.[125]

The Supreme Court has also made its fair share of references to the Court of Justice in Luxembourg for a preliminary ruling under what was originally Article 177 of the Treaty of Rome, later became Article 234 of the EC Treaty and is now Article 267 of the TFEU. Research has shown that between 1961 and 1995 the Supreme Court of Ireland made 14 references,[126] and Fennelly notes that between 1983 and 2005 there were 15.[127] Coincidentally the United Kingdom's Appellate Committee of the House of Lords made exactly the same number of references between 1961 and 1995.[128] By 2014 the average number of references made by all Irish courts or tribunals to the Court of Justice each year had fallen to ten while the UK average was just below 20.[129] Per head of population it can be seen that references are much more frequent from Ireland than they are from the United Kingdom, but there is no evidence that the Irish Supreme Court has in any way unduly exploited the reference procedure. As a percentage of the opportunities available to it (given its throughput of cases), the Supreme Court's reference rate must today be considerably less than that of the United Kingdom's Supreme Court. A recent example of a reference by the Irish Supreme Court is *M v Minister for Justice and Equality, Ireland*,[130] where in response to a request made in 2014 the Court of Justice ruled that when national legislation provides for two separate procedures, one after the other, for examining applications for refugee status and applications for subsidiary protection, the applicant for subsidiary protection does not have the right to be interviewed in relation to his or her claim for protection or the right to call or cross-examine witnesses when an interview does take place. The Supreme Court has since applied that ruling to the facts of the case, lamenting while doing so that this and other cases concerning migrants' rights are taking so long to resolve.[131]

Conclusion

In an interesting article published in 2011, Maria Cahill sought to explain what she described as 'the unusually supine approach of the Irish courts to European law', one which she contrasted with the approach demonstrated by constitutional courts in several other EU Member States, such as Germany, Italy and Spain, which 'assert the strength of the national constitutional legal order in the face of European law'.[132] She saw the Supreme Court's decision in *Maher* as quite significantly circumscribing the decision in *Meagher*, calling it an

[123] [2013] IESC 24, [2013] 4 IR 206 (Denham CJ, Murray, O'Donnell, McKechnie and MacMenamin JJ).

[124] *Francovich v Italy* Cases 6/90 and 9/90, [1993] 2 CMLR 66.

[125] [1997] 1 IR 1.

[126] Stone Sweet and Brunell (1997) 93. Two such references are those in the *SPUC* and *Bosphorus Airways* cases: see Chap 12 below, 281 and 291.

[127] Fennelly (2005) 59.

[128] Ibid, 94.

[129] Broberg and Fenger (2014), Figure 2.1.

[130] Case C-560/14, judgment of 9 February 2017.

[131] *M v Minister for Justice and Equality, Ireland* [2018] IESC 10, para 31 (per O'Donnell J). The applicant in this case had made his claim for protection on the last day of 2008. His case had previously been considered by the CJEU in an earlier preliminary ruling: C-277/11, judgment of 22 November 2012.

[132] Cahill (2011) 75.

'interpretive conversion—from the torpedo approach to the ripple approach'[133] and, relying for support on the views of Rossa Phelan,[134] she asked for a consistent interpretation of Article 29.4 of the Constitution which preserves the idea that EU law is to be respected because the Constitution has given it 'the force of law', not because EU law is in any sense anterior or superior to that Constitution. Sean O'Reilly, on the other hand, is of the view that Irish courts have not gone far enough in implementing EU law, particularly in the field of environmental issues. He objects, for instance, to the Supreme Court's decision in *Harding v Cork County Council*,[135] where he believes Kearns J wrongly prioritised the Irish approach to who has standing to bring judicial review proceedings: the judge correctly set out the extent of the interpretive obligation on Irish courts but then applied it 'in a manner not befitting its status as a fundamental duty imposed by Community law'.[136] O'Reilly also regrets that Irish courts do not submit more requests for preliminary rulings from the Luxembourg court.[137]

Such differences of opinion as to how faithfully EU law has been received, or transposed, into domestic law are not uncommon in EU Member States. There can still be little doubt that in Ireland generally, and in Irish courts in particular, including the Supreme Court, the applicability of EU law is now accepted as a 'given'. Ireland has benefited enormously, in economic and developmental terms, from its membership of the inter-governmental body and, paradoxically perhaps, its commitment to the EU 'project' has been strengthened by the prospect of Brexit, even if it is in Ireland's own best interests for the United Kingdom to strike a good deal with the other 27 EU States because the United Kingdom is far and away Ireland's leading trading partner. In 2016 the European Commission ruled that Ireland had improperly provided State aid, in the form of tax exemptions amounting to €13 billion, to the US company Apple Inc. While objecting strongly to the ruling, fearing that it might discourage other large companies from investing in Ireland in the future, the Irish government eventually burnished its EU credentials by promising to recoup the unpaid tax.[138] This is a good indication of how important EU membership is to the country and of what lengths it will go to in order to comply with EU law. We must remember as well that, in areas which are covered by European law, Ireland must now also abide by the requirements of the EU's Charter of Fundamental Rights, which has had effect in Ireland since the Treaty of Lisbon came into force on 1 December 2009. While the impact of the Charter has not been significant until now, it has the potential to become so.[139] Meanwhile the influence of another branch of European law—that of the European Convention on Human Rights—continues to play a huge role and it is to that which the next chapter turns.

[133] Ibid, 91. [134] Phelan (1997). [135] [2008] 2 ILRM 251. [136] O'Reilly (2009) 348.

[137] Ibid, 353. He calculates that 11 references were made by *all* Irish courts in the seven-year period 2000–07. See too Fahey (2007).

[138] 'Ireland forced to collect €13bn in tax from Apple that it doesn't want' *The Guardian*, 5 December 2017. The European Commission had threatened to take Ireland to the Court of Justice if it did not comply with the ruling.

[139] Dickson (2017); De Búrca (2013).

12

The Supreme Court and the European Convention on Human Rights

This chapter explores attitudes displayed by the Irish Supreme Court to the European Convention on Human Rights (the ECHR) as well as views expressed by the European Court of Human Rights on judgments of the Irish Supreme Court and on points of Irish law which somehow escaped the Supreme Court's attention.[1] By and large it examines the relevant cases in chronological order, with a view to charting how the two courts have developed their thinking concerning the protection of human rights in Ireland. More particularly, the chapter considers whether any change in the Supreme Court's thinking is yet discernible in the wake of the 'incorporation' of most of the ECHR into domestic Irish law by the European Convention on Human Rights Act 2003.[2]

The ECHR has been part of the domestic law of Ireland only since the last day of 2003, when the European Convention on Human Rights Act 2003 came into force. Prior to then the Supreme Court could not directly apply the ECHR if doing so would contradict the country's Constitution, its legislation or its common law. It could not, for example, hold a piece of legislation to be constitutional but then rule that it was somehow invalid because it was in violation of the ECHR. The only way in which the Supreme Court could allow the ECHR to intrude into domestic law was by using it as an aid to interpretation when construing an ambiguous piece of legislation or an unclear rule of the common law, just as was the case in the United Kingdom before the Human Rights Act 1998 came fully into effect on 2 October 2000. However, when Ireland ratified the ECHR on 25 February 1953 it immediately accepted that disaffected litigants in Ireland, if they believed that Irish law was violating their Convention rights, could lodge an application against Ireland at the European Commission on Human Rights in Strasbourg. If the case application was declared admissible and upheld on its merits it could then be referred by the Commission, by the Irish government or by any other State involved in the case, to the European Court of Human Rights. By ratifying Protocol 9 to the ECHR, Ireland accepted (from 1 October 1994) that the applicant who brought the application to the Commission could also refer the case to the European Court.

On at least 50 occasions an application to Strasbourg challenging a Supreme Court decision has been held to be inadmissible; 25 of these occurred while the European Commission was still in existence (up to 1 November 1998) and 25 thereafter, when the European Court assumed the task of deciding admissibility questions.[3] On a further 12 occasions the Commission (five times) or the Court (seven times) has struck out an application after the Irish government arrived at a friendly settlement with the applicant, usually involving the payment of compensation.[4] To date the European Court has considered the merits of specific

[1] The most prominent of the latter cases (which never came before the Supreme Court) are *Airey* (1979), *Johnston* (1987) and *A, B and C* (2011), all of which are discussed below.

[2] On the pre-incorporation status of the ECHR, see De Londras and Kelly (2010) 24–38. See too Paris (2015) 98–106; Egan (2014); Egan and Forde (2014).

[3] See App 5 below, Pt A.

[4] See App 5 below, Pt B.

decisions of Ireland's Supreme Court on 21 occasions. In seven of these no violation of the ECHR was found[5] and in the remaining 14 cases at least one violation was found.[6]

Of the total of 83 cases taken to Strasbourg from Ireland in which Supreme Court decisions have been challenged, 49 were dealt with by the European Commission or Court *before* the ECHR Act came into force domestically; they resulted in 31 declarations of inadmissibility, six friendly settlements, four findings of no violation on the merits and eight findings of violations. Since the ECHR Act came into force 34 applications have been dealt with by Strasbourg; these have led to 19 declarations of inadmissibility, six friendly settlements, three findings of no violation on the merits and six findings of violations. If we categorise declarations of inadmissibility and findings of no violation on the merits as unsuccessful applications, and friendly settlements and findings of a violation on ther merits as successful applications, the 'success rate' prior to the ECHR Act coming into force was 29 per cent (14 out of 49) while after that date it was 35 per cent (12 out of 34). This seems perverse, as one might have expected the Supreme Court to have been more successful at identifying violations of the ECHR *after* the Act came into force. But too much should not be read into these numbers. It may well be, for example, that before the Act came into force recourse to Strasbourg seemed an attractive proposition to applicants because arguments could be made there which could not have been made in the Supreme Court; this might have led to several 'hopeless' cases being taken to Strasbourg, including some which were obviously out of time (applications have to be submitted within six months of the final decision in the domestic courts). In addition, some cases were declared inadmissible because of a failure to exhaust domestic remedies. The Commission and Court have said on many occasions that a declaratory action before the High Court of Ireland, with a possibility of an appeal to the Supreme Court, constitutes the most appropriate method under Irish law of seeking to vindicate constitutional rights and unless an applicant has first pursued that route he or she is unlikely to get satisfaction in Strasbourg.[7]

At present though, it is too early to conclude that the Supreme Court has fully grasped the import of Strasbourg's approach to human rights. While it had an excuse for turning a blind eye to the ECHR before the end of 2003, its record since then has not been unblemished. In *Dublin City Council v Fennell*, reasonably enough, it ruled that the 2003 Act did not have retroactive effect and so could not affect past events.[8] But too often the Court has not been willing to adopt the 'dynamic and evolutive' approach to the ECHR which the European Court itself adheres to. At times it has failed to notice the inadequacies of Irish law in a particular context. The ECHR Act 2003 has certainly not had as great an impact on domestic Irish law as the Human Rights Act 1998 has had on UK law,[9] and the willingness of the Irish Supreme Court—and perhaps of the lawyers who plead before it—to engage with Convention jurisprudence is not yet as advanced as it is in the UK Supreme Court.[10] Understandably the Irish Supreme Court remains more focused on the Constitution than on the Convention. This was predicted by James MacGuill, who suggested that the kind of issue which arose in *Fennell* (whether a housing authority could evict a tenant without considering his or her Convention rights) could be more easily addressed as a constitutional issue, treating the legislation in question as having a continuing

[5] See App 5 below, Pt C. [6] See App 5 below, Pt D.

[7] eg *McDonnell v Ireland* App No 15141/89, (1990) 64 DR 203; *O'Hara v Ireland* App No 23156/94 (31 August 1994); *O'Reilly v Ireland* App No 24196/94 (22 January 1996); *LF v Ireland* App No 28154/95 (2 July 1997). For an apparent exception to this approach see *O'Keeffe v Ireland* (2014) 59 EHRR 15, discussed at 298-301 below.

[8] [2005] 1 IR 604; Hogan (2006). [9] For a comparison see Farrell (2007).

[10] On the UK Supreme Court's handling of human rights issues see Dickson (2013). UK judges occasionally fall back on provisions in the Bill of Rights 1688, but that legislation was never extended to Ireland: Osborough (1998).

effect.[11] But there should be more to human rights in Ireland than constitutional rights. The latter obviously constitute a special category because if legislation breaches constitutional rights it can be declared invalid and in most situations compensation is payable to the victim of the breach,[12] but other rights may give rise to remedies too, such as a declaration of incompatibility and damages under the 2003 Act[13] or an injunction and damages in a civil cause of action available under legislation or the common law.

The 1960s and the *Lawless* Case

Ireland and the United Kingdom were two of the ten original signatories to the Treaty of London in 1949 which established the Council of Europe. The European Convention for the Protection of Human Rights and Fundamental Freedoms was one of the first products of that Council, being opened for signature in 1950. Again, Ireland and the UK were amongst the first ten States to ratify the Convention,[14] and it therefore came into effect for both countries at the international level on 3 September 1953. At that time Ireland also became the first state to accept not just the competence of the European Commission of Human Rights to receive applications from applicants in Ireland but also the jurisdiction of the European Court of Human Rights to adjudicate upon cases in which Ireland was the respondent state. In the first of those two respects Ireland was several years ahead of the United Kingdom, which did not allow individual applications until 1966.[15] Moreover Ireland bought into the individual applications process indefinitely, whereas the United Kingdom initially limited its commitment to periods of five years at a time. Only in 1994, as a consequence of ratifying Protocol 11 to the ECHR, did the UK government agree to the process *sine die*.

Famously, the very first case ever decided by the European Court of Human Rights, in 1960–61, was brought against Ireland by an alleged member of the IRA who complained about being interned without trial under powers conferred on the Irish government and police by the Offences Against the State (Amendment) Act 1940.[16] Gerry Lawless had unsuccessfully challenged his detention in *habeas corpus* proceedings brought before Ireland's High Court and had equally unsuccessfully appealed to the Supreme Court, where he invoked not only the Constitution and laws of Ireland but also the ECHR.[17] This provided the Supreme Court with its first opportunity to grapple with the norms of the ECHR, a task which the United Kingdom's House of Lords did not undertake until more than 22 years later.[18] However Maguire CJ, speaking for the Court, gave short shrift to the

[11] MacGuill (2007) 52–4. He cites *Magee v Farrell* [2005] IEHC 388 (Gilligan J) as an example of this phenomenon, but this decision was overturned by the Supreme Court on appeal: [2009] 4 IR 703 (Murray CJ, Fennelly and Finnegan JJ).

[12] *Meskell v Coras Iompair Eireann* [1973] 1 IR 121; see Chap 8 above, 189.

[13] s 5(1) and (4).

[14] It was laid before the lower House of the Irish Parliament, Dáil Éireann, on 29 March 1954, in compliance with Art 29.5.1 of the 1937 Constitution.

[15] Italy did not accept individual applications or the jurisdiction of the Court until 1973; France delayed until 1974 before accepting the jurisdiction of the Court and until 1981 before allowing individual applications. See Bates (2010) 136.

[16] *Lawless v Ireland* (1979–80) 1 EHRR 1. The Court actually delivered three judgments in this case; the first two, in November 1960 and April 1961, dealt with Ireland's preliminary objections to the part played by the applicant's comments on the report on his application prepared by the Commission of Human Rights; only the third judgment, in July 1961, dealt with the merits of the application.

[17] The High Court and Supreme Court judgments were eventually reported more than two years after they were delivered, using the Irish version of the petitioner's name: *In re Ó Laighléis* [1960] IR 93 (High Court, 11 October 1957) and 110 (Supreme Court, 3 December 1957).

[18] Even then the treatment was very cursory: in *Attorney General v BBC* [1981] AC 303 Lord Scarman briefly considered the relevance of the decision of the European Court of Human Rights in *Sunday Times v UK* (1979–80)

series of arguments based on the ECHR put forward by Lawless's counsel, Seán MacBride SC.[19]

The learned Chief Justice enunciated five conclusions.[20] First, that the provision in the Constitution dealing with international relations (Article 29), which says that 'Ireland accepts the generally recognised principles of international law as its rule of conduct in its relations with other States',[21] refers only to relations between States and confers no rights on individuals. Second, that, if there is a principle that principles which are commonly accepted as binding by civilised nations become part of domestic law unless they can be shown to be contrary to it, it applies only to the parts of international law which are based on universally recognised custom and not the parts which depend upon treaties. Third, and most fundamentally, Article 15.2.1 of the 1937 Constitution makes it abundantly clear that 'the sole and exclusive power of making laws for the State is hereby vested in the Oireachtas: no other legislative authority has power to make laws for the State', and this is backed up by Article 29.6, which provides that 'no international agreement shall be part of the domestic law of the State save as may be determined by the Oireachtas'. Fourth, the Executive was not in any way estopped from relying upon domestic law even though it had previously pushed for Ireland's ratification of the ECHR. Fifth, and finally, it was unnecessary for the Court to decide that if Ireland wanted to keep in place the special powers authorised under the Offences Against the State (Amendment) Act 1940 it needed to derogate from the ECHR under Article 15 of the ECHR, and nor did the Court have to express an opinion on whether any provision of the 1940 Act was in violation of the ECHR.

This was a judgment deeply influenced by the notion of parliamentary sovereignty, a dualist approach to international law and a strict adherence to precedent. Moreover it was underpinned by the fact that when the 1940 Act had been a draft Bill it was referred to the Supreme Court under Article 26 of the Constitution for a judgment as to whether any of its provisions were repugnant to the Constitution. As we saw in Chapter 6, the Supreme Court ruled that it was not repugnant,[22] which meant that under Article 34.3.3 of the Constitution no court could later question the validity of the Act which the Supreme Court had already approved when it was a Bill.

Just two days after publication of the Supreme Court's decision, Mr Lawless lodged an application with the European Commission of Human Rights. Having first delegated responsibility for hearing the matter to a Sub-Commission, the Commission eventually adopted a report which revealed deep divisions between its 14 members.[23] Only nine thought that at the time of Lawless's internment there was a public emergency threatening the life of the nation, as required for a valid derogation under Article 15 of the ECHR. Furthermore, only eight Commissioners thought that internment was a measure strictly required by the exigencies of the situation, another requirement of Article 15.[24] But at the European Court of Human Rights, to which the Commission referred the case, the application was unanimously rejected by all seven judges.[25] They agreed that, because of a letter sent by the Irish

2 EHRR 245. The House of Lords could have discussed the ECHR in earlier cases but did not think it necessary to do so, given that the Convention was not then part of domestic law; see Dickson (2013) 17–34.

[19] As Ireland's Minister for External Affairs at the time, it was Seán MacBride who signed the ECHR on Ireland's behalf in 1950. On MacBride's role more generally see Schabas (2007).

[20] *In re Ó Laighléis* [1960] IR 110, 123–6. [21] Art 29(3).

[22] *In re Article 26 and the Offences Against the State (Amendment) Bill 1940* [1940] IR 470; see 109-10 above.

[23] The report is available in both English and French at ECHR, Series B, 1960–61 ('Lawless' Case) 9–184.

[24] The Commissioner who thought that there was a public emergency but that internment was not required was Professor Erim from Turkey. For full details of the Commission's involvement in this case see Doolan (2001), Chaps 5, 6 and 7.

[25] Counsel for the Irish government included two future Supreme Court judges—Mr A O'Keeffe (then the Attorney General of Ireland, also known as Aindrias Ó Caoimh) and Mr A J Hederman.

Minister for External Affairs to the Secretary-General of the Council of Europe on 20 July 1957, Ireland had validly derogated from the ECHR under Article 15. The letter stated that Part II of the Offences against the State (Amendment) Act 1940 had come into force on 8 July 1957 and continued:

> In so far as the bringing into operation of Part II of the Act, which confers special powers of arrest and detention, may involve any derogation from the obligations imposed by the Convention for the Protection of Human Rights and Fundamental Freedoms, I have the honour to request you to be good enough to regard this letter as informing you accordingly, in compliance with Article 15(3) of the Convention.

Had it not been for this derogation the European Court would have held Ireland to be in breach of Articles 5 and 6 of the ECHR, which protect the rights to liberty and a fair trial. The Court joined the Commission in rejecting the Irish government's alarming proposition that Mr Lawless could not claim his ECHR rights because he had somehow forfeited them as a result of Article 17 of that treaty.[26] Reliance on Article 17 suggests that the government was not adequately aware of the purpose of that provision, nor of the underlying fundamentality of the Convention rights in the preceding Articles of the Convention, although to be fair the government may have been misled in this regard by what had been said about Article 17 by the European Commission of Human Rights in its decision to declare inadmissible an application by the German Communist Party complaining of its dissolution by order of Germany's Federal Constitutional Court.[27]

At the time, the European Court's decision in *Lawless* does not seem to have prompted much legal debate within Ireland. As the years have gone by, however, those who have commented have tended to be very critical of it. Doolan, in his monograph on the case, suggests both in his sub-title and in his detailed analysis that it was an international miscarriage of justice.[28] One negative effect of the European Court's position may have been that it reinforced the Supreme Court's complacency concerning the compatibility of Irish law with the ECHR.

Failed Attempts to Challenge Supreme Court Decisions

Amazingly, it was to be another 27 years before the European Court would again have occasion to judge the merits of an application brought on the back of a decision by the Irish Supreme Court.[29] Before then, however, there were many unsuccessful attempts to persuade the European Commission to declare admissible applications impugning a decision of that court.

The first such case seems to have been *X v Ireland* in 1970,[30] which concerned an application by a stateless person who had been extradited from Scotland to Ireland and convicted of a murder which he was accused of having committed there. Amongst his many complaints were that the Supreme Court had not dealt with all his allegations concerning

[26] 'Nothing in this Convention may be interpreted as implying for any State, group or person any right to engage in any activity or perform any act aimed at the destruction of any of the rights and freedoms set forth herein or at their limitation to a greater extent than is provided for in the Convention.'

[27] App No 250/57, (1956–57) Ybk of the ECHR 222. The Commission was quite blunt in asserting that because of its aims and objectives the Communist Party of Germany was not entitled to the protection offered by Arts 9, 10 and 11 of the ECHR.

[28] Doolan (2001), esp Chap 10. Doolan, at 201, identifies the most disappointing feature of the judgment as its unanimity. See too Bates (2010) 205–7; Dickson (2010) 34–40; Maguire (2008) Chap 6 (143–72).

[29] This was in *Norris v Ireland* (1991) 13 EHRR 186, discussed below at 275-8.

[30] App No 3717/68, decision of 6 February 1970.

the way his case had been handled and had delayed for six months before delivering a judgment in an appeal he had lodged. The Commission could not see any substance in those complaints and declared them inadmissible. Similarly, in *X and Y v Ireland* in 1980,[31] the Commission rejected the applicants' allegations that they had been denied their 'right' to appeal to the Supreme Court: there is no right of appeal protected by the ECHR and in any event the Court of Criminal Appeal had considered the applicants' request for leave to appeal to the Supreme Court but rejected it on the ground that the point of law involved was not exceptional enough to make it desirable in the public interest to permit such an appeal to take place.[32] Moreover, as this request had been made several years after their conviction, the application to Strasbourg had not been brought within the six-month time limit required by what was then Article 26 of the Convention. The complaints were held to be inadmissible.

A year later, in 1981, the European Commission said that the opportunity to apply for permission to appeal from the Court of Criminal Appeal to the Supreme Court under the Courts of Justice Act 1924[33] was not an 'effective remedy' for the purposes of the ECHR: it therefore did not have to be exhausted before an application could be declared admissible in Strasbourg, but likewise the possibility of such an appeal did not interrupt the six-month time limit for lodging an application in Strasbourg.[34] A week after this decision the European Commission stated in yet another case called *X v Ireland*[35] that, for proceedings seeking leave to appeal out of time to be considered 'fair' for the purposes of Article 6 of the ECHR, it is not necessary that the court dealing with the request should have before it a transcript or a copy of the trial judge's note.

In a further case[36] the Supreme Court had rejected an applicant's allegation that he should not be extradited to the United Kingdom because Ireland's High Court had taken more than five years to issue a judgment responding to his allegations that the offences he was accused of committing were political in nature and had no equivalents in Irish law. The European Commission, adopting a position which might not be mirrored by the European Court today, held that such a delay was not excessive enough to breach Article 6, given the applicant's own conduct in going on the run since the rejection of his appeal by the Supreme Court. His application was therefore deemed to be an abuse of the right of petition under what was then Article 27(2) of the Convention.

The Supreme Court's compliance with Article 6 of the ECHR was challenged in a case arising out of the decision by Dublin Corporation to excavate a site of archaeological importance at Wood Quay, *FX Martin v Ireland*.[37] Mr Martin's appeal to the Supreme Court had

[31] App No 8299/78, 22 DR 51, decision of 10 October 1980.

[32] This is a little surprising, since the applicants' allegation was that Ireland's Extradition Act 1965 was unconstitutional, a matter which later came before the Supreme Court in several cases: Hogan et al (2018) 1934-5 and also *The State (Gilliland) v Governor of Mountjoy Prison* [1987] IR 201; see too Chap 7 above, 169. The two applicants in *X and Y v Ireland* alleged that, while they may have carried out an armed bank robbery in Dublin in 1972, they were acting at the time as British intelligence agents who had infiltrated the IRA.

[33] s 29 provides: 'The determination by the Court of Criminal Appeal of any appeal or other matter which it has power to determine shall be final, and no appeal shall lie from the Court to the Supreme Court. unless the Court or the Attorney General shall certify that the decision involves a point of law of exceptional public importance and that it is desirable in the public interest that an appeal should be taken to the Supreme Court, in which case an appeal may be brought to the Supreme Court, the decision of which shall be final and conclusive.'

[34] *X v Ireland*, App No 9136/80, decision of 10 July 1981. In a later case the Commission held that even if the Irish government was prepared to waive the six-month rule the Commission could not accept that: *K v Ireland* App No 10416/83, decision of 17 May 1984.

[35] App No 8315/78, decision of 15 July 1981. The applicant was a mother who was seeking an affiliation order from the High Court against the father of her illegitimate child, with a view to its maintenance. The Supreme Court refused to grant permission to appeal out of time because it thought the appeal had no chance of success.

[36] *X v Ireland* App No 9742/82, decision of 2 March 1983. From the facts it would seem that the applicant was Maurice Hanlon, on whom see Chap 7 above, 159-60.

[37] App No 8569/79, decision of 8 May 1985.

been rejected and he became liable to pay the Corporation's costs, amounting to IR£80,000. But the European Commission again declared this application inadmissible, on the basis that as Mr Martin's original claim had in effect been an *actio popularis*—one brought on behalf of society rather than on his own behalf—it did not qualify for Article 6 protection because it did not involve the determination of an individual's civil rights or obligations.

Likewise, in *O'Callaghan v Commissioners of Public Works*,[38] the Supreme Court held that a farmer who had bought land at Drumanagh in County Dublin had not suffered a breach of any of his constitutional rights when it transpired that he could not plough or build a house on the land because it was the subject of a preservation order issued by the Commissioners of Public Works.[39] Mr O'Callaghan's application to Strasbourg was declared inadmissible by the European Commission two years later, in *O v Ireland*,[40] because the restrictions on the use of the land were (as regards the right to peaceful enjoyment of one's possessions, guaranteed by Article 1 of Protocol 1 to the ECHR) proportionate to the aims pursued in the general interest and (as regards the rights guaranteed by Articles 8 and 14 of the ECHR) not arbitrary or discriminatory and not previously challenged on these grounds before the domestic courts. This decision re-emphasises the importance placed by the Strasbourg bodies on the State's margin of appreciation and on the need for applicants to exhaust their domestic remedies.

We have already noted in Chapter 9 that a complaint by a group of defendants who had been tried and convicted before the Special Criminal Court in Dublin for the murder of a police officer and who alleged that their trial had been unfair because it took place before judges alone, who were liable to be politically influenced, was rejected by the European Commission of Human Rights, because no evidence had been adduced to show that in practice judges serving on the Special Criminal Court were politically influenced.[41] This endorsed the view already expressed by the Irish Supreme Court in the same case three years earlier.[42]

The *Airey* and *Johnston* Cases

In the midst of the cases just considered the European Court had two other opportunities to consider the state of Irish law. The first of these arose in *Airey v Ireland*, in 1979, where the issue was whether Ireland's limited legal aid scheme meant that a woman who could not afford to apply for a decree of judicial separation from her husband had suffered a violation of her ECHR rights. The Supreme Court was not given an opportunity to decide this issue—nor was any other Irish court—because the European Commission accepted the application as admissible without insisting that 'domestic remedies' needed to be exhausted first: if Mrs Airey could not get legal aid to apply for a decree of judicial separation it was unlikely she would get legal aid to argue that her inaccessibility to legal aid was a breach of her right of access to justice. At that time ECHR rights were not directly part of domestic Irish law, and in view of the position adopted towards the ECHR by the Supreme Court in *Lawless*,[43] Mrs Airey's only hope would have been to rely on a constitutional right, or a common law right, to receive legal aid. In the event, the European Court found that Mrs Airey had suffered a violation of Articles 6 and 8 of the ECHR (the right to a fair trial and the right to a family life) and did not therefore find it necessary to consider whether other Convention

[38] [1985] ILRM 364; Dewhurst et al (2012) 250.
[39] Decision of 31 July 1984.
[40] App No 11446/85, decision of 3 March 1986.
[41] *Eccles, McPhillips and McShane v Ireland* App No 12839/87, 59 DR 212 (1988). See too Chap 9 above, 204.
[42] *Eccles v Ireland* [1986] ILRM 343.
[43] See above, 270-272.

rights (i.e. the right to an effective remedy in Article 13, or the right not to be discriminated against in Article 14) had been breached.[44] Possibly the most important consequence of the *Airey* case is that it cemented the European Court's commitment to ensure that Convention rights are guaranteed in ways that are 'practical and effective' rather than 'theoretical and illusory', a guiding principle which has been central to the Court's reasoning in countless subsequent judgments.[45]

A limited civil legal aid scheme was established in Ireland shortly after the announcement of this European Court decision.[46] A few years later an unsuccessful applicant for legal aid (who was defending himself against a claim brought by his wife relating to the custody of their children and maintenance) argued in the High Court that he should have a remedy because Ireland had failed to properly implement the judgment of the European Court in *Airey*.[47] The claim failed, for the simple reason that the High Court applied the reasoning used by the Supreme Court in *Lawless* concerning the status of the ECHR in Irish law, set out above.[48] Gerry Whyte has argued that it may be possible to make judgments issued by the European Court against Ireland enforceable in Ireland under Article 29.3 of the Constitution, which provides that 'Ireland accepts the generally recognised principles of international law as its rule of conduct in its relations with other States'.[49] But the difficulty with this, as the Supreme Court said in *Lawless*, is that a decision by an international court, even more so than a provision in a treaty, can hardly be categorised as *ipso facto* a 'generally recognized principle of international law'. To claim, as Whyte does, that the principle in question is *pacta sunt servanda* is surely stating the matter at too abstract a level.

The Supreme Court was also not involved in the next Irish case in which the European Court issued a judgment, *Johnston v Ireland*.[50] This is because the main complaint in the case was that two people could not get married as one of them was already married to someone else and Irish law did not allow a person to seek a divorce. The European Court accepted, therefore, that there were no domestic remedies to exhaust. It went on to hold, however, that the absence of any law permitting divorce, given the European Court's approach to a State's margin of appreciation, was not a violation of any Article in the ECHR.[51] The decision is an interesting pendant to *Airey*, since the latter dealt with the related matter of decrees of judicial separation, one step short of divorce.[52]

The *Norris* Case

By the time the European Court decided *Johnston* the Supreme Court had already had its second chance to display a more welcoming attitude towards the ECHR in the well-known case of *Norris v Attorney General*.[53] David Norris, then a lecturer in English at Trinity College Dublin and elected a few years later as a member of the Seanad Éireann representing that University, applied to the High Court for a declaration that legislation dating from 1861 which still criminalised homosexuality was in breach of his constitutional rights.[54] He lost

[44] *Airey v Ireland* (1979) 2 EHRR 305. [45] See eg Rainey et al (2017), 76–80; Bates (2010), 341–7.

[46] This was a non-statutory scheme established in 1979; there was no statutory scheme until the Civil Legal Aid Act 1995; see generally Byrne and McCutcheon (2014) 427–38. For relevant history see Carney (1979).

[47] *E v E* [1982] ILRM 497. [48] See 270-2 above. [49] Whyte (1982).

[50] (1987) 9 EHRR 203.

[51] But the Court found a breach of Art 8 in relation to the couple's child because she was not placed 'legally and socially, in a position akin to that of a legitimate child': ibid, para 74.

[52] See too Chap 10 above, 230. [53] [1984] IR 36 (22 April 1983); Gearty (1983).

[54] Offences Against the Person Act 1861, ss 61 and 62. He also complained about the Criminal Law Amendment Act 1885, s 11, which criminalised the commission by a male of an act of gross indecency with another male. One

in the High Court before McWilliam J and he lost again on appeal to the Supreme Court, where on the main issue O'Higgins CJ, Finlay P and Griffin J held against him while Henchy and McCarthy JJ held in his favour. The majority's decision is disappointing in a number of respects. First, it flies in the face of the decision of the European Court of Human Rights just 18 months earlier in *Dudgeon v UK*,[55] where 15 of the 19 judges held that *the very same legislative provisions*, as they applied in Northern Ireland, were in violation of the applicant's right to a private life under Article 8 of the ECHR. Second, it represents an overly cautious approach to the concept of unenumerated rights which in the 1960s the Supreme Court had been so proud to develop. Third, the Supreme Court's reasoning is at times based on religious and moral dogma which should find no place in the judgment of a national supreme court in any modern Western democracy.

In *Dudgeon v UK* the judge who sat in the European Court of Human Rights representing Ireland was Brian Walsh. He held that none of the applicant's rights had been breached and that Jeff Dudgeon should never have been considered as having victim status in the first place. Regrettably his partly dissenting judgment in that case is also heavily based on moral arguments and on what today, with respect, seems to be a rather naïve approach to the nature of homosexuality.[56] A measure of the lack of interest in the ECHR on the part of the Supreme Court judges who sat in *Norris* is that none of those who held against Mr Norris made any reference to Walsh J's provocative judgment in the earlier case (and there is only a fleeting reference to it in one of the minority judges' judgments too[57]). As far as the status of the ECHR in Irish law is concerned, it seems that in the eyes of the Supreme Court nothing at all had changed since the pronouncements it had made more than a quarter of a century earlier in *Ó Laighléis*. O'Higgins CJ rather dismissively rejected Mary Robinson's argument that the European Court's decision in *Dudgeon* should be regarded by the Supreme Court as more than just a persuasive precedent. He said: 'Neither the Convention on Human Rights nor the decision of the European Court in *Dudgeon v UK* is in any way relevant to the question which we have to consider in this case.'[58] The Chief Justice preferred to be guided only by the Irish Constitution, and in particular its Preamble:

The preamble to the Constitution proudly asserts the existence of God in the Most Holy Trinity and recites that the people of Ireland humbly acknowledge their obligation to 'our Divine Lord, Jesus Christ'. It cannot be doubted that the people ... were proclaiming a deep religious conviction and faith and an intention to adopt a Constitution consistent with that conviction and faith... Yet it is suggested that, in the very act of so doing, the people rendered inoperative laws which had existed for hundreds of years prohibiting unnatural sexual conduct which Christian teaching held to be gravely sinful. It would require very clear and express provisions in the Constitution itself to convince me that such took place.[59]

Henchy J, one of the dissenters in the case, also stressed that the ECHR forms no part of the domestic law of Ireland, but he qualified this by adding: 'That does not mean that this Court is not open to the persuasive influence that may be drawn from decisions of other

of the barristers representing Norris was Mary Robinson, future President of Ireland and UN High Commissioner for Human Rights.

[55] (1982) 4 EHRR 149. Amongst the lawyers acting for the UK government were Nicolas Bratza, a future judge and President of the European Court of Human Rights, and Brian Kerr, a future Lord Chief Justice of Northern Ireland, Law Lord and Justice of the UK Supreme Court.

[56] eg: 'A distinction must be drawn between homosexuals who are such because of some kind of innate instinct or pathological constitution judged to be incurable and those whose tendency comes from a lack of normal sexual development or from habit or from experience or from other similar causes but whose tendency is not incurable', ibid, at para 13 of Walsh J's partly dissenting judgment. For a review of Walsh J's service as a judge of the European Court of Human Rights see Hedigan (2001).

[57] [1984] IR 36, 101 (per McCarthy J). [58] Ibid, 67. [59] Ibid, 65.

courts, such as the European Court of Human Rights, which deal with problems similar or analogous to that now before us'.[60] Moreover on the use of moral arguments Henchy J was very clear in asserting that the case needed to be decided on the basis of evidence, not morality. He observed that:

> [W]e are not called upon in this case to express an opinion upon whether the law on this topic should be as it is or upon what the purpose of the law should be. Such considerations are for moral philosophers, legal theorists, lawmakers and the like.[61]

The learned judge then quoted extracts from some of the testimony of the ten witnesses who had been called before the High Court to show that the criminalisation of homosexuality was not for the public good and he stressed that the Attorney General had called no such witnesses to show that it was for the public good. While praising McWilliam J for dealing with the case 'with commendable thoroughness',[62] he criticised him for 'substituting his own conclusions on the personal and societal effects of the questioned provisions' and for stressing that sodomy was 'contrary to the standards of morality advocated by the Christian Churches in this State'.[63] Henchy J's view was that that factor should not be treated as a guiding consideration. To seek by criminal sanction to legislate the commission of any of the seven deadly sins out of existence in all circumstances was, he thought, 'neither constitutionally permissible nor otherwise desirable'.[64] Indeed, to do so 'would upset the necessary balance which the Constitution posits between the common good and the dignity and freedom of the individual'.[65]

McCarthy J's views were even more liberal than Henchy J's. For a start, he thought that David Norris did have standing to challenge the legislative provisions in question because they interfered with the privacy of marriage; Henchy J, on the other hand (along with the judges in the majority), made the wrong assumption that Mr Norris could never marry and so held that he had no standing on that basis.[66] Secondly, while finding it unnecessary to decide if Mr Norris's right to equality under Article 40.1 of the Constitution had been breached, McCarthy J said that he was 'not to be taken as agreeing with the view that the plaintiff's argument implies an over-wide interpretation of the scope of that constitutional guarantee'. Thirdly, McCarthy J went out of his way to say that the constitutionality of the provisions in question, which of course were enacted long before Ireland became a Dominion in 1922, let alone a full-blown Republic in 1949, should be judged against today's mores, not those which existed at the time when the 1937 Constitution was agreed.[67] Fourthly, he dissented from the suggestion that the source of personal rights in the Constitution was, apart from the democratic nature of the State, Christian theology rather than Christianity itself (which proclaims two great commandments—love of God and love of neighbour), and he added that:

> I would uphold the view that the unenumerated rights derive from the human personality and ... the actions of the State in respect of such rights must be informed by the proud objective of the people as declared in the preamble 'seeking to promote the common good, with due observance of prudence, justice and charity, so that the dignity and freedom of the individual maybe assured, true social order attained, the unity of our country restored, and concord established with other nations'. The dignity and freedom of the individual occupy a prominent place

[60] Ibid, 69. [61] Ibid, 70. [62] Ibid, 77. [63] Ibid.

[64] Ibid, 78. Presumably the deadly sin he had in mind was 'lust'. [65] Ibid.

[66] McCarthy J pointed out that Oscar Wilde, a prominent homosexual, had been married.

[67] The issue in *Norris* was whether the 1861 and 1885 legislative provisions were, under Art 50 of the 1937 Constitution, 'not inconsistent' with the Constitution.

in these objectives and are not declared to be subject to any particular exigencies but as forming part of the promotion of the common good.[68]

Fifthly, McCarthy J plainly asserted the role of the Supreme Court in developing the Constitution:

> At all events, since 1937, the concept of judicial dynamism in constitutional law has grown, thereby identifying more readily the role of the Courts and, in particular, this Court as the judicial organ of government, not merely by way of a supervisory jurisdiction on the actions of the legislative and executive branches of government but by way of legal interpretation—thus playing its part in 'seeking to promote the common good, with due observance of prudence, justice and charity, so that the dignity and freedom of the individual may be assured' as most strikingly evidenced by the decision in the *McGee* case.[69]

Finally, by detailing the different situations in which one person's masturbation of another would be lawful, McCarthy J made it clear that there was no compelling State interest in criminalising one man's masturbation of another. Even by the standards of today, 35 years later, such explicitness is startling.

As the Supreme Court judges could have no doubt predicted, two days after they pronounced their judgment Mr Norris lodged an application in Strasbourg. Although, depressingly, this took a further three years to process, the result of the application was something of a foregone conclusion, even if the victory for Mr Norris, by 8 v 6, was much narrower than one might have expected. The Court endorsed its own earlier judgment in *Dudgeon v UK* and was unconvinced that the margin of appreciation doctrine excused Ireland's criminalisation of homosexuality. Nor did the majority think that there was any pressing social need for such criminal laws.[70] Just as he had done in *Dudgeon*, the Irish judge, Brian Walsh, dissented, but he and five colleagues did so primarily on the narrow but convenient basis that they did not think Mr Norris was a 'victim' for the purposes of the Convention.[71] The European Court was brief, and remarkably uncritical, in relation to the views expressed by the Supreme Court's majority. It is regrettable that the Strasbourg judges were not more outspoken in their condemnation of the apex court of a member state of the Council of Europe which had paid so little regard to a prominent recent decision of the European Court on the very point at issue in the case. The Committee of Ministers of the Council of Europe must also shoulder some of the blame for allowing Ireland to take so long before fully implementing the *Norris* judgment: homosexuality was not decriminalised in the Republic until 1993.[72]

The *Pine Valley*, *Open Door* and *Keegan* Cases

The Supreme Court was involved on two separate occasions in the next Irish case to provoke a judgment from the European Court of Human Rights, *Pine Valley Developments Ltd v Ireland*.[73] In 1982 it ruled that outline planning permission given in relation to land at Clondalkin in County Dublin, which was later bought by two companies, had been invalid because it contravened the development plan for the area.[74] Bizarrely, while the Oireachtas

[68] [1984] IR 36, 99–100.

[69] Ibid, at 101. The *McGee* case is the decision concerning access to contraceptives, *McGee v Attorney General* [1974] 1 IR 284, discussed in Chap 10 above, 232-4.

[70] *Norris v Ireland* (1991) 13 EHRR 186. In its report of 12 March 1987 the Commission of Human Rights found by eight votes to five that there had been a violation of Art 8 of the ECHR.

[71] The UK judge, Sir Vincent Evans, formed part of the majority of eight.

[72] Criminal Law (Sexual Offences) Act 1993, s 2.

[73] (1992) 14 EHRR 319.

[74] *Pine Valley Developments Ltd v Dublin City Council* [1982] ILRM 169.

passed legislation to retrospectively validate the planning permission,[75] the two companies in question were excluded from the reach of the legislation because they had already begun compensation proceedings against the planning authorities.[76] Those compensation proceedings also reached the Supreme Court, but were unsuccessful.[77] The judges ruled that not only did the alleged negligence on the part of the planning authorities not fall within any of the acknowledged categories of *ultra vires* decisions which can be the basis of an action for damages in Irish law, but that it was also not unjust to deny compensation for breach of the plaintiffs' constitutional rights of property because granting immunity to persons vested with statutory powers of decisions who have acted without negligence or bad faith is reasonable. They did not think that there was any unlawful discriminatory treatment of the plaintiffs compared with other landowners who benefited from the retrospective validation of the planning permission. At no point did the Supreme Court consider the applicability of provisions in the ECHR.

The two companies then applied to Strasbourg, as did a third applicant, Mr Daniel Healy, the managing director and sole shareholder of both companies. At the Commission the majority view was that there had been no breach of Article 1 of Protocol 1 (nor of Article 13 of the ECHR itself, on the availability of an effective remedy) in relation to any of the applicants, but that there had been a breach of Article 14 taken in conjunction with Article 1 of Protocol 1 as far as the second and third applicants were concerned.[78] Before the Court the result was similar: the first applicant had suffered no breach of any Article but the second and third applicants had suffered a violation of Article 14 taken in conjunction with Article 1 of Protocol 1.[79] Article 1 of Protocol 1 had not been breached taken alone,[80] because the planning authorities' interference with the land was found to be justifiable in terms of protecting the environment and because the companies, as commercial enterprises, must always have known that there were financial risks involved when buying land for development. There had been a breach of Article 1 of Protocol 1 taken in conjunction with Article 14 because the retrospective legislation in question had not been applied to them. This part of the decision was in direct conflict with that reached by the Irish Supreme Court: the Irish government must itself have been unconvinced by the latter's reasoning on the point because it chose not to rely upon it when making its case to the European Court, somewhat to the latter's surprise.[81] The result in Strasbourg was a timely reminder to the Supreme Court that the reach of the non-discrimination provision in the ECHR is considerable, extending even to the realms of planning and property law.

Such is the time required to process an application through Strasbourg that, when the next case raising ECHR points came before the Supreme Court, the European Court had

[75] See the Local Government (Planning and Development) Act 1982.

[76] s 6(1) of the 1982 Act conferred retrospective validity on any *ultra vires* outline planning permission but s 6(2) said this did not apply if it conflicted with any person's constitutional rights. As the two companies in this case were attempting to exert their constitutional rights, they were deemed to be ineligible to benefit from s 6(1).

[77] *Pine Valley Developments Ltd v Minister for the Environment, Ireland and the Attorney General* [1987] ILRM 747, 753 (30 July 1986).

[78] *Pine Valley Developments Ltd v Ireland* App No 12742/87, decision of 3 May 1989. The first applicant company was held to have suffered no breach because it had sold the land to the second applicant company prior to the Supreme Court's first decision invalidating the outline planning permission. The Commissioner from Ireland, Jane Liddy, was the sole dissenter on this holding.

[79] *Pine Valley Developments Ltd v Ireland* (1992) 14 EHRR 319; a judgment on compensation was given later, awarding IR£1.2 million to the second and third applicants jointly and IR£50,000 to Mr Healy alone: (1993) 16 EHRR 379.

[80] Though three of the nine judges dissented on this point.

[81] At (1992) 14 EHRR 319, para 26, the European Court cited points made about the alleged discrimination by Henchy and Lardner JJ (at [1987] ILRM 747, 764 and 767 respectively).

still not issued its judgments in *Norris* or *Pine Valley*. This was unfortunate because the Supreme Court was still neglecting to absorb the full consequences of adherence to the ECHR. Like the House of Lords in the United Kingdom,[82] the Supreme Court was carrying on in blissful ignorance of how out of step its human rights thinking was compared to that of the European Court. Thus, when the important issue of the right of access to information about termination of pregnancy services came before the Supreme Court in *Attorney General v Open Door Counselling Ltd and Dublin Well Woman Centre Ltd* in March 1988 it was ill-equipped to apply the appropriate human rights principles. The proceedings were taken in the name of the Attorney General but were actually begun by the Society for the Protection of Unborn Children Ireland Ltd. The Attorney claimed that the two defendant organisations were acting unlawfully in giving information to pregnant women about a medical clinic in Great Britain where abortions were performed. The twin legal bases for the claim were that the provision of such information was contrary to Article 40.3.3 of the Constitution[83] and that it amounted to a conspiracy to corrupt public morals. In the High Court Hamilton P granted a declaration to the Attorney on the first of these grounds but rejected the second. He also issued an injunction restraining the two organisations from assisting pregnant women to obtain further advice on abortion. On appeal the Supreme Court unanimously endorsed Hamilton P's decisions.[84]

Interestingly, none of the counsel in the case referred to any decisions by the European Court of Human Rights.[85] This may have been in deference to the well-established view of the Supreme Court that the ECHR formed no part of Irish domestic law. Instead counsel agreed to argue about whether, if the activities of the defendants were illegal under Irish domestic law, they were nevertheless saved from such illegality by the law of the European Economic Community (as it was then known). However in the High Court Hamilton P chose not to consider EEC law because he concluded that all of the activities in question took place within Ireland and EEC law was therefore not applicable. The Supreme Court's view was that no question of the interpretation of EEC law arose because the defendants conceded that the Treaty of Rome did not confer any right on women to travel abroad and obtain the service of abortion there. It consequently refused to make a reference to the European Court of Justice (ECJ) for a preliminary ruling under Article 177 of the Treaty. But the defendants lodged an application with the European Commission of Human Rights in Strasbourg—not, of course, a body within the EEC, but rather an institution within the quite separate Council of Europe.

To complicate matters, prior to the Strasbourg Court delivering its judgment on this application, another case was taken to the Irish High Court on the same issue. The Society for the Protection of Unborn Children sought an injunction to prevent student associations in Ireland from distributing the kind of information which the clinics had been distributing in the *Open Door* case. The High Court, through Costello J, granted an interim injunction to SPUC[86] and when this appeared to be ignored by the students SPUC went back to the High Court to seek a further injunction, as well as an order for the committal of some individual

[82] Dickson (2012) 355–61 and 364–8.

[83] At the time this read in full: 'The State acknowledges the right to life of the unborn and, with due regard to the equal right to life of the mother, guarantees in its laws to respect, and, as far as practicable, by its laws to defend and vindicate that right.' The sub-section was later extended by two separate amendments made in 1992. See too Chap 10 above, 238.

[84] *Attorney General (SPUC) v Open Door Counselling Ltd* [1988] IR 593 (High Ct) and 618 (Sup Ct); the Supreme Court comprised Finlay CJ, Walsh, Henchy, Griffin and Hederman JJ, but only Finlay CJ gave a judgment (with which the other judges simply agreed).

[85] Counsel included Mary Robinson SC and three future Supreme Court judges, Frank Clarke SC, Adrian Hardiman SC and Hugh O'Flaherty SC.

[86] 'SPUC gets injunction against students' union over abortion guide' *Irish Times*, 4 October 1992, 10.

student leaders for breaching the interim injunction. On this occasion the judge, Carroll J, refused to issue an injunction or to commit the student leaders without first knowing the view of the ECJ on the matter and she consequently made a reference for a preliminary ruling from the ECJ concerning the compatibility of such an injunction with provisions of EEC law, more particularly on whether termination of a pregnancy fell within the definition of a 'service' for the purposes of Article 60 of the Treaty of Rome, which guarantees free movement of services.[87] On appeal, the Supreme Court granted the interim injunction but refused to overturn the reference to the ECJ.[88] The ruling on that reference was delivered on 4 October 1991 and was to the effect that an injunction would not violate EEC law because, although termination of pregnancy is a service, it is not contrary to EEC law for a member state in which medical termination of pregnancy is forbidden to prohibit the distribution of information about the location of clinics in another member state where it is lawful, provided those clinics are not involved in the distribution of that information.[89] Upon receipt of this ruling the Irish High Court made permanent the interim injunction issued by the Supreme Court.[90]

Then, a year later, the European Court of Human Rights delivered its judgment in *Open Door and Dublin Well Woman v Ireland*.[91] It held, by 15 v 8, that the applicants' right to freedom of expression, protected by Article 10 of the ECHR, had been violated and, by 17 v 6, that Ireland must pay Dublin Well Woman Ltd IR£25,000 by way of compensation.[92] The majority's attitude towards the Supreme Court's judgment was that the injunction it had authorised was disproportionate to the aims pursued.[93] Moreover, the right to freedom of expression extended to ideas that offend, shock or disturb the State: 'such are the demands of that pluralism, tolerance and broadmindedness without which there is no "democratic society"'.[94] The European Court noted that it was not a criminal offence under Irish law to travel abroad to have an abortion and that the Irish government had now conceded, in the wake of the *X* case,[95] that the injunction in this case could no longer be applied to women who were free to have an abortion in Ireland or abroad.[96] It added that the applicants had confined themselves to explaining options to pregnant women, that such counselling had been tolerated for many years prior to the Supreme Court's injunction, that the information being supplied was easily available elsewhere and that the injunction seemed largely ineffective because many women still travelled to Great Britain for an abortion.[97] The ad hoc Irish judge in the case, John Blayney, was one of the dissenters: he did not think the Supreme Court's injunction was disproportionate to the aims which it pursued and he thought that under Article 60 of the ECHR[98] the European Court could not find Ireland to be in breach of Article 10 because the right of the unborn is a human right guaranteed by

[87] [1989] IR 753. [88] Ibid, 760 (Finlay CJ, Walsh, Griffin, Hederman and McCarthy JJ).

[89] *SPUC v Grogan* Case C-159/90 [1991] ECR I-4685. The Advocate General had earlier provided an opinion that the injunction did violate EEC law. See too Phelan (1992), Wilkinson (1992), O'Leary (1992).

[90] Phelan (1992) 689.

[91] (1993) 15 EHRR 244, judgment of 29 October 1992. On 7 March 1991 the European Commission had already given its view (by 8 v 5) that the Supreme Court's injunction violated the applicants' rights under Art 10: (1991) 14 EHRR 131. The Irish Commissioner, Jane Liddy, dissented.

[92] Open Door Counselling Ltd had by then ceased to exist, having been made insolvent as a result of the costs order issued against it by the Supreme Court. Unfortunately the European Court unanimously agreed that it was not necessary to consider whether Arts 8 and 14 of the ECHR had also been violated.

[93] (1993) 15 EHRR 244, paras 68–70. [94] Ibid, para 71.

[95] *Attorney General v X* [1992] IR 1. This case is also discussed at Chap 10 above, 235-8.

[96] (1993) 15 EHRR 244, para 73. [97] Ibid, paras 75–6.

[98] This little known provision (now Art 53) reads: 'Nothing in this Convention shall be construed as limiting or derogating from any of the human rights and fundamental freedoms which may be ensured under the laws of any High Contracting Party or under any other agreement to which it is a Party.'

Article 40.3.3 of the Irish Constitution.[99] On this last point the majority said that 'it is not the interpretation of Article 10 but the position in Ireland as regards the implementation of the law that makes possible the continuance of the current level of abortions obtained by women abroad'.[100]

The judgment of the European Court of Human Rights in the *Open Door* case obviously caused quite a stir throughout Ireland, though less than it might have done had the *X* case not been decided earlier in the year[101] and had the government not already planned two referendums on the subject of abortion which were to occur just a month after the European Court's judgment was published. The *Irish Times* cautiously welcomed the decision, saying that 'it has nudged this State another few centimetres into the European mainstream on a vital matter of human rights and individual choice'.[102] The people of Ireland also clearly agreed with the European Court because in the referendum on the proposed Fourteenth Amendment to the Constitution there was a decisive 60 per cent to 40 per cent vote in favour of inserting the following words into Article 40.3.3 of the Constitution: 'This subsection shall not limit freedom to obtain or make available, in the State, subject to such conditions as may be laid down by law, information relating to services lawfully available in another state.'[103]

Compounding the shock of the European Court's decision in *Open Door*, less than six months later the European Commission of Human Rights (and later the European Court too) issued yet another damning verdict on Ireland's laws relating to children. Under the case name *K v W* the Supreme Court had held in December 1989 that section 6A of the Guardianship of Infants Act 1964[104] did not confer upon the natural father of a child the right to be the guardian of that child, only the right to apply to the court to be appointed the guardian; nor was a right to be a guardian conferred by the Constitution.[105] Moreover, the Supreme Court stressed that in deciding whether to appoint someone as a guardian judges had to have regard to the welfare of the child as the first and paramount consideration. In reaching these conclusions the Supreme Court seems to have paid no attention whatsoever to the ECHR, despite the involvement of some very expert counsel in the case.[106] It may therefore have come as a surprise to the Court when in February 1993 a 12-member Commission of Human Rights and in May 1994 a nine-judge Court[107] both unanimously held in *Keegan v Ireland* that the applicant's rights under the ECHR had been violated. This was because under Irish law Mr Keegan had been given no right to challenge the decision to place his child for adoption (a breach of Article 6(1), the right to a fair trial) and the decision had been taken without his knowledge or consent (a breach of Article 8, the right to a private and family life). The European Court awarded Mr Keegan IR£12,000 by way of non-pecuniary and pecuniary damages, but no doubt he would have much preferred to have received the custody of his child instead. He emphasised to the Court that he was not seeking to overturn the adoption order, but he contended, sadly, that it was unlikely that he would ever be re-united with his daughter.[108]

[99] (1993) 15 EHRR 244, 283–4.

[100] Ibid, para 79.

[101] [1992] 1 IR 1 (5 March 1992); for comments on the two European cases and the *X* case see Lawson (1994).

[102] *Irish Times*, 30 October 1992, 15 (editorial).

[103] This became the second paragraph of Art 40.3.3.

[104] Inserted by s 12 of the Status of Children Act 1987.

[105] *JK v VW* [1990] 2 IR 437.

[106] Such as Susan Denham SC for the adoptive parents, Frank Clarke SC and Catherine McGuinness for the natural mother (all future Supreme Court judges) and Mary Robinson SC for the natural father.

[107] *Keegan v Ireland* (1994) 18 EHRR 342; the Commission's report is at 353–8 within that judgment. The Irish judge was Judge Blayney, as Judge Walsh withdrew pursuant to rule 24(2): see para 4 of the judgment; the Irish Commissioner was Jane Liddy.

[108] Ibid, 365 (para 66).

The *Heaney, DG* and *McElhinney* Cases

The attitude of the Irish Supreme Court to the country's anti-terrorism (or 'emergency') laws was again scrutinised by the European Court of Human Rights at the turn of the century. In *Heaney and McGuinness v Ireland*[109] the simple question at issue was whether section 52 of the Offences Against the State Act 1939 constituted a violation of the rights guaranteed by Articles 6, 8 and 10 of the ECHR, namely the rights to a fair trial, to respect for private and family life and to freedom of expression. Section 52 reads in full as follows:

> (1) Whenever a person is detained in custody under the provisions in that behalf contained in Part IV of this Act, any member of the Gárda Síochána may demand of such person, at any time while he is so detained, a full account of such person's movements and actions during any specified period and all information in his possession in relation to the commission or intended commission by another person of any offence under any section or sub-section of this Act or any scheduled offence.
>
> (2) If any person, of whom any such account or information as is mentioned in the foregoing sub-section of this section is demanded under that sub-section by a member of the [police], fails or refuses to give to such member such account or any such information or gives to such member any account or information which is false or misleading, he shall be guilty of an offence under this section and shall be liable on summary conviction thereof to imprisonment for a term not exceeding six months.

In 1990, a day after a terrorist attack in Northern Ireland, in which five British soldiers and a local civilian were killed, two men were arrested in the Republic of Ireland in incriminating circumstances. They refused to give an account of their movements around the time of the incident and were then brought to the Special Criminal Court in Dublin and charged with failing to account for their movements as well as with membership of an unlawful organisation, the IRA. They were acquitted of the latter offence but convicted of the former, and sentenced to six months' imprisonment. In subsequent challenges to the constitutionality of section 52, both the High Court and the Supreme Court held that it was constitutional.[110] In the High Court Costello J focused on whether section 52 was repugnant to Article 38.1 of the Constitution, which provides that 'No person shall be tried on any criminal charge save in due course of law.' The Supreme Court, on the other hand, analysed the right to silence as being a corollary to the right to freedom of expression, which is guaranteed by Article 40.6.1.i of the Constitution and is explicitly conferred 'subject to public order and morality'. The issue in both courts was whether the restriction on the right to silence contained in section 52 was proportionate and both courts held that it was.[111] The Supreme Court noted that an innocent person had nothing to fear from giving an account of his or her movements and that the entitlement of those with something relevant to disclose concerning the commission of a crime to remain silent had to yield to the right of the State to protect itself. However the Supreme Court stopped short of approving an earlier decision by the Court of Criminal Appeal[112] that information lawfully obtained under section 52 could later be used in evidence. In *Re National Irish Bank Ltd*[113] it had already held that

[109] [1996] IR 580. The Willie McGuinness in this case was the brother of the late Martin McGuinness, former Deputy First Minister of Northern Ireland from 2007 to 2017.

[110] [1994] 3 IR 593 (High Ct); [1996] I IR 580 (Sup Ct).

[111] See further O'Malley (2009) 778–9.

[112] *The People (Director of Public Prosecutions) v McGowan* [1979] IR 45.

[113] [1999] 3 IR 145. Here the Supreme Court ruled that a confession by a bank official, obtained by inspectors under powers conferred by s 10 of the Companies Act 1990, would not generally be admissible at the trial of that official unless the judge was satisfied that the confession was voluntary. However the Court also ruled that any

section 52 did need to be considered in the light of fair trial rights under Article 38 of the Constitution,[114] but in *Heaney* it postponed further discussion of the matter until another day. Again no reference was made by the Supreme Court to the ECHR, even though in the High Court Costello J had gone out of his way to expound the proportionality test adopted by the European Court of Human Rights.[115] The Supreme Court's judgment, delivered by O'Flaherty J and concurred with by Hamilton CJ and Blayney, Denham and Barrington JJ, was a mere eight pages.

The European Court, giving judgment in the case more than four years later, preferred to analyse the issue as relating more to the right to a fair trial than to the right to freedom of expression.[116] It ruled that Ireland's Supreme Court had failed to apply the ECHR's standards on a fair trial in two important respects. First, it had not seen that, given the uncertainty over whether things said by detainees as a result of pressure placed on them by section 52 could later be used as evidence against them, the degree of compulsion 'in effect destroyed the very essence of their privilege against self-incrimination and their right to remain silent'.[117] Second, it had miscalculated in holding that the security and public order concerns relied on by the Irish government did not extinguish the very essence of the applicants' rights.[118] As a result, the European Court found unanimously that there had been a violation of Articles 6(1) and (2) of the ECHR,[119] and awarded each of the applicants IR£4,000 in compensation (they had claimed at least IR£50,000). The same Chamber of the European Court reached a similar conclusion on the same day in another case concerning section 52, *Quinn v Ireland*.[120] The European Court's decisions were a resounding rebuff to the Irish Supreme Court's stance on its own Constitution.

In the wake of these two European Court judgments section 52 has not been explicitly amended. Instead, prior to the decisions, the Irish government secured the enactment of the Offences Against the State (Amendment) Act 1998 which provides, amongst many other things, that section 52 of the 1939 Act has no effect in relation to a person detained under Part IV of that Act 'unless, immediately before a demand is made of him or her under that subsection, he or she is informed in ordinary language by a member of the Garda Síochána of (a) the fact that the demand is being made under the said section 52, and (b) the consequences provided by that section for a failure or refusal to comply with such a demand or for the giving of any account or information in purported compliance with such a demand which is false or misleading'.[121] In effect the provision has been 'read down', as British lawyers might put it, so as to be compatible with the ECHR. But, even as so qualified, section 52 still sails close to the wind as far as its compatibility with Article 6 of the ECHR is

other evidence obtained as a result of information provided under s 52 of the 1939 Act would be admitted in evidence if the judge found that it would be just and fair to do so.

[114] Art 38.1 reads: 'No person shall be tried on any criminal charge save in due course of law.'

[115] *Heaney v Ireland* [1994] 3 IR 593, 607.

[116] *Heaney and McGuinness v Ireland* (2001) 33 EHRR 12; McGuckian (2004).

[117] Ibid, para 55.

[118] Ibid, para 58.

[119] Art 6(1) protects the right to a fair trial; Art 6(2) protects the right to be presumed incident. The Court found it was unnecessary to consider the claims that Arts 8 and 10 had also been breached. Unusually, there was no judge from the respondent state sitting in this case: John Hedigan had for some unstated reason withdrawn and, rather than appoint a domestic judge as an ad hoc judge, the Irish government nominated Croatia's judge at Strasbourg to sit in his place.

[120] App No 36887/97, judgment of 21 December 2000. The applicant had not taken his case beyond the Circuit Court in Ireland.

[121] Offences Against the State (Amendment) Act 1998, s 13. In *Sweeney v Ireland* [2017] IEHC 702 Baker J declared unconstitutional s 9(1)(b) of the 1998 Act, which says that a person shall be guilty of an offence if he or she has information which he or she believes might be of material assistance in securing the apprehension or conviction of any other person for a serious offence and fails without reasonable excuse to disclose that information as soon as practicable to a police officer.

concerned. It is by no means clear that the restrictions it upholds on the right to silence do not undermine its essence in a manner which the European Court thought was unacceptable in both *Heaney* and *Quinn*.

The Supreme Court's protection of the right to liberty was at issue in judicial review proceedings brought by a troubled young man from a dysfunctional family who complained that, after being released from detention in St Patrick's Institution as a 16-year-old, he had not been provided with suitable care and accommodation. The High Court, exercising its 'inherent' jurisdiction, ordered that he be sent back to St Patrick's, even though he had not been found guilty of any offence; in the Court's view, there was no other better option. The Supreme Court, by 4 v 1, upheld this decision, but again without any reference whatsoever to the ECHR.[122] The Chief Justice noted the young man's conflicting constitutional rights: his right to liberty (Article 40) and his unenumerated rights 'to be fed and to live, to be reared and educated, to have the opportunity of working and of realising his or her personality and dignity as a human being'.[123] Accepting, along with all parties to the case, that the applicant's welfare was of paramount importance, the Chief Justice concluded that the High Court judge had acted lawfully in ordering the applicant's detention in a penal institution, but he stressed that the State should continue to make efforts to fulfil its statutory obligation to find suitable alternative arrangements consistent with the needs of the applicant. For Denham J, dissenting, the detention of the young man was 'a step too far'; she would have ordered the Health Board to address its statutory duties and provide some other means of caring for the child.[124]

When the case reached Strasbourg, as *DG v Ireland*,[125] the European Court found unanimously that there had been a breach both of the right to liberty, guaranteed by Article 5(1) of the ECHR, and of the right to be compensated for that breach, guaranteed by Article 5(5). But there had been no breach of Article 3 (the right not to be ill-treated) and no separate issue under Article 8 (the right to a private and family life). The applicant was awarded €5,000 in compensation. The Irish judge on the Court, Hedigan J, concurred with the decision. The case is a further illustration of the inadequacy of the Irish Constitution in protecting all the rights set out in the ECHR and of the unwillingness of the Supreme Court even to take the ECHR under its notice. It provided a further justification for incorporating the Convention into Irish law some 20 months after the European Court's judgment.[126]

In *McElhinney v Williams* the plaintiff, who was a policeman, brought a claim in the Irish courts for personal injury damages against a soldier who lived in Northern Ireland and against the Secretary of State for Northern Ireland, who was said to be the person ultimately responsible for the actions of British soldiers based in Northern Ireland. The plaintiff alleged that when he was driving through a vehicle checkpoint from County Londonderry in Northern Ireland into County Donegal in the Republic of Ireland a British soldier somehow attached himself to the truck his car was trailing and then, when across the border, jumped off the car and attempted to fire a gun at the plaintiff (but it jammed). In answer to the claim the defendants pleaded sovereign immunity, arguing that soldiers and the States they represent cannot be sued in a foreign jurisdiction when they are acting within the sphere of governmental activity. In the High Court and Supreme Court the issue was simply whether

[122] *DG v Eastern Health Board* [1997] 3 IR 511. Hamilton CJ gave the leading judgment, with which O'Flaherty and Keane JJ simply concurred; Murphy J added a short judgment reaching the same conclusion; Denham J added a long dissent.

[123] This is a quotation from the judgment of O'Higgins CJ in *G v An Bord Uchtála* [1980] IR 32, 56.

[124] [1997] 3 IR 511, 538.

[125] App No 39474/98, judgment of 16 May 2002.

[126] Through the European Convention on Human Rights Act 2003.

the principle of sovereign immunity applied in the circumstances of the case or whether it was displaced either because of an exception to the principle recognised under public international law[127] or because of the Irish Constitution's guarantee of the rights to bodily integrity and to reclaim redress in the courts.[128] Both courts held against the plaintiff on all counts.[129] The Supreme Court distinguished its own earlier decision in *Government of Canada v Employment Appeals Tribunal*,[130] which had been relied upon by the plaintiff, on the basis that there it had held only that the doctrine of sovereign immunity did not apply in respect of commercial or trading activities carried out by a foreign government, while here the activities alleged were definitely not of that character but were of a sovereign nature (*de iure imperii*).

Undaunted, Mr McElhinney pursued his case in Strasbourg, bringing it against both the Irish government and the UK government (and dropping his case against the individual soldier). The case was deemed important enough to be referred by the Chamber to the Grand Chamber. In *McElhinney v Ireland and UK* the European Court declared admissible the applicant's complaints against Ireland that he had been denied access to a court and discriminated against (in that other people claiming personal injury damages in Ireland against other types of defendants did not have to face a defence of sovereign immunity), but it declared inadmissible the applicant's complaints against the United Kingdom because the applicant had not pursued the remedy open to him to sue within Northern Ireland for the injuries allegedly caused to him.[131] When the admissible claims were eventually heard on their merits the European Court held by 12 v 5 that there had been no violation of Article 6(1) of the ECHR.[132] It noted the apparent trend in international and comparative law towards limiting State immunity for injuries caused within the forum State, but it did not consider this trend to be very definite. It could not be said that Ireland was alone or acting outside currently accepted international standards in allowing immunity to attach to tortious claims committed *de iure imperii*. The European Court therefore agreed with the Irish Supreme Court that it was not possible to conclude that in this matter Irish law conflicted with general principles of international law. This was an oblique reference to Article 29.3 of the Irish Constitution, which declares that 'Ireland accepts the generally recognised principles of international law as its rule of conduct in its relations with other states'. Unfortunately the European Court has continued to maintain its support for the doctrine of sovereign immunity. It has even held that the doctrine justifies preventing the victim of torture from being able to sue the representatives of the State where the torture occurred.[133]

The *Murphy* and *Independent News* Cases

The compatibility of Irish law with Article 10 of the ECHR returned to the European Court in Strasbourg in 2003, when it had to consider whether the Supreme Court had been correct in ruling that a complaint by Pastor Murphy about Ireland's law on religious broadcasting should not be upheld. Pastor Murphy wished to advertise on radio an event being organised by the Irish Faith Centre, during which a one-hour video would be presented on evidence

[127] eg through Art 11 of the European Convention on State Immunity 1972, under which a State cannot claim immunity in proceedings in another State if these relate to redress for personal injuries.

[128] These are guaranteed by, respectively, Arts 40.3.2 and 40.3.1 of the 1937 Constitution.

[129] *McElhinney v Williams* [1995] 3 IR 382 (Costello J in the High Court, Hamilton CJ in the Supreme Court, with whom O'Flaherty and Blayney JJ agreed).

[130] [1992] 2 IR 484.

[131] App No 31253/96, admissibility decision of 9 February 2000 (GC).

[132] *McElhinney v Ireland* (2002) 34 EHRR 13, judgment of 21 November 2001.

[133] *Jones v UK* (2014) 59 EHRR 1.

for the resurrection of Christ. The advertisement had been banned by the Independent Radio and Television Commission (IRTC) under section 10(3) of the Radio and Television Act 1988, which provided that: 'No advertisement shall be broadcast which is directed towards any religious or political end or which has any relation to an industrial dispute.' Affirming the decision by the High Court, where Geoghegan J did explicitly consider the compatibility of the ban in question with Article 10 of the ECHR,[134] though focusing much more on the constitutionality of the impugned statutory provision, the Supreme Court ruled that the restriction on religious broadcasting imposed by section 10(3), although absolute, was proportionate to the legitimate aim of controlling what was presented to people through their television sets.[135] In the words of the Court:

> All three kinds of banned advertisement relate to matters which have proved extremely divisive in Irish society in the past. The Oireachtas was entitled to take the view that the citizens would resent having advertisements touching on these topics broadcast into their homes and that such advertisements, if permitted, might lead to unrest.[136]

In relation to Article 10, the Supreme Court squashed any suggestion that the constitutionality of an Irish statutory provision could be determined by whether it offended the ECHR:

> Whatever methodology may be adopted by the European Court of Human Rights in deciding its cases we are bound to presume that a statute passed since the enactment of the Constitution does not violate the Constitution and we can only rule such an act unconstitutional if that presumption has been rebutted. In the present case, it has not been rebutted ...[137]

On this occasion the European Court of Human Rights agreed with the Supreme Court's approach and conclusions.[138] Perhaps surprisingly, it readily accepted that the Irish government had a legitimate aim in adopting section 10(3), namely, 'public order and safety together with the protection of the rights and freedoms of others',[139] and it went on to hold that Ireland's reasons for the restrictions in question were 'relevant and sufficient'. These reasons were, essentially, that Irish people with religious beliefs might be offended by religious advertising from a different church and interpret it as proselytism, that the prohibition concerned only the audio-visual media and only advertising, and that it was likely that even a limited freedom to advertise would benefit a dominant religion, thereby jarring with the objective of promoting neutrality in broadcasting.[140]

For once, then, the European Court's preparedness to apply a margin of appreciation chimed with the Supreme Court's conservatism, though questions surely need to be asked today, a decade later, whether such extreme sensitivity is still justifiable, especially in view of the rise of social media, of private television services and of a much more liberally-minded and discriminating younger generation. In 1999 Fine Gael tried to have the 1988 Act amended to facilitate religious advertising, but the government was opposed to the amendment and the proposed Bill failed to get passed.[141] Two years later the government did secure the passing of the Broadcasting Act 2001, section 65 of which relaxed the prohibition imposed by section 10(3) of the 1988 Act by providing that it does not prevent the broadcasting of the fact that a particular religious publication is available for supply or that an event associated with a particular religion will be taking place, so long as the broadcast

[134] *Murphy v Independent Radio and Television Commission* [1997] 2 ILRM 467, 476–9; Cannon (1998).

[135] *Murphy v Independent Radio and Television Commission* [1999] 1 IR 12.

[136] Ibid, 22 (per Barrington J, for the Court).

[137] Ibid, 27 (per Barrington J, for the Court).

[138] *Murphy v Ireland* (2004) 38 EHRR 13.

[139] Ibid, para 63.

[140] Ibid, paras 73, 74 and 78.

[141] Radio and Television (Amendment) Bill 1999.

does not address the merits or otherwise of adhering to any religious faith. That was hardly a huge step forward for freedom of speech.

The Supreme Court's adherence to the ECHR's approach to the right to freedom of expression came under further scrutiny in litigation flowing from the publication in 1992 of an article in the *Sunday Independent*, a paper which was at that time read by over a million people each week. A prominent politician, Proinsias de Rossa, alleged that he had been libeled in the article, so he brought defamation proceedings against the newspaper's owners. In the High Court a jury found that the impugned words did imply that Mr de Rossa had been involved in or had tolerated serious crime and that he had personally supported anti-semitism and violent communist oppression. It consequently awarded him IR£300,000 in compensation, a sum which was more than three times higher than any previously approved by the Supreme Court.[142] The newspaper owners duly appealed to the Supreme Court, denigrating the practice in Ireland whereby the trial judge could not give the jury any guidance as to what might be an appropriate level of damages; they argued that this ran contrary to the European Court's judgment in *Tolstoy Miloslavsky v UK*.[143] However, with one dissent (that of Denham J) the Supreme Court rejected the newspaper's appeal and held that existing law and practice, as approved by the Supreme Court in previous cases,[144] was neither unconstitutional[145] nor inconsistent with the ECHR.[146] Denham J, on the other hand, could see no objection to giving some guidance to juries. Citing the Supreme Court's judgment in *McDonagh v News Group Newspaper Ltd*,[147] she would have reduced the jury's award by 50 per cent, to IR£150,000.

When the newspaper took the matter to Strasbourg the European Court closely analysed the Supreme Court's judgments and concluded, by 6 v 1, that the majority's view did not violate Article 10 of the ECHR.[148] It carefully distinguished the case from *Tolstoy Miloslavsky v UK*.[149] In the latter it had found inadequate a court's review of a jury award which asked whether it was 'so unreasonable that it could not have been made by sensible people and must have been arrived at capriciously, unconscionably or irrationally'.[150] In the *Independent Newspapers* case, by contrast, the Irish Supreme Court's role was 'more

[142] But in *Denny v Sunday News, Irish Times*, 14 November 1992, a jury in the High Court awarded IR£275,000 and the newspaper did not appeal to the Supreme Court.

[143] (1995) 20 EHRR 442.

[144] Namely, *Barrett v Independent Newspapers Ltd* [1986] IR 13 (where a jury's award of IR£65,000 for a defamatory allegation that a politician had pulled a journalist's beard when leaving Parliament was set aside as disproportionate) and *Hynes-O'Sullivan v O'Driscoll* [1988] IR 436 (where the defendant's solicitor had complained about a psychiatrist to the Irish Medical Association rather than to the Medical Council and the Supreme Court held that the defendant's honest belief that the IMA had an interest in receiving the complaint did not make it a privileged communication—but there was no damages point in this case). See too *Dawson and Dawson v Irish Brokers Association*, judgment of 27 February 1997, unreported, where the Supreme Court overturned an award of IR£515,000 (at a retrial the jury awarded IR£135,000), and *O'Brien v MGN Ltd* [2001] 1 IR 1, where the Supreme Court refused to change the position it had followed in *de Rossa* but nevertheless overturned a jury's award of IR£250,000 to a well-known businessman whom a newspaper suggested had bribed politicians to secure radio licences and been involved in other corrupt practices (Denham J agreed with this result but would still have preferred to change the position adopted by the majority in *de Rossa*, while Geoghegan J took the converse view).

[145] Art 40.6.1.i provides that 'The State guarantees liberty for the exercise of … the right of the citizens to express freely their convictions and opinions.'

[146] *De Rossa v Independent Newspapers plc* [1999] 4 IR 6.

[147] Judgment of 23 November 1993 (Finlay CJ), unreported (where the Supreme Court upheld a jury's award of IR£90,000 to a barrister who had been alleged to be a sympathiser with terrorist causes and incapable of performing his duties objectively).

[148] *Independent News and Media and Independent Newspapers Ireland Ltd v Ireland* (2005) 42 EHRR 46; the dissenter was Judge Cabral Barreto from Portugal.

[149] (1995) 20 EHRR 442.

[150] Ibid, para 38; this was the test that had been laid down by the House of Lords in *Broome v Cassell & Co Ltd* [1972] AC 1027, 1135 (per Lord Kilbrandon).

robust' in that it had asked whether a jury's award in a libel case was proportionate. The trial judge had given the jury two concrete indications as to the level of damages that might be awarded, namely, the example of a relatively minor defamatory comment to allow the jury to assess the relative seriousness of the defamatory article in this case and an example indicating that, if the jury was to award damages, they would have to be substantial. The difference between the non-ECHR-compliant UK law and the ECHR-compliant Irish law may be a very fine one, but on this occasion the Irish Supreme Court was found to have fulfilled its international human rights obligations.

However the very same issue was to return to both the Supreme Court and the European Court of Human Rights two decades later. Another paper owned by Independent Newspapers (Ireland) Ltd, the *Evening Herald*, had, over the course of two weeks, published 11 articles and a number of doctored photographs suggesting that Martin Cullen, a government minister, had granted preferential treatment to Monica Leech, a consultant who had applied for government contracts. There were insinuations that the couple were having an extra-marital affair. Ms Leech brought defamation proceedings against the newspaper and O'Neill J, obeying the instructions given by the Supreme Court in the *Barrett* case[151] and reaffirmed in the *De Rossa* case,[152] indicated to the jurors what factors they should take into account when assessing appropriate compensation but did not suggest any particular figures for them to think about. The jury awarded €1,872,000 and the newspaper appealed to the Supreme Court claiming that that sum was disproportionately high and violated its rights under both the Constitution and the ECHR. In 2004 a three-judge Supreme Court allowed the appeal; two of the judges (Dunne and Murray JJ) thought that an award of €1,200,000 should be substituted, while the third judge (McKechnie J) would have awarded €1,000,000.[153] All three believed they were applying the principle laid down by the European Court itself in *Independent News and Media and Independent Newspapers Ireland Ltd v Ireland*, but when the newspaper took its case to Strasbourg the judges there did not agree with the Supreme Court.[154] The awards issued, whether by the High Court or the Supreme Court, were larger than any previous awards for defamation and, unlike in the earlier case just cited, the High Court judge had given no specific indications at all as to what amount of compensation might be awardable. As for the Supreme Court's award, the European Court found that the Court had not clarified why it had made the highest ever award even though it had not categorised the defamation in question as one of the gravest and most serious:

> the quite legitimate but exceptional exercise by the Supreme Court of its power to substitute its own assessment of damages for that of the jury ... along with the exceptional nature of the final award from a domestic perspective pointed to a need for comprehensive reasons explaining the final award. As the applicant company and third parties explained, that award had the capacity to act as a benchmark for future defamation awards and out-of-court settlements.[155]

The facts of this case arose before the Defamation Act 2009 came into force. That Act permits trial judges to give more detailed directions to juries as to how to assess damages; if they continue not to do so and the Supreme Court has to consider an appeal in a case, it will

[151] See n 144 above. [152] See n 146 above.

[153] *Leech v Independent Newspapers (Ireland) Ltd* [2014] IESC 79, [2015] 2 IR 214.

[154] *Independent Newspapers (Ireland) Ltd v Ireland*, App No 28199/15, judgment of 15 June 2017.

[155] Ibid, para 100. Remarkably, the European Court refused to award any compensation to the newspaper for the breach of its Art 10 right, which presumably means that it cannot recover any of the (unquantified) excess compensation paid to the woman libeled in the case.

have to have regard to the strictures laid down by the European Court in its most recent pronouncement on the matter.

The *Bosphorus Airways* Case

Strasbourg's next opportunity to consider a decision of the Irish Supreme Court arose in the strange context of European Community law and the impounding of aircraft. The applicant was a Turkish company which in 1992 had taken out a four-year lease on a Boeing 737-300 from Yugoslav Airlines (JAT). In 1993 it arranged for the plane to be maintained by a company in Ireland but while the plane was there it was impounded by the Irish government in compliance with UN Security Council Resolution 820 (1993) which, in the context of the on-going war in Bosnia-Herzegovina, required States to impound all aircraft in their territories 'in which a majority or controlling interest is held by a person or undertaking in or operating from [Serbia and Montenegro]'. This Resolution was implemented in the European Community by Regulation EEC/990/93. In judicial review proceedings a High Court judge held on two occasions that the government's interpretation and application of Regulation 990/93 was unlawful.[156] When the first of these decisions was appealed to the Supreme Court a reference was made to the European Court of Justice in Luxembourg for a preliminary ruling on how Regulation 990/93 should be interpreted and in July 1996 the ECJ ruled that Ireland's impounding of the aircraft was entirely lawful.[157] It therefore rejected the Turkish company's argument that Ireland had infringed its right to peaceful enjoyment of its possessions and its freedom to pursue a commercial activity.[158] The Irish Supreme Court, in response to this preliminary ruling, upheld the Irish government's appeal against the High Court's decision.[159] It was this decision which the applicant then challenged in Strasbourg.

The Grand Chamber of the European Court of Human Rights held that the Supreme Court had had no choice but to follow the ECJ's preliminary ruling and that it was acceptable under the ECHR for a State to transfer sovereign power to an international or supranational organisation, such as the European Community, in order to pursue co-operation in certain fields of activity so long as that organisation protected fundamental rights 'in a manner which can be considered at least equivalent to that for which the Convention provides'.[160] The Strasbourg Court did not therefore examine whether the ECJ had itself properly decided that the impounding of the airplane was not disproportionate. It deemed it enough to conclude that the important general interest in national compliance with

[156] *Bosphorus Hava Yollari Turizm v Minister for Transport, Energy and Communications* [1994] 2 ILRM 551 (Murphy J) and [1997] 2 IR 1 (Barr J). The first case related to the application of Art 8 of Regulation EEC/990/93, while the second related to the application of Art 9. The latter decision was approved by the Supreme Court: [1997] 2 IR 1, 18.

[157] Case C-84/95, *Bosphorus Airways* [1996] ECR I-3953, judgment of 30 July 1996.

[158] See para 26: 'As compared with an objective of general interest so fundamental for the international community, which consists in putting an end to the state of war in the region and to the massive violations of human rights and humanitarian international law in the Republic of Bosnia-Herzegovina, the impounding of the aircraft in question, which is owned by an undertaking based in or operating from [Yugoslavia], cannot be regarded as inappropriate or disproportionate.'

[159] Judgment of 29 November 1996 (unreported); in May 1998 the Supreme Court also allowed the government's appeal from the second High Court decision, but in view of the intervening rulings by the ECJ and the Supreme Court itself, this 1998 appeal was hypothetical only.

[160] *Bosphorus Hava Yollari Turizm Ve Ticaret Anonim Şirketi v Ireland* (2006) 42 EHRR 1, judgment of 26 June 2005 (GC), para 155, citing *M & Co v Federal Republic of Germany*, App No 13258/87, Commission decision of 9 February 1990, 64 DR 138, 145. For comments on the European Court's decision see Hoffmeister (2006) and Schorkopf (2005).

European Community obligations justified Ireland's interference with the company's property rights because, as the European Community was an organisation which in general protected fundamental rights in a comparable way to that required by the ECHR, there was a presumption that Ireland had not breached the ECHR when implementing legal obligations flowing from its membership of the European Community.[161]

This case laid down an important precedent for the European Court of Human Rights and has been respected ever since. It helps to define the relationship between Europe's two highest courts. In addition the Strasbourg Court's strong endorsement of the way in which the Irish Supreme Court had dealt with the matters before it in this case must undoubtedly have pleased the Irish judges. Strasbourg said that the Supreme Court was required to make the preliminary reference to the ECJ because the interpretation of the Regulation in question was not obvious (the views of the UN Sanctions Committee and of Ireland's Minister for Transport were in conflict with those of the Irish High Court) and the question was of central importance to the case. Moreover there had been no previous ruling by the ECJ on the point and the ruling now provided was binding on the Supreme Court. In effect it resolved the domestic proceedings and it would have been inappropriate for the Supreme Court to issue supplementary rulings or make a second preliminary reference because the Turkish company had not developed these points in any detail when pleading before the Supreme Court. One can hardly blame the Supreme Court for not paying greater attention to the company's claim that its right to peaceful enjoyment of its possessions had been disproportionately interfered with, because neither the ECJ nor the Strasbourg Court queried the legality of the interference. Subsequent case law from both courts have revealed that in cases where UN sanctions are being implemented the right to a fair hearing needs to be taken more seriously into account than perhaps was the case vis-à-vis Bosphorus Airways.[162]

Further Cases on Delay and Unfairness

In *Doran v Ireland*[163] the European Court found a violation of Articles 6 and 13 as regards the length of time taken to deal with civil proceedings which the applicants had brought in relation to the purchase of land that turned out not to have access to a road. The Court awarded €25,000 in compensation. The applicants had begun High Court proceedings in July 1991[164] and in March 1998 the Supreme Court finally upheld their appeal,[165] holding that the vendors' solicitors were liable to them in negligence. The European Court found that the State was responsible for delays amounting to some three years, caused by the High Court judge in question. This was Hamilton J, as he then was, who while dealing with this litigation was also chairing the so-called Beef Tribunal.[166] The hearing at first instance took one year, there was a further delay of almost one year between the end of the hearing and the delivery of judgment, and almost a further year passed between the date when the

[161] Ibid, paras 151–66.

[162] See eg *Kadi I* Joined Cases C-402/05 P and C-415/05, 3 September 2008; *Kadi II* Joined Cases C-584/10P, C-593/10 P and C-595/10P, 18 July 2013; *Nada v Switzerland* App No 10593/08, 12 September 2012 (GC); *Al-Dulimi and Montana Management Inc v Switzerland* App No 5809/08, 21 June 2016 (GC).

[163] (2006) 42 EHRR 13, judgment of 31 July 2003.

[164] These concluded in September 1995: *Doran v Delaney* [1996] 1 ILRM 490.

[165] *Doran v Delaney* [1998] 2 IR 61.

[166] The Beef Tribunal was an inquiry into malpractices within Ireland's beef processing industry and allegations that a government Minister had granted special dispensations to a particular individual. It ran from June 1991 to July 1994 and was the longest inquiry in Ireland's history up to that time.

Supreme Court directed the trial judge to settle the note of evidence and his finalising a six-page report on that note. In relation to the applicants' claim based on Article 13 (the right to an effective remedy), the European Court rejected the Irish government's argument that the applicants could have begun an action in the courts based on their unenumerated constitutional right to constitutional justice. Even if a right to a determination of proceedings within a reasonable period of time was a guarantee flowing from Article 40.3.1 of the Constitution, it had not been demonstrated that the remedy to which the government referred was 'effective, adequate or accessible' for the purposes of Article 13 of the ECHR.[167] This was because the government had not been able to cite a single case where an individual's complaint to a domestic tribunal about delay had resulted in the prevention of its continuation or in damages for delay that had already occurred, nor to a case where the domestic courts had relied on the European Court's judgments about delay to recognise a further unenumerated constitutional right and to develop a domestic remedy for its breach.[168] The European Court's judgment again casts an unflattering light on Ireland's judicial processes.

In *O'Reilly v Ireland*[169] the European Court declared admissible an application by eight applicants who alleged that their rights under Articles 6 and 13 of the ECHR had been violated because they had to wait nearly five years before getting a definitive court ruling on whether they could require Cavan County Council to repair the road on which they were living. Having ruled that the dispute in question was one which was covered by Article 6, the European Court noted that the applicants' court proceedings in Ireland had begun with their motion for leave to apply for judicial review in July 1994 and ended when the Supreme Court made its final orders in June 1999. More particularly, the High Court hearing had occurred in April 1995 but judgment was not delivered until December 1996, and in the Supreme Court the appeal hearing was adjourned from February 1998 to February 1999. When it later considered the merits of the case the European Court held that both Article 6 and Article 13 had indeed been violated. In relation to Article 6, the Court stressed that it was up to Ireland to organise its own court system in a way which did not lead to unreasonable delays:

> As regards the Government's submission that the applicants did not pursue the speedy resumption of the Supreme Court proceedings after February 1998, the Court recalls that States are obliged to organise their legal systems so as to allow the courts to comply with the reasonable time requirement of Article 6 so that even a principle of domestic law or practice requiring the parties to take initiatives to advance the proceedings does not dispense the State from this obligation ...[170]
>
> ... While the High Court judge had other judicial commitments, while an urgent case and other court business combined to delay the Supreme Court hearing and even if the parties incorrectly estimated the appeal hearing time, the Court reiterates that it is for the State to organise its legal systems as to comply with the reasonable time aspect of Article 6 of the Convention.[171]

As regards the violation of Article 13, the European Court applied what it had said in *Doran v Ireland* just five weeks earlier and added that it made no difference that towards the end of November 1996 the President of the High Court (Costello P) had issued general directions

[167] Note 163 above, para 64. [168] Ibid, paras 67–8.

[169] (2005) 40 EHRR 40, judgment of 5 September 2003.

[170] Here the Court cited *Süßmann v Germany,* App No 20024/92, judgment of 16 September 1996 (GC); *Mitchell and Holloway v UK* App No 44808/98, 17 December 2002; *Price and Lowe v UK,* App Nos 43185/98 and 43186/98, 29 July 2003.

[171] (2005) 40 EHRR 40, judgment of 29 July 2004, paras 32 and 33.

that all complaints about delays in proceedings should be forwarded to him, including complaints about delays in delivering reserved judgments (which was allegedly due to the shortage of judges). The fact remains that in *O'Reilly v Ireland* the Supreme Court itself was found to have contributed to the inordinate delays, in violation of Article 6 of the ECHR.

On the same day that it decided *O'Reilly* the European Court gave judgment in a comparable application brought against Ireland, *McMullen v Ireland*.[172] In 1988 Mr McMullen had issued negligence proceedings against a firm of solicitors which had represented him in an earlier court case. He eventually lost the case against the solicitors in the High Court[173] and unsuccessfully challenged the dismissal of his claim concerning the costs awarded against him.[174] The solicitors then sought to recover their costs against the applicant and successfully applied for him to be declared bankrupt when he refused to pay. The application by Mr McMullen to Strasbourg alleged a breach of Article 6 as regards the duration of the negligence proceedings, and was successful, with compensation of €8,000 being awarded. Although the European Court attributed some of the delays to the applicant himself, it drew particular attention to specific and lengthy delays attributable to the domestic authorities: more than a year elapsed between the High Court's hearings and the delivery of its judgment, almost two years elapsed between the applicant's confirmation that all appeal documents had been filed and the first hearing date for the appeal, and a period of six months elapsed for the Supreme Court to re-constitute and fix a hearing date for the relevant appeal. As in *Doran*, the European Court took the period during which costs were taxed as part of the original proceedings (so the period was ongoing at the date of the Court's judgment).

Delay in Criminal Cases

Taken together, *Doran*, *O'Reilly* and *McMullen* were clear signals to the Irish legislature and government that, notwithstanding the value attributed to the enumerated and unenumerated rights in the Irish Constitution, there were still respects in which these fell short of the guarantees required by the ECHR as regards the right to a fair hearing, even within the Supreme Court.[175] As Brown points out,[176] the trio of defeats for the Irish government served to focus the minds of domestic courts in subsequent civil cases. But delays in criminal cases were also condemned by Strasbourg. In *Barry v Ireland*[177] a doctor was prosecuted for allegedly sexually assaulting a number of female patients. The proceedings against him began when his home, clinic and consulting rooms were searched in June 1995, but by the date of the European Court's judgment in December 2005 the proceedings against him had still not been completed. Again, while attributing part of the delay to the applicant himself, the Court criticised the authorities for being partly responsible for delays amounting to 88 months. Although the Supreme Court had been involved on three occasions in considering aspects of the case, no particular blame was allocated to it for the delays, but the High Court was said to be responsible for a 13-month gap between a hearing in the case and the delivery of a judgment on that hearing. Interestingly, during the course of the disciplinary proceedings against Dr Barry he sought judicial review of a decision by the Fitness to Practise Committee of the Medical Council to hold a *private* inquiry about

[172] App No 42297/98, judgment of 29 July 2004.

[173] *McMullen v Farrell* [1993]1 IR 123.

[174] *McMullen v Farrell (No 2)* [2004] 2 IR 328.

[175] See too Coen (2015) 333–4. As regards Irish law's consistency with Art 6 more generally, see O'Donnell (2004); Dewhurst et al (2012) Chap 6.

[176] Brown (2009) 118.

[177] App No 18273/04, judgment of 15 December 2005. The Court found breaches of Arts 6(1) and 13 of the ECHR and awarded compensation of €8,000

his conduct. He alleged that this was in breach not only of his rights under Article 40.3 of the Constitution but also of his rights under Article 6(1) of the ECHR, a bold attempt to claim that by 1997 the Convention had somehow become part of domestic Irish law. Both the High Court and, on appeal, the Supreme Court rejected Dr Barry's request[178] but, while the Supreme Court, through Barrington J, accepted that the ECHR was not part of Irish law, it did nevertheless take time to consider the requirements of Article 6,[179] eventually distinguishing the facts of a relevant European Court decision[180] from that before the Supreme Court in *Barry*.

An excellent opportunity for the Supreme Court to consider and apply the European Court's jurisprudence on fair trials arose in a case involving a suspected member of the IRA, Brendan McFarlane. He had been imprisoned in Northern Ireland in 1975 for his involvement in a bomb explosion which killed five people, but he escaped in 1983. He was returned to prison in 1986, having been extradited from the Netherlands, and was eventually released in 1998. While he was on the run between 1983 and 1986 his fingerprints were found at the scene of a kidnapping incident in the Republic of Ireland (involving Mr Don Tidey) in which a policeman and a soldier were killed. Upon his release from prison in Northern Ireland he was almost immediately arrested while on a visit to the Republic, questioned by the police and charged with involvement in the kidnapping. Eight days later he was granted bail. While awaiting trial McFarlane challenged the lawfulness of the process being used against him, first on the basis that the fingerprint samples found at the scene of the kidnapping had since been lost and second on account of the many years' delay between the occurrence of the incident in 1983 and his being questioned about it in 1998. These issues reached the Supreme Court but the judges unanimously found against McFarlane.[181] His trial was fixed for October 2006, but again he entered a challenge, this time arguing that the delay resulting from the time taken to deal with his earlier judicial review application meant that his constitutional right to a trial with reasonable expedition had been violated, exposing him to a real and serious risk of an unfair trial,[182] and that his right to a fair trial under Article 6 of the ECHR had been violated. By this time the ECHR was part of the domestic law of Ireland.[183]

These challenges also failed, both in the High Court[184] and in the Supreme Court.[185] In holding that there had been no objectionable delay both Fennelly and Kearns JJ pointed out that the question the Supreme Court had to ask itself was different from that which confronted the European Court: the latter had simply to consider whether there had been an unreasonable delay and, if so, whether any compensation should be paid as a result, whereas the Supreme Court had to weigh the delay against the public interest in pursuing serious crime. The judges referred to the European Court's judgments in *McMullen* and *Barry*, discussed above, but were able to distinguish them, mainly on the basis that McFarlane had

[178] *Barry v The Medical Council* [1998] 3 IR 368. [179] Ibid, 392–6.

[180] *Diennet v France* (1995) 21 EHRR 554.

[181] *McFarlane v DPP* [2006] IESC 11, [2007] 1 IR 134. At the High Court hearing Ó Caoimh J had held that the police's failure to retain the fingerprint samples would have made the trial unfair, but the Supreme Court thought it was sufficient that photographs of the prints had been preserved and that the results of the forensic analysis of the prints were still available for McFarlane to try to rebut if he so wished. Keane J dissented on this point.

[182] Under Art 38(1) of the 1937 Constitution.

[183] The European Convention on Human Rights Act 2003 came into effect on 31 December 2003. Section 4 requires judicial notice to be taken of (amongst other things) the Convention provisions, judgments of the European Court and decisions of the European Commission of Human Rights. It also requires a court, when interpreting and applying the Convention provisions, to 'take due account of the principles laid down by' those judgments and decisions. The section is similar, but not identical, to the UK's Human Rights Act 1998, s 2(1).

[184] [2006] IEHC 389 (Quirke J). [185] *McFarlane v DPP* [2008] IESC 57, [2008] 4 IR 117.

failed to demonstrate that he himself had not been the cause of much of the delay in processing the earlier judicial review proceedings and that the delays in his case had been well outside the norm.[186] Geoghegan J differed from his colleagues in suggesting that if an applicant complained of systemic delay caused by failures in the criminal justice system he or she would have to show 'a positively negligent system or negligent failure of system within the resources that exist of (*sic*) administering criminal justice'.[187] While finding no violation of the Irish Constitution the Supreme Court left open the question whether, if the right to a trial with reasonable expedition is breached, a remedy in damages should be available.

The date of McFarlane's trial was then fixed for June 2008. Ironically, in view of all the time taken to deal with the challenges up to that point, the Special Criminal Court quickly ruled that the main evidence against the defendant, namely the admission he had allegedly made during police questioning in 1998, was inadmissible and that, as the prosecution did not wish to adduce any further evidence, the charges should be dismissed.[188] No doubt buoyed by this victory, McFarlane lodged an application with the European Court of Human Rights which, by 12 v 5, held that he had suffered a violation of both Article 6 and Article 13 of the Convention.[189] It rejected the government's argument that the applicant had not himself actively pursued the litigation and it criticised the Irish courts for delays totaling 57 months.[190] As regards Article 13, the Court repeated what it had said in its *Barry* judgment, namely that the right under Irish law to claim damages for breach of the right to reasonable expedition in a trial was not an effective remedy within the meaning of Article 13 of the Convention. The Irish government had not requested the referral of the *Barry* judgment to the Grand Chamber; that did not mean that the government was estopped from raising the point in *McFarlane*, but the Chamber was content to adhere to its previous position. *McFarlane v Ireland* shows that even in 2008 the Irish Supreme Court had still not internalised the required approach to the right to a fair trial set out in Article 6 of the ECHR and as interpreted by the Court in Strasbourg. It was reluctant to admit that the delays in Ireland's judicial processes meant that the system was fundamentally flawed in human rights terms.

In *Donohoe v Ireland*[191] the European Court, however, found no violation of Article 6 in a case where the applicant complained that relevant material had not been disclosed to him by the prosecution. He had been convicted of membership of the Irish Republican Army, partly on evidence from a chief superintendent of police that he believed Mr Donohoe to be such a member, but the evidential sources for this belief were not revealed to the applicant.[192] He applied to the Court of Criminal Appeal (CCA) under section 29 of the Courts of Justice Act 1924 Act, requesting that court to certify that the decision it had taken on his appeal from the Special Criminal Court involved a point of law of exceptional public

[186] [2008] 4 IR 17, paras 81–91 (per Fennelly J) and 146–56 (per Kearns J).

[187] Ibid, para 10.

[188] www.irishtimes.com/news/mcfarlane-trial-over-tidey-kidnap-collapses-1.824978.

[189] *McFarlane v Ireland* (2011) 52 EHRR 20, judgment of 10 September 2010 (GC). The Court also awarded €5,500 by way of compensation. The same applicant lodged a second application in April 2008 (App No 25100/08), which complains mainly about delays involved in his first challenge to the trial process, but for some reason that application was not joined to this one (see para 46 of the judgment) and it does not yet appear to have resulted in any decision by the Court.

[190] Ibid, paras 147–51.

[191] App No 19165/08, judgment of 12 December 2013. The Irish Human Rights Commission submitted detailed views on the compatibility of the Irish legislation with the ECHR.

[192] Such evidence is admissible because of the Offences Against the State (Amendment) Act 1972, s 3(2), which reads: 'Where an officer of the Garda Síochána, not below the rank of Chief Superintendent, in giving evidence in proceedings relating to an offence under [section 21 (membership of an unlawful organisation)], states that he believes that the accused was at a material time a member of an unlawful organisation, the statement shall be evidence that he was then such a member.'

importance and that it was therefore desirable in the public interest that he be allowed a further appeal to the Supreme Court, the question for consideration being whether he had received a fair trial pursuant to Article 6 of the ECHR and Article 38 of the Constitution. In 2007 the CCA refused the application for a section 29 certificate,[193] so the Supreme Court was denied an opportunity to give its view on the issue.

On his application to Strasbourg the Court there carefully reviewed its case law on the fairness of trials in which the defendant is unable to cross-examine the sources of evidence, but held that in this case that there was plenty of other evidence to justify the applicant's conviction and several safeguards in place to prevent improper reliance on the police officer's belief. The Court no doubt opted to look at the merits of this application because of its recent case law concerning evidence from anonymous or deceased witnesses.[194] In an earlier application against Ireland, again following a decision by the Irish Supreme Court upholding the admissibility of a senior police officer's evidence in the Special Criminal Court as to his or her 'belief', the European Court declared it inadmissible.[195] It is worth noting that in 2009, when the prosecuting authorities were trying to convict Colm Murphy of membership of the IRA, the Supreme Court held that it would be unfair to proceed with the trial given (amongst other things) the delay caused by the prosecution of two police witnesses for perjury alleged to have been committed at his original trial.[196] This conclusion was reached, however, without any significant reference to the ECHR.

Delay Today

A further embarrassment to the Supreme Court was the judgment issued by a three-judge committee of the European Court in *Rooney v Ireland* in 2013.[197] Mr Rooney, who was both a farmer and a barrister (representing himself in court), brought various challenges against the constitutionality of Ireland's scheme for dealing with bovine tuberculosis. He initiated, and lost, so many court actions that in 2001 the Supreme Court declared him to be a vexatious litigant.[198] In 2010, however, he persuaded the Supreme Court that, due to a clear 'oversight', his 1990 appeal in relation to a decision of the High Court not to issue him with a judgment in default of defence had never been determined.[199] In the same year he finally got a decision from the Supreme Court that a different appeal lodged by him in 2004 had been unsuccessful.[200] He duly complained to the European Court of Human Rights that there had been unacceptable delays in the processing of these two appeals. Not surprisingly, and after referring to the Grand Chamber's decision in *McFarlane v Ireland,* the European Court wasted little time in agreeing with him and awarded him compensation of €26,000 (to include his costs and expenses), though this was far short of the €600,000 he was demanding. During the course of his 2004 appeal the Supreme Court's registrar notified Mr Rooney that there was then a 31-month waiting time for a hearing to take place after a case

[193] [2007] IECCA 97, available at www.bailii.org/ie/cases/IECCA/2007/C97.html. The decision to convict Mr Donohoe is reported at [2006] IECCA 147, available at www.bailii.org/ie/cases/IECCA/2006/C147.html.

[194] eg *Al-Khawaja and Tahery v UK* (2012) 54 EHRR 23.

[195] *Kelly v Ireland*, App No 41130/06, decision of 14 December 2010. The Supreme Court's decision is reported as *DPP v Kelly* [2006] IESC 20, [2006] 3 IR 115.

[196] *Murphy v DPP* [2009] IESC 53, [2009] 3 IR 821. Murphy had previously been acquitted (on appeal) of involvement in the bomb in Omagh, County Tyrone, in 1998, which killed 29 people and unborn twins.

[197] App No 32614/10, judgment of 31 October 2013.

[198] For an earlier Supreme Court decision rejecting his claim that the extra-statutory bovine tuberculosis scheme was invalid see *Rooney v Minister for Agriculture and Food* [1991] 2 IR 539.

[199] *Rooney v Minister for Agriculture and Food* [2010] IEHC 12.

[200] *Rooney v Minister for Agriculture and Food* [2010] IESC 55.

had been certified as ready; this was bad enough, but for the Supreme Court then to lose track altogether of not just one appeal but two made it look all the more inefficient.

A corner, however, may now have been turned. The most recent case from Ireland to reach the European Court of Human Rights, *Brennan v Ireland*,[201] is another relatively simple one where a plaintiff was seeking compensation from those responsible for serious defects in a building she had bought. The proceedings went on interminably, from 10 February 2003 to 29 July 2015; having won at first instance, she lost on appeal. On the specific facts the European Court did not think that there had been a violation of Article 6 because most of the delays were due to the applicant. In the course of its judgment the Court gave credit to Ireland for dealing with the backlog in Supreme Court cases by creating a Court of Appeal in October 2014 and transferring a number of cases to that forum, including Ms Brennan's. It observed that the two appeals in the case had been heard by the Court of Appeal within five months of being transferred, with decisions being announced very soon thereafter and no more than 23 months after the decisions being appealed against. That, apparently, is an acceptable period of delay for appeals, even in a rather mundane and not particularly valuable case such Ms Brennan's. The Court stated: 'It is clear from the manner in which the appeals were dealt with by the Court of Appeal after they were transferred that it was alive to the issue of delay and prepared to take steps in order to dispose rapidly of the proceedings to the extent possible ... The final stage, regarding this aspect of the litigation—the Supreme Court's refusal of leave to appeal—was concluded without delay.'[202] With luck this will see an end to the unfortunate litany of cases in Strasbourg highlighting how sclerotic the Irish judicial system had become prior to 2014.

The *A, B and C* Case

The Supreme Court's decisions on abortion have been examined elsewhere in this book.[203] The first opportunity for the European Court of Human Rights to pronounce directly on the matter arose in *A, B and C v Ireland*.[204] The first two applicants (who were Irish citizens) complained about the prohibition of abortion on health and well-being grounds, while the third applicant (a Lithuanian citizen) complained about the lack of legislation on the right to abortion in Ireland when there is a risk to a woman's life. As in *Airey* and *Johnston*,[205] the applications came before the European Court without first having been considered by any domestic Irish court, let alone the Supreme Court, so naturally the Irish government argued that the applicants had not exhausted their domestic remedies. The judges in Strasbourg affirmed what had been said in an earlier case against Ireland where an application had been declared inadmissible, *D v Ireland*,[206] namely that:

> ... in a legal system providing constitutional protection for fundamental rights it is incumbent on the aggrieved individual to test the extent of that protection and, in a common-law system, to allow the domestic courts to develop those rights by way of interpretation. In this respect, it is noted that a declaratory action before the High Court, with a possibility of an appeal to the

[201] App No 44360/15, judgment of 2 November 2017.

[202] Ibid, para 55.

[203] See Chap 10 above, 235-9.

[204] (2011) 53 EHRR 13, judgment of 16 December 2010 (GC). See Wicks (2011) and (2012).

[205] See above, 274-5.

[206] App 26499/02, decision of 27 June 2006. In this case the European Court found that the applicant could have argued in an Irish court, with some prospect of success, that the relevant balance of competing interests was in her favour since one of the twin foetuses she was carrying was already dead and the other had a confirmed fatal abnormality.

Supreme Court, constitutes the most appropriate method under Irish law of seeking to assert and vindicate constitutional rights.[207]

Nevertheless, after considering the current state of Irish constitutional law, as developed by the Supreme Court in 'the seminal *X* case',[208] the European Court unanimously ruled that any attempt by the first and second applicants to obtain an effective remedy in Ireland would have had no prospect of success. They reiterated the underlying principle that, for an application to be declared inadmissible for non-exhaustion of domestic remedies, the existence of such remedies 'must be sufficiently certain not only in theory but also in practice, failing which they will lack the requisite accessibility and effectiveness'.[209] The Irish government had tried to convince the Strasbourg Court that a declaration of incompatibility, now available under the ECHR Act 2003, was an effective remedy, citing the Supreme Court's explanation of that remedy in *Carmody v Minister for Justice, Equality and Law Reform Ireland*,[210] but the European Court responded by saying that a declaration, and any associated *ex gratia* award of damages, was not an effective remedy since '[t]he rights guaranteed by the 2003 Act would not prevail over the provisions of the Constitution' and a declaration did not oblige the State to amend domestic law.[211]

As regards the third applicant, the European Court ruled that her complaint, about the lack of any legislation specifying more precisely when a woman's life might be at risk, was so tied up with the merits of her claim that it needed to be considered alongside those merits.[212] The Court did, however, declare all of the applicants' claims under Articles 2 and 3 of the ECHR inadmissible, since there was no evidence of either a real risk to life (the third applicant could have gone to England to get an abortion) or of inhuman or degrading treatment.[213] As regards Article 8, the European Court held by 11 v 6 that it had not been violated as far as the first and second applicants were concerned[214] but by 17 v 0 that it had been violated in the case of the third applicant, to whom they awarded €15,000 in compensation. The *A, B and C* case has not since been cited by the Irish Supreme Court but it was instrumental in leading the Oireachtas to pass the Protection of Life During Pregnancy Act 2013 and to the 'Repeal the Eighth' petition, which ultimately led to the referendum in May 2018 and to the resulting changes to Ireland's abortion law.[215]

The *O'Keeffe* Case

The most recent occasion on which the views of the Supreme Court have been considered by the Grand Chamber of the European Court of Human Rights is *O'Keeffe v Ireland*.[216] The

[207] (2011) 53 EHRR 13, para 142, citing *D v Ireland*, para 85, which in turn cites *Patrick Holland v Ireland* App No 24827/94, Commission decision of 14 April 1998, 93 DR 15, and *Independent News and Media and Independent Newspapers Ireland Ltd v Ireland* (2005) 42 EHRR 46.

[208] Ibid, para 147. [209] Ibid, para 142.

[210] [2009] IESC 71, [2010] 1 IR 635. See too de Londras (2014b); Hogan (2006).

[211] (2011) 53 EHRR 13, para 150; here the European Court cited two of its decisions relating to declarations of incompatibility under the UK's Human Rights Act 1998: *Hobbs v UK* (2007) 44 EHRR 54 and *Burden v UK* (2008) 47 EHRR 38.

[212] Ibid, para 155. This also occurred in *Tysiąc v Poland* App No 5410/03, decision of 7 February 2006.

[213] On this aspect of the admissibility decision the Court was not unanimous, but the judgment does not reveal the identity or number of dissenters.

[214] The dissenters were the judges from Greece, Belgium, Sweden, Finland, Switzerland and Moldova. The ad hoc judge from Ireland, Mary Finlay Geoghegan (a Supreme Court judge since December 2017, a High Court from 2002 to 2017 and a member of the Constitution Review Group which sat from 1995–96) agreed with the majority.

[215] See Chap 10 above, 239.

[216] App No 35810/09, judgment of 28 January 2014 (GC). Again the Irish Human Rights Commission intervened with third party submissions.

applicant had been the victim of repeated sex abuse committed by a teacher at a primary school she attended in 1973, when she was nine years old. The school was owned and run by the Catholic Church but was recognised and inspected by the State as a national school. The teacher responsible for the abuse was later prosecuted and convicted; he was also successfully sued by the applicant and ordered to pay her €305,000, which he was doing at the rate of €400 per month. But the applicant also sued the Irish government, claiming it was directly and/or vicariously liable for what had happened to her (strangely, she did not sue the Catholic Church). On the direct liability point the applicant lost in the High Court and did not pursue the claim on appeal to the Supreme Court: her argument that she had a right to damages because the State had broken its duty under Article 42.4 of the Constitution to provide her with free primary education did not appeal to De Valera J.[217] On the vicarious liability point the claimant lost in both Courts, with Geoghegan J dissenting in the Supreme Court.[218] The prevailing view was that there was not the kind of close connection between the government and the running of the school, and certainly no employment relationship, to justify the imposition of vicarious liability. In so holding the Supreme Court gave careful consideration to a number of decisions reached by top courts in Australia, Canada and the United Kingdom but could not deduce from any of them a sound reason for imposing liability on the State here. In the words of Hardiman J:

> It seems to me ... lacking in fundamental justice to impose a liability on a person simply because he is, or is thought to be, in a position to pay compensation. Equally, and perhaps even more obviously, it is wrong to impose the status of wrongdoer and the liability to pay compensation without fault for acts outside the scope of employment on the basis of *pour encourager les autres*.[219]

Geoghegan J simply disagreed. For him, given the circumstances of the relationship between Church and State, exemption from vicarious liability by the State was not just.[220] Overall, the position of the Supreme Court in this case was a conservative one, which is all the more startling in view of the revelations which have been brought to light in recent years concerning the extent of child abuse at official institutions in Ireland, most starkly exposed in the report of the Ryan Commission in 2009.[221]

The ECHR does not seem to have been mentioned in the domestic proceedings. Presumably this was because, even though the European Convention on Human Rights Act 2003 was in force when Ms O'Keeffe began her case, the facts she was relying upon to justify her claim had occurred many years earlier, and the Act was not retrospective to that extent.[222] Section 2(1) of the 2003 Act imposes on courts, and only on courts,[223] a duty to interpret and apply any statutory provision or rule of law, 'in so far as is possible, subject to the rules of law relating to such interpretation and application, in a manner compatible with the State's obligations under the Convention provisions' but Article 42.4 is not a

[217] [2006] IEHC 13; the judge was a grandson of the former Taoiseach and President.

[218] *O'Keeffe v Hickey* [2008] IESC 72, [2009] 2 IR 302. The High Court judgment is at [2006] IEHC 13.

[219] Ibid, [121]. [220] Ibid, [180].

[221] This body was established under the Commission to Inquire into Child Abuse Act 2000; it confined itself to occurrences of abuse in industrial and reformatory schools. A summary of relevant investigations of child abuse in Ireland is set out in the European Court's judgment, n 224 below, paras 69–90. It was initially chaired by Mary Laffoy, later a Supreme Court judge, and then by Seán Ryan, President of the Court of Appeal from 2014–18.

[222] Under s 3(5) of the Act, proceedings cannot be brought in respect of any contravention by an organ of the State of its duty to perform its functions compatibly with the ECHR if the contravention arose more than one year before the Act's commencement. Again, the UK's Act was worded differently, and more ambiguously; see Amos (2014) 67–71.

[223] In contrast with s 3 of the UK's Human Rights Act 1998.

statutory provision nor (though this is more controversial) a 'rule of law'. When it comes to the common law concept of vicarious liability the High Court and Supreme Court may well have been conscious (though if so they did not admit it) of the fact that section 1(1) of the 2003 Act excludes courts from the definition of 'organs of the state', thereby exonerating them from the duty imposed by section 3(1) to 'perform [their] functions in a manner compatible with the State's obligations under the Convention provisions'.

When the case reached the European Court of Human Rights the arguments were of course entirely about human rights liability and not at all about tortious liability. By 11 v 6 the Grand Chamber held that Ireland had violated the applicant's right under Article 3 of the ECHR not to be subjected to torture or to inhuman or degrading treatment or punishment, and also her right under Article 13 to have an effective remedy for the breach of Article 3.[224] It awarded the applicant €30,000 in compensation, as well as €85,000 for her legal costs. Amongst the six dissenters was the ad hoc judge from Ireland, Peter Charleton (then a judge of the High Court, now of the Supreme Court). His main objection was that Ireland was inappropriately being held responsible for not behaving in 1973 in ways which only recently had come to be regarded as necessary. He approved of the conclusion reached by the applicant's expert witness, Professor Ferguson, who, having reviewed how child abuse might have been prevented in the mid-1970s, said there was no basis on which he could testify that Ireland had failed in its duty of care towards school children. Judge Charleton agreed that 'it was not possible to project onto the past the knowledge and systems of accountability of the present day'.[225] There is an initial attractiveness in such a position, but it is difficult to reconcile with the common law tradition of creating new law and applying it retrospectively. Moreover the European Court has emphasised time and time again that the Convention must be interpreted in a dynamic and evolutive manner. Here it stressed that, having regard to the particularly vulnerable nature of children, 'it is an inherent obligation of government to ensure their protection from ill-treatment, especially in a primary education context, through the adoption, as necessary, of special measures and safeguards'.[226] What's more, this obligation existed even at the time when the abuse in this case was taking place, 1973.[227] The Court dismissed Professor Ferguson's evidence as 'not an expert investigation report but rather pre-litigation advice and thus inevitably also concerned with issues such as chances of success and costs exposure'.[228]

The European Court's decision has been criticised extra-judicially by both Adrian Hardiman and Ronan Keane.[229] The former upbraids the Court for dealing with the applicant's claim of direct state responsibility even though, having lost on that ground in the High Court she did not seek to appeal the point to the Supreme Court. In Hardiman J's words, the European Court 'thus assumed a jurisdiction, and made a finding adverse to the State, in a case where domestic remedies have not even been attempted to be exhausted'.[230] He politely suggests that the Court might have been confused or expressed itself ambiguously.[231] Keane likewise observes that the majority judgment in the European Court 'proceeded on a legal basis which had never been presented to the Supreme Court'[232] and he suggests that the European Court effectively contradicted its margin of appreciation

[224] *O'Keeffe v Ireland* (2014) 59 EHRR 15, judgment of 28 January 2014 (GC).

[225] Dissenting judgment, para 24. He added (at para 2): 'In 1973, no one would have suspected that a senior head teacher could be a source of sexual violence to his child pupils. Without proof that Ireland in the 1970s should have taken the precautions that bitter experience and decades of official reports now demonstrate is appropriate, the case that Ireland failed in human rights obligations is not made out.'

[226] Note 224 above, para 146. [227] Ibid, para 147. [228] Ibid, para 167.

[229] Hardiman (2017); Keane (2015). [230] Ibid, 100.

[231] Ibid, 106. [232] Keane (2015) 173.

doctrine, under which States are allowed to devise their own system for managing the provision of education.[233] The European Court's judgment was defended by Conor O'Mahony[234] but Keane challenges both the latter's understanding of Supreme Court practice in dealing with appeals against High Court decisions and his suggestion that a claim for direct state responsibility was not a recognised cause of action in Irish law. But the European Court was merely adhering to its established position that, if there are a number of domestic remedies which an applicant could have pursued, he or she is entitled to say that the remedy chosen satisfies the requirements of the exhaustion of remedies rule.[235] It is also likely that if the Supreme Court was not persuaded that the State was vicariously liable for the abuse of this child it was hardly going to be persuaded that the State was directly liable. On balance the European Court's position in *O'Keeffe* seems a reasonable one.

The Impact of the European Convention on Human Rights Act 2003

The 2003 Act was obviously an important development in Irish law and there is a substantial literature on its impact to date, including a comprehensive report compiled by Suzanne Kingston and Liam Thornton for the Law Society of Ireland and the Dublin Solicitors Bar Association.[236] The report lists many cases where the Act has been pleaded and shows how it can add value to the protection of human rights in existing Irish law. A common view, however, is that the Act has not yet impacted in the way that it might have done. To date only three declarations of incompatibility have been issued, two by the High Court and one by the Supreme Court. One of the High Court cases concerned transgender rights and led to the passing of the Gender Recognition Act 2015,[237] while the other two cases related to the eviction of tenants from social housing and led to a provision in the Housing (Miscellaneous Provisions) Act 2014.[238] Amongst the challenges to Supreme Court judgments which have failed in Strasbourg since 2003[239] the most prominent are perhaps *Lynch and Whelan v Ireland*,[240] where Ireland's law on life sentences survived scrutiny; *MD v Ireland*,[241] where the European Court ruled that Ireland had acted within its margin of appreciation in exempting girls under the age of 17 who had sex with boys under that age from being prosecuted for having sexual intercourse; and *Irish Congress of Trade Unions v Ireland*,[242] where the ICTU's application was held inadmissible because the Congress had not first sought a domestic remedy for the alleged violation of the ECHR resulting from non-registration of collective labour agreements. In three further cases alleging undue delay in domestic court proceedings the applications were also declared inadmissible.[243]

[233] Ibid, 184.

[234] O'Mahony (2017). See too Paris (2015), who (at 101–2) considers the Irish government's response to the judgment.

[235] (2014) 59 EHRR 15, para 109, citing *O'Reilly v Ireland* App No 24196/94, decision of 22 January 1996.

[236] Kingston and Thornton (2015), available online. See too Hogan et al (2018) 635-40; De Londras (2014a) and (2014b); Doyle and Ryan (2011); Carney (2010); De Londras and Kelly (2010); O'Connell (2009); Whelan (2006); Ní Raifeartaigh (2004); Egan (2003); Bacik (2001).

[237] *Foy v An tArd Chláraitheoir* [2007] IEHC 470, [2012] 2 IR 1.

[238] s 18(3). The cases were *Dublin City Council v Gallagher* [2008] IEHC 354 (O'Neill J) and *Donegan v Dublin City Council* [2012] IESC 18, [2012] 3 IR 600 (Laffoy J).

[239] For the full list see App 5 below, Pt A (nos 32–50) and Pt C.

[240] Apps Nos 70495/10 and 74565/10, decision of 18 June 2013.

[241] App No 50936/12, decision of 16 September 2014.

[242] App No 72596/13, decision of 2 December 2014.

[243] *Lopes v Ireland* App No 14349/13 (decision of 30 September 2014); *Enright v Ireland* App No 75116/12 (decision of 30 September 2014); and *PH v Ireland* App No 45046/16 (decision of 10 October 2017).

The challenges to post-2003 judgments of the Supreme Court which have succeeded in Strasbourg, apart from the judgments by the European Court already alluded to (*McMullen, McFarlane, Rooney, O'Keeffe, Leech, Brennan*), have included several where the Irish government has conceded the correctness of the complaint before the European Court was able to rule on the matter. This occurred in *JB v Ireland*,[244] where a friendly settlement led to the State paying €13,000 to an applicant who was complaining about the delays in prosecuting him for sexual offences; *Magee v Ireland*,[245] where the State agreed to grant legal aid to the applicant so that she could attend the inquest into the death of her son, who had died while in police custody; *Kieran v Ireland*,[246] where the State paid the applicant €6,000 in compensation for the interest she had lost in a house bought for her by a former partner; and *Blehein v Ireland*,[247] where the State paid compensation and admitted its liability for delays in a case concerning access to justice by people detained on account of mental illness. In a case not involving a challenge to a Supreme Court decision the government admitted that there had been a failure to comply with Article 2 of the ECHR in the investigation of the death of Ronan O'Lochlainn, who had been shot by the police in 1998.[248] The government paid compensation to the victim's mother. In striking out the application the European Court held that the non-retrospective nature of the ECHR Act 2003 did not of itself violate any Articles in the Convention, another feature which the 2003 Act shares with its 1998 counterpart in the United Kingdom.[249]

Conclusion

This chapter has told the story of how the European Commission and Court of Human Rights have reacted to decisions of the Irish Supreme Court, a process which began as far back as 1960. It has not systematically examined the attention paid by the Supreme Court to decisions and judgments of the European Commission and Court. The story reveals that on many occasions the position adopted by the Supreme Court has been held not to violate the ECHR, but there are at least 26 occasions on which such a violation *has* been identified.[250] Until incorporation of the ECHR into domestic Irish law at the end of 2003 issues were taken to Strasbourg time and time again which had not been seen by the Supreme Court as raising any Convention issues. Since the enactment of the ECHR Act 2003 the Supreme Court has continued to be on a learning curve in this regard, much as the United Kingdom's top court has been since 2000.[251] To some extent this quasi-Nelsonian approach to the ECHR must be a consequence of the failure of barristers to present judges with sound arguments based on Convention points, but it must always be remembered that both before and after 2003 the primary source for protection of human rights in Ireland has been the country's Constitution, a document with which the Irish Supreme Court continues to rigorously engage. That is something which the United Kingdom's judges cannot emulate. The suspicion persists, however, that the Supreme Court does not always examine Convention points as thoroughly as it might once it is satisfied that there has been no unconstitutionality in a case.

244 App No 9519/07, decision of 21 June 2011.

245 App No 53743/09, struck out 20 November 2012.

246 App No 73886/11, struck out 28 May 2013.

247 App No 14704/16, decision of 25 April 2017.

248 *Nic Gibb v Ireland* App No 17707/10, struck out 25 March 2014.

249 *R v Lambert* [2001] UKHL 37, [2002] 2 AC 545; *R v Kansal (No 2)* [2001] UKHL 62, [2002] 2 AC 69.

250 See above, 269.

251 Dickson (2013), *passim*. The UK's Human Rights Act 1998 came fully into effect on 2 October 2000.

Other commentators have also been censorious of the way in which Irish courts in general, and the Supreme Court in particular, have failed to uphold Convention rights. De Londras concludes that 'it is difficult to tell a particularly optimistic story of the effectiveness of the European Convention on Human Rights Act 2003'; she thinks its impact has been limited, although its potential is not.[252] Paris, likewise, argues that the 2003 Act needs to be better entrenched in Irish law, finding that it is 'still underused in domestic legal practice' and 'yet to be regarded as part and parcel of the politico-legal culture'.[253] A similar point has been made in relation to the impact of the ECHR Act on Irish criminal law.[254] I venture to suggest that the current state of affairs is not because of a lack of training in the jurisprudence of the Strasbourg Court but because of an entrenched tradition of adjudicating human rights cases by reference to domestic law alone, and in particular the 1937 Irish Constitution.[255] European Convention law, unlike European Union law, has not been viewed by judges as a binding set of norms which must always be taken into account even when the lawyers in a case do not advert to it. It is to be hoped that this attitude will change, so that application of the standards set by the ECHR will become second nature to all who are working within the legal system of Ireland, especially the Supreme Court judges.

[252] De Londras (2014a) 53. [253] Paris (2015) 88 and 106.
[254] McDermott and Murphy (2008); see too Ní Raifeartaigh (2007); O'Connell (2009).
[255] A point stressed by O'Connell (2008).

13

Conclusion

A Summing Up

Compiling this study has been a major challenge because the book has had to strike a balance between attempting, on the one hand, to explain and comment on a large number of Supreme Court decisions across a wide range of legal fields and, on the other, to analyse what the Court as an institution has achieved (or not) during its almost 100 years of existence. Some readers will no doubt cavil at the omission of several decisions which they expected to see examined; others will perhaps regret that a more metrics-based approach was not adopted, one that looked at how often the Supreme Court has overruled its own previous decisions or relied heavily on judgments issued by top courts in other jurisdictions. Those who believe that what most determines the achievements of an apex court is the leadership provided by its Chief Justice or President will be disappointed that the text has not included any sections comparing the skills of the 12 Chief Justices who have so far had the privilege of leading the Irish Supreme Court.

There are many perspectives from which the performance of a Supreme Court can be assessed and a truly comprehensive evaluation of Ireland's Court would clearly be a multi-volume endeavour. What has been presented here is a snapshot, albeit one which encompasses at least six major areas of law and portrays the development of the Court as an institution from its inception in 1924, through the adoption of a new national Constitution in 1937 and the creation of a 'new' Supreme Court in 1961, to the radical scaling down of the workload of the Court in 2014 as a result of the creation of the Court of Appeal in that year. The picture has been painted in words, with each chapter seeking to tell the story of how the Supreme Court has coped with the challenges brought to it at various times and in various fields. This has entailed some close consideration of particular judgments, which in turn has required a high degree of selectivity within each chapter. Chapters 6 and 9, on constitutional law and criminal justice respectively, have been most affected by this selectivity but they nevertheless purport to convey a flavour of how the Court has responded to key issues which have confronted it.

In Chapter 1 a case was made for assessing the work of a Supreme Court against four main criteria—clarity, fairness, efficiency and respect. Each subsequent chapter has sought to highlight problems that have been encountered on these fronts at different times and in different fields. At several junctures we have noted how the Court could have expressed itself more clearly (eg in administrative law) or with more regard for the rights of individuals (eg in the realm of personal and family life). In Article 26 references and in posterior constitutional reviews, the 'one judgment rule' may at times have improved the clarity of the ruling but this has been at the expense of a richness of argumentation. Some more recent decisions, in contrast, have included so many and such long judgments that even a dedicated scholar of the Court's output would find it difficult to internalise and reconcile all that has been said. Although the Court's website is quick to upload recently issued judgments, it does not supply summaries of them in the way that the UK Supreme Court website does. As regards fairness, we have seen that the Supreme Court has moved from a rigid to a more flexible approach in criminal law, that it has taken quite some time to develop the concept in

The Irish Supreme Court: Historical and Comparative Perspectives. Brice Dickson.
Published 2019 by Oxford University Press.

the field of family law, and that it is still behind the curve as regards ensuring that standards contained in the European Convention on Human Rights, as interpreted by the European Court of Human Rights, are faithfully upheld throughout the domestic legal system.

Acting efficiently, it has to be admitted, has until recently been a real struggle for the Supreme Court. In the 25 years or so leading up to 2014 the Court was undoubtedly incapacitated because it had far too many cases to deal with. The creation of the Court of Appeal in that year looks like being the Supreme Court's salvation because it has freed up the top judges to focus on fewer, more significant, cases. The determination of Chief Justice Susan Denham in pushing for this reform over many years is greatly to be admired and there are now signs that with a slimmed-down Court and a more strategic approach to case selection and case management the Supreme Court will be able to take its place alongside the great Supreme Courts of other common law countries. That, in turn, will do much to enhance respect for the Court, both nationally and internationally. This is not to suggest that the Court has failed to command such respect in the past, although decisions such as those in *The State (Ryan) v Lennon*,[1] *In re Article 26 and the Offences Against the State (Amendment) Bill 1940*,[2] *In re Ó Laighléis*,[3] *State (Nicolaou) v An Bord Uchtála*[4] and *Norris v Attorney General*[5] did leave the distinct impression that for most of the twentieth century the Court was unduly deferential to government assertions as to what was required in the public interest or the common good and not respectful enough of the rights of individuals. Respect was also damaged by Hugh O'Flaherty's resignation in 1999 and by the unseemly public row over judges' salaries and pensions in the period 2009 to 2013. Amongst the liberal elite the prestige of the Court has been diminished as a result of its refusal to frame socio-economic issues in human rights terms, notably in *Sinnott v Minister for Education*[6] and *TD v Minister for Education*.[7] Others may see this judicial disinclination to constrain the way elected politicians choose to deal with socio-economic issues as a more democratic stance, one designed to enhance the credibility of the judges rather than undermine it.

Constraints on the Supreme Court's Decision-Making

The most significant constraint on the Supreme Court was removed in 2014 when it gained a much greater right to decide for itself which cases it would like to hear. While it is still possible for cases to be appealed directly from the High Court to the Supreme Court, in both civil and criminal cases, this is now the exception rather than the rule, with most cases now passing through the new Court of Appeal first. The Supreme Court is no longer restricted by the one judgment rule when considering the constitutionality of post-1937 primary legislation, but concurrent and dissenting judgments are still prohibited in cases referred to the Court by the President under Article 26 of the Constitution. Likewise the Court cannot examine the constitutionality of a provision in an Act if it has previously given a clean bill of health to the whole of the legislation when it was previewed by the Court in an Article 26 reference, even if the precise issue which subsequently arises was not specifically considered during the Article 26 reference. So, while the Court rightly abandoned its strict adherence to the doctrine of precedent as far back as 1964,[8] it still clings to the 'immutability' rule in one of the most important contexts of all, that of the constitutionality of legislation.

[1] [1935] IR 170. [2] [1940] IR 470. [3] [1960] IR 110. [4] [1966] IR 567.
[5] [1984] IR 36. [6] [2001] 2 IR 545. [7] [2001] 4 IR 259.
[8] *The State (Quinn) v Ryan* [1965] IR 110 and (decided a week later, in December 1964) *Attorney General v Ryan's Car Hire Ltd* [1965] IR 642.

A changing approach to its attitude to previous decisions is within the Court's own competence to adopt. On the face of it this is not the case as regards the non-cognisability by it or any other court of the directive principles of social policy set out in Article 45 of the Constitution. There are still ways, however, in which the Supreme Court could, if it wished, incorporate some of the values implicit in those directive principles when deciding cases under the common law, and even when it is interpreting legislation. When Article 45.1 indicates that the State should strive to secure a social order 'in which justice and charity shall inform all the institutions of the national life', this does not disqualify the Supreme Court from seeking to procure justice and charity by basing its decisions on cognate concepts such as clarity and fairness. Again, when Article 45.2.2 requires the State to direct its policy towards securing the distribution of the control of material resources 'amongst private individuals and the various classes as best to subserve the common good', this does not preclude the Supreme Court from using ideas such as reasonableness and proportionality when determining issues in fields such as planning law and public liability law (in the context of vicarious liability, for example). Moreover the Preamble to the Constitution, which the Supreme Court is perfectly at liberty to refer to when it is clarifying the law, states that in adopting the Constitution the people of Ireland are 'seeking to promote the common good, with due observance of Prudence, Justice and Charity, so that the dignity and freedom of the individual may be assured [and] true social order attained ...'.[9] Nor is there anything to prevent the Supreme Court from developing Irish law by citing precedents from other apex courts in the common law world, even if those precedents are in turn based on principles which coincide with those in Article 45.

As a dedicated member of both the European Union and the Council of Europe, Ireland is obliged to adhere to the Charter of Fundamental Rights when implementing EU law and to the European Convention on Human Rights in every context. The Supreme Court, like other courts in Ireland, is not specifically obliged under section 3(1) of the ECHR Act 2003 to 'perform its functions in a manner compatible with the State's obligations under the Convention provisions',[10] but it is still obliged under section 2(1) to interpret and apply any statutory provision or rule of law, 'in so far as is possible, subject to the rules of law relating to such interpretation and application, ... in a manner compatible with the State's obligations under the Convention provisions'. It is therefore acceptable for the Supreme Court to decide cases by reference to the way in which the EU Charter and the ECHR have been interpreted by the Court of Justice of the EU and the European Court of Human Rights, just so long as the interpretation arrived at does not violate the Irish Constitution. We have seen how the Supreme Court, in *Crotty v An Taoiseach* for example,[11] has subordinated EU law to Irish constitutional law, and the ECHR Act 2003 clearly incorporates the ECHR at a sub-constitutional level, but neither of these realities takes away from the Supreme Court's freedom, if it wishes to exercise it, to develop domestic law in ways which it might not otherwise have found it possible to do by relying only on Irish precedents and principles.

The Principle of Consistency

Across the common law world there has been a huge debate about how senior judges should go about their role of adjudication in situations where there are competing interests, values

[9] The capital letters are in the original.

[10] This is because s 1(1) of the Act defines 'organ of the State' as excluding a court (as well as the President, the two Houses of the Oireachtas and any committee of either of those Houses).

[11] [1987] IR 713.

or policies. In disputes between private parties they do this day and daily without anyone exhibiting much interest in the choices they make, such as when they consider whether a commercial contract should be interpreted in the light of oral statements made before or after a written form of the contract has been settled,[12] or whether a limitation period for personal injury claims gives too much weight to the interests of administrators of deceased persons' estates.[13] But when disputes involve communities, or the country as whole, questions are often asked about the entitlement of judges to take decisions which could have implications for thousands if not millions of people. Most commentators agree that in such cases the judges should be allowed some leeway to *interpret* whatever legal documents are in play—the Constitution, legislation or some non-binding guidance—because a strict formalism, while allowing the law to be certain and predictable, can easily lead to what the majority of people would see as injustice. Those of a conservative disposition are inclined to stick to given rules, citing the adage that 'hard cases make bad law', that is, that changing a rule to cater for some exceptional circumstances will end up reducing respect for the rule in the future. Those who are more liberal tend to want judges to operate more flexibly in such cases.

Siobhan Mullaly has helpfully explored what the prevailing attitude within the Irish Supreme Court has been to these more controversial situations.[14] She criticises the Constitution Review Group's report of 1996 for advocating a return to a more formalist approach, such as in its suggestion that the unenumerated constitutional rights should be codified, and she also expresses reservations concerning the two most prominent schools of thought on this issue within the liberal camp. One is the school inspired by Ronald Dworkin's 'rights thesis', whereby he urges judges to arrive at the correct answer by carefully weighing up the parties' competing arguments and arriving at a conclusion which is best from a human rights point of view. The other is the school constructed around the work of John Rawls, who sees justice as 'fairness' in that it promotes a society of individuals who are free, who have equal rights and who are treated in an egalitarian way by the economic system within which they live. This is not the place in which to examine whether the output of the Irish Supreme Court fits more neatly into one or other of these two schools of thought. Suffice it to say that the schools have much in common but were constructed at a time when the world was not as globalised, and nations not as inter-dependent, as is the case today.

In Chapter 6 we looked briefly at the role which a 'natural law' approach to the adjudicative process has played in the jurisprudence of the Irish Supreme Court. Writing in 1998 Mullaly could still see some vestiges of that approach in the Court's work, although she designates it as 'relativist'.[15] She herself prefers to adhere to what has been labelled 'the principle of generic consistency',[16] by which is meant that judges should decide cases 'in accord with the generic rights of [their] recipients as well as of [themselves]',[17] with 'generic

[12] As in *Law Society of Ireland v Motor Insurers' Bureau of Ireland* [2017] IESC 31.

[13] As in *Moynihan v Greensmyth* [1977] IR 55, where a two-year time limit was held not to be an 'unjust attack' on the plaintiff's property rights. Osborough (1979–80), at 101, sees this decision (and that of the Supreme Court in *Crowley v Ireland* [1980] IR 102, on the right to be provided with free primary educations) as evidence that 'the work of constitutional expansionism intimately associated with Mr Justice Walsh and the late Cearbhall Ó Dálaigh is now at an end. Either that or the rate of expansion is being considerably slowed down'.

[14] Mullaly (1998).

[15] In support she cites the Supreme Court's judgment in *In re Article 26 and the Regulation of Information (Services outside the State for Termination of Pregnancies) Bill 1995* [1995] 1 IR 1. Another commentator, on the other hand, sees this decision as signifying 'the death of natural law': Twomey (1995).

[16] Developed by Beyleveld and Brownsword (1994) but coined by Gewirth (1978).

[17] Beyleveld and Brownsword (1994) 133.

rights' embracing rights to freedom as well as rights to well-being. There is a superficial attractiveness to this theory, but it is difficult to see how its applicability can be predicted with any degree of certainty in new situations. It has also been rejected at the theoretical level by Robert Alexy.[18]

There can be no doubting, however, that the idea of 'consistency' has a ring to it which chimes with most people's thinking around justice. Like cases should be treated alike, and if two cases are to be treated differently the differences between them should be clearly articulated and supported with evidence. In recent years the Irish Supreme Court seems more aware than ever that to maintain the public's confidence in the institution it must engage in substantial justification processes. This may be one reason why some of the judgments issued by members of the Court have been so long.

Of course an awareness of the need to provide detailed justification for conclusions does not necessarily lead to greater unanimity amongst judges; indeed the converse is likely to be the case. In 2013 Mac Cormaic claimed that in the five-year period from July 2008 to June 2013 the Supreme Court was unanimous in 90 per cent of all cases in which its judgments were published.[19] The dissent rate of 10 per cent was doubled to 20 per cent when the Court was dealing with constitutional arguments or 'a fundamental point of law', which is not altogether surprising given that most if not all of those cases will have involved five or seven judges, thereby increasing the possibility of dissent. In the United Kingdom Supreme Court, where there are always at least five judges, the average annual dissent rate in the six-year period from 2012 to 2017 was 20 per cent.[20] In the US Supreme Court the dissent rate is consistently much higher still,[21] while in Canada there was at least one dissent in 50 per cent of the decisions reached by the Supreme Court in 2015, not a wholly untypical year.[22] The Irish Supreme Court is therefore more consensus-orientated than comparable courts elsewhere, which is itself an indicator of internal consistency.

What Ireland still lacks is research into how exactly the Supreme Court judges go about discussing and finalising their views on cases once the arguments have been heard in court.[23] It may be that pressure of time, given the throughput of cases, militates against any lengthy confabulations. That may also be a factor reducing the number of extra-judicial lectures which the Supreme Court judges are able to give, an activity which Justices of the UK Supreme Court now indulge in with alacrity. The more light that can be shone on how the Irish Supreme Court operates in practice the more likely it is that its legitimacy will endure and the quality of its law-making excel.

[18] Alexy (2006).

[19] Including 3 per cent where the Court was required to adhere to the single judgment rule. There were 332 judgments in all. See Mac Cormaic, 'Supreme Court judges seldom dissent', *Irish Times*, 8 July 2013.

[20] This is based on my own calculations after reviewing all 438 decisions during that period.

[21] See the figures in Adam Feldman, 'King of dissents', 22 June 2016, available at https://empiricalscotus.com/2016/06/22/king-of-dissents/.

[22] Perrin (2016) 14–5.

[23] For studies of the House of Lords and UK Supreme Court of this nature see Paterson (1982) and (2013).

APPENDIX 1

Office Holders, 1922–2018

Governor General / President

Governor General

Timothy Healy 1922–28
James McNeill 1928–32
Domhnall Ua Buachalla 1932–36

President

Douglas Hyde 1938–45
Seán O'Kelly 1945–59
Éamon de Valera 1959–73
Erskine Childers 1973–74
Cearbhall Ó Dálaigh 1974–76
Patrick Hillery 1976–90
Mary Robinson 1990–97
Mary McAleese 1997–2011
Michael Higgins 2011–

Taoiseach (Prime Minister) and main governing party

William Cosgrave, Cumann na nGaedheal 1922–32
Éamon de Valera, Fianna Fáil 1932–48
John Costello, Fine Gael 1948–51
Éamon de Valera, Fianna Fáil 1951–54
John Costello, Fine Gael 1954–57
Éamon de Valera, Fianna Fáil 1957–59
Seán Lemass, Fianna Fáil 1959–66
Jack Lynch, Fianna Fáil 1966–73
Liam Cosgrave, Fine Gael 1973–77
Jack Lynch, Fianna Fáil 1977–79
Charles Haughey, Fianna Fáil 1979–81
Garret FitzGerald, Fine Gael 1981–82
Charles Haughey, Fianna Fáil 1982
Garret FitzGerald, Fine Gael 1982–87
Charles Haughey, Fianna Fáil 1987–92
Albert Reynolds, Fianna Fáil 1992–94
John Bruton, Fine Gael 1994–97
Bertie Ahern, Fianna Fáil 1997–2008
Brian Cowen, Fianna Fáil 2008–11
Enda Kenny, Fine Gael 2011–17
Leo Varadkar, Fine Gael 2017–

Attorney General

Hugh Kennedy 1922–24
John O'Byrne 1924–26
John Costello 1926–32
Conor Maguire 1932–36
James Geoghegan 1936
Patrick Lynch 1936–40
Kevin Haugh 1940–42
Kevin Dixon 1942–46
Cearbhall Ó Dálaigh 1946–48
Cecil Lavery 1948–50
Charles Casey 1950–51
Cearbhall Ó Dálaigh 1951–53
Thomas Teevan 1953–54
Aindrias Ó Caoimh 1954
Patrick McGilligan 1954–57
Aindrias Ó Caoimh 1957–65
Colm Condon 1965–73
Declan Costello 1973–77
John Kelly 1977
Anthony Hederman 1977–81
Peter Sutherland 1981–82
Patrick Connolly 1982
John Murray 1982
Peter Sutherland 1982–84
John Rogers 1984–87
John Murray 1987–91
Harry Whelehan 1991–94
Eoghan Fitzsimons 1994
Dermot Gleeson 1994–97
David Byrne 1997–99
Michael McDowell 1999–2002
Rory Brady 2002–07
Paul Gallagher 2007–11
Máire Whelan 2011–17
Séamus Woulfe 2017–

President of the Supreme Court / Chief Justice

Hugh Kennedy 1924–36
Timothy Sullivan 1936–46
Conor Maguire 1946–61
Cearbhall Ó Dálaigh 1961–73
William FitzGerald 1973–74
Tom O'Higgins 1974–85

Tom Finlay 1985–94
Liam Hamilton 1994–2000
Ronan Keane 2000–04
John Murray 2004–11
Susan Denham 2011–17
Frank Clarke 2017–

President of the Court of Appeal

Seán Ryan 2014–
George Birmingham 2018–

President of the High Court

Timothy Sullivan 1924–36
Conor Maguire 1936–46
Cahir Davitt 1951–66
Aindrias Ó Caoimh 1966–74
Tom Finlay 1974–85
Liam Hamilton 1985–94
Harold Whelehan 1994
Declan Costello 1995–98
Frederick Morris 1998–2001
Joseph Finnegan 2001–06
Richard Johnson 2006–09
Nicholas Kearns 2009–15
Peter Kelly 2015–

APPENDIX 2

A Chronology of Supreme Court Appointments

Judges appointed to the Supreme Court (with life-span and years served)

1 Hugh Kennedy (1879–1936), 1924–36
2 Charles O'Connor (1854–1928), 1924–25
3 Gerald FitzGibbon (1866–1942), 1924–38
4 James Murnaghan (1881–1973), 1925–53
5 Timothy Sullivan (1874–1949), 1936–46
6 James Geoghegan (1886–1951), 1936–50
7 James Creed Meredith (1875–1942), 1936–42
8 William Johnston (1868–1940), 1939–40
9 John O'Byrne (1884–1954), 1940–54
10 William Black (1879–1967), 1942–51
11 Conor Maguire (1889–1971), 1946–61
12 Cecil Lavery (1894–1973), 1950–66
13 Theodore Kingsmill Moore (1893–1979), 1951–66
14 Cearbhall Ó Dálaigh (1911–78), 1953–72
15 Martin Maguire (1889–1962), 1954–61
16 Kevin Haugh (1901–69), 1961–69
17 Brian Walsh (1918–98), 1961–90
18 Aindrias Ó Caoimh (1912–94), 1965–66
19 Frederick Budd (1904–76), 1966–75
20 William FitzGerald (1906–74), 1966–74
21 Richard McLoughlin (1902–72), 1969–72
22 Seamus Henchy (1918–2009), 1972–98
23 Frank Griffin (1918–2016), 1973–91
24 Tom O'Higgins (1916–2003), 1974–85
25 John Kenny (1917–87), 1975–82
26 Weldon Parke (1912–81), 1976–81
27 Anthony Hederman (1921–2014), 1981–93
28 Niall McCarthy (1925–91), 1982–92
29 Thomas Finlay (1922–2017), 1985–94
30 Hugh O'Flaherty (b 1938), 1990–99
31 Seamus Egan (1923–2004), 1991–95
32 John Blayney (1925–2018), 1992–97
33 Susan Denham (b 1945), 1992–2017
34 Liam Hamilton (1928–2000), 1994–2000
35 Donal Barrington (1928–2017), 1996–2000
36 Ronan Keane (b 1932), 1996–2004
37 Frank Murphy (b 1932), 1996–2002

38 Kevin Lynch (1927–2013), 1996–99
39 Henry Barron (1928–2010), 1997–2000
40 John Murray (b 1943), 1999–2011
41 Nial Fennelly (b 1942), 2000–14
42 Catherine McGuinness (b 1934), 2000–06
43 Adrian Hardiman (1951–2016), 2000–16
44 Hugh Geoghegan (b 1938), 2000–10
45 Brian McCracken (b 1934), 2002–06
46 Nicholas Kearns (b 1946), 2004–09
47 Fidelma Macken (b 1945), 2005–12
48 Joseph Finnegan (b 1942), 2006–12
49 Donal O'Donnell (b 1958), 2010–
50 Liam McKechnie (b 1951), 2010–
51 John MacMenamin (b 1952), 2012–
52 Frank Clarke (b 1951), 2012–
53 Mary Laffoy (b 1945), 2013–17
54 Elizabeth Dunne (b 1956), 2013–
55 Peter Charleton (b 1956), 2014–
56 Iseult O'Malley (b 1964), 2015–
57 Mary Finlay Geoghegan (b 1951), 2017–

The changing composition of the Supreme Court (Chief Justice in bold)

1924 **Kennedy**, O'Connor, FitzGibbon
1925 **Kennedy**, FitzGibbon, Murnaghan
1936 **Sullivan**, FitzGibbon, Murnaghan
1936 **Sullivan**, FitzGibbon, Murnaghan, Geoghegan, Meredith
1939 **Sullivan**, Murnaghan, Geoghegan, Meredith, Johnston
1940 **Sullivan**, Murnaghan, Geoghegan, Meredith, O'Byrne
1942 **Sullivan**, Murnaghan, Geoghegan, O'Byrne, Black
1946 **Maguire C**, Murnaghan, Geoghegan, O'Byrne, Black
1950 **Maguire C**, Murnaghan, O'Byrne, Black, Lavery
1951 **Maguire C**, Murnaghan, O'Byrne, Lavery, Kingsmill Moore
1953 **Maguire C**, O'Byrne, Lavery, Kingsmill Moore, Ó Dálaigh
1954 **Maguire C**, Lavery, Kingsmill Moore, Ó Dálaigh, Maguire M
1961 **Maguire C**, Lavery, Kingsmill Moore, Ó Dálaigh, Haugh
1961 **Ó Dálaigh**, Lavery, Kingsmill Moore, Haugh, Walsh
1965 **Ó Dálaigh**, Lavery, Haugh, Walsh, Ó Caoimhe
1966 **Ó Dálaigh**, Lavery, Haugh, Walsh, Budd
1966 **Ó Dálaigh**, Haugh, Walsh, Budd, FitzGerald
1969 **Ó Dálaigh**, Walsh, Budd, FitzGerald, McLoughlin
1972 **Ó Dálaigh**, Walsh, Budd, FitzGerald, Henchy
1973 **FitzGerald**, Walsh, Budd, Henchy, Griffin
1974 **O'Higgins**, Walsh, Budd, Henchy, Griffin
1975 **O'Higgins**, Walsh, Henchy, Griffin, Kenny
1976 **O'Higgins**, Walsh, Henchy, Griffin, Kenny, Parke
1981 **O'Higgins**, Walsh, Henchy, Griffin, Kenny, Hederman
1982 **O'Higgins**, Walsh, Henchy, Griffin, Hederman, McCarthy
1985 **Finlay**, Walsh, Henchy, Griffin, Hederman, McCarthy
1988 **Finlay**, Walsh, Griffin, Hederman, McCarthy

1990 **Finlay**, Griffin, Hederman, McCarthy, O'Flaherty
1991 **Finlay**, Hederman, McCarthy, O'Flaherty, Egan
1992 **Finlay**, Hederman, O'Flaherty, Egan, Blayney
1992 **Finlay**, Hederman, O'Flaherty, Egan, Blayney, Denham
1993 **Finlay**, O'Flaherty, Egan, Blayney, Denham
1994 **Hamilton**, O'Flaherty, Egan, Blayney, Denham
1996 **Hamilton**, O'Flaherty, Blayney, Denham, Barrington
1996 **Hamilton**, O'Flaherty, Blayney, Denham, Barrington, Keane, Murphy, Lynch
1997 **Hamilton**, O'Flaherty, Denham, Barrington, Keane, Murphy, Lynch, Barron
1999 **Hamilton**, Denham, Barrington, Keane, Murphy, Lynch, Barron, Murray
2000 **Hamilton**, Denham, Barrington, Keane, Murphy, Lynch, Murray, Fennelly
2000 **Keane**, Denham, Barrington, Murphy, Murray, Fennelly, McGuinness, Hardiman
2000 **Keane**, Denham, Murphy, Murray, Fennelly, McGuinness, Hardiman, Geoghegan
2002 **Keane**, Denham, Murray, Fennelly, McGuinness, Hardiman, Geoghegan, McCracken
2004 **Murray**, Denham, Fennelly, McGuinness, Hardiman, Geoghegan, McCracken, Kearns
2005 **Murray**, Denham, Fennelly, McGuinness, Hardiman, Geoghegan, McCracken, Kearns, Macken
2006 **Murray**, Denham, Fennelly, Hardiman, Geoghegan, Kearns, Macken, Finnegan
2010 **Murray**, Denham, Fennelly, Hardiman, Geoghegan, Macken, Finnegan, O'Donnell
2010 **Murray**, Denham, Fennelly, Hardiman, Macken, Finnegan, O'Donnell, McKechnie
2011 **Denham**, Murray Fennelly, Hardiman, Macken, Finnegan, O'Donnell, McKechnie
2012 **Denham**, Murray, Fennelly, Hardiman, O'Donnell, McKechnie, MacMenamin, Clarke
2013 **Denham**, Murray, Fennelly, Hardiman, O'Donnell, McKechnie, MacMenamin, Clarke, Dunne, Laffoy
2014 **Denham**, Murray, Hardiman, O'Donnell, McKechnie, MacMenamin, Clarke, Dunne, Laffoy, Charleton
2015 **Denham**, Hardiman, O'Donnell, McKechnie, MacMenamin, Clarke, Dunne, Laffoy, Charleton, O'Malley
2016 **Denham**, O'Donnell, McKechnie, MacMenamin, Clarke, Dunne, Laffoy, Charleton, O'Malley
2017 **Denham**, O'Donnell, McKechnie, MacMenamin, Clarke, Dunne, Charleton, O'Malley
2017 **Clarke**, O'Donnell, McKechnie, MacMenamin, Dunne, Charleton, O'Malley
2017 **Clarke**, O'Donnell, McKechnie, MacMenamin, Dunne, Charleton, O'Malley, Finlay Geoghegan

APPENDIX 3

Biographies of the Judges of the Supreme Court 1924–2018[1]

Barrington, Donal (1928–2018; served 1996–2000)

Born in Dublin. Attended Belvedere College. First class honours degree in Legal and Political Science at UCD in 1950, an LLB in 1951 and an MA in 1952. Called to the Bar in 1951, becoming SC in 1967. Involved in several leading cases in the 1960 and 1970s. Helped to set up the influential society 'Tuairim' ('View') as well as the Irish Council for Civil Liberties. Appointed to the High Court in 1979. Chaired the Stardust Victims Compensation Tribunal from 1985–87. Ireland's judge at the Court of First Instance in Luxembourg from 1989 to 1996. Appointed in 2001 as the first President of the Irish Human Rights Commission.

Barron, Henry (1928–2010; served 1997–2000)

Educated at St Columba's College, Dublin, and TCD, where he obtained a first class degree in legal science in 1950. Called to the Bar in 1951 and appointed SC in 1970. Made a judge of the High Court in 1982 and promoted to the Supreme Court in 1997. The first person of Jewish faith to be appointed to either of those courts. The first judge to grant a divorce in Ireland, on 17 January 1977. In retirement he completed the inquiry into the Dublin and Monaghan bombings of 1974 begun by Liam Hamilton.

Black, William (1879–1967; served 1942–51)*

The son of a Methodist minister from Holywood, County Down. Educated at Methodist College Belfast and TCD. Called to the Bar in 1901, taking silk in 1935. A supporter of Sinn Féin and then of Fianna Fáil, he stood for the latter in the Dáil election of 1938 but lost. Served as a High Court judge from 1939 to 1942. Elected in 1954 as Ireland's representative on the European Commission of Human Rights in Strasbourg.

Blayney, John (1925–2018 ; served 1992–97)

Born in Dublin, the son of a surgeon from Ulster. Attended Belvedere and Glenstal schools and studied classics at UCD. Called to the Bar in 1948, taking silk in 1973. Brother-in-law of Tom Finlay, the seventh Chief Justice of Ireland. A notable rugby player, he obtained one cap for Ireland in 1950. Staunch Catholic who supported the Eighth Amendment on abortion in 1983. Appointed to the High Court in 1986 and, although a supporter of Fine Gael, promoted to the Supreme Court by a Fianna Fáil Taoiseach in 1992, shortly after the decision in the *X* case on abortion. Chaired an inquiry into the conduct of a number of accountants in Ireland, published in 2003.

[1] An asterisk against a name indicates that an entry for that individual appears in *The Dictionary of Irish Biography*, CUP, 2009 (the *DIB*), the richness of which as a source for this appendix is duly acknowledged; also useful were Cairnduff (1991), Boylan (1998), Ferguson (2005) and Mac Cormaic (2013). Abbreviations: CBS = Christian Brothers School; CJ = Chief Justice; ECJ: Court of Justice of the European Union; JP = Justice of the Peace; KC = King's Counsel; LLB = Bachelor of Laws; LLD = Doctor of Laws; MA = Master of Arts; NUI = National University of Ireland; SC = Senior Counsel; TCD = Trinity College Dublin; UCC = University College Cork; UCD = University College Dublin.

Budd, Frederick (1904–76; served 1966–75)*

Born in Ennis, County Clare. Educated at Manor School, Fermoy, and Felsted, Essex. A member of the Church of Ireland. Graduated from TCD in 1925 with a BA in history and political science, in 1926 with an LLB and in 1928 with an LLD. Called to the Bar in 1927, becoming SC in 1943. Elected as independent senator for TCD in 1951 but resigned when appointed to the High Court a month later. Died less than two months after retiring. His son Declan served as a High Court judge from 1991 to 2011.

Charleton, Peter (b 1956; appointed 2014)

Born in Dublin and educated at TCD. Called to the Bar in 1979, becoming SC in 1995. From 2002 to 2006 was counsel to the Morris Tribunal, which inquired into allegations of police corruption in Donegal. Served as a judge of the High Court from 2006 to 2014, specialising in commercial cases. A prolific writer in fields such as criminal law, family law and constitutional law. In 2017 he was appointed to head the Disclosures Tribunal, which is inquiring into allegations of police malpractice. A founder member of the RTÉ Philharmonic Choir.

Clarke, Frank (b 1951; appointed 2012)

Born in Dublin, and educated at Drimnagh Castle CBS and UCD, where he graduated in mathematics and economics. Called to the Bar in 1973 and became SC in 1985, focusing mainly on commercial and constitutional cases. Supporter of Fine Gael, writing speeches for Garret FitzGerald. Stood unsuccessfully for election to the Seanad in the 1980s. Was counsel to the Commission of Inquiry into Child Abuse. Appointed to the High Court in 2004 by the coalition government of Fianna Fáil and Progressive Democrats. Has served as an honorary professor at Griffith College and TCD. Promoted to the Supreme Court in 2012 and succeeded Susan Denham as Chief Justice in 2017.

Denham, Susan (b 1945; served 1992–2017)

Educated at Alexandra College, Dublin, and at TCD and Columbia University, New York. Daughter of the former editor of the Irish Times, Douglas Gageby, and grand-daughter of the last Secretary General to the League of Nations, Seán Lester. Called to the Bar in 1973, eventually specialising in public law. Appointed SC in 1987 and as a High Court judge in 1991. The first woman appointee to the Supreme Court. Chaired the working group which eventually led to the establishment of the Courts Service in 1999 and argued strongly for the creation of a Court of Appeal and a Judicial Council.

Dunne, Elizabeth (b 1956; appointed 2013)

Born in Galway; educated at UCD; called to the Bar in 1977. Served as a judge of the Circuit Court from 1996 to 2004 and of the High Court from 2004 to 2013. Appointed to the Supreme Court on the same day as Mary Laffoy, thereby completing the complement of nine ordinary judges plus the Chief Justice.

Egan, Seamus (1923–2004; served 1991–95)

Born in Tuam, County Galway, but moved with his family to Dublin and attended Synge Street School and Blackrock College. Studied law at UCD, being called to the Bar in 1945 and becoming SC in 1962. Appointed to the High Court in 1984, despite having no significant political ties. After retiring he served as Chair of the Hepatitis B Compensation Tribunal from 1995 to 2003.

Fennelly, Nial (b 1942; served 2000–14)

Originally from Kilkenny. Educated at Clongowes Wood College and UCD, where he primarily studied economics. Called to the Bar in 1964 and made SC in 1995. Never actively engaged in politics but thought to be a supporter of Fine Gael. The first person from Ireland to serve as an Advocate General at the ECJ, from 1995 to 2000. Appointed in 2014 to investigate controversial aspects of Garda activity, such as the unauthorised recording of phone calls, alleged misconduct during the investigation of the murder of Sophie Toscan du Plantier in 1996, and the circumstances surrounding the retirement of Garda Commissioner Martin Callinan in 2014.

Finlay, Thomas (1922–2017; served 1985–94)

Born in 1922, son of a Cummann na nGaedhael TD and SC who died when Tom was aged 10. Educated at Clongowes Wood College and UCD. Called to the Bar in 1944. Elected as Fine Gael TD for Dublin-South Central in 1954 but not re-elected in 1957. Appointed SC in 1961. Defended Capt Kelly in the Haughey arms trial. Made a High Court judge in 1971, becoming President of that Court in 1974. Succeeded Tom O'Higgins as CJ in 1985, serving until reaching retirement age in 1994. In 1992 he gave the leading judgment in the *X* case on abortion. Chaired the tribunal of inquiry into the Blood Transfusion Service Board, reporting in 1997. His daughter, Mary Finlay Geoghegan, was sworn in as a Supreme Court judge in 2017 two days before his death at the age of 95.

Finlay Geoghegan, Mary (b 1951; appointed 2017)

Educated at UCD and at the College of Europe in Bruges. Fist qualified as a solicitor in 1973 but switched to the Bar in 1980, becoming SC just eight years later. Appointed to the High Court in 2002 and was assigned to handle commercial cases there from 2004. Promoted to the Court of Appeal in 2014 when that court was first established. The daughter of the former Chief Justice Tom Finlay and the wife of former Supreme Court judge Hugh Geoghegan whose father was also a Supreme Court judge.

Finnegan, Joseph (b 1942; served 2006–12)

Educated at Synge Street, CBS and St Mary's College, Dundalk. Studied law at University College Dublin and became a solicitor in 1966. Twelve years later he changed to practise at the Bar and became Senior Counsel in 1990. He was made a High Court judge in 1999, becoming President of that court in 2001. Remained in that post until promotion to the Supreme Court in 2006. In retirement he has chaired some prominent mediation processes such as those relating to Priory Hall in Dublin and the businessman Seán Quinn.

FitzGerald, William ['Billy'] (1906–74; served 1966–74)*

Born in Cork but educated at Belvedere College, Dublin, and UCD. Called to the Bar in 1927, practising initially in the Cork area, and became SC in 1944. Specialised in road accident cases. Chaired the Bar Council for three years in the 1950s. A member of Fine Gael, but not actively so, yet was appointed directly to the Supreme Court in 1966 by a Fianna Fáil government. A surprise choice to succeed Cearbhall Ó Dálaigh as Chief Justice in 1973. Dissented in *Byrne v Ireland* (1972) and in *McGee v Attorney General* (1974). Died in office in October 1974, after less than two years in post. He was the father of nine children.

FitzGibbon, Gerald (1866–1942; served 1924–38)

Gerald FitzGibbon was the son of a Lord Justice of Appeal of the same name and the grandson, through his mother, of Baron FitzGerald of the Court of Exchequer. His great-grandfather was a farmer who had left the Catholic Church for the established church and whose descendants maintained a strong interest in the vitality of the Church of Ireland. Born in Dublin and attended Clifton College, Bristol, and TCD. Called to the Bar in 1887, taking silk in 1908. Elected unopposed as an independent unionist representative of TCD in the House of Commons of Southern Ireland in

1921. One of the first three members of the Supreme Court. Delivered a rather embittered judgment in *The State (Ryan) v Lennon* in 1934, suggesting that the Free State did not protect rights to the same extent as English law did.

Geoghegan, Hugh (b 1938; served 2000–10)

Son of James Geoghegan (see below). Educated at Clongowes Wood College and UCD. Called to the Bar in 1962, becoming SC in 1977. Served as a judge of the High Court from 1992 to 2000. A strong supporter of the proposal to create a Court of Appeal as a way of lessening the workload of Supreme Court judges. Married to Mary Finlay Geoghegan, who was herself the daughter of Chief Justice Tom Finlay and was appointed to the Supreme Court in 2017.

Geoghegan, James (1886–1951; served 1936–50)*

Born in Walshestown, County Westmeath, the son of farmers. Educated at CBS in Mullingar. Qualified as a solicitor in 1907 but was called to the Irish Bar in 1915 and the English Bar in 1923. Became SC in 1925. Took no part in hostilities and joined Cumann na nGaedheal in the early 1920s, switching to Fianna Fáil in 1930. Elected TD for Longford-Westmeath that year. Served as Minister of Justice 1932–33 and as Attorney General for less just 51 days in 1936. Appointed directly to the Supreme Court that year and retired early on health grounds. Father of Hugh Geoghegan (see above). Remained a strict Catholic all his life.

Griffin, Frank (1918–2016; served 1973–91)

Born in Limerick, the son of an insurance agent father. Educated in Drogheda and entered his father's business before turning to the study of law at UCD. Called to the Bar in 1946, practising mainly in Counties Louth and Meath. Appointed to the High Court in 1971 and became the first presiding judge of the new Special Criminal Court in 1972. Promoted to the Supreme Court just one year later. With Finlay CJ he dissented in the *Crotty* case on the Single European Act. Lived to the age of 97. His son Gerard is a Circuit Court judge.

Hamilton, Liam (1928–2000; served 1994–2000)*

Born in Mitchelstown, County Cork. Educated at the CBS, Mitchelstown. Worked as a civil servant in the Central Office of the High Court before studying law at UCD. Called to the Bar in 1956, coming first in the final Bar examinations. Joined the Labour Party in 1958 and specialised in employment and personal injury cases. Became SC in 1968. Made a judge of the High Court in 1974 and became President in 1985. Often sat in the Special Criminal Court. Chaired the Inquiry into the Beef Industry 1991–94 and was criticised for producing a report which appeared to exonerate politicians. Appointed CJ by Albert Reynolds in 1994, succeeding Tom Finlay. Reported on the conduct of his colleague on the Supreme Court, Hugh O'Flaherty, who then resigned. Began an inquiry in 2000 into the 1974 bombs in Dublin and Monaghan but died in November after a short illness.

Hardiman, Adrian (1951–2016; served 2000–16)

Educated at Belvedere College, Dublin and UCD, where he graduated in history. Son of a teacher who served as President of the Association of Secondary Teachers Ireland. Called to the Bar in 1974 and appointed SC in 1989. Stood unsuccessfully as a Fianna Fáil candidate for the local council in Dun Laoghaire in 1985 but later that year helped to found the Progressive Democrats. A keen legal historian and noted speaker and writer, fluent in Irish. Appointed directly to the Supreme Court in 2000, aged 49. Known for his conservative approach to judicial activism. Married to Yvonne Murphy, who was a Circuit Court judge from 1998 to 2012. Died suddenly in 2016.

Haugh, Kevin (1901–69; served 1961–69)*

Born and educated in Dublin, at Belvedere College and then Blackrock College, where his father was a teacher of mathematics. Studied legal and political science at UCD, graduating in 1922 and being called to the Bar in 1925, where he became a leading prosecutor. Involved in republican politics, protesting in particular at the execution of Kevin Barry in 1920. Became SC in 1938 and in 1940 was appointed Attorney General by Éamon de Valera. Served as a judge of the High Court from 1942 to 1961. Chaired the Censorship Appeal Board and the Irish Red Cross. His son served as a judge of the High Court from 1996 until his death in 2009.

Hederman, Anthony (Tony) (1921–2014; served 1981–93)

The son of drapers; educated at Castleknock College in Dublin and UCD; called to the Bar in 1944, becoming SC in 1965 and specialising in criminal law. Represented the State in *Lawless v Ireland* and *Ireland v UK*. Served on Fianna Fáil's national executive 1948–73 and as Attorney General 1977–81. Then appointed straight to the Supreme Court. The only judge to dissent in the *X* case on abortion in 1992. Chaired the Irish Law Reform Commission 1992–98 and the Committee to Review the Offences Against the State Acts 1930–1998, reporting in 2002; he was one of three dissenters to the recommendation that the Special Criminal Court be retained.

Henchy, Seamus (1918–2009; served 1972–88)*

Graduated in Irish from University College Galway, and took a first in law from UCD in 1939 before acquiring a doctorate in mediaeval Irish studies from UCD in 1943. While practising at the Bar he was a part-time professor of Roman law, jurisprudence and legal history at UCD from 1948 to 1962. Became SC in 1959 and was appointed a judge of the High Court in 1962. Had Fianna Fáil leanings but presided in the arms trial in which Charles Haughey and others were acquitted of gun-running. Elevated to the Supreme Court in 1972, where he had a tense relationship with Brian Walsh. Renowned for his eloquent and persuasive writing style. In 1965 he presided over an International Commission of Jurists' Inquiry in British Guiana. For a while he chaired the Censorship of Publications Board and he resigned as a judge two years early to chair the Independent Radio and Television Commission.

Johnston, William (1869–1940; served 1939–40)*

Born near Magherafelt, in County Londonderry. Educated at Methodist College and Queen's College, Belfast, obtaining his MA in 1889 and LLB in 1891. Called to the Bar in 1892. Later edited both the *New Irish Jurist* and the *Irish Law Times and Solicitors' Journal*. Served as a county court judge from 1911 and was a member of the Judiciary Committee in 1923. Was the longest-serving of the first six appointees to the High Court in 1924. Died unexpectedly within a year of being appointed to the Supreme Court. His last judgment was his dissent in *The State (Burke) v Lennon*.

Keane, Ronan (b 1932; served 1996–2004)

Educated at Blackrock College, Dublin and UCD, where he studied history. Called to the Bar in 1954 and became SC in 1970. Appointed a High Court judge in 1979 and chaired the inquiry into the fire at the Stardust nightclub in Dublin in 1981. President of the Irish Law Reform Commission from 1987 to 1992. After four years as an ordinary Supreme Court judge he was made Chief Justice in 2000 in succession to Liam Hamilton, retiring four years later. A keen academic and writer, still serving as an Adjunct Professor at TCD.

Kearns, Nicholas (b 1946; served 2004–09)

Born in Dublin and educated at St Mary's College, Rathmines and UCD. Called to the Bar in 1968 and became SC in 1982. Appointed to the High Court in 1998, where he focused on competition law. In 2001 he sat as an ad hoc judge in the European Court of Human Rights and in 2004 he chaired the Referendum Commission during the referendum on citizenship. From 2005 he was a member of the Permanent Court of Arbitration at The Hague. In 2009 he resigned from his post as an ordinary judge of the Supreme Court to become President of the High Court, where he remained until retiring in 2015.

Kennedy, Hugh (1879–1936; served 1924–36)*

Educated privately and at UCD, where he co-founded a student magazine. Called to the Bar in 1902 and became KC in 1920. Served as Honorary Secretary of the Gaelic League and was one of the few lawyers to actively support Sinn Féin. Advised the Irish team which negotiated the Anglo-Irish Treaty of 1921. Served as Attorney General in the Provisional Government of Southern Ireland (1921–22) and the Executive Council of the Irish Free State (1922–24), being a member of both the Constitution Commission and the Judiciary Committee. Not elected to the Dáil until October 1923, as a representative of Cumann na nGaedheal. Resigned his seat eight months later when appointed as the first Chief Justice of the Irish Free State, where he served until dying in office a year before the new Constitution came into effect. Still the youngest person ever appointed to the Supreme Court, at the age of 44.

Kenny, John (1917–87; served 1975–82)*

Born into a working class family in Dublin. Educated at the Catholic University School, Dublin and at UCD, graduating with a BA in 1938 and LLB in 1941. Also obtained a Diploma in Vienna. Called to the Bar in 1940, taking silk in 1957. Taught law at UCD, where he challenged the way in which academic appointments were being made at the University. Served as a judge of the High Court from 1961 to 1975, where in *Ryan v Attorney General* he laid the foundation for the idea that the 1937 Constitution contains 'unenumerated' rights.

Kingsmill Moore, Theodore (TC) (1893–1979; served 1951–66)*

Son of the head of the training college for the Church of Ireland. Educated at Marlborough College in England and studied classics and legal and political science at TCD, graduating in 1916. Served in the Royal Flying Corps during World War I. Called to the Bar in 1918. Journalist for the *Irish Times* during the civil war of 1922-23. Became SC in 1935. Was elected an independent member of the Seanad for TCD in 1943. Served as a judge of the High Court from 1947 to 1951. Known for his refined writing style.

Laffoy, Mary (b 1945; served 2013–17)

Educated at UCD and called to the Bar in 1971, becoming SC in 1987. Served as a High Court judge from 1995 to 2013, mainly handling civil litigation, especially Chancery matters. Chaired the Commission to Inquire into Child Abuse from 1999 to 2003, when she resigned because of her dissatisfaction with the way the government was cooperating with the Commission. Judge Seán Ryan took over as chair of the Commission. In 2016 she was appointed by the Taoiseach to chair the Citizens Assembly, which comprises 99 other citizens who have been asked to consider a range of important societal issues, including the law on abortion.

Lavery, Cecil (1894–1967, served 1950–66)*

Born in Armagh and educated at Castleknock College, Dublin and UCD. Elected as Fine Gael TD for Dublin County in 1935 and 1937, but lost the seat in 1938. In 1948 he was chosen to be a member of the Seanad and appointed as Attorney General, being permitted to continue his private practice while serving in that role. Assisted in the drafting of the ECHR at the Council of Europe. Appointed directly to the Supreme Court in 1950. Was a favourite for appointment as Chief Justice when Conor Maguire retired in 1961, but lost out to the more experienced Cearbhall Ó Dálaigh, who had preceded Cecil Lavery as Attorney General.

Lynch, Kevin (1928–2013; served 1996–99)

Born in Dublin and educated at St Mary's College, Rathmines, and UCD. Called to the Bar in 1949, becoming SC in 1970. Served as a High Court judge from 1984 to 1996, during which time he chaired the inquiry into the 'Kerry babies' case, which concerned police behaviour after a baby's body was found on a beach in 1984.

Macken, Fidelma (b 1945; served 2005–12)

Educated at TCD. Called to the Bar in 1972 but began practising in 1979, specialising in intellectual property law and medical law. Became SC in 1995. Appointed to the High Court in 1998 and in 1999 succeeded John Murray as Ireland's judge on the European Court of Justice, the first woman from any country to serve on that Court. Returned to the High Court in 2004 but was promoted to the Supreme Court a year later. Retired when 67.

MacMenamin, John (b 1952; appointed 2012)

Born in Dublin and educated at Terenure College and UCD (where he studied history), a contemporary of Frank Clarke, who was appointed to the Supreme Court on the same day in 2012. Called to the Bar in 1975 and became SC in 1991. Chaired the Bar Council from 1997-99. Like Clarke, he specialised in commercial law and supported Fine Gael, but was appointed to the High Court bench by a Fianna Fáil/Progressive Democrat government in 2004 and dealt mainly with judicial review applications. Has published articles in fields such as family law and the law on children.

Maguire, Conor (1889–1971; served 1946–61)*

Son of a doctor in County Mayo. Graduated from NUI and qualified as a solicitor in 1915 and then as a barrister in 1922. An active member of Sinn Féin, imprisoned for six months in 1919 for publicising so-called Dáil bonds. Appointed as a judge of the Republican Courts and Dáil Land Settlement Commission 1920–22 but was dismissed for his anti-Treaty stance. Became SC in 1932. Elected TD for the NUI in 1932–36, during which time he served as Attorney General. President of the High Court from 1936–46 and CJ from 1946–61, the longest period any CJ has served.

Maguire, Martin (1889–1962; served 1954–61)

Born in 1889, the son of a JP in County Fermanagh. Educated at St Macartan's College in County Monaghan, Blackrock College in Dublin and TCD. Called to the Bar in 1911 and made SC in 1925, serving as leading SC from 1932. Succeeded John O'Byrne when the latter was promoted from the High Court to the Supreme Court in 1940, and succeeded him again in the Supreme Court when O'Byrne died in 1954.

McCarthy, Niall ('Neil') (1925–92; served 1982–92)*

The son of a Circuit Court judge; educated at the CBS in Dun Laoghaire, Clongowes Wood College and UCD. Called to the Bar in 1949, becoming SC in 1959. Defended Charles Haughey during the arms trial. Supposedly the top earner before being appointed directly to the Supreme Court in 1982. Dissented in the *Norris* case on homosexuality, together with Henchy J. Died with his wife in a car crash in Spain while still in office.

McCracken, Brian (b 1934; served 2002–06)

Born in Cork and educated at the High School, Dublin and TCD. Called to the Bar in 1957 and made SC in 1975. Practised mainly in land law, intellectual property law and commercial law. Served in the High Court from 1995 to 2002. In 1997 he chaired a tribunal of inquiry into allegations that the entrepreneur Ben Dunne made secret payments to politicians Charles Haughey and Michael Lowry. He found that Haughey had given untrue evidence and that Dunne had helped Lowry to evade tax. The report led to the more extensive Moriarty Tribunal.

McGuinness, Catherine (b 1934; served 2000–06)

Born into a Church of Ireland family in Northern Ireland. Educated at Alexandra College, Dublin and TCD, where she studied French and Irish. Worked as a teacher, writer and parliamentary officer for the Labour Party. Chaired the National Social Service Council and was a member of the Adoption Board from 1970 to 1977. Called to the Bar in 1977, specialised in family law, and became SC in 1989. Member of Seanad Éireann for TCD from 1979 to 1987 and Chair of the Employment Equality Agency from 1988 to 1993. Member of the Council of State from 1988 to 1991. Chaired the Kilkenny Inquest Inquiry in 1993 and the Forum for Peace and Reconciliation from 1994 to 1996. First woman to be appointed to the Circuit Court (1994–96) and served in the High Court from 1996 to 2000. After retirement she was made President of the Irish Law Reform Commission and she currently chairs NUI Galway's Governing Authority.

McKechnie, William (Liam) (b 1951; appointed 2010)

Born in Cork. Attended Presentation Brothers College and studied law at UCC. Called to the Bar in 1972 and appointed SC in 1987. Practised mainly in commercial law, chancery law and local authority law, also developing interests in medical negligence law and competition law. Chair of the Bar Council in 1999 and served in the High Court from 2000 to 2010; also Chairman of the Valuation Tribunal from 1995 to 2000. Issued the first declaration that a piece of Irish legislation was incompatible with the European Convention on Human Rights, in *Foy v An tArd Chláraitheoir*, 9 July 2002.

McLoughlin, Richard (1901–72; served 1969–72)

The son of a solicitor, he was called to the Bar in 1923 and became SC in 1938. He served as a judge of the High Court from 1952 to 1969 before being elevated to the Supreme Court. A conservative, he often sided with FitzGerald J in decisions where Ó Dálaigh CJ and Walsh and Budd JJ were in the majority. He died in office and his seat on the Court was taken by Seamus Henchy.

Meredith, James Creed (1875–1942, served 1936–42)*

Son of the secretary of the Royal University of Ireland (1880–1909) and a Protestant. Successful athlete and scholar at TCD. Called to the Bar in 1901 and became KC in 1918. Active in the Irish Volunteers from its foundation in 1913 and engaged in the smuggling of weapons into Ireland in 1914. Appointed President of the Dáil Éireann courts in 1919 and oversaw their winding-up in 1924, when he was one of the first six judges to be appointed to the High Court. Was given one of the two new positions on the Supreme Court in 1936, along with James Geoghegan. Translated the works of Immanuel Kant. Also wrote plays and a novel. Was a Quaker when he died in office in 1942.

Murnaghan, James (1881–1973; served 1925–53)*

Born in the USA but brought to Omagh in County Tyrone as a young child. Father was an Irish Party MP for Mid-Tyrone from 1885 to 1900. Educated at the Royal University (now UCD), obtaining a BA and LLD. Called to the Bar in 1903. Also worked as part-time professor of jurisprudence, Roman law and international law at UCD. Took no active part in nationalist politics but was appointed to the committee which drafted the Constitution of the Irish Free State in 1921. Appointed to the High Court in 1924 even though not yet a KC and chosen to succeed Charles O'Connor on the Supreme Court a year later. Served for 28 years, the second longest period (after Brian Walsh). A conservative judge, though a keen nationalist. A grand-niece, Sheelagh Murnaghan (1924–93), served as an Ulster Liberal Party MP for Queen's University in the Northern Ireland House of Commons from 1961 to 1969. A nephew was a High Court judge from 1954 to 1979.

Murphy, Francis (b 1932; served 1996–2002)

Educated at St Mary's College, Rathmines and UCD. Called to the Bar in 1953 and became SC in 1969, specialising in company law and taxation law. Served as a judge of the High Court from 1982 to 1996. In 2000 he conducted an inquiry into alleged misconduct by a District Judge, Donnchadh O'Buachalla. In 2002 he dissented, along with Keane CJ, in *Maguire v Ardagh* (the Abbeylara Inquiry case).

Murray, John (b 1943; served 1999–2015)

Born in Limerick and educated at Rockwell College, County Tipperary. Called to the Bar in 1967 after graduating from UCD. President of the Union of Students in Ireland, 1966–67. Became SC in 1981. Served as Attorney General in Charles Haughey's Fianna Fáil government for four months in 1982 and again from 1987 to 1991. Appointed as Ireland's judge at the European Court of Justice in 1992, remaining there until 1999. He then transferred to the Supreme Court and in 2004 succeeded Ronan Keane as Chief Justice. His term ran out in 2011 but he reverted to being an ordinary judge of the Supreme Court, not retiring until 2015. Married to the daughter of the former Supreme Court judge, Brian Walsh.

O'Byrne, John (1884–1954; served 1940–54)*

Educated at the Patrician Monastery in Tullow, County Carlow and at UCD. Worked as a civil servant before turning to the law, being called to the Bar in 1911. Active in Sinn Féin and the Gaelic League. Like Hugh Kennedy, he advised the Irish delegation during negotiations leading to the Anglo-Irish Treaty in 1921 and was a member of the Committee which drafted the Constitution of the Irish Free State in 1922 and of the Judiciary Committee in 1923. Became SC when appointed Attorney General in succession to Hugh Kennedy in 1924. Appointed to the High Court in 1926. Notwithstanding his former service for a Cummann na nGaedheal government, he was nominated for the Supreme Court by a Fianna Fáil government in 1940. Died in office and his widow then pursued an unsuccessful legal action claiming that it was unconstitutional to tax a judge's salary: *O'Byrne v Minister for Finance* (1959).

Ó Caoimh, Aindrias (1912–94; served 1965–66)*

Also styled as Andreas O'Keeffe and Ayindries Ó Cuiv. A Dubliner, educated at the O'Connell schools and UCD. Called to the Bar in 1935. A strong supporter of Fianna Fáil, he served as Attorney General in governments formed by that party in 1954 and 1957–65, succeeding Cearbhall Ó Dálaigh. Represented the government in *Lawless v Ireland* at Strasbourg. Like Ó Dálaigh he was appointed straight to the Supreme Court after his last spell as Attorney General, but after just one year he was appointed as President of the High Court. He recused himself from the trial of Charles Haughey and others for allegedly importing arms into Ireland. Left the High Court in 1974, when he succeeded Ó Dálaigh as the Irish judge on the ECJ. His younger brother married the daughter of Éamon de Valera. His son served as a High Court judge from 1999 to 2004 and as Ireland's judge at the ECJ from 2004 to 2015.

O'Connor, Charles (1854–1928; served 1924–25)*

Educated at St Stanislaus College, Tullabeg and at TCD. Called to the Bar in 1878, developing a successful Chancery practice mostly on the Connaught circuit. Became a QC in 1894. A firm supporter of Home Rule for Ireland but did not stand for election. Appointed Solicitor General for Ireland in 1909 and Attorney General for Ireland in 1911. Appointed straight to the Court of Appeal of Ireland, as Master of the Rolls, in 1912. In 1924 he turned down the position of President of the High Court, choosing instead to be one of the three first judges of the Supreme Court, but he retired the following year at the age of 70.

Ó Dálaigh, Cearbhall (1911–78; served 1953–72)*

Born in Bray, County Wicklow, son of a manager of a fish shop. Attended the CBS in Synge Street, Dublin, and graduated in Celtic Studies from UCD. While working as the Irish editor of the *Irish Press* he was called to the Bar in 1934. Stood twice, unsuccessfully, as a Fianna Fáil candidate for the Dáil. Became SC in 1944 and the youngest ever Attorney General in 1946. Served in that role until 1948 and again from 1951 to 1953, when he was appointed straight to the Supreme Court. Became Chief Justice in 1961, in preference to Cahir Davitt, the President of the High Court, and Cecil Lavery, the longest serving ordinary judge in the Supreme Court. A strong defender of personal rights, including unenumerated rights, and a staunch upholder of the courts' powers to check the excesses of both the Oireachtas and the government. On 1 January 1973 he became Ireland's first judge at the ECJ. After the sudden death of President Erskine Childers in 1974, he stood unopposed for the Presidency. In 1976, after being described as 'a thundering disgrace' by a government Minister for his referral of the Emergency Powers Bill to the Supreme Court under Article 26 of the Constitution, he resigned from the Presidency. Died suddenly on 21 March 1978.

O'Donnell, Donal (b 1958; appointed 2010)

Born in Belfast, where his father, Turlough O'Donnell, was a High Court judge from 1971 to 1979 and a Lord Justice of Appeal from 1979 to 1900. Educated at St Mary's CBS in Belfast, UCD and the University of Virginia. Called to the Bar in 1982 (and to the Northern Ireland Bar in 1989) and became SC in 1995. A member of the Irish Law Reform Commission from 2005 to 2112, his father having also served there. Appointed straight to the Supreme Court in 2010.

O'Flaherty, Hugh (b 1938; served 1990–99)

Educated at the CBS in Cahirciveen, St Brendan's College in Killarney and UCD; called to the Bar in 1959, becoming SC in 1976. Represented the McGimpsey Brothers in their challenge to the Anglo-Irish Agreement 1985. Appointed directly to the Supreme Court in 1990. Chairman of the Valuation Tribunal and a member of the Stardust Victims Compensation Tribunal. Resigned from his position in 1999 after being accused of improperly interfering in a criminal appeal.

O'Higgins, Thomas (1916–2003; served 1973–85)

A great-nephew of Tim Sullivan, Ireland's second Chief Justice, and a nephew of Kevin O'Higgins, the Minister for Justice who was assassinated by anti-treaty paramilitaries in 1927. His father was a doctor and a Fine Gael politician. Born in Sunday's Well, County Cork and educated at St Mary's College in Rathmines and from 1930–34 at Clongowes. Graduated from UCD with a first-class honours degree in law and political science and was a prize-winner at King's Inns. Called to the Bar in 1938, taking silk in 1954. Stood as an unsuccessful Fine Gael candidate for Dublin South in the 1943 general election. Elected in 1948 for his father's former seat, Laois–Offaly, and remained the representative until 1969. Served as Minister of Health in the coalition government headed by John Costello from 1954–57. Stood in 1966 as the Fine Gael candidate for the Presidency of Ireland, losing to Éamon de Valera by less than one per cent of the vote. Successfully stood in the general election in 1969 for Dublin County South. Became deputy leader of Fine Gael, under Liam Cosgrave, but stood again for the Presidency in 1973 and lost to Erskine Childers. Left politics later that year to become a High Court judge and just 10 months later, in 1974, took over as

Chief Justice following the sudden death of 'Billy' FitzGerald, retiring in 1985. Served from 1985 to 1991 as Ireland's judge on the ECJ. His memoirs, *A Double Life*, were published in 1996.

O'Malley, Iseult (b 1964; appointed 2015)

Born in 1964, the granddaughter of Kevin O'Higgins, the Minister for Justice assassinated in 1927, and cousin of Tom O'Higgins, Ireland's sixth Chief Justice. Educated at TCD, called to the Bar in 1987 and became SC in 2007. Focused mainly on criminal law cases but also served as Director and Chair of the Free Legal Advice Centre from 1985 to 2012, maintaining strong links to the Labour Party. In 2012 she was appointed to the High Court and was elevated to the Supreme Court three years later, taking the seat vacated by a former Chief Justice, John Murray.

Parke, Weldon (1912–81; served 1976–81)

Educated at TCD and called to the Bar in 1939, becoming SC in 1963. Appointed to the High Court in 1974 before being promoted to the Supreme Court in 1976 as an additional sixth judge to allow Brian Walsh to devote more time to his role as Chairman of the Irish Law Reform Commission. The composition of the Supreme Court remained unchanged until he died suddenly in 1981.

Sullivan, Timothy (1874–1949; served 1936–46)*

One of 17 children of an Irish nationalist MP and poet; his cousin was Tim Healy, the first governor-general of the Irish Free State and he later married Healy's daughter but had no children; he was also the uncle of Kevin O'Higgins (assassinated in 1927) and the great uncle of Tom O'Higgins, a future Chief Justice. Educated at Belvedere College in Dublin and called to the Bar in 1895, practising mainly in Munster. Took silk in 1918. Did legal work for the provisional government of the Irish Free State, opposing the *habeas corpus* application by Erskine Childers in 1922. Was a member of the Judiciary Committee in 1923. Became the first President of the new High Court of Ireland in 1924, serving until 1936, when he succeeded Hugh Kennedy as Chief Justice. He rejected the appeal against a writ of *habeas corpus* in *The State (Burke) v Lennon* but then maintained a deferential attitude in the Article 26 reference concerning the Offences Against the State (Amendment) Act 1940.

Walsh, Brian (1918–98; served 1961–90)*

Born in Dublin. Called to the Bar in 1941, becoming SC in 1954. Appointed to the High Court in 1959 and promoted just two years later to the Supreme Court, on the same day as Cearbhall Ó Dálaigh became Chief Justice. In 1962 he chaired a committee of inquiry into the operation of the courts, including the cost of litigation. Served as President of the Irish Law Reform Commission from 1975 to 1985 and as a judge at the European Court of Human Rights from 1980 to 1998. Through a series of judgments in the 1960s and 1970s he established himself as one of the most activist judges ever to have served on the Supreme Court, notably in *Byrne v Ireland, The People (Attorney General) v O'Callaghan* and *McGee v Attorney General.* Led the Irish side on the Anglo-Irish Law Enforcement Commission in 1974 and was reluctant to extradite suspects to Northern Ireland. A supporter of individual rights but conservative on some issues, such as abortion and homosexuality.

APPENDIX 4

References to the Supreme Court under Article 26 of the Constitution

	Name of case, law report reference, date of decision, length of hearing and of the judgment	**The President who made the reference and the judges who responded to it**	**The issues raised and conclusions reached**
1	*In re Article 26 and the Offences Against the State (Amendment) Bill 1940* [1940] IR 470 9 February 1940 5 day hearing 9 pages	Douglas Hyde Sullivan CJ Maguire P Murnaghan J Geoghegan J O'Byrne J	None of the provisions (on arresting, indefinitely detaining, searching, photographing and fingerprinting) were repugnant to the Constitution: they did not permit the Minister to administer justice, to punish someone or to violate the personal rights of the citizen. See Chap 4, 109-10 and 119.
2	*In re Article 26 and the School Attendance Bill 1942* [1943] IR 334 15 April 1943 4 day hearing 9 pages	Douglas Hyde Sullivan CJ Murnaghan J Geoghegan J O'Byrne J Black J	Section 4 of the Bill was repugnant to Art 42.3.2 of the Constitution because it permitted the Minister to prescribe for children educated at home or at a private school more than the minimum standard of education required by the Constitution; it also required the manner of the education to be certified and there would inevitably be a time gap before a Minister could provide a certificate, leaving the parent in default in the meantime. See Chap 6, 120.
3	*In re Article 26 and the Electoral (Amendment) Bill 1961* [1961] IR 169 14 July 1961 4 day hearing 6 pages	Éamon de Valera Maguire CJ Lavery J Kingsmill Moore J Ó Dálaigh J Haugh J	The 1961 Bill had been passed after a 1959 Bill was declared invalid in part by Budd J in *O'Donovan v AG* [1961] IR 114.The 1961 Bill was held to be constitutional in using the 1956 census as the basis for assessing the population for election purposes, even though the 1961 census was in the course of completion at the time of the Bill's passing. On the 1956 figures the total number of Dáil members did not exceed that which was permitted by Art 16.2.2, but the permitted number would have been exceeded had the election been based on the (lower) estimated 1961 figures.

4	*In re Article 26 and the Criminal Law (Jurisdiction) Bill 1975* [1977] IR 129 6 May 1976 5 day hearing 17 pages	Cearbhall Ó Dálaigh O'Higgins CJ Finlay J Griffin J Kenny J Parke J	The Bill was held to be constitutional, despite Art 3 of the Constitution saying that the laws of the Oireachtas 'shall have the like area and extent of application ... and the like extra-territorial effect' as laws of the Irish Free State. See Chap 7, 157-9.
5	*In re Article 26 and the Emergency Powers Bill 1976* [1977] IR 159 15 October 1976 3 day hearing 8 pages	Cearbhall Ó Dálaigh O'Higgins CJ Walsh J Henchy J Griffin J Kenny J	The Supreme Court held that the President had the power to refer this Bill, even though Art 28.3.3 of the Constitution provides that nothing in the Constitution shall be invoked to invalidate any law expressed to be for the purpose of securing public safety in the time of armed rebellion etc. But because of Art 28.3.3 the Court could not declare any provision in the Bill to be unconstitutional. No evidence was presented suggesting that the relevant resolutions passed by the Houses of the Oireachtas were based on incorrect facts. See Chap 6, 111-12.
6	*In re Article 26 and the Housing (Private Rented Dwellings) Bill 1982* [1983] IR 181 19 February 1982 4 day hearing 7 pages	Patrick Hillery O'Higgins CJ Walsh J Henchy J Griffin J Hederman J	The Bill was held to be repugnant to the Constitution, the first time a Bill passed to replace legislation already declared unconstitutional (in *Blake v Attorney General* [1982] IR 117) was itself held to be unconstitutional. Contrary to Art 40.3.2 of the Constitution, s 9 of the Bill deprived landlords of substantial proportions of their proper rents. See Chap 6, 113.
7	*In re Article 26 and the Electoral (Amendment) Bill 1961* [1961] IR 169 14 July 1961 4 day hearing 6 pages	Patrick Hillery O'Higgins CJ Finlay P Henchy J Grifffin J McCarthy J	The Bill was held to be repugnant to Art 16 of the Constitution in that it purported to allow British citizens (i.e. non-Irish citizens) to vote at elections for members of Dáil Éireann. Later the same year a new Art 16.1.2 was inserted into the Constitution after a referendum.
8	*In re Article 26 and the Adoption (No 2) Bill* [1989] IR 656 26 July 1988 2 day hearing 9 pages	Patrick Hillery Finlay CJ Walsh J Henchy J Griffin J Hederman J	The Bill was held to be constitutional. It did not violate the rights of the family under Arts 41 or 42 of the Constitution. See Chap 10, 221-2.
9	*In re Article 26 and the Matrimonial Home Bill 1993* [1994] 1 IR 305 24 January 1994 3 day hearing 9 pages	Mary Robinson Finlay CJ O'Flaherty J Egan J Blayney J Denham J	The Bill was held to be repugnant to the Constitution as, by cancelling the joint decision of some spouses relating to the ownership of their matrimonial home made prior to the legislation, it did not constitute proportionate intervention by the State with the rights of the family as guaranteed by Art 41. See Chap 10, 230-1.

10	*In re Article 26 and the Regulation of Information (Services outside the State for Termination of Pregnancies) Bill 1995* [1995] 1 IR 1 12 May 1995 4 day hearing 36 pages	Mary Robinson Hamilton CJ O'Flaherty J Egan J Blayney J Denham J	The Bill was held not to be repugnant to the Constitution. The Oireachtas had been engaged in balancing constitutional rights and duties and the Court should not impose its view of the correct or desirable balance in substitution for that of the legislature; rather it should determine whether the provisions represented a fair and reasonable balance and were not an unjust attack on some individual's constitutional rights (applying *Tuohy v Courtney* [1994] 3 IR 1). Moreover the Constitution was the fundamental and supreme law of the State, not natural law. See Chap 6, 114-5.
11	*In re Article 26 and the Employment Equality Bill 1996* [1997] 2 IR 321 15 May 1997 6 day hearing 57 pages	Mary Robinson Hamilton CJ O'Flaherty J Denham J Barrington J Keane J	The provisions allowing for positive discrimination on the ground of disability constituted a delimitation of the exercise by employers of their right under Arts 40.3 and 43 to carry on a business and earn a livelihood by imposing so onerous a burden as to amount to a failure to adequately protect those rights. Section 15 of the Bill, on vicarious liability, including criminal liability, was contrary to Arts 38.1 and 40.1 of the Constitution, and s 63(3), on the use of a certificate to prove guilt, was also contrary to Art 38.1 (the right not to be charged with any criminal offence save in due course of law). See Chap 6, 115-6.
12	*In re Article 26 and the Equal Status Bill 1997* [1997] 2 IR 387 19 June 1997 2 day hearing 14 pages	Mary Robinson Hamilton CJ O'Flaherty J Denham J Barrington J Keane J	Given that ss 40(3) and 71 of this Bill were very similar to ss 63(3) and 15 of the Employment Equality Bill, already declared repugnant to the Constitution, the Supreme Court held there was no justiciable issue concerning the remaining provisions of the Equal Status Bill. See Chap 6, 116.
13	*In re Article 26 and Part V of the Planning and Development Bill 1999* [2000] 2 IR 321 28 August 2000 3 day hearing 36 pages	Mary McAleese Keane CJ Murphy J Murray J McGuinness J Geoghegan J	Part V was held not to be repugnant to the Constitution because ensuring the availability of affordable housing by imposing a condition on applicants for planning permission to develop land for residential purposes, whereby the owner was required to cede some part of the land to the housing authority, was an objective of sufficient importance to warrant interference with the constitutionally protected right to property and impaired that right as little as possible and in a way that was proportionate to the objective (following *Heaney v Ireland* [1994] 3 IR 593). See Chap 6, 117.

14	*In re Article 26 and Sections 5 and 10 of the Illegal Immigrants (Trafficking) Bill 1999* [2000] 2 IR 360 28 August 2000 2 day hearing 51 pages	Mary McAleese Keane CJ Murphy J Murray J McGuinness J Geoghegan J	The sections were held not to be repugnant to the Constitution. Section 5, in placing restrictions on how certain orders etc could be challenged by non-nationals, did not deny the right of access to the courts or the right to equality. Nor was there any requirement that a restriction imposed by the Oireachtas on an appeal from the High Court to the Supreme Court had to be objectively justified. Section 10, in extending the Minister's powers to make deportation orders etc, did not result in any unfair or unconstitutional hardship. The safeguards in place in relation to preventative detention were adequate to satisfy the Constitution and there was no conflict with Art 5 of the ECHR. See Chap 6, 117-8.
15	*In re Article 26 and the Health (Amendment) (No 2) Bill 2004* [2005] IESC 7, [2005] 1 IR 105 16 February 2005 3 day hearing 55 pages	Mary McAleese Murray CJ Denham J McGuinness J Hardiman J Geoghegan J Fennelly J McCracken J	The retrospective provisions in s 1(b) of the Bill, which abrogated the right of persons, otherwise entitled to do so, to recover monies for charges unlawfully imposed upon them in the past for the provision of in-patient hospital services, were repugnant to the Constitution, in particular Arts 43 and 40.3.2. But the requirement to pay charges for such services in the future could not be considered an infringement of the constitutional right to life or the right to bodily integrity as derived from Art 40.3 of the Constitution. See Chap 6, 118-9.

APPENDIX 5

Supreme Court Decisions reviewed in Strasbourg

Part A: Challenges which were found inadmissible (i.e. not given a full consideration on their merits)

No	The case in the Supreme Court (apparently unreported unless otherwise stated)	The case in Strasbourg
1	Judgments of 11 November 1968 and July 1969.	*X v Ireland* App No 3717/68 (6 February 1970). Application based on Arts 6 and 14 manifestly ill-founded. No evidence of judicial bias, conspiracy or undue delay in trial of stateless person for murder.
2	Judgment of March 1976 dismissing the brothers' appeal against conviction.	*X and Y v Ireland* App No 8299/78 (15 July 1980). Applications concerning unfairness under Art 6 relating to extradition proceedings against two brothers in England and their subsequent trial before the Special Criminal Court in Ireland. Both inadmissible. See too *Eccles v Ireland*, no 10 below.
3	No unfairness where the Supreme Court, with the parties' consent, hear an appeal without any note of the High Court proceedings.	*X v Ireland* App No 8315/78 (15 July 1981). Inadmissible because no violation of Art 6.
4	Judgment of October 1981 rejecting the applicant's appeal, because his breaking of bail in the UK in 1972 was the initial cause of the delay in his trial there.	*X v Ireland* App No 9742/82 (2 March 1983). Application concerning the length of extradition proceedings (nearly seven years) was an abuse of process, since the applicant had himself fled justice.
5	Judgment of 29 October 1982, dismissing the applicant's appeal for an armed mail train robbery.	*K v Ireland* App No 10416/93 (17 May 1984). Application complaining of ill-treatment by the police was out of time.
6	Judgment of the Supreme Court in 1987 discharging an interlocutory injunction obtained by the applicant in the High Court, hearing the substantive issue against the applicant and thereby triggering his undertaking to pay Dublin Corp's costs.	*FX v Martin* App No 8569/79 (8 May 1985). Inadmissible because Art 6 was not engaged as bringing an *actio popularis* against a decision by Dublin Corporation to build over Viking remains at Wood Quay in Dublin did not engage 'civil rights or obligations'.
7	*O'Callaghan v Commissioner of Public Works* [1985] ILRM 364 (31 July 1984). Purchaser of land unsuccessful in challenging restrictions relating to the land.	*O v Ireland* App No 11446/85 (3 March 1986). Application manifestly ill-founded concerning Art 1 of Prot 1 and also Arts 8 and 14.

8	*Neal Duggan v Mr Justice Griffin* et al (24 November 1982, 12 March 1984 and 11 March 1986).	*D v Ireland* App No 12234/86 (2 December 1986). Application concerning bias by a judge on the Supreme Court (Hederman J, a stockholder in the Bank of Ireland) inadmissible for non-exhaustion of domestic remedies and otherwise manifestly ill-founded.
9	Judgments of 21 January 1983, 7 February 1983 and 28 March 1984.	*D v Ireland* App No 11489/95 (3 December 1986). Application concerning judicial bias (as Hederman J had shares in a newspaper group) manifestly ill-founded.
10	*Eccles v Ireland* [1985] IR 545 (1 November 1985).	*Eccles v Ireland* App No 12839/87 (9 December 1988). Application manifestly ill-founded. The Commission had previously found the Special Criminal Court to be an independent and impartial tribunal although the applicants in that case did not question the independence of the Court with reference to the removability of the judges or to their remuneration (*X and Y v Ireland*, App No 8299/78, 22 DR 551, decision of 10 December 1980; see too no 2 above).
11	Four judgments between 29 June 1993 and 29 July 1994 on the applicant's complaints about censorship of prisoner correspondence and his inability to vote in a Presidential election.	*Holland v Ireland* App No 24827/94 (3 May 1989). Applications inadmissible for failure to exhaust domestic remedies and because manifestly ill-founded.
12	*McGlinchey v Governor of Portlaoise Prison* [1988] 1 IR 671 (20 July 1988) and 21 December 1989.	*McGlinchey v Ireland* App No 16751/90 (5 March 1991). Application manifestly ill-founded because of lack of evidence of discrimination or of illegal detention. Also out of time in one respect.
13	No Supreme Court judgment directly at issue, but the European Court considered *The State (Lynch) v Cooney* [1982] IR 337 (28 July 1981).	*Purcell v Ireland* App No 15404/89 (16 April 1991). A challenge to 'the broadcasting ban' targeted at supporters of paramilitary violence. Application under Arts 10, 13 and Art 3 of Prot 1 all manifestly ill-founded.
14	Judgment of 19 December 1990 involving the custody of children.	*O v Ireland* App No 15601/89 (10 October 1991). Application that the applicant's Art 6 rights were violated because he had to represent himself was manifestly unfounded.
15	Judgment of 13 June 1989.	*McLoughlin v Ireland* App No 15967/90 (6 July 1992). Application manifestly ill-founded in so far as it alleged a violation of Art 6 in that the applicant was supposedly convicted of a criminal offence in civil proceedings relating to non-payment of tax.

16	*Goodman International v Mr Justice Hamilton* [1992] 2 IR 542 (5 November 1991).	*Goodman International v Ireland* App No 19538/92 (12 January 1993). Applications based on Arts 3, 13, 14 and Art 1 of Prot 1 all manifestly ill-founded, mostly because there was no evidence to support them.
17	*Hardy v Ireland* [1994] 2 IR 550 (18 March 1993), on the burden of proof in a case concerning suspected possession of explosive substances.	*Hardy v Ireland* App No 23456/94 (29 June 1994). Application manifestly ill-founded under Art 6.
18	No Supreme Court judgment directly at issue, but in the High Court Geoghegan J followed the guidelines set out by the Supreme Court in *The Adoption (No 2) Bill 1987* [1989] IR 656 (26 July 1988).	*ED v Ireland* App No 25054/94 (18 October 1995). Application manifestly ill-founded under Arts 8 and 14 regarding the Adoption Board's decision to place the child of a couple from the Travelling community with adopting parents.
19	*Tuohy v Courtney* [1994] 3 IR 1 (26 July 1994), disallowing the applicant's claim for negligence against a solicitor because of the limitation period.	*Tuohy v Ireland* App No 26270/95(16 October 1996). Application under Arts 6, 14 and Art 1 of Prot 1 manifestly ill-founded.
20	At least four judgments on 22 April 1993, 28 July 1994, 19 May 1995 and 29 March 1996.	*Ó Cathail v Ireland* App No 27348/95 (9 April 1997). Application manifestly ill-founded as regards its allegations that the applicant's rights as a father concerning access to his two sons had been violated.
21	Judgments of 20 July 1993 and 21 December 1994.	*Dublin Well Woman Centre Ltd v Ireland* App No 28177/95 (9 April 1997). Application manifestly ill-founded because no lack of a fair hearing and no discrimination when the Irish courts did not discharge the injunction granted against the applicant company after the European Court of Human Rights judgment of 29 October 1992. The Committee of Ministers had already adopted its Resolution DH(96) 368 of 25 June 1996.
22	*McKone Estates Ltd v Dublin City Council* [1995] 2 ILRM 283 (19 May 1993).	*McKone Estates Ltd v Ireland* App No 28892/95 (10 September 1997). Application manifestly ill-founded under Arts 6, 13 and 14 and Art 1 of Prot 1. The applicant company knew that its original planning permission was time-limited and could be subject to conditions.
23	*H v Director of Public Prosecutions* [1994] 2 IR 589 (19 May 1994), disallowing judicial review proceedings against the DPP because there was no evidence of bad faith. A child's mother alleged the father was a paedophile.	*Herron v United Kingdom and Ireland* App No 36931/97 (3 December 1997). Application relying on Art 8 inadmissible because the interference was justifiable; otherwise the application was manifestly ill-founded.

24	No Supreme Court judgment directly at issue, but reference made to the judicial review case of *Hutchinson v Minister for Justice* [1993] 3 IR 567 (16 October 1992).	*O'Hara v Ireland* App No 26667/95 (14 April 1998). Application concerning the alleged censorship of a prisoner's mail inadmissible for non-exhaustion of domestic remedies.
25	*McHugh v Minister for Justice* [1997] 1 IR 245 (7 June 1996), denying the applicant a trip from Portlaoise Prison to his mother in Dundalk, such a visit being entirely up to the Minister's discretion.	*McHugh v Ireland* App No 34486/97 (16 April 1998). Application based on Arts 8 and 11 inadmissible partly for being out of time, partly for non-exhaustion of domestic remedies and partly *ratione materiae*.
Note: After 1 November 1998 decisions on admissibility were taken by the European Court rather than the European Commission		
26	*Dempsey v An Bord Uachtála*, 17 May 1996	*Dempsey v Ireland* App No 41382/98 (6 April 2000). Application manifestly ill-founded because no denial of access to justice due to unavailability of legal aid to fight an adoption order.
27	*Rock v Ireland* [1997] 3 IR 484 (19 November 1997).	*Rock v Ireland* App No 41525/98 (11 May 2000). Application manifestly ill-founded because there was no evidence that any negative inferences had been drawn from the applicant's silence.
28	*Barry v The Medical Council* [1998] 3 IR 368 (16 December 1997).	*Barry v Ireland* App No 41957/98 (6 July 2000). Application inadmissible because premature. A later application by the same applicant was successful in 2005: see App 18273/04 in Part D, no 10, below.
29	*O'B v S* [1984] IR 316 (20 January 1984). The Supreme Court ruled that 'issue' in the Succession Act 1965, s 67, excluded illegitimate children but that this was not a breach of the principle of equality in Art 40.1 of the Constitution.	*Nee v Ireland* App No 52787/99 (30 January 2003). Application inadmissible because out of time.
30	*Dawson v Irish Brokers Association*, 27 February 1997; 6 November 1998; 8 May 2002.	*Dawson v Ireland* App No 21826/02 (8 July 2004). Application manifestly ill-founded as regards alleged delays, exclusion of evidence and award of costs.
31	*Attorney General v X* [1992] 1 IR 1 (5 March 1992). The Supreme Court allowed a 14-year-old girl to travel to England for an abortion but left it unclear as to exactly when an abortion could be obtained in Ireland.	*D v Ireland* App No 26499/02 (27 June 2006) Application inadmissible because of failure to seek a domestic ruling on whether a woman could get an abortion in a situation of fatal foetal abnormality. The Court said it was possible the Irish courts would permit an abortion in such a case even under its existing legal regime.

<table>
<tr><td colspan="3">Note: The European Convention on Human Rights Act 2003 came into force in Ireland on 31 December 2003</td></tr>
<tr><td>32</td><td>Minister for Justice, Equality and Law Reform v Stapleton
[2007] IESC 30 (26 July 2007)</td><td>Stapleton v Ireland App No 56588/07 (4 May 2010).
A case on surrendering a person to the UK under a European Arrest Warrant. Application manifestly ill-founded.</td></tr>
<tr><td>33</td><td>Director of Public Prosecutions v Kelly
[2006] IESC 20, [2006] 3 IR 115 (4 April 2006).</td><td>Kelly v Ireland App No 41130/06 (14 December 2010).
Application concerning the admission of, and reliance upon, the evidence of a Chief Superintendent against the applicant was manifestly ill-founded as regards Arts 6 and 13.</td></tr>
<tr><td>34</td><td>Adio v the Minister for Justice, Equality and Law Reform
[2007] IESC 63 (20 December 2007), applying the Supreme Court's decision in Bode v Minister for Justice, Equality & Law Reform [2007] IESC 62, [2008] 3 IR 663 (20 December 2007).</td><td>Adio v Ireland App No 8596/08 (17 May 2011).
Application inadmissible ratione personae because the applicant and her child had not taken any steps, whether prior to entry or subsequent thereto, to apply for an entry visa or residence permit or to request leave to remain in Ireland.</td></tr>
<tr><td>35</td><td>Izevbekhai v Minister for Justice Equality and Law Reform
[2010] IESC 303 (9 July 2010).</td><td>Izevbekhai v Ireland App No 43408/08 (17 May 2011).
Application manifestly ill-founded because the first applicant and her husband could protect their two daughters from FGM if returned to Nigeria. No grounds for complaint under Arts 6, 13 and 14 also.</td></tr>
<tr><td>36</td><td>Brennan v Governor of Portlaoise Prison
[2008] IESC 12 (12 March 2008).</td><td>Birney v Ireland App No 52054/08 and Troy and Brennan v Ireland App No 52079/08 (10 January 2012).
Applications rejected on grounds of failure to exhaust domestic remedies in relation to challenges that they had not brought before the Special Criminal Court 'forthwith' as required by O'Brien v Special Criminal Court [2007] IESC 45.</td></tr>
<tr><td>37</td><td>No Supreme Court judgment directly at issue, but reference was made by the European Court of Human Rights to the Supreme Court's rejection of the claim for compensation for nervous shock in The State (Keegan) v The Stardust Victims Compensation Tribunal
[1986] 1 IR 642 (16 December 1986).</td><td>McDermott v Ireland; Keegan v Ireland App Nos 23213/09 and 62652/09 (25 September 2012).
Applications inadmissible because out of time. The applicants complained under Arts 1, 2, 6, 8, 13, 14 and 17 that there were deficiencies in the investigation into the deaths of their children in the Stardust fire in 1981 and that those responsible had therefore not been punished.</td></tr>
</table>

38	*The People (Director of Public Prosecutions) v Boyce* [2008] IESC 62, [2009] 2 IR 124 (18 November 2008).	*Boyce v Ireland* App No 8428/09, (2013) 56 EHRR SE11 (27 November 2012). Application concerning the taking, retention and use of a blood sample provided by a person in police custody inadmissible as regards Art 8 for failure to exhaust domestic remedies and as regards Art 6 because it was manifestly ill-founded.
39	*Lynch and Whelan v Minister for Justice, Equality and Law Reform* [2010] IESC 34 (14 May 2010).	*Lynch and Whelan v Ireland* Apps Nos 70495/10 and 74565/10 (18 June 2013). Applications manifestly ill-founded because a life sentence for murder was not 'unfixed' just because a Minister had a discretion to allow temporary release.
40	*Smith v Minister for Justice and Equality* [2013] IESC 4 (1 February 2013).	*Smith v Ireland* App No 52223/13 (24 June 2014). Application manifestly ill-founded as regards its claim that deporting the father of a family to Nigeria would breach Art 8.
41	*MD (A Minor) v Ireland* [2012] IESC 10 (23 February 2012).	*MD v Ireland* App No 50936/12 (16 September 2014). Application manifestly ill-founded because the State had acted within its margin of appreciation in exempting girls under the age of 17 who had sex with boys under that age from being prosecuted just for having sexual intercourse.
42	*Reilly v Devereux* [2009] IESC 22, [2009] 3 IR 660 (24 March 2009).	*Reilly v Ireland* App No 51083/09 (23 September 2014). Application manifestly ill-founded because the sergeant major's alleged abuse could not be attributed to the State, there was no failure to protect the applicant under Art 3, and the denial of vicarious liability was a permissible limitation to access to justice under Art 6.
43	*Lopes v Minister for Justice, Equality and Law Reform* decisions in July 1997, July 1999 and 27 March 2014 ([2014] IESC 21).	*Lopes v Ireland* App No 14349/13 (30 September 2014). Application manifestly ill-founded concerning delay and racial bias (Arts 6 and 13).
44	*Mahon v Keena* [2009] IESC 64 and 78 [2010] 1 IR 336 (26 November 2009).	*Keena and Kennedy v Ireland* App No 29804/10 (30 September 2014). No violation of Art 10 or other Arts when Supreme Court ordered the applicants to pay the costs of a Tribunal's action against them. Application manifestly ill-founded.

45	*Enright v Director of Public Prosecutions* [2012] IESC 54 (26 October 2012).	*Enright v Ireland* App No 75116/12 (30 September 2014). Application concerning delay, under Arts 6 and 13, manifestly ill-founded. Patrick Enright had earlier agreed a friendly settlement over a previous claim concerning delay: App No 61138/08, struck out 21 June 2011 (see Part B, no 7, below).
46	*McGowan v Labour Court* [2013] IESC 21, [2013] 3 IR 718 (9 May 2013).	*Irish Congress of Trade Unions v Ireland* App No 72596/13 (2 December 2014). Application inadmissible for non-exhaustion of domestic remedies. The applicant could have raised the compatibility of an approach to non-registration of collective labour agreements in domestic litigation.
47	*Minister for Justice, Equality and Law Reform v Tobin* [2008] IESC 3 (25 February 2008, giving reasons for a decision on 3 July 2007) and [2012] IESC 37 (19 June 2012).	*Zoltai v Hungary and Ireland*, App No 61946/12 (29 September 2015). Application manifestly ill-founded because Ireland had not breached Art 2 in the way that it had prevented, or delayed, Mr Tobin's surrender to Hungary to serve a sentence for causing the death of two children by careless driving.
48	*Adigun v The Equality Tribunal* [2015] IESC 91 (8 Decmber 2015).	*Adiguin v Ireland* App No 19673/16 (31 January 2017). Application inadmissible *ratione materiae* because the Equality Tribunal and judicial review proceedings could not deal with the applicants' alleged grievances.
49	No Supreme Court judgment directly at issue, just one by the Court of Appeal: *Hegarty v Mercy University Hospital Cork Ltd* [2016] IECA 24 (10 February 2016).	*PH v Ireland* App No 45046/16 (10 October 2017). Application manifestly ill-founded because Ireland had taken steps to deal with the backlog of cases at the Supreme Court by creating the Court of Appeal, referring to *Brennan v Ireland* App No 44360/15, decision of 2 November 2017 (*sic*), paras 54-55 (see Part C, no 7, below).
50	Judgment denying leave to appeal against the Court of Appeal's decision in *Director of Public Prosecutions v Campion* [2015] IECA 274 (30 November 2015).	*Campion v Ireland* App No 29276/17 (10 October 2017). Application concerning unfairness under Art 6 was manifestly ill-founded and allegation that s 16 of the Criminal Justice Act 2006, on admissibility of previous inconsistent witness statements, was incompatible with Art 6 was inadmissible for non-exhaustion of domestic remedies.

Part B: Challenges which were terminated because Ireland accepted the Commission's finding of a violation or because a friendly settlement was reached

1	Judgment of 20 January 1984. The applicant was not entitled to succeed on intestacy, not being 'issue' within s 67 of the Succession Act 1965. Nor did ss 67 or 69 of the Act infringe the principle of equality before the law guaranteed under Art 40.1 of the Constitution.	*Stoutt v Ireland* App No 10978/84 (14 October 1986). Declared admissible the applicant's complaints under Art 14 in conjunction with Art 8 concerning the absence of inheritance rights on intestacy over the estates of her father and her parents' near relatives. Friendly settlement adopted by the Commission on 17 December 1987 whereby the government paid Mrs Stoutt IR£10,000 and the Court noted that the Status of Children Bill, reforming succession law, was going through the Oireachtas.
2	*Dreher v Irish Land Commission* [1984] ILRM 94 (1 July 1983), where the constitutionality of payment for compulsorily acquired land in Irish Land Bonds under the Land Bond Act 1934 was upheld.	*Dreher v Ireland* App No 11048/84 (6 July 1987). Application based on Art 1 of Prot 1 struck out after the government agreed that the applicant's land could be restored to him despite the Supreme Court's decision that reasonable compensation had been paid to him for its compulsory acquisition.
3	*The People (Director of Public Prosecutions) v Quilligan and O'Reilly* [1986] 1 IR 495 (25 July 1986), the first ever appeal against a murder acquittal in the Central Criminal Court, and *(No 2)* [1989] 1 IR 46 (29 July 1988), the first ever application to re-try someone already acquitted of murder, and also judgments of 14 and 30 July 1992.	*O'Reilly v Ireland* App No 21624/93, Report of Commission adopted 22 February 1995. Violation of Art 6(1) because Patrick O'Reilly's trial for murder and burglary lasted 7 years and 7 months (by 8 v 1). Led to Committee of Ministers' Resolution DH (97) 7 on 28 January 1997. IR£3,000 was paid in compensation.
4	Judgment of 16 November 1993.	*O'Reilly v Ireland* App No 24196/94, Report of Commission adopted 3 December 1996. Friendly settlement of the applicant's complaints under Arts 5, 6, 8 and 13 as regards her detention in a psychiatric institution. The government agreed to pay the applicant IR£14,000 in compensation.
5	Judgments of 9 February 1994 and 12 July 1994.	*McMullen v Ireland* App No 25353/94, Report of Commission adopted 21 October 1998. Violation of Art 6(1) because negligence claims against various solicitors had lasted 8 years and 9 months. Led to Committee of Ministers' Final Resolution ResDH(2001)31. IR£1,000 was paid in compensation.

<table>
<tr><td colspan="3">Note: On 1 November 1998 the European Commission ceased considering new applications, but for one year it continued to work on applications already declared admissible</td></tr>
<tr><td>6</td><td>Croke v Smith
[1998] 1 IR 101 (31 July 1996), ruling that s 172 of the Mental Treatment Act 1945 was not unconstitutional.</td><td>Croke v Ireland, App No 33267/96, struck out 21 December 2000. Friendly settlement reached over need for an independent formal review of detention under the Mental Health Acts. See now Mental Health Act 2001, ss 17 and 18.</td></tr>
<tr><td colspan="3">Note: The European Convention on Human Rights Act 2003 came into force in Ireland on 31 December 2003</td></tr>
<tr><td>7</td><td>See Part A, no 45, above.</td><td>Enright v Ireland App No 61138/08 (21 June 2011).
Application struck out after the government promised to pay €9,500 on account of delay in the prosecution of the applicant for forgery.</td></tr>
<tr><td>8</td><td>JB v Director of Public Prosecutions
[2006] IESC 66 (29 November 2006), rejecting an appeal against a failed judicial review alleging delay in prosecutions of sexual offences.</td><td>JB v Ireland App No 9519/07 (21 June 2011).
Application struck out after the government promised to pay €13,000.</td></tr>
<tr><td>9</td><td>Magee v Farrell
[2009] IESC 60, [2009] 4 IR 703 (28 July 2009).</td><td>Magee v Ireland, App No 53743/09, struck out 20 November 2012.
Friendly settlement over legal aid for mother at inquest of son who died in police custody.</td></tr>
<tr><td>10</td><td>Stanley v Kieran
[2011] IESC 19 (7 June 2011), denying the applicant any interest in a house bought for her by a former partner, in whose favour a resulting trust arose.</td><td>Kieran v Ireland App No 73886/11 (28 May 2013).
Application struck out after the government offered to pay the applicant €6,000.</td></tr>
<tr><td>11</td><td>No Supreme Court judgment directly at issue: High Court proceedings were still in train. But in Dublin City Council v Fennel [2005] 1 IR 604 the Supreme Court had held that the ECHR Act 200 could not be seen as having retroactive effect or as affecting past events.</td><td>Nic Gibb v Ireland App No 17707/10 (25 March 2014).
Application struck out after the government unequivocally admitted a violation of Art 2 in relation to the investigation of the death of Ronan O'Lochlainn on 1 May 1998 and offered adequate compensation to the applicant as well as an Art 2 compliant investigation. No violation of Arts 2, 6, 8 or 13 as regards the non-retrospective nature of the ECHR Act 2003.</td></tr>
<tr><td>12</td><td>Blehein v Minister for Health and Children [2008] IESC 40, [2009] 1 IR 275 (10 July 2008), holding that the limitation in s 260 of the Mental Treatment Act 1945, as amended, on access to the courts on two specified grounds constituted an impermissible interference by the legislature in the judicial domain.</td><td>Blehein v Ireland App No 14704/16 (25 April 2017).
Application struck out because of unilateral declaration made by Ireland concerning compensation and admissions about delay.</td></tr>
</table>

Part C: Challenges which were found admissible but no violations were then found on the merits

No	The case in the Supreme Court	The case in Strasbourg
1	*In re Ó Laighléis* [1960] IR 110 (3 December 1957).	*Lawless v Ireland (No 3)* (1978) 1 EHRR 15 (1 July 1961). Supreme Court decision approved.
2	*McElhinney v Williams* [1995] 3 IR 382 (15 December 1995).	*McElhinney v Ireland* (2002) 34 EHRR 13 (21 November 2001) (GC) Supreme Court decision approved.
3	*Murphy v Independent Radio and Television Commission* [1999] 1 IR 12 (28 May 1998).	*Murphy v Ireland* (10 July 2003) Supreme Court decision approved.
4	*DPP v Ward* [1999] 1 IR 60 *DPP v Kelly* [2006] 3 IR 115 *Redmond v. Ireland* [2009] 2 ILRM 419 *DPP v. Donnelly, McGarrigle and Murphy* [2012] IECCA 78 These decisions upheld the constitutionality of the Offences Against the State (Amendment) Act 1992, s 3(2), allowing a statement of belief from a Chief Superintendent relating to a person's membership of an illegal organization to be evidence of that membership.	*Donohoe v Ireland* App No 19165/08 (12 December 2013). No violation of Art 6 because the weight of the evidence other than the belief evidence, combined with the counterbalancing safeguards and factors, was sufficient to conclude that the grant of privilege regarding the sources of the Chief Superintendent's belief did not render the applicant's trial unfair.
Note: The European Convention on Human Rights Act 2003 came intoforce in Ireland on 31 December 2003		
5	*De Rossa v Independent Newspapers plc* [1999] 4 IR 6 (30 July 1999).	*Independent News and Media v Ireland* (2005) 42 EHRR 46 (16 June 2005) Supreme Court decision approved.
6	Judgment of 29 November 1996.	*Bosphorous Hava Yollari Turizm Ve Ticaret Anonim Şirketi v Ireland* (30 June 2005; GC) 17 v 0: no violation of Art 1 of Prot 1. Supreme Court decision approved.
7	On 29 July 2015 the Supreme Court refused to grant leave to the applicant to appeal against the Court of Appeal's decision in *Brennan v Flannery* [2015] IECA 78 (9 March 2015).	*Brennan v Ireland* App No 44360/15 (2 November 2017) No violation of Art 6(1) as regards delays in the civil proceedings (12 years and five months).

Part D: Challenges which were found admissible and violations were then found on the merits

No	The case in the Supreme Court	The case in Strasbourg
1	*Norris v Attorney General* [1984] IR 36 (22 April 1983).	*Norris v Ireland* (1991) 13 EHRR 186 (26 October 1988): 8 v 6: Norris could claim to be a victim 8 v 6: violation of Art 8 14 v 0: no award of compensation
2	*Pine Valley Developments Ltd v Minister for the Environment, Ireland and the Attorney General* [1987] ILRM 753 (30 July 1986).	*Pine Valley Developments Ltd v Ireland* (1992) 14 EHRR 319 (29 November 1991) and (No 2) (1993) 16 EHRR 379 (9 February 1993): 9 v 0: no violation of A1P1 taken alone or with Art 14 regarding Pine Valley 6 v 3: no violation of Art 1 regarding Healy Holdings or Mr Healy 9 v 0: violation of Art 14 taken with A1P1 regarding Healy Holdings and Mr Healy 9 v 0: no violation of art 13 9 v 0: Ireland to pay IR£1.2 million to Healy Holdings and Mr Healy jointly and IR£50,000 to Mr Healy
3	*Attorney General v Open Door Counselling Ltd and Dublin Well Woman Centre Ltd* [1988] IR 618 (16 March 1988).	*Open Door Counselling Ltd and Dublin Well Woman Centre Ltd v Ireland* (1991) 14 EHRR 131 (Cm; 7 March 1991) (1992) 15 EHRR 244 (Ct; 29 October 1992) 15 v 8: violation of Art 10 23 v 0: unnecessary to consider other complaints 17 v 6: Ireland to pay Dublin Well Woman Centre IR£25,000
4	*K v W* [1990] 2 IR 437 (1 December 1989).	*Keegan v Ireland* (1994) 18 EHRR 352–8 (Cm; 17 February 1993) 12 v 0: violation of Arts 8 and 6(1) 11v 1: unnecessary to consider Art 14 (1994) 18 EHRR 342 (Ct; 26 May 1994) 9 v 0: violation of Art 8 9 v 0: violation of Art 6(1) 9 v 0: unnecessary to consider Art 14 9 v 0: Ireland to pay IR£12,000
5	*Heaney and McGuinness v Ireland* [1996] IR 580 (23 July 1996).	*Heaney v Ireland* (2001) 33 EHRR 12 (21 December 2000) Violation of Arts 6(1) and 6(2) because of breaches of the right to remain silent and to not incriminate oneself. IR£4,000 awarded in compensation.
6	*DG v Eastern Health Board* [1997] 3 IR 511 (16 July 1997), finding no breach of the constitutional right to liberty when a 16-year-old was confined in a detention centre even though he had committed no crime.	*DG v Ireland* App No 39474/98 (16 May 2002) Violation of Arts 5(1) and 5(5), but not of Arts 3 or 8. Compensation of €5,000 awarded.

7	*Doran v Delaney* [1998] 2 IR 61 (9 March 1998). Supreme Court upheld claim for negligence against the solicitors of vendors of land.	*Doran v Ireland* (2006) 42 EHRR 13 (31 July 2003) Violations of Arts 6 and 13 because of three-year delay at High Court level and lack of effective remedy for this.
8	*Brady v Cavan County Council* [1999] 4 IR 99 (17 and 22 June 1999). Supreme Court refused to grant an order of mandamus requiring the Council to repair a road.	*O'Reilly v Ireland* (2005) 40 EHRR 40 (29 July 2004) Violations of Arts 6 and 13 because of delays at High Court and Supreme Court levels.
Note: The European Convention on Human Rights Act 2003 came into force in Ireland on 31 December 2003		
9	*McMullen v Farrell (No 2)* [2004] IESC 6, [2004] 2 IR 328 (29 January 2004), ruling that McMullen's negligence claim against his solicitors should fail.	*McMullen v Ireland* App No 42297/98 (29 July 2004) Violation of Art 6 because of undue delay in the proceedings. Compensation of €8,000 awarded.
10	*Barry v The Medical Council* [1998] 3 IR 368 (16 December 1997).	*Barry v Ireland* App No 18273/04 (15 December 2005) Violation of Art 6 because of undue delay in criminal proceedings against the applicant, partly due to the High Court's inaction.
11	*McFarlane v DPP* [2008] IESC 7, [2008] 4 IR 117 (5 March 2008), finding no breach of the Constitution or of the ECHR as a result of delays in criminal proceedings.	*McFarlane v Ireland* (2011) 52 EHRR 20 (10 September 2010; GC) Violations of Arts 6 and 13. €5,000 paid in compensation.
12	*Rooney v Minister for Agriculture and Food* [2010] IESC 55 (18 November 2010).	*Rooney v Ireland* App No 32614/10 (31 October 2013) Violation of Art 6 because of undue delay in the processing of two appeals by the applicant.
13	*O'Keeffe v Hickey* [2008] IESC 72, [2009] 2 IR 302 (19 December 2008), finding no vicarious liability on the part of the State.	*O'Keeffe v Ireland* App No 35810/09 (28 January 2014, GC). Violation of Arts 3 and 13 and €30,000 awarded as compensation.
14	*Leech v Independent Newspapers (Ireland) Ltd* [2014] IESC 79, [2015] 2 IR 214 (19 December 2014).	*Independent Newspapers (Ireland) Ltd v Ireland* App No 28199/15 (15 June 2017) Violation of Art 10 because the Supreme Court had not properly explained why it had awarded such a very large amount of libel damages.

Bibliography

Abrahamson, Max W, (1963) 'Current constitutional interpretation in Ireland' 12 *International and Comparative Law Quarterly* 312.

Aletras, Nikolaos et al (2016) 'Predicting judicial decisions of the European Court of Human Rights: a Natural Language Processing perspective' *PeerJ Computer Science 2:e93*.

Alexy, Robert (2006) 'Effects of defects—action or argument? Thoughts about Deryck Beyleveld and Roger Brownsword's *Law as a Moral Judgment*' 19 *Ratio Juris* 170.

Amos, Merris (2014) *Human Rights Law*, Oxford and Portland, Hart Publishing, 2nd ed.

Anon (1950) 'The recruitment of the judiciary' 16 *Irish Jurist* 35.

Anthony, Gordon (2014) *Judicial Review in Northern Ireland*, Oxford and Portland, Hart Publishing, 2nd ed.

Aughey, Arthur and Cathy Gormley-Heenan (eds) (2013) *The Anglo-Irish Agreement: Re-thinking Its Legacy*, Manchester, Manchester University Press.

Bacik, Ivana (2001) 'Incorporation of the European Convention on Human Rights' 11 *Irish Journal of Criminal Law* 18.

Bacik, Ivana (2004) *Kicking and Screaming: Dragging Ireland into the 21st Century*, Dublin, O'Brien Press.

Bacik, Ivana and Mary Rogan (2016) *Legal Cases that Changed Ireland,* Dublin, Clarus Press.

Ball, F Elrington (1927) *The Judges in Ireland*, 1221–1921, London, John Murray.

Barnes, Robert et al (2016) *Symposium Panel on Supreme Court Transparency in the Age of Social Media* 32(4) *Georgia State University LR* 927–51.

Barrett, Gavin (2009) 'Building a Swiss chalet in an Irish legal landscape? Referendums on European Union treaties in Ireland and the impact of Supreme Court jurisprudence' 5 *European Constitutional Law Review* 32.

Barrett, Gavin (2012) 'The evolving door to Europe: reflections on an eventful forty years for Article 29.4 of the Irish Constitution' 48 *Irish Jurist ns* 132.

Barrington, Dónal (1952) 'The Irish Constitution – IV The Judiciary' *Irish Monthly*, vol 80, no 947, 191–9.

Barrington, Donal (1987) 'The Constitution in the Courts' in Litton (ed), below, 110–27.

Barrington, Dónal (1988) 'The North and the Constitution' in Brian Farrell (ed), *De Valera's Constitution and Ours*, Dublin, Gill and Macmillan, Chap 5.

Bartholomew, Paul C (1971) *The Irish Judiciary*, The Institute of Public Administration and University of Notre-Dame Press, Dublin.

Bates, Ed (2010) *The Evolution of the European Convention on Human Rights: From its Inception to the Creation of a Permanent Court of Human Rights*, Oxford, Oxford University Press.

BCLRG (2007), Balance in the Criminal Law Review Group: *Final Report*, Dublin, Department of Justice, Equality and Law Reform.

Belinskij, Antti, Louis Kotze and Oliver Fuo (2017) 'Domestic manifestations of international law's right to water: a comparative analysis of emerging rights obligations in Finland and South Africa' 25 *African Journal of International and Comparative Law* 261.

Bell, Evan (2008) 'Judicial qualities: illustrations from past lives' 8(2) *Irish Judicial Studies Journal* 18.

Beth, Loren P (1967) *Development of Judicial Review in Ireland, 1936-1966*, Dublin, Institute of Public Administration.

Beyleveld, Deryck and Roger Brownsword (1994) *Law as a Moral Judgment*, Sheffield, Sheffield Academic Press, 2nd ed.

Beytagh, Francis X (1983) 'Equality under the Irish and US Constitutions' 18 *Irish Jurist ns* 56 and 219.

Beytagh, Francis X (1997) *Constitutionalism in Ireland: An American Perspective*, Dublin, Round Hall Sweet & Maxwell.

Biehler, Hilary (2013a) 'Curial deference in the context of judicial review of administrative action post-*Meadows*' 49 *Irish Jurist ns* 29.

Biehler, Hilary and Catherine Donnelly (2014), 'Proportionality in the Irish Courts: the need for guidance' *European Human Rights Law Review* 272.

Binchy, William (1977) 'Marital privacy and family law: a reply to Mr O'Reilly' *Studies* 330.

Binchy, William (1992) 'Constitutional remedies and the law of torts' in James O'Reilly (ed), *Human Rights and Constitutional Law*, Dublin: Round Hall, 201–25.

Binchy, William (2007) 'The Supreme Court of Ireland' in Brice Dickson (ed), *Judicial Activism in Common Law Supreme Courts*, Oxford, Oxford University Press, Chap 5, 169–215.

Binchy, William (2008) 'Dignity as a constitutional concept' in Eoin Carolan and Oran Doyle (eds), Chap 17.

Binchy, William (2011) '*Meskell*, the Constitution and tort law' 33 *Dublin University Law Journal* 339.

Binchy, William (2016) 'Tort law in Ireland: a half-century review' 51 *Irish Jurist ns* 199.

Blackshield, Tony, Michael Coper and George Williams (eds) (2001) *The Oxford Companion to the High Court of Australia*, Oxford, Oxford University Press.

Blom-Cooper, Louis and Gavin Drewry (1972) *Final Appeal: A Study of the House of Lords in its Judicial Capacity*, Oxford, Clarendon Press.

Blom-Cooper, Louis, Brice Dickson and Gavin Drewry (eds) (2009) *The Judicial House of Lords 1876–2009*, Oxford, Oxford University Press.

Bloom, Robert M and Erin Dewey (2011) 'When rights become empty promises: promoting an exclusionary rule that vindicates personal rights' 46 *Irish Jurist ns* 38.

Böss, Michael 2002, 'Constitutional and legal reform in Ireland, 1937–1998: the American context' 1 *Nordic Irish Studies* 121.

Boylan, Henry (1998) *A Dictionary of Irish Biography*, Dublin, Gill and Macmillan, 2nd ed.

Bradley, Conleth (2000) *Judicial Review*, Dublin, Round Hall Ltd.

Bradley, Kieran, Noel Travers and Anthony Whelan (eds) (2014) *Of Courts and Constitutions: Liber Amicorum in Honour of Nial Fennelly*, Oxford and Portland, Oregon, Hart Publishing.

Brady, Alan (2010) 'Proportionality, deference and fundamental rights in Irish administrative law: the aftermath of *Meadows*' 32 *Dublin University Law Journal* 136.

Brittain, Stephen (2010) 'The case for an originalist approach to constitutional interpretation in Ireland' 13 *Trinity College Law Review* 71.

Broberg, Morten and Niels Fenger (2014) *Preliminary References to the European Court of Justice*, Oxford, Oxford University Press, 2nd ed.

Brown, Eimear (2009) 'Article 6 and Civil Cases', in Kilkelly (2009), below, Chap 4.

Buckley, Lucy-Ann (2017) in Enright, McCandless and O'Donoghue (eds), below, 163–75.

Buckley, Niall (2004) 'Merging principles of public law: towards proportionality in an Irish context' 39 *Irish Jurist ns* 161.

Burley, Jenny and Francis Regan (2002) 'Divorce in Ireland: the fear, the floodgates and the reality' 16 *International Journal of Law Policy Family* 202.

Butler, Andrew and Rory O'Connell (1998) 'A critical analysis of Ireland's Constitutional Review Group' 33 *Irish Jurist* 237.

Byrne, Anne (1997) 'Single women in Ireland' in A Byrne and M Leonard (eds), *Women and Irish Society: A Sociological Reader*, Dublin, Beyond the Pale Publications, Chap 25.

Byrne, Colm Scott (2013) 'A time to change the law on euthanasia and assisted suicide in Ireland' 16 *Trinity College Law Review* 15.

Byrne, Raymond and J Paul McCutcheon (2014) *Byrne and McCutcheon on the Irish Legal System*, Dublin, Bloomsbury Professional, 6th ed (with Claire Bruton and Gerard Coffey).

Cahill, Maria (2010) '*McD v L* and the incorporation of the European Convention on Human Rights' 45 *Irish Jurist ns* 221.

Cahill, Maria (2011) 'Constitutional exclusion clauses, Article 29.4.6, and the constitutional reception of European law' 34 *Dubin University Law Journal* 74.

Cahillane, Laura (2011) 'The influence of the post-war European constitutions on the Constitution of the Irish Free State' 15.1 *Electronic Journal of Comparative Law.*

Cahillane, Laura (2015) 'Ireland's system for disciplining and removing judges' 38 *Dubin University Law Journal* 55.

Cahillane, Laura (2017) 'Judicial appointments in Ireland: the potential for reform' in Cahillane, Gallen and Hickey (eds), below, Chap 8.

Cahillane, Laura, James Gallen and Tom Hickey (eds) (2017) *Judges, Politics and the Irish Constitution*, Manchester, Manchester University Press.

Cairnduff, Maureen (ed) (1991) *Who's Who in Ireland*, Dublin, Hibernian Publishing Co, 2nd ed.

Cameron, Edwin and Max Taylor (2017) 'The untapped potential of the Mandela Constitution' *Public Law* 382.

Campbell, Colm (1989) 'Extradition to Northern Ireland: prospects and problems' 52 *Modern Law Review* 585.

Campbell, Colm (1994) *Emergency Law in Ireland, 1918-1925*, Oxford, Clarendon Press.

Cannon, Robert (1998) 'Does expression have any freedom left? *Murphy v Independent Radio and Television Commission*' 1 *Trinity College Law Review* 126.

Carlson, Keith, Michael Livermore and Daniel Rockmore (2015), 'A Quantitative Analysis of Writing Style on the US Supreme Court' 93(6) *Washington University Law Review* 1461.

Carney, Caroline et al (2010) '*I can't get no satisfaction*: an analysis of the influence of the European Convention on Human Rights on the repossession of public housing in Ireland' 13 *Trinity College Law Review* 55.

Carney, Claire (1979) 'The growth of legal aid in the Republic of Ireland' *Irish Jurist ns* Part I, 61; Part II, 221.

Carolan, Bruce (2005) 'Consideration of foreign judgments by the Irish Supreme Court: an extra-constitutional analysis of several select cases' 12 *Irish Journal of European Law* 115.

Carolan, Eoin (2011) 'The relationship between judicial remedies and the separation of powers: collaborative constitutionalism and the suspended declaration of invalidity' 46 *Irish Jurist ns* 180.

Carolan, Eoin and Oran Doyle (eds) (2008) *The Irish Constitution: Governance and Values*, Dublin, Thomson Round Hall.

Carroll, Jennifer (2005) 'You Be the Judge: Part I—A Study of the Backgrounds of Superior Judges in Ireland in 2004' and 'Part II—The Politics and Processes of Judicial Appointments in Ireland' 10 *Bar Review* 153 and 182.

Carroll MacNeill, Jennifer (2016) *The Politics of Judicial Selection in Ireland*, Dublin, Four Courts Press.

Casey, E (ed) (1990) *Judgments of the Court of Criminal Appeal 1984–1989*, Dublin, Round Hall Sweet & Maxwell.

Casey, James P (1970) 'Republican Courts in Ireland 1919–1922' 5 *Irish Jurist ns* 321.

Casey, James P (1974) 'The genesis of the Dáil courts' 9 *Irish Jurist ns* 326.

Casey, James P (1975) 'Confusion in criminal appeals—the legacy of *Conmey*' 10 *Irish Jurist ns* 300.

Casey, James P (1978) 'The development of constitutional law under Chief Justice Ó Dálaigh' 3 *Dublin University Law Journal* 3.

Casey, James P (1979) 'The Constitution and the legal system' 14 *Irish Jurist ns* 14.

Casey, James P (1979–80) 'Constitutional law—natural and constitutional justice- the policeman's lot' 4 *Dublin University Law Journal 95.*

Casey, James P (1986) 'The development of constitutional law under Chief Justice O'Higgins' 21 *Irish Jurist ns* 7.

Casey, James P (2000) *Constitutional Law in Ireland*, Dublin, Round Hall Sweet and Maxwell, 3rd ed.

Cheffins, Ronald (1966) 'The Supreme Court of Canada: The Quiet Court in an Unquiet Country' 4 *Osgoode Hall Law Journal* 259.

Chemerinsky, Erwin (2014) *The Case against the Supreme Court*, New York, Viking Penguin.

Choo, Andrew (2008) *Abuse of Process and Judicial Stays of Criminal Proceedings*, 2nd ed, Oxford, Oxford University Press.

Christoffersen, Jonas and Mikael Madsen (eds) (2011) *The European Court of Human Rights between Law and Politics*, Oxford, Oxford University Press.

Clarke, Desmond M (1977) 'Emergency legislation, fundamental rights and Article 28.3.3 of the Irish Constitution' 12 *Irish Jurist ns* 217.

Clarke, Desmond (1982) 'The role of natural law in Irish constitutional law' 17 *Irish Jurist ns* 187.

Clarke, Desmond (2008) 'Interpreting the Constitution: essentially contested concepts' in Eoin Carolan and Oran Doyle (eds), above, Chap 4.

Clarke, Desmond (2011a) 'Unenumerated rights in constitutional law' 34 *Dublin University Law Journal* 101.

Clarke, Desmond (2011b) 'Judicial reasoning: logic, authority, and the rule of law in Irish courts' 46 *Irish Jurist ns* 152.

Cleary, Niamh (2011) 'Public and private law principles: *Murphy v Attorney General* reassessed' 34 *Dublin University Law Journal* 155.

Coakley, John (2001) 'The Belfast Agreement and the Republic of Ireland' in Rick Wilford (ed) *Aspects of the Belfast Agreement*, Oxford, Oxford University Press, Chap 12.

Coen, Mark (2009) 'Fair procedures, local authority housing, the Constitution and the European Convention on Human Rights' 31 *Dublin University Law Journal* 423.

Coen, Mark (2015) 'International human rights law: a flavour of its impact on the Irish criminal justice system' in Egan (ed), below, Chap 16.

Coffey, Donal (2011) 'The judiciary of the Irish Free State' 33 *Dublin University Law Journal* 61.

Coffey, Donal (2012) 'The need for a new constitution: Irish constitutional change 1932-1935' 48 *Irish Jurist ns* 275.

Collins, Anthony and James O'Reilly (2003) *Civil Proceedings and the State*, Dublin, Round Hall Press Ltd, 2nd ed.

Collins, Diarmuid (2009) 'The exclusionary rule – back on the agenda?' 19 *Irish Criminal Law Journal* 98.

Commission on the Status of Women (1993) *Second Commission on the Status of Women: Report to the Government*, Dublin, Stationery Office.

Committee on Court Practice (1972) *The Jurisdiction and Practice of the Supreme Court*, Dublin, Committee on Court Practice and Procedure, 11th Interim Report, Prl 1835.

Connelly, Alpha (1982) 'Non-extradition for political offences: a matter of legal obligation or simply a policy choice?' 17 *Irish Jurist ns* 59.

Connelly, Alpha (1997) 'Ireland and the European Convention' in Brice Dickson (ed) *Human Rights and the European Convention*, London, Sweet & Maxwell.

Coonan, Genevieve (2006) 'The role of judicial research assistants in supporting the decision-making role of the Irish judiciary' 6 *JSIJ* 171.

Corcoran, Donal P (2013) *Freedom to Achieve Freedom: The Irish Free State 1922–1932*, Dublin, Gill and Macmillan.

Corder, Hugh (2007) 'Judicial Activism of a Special Type: South Africa's Top Courts Since 1994' in Dickson (2007), above, 323–62.

Costello, Declan (1956) 'The natural law and the Irish Constitution' 45 *Studies* 403.

Costello, Declan (1962) *Studies*, vol 51, no 201, 201–3.

Costello, Francis (2003) *The Irish Revolution and its Aftermath, 1916–1923: Years of Revolt*, Dublin, Irish Academic Press.

Costello, Kevin (1997) 'The expulsion of prerogative doctrine from Irish law: quantifying and remedying the loss of the royal prerogatives' 32 *Irish Jurist ns* 145.

Cox, Archibald (1987) *The Court and the Constitution*, Boston, Houghton Mifflin.

CRG (1966) *Report of the Constitution Review Group*, Dublin, The Stationery Office, Pn 2632.

Crossland, Gerald (1994) 'Three major decisions given by the *Bundersverfassungsgericht* (Federal Constitutional Court)' 19 *European Law Review* 202.

Crowe, Michael Bertram (1971-72) 'Human rights, the Irish Constitution and the courts' 47 *Notre Dame Lawyer* 281.

Crowley, Louise (2013) *Family Law*, Dublin Round Hall Thomson Reuters.

Crowley, Louise (2017) 'Commentary on the *Matrimonial Homes Bill*' in Enright, McCandless and O'Donoghue (eds), below, 157–62.

Curran, Joseph M (1980) *The Birth of the Irish Free State, 1921-1923*, Tuscaloosa, Alabama, University of Alabama Press.

Curtin, Deirdre (1989) 'Some reflections on European Community law in Ireland' 11 *Dublin University Law Journal* 207.

Curtin, Deirdre and David O'Keeffe (1992) (eds): *Constitutional Adjudication in European Community and National Law: Essays for the Hon Mr Justice T. F. O'Higgins*, Dublin, Butterworths.

Daly, Eoin and Tom Hickey (2015) *The Political Theory of the Irish Constitution: Republicanism and the Basic Law*, Manchester, Manchester University Press.

Daly, Mary (2016) *Sixties Ireland: Reshaping the Economy, State and Society, 1957-1973*, Cambridge, Cambridge University Press.

Daly, Paul (2008) 'Political questions and judicial review in Ireland' 8(2) *Irish Judicial Studies Journal* 116.

Daly, Paul (2010) 'Standards of review in Irish administrative law after *Meadows v Minister for Justice, Equality and Law Reform*' 32 *Dublin University Law Journal* 379.

Daly, Yvonne (2009b) 'Unconstitutionally obtained evidence in Ireland: protectionism, deterrence and the winds of change' 19 *Irish Criminal Law Journal* 40.

Davis, Fergal (2007) *The History and Development of the Special Criminal Court 1922-2005*, Four Courts Press, Dublin and Portland, Oregon.

Davitt, Cahir (1968) 'Some aspects of the Constitution and the law in relation to marriage' 57 *Studies* 6.

Dawson, Mark, Bruno de Witte and Elise Muir (eds) (2013) *Judicial Activism at the European Court of Justice*, Cheltenham, Edward Elgar.

De Blácam, Mark (1997) 'Justice and natural law' 32 *Irish Jurist* 323.

De Blácam, Mark (2009) *Judicial Review*, Haywards Heath and Dublin, Tottel Publishing, 2nd ed.

De Búrca, Grainne (2013) 'The domestic impact of the EU Charter of Fundamental Rights' 49 *Irish Jurist ns* 49.

Delany, Hilary and Gerard Hogan (1993) 'Anglo-Irish extradition viewed from an Irish perspective' *Public Law* 93.

Delany, VTH (1952) 'The Irish Court of Criminal Appeal: the first thirty years' 18 *Irish Jurist* 33.

Delany VTH (1957-58) 'The Constitution of Ireland: its origin and development' 12 *University of Toronto Law Journal* 1.

De Londras, Fiona and Cliona Kelly (2010) *European Convention on Human Rights Act: Operation, Impact and Analysis*, Dublin, Round Hall.

De Londras, Fiona (2014a) 'Neither herald nor fanfare: the limited impact of the ECHR Act 2003 on rights infrastructure in Ireland', in Egan, Thornton and Walsh (below), Chap 12.

De Londras, Fiona (2014b) 'Declarations of incompatibility under the European Convention on Human Rights Act 2003: a workable transplant?' 35 *Statute Law Review* 50.

Denham, Susan (2006) 'Proposal for a Court of Appeal' 6 *Irish Judicial Studies Journal* 1.

Denham, Susan and Genevieve Burke (2009) 'Constitutional courts and the Lisbon Treaty' 16 *Irish Journal of European Law* 93.

Dewhurst, Elaine (2013) 'Exclusionary or inclusionary constitutional protection: protecting the rights of citizens, non-citizens and irregular immigrants under Articles 40-44 of the Irish Constitution' 49 *Irish Jurist ns* 98.

Dewhurst, Elaine, Noelle Higgins and Los Watkins (2012) *Principles of Irish Human Rights Law*, Dublin; Clarus Press.

De Witte, Bruno and Thomas Beukers (2013) 'The Court of Justice approves the creation of the European Stability Mechanism outside the EU legal order: *Pringle*' 50 *Common Market Law Review* 805.

Dickson, Brice (2004) 'A Constitutional Court for Northern Ireland?' in A Le Sueur (ed), *Building the UK's New Supreme Court: National and Comparative Perspectives*, Oxford, Oxford University Press, 49–66.

Dickson, Brice (2006) 'The House of Lords and the Northern Ireland conflict – a sequel' 69 *Modern Law Review* 383.

Dickson, Brice (ed) (2007) *Judicial Activism in Common Law Supreme Courts*, Oxford, Oxford University Press.

Dickson, Brice (2010) *The European Convention on Human Rights and the Conflict in Northern Ireland*, Oxford, Oxford University Press.

Dickson, Brice (2012) 'The Record of the House of Lords in Strasbourg' 128 *Law Quarterly Review* 354.

Dickson, Brice (2013) *Human Rights and the United Kingdom Supreme Court*, Oxford, Oxford University Press.

Dickson, Brice (2017) 'The Charter of Fundamental Rightsb within Ireland' in Laurence Burgorgue-Larsen (ed), *La Charte des Droits Fondamentaux saisie par les Juges en Europe*. Burgorgue-Larsen, Paris, Éditions Pedone, 465–74.

Doherty, Barry (2004) 'Land, milk and freedom – implementing Community law in Ireland' 11 *Irish Journal of European Law* 141.

Donaldson, Alfred (1957) *Some Comparative Aspects of Irish Law*, Durham (NC), Duke University Press and London, Cambridge University Press.

Donnelly, Catherine and Hilary Delany (2011) 'The Irish Supreme Court inches towards proportionality review' *Public Law* 19.

Donnelly, Joan (2009) 'Inherent jurisdiction and inherent powers of the Irish courts' 9(2) *Irish Judicial Studies Journal* 122.

Donohue, Laura (2001) *Counter-Terrorist Law and Emergency Powers in the United Kingdom 1922–2000*, Dublin, Irish Academic Press.

Doolan, Brian (2001) *Lawless v Ireland (1957–1961)—The First Case before the European Court of Human Rights: An International Miscarriage of Justice?* Aldershot and Burlington VT, Ashgate Publishing.

Dothan, Shai (2011–12) 'Judicial tactics in the European Court of Human Rights' (2011–12) 12 *Chicago Journal of International Law* 115.

Dothan, Shai (2015) *Reputation and Judicial Tactics: A Theory of National and International Courts*, Cambridge, Cambridge University Press.

Doyle, Oran (2003) 'Legal validity: reflections on the Irish Constitution' 25 *Dublin University Law Journal* 56.

Doyle, Oran (2008) *Constitutional Law: Text, Cases and Materials*, Dublin, Clarus Press.

Doyle, Oran (2009) 'Legal positivism, natural law and the Constitution' 31 *Dublin University Law Journal* 206.

Doyle, Oran and Desmond Ryan (2011) 'Judicial interpretation of the European Convention on Human Rights Act 2003: reflections and analysis' 33 *Dublin University Law Journal* 369.

Duffy, Timothy (1991) 'The law v the IRA: The effect of extradition between the United Kingdom, the Republic of Ireland and the United States in combating the IRA' 9 *Penn State International Law Review* 293.

Dugard, Jackie (2016) 'Testing the transformative premise of the South African Constitutional Court: a comparison of High Courts, Supreme Court of Appeal and Constitutional Court socio-economic rights decisions, 1994–2015' 20 *International Journal of Human Rights* 1132.

Duncan, William (1986) 'Family law – the child's right to a family – parental rights in disguise' 8 *Dublin University Law Journal* 76.

Duncan, William (1996) 'The constitutional protection of parental rights' in *Report of the Constitution Review Group*, Dublin, The Stationery Office, Pr 9817, Appendix 22.

Dunne, Gerald (1970) *Justice Joseph Story and the Rise of the Supreme Court*, New York, Simon & Schuster.

Dzehtsiarou, Kanstantsin (2015) *European Consensus and the Legitimacy of the European Court of Human Rights*, Cambridge, Cambridge University Press.

ECAS (2017) *Brexit and the European Arrest Warrant: How Will Change Affect the Interests of Citizens*, Brussels, European Citizen Action Service.

Egan, Suzanne (2003) 'The European Convention on Human Rights Act 2003: a missed opportunity for domestic human rights litigation' 25 *Dublin University Law Journal* 230.

Ega, Suzanne (2014) 'Introduction' in Egan, Thornton and Walsh (eds), below, Chap 1.

Egan, Suzanne (ed) (2015) *International Human Rights: Perspectives from Ireland*, Dublin, Bloomsbury.

Egan, Suzanne and Aidan Forde (2014), 'From judgment to compliance: domestic implementation of the judgments of the Strasbourg Court' in Egan, Thornton and Walsh (eds), below, Chap 2.

Egan, Suzanne, Liam Thornton and Judy Walsh (eds) (2014) *Ireland and the European Convention on Human Rights: 60 Years and Beyond*, Dublin; Bloomsbury Professional.

Elgie, Robert, Adam McAuley and Eoin O'Malley (2018) 'The (not-so-surprising) non-partisanship of the Irish Supreme Court' 33 *Irish Political Studies* 88.

Enright, Máiréad, Julie McCandless and Aoife O'Donoghue (eds) (2017), *Northern/Irish Feminist Judgments: Judges' Troubles and the Gendered Politics of Identity*, Oxford and Portland, Hart Publishing.

Epstein, Lee, Valerie Hoeksra, Jeffrey Segal and Harold Spaeth (1998) 'Do Political Preferences Change? A Longitudinal Study of US Supreme Court Justices' 60 *Journal of Politics* 801.

Epstein, Lee, Andrew Martin, Kevin Quinn and Jeffrey Segal (2007) 'Ideological Drift Among Supreme Court Justices: Who, When, and How Important' 101 *Northwestern University Law Review* 1483.

Fahey, Elaine (2007) *Practice and Procedure in Preliminary References to Europe: 30 Years of Article 234 EC Caselaw from the Irish Courts*, Dublin, First Law.

Fanning, Bryan (2008) *The Quest for Modern Ireland: The Battle of Ideas 1912–1986*, Dublin and Portland, Oregon, Irish Academic Press.

Fanning, Ronan (1983), *Independent Ireland*, Dublin, Helicon Ltd.

Fanning, Rossa (2005) 'Hard case; bad law? The Supreme Court decision in *A v The Governor of Arbour Hill Prison*' 40 *Irish Jurist ns* 188.

Farrell, Brian (1970–71) 'The drafting of the Irish Free State Constitution:' I 5 *Irish Jurist* 115; II 5 *Irish Jurist* 343; III 6 *Irish Jurist* 111; IV 6 *Irish Jurist* 345.

Farrell, Brian (ed) (1988) *De Valera's Constitution and Ours*, Dublin, Gill and Macmillan.

Farrell, Michael (2007) 'The challenge of the ECHR' 7(2) *Irish Judicial Studies Journal* 76.

Fasone, Cristina (2013) 'The Supreme Court of Ireland and the use of foreign precedents: the value of constitutional history' in T Groppi and M-C Ponthoreau, *The Use of Foreign Precedents by Constitutional Judges*, Oxford and Portland, Oregon, Hart Publishing, 97–127.

Feenan, Dermot (2008) 'Judicial appointments in Ireland in comparative perspective' 8 *Irish Judicial Studies Journal* 37.

Feeney, Brian (2002) *Sinn Féin: A Hundred Turbulent Years*, Dublin, O'Brien Press.

Fennelly, Nial (1996) 'Reflections of an Irish Advocate General' 5 *Irish Journal of European Law* 5.

Fennelly, Nial (1998) 'Where power now lies—institutional reform' 7 *Irish Journal of European Law* 10.

Fennelly, Nial (2005) 'Preliminary reference procedure: a factual and legal review' 13 *Irish Journal of European Law* 55.

Fennelly, Nial (2017) 'The judicial legacy of Mr Justice Adrian Hardiman' 58 *Irish Jurist* 81.

Ferguson, Kenneth (ed) (2005) *King's Inns Barristers 1868–2004*, Dublin, The Honourable Society of King's Inns and Irish Legal History Society.

Ferriter, Diarmaid (2005) *The Transformation of Ireland*, London, Profile Books.

Ferriter, Diarmaid (2013) *Ambiguous Republic: Ireland in the 1970s*, London, Profile Books Ltd.

Finegan, Thomas (2010) 'An unmarried father's right to guardianship of his child and a child's right to the support of his/her father: a Hohfeldian view of the Irish Constitution' 32 *Dublin University Law Journal* 320.

Finlay, Tom (2005) 'The role of the judge' 5(1) *Irish Judicial Studies Journal* 1.

Fitzgerald, Garrett (1991) *All in a Life: Garrett Fitzgerald, An Autobiography*, Dublin, Gill & Macmillan.

Fitzgerald, Oliver (2008-09) 'The constitutional protection of children in Ireland – assessing the need for reform and the available alternatives' 8 *Hibernian Law Journal* 33.

Fitzpatrick, David (1998) *The Two Irelands 1912–1939*, Oxford and New York, Oxford University Press.

Flogaitis, Spyridon, Tom Zwart, and Julie Fraser (eds) (2013) *The European Court of Human Rights and its Discontents*, Cheltenham, Edward Elgar.

Flynn, Leo (1994) 'The significance of the European Convention on Human Rights in the Irish legal order' *Irish Journal of European Law* 4.

Flynn (1998) 'To be an Irish man—constructions of masculinity within the Constitution' in Tim Murphy and Patrick Twomey (eds), below, Chap 11.

Foley, Anthony and Stephen Lawlor (eds) (1995) *Gill & Macmillan Annotated Constitution of Ireland, With Commentary*, Dublin, Gill and Macmillan.

Foley, Brian (2006) 'Interpretative and deference based models of judicial restraint in the Irish Constitution' 6 *Hibernian Law Journal* 65

Foley, Brian (2007) 'Presuming the legislature acts constitutionally: legislative process and constitutional decision-making' 29 *Dublin University Law Journal* 141.

Foley, Brian (2008) *Deference and the Presumption of Constitutionality*, Dublin, Institute of Public Administration.

Forde, Michael (1982) 'Equality and the Constitution' 17 *Irish Jurist ns* 295.

Forde, Michael (2005) *Extradition Law in Ireland*, Dublin, Thomson Round Hall, 2nd ed.

Forde, Michael and David Leonard (2013) *Constitutional Law in Ireland*, Haywards Heath and Dublin, Bloomsbury Professional.

Foster, Roy F (2007) *Luck and the Irish: A Brief History of Change c. 1970–2000*, London, Allen Lane.

Foxton, David (2008) *Revolutionary Lawyers: Sinn Féin and Crown Courts in Ireland and Britain, 1916–1923*, Dublin, Four Courts Press.

Frewen, Gerard (1979 and 1984) (ed) *Judgments of the Court of Criminal Appeal 1924–1978* and *1979–1983*, Dublin, Incorporated Council of Law Reporting.

Gadbois, George (2011) *Judges of the Supreme Court of India: 1950–1989*, New Delhi, Oxford University Press.

Gaetz, Michael and Linda Greenhouse (2016) *The Burger Court and the Rise of the Judicial Right*, New York, Simon & Schuster.

Gageby, Patrick (1991) 'Changes in the political offence under Part III of the Extradition Act 1965' 1 *Irish Criminal Law Journal* 105.

Gallagher, Paul (2010) 'The Irish Constitution – its unique nature and the relevance of international jurisprudence' 45 *Irish Jurist ns* 22.

Gamper, Anna and Francesco Palermo (2009) 'The Constitutional Court of Austria: Modern Profiles of an Archetype of Constitutional Review' in Andrew Harding and Peter Leyland (eds), *Constitutional Courts: A Comparative Study*, London, Wildy, Simmonds and Hill Publishing, 31–51.

Gearty, Conor (1983) 'Constitutional law – homosexuals and the criminal law – the right to privacy' 5 *Dublin University Law Journal* 264.

Geoghegan, Hugh (2013) 'The three judges of the supreme court of the Irish Free State, 1925–36: their backgrounds, personalities and mindsets' in Felix M Larkin and NM Dawson (eds), *Lawyers, the Law and History*, Dublin, Four Court Press in association with the Irish Legal History Society, 29–53.

Geoghegan, Hugh (2014) '*Crotty* put to sleep by *Pringle*' in Bradley et al (2014), above, Chap 13.

Gewirth, Alan (1978) *Reason and Morality*, Chicago, University of Chicago Press.

GH (1990) 'Mr Justice Brian Walsh' 12 *Dublin University Law Journal* 106.

GH (1992) 'Mr Justice Niall McCarthy' 14 *Dublin University Law Journal* (opening page).

Gilbert, Geoff (1992) 'The Irish interpretation of the political offence exception' 41 *International & Comparative Law Quarterly* 66.

Girvin, Brian and Gary Murphy (2005), *The Lemass Era: Politics and Society on the Ireland of Seán Lemass*, Dublin, University College Dublin Press.

Grant, JAC (1934) 'Judicial review of legislation under the Austrian Constitution of 1920' 28 *American Political Science Review* 670.

Gray, Tony (1994) *Ireland This Century*, London, Little, Brown and Co.

Greenhouse, Linda (2005) *Becoming Justice Blackmun: Harry Blackmun's Supreme Court Journey*, New York, Times Books and Henry Holt & Co.

Griffith, John (1997) *The Politics of the Judiciary*, London, Fontana Press, 5th ed.

Grogan, Vincent (1951) 'Irish constitutional development' 40 *Studies* 385.

Gwynn, Denis (1928), *The Irish Free State 1922–1927*, London, Macmillan.

Hadden, Tom and Kevin Boyle (1989) *The Anglo-Irish Agreement: Commentary, Text and Official Review*, London, Edwin Higel Ltd and Sweet and Maxwell Ltd.

Hadjigeorgiu, Anastasia (2014) Review of Roux (2013) below, 12 *International Journal of Constitutional Law* 1076.

Hall, Kermit (ed) (2005) *The Oxford Companion to the Supreme Court of the United States*, New York, Oxford University Press, 2nd ed.

Hardiman, Adrian (2004) 'The role of the Supreme Court in our democracy' in Joe Mulholland (ed), *Political Choice and Democratic Freedom in Ireland: 40 Leading Irish Thinkers*, Dublin, MacGill Summer School, 32.

Hardiman, Adrian (2007) 'Weasel words and doubtful meanings: a study in the language of law reform' 7(2) *Irish Judicial Studies Journal* 1.

Hardiman, Adrian (2017) 'The jurisdiction of the European Court of Human Rights and the case of *O'Keeffe v Hickey*' in Cahillane, Gallen and Hickey (eds), Chap 6.

Hardy, ER Review of James O'Connor, *History of Ireland, 1798-1924* (1927) 42 *Political Science Quarterly* 145.

Harkness, David W (1969) *The Restless Dominion: The Irish Free State and the British Commonwealth of Nations*. London, Macmillan.
Harrington, Paul (1995) 'Constitutional law—withdrawal of treatment from an incompetent patient' 17 *Dublin University Law Journal* 120.
Harris, Bruce (2007) 'Judicial Activism and New Zealand's Appellate Courts' in Dickson (ed) (2007), above, 273–322.
Hart, A R (2013) *A History of the Bar and Inn of Court of Northern Ireland*, Belfast, General Council of the Bar of Northern Ireland.
Healy, John (2006) *Principles of Irish Torts*, Dublin, Clarus Press.
Hederman, Anthony (2002) *Report of the Committee to Review the Offences Against the State Acts 1939-98 and Related Matters*, Dublin, Department of Justice and Equality.
Hedigan, John (2001) 'Brian Walsh and the European Convention on Human Rights—the Strasbourg years' 10 *Irish Journal of European Law* 22.
Henchy, Seamus (1962) 'Precedent in the Irish Supreme Court' 25 *Modern Law Review* 544.Henchy, Seamus (1977) 'The Irish Constitution and the EEC' 1 *Dublin University Law Journal* 20.
Henchy, 'Contempt of Court and Freedom of Expression' (1982) 33 *Northern Ireland Legal Quarterly* 326.
Heuston, RFV (1964) *Essays in Constitutional Law*, London, Stevens, 2nd ed.
Heuston, RFV (1976) 'Personal rights under the Irish Constitution' 11 *Irish Jurist ns* 205.
Hoffmann, Lord (1997) 'A sense of proportion' 32 *Irish Jurist ns* 49.
Hoffmeister, Frank (2006) *Bosphorus Hava Yollari Turzim v Ireland, App No 45036/98* 100 *American Journal of International Law* 442.
Hogan, Claire (2010) '*JMcD v PL and BM*: Sperm Donor Fathers and De Facto Families' 13 *Irish Journal of Family Law* 83.
Hogan, Gerard (1979) 'Procedural rights under natural justice' 14 *Irish Jurist ns* 106.
Hogan, Gerard (1984) 'Natural law and constitutional justice – *adieu* to *laissez-faire*' 19 *Irish Jurist ns* 309.
Hogan, Gerard (1986) 'Irish nationalism as a legal ideology' 75 *Studies* 528.
Hogan, Gerard (1987b) 'The Supreme Court and the Single European Act' 22 *Irish Jurist ns* 55.
Hogan, Gerard (1988) 'Chief Justice Kennedy and Sir James O'Connor's Application' 23 *Irish Jurist ns* 144.
Hogan, Gerard (1990-92) 'Unenumerated personal rights: *Ryan's* case re-evaluated' 25–7 *Irish Jurist ns* 95.
Hogan, Gerard (1992a) 'Some reflections on the role of the Attorney General and the Patrick Ryan affair' 2 *Irish Criminal Law Journal* 128.
Hogan, Gerard (1992b) 'The early judgments of Mr Justice Brian Walsh' in James O'Reilly (ed), *Human Rights and Constitutional Law: Essays in Honour of Brian Walsh*, Dublin, Round hall Press.
Hogan, Gerard (1994a) 'Constitutional law—the Matrimonial Homes Bill Reference' 16 *Dublin University Law Journal* 175.
Hogan, Gerard (1994b) 'The implementation of European Union law in Ireland: the *Meagher* case and the democratic deficit' 2 *Irish Journal of European Law* 190.
Hogan, Gerard (1994c) 'The *Meagher* case and the executive implementation of European Directives in Ireland' 1 *Maastricht Journal of European Law* 174.
Hogan, Gerard (1996) 'Hugh Kennedy, the Childers *habeas corpus* application and the return to the Four Courts' in Caroline Costell (ed) *The Four Courts: 200 Years—Essays to Commemorate the Bicentenary of the Four Courts*, Dublin, Incorporated Council of Law Reporting for Ireland, 177–219.
Hogan, Gerard (1997) 'The Sinn Féin Funds judgment fifty years on' 2 *Bar Review* 375.
Hogan, Gerard (2000a) 'The Supreme Court and the reference of the Offences against the State (Amendment) Bill 1940' 35 *Irish Jurist ns* 238.
Hogan, Gerard (2000b) 'A desert island case set in the silver sea: *The State (Ryan) v Lennon* (1934)' in Eoin O'Dell (ed), *Leading Cases of the Twentieth Century*, Dublin, 80–103.
Hogan, Gerard (2001) 'Directive principles, socio-economic rights and the Constitution' 36 *Irish Jurist ns* 174.
Hogan, Gerard (2006) 'The value of declarations of incompatibility and the rule of avoidance' 28 *Dublin University Law Journal* 408.

Hogan, Gerard (2008), 11 *Trinity College Law Review*, Foreword.

Hogan, Gerard (2011a) 'The judicial thought and prose of Mr Justice Seamus Henchy' 46 *Irish Jurist ns* 96.

Hogan, Gerard (2011b) 'John Hearne and the plan for a Constitutional Court' 33 *Dublin University Law Journal* 75.

Hogan, Gerard (ed) (2012) *The Origins of the Irish Constitution, 1928–1941*, Dublin, Royal Irish Academy.

Hogan, Gerard (2014a) '*Elegantia juris*: Mr Justice Seamus Henchy—Some thoughts on two leading judgments', Inaugural Justice Henchy Memorial Lecture, available at https://ulsites.ul.ie/law/inaugural-justice-henchy-memorial-lecture.

Hogan, Gerard (2014b) 'Declarations of incompatibility, inapplicability and invalidity: rights, remedies and the aftermath' in Bradley et al (2014) above, Chap 15.

Hogan, Gerard (2017) 'Mr Justice Brian Walsh: the legacy of experiment and the triumph of judicial imagination' 57 *Irish Jurist ns* 1.

Hogan, Gerard, David Kenny and Rachael Walsh (2015) 'An anthology of declarations of unconstitutionality' 54 *Irish Jurist ns* 1.

Hogan, Gerard and David Gwynn Morgan (2010) *Administrative Law in Ireland*, Dublin, Round Hall, 4th ed.

Hogan, Gerard and Clive Walker (1989) *Political Violence and the Law in Ireland*, Manchester, Manchester University Press.

Hogan, Gerard and Anthony Whelan (1995) *Ireland and the European Union: Constitutional and Statutory Texts and Commentary*, London, Sweet and Maxwell.

Hogan, Gerard, Gerry Whyte, David Kenny and Rachel Walsh (2018) *Kelly: The Irish Constitution*, 4th ed.

Hogg, Peter (2006) 'Canada: from Privy Council to Supreme Court' in Jeffrey Goldsworthy (ed) *Interpreting Constitutions: A Comparative Study*, Oxford, Oxford University Press, Chap 2.

Hogg, Peter (2012) *Constitutional Law of Canada, Student edition*, Toronto, Carswell, Chap 8.

Holland, Ailsa C (1989) 'The papers of Hugh Kennedy: a research legacy for the foundation of the State' 24 *Irish Jurist ns* 279

Hollenberg, Stephan (2015) 'The diverging approaches of the European Court of Human Rights in the cases of *Nada* and *Al-Dulimi*' 64 *International & Comparative Law Quarterly* 445.

Hood Phillips, Owen (1936) '*Ryan's* case' 52 *Law Quarterly Rewiew* 241.

Houghton, Ruth Alice (2017), *McGimpsey v Ireland*, in Enright, McCandless and O'Donoghue (eds), above, 221–8.

Howlin, Niamh and Kevin Costello (eds) (2017), *Law and the Family in Ireland, 1800–1950*, Basingstoke, Palgrave Macmillan.

Humphreys, Richard (1990) 'Constitutional law—reflections on the role and functioning of the Supreme Court' 12 *Dublin University Law Journal* 127.

Humphreys, Richard (1993) 'Constitutional interpretation' 15 *Dublin University Law Journal* 59.

Humphreys, Richard (1993–95) 'Interpreting natural rights' 28–30 *Irish Jurist ns* 221.

Humphreys, Richard (2008) 'Constitutional contradictions: accommodating multiple identities after the Good Friday Agreement' in Eoin Carolan and Oran Doyle (eds), above, Chap 5.

Hunt, Murray (2003) 'Sovereignty's blight: why contemporary public law needs the concept of "due Deference"' in N Bamforth and P Leyland (eds), *Public Law in a Multi-Layered Constitution, Oxford*, Hart, 2003, 337.

Hussey, Gemma (1993) *Ireland Today: Anatomy of a Changing State*, Dublin, Townhouse and Viking.

Iacobucci, Frank (2002) 'The Supreme Court of Canada: its history, powers and responsibilities' 4 *Journal of Appellate Practice and Process* 27.

ICCL (2009) *Combating Organised Crime and Respecting the Rule of Law: Human Rights Based Alternatives to the Criminal Justice (Amendment) Bill 2009*, Dublin, Irish Council for Civil Liberties.

IHRC (2005) *Economic, Social and Cultural Rights: Discussion Document*, available at https://www.ihrec.ie/download/pdf/escrdiscussiondocument.pdf

IHREC (2017) *Ireland and the Convention on the Elimination of All Forms of Discrimination Against Women: Submission to the United Nations Committee on the Elimination of Discrimination Against*

Women on Ireland's Combined Sixth and Seventh Periodic Reports, Dublin, Irish Human Rights and Equality Commission.
Irons, Peter (2006) *A People's History of the Supreme Court*, New York, Penguin Books.
Iyer, Venkat (2007) 'The Supreme Court of India' in Dickson (ed) (2007), above, 121–68.
JAAB (2016) Judicial Appointment Advisory Board, *Annual Report 2015*, Dublin.
Jackson, John and Seán Doran (1995) *Judge Without Jury: Diplock Trials in the Adversary System*, Oxford, Clarendon Press.
Jackson, John and Seán Doran (2003) *A study of the jurisdiction of the criminal courts in Ireland*, Dublin, Stationery Office.
Jackson, Nuala (1992) 'Family law – the Constitution and beneficial ownership of the family home' 14 *Dublin University Law Journal* 153.
Jaconelli, Joseph (1983) 'Reference of Bills to the Supreme Court – a comparative perspective' 18 *Irish Jurist ns* 322.
Jaconelli, Joseph (1987) 'The European Convention on Human Rights as Irish municipal law' 22 *Irish Jurist ns* 13.
Jones, David Lewis (2009) 'The Judicial Role of the House of Lords before 1870' in Blom-Cooper, Dickson and Drewry, above, 1–12.
Joseph, Sarah (2007) 'Human Rights Committee: Recent Jurisprudence' 7 *Human Rights Law Review* 567.
Kahn, Ellison (1960) *The Union of South Africa: The development of its Laws and Constitution*, London, Stevens.
Kavanagh, Aileen (1997) 'The quest for legitimacy in constitutional interpretation' 32 *Irish Jurist ns* 195.
Kavanagh, Aileen (2008) 'Deference or defiance? The limits of the judicial role in constitutional adjudication' in G Huscroft (ed), *Exponding the Constitution: Essays in Constitutional Theory*, Cambridge, Cambridge University Press, 184.
Kavanagh, Aileen (2012) 'The Irish Constitution at 75 years: natural law, Christian values and the ideal of justice' 48 *Irish Jurist ns* 71.
Keane, Ronan (1967) 'Preventive justice' 2 *Irish Jurist ns* 233.Keane, Ronan (1987) 'Law reform in Ireland – the European perspective' 22 *Irish Jurist ns* 1.
Keane, Ronan (1990–92a) 'John Kelly and the Constitution' 25–7 *Irish Jurist ns* 4.
Keane, Ronan (1990–92b) '"The will of the general": martial law in Ireland, 1535–1924' 25–7 *Irish Jurist ns* 151.
Keane, Ronan (1996) 'The voice of the Gael: Chief Justice Kennedy and the emergence of the new Irish court system 1921–36' 31 *Irish Jurist ns* 205.
Keane, Ronan (2000) 'Across the Cherokee frontier of Irish constitutional jurisprudence: the *Sinn Féin Funds* case: *Buckley v Attorney General* (1950)' in Eoin O'Dell (ed) *Leading Cases of the Twentieth Century*, Dublin, Round Hall Sweet & Maxwell, 185.
Keane, Ronan (2001) 'The Irish courts system in the 21st century: planning for the future' 1 *JSIL* 1.
Keane, Ronan (2004) 'Judges as lawmakers: the Irish experience' 4(2) *Irish Judicial Studies Journal* 1.
Keane, Ronan (2004–06) 'Reflections on the Irish Constitution' 5–7 *Radharc* 135.
Keane, Ronan (2006) 'The "one-judgment rule" in the Supreme Court' in NM Dawson (ed) *Reflections on law and History: Irish Legal History Society Discourses and Other Papers*, 2000–2005, Dublin, Four Courts Press in association with the Irish Legal History Society, 307–19.
Keane, Ronan (2014) 'Reconciling Ireland's sovereignty with membership of the European Union: the lessons of *Crotty* and *Pringle*' in Bradley et al (2014) above, Chap 12.
Keane, Ronan (2015) 'O'Keeffe v Ireland in Strasbourg: punishing the guilty?' 38 *Dublin University Law Journal* 172.
Keane, Ronan (2018) 'Mr Justice Donal Barrington' 23(1) *Bar Review* 25.
Kelly, JM (1966a) 'Revision of the Constitution of Ireland' 1 *Irish Jurist ns* 1.
Kelly, JM (1966b) 'Administrative discretion and the courts' 1 *Irish Jurist ns* 209.
Kelly, JM (1967) *Fundamental Rights in the Irish Law and Constitution*, 2nd ed. [1st ed, 1961], Dublin, Allen Figgis & Co Ltd.
Kelly, JM (1971) 'Judicial Review of Administrative Action: New Irish Trends' 6 *Irish Jurist ns* 40.
Kelly, JM (1988a) 'Hidden treasure and the Constitution' 10 *Dublin University Law Journal* 5.

Kelly, JM (1988b) 'Fundamental rights and the Constitution' in Brian Farrell (ed), *De Valera's Constitution and Ours*, Dublin, Gill and Macmillan, Chap 12.

Kelly, Ruth (2007) 'Baby Ann's constitutional rights' 10(3) *Irish Journal of Family Law*.

Kennedy, Hugh (1928a) 'Character and sources of the Constitution of the Irish Free State' 14 *American Bar Association Journal* 437.

Kennedy, Hugh (1928b) 'The association of Canada with the Constitution of the Irish Free State' 6 *Canadian Bar Review* 747.

Kennedy, Rónán et al (eds) (2003) *The Supreme Court of Ireland: A History*, Dublin, Courts Service.

Kennedy, Rónán (2005) 'Extra-judicial comment by judges' 5(1) *JSIJ* 199.

Kennedy, Rónán (2011) 'The Judiciary in Public Debates' 29 *Irish Law Times* 198–201.

Kenny, Colum (2005) *Moments That Changed Us*, Dublin, Gill and Macmillan.

Kieran, Francis (2004) '*TD* re-considered: constructing a new approach to enforcement of rights' 7 *Trinity College Law Review* 62.

Kieran, Francis (2012) 'Implications of *Damache v DPP* and its progeny' 22 *Irish Criminal Law Journal* 116.

Kilcommins, Shane and Barry Vaughan (2014) 'A perpetual state of emergency: subverting the rule of law in Ireland' 35 *Cambrian Law Review* 55.

Kilcommins, Shane, Ian O'Donnell, Eoin O'Sullivan and Barry Vaughan (2014) *Crime, Punishment and the Search for Order in Ireland*, Dublin, Institute of Public Administration.

Kilkelly, Ursula (2002) 'Children's rights—*DG v Ireland*: protecting the rights of children at risk—lazy government and unruly courts' 24 *Dublin University Law Journal* 268.

Kilkelly, Ursula (ed) (2009) *ECHR and Irish Law*, Bristol, Jordan Publishing Ltds, 2nd ed.

Kingston, Suzanne and Liam Thornton (2015) *A Report on the Application of the European Convention on Human Rights Act 2003 and the European Charter of Fundamental Rights: Evaluation and Review*, Dublin, Law Society of Ireland's Human Rights Committee and the Dublin Solicitor's Bar Association.

Kirby, M (2007) 'Judicial dissent: common law and civil law traditions' 123 *Law Quarterly Review* 379.

Kirk, Linda (2001) 'Judicial power' in T Blackshield, M Coper and G Williams (eds), *The Oxford Companion to the High Court of Australia*, Oxford University Press, Melbourne, 372–3.

Kirwan, Brendan (2008) '*Campus Oil* turns twenty-five: is there much to celebrate?' 30 *Dublin University Law Journal* 325.

Klarman, Michael (2004) *From Jim Crow to Civil Rights: The Supreme Court and the Struggle for Racial Equality*, New York, Oxford University Press.

Klug, Heinz (2009) 'South Africa's Constitutional Court: Enabling Democracy and Promoting Law in the Transition from Apartheid' in Andrew Harding and Peter Leyland (eds), *Constitutional Courts: A Comparative Study*, Wildy, Simmonds and Hill Publishing, 263–88.

Knight, Michael (1969) 'The Irish Court of Criminal Appeal' 4 *Irish Jurist ns* 91 and 247.

Kohn, Leo (1932) *The Constitution of the Irish Free State*, London, Allen and Unwin.

Kotsonouris, Mary (1994) *Retreat from Revolution: The Dáil Courts, 1920-24*.

Kotsonouris, Mary (2002) 'Criticising judges in Ireland' 2(1) *Irish Judicial Studies Journal* 79.

Kotsonouris, Mary (2004) *The Winding-Up of the Dáil Courts, 1922–25: An Obvious Duty*, Dublin: Four Courts Press.

Landau, Leslie (1981-82) 'Gender-based statutory rape law does not violate the equal protection clause: *Michael M v Sonoma County Superior Court*' 67 *Cornell Law Review* 1109.

Langwallner, David (2008) 'Separation of powers, judicial deference and the failure to protect the rights of the individual' in Eoin Carolan and Oran Doyle (eds), above, Chap 14.

Laskin, Bora (1964) 'The Supreme Court of Canada: a final court of appeal of and for Canadians' in Lederman, below, 125–51.

Lawson, Rick (1994) 'The Irish Abortion Cases: European Limits to National Sovereignty' 1 *European Journal of Health Law* 167.

Lazarus, Edward (2005) *Close Chambers: The Rise, Fall, and Future of the Modern Supreme Court'* New York, Penguin Random House.

Le Roux-Kemp, Andra (2016), 'The recognition of health rights in Constitutions on the African continent: a systematic review' 24 *African Journal of International and Comparative Law* 142.

Le Sueur, Andrew (2004) (ed) *Building the UK's New Supreme Court: National and Comparative Perspectives*, Oxford, Oxford University Press.

Lederman, W R (ed) (1964) *The Courts and the Canadian Constitution*, Toronto, McClelland and Stewart Ltd.

Lee, James (ed) (2011) *From House of Lords to Supreme Court: Judges, Jurists and the Process of Judging*, Oxford and Portland, Hart Publishing.

Lee, Simon (1988) *Judging Judges*, London, Faber and Faber.

Lenihan, Niall (1989) 'Royal prerogatives and the Constitution' 24 *Irish Jurist ns* 1.

Litton, Frank (ed) (1988) *The Constitution of Ireland 1937–1987*; also special issue of *Administration*, 1987, vol 35(4), Dublin, Institute of Public Administration.

Lowry, Robert (2001) 'The Irish lords of appeal in ordinary' in DS Greer and NM Dawson (eds) *Mysteries and Solutions in Irish Legal History: Irish Legal History Society Discourses and Other Papers, 1996-1999*, Dublin, Four Courts Press in association with the Irish Legal History Society, 193–16.

Luquiens, Corinne et al (2017) 'Developments in French Constitutional Law: The Year 2016 in Review', I-CONnect Blog, 11 November 2017.

Lyall, Andrew (1993–95) 'The Irish House of Lords as a judicial body, 1783–1800' 28–30 *Irish Jurist ns* 314.

Lynch, Kathleen (1996) 'Defining the family and protecting the caring functions of both traditional and non-traditional families' in *Report of the Constitution Review Group*, Dublin, The Stationery Office, Pr 9817, Appendix 23.

Lyne, Anne (2011) 'Judicial review, proportionality and the employment relationship post *Meadows v Minister for Justice, Equality and Law Reform*' 8 *Irish Employment Law Journal* 109.

Lyons, FSL (1973) *Ireland Since the Famine*, London, Fontana (rev ed).

Mac Cormaic, Ruadhán (2013), 'Inside Ireland's Supreme Court', *Irish Times*, 6–10 July.

Mac Cormaic, Ruadhán (2016) *The Supreme Court*, Dublin, Penguin Ireland.

MacGuill, James (2007) 'The impact of recent ECHR changes on the Constitution' 7(2) *Irish Judicial Studies Journal* 50.

MacKinnon, Frank (1964) 'The establishment of the Supreme Court of Canada' in Lederman, above, 106–24.

MacNeill, JG Swift (1925) *Studies in the Constitution of the Irish Free State*, Dublin, Talbot Press.

Maguire, John (2008) *IRA Internments and the Irish Government: Subversives and the State 1939–1962*, Dublin and Portland, Or, Irish Academic Press.

Makowski, Kevin (1995) 'Solange III: the German Federal Constitutional Court's decision on accession to the Maastricht Treaty of European Union' *University of Pennsylvania Journal of International Law* 155

Manning, Maurice (1970) *The Blueshirts*, Dublin, Gill and Macmillan.

Mansergh, Nicholas (1934) *The Irish Free State: Its Government and Politics*, London, Allen and Unwin.

Mansergh, Nicholas (1991) *The Unresolved Question: The Anglo-Irish Settlement and Its Undoing 1912–72*, New Haven and London, Yale University Press.

Margulies, Martin B (2002) 'Standards of review and state action under the Irish Constitution' 37 *Irish Jurist ns* 23.

Marsh, Michael, Jane Suiter and Theresa Reidy (2012). *Report on reasons behind voter behaviour in the Oireachtas inquiry referendum 2011*, Dublin, Department of Public Expenditure and Reform.

Martin, Frank (1998) 'The family in the Constitution: principle and practice' in Tim Murphy and Patrick Twomey (eds), *Ireland's Evolving Constitution 1937–1997: Collected Essays*, Oxford, Hart Publishing, Chap 7.

Martin, Frank (2005) 'The changing face of family law in Ireland' 5(1) *Irish Judicial Studies Journal* 16.

Mason, Sir Anthony (2003) 'High Court of Australia: a personal impression of its first 100 years' 27 *Melbourne University Law Review* 864.

McCarthy, Niall (1992) 'Observations on the protection of fundamental rights in the Irish Constitution' in Curtin and O'Keefe (eds), above, 179.

McCormick, Peter (1993) 'Assessing Leadership on the Supreme Court of Canada: Towards a Typology of Chief Justice Performance' 4 *Supreme Court Law Review* (2nd Ser) 409.

McCormick, Peter (2000) *Supreme At Last: The Evolution of the Supreme Court of Canada*, James Lorimer & Co Ltd, Toronto.

McCutcheon, J Paul and Laraine Hanlon (2005) 'A review of the jurisprudence of the Court of Criminal Appeal 2002–2004: principles and general themes' 5(1) *Irish Judicial Studies Journal* 213.
McDermott, Paul (2000a) 'The separation of powers doctrine and the doctrine of non-justiciabililty' 35 *Irish Jurist ns* 280.
McDermott, Paul and Mark Murphy (2008) 'No revolution: the impact of the ECHR Act 2003 on Irish criminal law' 30 *Dublin University Law Journal* 1.
McGrath, Declan (2004) 'The exclusionary rule in respect of unconstitutionally obtained evidence' 26 *Dublin University Law Journal* 108.
MacGuckian, Síle (2004) 'Confessions and the Constitution' 26 *Dublin University Law Journal* 272.
MacGuckian, Síle (2005) 'Judge or politician? The political role of the judiciary in society' 27 *Dublin University Law Journal* 302.
McGuinness, Catherine (2002) 'Recent developments in family law' 2(2) *Irish Judicial Studies Journal* 68.
McInerney, Pat (2010) '"Equality of arms" between the suspect interrogated in Garda custody and the Gardaí?' 10(1) *Irish Judicial Studies Journal*1.
McKittrick, David, Seamus Kelters, Brian Feeney, Chris Thornton, and David McVea (2006), *Lost Lives*, Edinburgh, Mainstream Publishing, rev ed.
McWhinney, Edward (1954–55) 'The courts and the Constitution in Catholic Ireland' 29 *Tulane Law Review* 69.
Mohr, Thomas (2002) 'Law without loyalty: the abolition of the Irish appeal to the Privy Council' 37 *Irish Jurist ns* 187.
Mohr, Thomas (2008) 'The Colonial Laws Validity Act and the Irish Free State' 43 *Irish Jurist ns* 21.
Mohr, Thomas (2011) 'A British Empire Court: A Brief Appraisal of the History of the Judicial Committee of the Privy Council' in Anthony McElligott et al (eds), *Power in History*, Historical Studies XXVII, Dublin, Irish Academic Press, Chap 7.
Mohr, Thomas (2016) *Guardian of the Treaty: The Privy Council Appeal and Irish Sovereignty*, Dublin, Four Courts Press.
Mohr, Thomas (2018) 'Law and the foundation of the Irish State on 6 December 1922' 59 *Irish Jurist ns* 31.
Moore, Anthony (2001) 'Isaac Wunder orders' 1 *Judicial Studies Institute Journal* 137.
Moran, Michael JS (2007) 'Impartiality in judicial appointments: *an absent concept*?' 10 *Trinity College Law review* 5.
Morgan, David Gwynn (1978–79) 'The Emergency Powers Bill reference' I: 13 *Irish Jurist ns* 67 and II: 14 *Irish Jurist ns* 252.
Morgan, David Gwynn (1988) 'Constitutional interpretation' 10 *Dublin University Law Journal* 24.
Morgan, David Gwynn (2001) *A Judgment Too Far? Judicial Activism and the Constitution*, Cork, Cork University Press.
Morgan, David Gwynn (2004a) 'Selection of superior judges' 22 *Irish Law Times* 42.
Morgan, David Gwynn (2004b) '"Judicial-o-centric" separation of powers on the wane?' 39 *Irish Jurist ns* 142.
Mullaly, Siobhán (1998) 'Searching for foundations in Irish constitutional law' 33 *Irish Jurist ns* 333.
Mulligan, Andrea (2010) '*Roche v Roche*: some guidance for frozen embryo disputes' 13 *Trinity College Law Review* 168.
Mulligan, Andrea (2011) 'Frozen embryo disposition in Ireland after *Roche v Roche*' 46 *Irish Jurist ns* 202.
Mulligan, Andrea (2012) 'From *Murray v Ireland* to *Roche v Roche*: re-evaluating the constitutional right to procreate in the context of assisted reproduction' 35 *Dublin University Law Journal* 261.
Murnaghan, James (1912) 'The development of supreme judicature in Ireland' 1 *Studies* 130.
Murphy, Cathal (2002) 'Inquiries and tribunals after Abbeylara' 7(7) *Bar Review* 355.
Murphy, Mark William (2007) 'The problem of unconstitutionality and retroactivity in criminal law: Ireland, the US and Canada compared' 42 *Irish Jurist ns* 63.
Murphy, T and P Twomey (eds) (1998) *Ireland's Evolving Constitution 1937–1997: Collected Essays*, Oxford, Hart Publishing.
Murray, Thomas (2016) *Contesting Economic and Social Rights in Ireland: Constitution, State and Society, 1848–2016*, Cambridge, Cambridge University Press.

Muttart, Daved (2007) *The Empirical Gap in Jurisprudence: A Comprehensive Study of the Supreme Court of Canada*, Toronto, University of Toronto Press.

Ní Raifeartaigh, Úna (2004) 'The European Convention on Human Rights and the Irish criminal justice system' 4(2) *Irish Judicial Studies Journal* 20.

Ní Raifeartaigh, Úna (2007) 'The ECHR and the criminal justice system' 7(2) *Irish Judicial Studies Journal* 18.

Noctor, Cathleen (1996) 'Adoption, consent and the Constitution' 18 *Dublin University Law Journal* 50.

Noonan, Robert (2007) 'Stare decisis, overruling and judicial law-making: the paradox of the *JC* case' 57 *Irish Jurist ns* 119.

O'Brien, Justin (2000) *The Arms Trial*, Dublin, Gill and Macmillan.

O'Brien, Zeldine (2004) 'The courts make a new friend? *Amicus curiae* jurisdiction in Ireland' 7 *Trinity College Law Review* 5.

O'Cinneide, Colm (2003) 'Taking horizontal effect seriously: private law, constitutional rights and the European Convention on Human Rights' 3 *Hibernian Law Journal* 77.

O'Cinneide, Colm (2007) 'Irish constitutional law and direct horizontal effect – a successful experiment?' in Dawn Oliver and Jörg Fedtke (eds), *Human Rights in the Private Sphere: A Comparative Study*, Abingdon, Routledge-Cavendish, Chap 7.

O'Connell, Donncha (2008) 'The added value of sub-constitutional incorporation: ECHR Act 2003' in Eoin Carolan and Oran Doyle, above, Chap 28.

O'Connell, Donncha (2009) 'Watched kettle boil slowly: the impact of the ECHR Act 2003' in Ursula Kilkelly (ed), *ECHR and Irish Law*, Bristol, Jordan Publishing Ltd.

O'Connell, Rory (1999) 'Guardians of the Constitution: unconstitutional constitutional norms' in 4 *Journal of Civil Liberties* 48.]

O'Connell, Rory (2008) 'From equality before the law to the equal benefit of the law: social and economic rights in the Irish Constitution' in Eoin Carolan and Oran Doyle (eds), above, Chap 18.

O'Connor, Cian, Laurence Kelly and Eoghan McSwiney (2012) 'Natural law: a Bible for judicial reasoning?' 15 *Trinity College Law review* 75.

O'Connor, Paul (1982) 'The admissibility of unconstitutionally obtained evidence in Irish law' 17 *Irish Jurist ns* 257.

O'Connell, Paul (2008-09) '"Anxious scrutiny" in the Irish courts: too little, too late?' 8 *Hibernian Law Journal* 75.

O'Dell, Eoin and Gerry Whyte (2005) 'Is this a country for old men and women? – *In re Article 26 and the Health (Amendment) (No 2) Bill 2004*' 27 *Dublin University Law Journal* 368.

O'Donnell, Donal (2004) 'A comparison of Article 6 of the European Convention on Human Rights and the due process requirements of the Constitution of Ireland' 4(2) *JSIL* 37.

O'Donnell, Donal (2014) 'Nial Fennelly: *Mallak* and the rule of reasons' in Bradley et al (2014) Chap 14.

O'Donoghue, Aoife (2017) in Enright, McCandless and O'Donoghue (eds), above, 229–40.

O'Dowd, John (2003) 'Knowing how way leads on to way: some reflections on the *Abbeylara* decision' 38 *Irish Jurist ns* 162.

O'Dowd, John (2012) 'Judges in whose cause? The Irish bench after the judges' pay referendum' 48 *Irish Jurist ns* 102.

O'Flaherty, Hugh (1996-97) 'An introduction to the relationship between European Community law and national law in Ireland' 20 *Fordham International Law Journal* 1151.

O'Flaherty, Hugh (1998) 'Obituary of Brian Walsh 1918–1998' 7 *Irish Journal of European Law* 1.

Ó Floinn, Benedict (2008) *Practice and Procedure in the Superior Courts*, Dublin, Bloomsbury Professional, 2nd ed.

O'Hanlon, Roderick J (1965) 'Special courts and military tribunals under the Constitution of Ireland: powers of the President in relation to emergency legislation' 31 *Irish Jurist* 1.

O'Hanlon, Roderick (1958) 'Irish Extradition and Practice' 34 *British Yearbook of International Law* 274.

O'Higgins, Paul (1958) 'Irish Extradition and Practice' 34 *British Yearbook of International Law* 274.

O'Higgins, Thomas (1996) 'The Irish legal system' 31 *Irish Jurist ns* 1.

O'Keeffe, David (1983) 'EEC law – preliminary deference: the Supreme Court and Community law' 5 *Dublin University Law Journal* 286.

O'Keeffe, David (1984) 'Appeals against an order to refer under Article 177 of the EEC Treaty' 9 *European Law Review* 87.

O'Leary, Siofra (1992) 'Freedom of establishment and freedom to provide services: the Court of Justice as a reluctant constitutional adjudicator: an examination of the abortion information case' 17 *European Law Review* 138.

Ó Longaigh, Seosamh (2006) *Emergency Law in Independent Ireland 1922-1948*, Dublin, Four Courts Press.

O'Mahony, Conor (2002) 'Education, remedies and the separation of powers' 24 *Dublin University Law Journal* 57.

O'Mahony, Conor (2003) 'Extra-marital families and education rights under the Irish Constitution' *Irish Journal of Family Law* 21.

O'Mahony, Conor (2005) 'A new slant on education rights and mandatory injunctions?' 27 *Dublin University Law Journal* 363.

O'Mahony, Conor (2017) 'Subsidiarity of ECHR and *O'Keeffe v Ireland*: a response to Mr Justice Hardiman' in Cahillane, Gallen, and Hickey (eds), above, Chap 7.

O'Malley, Thomas (2009) *The Criminal Process*, Dublin, Thomson Round Hall.

O'Neill, Ailbhe (2007) 'The effect of a finding that legislation is unconstitutional: the approach of the Irish Supreme Court' 36 *Common Law World Review* 220.

O'Reilly, James (ed) (1992) *Human Rights and Constitutional Law: Essays in Honour of Brian Walsh*, Dublin, Round Hall Press.

O'Reilly, Seán (2009) 'The private enforcement of European Community law in the Irish superior courts' 31 *Dublin University Law Journal* 324.

Orentlicher, David (2018) 'Politics and the Supreme Court: The Need for Ideological Balance' 79(3) *University of Pittsburgh Law Review* 411.

Osborough, W Nial (1972) 'Law in Ireland, 1916–1926', 23 *Northern Ireland Legal Quarterly* 48.

Osborough, W Nial (1973a) 'Supreme Court Report' 8 *Irish Jurist ns* 78.

Osborough, W Nial (1973b) 'The demise of the State's immunity in tort' 8 *Irish Jurist ns* 275.

Osborough, W Nial (1974) 'The title of the last Lord Chief Justice of Ireland' 9 *Irish Jurist ns* 87.

Osborough, W Nial (1975) Review of Mary Robinson (1974), below, 10 *Irish Jurist ns* 369.

Osborough, W Nial (1976) 'The State's tortious liability: further reflections on *Byrne v Ireland*' (I) 11 *Irish Jurist ns* 11, and (II) 11 *Irish Jurist ns* 279.

Osborough, W Nial (1979–80) 'Constitutional law – a waning of judicial activism?'4 *Dublin University Law Journal* 101.

Osborough, W Nial (1996) 'The Irish Legal System, 1796–1877' in Caroline Costello (ed) *The Four Courts: 200 Years*, Dublin, Four Courts Press, 33–79.

Osborough, W Nial (1998) 'The failure to enact an Irish Bill of Rights: a gap in Irish constitutional history' 33 *Irish Jurist ns* 392.

Osborough, W Nial (2011) 'The Law School's early professoriate' 46 *Irish Jurist ns* 1.

Ostberg CL and Matthew Wetstein (2007) *Attitudinal Decision Making in the Supreme Court of Canada*, Vancouver, UBC Press.

Paris, Marie-Luce (2015) 'The ECHR in Irish law: compliance and implementation' in Egan (ed) above, Chap 6.

Parker, J Wilson (1997) 'Must constitutional rights be specified? Reflections on the proposal to amend Article 40.3.1' 32 *Irish Jurist ns* 102.

Paterson, Alan (1982) *The Law Lords*, London, Palgrave Macmillan.

Paterson, Alan (2013) *Final Judgment: The Last Law Lords and the Supreme Court*, Oxford and Portland, Hart Publishing.

Paton, GW (1952) (ed) *The Commonwealth of Australia: The Development of its Laws and Constitution*, Stevens & Sons Ltd, London.

Patterson, Henry (2006) *Ireland Since 1939: The Persistence of Conflict*, Dublin, Penguin Ireland.

Perrin, Benjamin (2016), *Dissent from Within at the Supreme Court of Canada*, Ottawa, Macdonald-Laurier Institute.

Phelan, Diarmuid Rossa (1992) 'Right to life of the unborn v promotion of trade in services: the European Court of Justice and the normative shaping of the European Union' 35 *Modern Law Review* 670.

Phelan, Diarmuid Rossa (1994) 'The concept of social rights' 16 *Dublin University Law Journal* 105–46.

Phelan, Diarmuid Rossa (1997) *Revolt or Revolution: The Constitutional Boundaries of the European Community*, Dublin, Round Hall and Sweet and Maxwell.

Phelan, Diarmuid Rossa and Anthony Whelan (1997) 'National constitutional law and European integration: FIDE report' 6 *Irish Journal of European Law* 24.

Poole, Thomas and Sangeeta Shah (2009) 'The impact of the Human Rights Act on the House of Lords' *Public Law* 347.

Poole, Thomas and Sangeeta Shah (2011) 'The Law Lords and Human Rights' 74 *Modern Law Review* 79.

Power, Conor (2003) '*T v T*, an Irish solution to an international problem' *Irish Journal of Family Law* (3)1.

Prendergast, David (2011a) 'The constitutionality of strict liability in criminal law' 33 *Dublin University Law Journal* 285.

Prendergast, David (2011b) 'Strict liability and the presumption of mens rea after *CC v Ireland*' 46 *Irish Jurist ns* 211.

Price, Daniel (2013) '*Meadows v The Minister for Justice, Equality and Law Reform*: an unreasonable lack of clarity?' 16 *Trinity College Law Review* 183.

Quinlivan, Shivaun and Mary Keys (2002) 'Official indifference and persistent procrastination: an analysis of *Sinnott*' 2(2) *Irish Judicial Studies Journal* 163.

Rainey, Bernadette, Elizabeth Wicks and Clare Ovey (eds) (2017) *Jacobs, White and Ovey: The European Convention on Human Rights*, Oxford, Oxford university Press, 7th edn.

Rasmussen, Hjalte (1986) *On Law and Policy in the European Court of Justice: A Comparative Study in Judicial Policy-Making*, Dordrecht, Martinus Nijhoff.

Redmond, Mary (1978) 'The Criminal Law (Jurisdiction) Act 1976 and the Constitution' 13 *Irish Jurist ns* 1.

Redmond, Mary (1979–80a) 'Towards an Hohfeldian view of the rights and freedoms in the Irish Constitution' 4 *Dublin University Law Journal* 52.

Redmond, Mary (1979–80b) 'Constitutional law—waiver of rights' 4 *Dublin University Law Journal* 104.

Requa, Marny (2015) 'Revisiting the Past; Miscarriages of Justice, the Courts and Transition' in Anne-Marie McAlinden and Clare Dwyer (eds), *Criminal Justice in Transition: The Northern Ireland Context*, Oxford and Portland, Hart Publishing, Chap 12.

Ring, Sinead (2010) '*Carlin v DPP*: prosecutorial discretion and the decision (not) to prosecute', *Human Rights in Ireland Blog*, 24 March 2010.

Roach, Kent (2007) 'Judicial Activism in the Supreme Court of Canada' in Dickson (ed) (2007), above, 60–119.

Roach, Kent (2016) *The Supreme Court on Trial: Judicial Activism or Democratic Dialogue*, Toronto, Irwin Law, rev ed.

Robertson, David (1998) *Judicial Discretion in the House of Lords*, Oxford, Clarendon Press.

Robinson, Mary T W (1974) *The Special Criminal Court*, Dublin, Dublin University Press.

Robinson, Mary T W (1976), 'Reform of the law relating to family planning in Ireland' 2 *Dublin University Law Journal* 12.

Rogers, Jonathan (2008) 'The boundaries of the abuse of process in criminal trials' 61 *Current Legal Problems* 289.

Roux, Theunis (2013), *The Politics of Principle: The First South African Constitutional Court, 1995–2005*, Cambridge University Press.

Ruane, Blathna (1994) *An assessment of the independence of the Irish Supreme Court in the context of constitutional law with particular reference to the system of judicial appointments*, doctoral dissertation at the University of Cambridge.

Ruane, Blathna (2015) 'Regime change: the fate of the senior Crown judiciary following the Anglo-Irish Treaty 1921' 54 *Irish Jurist ns* 96.

Ryan, Andrea (2003) 'Avoiding the hard question: *DPP v Buck* and the constitutional right of access to legal advice' 25 *Dublin University Law Journal* 257.

Ryan, Desmond (2009) 'Connections without consensus: approaches to vicarious liability in the Irish Supreme Court' 31 *Dublin University Law Journal* 457.

Ryan, Fergus (2000) 'Family law—reversal of fortune—nullity law in the age of divorce' 22 *Dublin University Law Journal* 224.

Ryan, Fergus (2002) 'Disability and the right to education: defining the constitutional "child"' 24 *Dublin University Law Journal* 96.

Ryan, Ray and Desmond Ryan (2004) 'Some comments about "caution": emerging trends in Irish negligence law' 7 *Trinity College Law Review* 114.

Rynder, Constance, 'Sheelagh Murnaghan and the struggle for human rights in Northern Ireland' (2006) 14 *Irish Studies Review* 447.

Salzberger, Eli (2007) 'Judicial Activism in Israel' in Dickson (2007), above, 217–71.

Sawer, Geoffrey (1948) 'The Judicial Power of the Commonwealth' 1(1) *University of Western Australia Law Review* 29.

Schabas, William (2007) 'Ireland, the European Convention on Human Rights, and the Personal Contribution of Seán McBride' in J Morison, K McEvoy and G Anthony (eds) *Judges, Transition and Human Rights*, Oxford, Oxford University Press, Chap 13.

Schauer, Frederick (2017) 'The Supreme Court as Public Educator?' 88(2) *University of Colorado Law Review* 333.

Schertzer, Robert (2016) *The Judicial Role in a Diverse Federation: Lessons from the Supreme Court of Canada*, Toronto, University of Toronto Press.

Schorkopf, Frank (2005) 'The European Court of Human Rights' judgment in the case of *Bosphorus Hava Yollari Turizm v Ireland*' 6 *German Law Journal* 1255.

Schwartz, Bernard (1993) *A History of the Supreme Court*, New York, Oxford University Press.

Schwartz, Herman (ed) (2002) *The Rehnquist Court*, New York, Hill & Wang.

Scott, Maria (2010) 'The house that the Supreme Court built: the rulings in *Coughlan* and *McKenna*, the Lisbon Treaty and the constitutional referendum in Ireland' 9 *Hibernian Law Journal* 219.

Shah, Sangeeta, Thomas Poole and Michael Blackwell (2014) 'Rights, interveners and the Law Lords' 34 *Oxford Journal of Legal Studies* 295.

Shannon, Geoffrey (2005) 'The internationalisation of Irish family law' 5(1) *Irish Judicial Studies Journal* 42.

Shapiro, Carolyn and Christopher Schmidt (eds) (2013) *Symposium on the Supreme Court and the American Public* 88(2) *Chicago-Kent Law Review* 287–526.

Sherlock, Ann (1987) 'Constitutional law—sovereignty, the Constitution and the Single European Act' 9 *Dublin University Law Journal* 101.

Sherlock, Ann (1989) 'The right to life of the unborn and the Irish Constitution' 24 *Irish Jurist ns* 13.

Sherry, Suzanna et al (2016) *Symposium on Erwin Chemerinsky's Case against the Supreme Court* 69(4) *Vanderbilt Law Review* 909–1158.

Smyth, Claire-Michelle (2017) *Social and Economic Rights in Ireland*, Dublin, Clarus Press.

Songer, Donald (2008) *The Transformation of the Supreme Court of Canada: An Empirical Examination*, Toronto, University of Toronto Press.

Stafford, Caoimhe (2017) 'The case for a judicially enforceable right to housing' 16 *Housing Law Journal* 42.

Staines, Michael (1976) 'The concept of "the family" under the Irish Constitution' 11 *Irish Jurist ns* 223.

Stevens, Robert (1979) *Law and Politics: The House of Lords as a Judicial Body, 1800–1976*, London, Weidenfeld & Nicolson.

Stoebuck, William B (1968–69) 'Reception of English common law in the American colonies' 10 *William & Mary Law Review* 393.

Stone Sweet, Alec and Thomas Brunell (1998) *The European Court and the National Courts: A Statistical Analysis of Preliminary References, 1961-95*, 5 *Journal of European Public Policy* 66, also available online.

Street, Amy and Richard Gordon (2012), *Select Committees and Coercive Powers—Clarity or Confusion?*, London, The Constitution Society.

Supperstone, Sir Michael, James Goudie and Sir Paul Walker (2014) *Judicial Review*, London, Butterworths LexisNexis, 5th ed.

Symmons, Clive R (1973) 'The Law Enforcement Commission Report and Article 29 of the Irish Constitution' 8 *Irish Jurist ns* 33.

Symmons, Clive R (1978) 'The Criminal Law (Jurisdiction) Act 1976 and international law' 13 *Irish Jurist ns* 36.
Temple Lang, John (1987) 'The Irish court case which delayed the Single European Act: *Crotty v An Taoiseach and others*' 24 *Common Market L Rev* 709.
Thomas, George (2008) *The Supreme Court on Trial: How the American Justice System Sacrifices Innocent Defendants*, Ann Arbor (ML), University of Michigan Press.
Thompson, Brian (1991) 'Living with a Supreme Court in Ireland' 44 *Parliamentary Affairs* 33.
Thornton, Liam (2015) 'Socio-Economic Rights in Ireland' in Egan (ed) above, Chap 9 (171–98).
Thornton, Liam (2014) 'The European Convention on Human Rights: a socio-economic rights Charter?' in Egan, Thornton and Walsh (eds), Chap 14 (227–56)
Tobin, Brian (2014) 'The Revised General Scheme of the Children and Family Relationships Bill 2014: Cognisant of the Donor-Conceived Child's Constitutional Rights' 52 *Irish Jurist ns* 153.
Tobin, Fergal (1984) *The Best of Decades: Ireland in the 1960s*, Dublin, Gill and Macmillan.
Tóibin, Colm (1985) *Magill*, vol 8, no 7, February.
Tomkins, Adam (2003) *Public Law*, Oxford, Clarendon Press.
Toobin, Jeffrey (2007) *The Nine: Inside the Secret World of the Supreme Court*, New York, Doubleday.
Towey, T (1977) 'Hugh Kennedy and the constitutional development of the Irish Free State 1922–23' 12 *Irish Jurist ns* 355.
Travers, Noel (1994) 'The constitutionality of the implementation of EC Directives into law re-visited' 88 *Gazette of the ILSI* 99.
Travers, Noel (1998) 'Community Directives: effects, efficiency, justiciability' 7 *Irish Journal of European Law* 165.
Travers, Noel (2003) 'The reception of community legislation into Irish law and related issues re-visited' 38 *Irish Jurist ns* 58.
Twomey, Adrian (1995) 'The death of natural law' 13 *Irish Law Times* 270.
Verma SK and K Kusum (eds) (2004) *Fifty Years of the Supreme Court of India: Its Grasp and Reach*, New Delhi, Indian Law Institute.
Vilhena de Freitas, L (2015) 'The Judicial Activism of the European Court of Justice' in LP Coutinho, M La Torre and SD Smith, *Judicial Activism: An Interdisciplinary Approach to the American and European Experiences*, Chem, Switzerland, Springer, Chap 12.
Voeten, Eric (2008) 'The impartiality of international judges: evidence from the European Court of Human Rights' 102 *American Political Science Review* 417.
Von Prondzynski, Franz Ferdinand (1976) 'The Emergency Powers Bill' 1(2) *Dublin University Law Journal* 47.
Von Prondzynski, Franz Ferdinand (1977) 'Natural law and the Constitution' 2 *Dublin University Law Journal* 33.
Von Prondzynski, Franz Ferdinand (1978–80) 'The protection of constitutional rights: comparisons between Germany and Ireland' 2 *Dublin University Law Journal* 14.
Wallace, Stuart (2011) 'Tackling *Jarndyce and Jarndyce*: delay, *McFarlane v Ireland* and the European Court of Human Rights' 21 *Irish Criminal Law Journal* 31.
Walsh, Brian (1977) 'The judicial power and the protection of the right to privacy' 2 *Dublin University Law Journal* 3.
Walsh, Brian (1988a) 'The Constitution and Constitutional Rights' in Litton (ed), above, 86–109.
Walsh, Brian (1988b) 'The Constitution: a view from the bench' in Brian Farrell (ed), *De Valera's Constitution and Ours*, Dublin, Gill and Macmillan, Chap 14.
Walsh, Dermot (2013) 'Liability for Garda negligence in the prevention and investigation of crime' 49 *Irish Jurist ns* 1.
Walsh, Dermot (2016) *Walsh on Criminal Procedure*, Dublin, Round Hall Thomson Reuters, 2nd ed.
Walsh, Ian (2005) 'Precedent in former Irish superior courts' 40 *Irish Jurist ns* 160.
Ward, Alan J (1994) *The Irish Constitutional Tradition: Responsible Government and Modern Ireland, 1782–1992*, Dublin, Irish Academic Press.
Ward, Artemus, Christopher Brough and Robert Arnold (2015) *Historical Dictionary of the US Supreme Court*, Lanham, Maryland and London, Rowman & Littlefield.
Ward, Tanya (2007) *Justice Matters: Independence, Accountability and the Irish Judiciary*, Dublin, Irish Council for Civil Liberties.

Ward, Tanya (2008) 'Independence, accountability and the Irish judiciary' (2008) 8(1) *Irish Judicial Studies Journal* 1.

Weiler, Paul (1974) *In the Last Resort: A Critical study of the Supreme Court of Canada*, Toronto, Carswell/Methuen.

Wendel, Mattias (2013) 'Judicial restraint and the return to openness: the decision of the German Federal Constitutional Court on the ESM and the Fiscal Treaty of 12 September 2012' 14 *German Law Journal* 21.

Wheeler, Fiona and John Willaims (2007), 'Restrained Activism in the High Court of Australia' in Dickson (ed) (2007), above, Chap 2.

Whelan, Anthony (1992) 'Article 29.4.3 and the meaning of "necessity"' 2 *Irish Students Law Review* 60.

Whelan, Anthony (1993) 'Constitutional law—*Meagher v Minister for Agriculture*' 15 *Dublin University Law Journal* 152.

Whelan, Emmet (2006) 'The right to family life v immigration control: the application of Article 8 of the European Convention on Human Rights in Ireland' 6 *Hibernian Law Journal* 93.

Whyte, Gerry (1982) 'Application of the European Convention on Human Rights before the Irish courts' 31 *International & Comparative Law Quarterly* 856.

Whyte, Gerry (1983) 'Constitutional law—the one judgment rule in action' 5 *Dublin University Law Journal* 273.

Whyte, Gerry (1996) 'Natural law and the Constitution', 14 *Irish Law Times* 8.

Whyte, Gerry (2006) 'The role of the Supreme Court in our democracy: a response to Mr Justice Hardiman' 28 *Dublin University Law Journal* 1.

Whyte, Gerry (2010) 'A tale of two cases—divergent approaches of the Irish Supreme Court to distributive justice' 32 *Dublin University Law Journal* 365.

Whyte, Gerry (2012) 'Constitutional litigation and disability rights' 48 *Irish Jurist ns* 303.

Whyte, John (1970) 'Church, State and Society' in J J Lee (ed), *Ireland 1945-1970*, Dublin, Gill and Macmillan, 73-82.

Wicks, Elizabeth (2011) '*A, B, C v Ireland*: Abortion Law under the European Convention on Human Rights' 11 *Human Rights Law Review* 556.

Wicks, Elizabeth (2012) 'The meaning of "life": dignity and the right to life in international human rights treaties' 12 *Human Rights Law Review* 199.

Wieland, Joachim (1994) 'Germany in the European Union—the Maastricht decision of the *Bundesverfassungsgericht*' 5 *European Journal of International Law* 259.

Wilkinson, Brian (1992) 'Abortion, the Irish Constitution and the EEC' *Public Law* 20.

Williams, Michael (2015) *Serving the People? The Need for Reform in the Irish Legal System*, Dublin, Liffey Press.

Woodward, Bob and Scott Armstrong (1979) *The Brethren: Inside the Supreme Court*, New York, Simon & Schuster.

Working Group (2003) *The Criminal Jurisdiction of the Courts*, Report of the Working Group on the Jurisdiction of the Courts, Dublin, Courts Service.

Working Group (2009) *Report of the Working Group on a Court of Appeal*, Dublin, Courts Service.

Yusuf, Hakeem (2014) *Colonial and Post-colonial Constitutionalism in the Commonwealth: Peace, Order and Good Government*, Abingdon, Routledge.

Index

The manufacturer's authorised representative in the EU for product safety is Oxford University Press España S.A. of el Parque Empresarial San Fernando de Henares, Avenida de Castilla, 2 – 28830 Madrid (www.oup.es/en or product.safety@oup.com). OUP España S.A. also acts as importer into Spain of products made by the manufacturer.

www.ingramcontent.com/pod-product-compliance
Lightning Source LLC
LaVergne TN
LVHW062205200926
848484LV00006B/1320

* 9 7 8 0 1 9 8 7 9 3 7 3 1 *